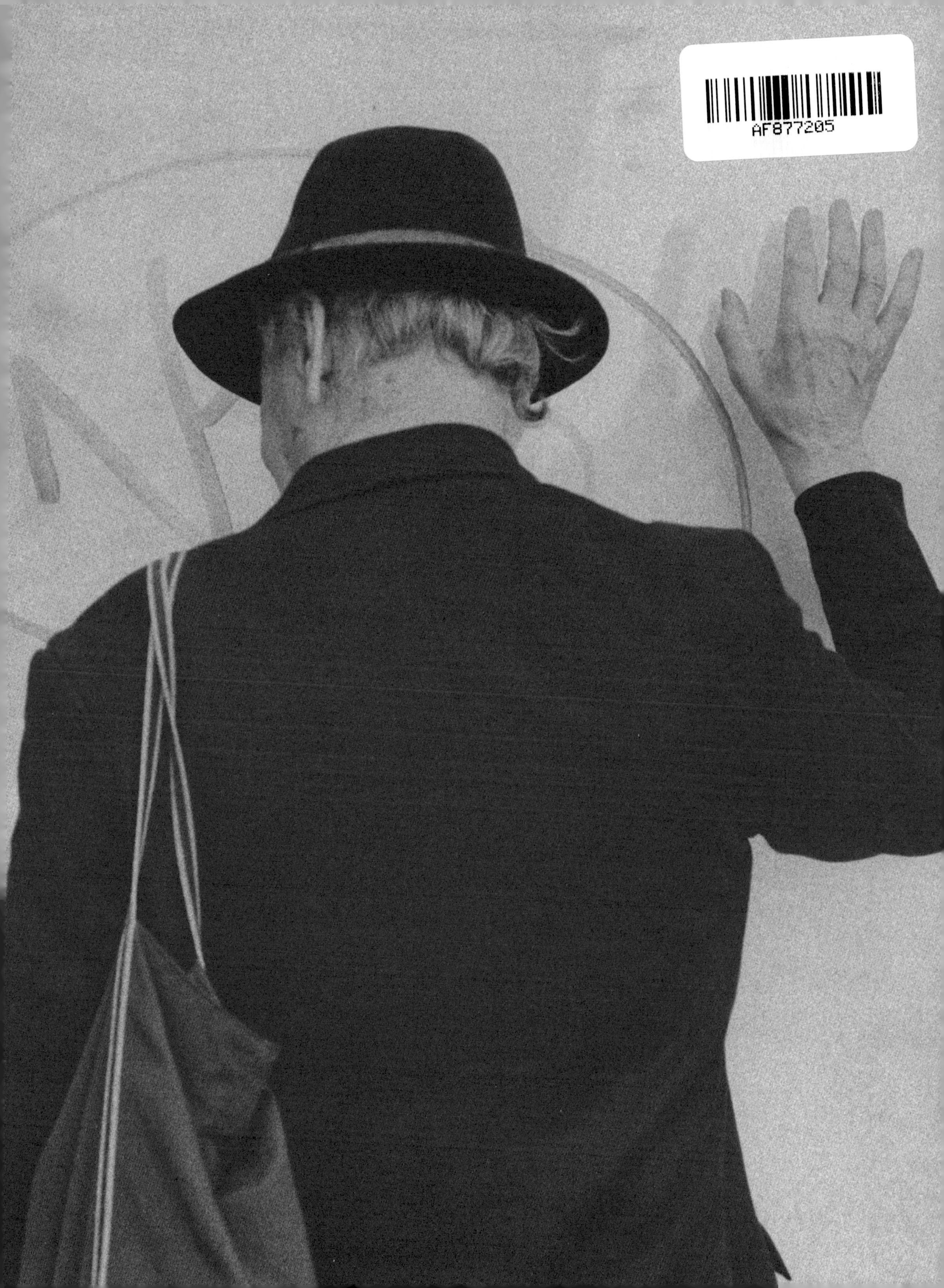

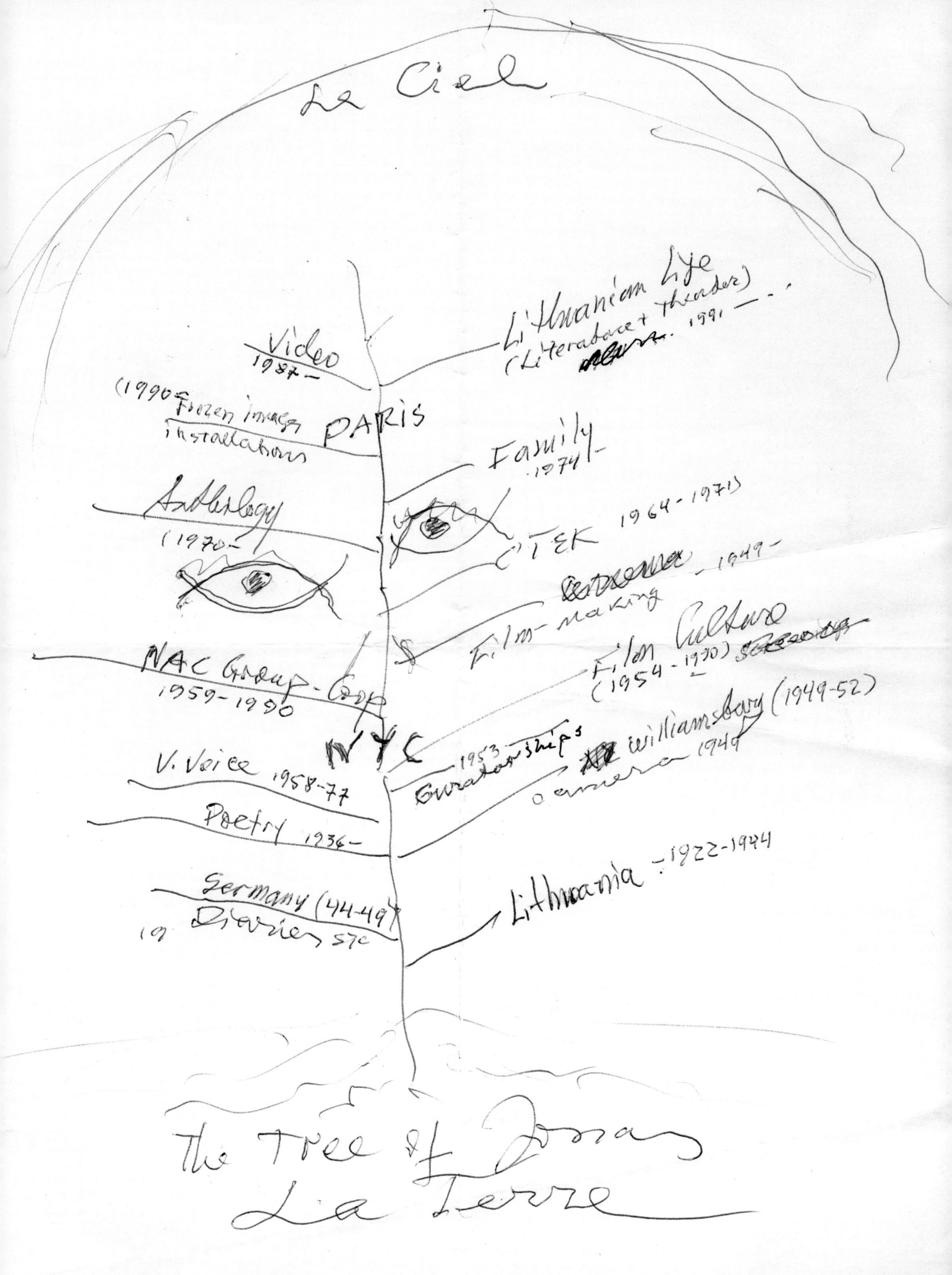
Le Ciel
Lithuanian Life (Literature + theater) 1991 —
Video 1987–
(1990 Frozen images installations
PARIS
Family 1974–
Anthology (1970–
OTEK 1964–1971
Film-making 1949–
Film Culture (1954–1970)
NAC Group - Coop 1959–1990
NYC
Williamsburg (1949-52)
camera 1949
1953 Curatorships
V. Voice 1958-77
Poetry 1936–
Lithuania 1922-1944
Germany (44-49)
Diaries etc
The Tree of Jonas
La Terre

DONORS AND LENDERS

Jonas Mekas and the New York Avant-Garde, at the National Gallery of Art, Vilnius, is made possible by the Lithuanian Council for Culture and other generous supporters.

Jonas Mekas: The Camera Was Always Running, at the Jewish Museum, New York, is made possible by the Andy Warhol Foundation for the Visual Arts, Art Mentor Foundation Lucerne, Lithuanian Council for Culture, the Lithuanian Foundation, a gift from the estate of Gaby and Curtis Hereld, Kazickas Family Foundation, Paul Pincus, the Lithuanian Culture Institute, and other generous donors.

Additional support is provided by the Melva Bucksbaum Fund for Contemporary Art and the Peter Jay Sharp Exhibition Fund.

The Andy Warhol Foundation for the Visual Arts

ART FOUNDATION MENTOR LUCERNE

LITHUANIAN COUNCIL FOR CULTURE

LIETUVIŲ FONDAS · LITHUANIAN FOUNDATION, INC.

Lithuanian Culture Institute

All works and objects in the New York exhibition are loaned by the Estate of Jonas Mekas.

JONAS MEKAS

THE CAMERA WAS ALWAYS RUNNING

Edited by Inesa Brašiškė,
Lukas Brasiskis, and Kelly Taxter

With essays by Ed Halter,
Melissa Ragona, Kelly Taxter,
and Andrew V. Uroskie

Jewish Museum, New York
Under the auspices of the Jewish Theological Seminary of America

The Lithuanian National Museum of Art, Vilnius

Yale University Press
New Haven and London

CONTENTS

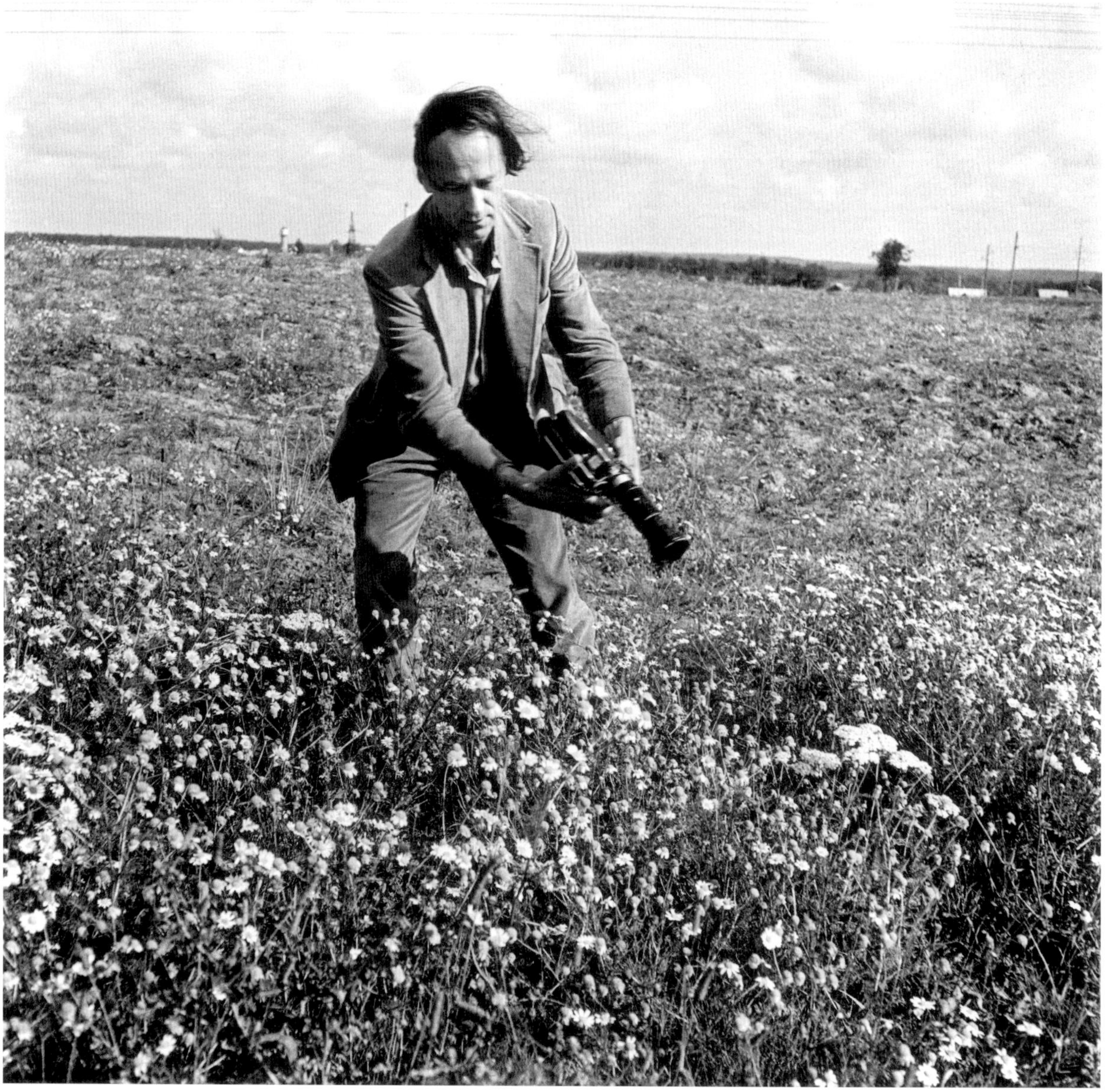

Jonas Mekas photographed by Antanas Sutkus in Semeniškiai, Lithuania, 1971.

THE MEKAS PARADOX

Is Jonas Mekas a figure of which every art-loving Lithuanian is proud? Are Mekas's works well known in Lithuania? Can you see them in major art museums of his native country? Yes and no. *Lost, Lost, Lost*, his emblematic film of 1976, was acquired by The Lithuanian National Museum of Art only in 2020, a year after the artist's death. True, in 2007 the Vilnius city council had purchased the Fluxus Collection from Jonas Mekas and established the Jonas Mekas Visual Arts Center, but the Center's activities were driven by the energy and enthusiasm of three or four dedicated people. Despite organizing important shows and presentations, the Center never achieved great visibility or gained more substantial state support, and today it is likely to merge with a larger institution. Thankfully, Jonas Mekas represented Lithuania in the Venice Biennale of 2005, to great acclaim.

Mekas is probably better known to people in Lithuania as a poet than as a member of the international avant-garde or founder of Anthology Film Archives. In the late 1990s, a commercial television network created a comic version of Jonas Mekas that mocked the way he was "preaching his wisdom" by filming his "life lessons" to Lithuania and broadcasting them on LRT, the national broadcaster; in the satire, his "lessons" were appreciated by one, completely misunderstood by another, and ridiculed by a third. In the minds of many Lithuanians, it was virtually impossible to connect the Jonas Mekas from Semeniškiai, the modest youth speaking the local dialect, with Jonas Mekas, the major New York art figure, friend and comrade of George Maciunas, Yoko Ono, Nam June Paik, and Andy Warhol.

On January 24, 2019, I was invited by LRT to discuss the topic of the day, "The Death of J. Mekas: Has Lithuania Understood Whom It Has Just Lost?" It was not a very easy discussion as far as I can remember. Later, I was widely quoted as having said that "[by his Art and activities] Mekas was rubbing American society the wrong way." But Mekas was also harshly critical of the post-Soviet Lithuania that he rediscovered after the fall of the Berlin Wall, just as he had been critical of other societies he experienced throughout his life. Jonas Mekas's creative ideas, works, and organizational activities originated in a postwar environment that was prosperous for the United States but very difficult for Europe—catastrophic, even, for Eastern Europe—or the "Bloodlands," as the prominent American historian Timothy Snyder has called Europe between Hitler and Stalin in a recent book of the same name. These stark differences of postwar geopolitical, economic, social, and cultural configurations make "the Mekas paradox" an even more complicated phenomenon to decipher.

Mekas's views and his art were outside the cultural mainstream, and there are still many indications that "the father of American avant-garde cinema" must be rediscovered—indeed, rediscovered and reanalyzed—every time his life and works are addressed. And his native Lithuania is—first and foremost—the country that must do this work as a regular spiritual exercise.

Therefore, I was delighted to learn of the collaboration between the Jewish Museum in New York and The Lithuanian National Museum of Art in Vilnius to organize two parallel exhibitions and publish a joint catalogue with Yale University Press. I am very much looking forward to readdressing, together with art-loving audiences, this major figure of the avant-garde—Jonas Mekas—from two different perspectives, the American and the Lithuanian. I would like to express my heartfelt thanks to the key individuals behind this initiative—Darsie Alexander, Ruth Beesch, Kelly Taxter, Inesa Brašiškė, Lukas Brasiskis, and Giedrius Gulbinas—as well as my dear colleague, the chief curator of the National Gallery of Art in Vilnius, Lolita Jablonskienė. I sincerely thank Claudia Gould, director of the Jewish Museum, for granting her support to a project that is not only important for presenting an international artist but also for revisiting the cultural and political landscape of two countries, completely different in their histories but very close in their shared values.

The photograph by the renowned photographer Antanas Sutkus of Jonas Mekas in Semeniškiai hangs in my living room, and every day it is before my eyes. I have no doubt his image will be enriched by the insights and the discoveries provided by the curators and scholars of the Jewish Museum in New York and The Lithuanian National Museum of Art in Vilnius.

Dr. Arūnas Gelūnas
Director
The Lithuanian National Museum of Art, Vilnius

MEKAS UPTOWN AND DOWNTOWN

Each of us who comes to New York from another place discovers his or her own city. When I arrived in late 1978 I was some years younger than Jonas Mekas had been in 1949. Like him, and so many others, I knew immediately that I would stay.

Downtown New York City in the 1970s has been mythologized as an almost utopian moment for artists—a place of endless ferment, creativity, danger, and excitement. The reality was, of course, more prosaic. New York was broke and downtown Manhattan was cheap. Its crumbling nineteenth-century tenements, storefronts, and factory buildings made great work and living spaces for artists and affordable small venues for music, theater, and film. The consequence of low rents, plenty of raw space, and a dense concentration of people produced extraordinary creative fertility.

This social aspect of the downtown art scene played out in the many small art and performance spaces that sprang up in the neighborhood in the seventies and early eighties—the Kitchen, Artists Space, the Clocktower, White Columns, Franklin Furnace, ABC No Rio, PS 122, Squat Theatre—not only nurturing careers and building audiences, but fostering a culture of participation and collaboration.

One place where everyone met everyone else was Anthology Film Archives, presided over by a magnetic man named Jonas Mekas. Anthology screened films of all kinds, and was a place for holding events, meetings, and lectures, as well as informal gatherings. The films and videos that were a revelation to me were the experimental works that no other theater was showing. Anthology was where I discovered the works of Ericka Beckman, Stan Brakhage, Tony Conrad, Maya Deren, Yoko Ono, Jack Smith, Michael Snow, and many others, as well as Mekas's own breathtaking films.

But even more revelatory was Mekas's ability to dismantle walls and reject categories. In this he exemplified the Zeitgeist of the late sixties, seventies, and early eighties, operating within an atmosphere in which artists were defying the established assumptions of the art world—that painting was separate from sculpture, that music occupied a different realm from poetry, that film was a medium of mere entertainment. Artists were making film, video, audio art, working in prints, music, painting, performance, installation, all at once, seeking to be creative in multiple dimensions.

It is no accident that Mekas brought this spirit of creative flux uptown, when he programmed film events at the Jewish Museum between 1968 and 1970. Revisiting his work and career now, I am reminded not only of his importance to the world of avant-garde art, but also of his particular skill in breaking down artificial divisions, including the uptown / downtown dichotomy. Today his art and career remain a touchstone.

From day one of her time at the Jewish Museum, Kelly Taxter advocated for a Mekas survey. When I saw Douglas Gordon's exquisite film on Mekas, *I Had Nowhere to Go,* screened outdoors at Documenta in Athens in 2017, the moment was pivotal for me and I knew she was right; I thank her for her incisive curatorial vision.

The present project could not have come about without the invaluable support of many. In Mekas's spirit, this book is a collaboration of the Jewish Museum and The Lithuanian National Museum of Art in Vilnius, and is designed to accompany two distinct, complementary exhibitions. In Lithuania I am deeply grateful to Dr. Arūnas Gelūnas, director of the National Museum, Lolita Jablonskienė, chief curator of the National Gallery of Art, Vilnius, Giedrius Gulbinas, its head of exhibitions, and the astute curators, Inesa Brašiškė and Lukas Brasiskis, as well as to the Lithuanian Council for Culture and Lithuanian Culture Institute. In New York I extend my warm thanks to Sebastian Mekas, who has been a close collaborator in both book and exhibition, and to the superb Jewish Museum staff. As ever, I am indebted to the supportive leadership of our Board of Trustees, led with boundless commitment by Robert A. Pruzan and Stephen M. Scherr.

Claudia Gould
Helen Goldsmith Menschel Director
Jewish Museum

ACKNOWLEDGMENTS

Jonas Mekas inspired us to pursue our exhibitions and this publication. We are profoundly grateful to have had his blessing at the outset of the project. In his deeply felt absence, his family's generosity has been invaluable. His son, Sebastian Mekas, provided access to Jonas's extraordinary archive, trusted us with irreplaceable documents, and gave us the opportunity to explore his father's importance and influence. We are indebted to the Mekas family: Sebastian, Jonas's daughter, Oona Mekas, and their mother, Hollis Melton.

Jonas's chosen family members were as important to him as they have been to our work. We are thankful to Gražina Michnevičiūtė, Cultural Attaché of the Consulate General of the Republic of Lithuania in New York, who created a thriving nexus of support for our projects. Many others from Jonas's circle of friends and collaborators were crucial to us. We are grateful to Elle Burchill, Phong Bui, Olivia Casa, Pip Chodorov, Thomas Dozol, James Fuentes, Ken and Flo Jacobs, Robert Beavers, Johan Kugelberg, Babette Mangolte, Benn Northover, Liutauras Psibilskis, Michael Stipe, Francesco Ragazzi, Chiara Rusconi, Hans Ulrich Obrist, Amy Taubin, and Francesco Urbano. Several institutions and their staffs were crucial to our efforts: at Anthology Film Archives, John Mhiripiri and staff; M. M. Serra and the staff of the Film-Makers' Cooperative; at the Andy Warhol Foundation for the Visual Arts, Joel Wachs, James Bewely, Greg Pierce, and Rachel Bers; Dennis Lim of Film at Lincoln Center; and the staffs of the Lithuanian Film Center, Skalvija Cinema Center, Lithuanian Culture Institute, Baltic-American Freedom Foundation, and Electronic Arts Intermix.

A warm thank-you goes to Ed Halter, Melissa Ragona, and Andrew V. Uroskie, whose superb scholarship has expanded our understanding of Jonas Mekas. Mark Owens of Life of the Mind, assisted by David Wise of Forthcoming Studio, created a book that captures Jonas's singular aesthetic.

At The Lithuanian National Museum of Art, Vilnius, we extend our thanks to Dr. Arūnas Gelūnas, Director; Gediminas Mikelaitis, Head of the Publishing Department; and Lina Paukštė, Head of the Communication and Marketing Department. At the National Gallery of Art we thank Lolita Jablonskienė, Chief Curator; Giedrius Gulbinas, Head of Exhibitions; Goda Aksamitauskaitė, Curator of Public Programs; Ieva Mazūraitė, Head of the Department of Information and Communication, and staff members Eglė Juocevičiūtė and Ernestas Parulskis; and Eglė Nedzinskaitė, Austėja Tavoraitė, Renata Mažeikaitė, and Povilas Šnaras in the Education Center. We offer our great appreciation to the exhibition architect, Mindaugas Reklaitis, and graphic designer, Laura Grigaliūnaitė; Ona Lozuraitytė and Petras Išora, exhibition architects; Kristijonas Gukauskas, intern; and many others.

At the Jewish Museum, New York, we thank Claudia Gould, Helen Goldsmith Menschel Director; Darsie Alexander, Susan and Elihu Rose Chief Curator; Kristina Parsons, Leon Levy Curatorial Assistant; Swagato Chakravorty, Blanksteen Intern; Saga Beus and Emily Stein, Curatorial Interns; staff members Elizabeth Abbarno, Lyndsey Anderson, Sabina Avanesova, Ruth Beesch, Nelly Silagy Benedek, Taylor Catalana, Allison

Curran, Will Fitzgerald, Collin Garrett, Chris Gartrell, Amelia Kutschbach, Julija Lazutkaite, Julie Maguire, Yael Miller, Jonah Nigh, Julie Maguire, Val Ognev, Jennifer Roberts, Anne Scher, Yeliz Secerli, Matthew Shattuck, Eve Sinaiko, Daniela Stigh, Sarah Supcoff, Aviva Weintraub, and Jenna Weiss; and the exhibition designers Jaffer Kolb and Ivi Diamantopoulou of New Affiliates.

The curators express personal gratitude to Vilma Levickaitė, Mary Frank, President, and her Co-Chair Mark Renton of the Parrish Art Museum, Rob Davis, Jane Hait and Justin Beal, Eleanor Cayre, and Marty and Rebecca Eisenberg for their support, guidance, and friendship. Above all, we thank each other for a collaboration that, in the spirit of Jonas Mekas, offered insights and delights in equal measure.

Inesa Brašiškė, Lukas Brasiskis, and Kelly Taxter
Curators

INTRODUCTION
Jonas Mekas Expanded

Inesa Brašiškė, Lukas Brasiskis, and Kelly Taxter

This publication marks the first survey exhibitions of the poet, filmer, and institution-builder Jonas Mekas in both his native Lithuania and his adopted hometown of New York City. *Jonas Mekas and the New York Avant-Garde* at the National Gallery of Art, Vilnius, and *Jonas Mekas: The Camera Was Always Running* at the Jewish Museum in New York bridge the spatial and temporal coordinates of Mekas's life. They reveal a circuit of consequential friendships and collaborations, and shed light on the entanglement of his art, organizational work, and critical voice. Perhaps most profoundly, this book binds together the two places Mekas called home, elucidating the connectivity of exile and reinvention, longing and creativity that propelled him.

Jonas Mekas arrived in New York City on October 29, 1949, with his younger brother, Adolfas. Penniless and war-weary, the two men nonetheless swiftly integrated into the city's thriving counterculture. Jonas became a prolific moving-image artist and central organizer within the avant-garde community, and a visionary maker and promoter of American independent film. Alongside—and often at the expense of—his creative work, he united and stabilized the experimental film community.

Mekas's lifelong commitment to artistic and cultural labor outside the mainstream brought together and forged creative alliances among generations of filmmakers, artists, and institutions, and an extensive network of family, friends, and colleagues emerges across his oeuvre, testifying not merely to his central position within the New York art world but also to the rich cultural fabric woven together by his life and work.

His contributions were many and lasting: in 1954 Mekas cofounded *Film Culture*, the first journal devoted to what he defined as the New American Cinema; in 1958 he began writing "Movie Journal," the first film-review column in the *Village Voice*; in 1961 he helped to establish the New American Cinema Group with other New York artists and filmmakers, including Shirley Clarke, Andy Warhol, and Jack Smith; in 1962 he cofounded the Film-Makers' Cooperative, a new distribution channel for experimental film; in 1964—under the auspices of the Coop—he initiated the Film-Makers' Cinematheque, a screening series hosted by a succession of independent theaters and cultural institutions throughout the city, including, between 1968 and 1970, the Jewish Museum; and in 1970 he opened the first iteration of Anthology Film Archives, the first and still leading institution for avant-garde cinema in the United States.

Mekas's primary artistic contribution was the "diary film," an intensely personal idiom that emerged from his extensive journals and poetry. Like many émigrés after World War II—and for so many across the globe today—he was profoundly marked by the refugee experience: the

1 *Walden* premiered at New York's Elgin Theater on December 20, 1969.

loss, memory, and yearning for a home he permanently left behind in 1944. Through his entwined forms of first-person accounting, Mekas centered his outsiderness and upturned his marginalized status as a displaced person, then immigrant, and finally artist. He began filming in 1950, not yet sure what he wanted to achieve but committed to the act itself, using the camera as a tool to fight against the wrenching loneliness of exile and to resist the violent erasures of being "other." He emerged as a filmmaker in 1964 with the release of *The Brig*, which won the grand prize for Best Documentary at that year's Venice Film Festival. But it was *Walden (Diaries, Notes, and Sketches)*, which premiered in 1969, that introduced his signature style. In *Walden*, comprising footage shot between 1964 and 1968, as in his subsequent diary films, Mekas eschews both linearity and hierarchy, instead presenting a churning whirlpool of times past and present; places urban and pastoral; quotidian moments and watershed events; family members, cultural icons, and public figures. Mekas seamlessly orchestrates collisions of disparate material, suggesting a radical interconnectedness that allows for even small and seemingly inconsequential moments to change the course of history.

During his seventy-year career, Mekas made more than one hundred films and videos, amassing footage that was both a record of his life and a resource for his art. *As I Was Moving Ahead Occasionally I Saw Brief Glimpses of Beauty*, Mekas's last 16mm film, completed in 2000, was edited from reels that spanned forty years. *Requiem* (2019), his final work, contains material recorded for over a decade. These works are profoundly concerned with the passage of time. Their flickering rhythms destabilize continuity and gesture toward the contingent nature of reality, identity, and belonging; altogether, his is a fundamentally immigrant cinema. Kelly Taxter delves into this notion and draws on contemporary theories about trauma and exile to investigate an interesting paradox in Mekas's work; in her essay, she proposes that while he invoked his exilic narrative to express an unquenchable, existential loss that he carried his entire life, his forced flight—its upheavals, disruptions, and losses—allowed him to evolve as an artist.

The exhibition *Jonas Mekas: The Camera Was Always Running* at the Jewish Museum, curated by Kelly Taxter, is centered on the notion of displacement, how it manifests aesthetically and conceptually in Mekas's work and extends to its reception. His diary films are at the heart of this exploration, a focus that strives to elucidate the particular ways he crystallized the stuff of lived experience. Drawing on Mekas's own structural logic, multiple screens each present a chapter from a single work. For example, the six chapters that constitute *Walden* run simultaneously across six screens. In the program notes for its premiere, Mekas wrote, "This film being what it is, i.e. a series of personal notes on events, people (friends) and Nature (seasons)—the Author won't mind (he is almost encouraging it) if the Viewer will choose to watch only certain parts of the work (*film*), according to the time available to him, according to his preferences, or any other good reason" (see pages 168–69).[1] Thus he grants the viewer license to enter and exit his film at any point (which also intuits a

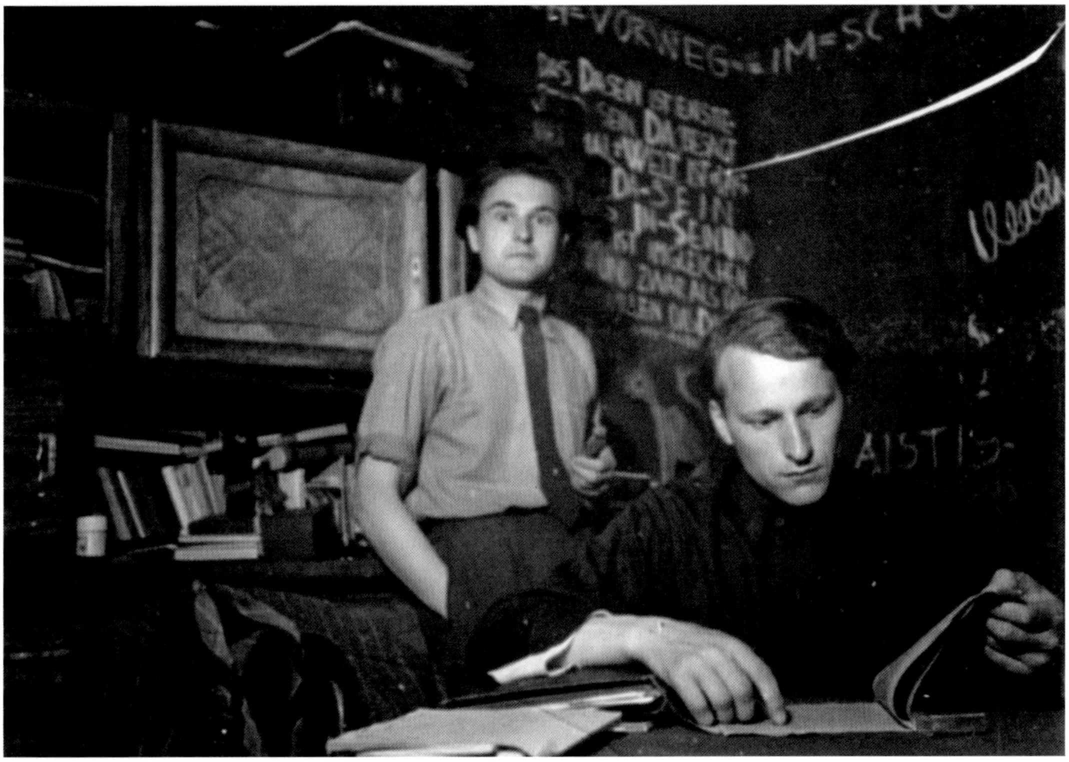

Jonas and Adolfas Mekas, Kassel/Mattenberg D.P. camp, 1947 or 1948.

not-so-distant future when filmmakers would screen their works in exhibition spaces rather than cinemas). And he makes plain that a consciousness of time is fundamental to his work.

As Mekas suggested on multiple occasions, the diaristic content and idiosyncratic, fragmentary form of his films were a result, at least to some extent, of a *lack* of time. A diary entry dated November 29, 1966, encapsulates his busy schedule:

8:15AM	Session with G. Maciunas at the Co-op re. Film Culture, Mixed Media catalog, etc.
9:30–12:30	Working on the Mixed Media catalog
12:30PM	Co-op—splicing titles to the AMERICA TODAY program; other business
2:30PM	Press screening of AMERICA TODAY, at the Tek. Arrangements made, contracts signed with Ackerman for the Rendezvous theatre for Chelsea Girls
5:30PM	reception for Ledoux at the Museum of Modern Art (meeting about money in Museum's back room, Shirley, Louis, Schectman, myself, Storm)
7:30PM	Back at the Tek advertisement prepared for the Chelsea Girls
12:30AM	back home

The exhibition *Jonas Mekas and the New York Avant-Garde* at the National Gallery of Art, Vilnius, curated by Inesa Brašiškė and Lukas Brasiskis, looks at Mekas's work in the expanded sense. It surrounds Mekas's filmic corpus with his critical writing, curated programs, institutional paperwork, and other archival ephemera, situating his films and videos alongside his central role in creating and maintaining infrastructure dedicated to advocating, producing, distributing, promoting, and preserving the filmic avant-garde. Mekas's organizational impulse—work that both drove him crazy *and* kept him going—falls within an alternative arts movement that sprang up across New York in the postwar years. Artist-run spaces, groups, and cooperatives constituted a new cultural and social sphere, set up in reaction against mainstream institutional structures and official cultural politics. In deploying both his art and his intellectual and often bluntly administrative labor to build and lead multiple organizations, Mekas fostered new habits of looking at film as an art form.

To look at Mekas's *work* in the expanded sense is also to follow the threads of innumerable personal and professional connections, friendships, and collaborations. An important part of the Vilnius exhibition is a selection of films and videos by other avant-garde filmmakers and artists, including Marie Menken, Andy Warhol, Ken Jacobs, and others, that captures the radical spirit of the invigorating milieu in which Mekas moved from his early days in New York, and that he was so instrumental in encouraging.

And so the long list of his projects must be seen in tandem with his explorations of cinematic style and meaning, beginning with the first event he organized, at Gallery East in October 1953. The next year, together with Adolfas Mekas and a fellow filmmaker, George Capsis, he initiated Film Forum, a group for the advancement of the art of film. Gradually, Mekas became an opinionated observer and commentator, and with his brother began publishing *Film Culture* magazine in 1954. He soon joined the *Village Voice* as a staff film critic. The next decade marked Mekas's full embrace of the avant-garde spirit, sealed by the establishment of the Film-Makers' Cooperative and the Film-Makers' Cinematheque. By the mid-1960s, Mekas's loft became a headquarters for these converging activities, a sleepless hub frequented by filmmakers and artists alike. His purchase in 1979 of a defunct courthouse on Second Avenue in downtown Manhattan as the permanent home of Anthology Film Archives was the culmination of these efforts.

Mekas's artistic and professional approach took shape while in relation to other people. As Ed Halter points out in his contribution to this volume, Mekas advocated for a social and collective practice of cinema in a double sense: as a shared viewing experience and as a matrix of personal relationships that helped him to sustain the independent, anti-institutional, and antisystemic cultural avant garde. Therefore, to look at Mekas's *work* in the expanded sense is also to follow the threads of innumerable personal and professional connections, friendships, and collaborations.

This publication acknowledges Mekas's connection to the emergent interdisciplinary art scene, in which experimental theater, music, and dance merged with elements of sculpture, painting, and drawing within the context of live performance. Melissa Ragona details how Mekas borrowed experimental composition techniques from John Cage and the avant-garde sounds of John Cale's drone-based music. Mekas used the sound of his own voice—the ever-present narrator—to both underscore and complicate notions of identity. Mekas's collaboration with the Living Theatre, discussed in Andrew V.

2 *Village Voice*, June 3 and November 11, 1965.

Uroskie's essay, further elucidates his broader scope of interest. Showcasing the unconventional documentation of the Living Theatre's performance of *The Brig*, Uroskie highlights Mekas's interest in developing novel aesthetic forms, establishing new norms of exhibition and spectatorship, and, ultimately, facilitating the critical discourse surrounding late modernist art. To describe the unorthodox spirit thriving in the 1960s and 1970s art world and its relation to the medium of film, Mekas coined the term "new American cinema" and was at the forefront of organizing the first New Cinema Festival, a series of multimedia events in New York. The festival featured genre-bending works by Stan VanDerBeek, Nam June Paik, La Monte Young, Robert Rauschenberg, Claes Oldenburg, Robert Whitman, and others that Mekas defined as "new uses of cinema" that "dissolved the edges of this art."[2]

Finally, the biographical, creative, and administrative milestones of Mekas's long career are marked and contextualized in a timeline that sketches the interwar political history of Lithuania, offering insight into the conditions under which Jonas and Adolfas were compelled to flee their home. The brothers' years as displaced persons, between 1944 and 1949, are traced through their movements from one refugee camp to another and the creative work they undertook while stateless and homeless, underscoring the fierce optimism and growing commitment to the arts that ultimately led them to New York City. Beginning with his arrival in Manhattan in October 1949, Jonas's development as a filmmaker and institution-builder is plotted out to intersect with the emergence of avant-garde cinema and the individuals essential to its development. The social and political climate of the 1960s and 1970s that accompanied these beginnings—the civil rights movement, the Vietnam War, the women's liberation movement—is not explicitly present, but its energy, tragedies, and triumphs were key to Mekas's antiestablishment and anticapitalist ethos and that of the creative avant-garde.

The accounting ends with Mekas's death on January 23, 2019, as he was editing his last work, *Requiem*. Over the course of that video's one hour and twenty-four minutes, we see a barrage of flowers: the trees and community gardens that surrounded his home in Clinton Hill, Brooklyn, and the East Village neighborhood around Anthology, as well as vast fields of wildflowers across Europe. This swing between the urban and pastoral is quintessential Mekas, who always had one foot in New York City and the other on the grounds of his childhood farm in Semeniškiai. Brutal, tragic images interrupt these movements, pictures that tell the story of the twentieth—and now twenty-first—century's wars, humanitarian and climate crises, and the massive losses and displacements that follow in their wakes. These brief instants collide with passages of great beauty, what Jonas called "moments of ecstasy." While his achievements were vast, they were not without struggle and hardship; yet, it was impossible to shake his commitment to friendship, celebration, and beauty. Like his voluminous oeuvre, this timeline, these essays, the archival ephemera, and the film and video stills collected here tell us that Jonas Mekas never ceased moving forward; he always—as he was known to say—kept going.

IN PRAISE OF HEAT

Ah, the summers of
New York!
Adrenalin of 95 degrees! 100!
Happy I walk the streets of New
World, panicking about the next
bill, on top of all the others—
banks, Ft.Lee, and the Fluxus artists
of last October, still not paid—
I don't open Jackson Mac Low's
letters—

ah, I need it all, it drives me mad
and keeps me going, these debts and these
constant emergencies, threatenings,
each worse than the other,
since . . . since winter 1953 on
Avenue A, Gallery East—not far from where
I met Lilly—
no, I didn't move far away, my friends,
not far at all—

and, I tell you, you get used to it all
and it's just another heat, another
day and 95 degrees and then maybe
goes up to 100 and everything seems to
about to crash or, say, melt, and Robert,
even Robert seems to lose his cool—I wish
he'd eat some chocolate, but he's forbidden to do
so—so we write some desperate irrational
letters and sit on phones and,
I tell you, it's very very hot and
we sleep horribly and sweat—it goes up to
105 and more, maybe 120.

Ah, no end to our summer heat, but that's
adrenalin we need to live, it's our way
of living, it seems, and if, imagine!
suddenly everything would get normal and
cool and suddenly no angry calls
and threats to turn off electricity
and phones, and close the Ft.Lee vault,
and Nat West, three months behind
by now in payments—and what's her
name, calling for her $75 from four
years ago—
the heat would drop to maybe 70
and we'd look around and listen in disgust:

ah, how normal, disgustingly, and how like
everybody else's
our lives have become, with no
threats and no crashes and no emergencies
and no crazy woman coming to our door about
the street lamps with no bulbs because we have
no three dollars to buy them—.

Ah! I like this heat! I think it's
reaching one hundred, it's going up,
I am all excited—the rats are leaving the
ship—they think it will sink—Ah, you
little ratties, you don't know we are the
super rats, Jack knew it!—and no hurricane
no heat will sink us!
It's in our blood, the disasters, shipwrecks and
supper heats & constant sinkings—it's
our very nature! So let's go to Sophie,
Julius, let's have a beer—later
we'll stop at Max Fish, to see Gloria
who just shaved her head & put her hair in
a jar of formaldehyde, in a Gallery—
Ludlow street, just a door from Gallery
East, anno 1953—
she serves us beer for free, and we'll
play pool, maybe—

"It hits you like a hot hair dryer, this heat,"
said Raimund. "This is what Peter said,"
he continued, as we were driving
in his happy jeep through the 110 degrees
of New York evening. "He said 'when
the lemmings are marching towards their mass
suicide, the avantgarde stays
in the back,'"
and we laughed. Ah, Peter, we wish you'd be
here with us this evening and
P.Adams, and Gozo, Istvan, Giuseppe,
Hermann, and DoDo Jin Ming—

So be calm, be calm, dear friends, be calm
in the very eye of
storm: we do not budge, we enjoy the sweat,
we like the scorching heat, we like
when it hits 100 and
more—

go, heat, go go go, rise up and up and
up—we are the junkies of the constant
heat! we are the Super Rats of
cinema—

go up, heat,
Go!

—JONAS MEKAS, JULY 1995

EPHEMERA

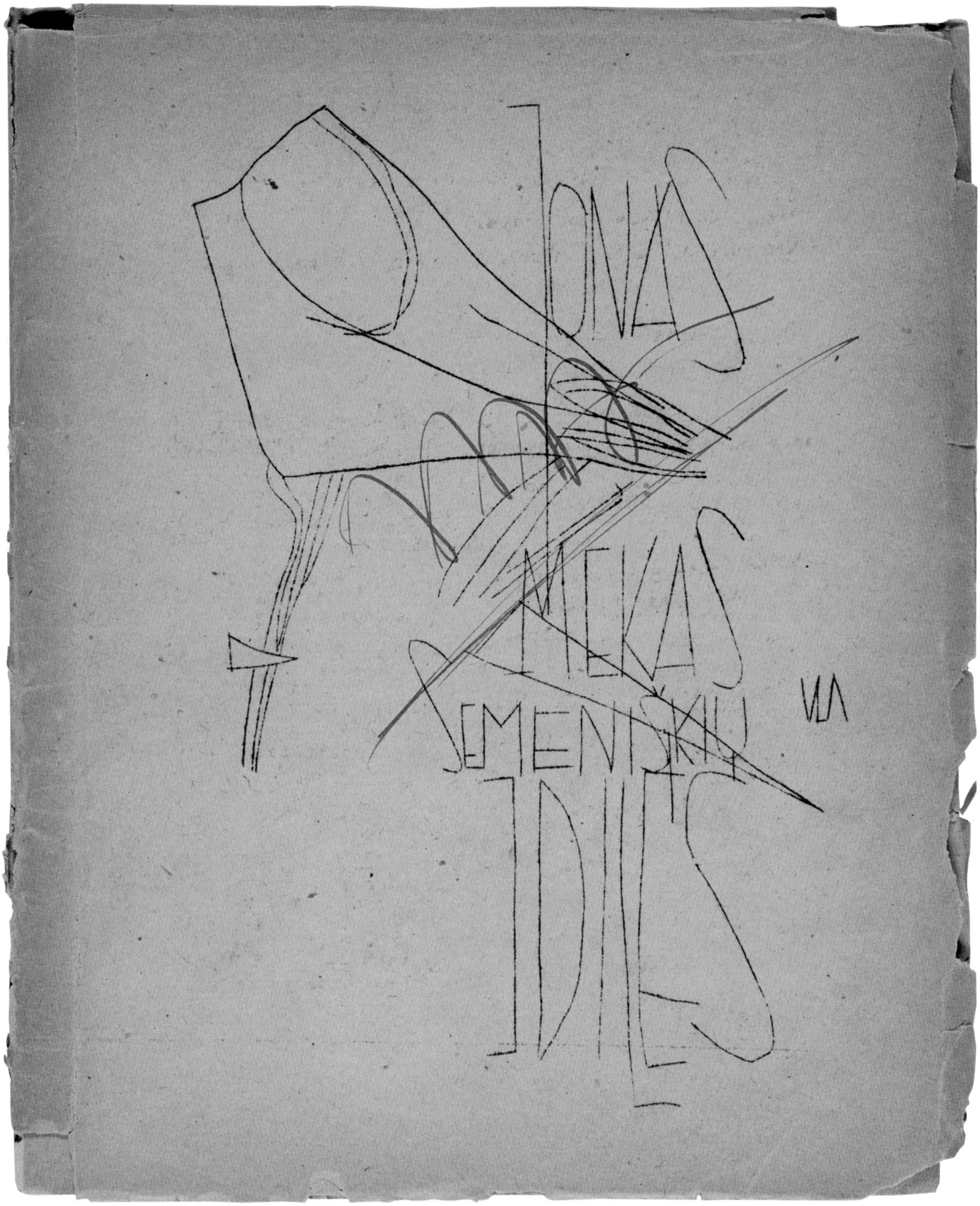

Cover of the first edition of *Semeniškių idilės* (Idylls of Semeniškiai), poems by Jonas Mekas, published while he was in the D.P. camp in Kassel, Germany, 1948.

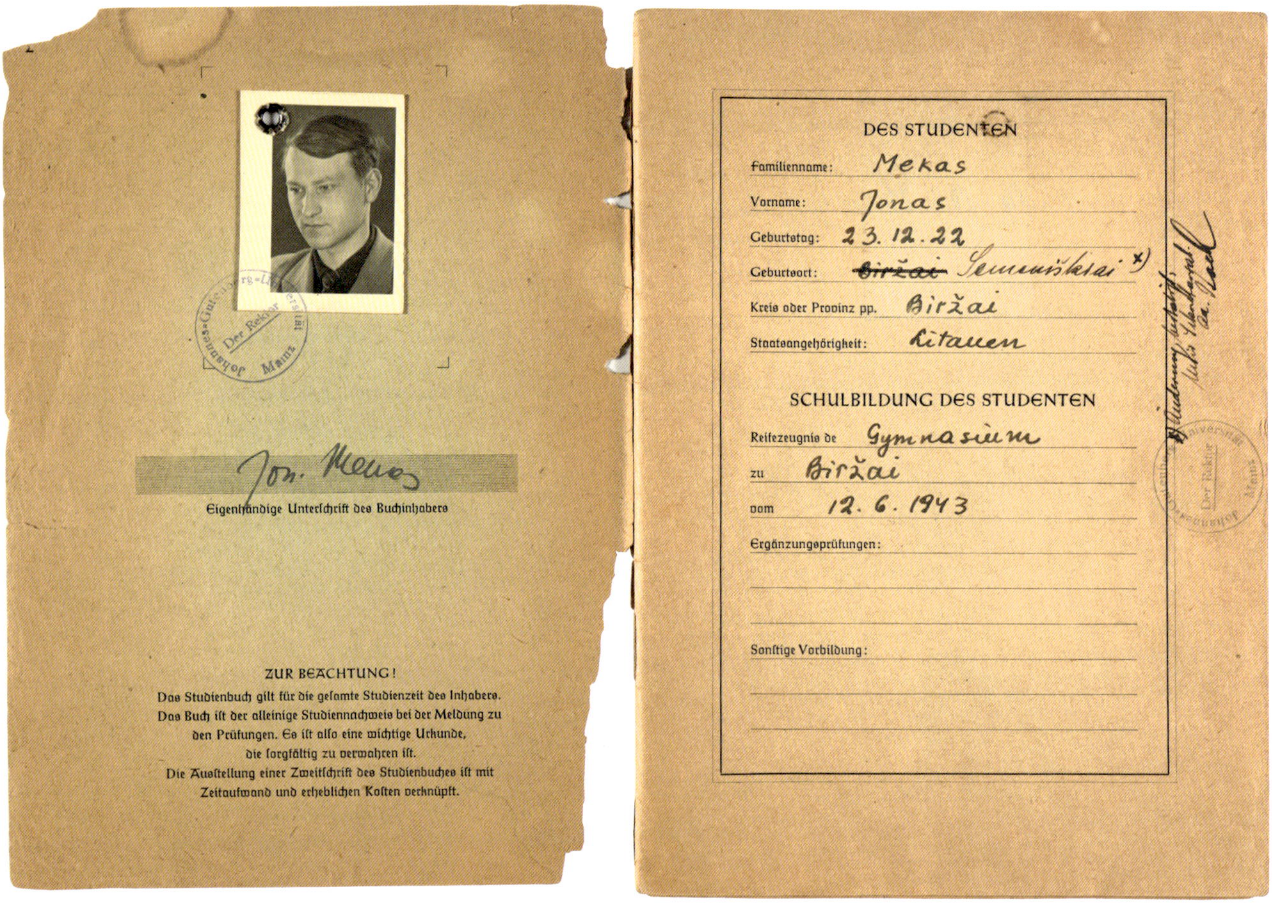

Jon. Mekas

Eigenhändige Unterschrift des Buchinhabers

ZUR BEACHTUNG!

Das Studienbuch gilt für die gesamte Studienzeit des Inhabers. Das Buch ist der alleinige Studiennachweis bei der Meldung zu den Prüfungen. Es ist also eine wichtige Urkunde, die sorgfältig zu verwahren ist. Die Ausstellung einer Zweitschrift des Studienbuches ist mit Zeitaufwand und erheblichen Kosten verknüpft.

DES STUDENTEN

Familienname: Mekas

Vorname: Jonas

Geburtstag: 23.12.22

Geburtsort: ~~Biržai~~ Semeniškiai *)

Kreis oder Provinz pp. Biržai

Staatsangehörigkeit: Litauen

SCHULBILDUNG DES STUDENTEN

Reifezeugnis de Gymnasium

zu Biržai

vom 12.6.1943

Ergänzungsprüfungen:

Sonstige Vorbildung:

Academic transcript of Jonas Mekas for the University of Mainz, issued in May 1946 and with entries until the summer of 1947.

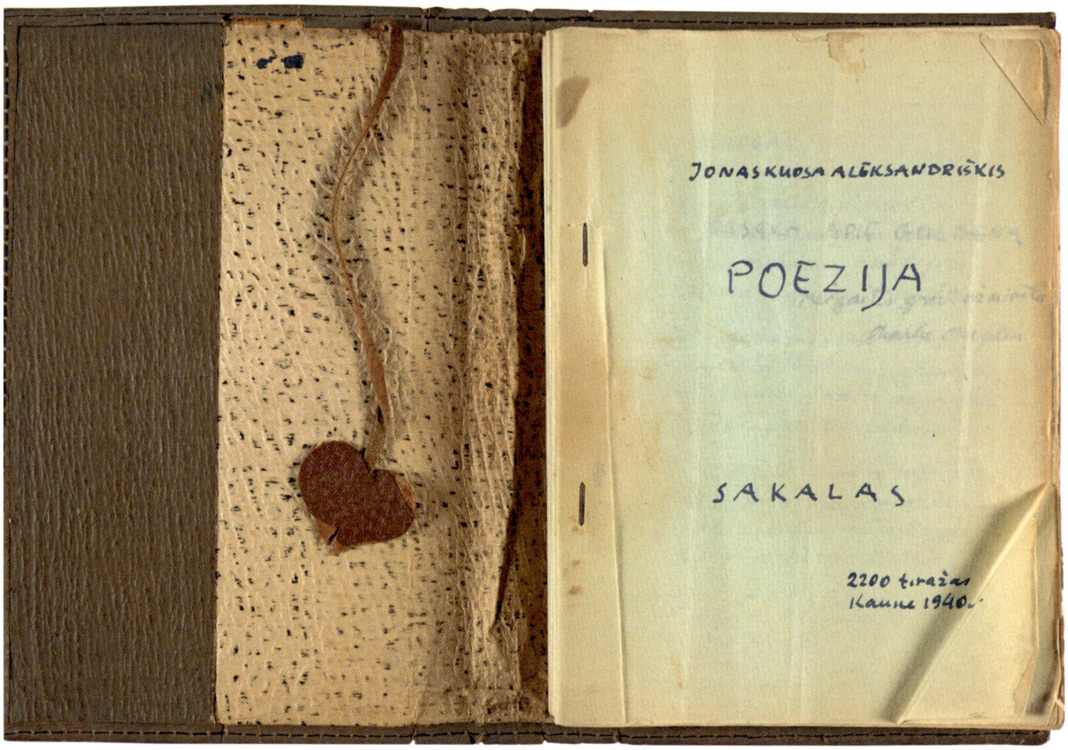

Notebook of poems by Jonas Kudsa Aleksandriskis, published in Kaunas in 1940, hand-transcribed by Jonas Mekas.

Jonas Mekas was a voracious reader and writer throughout his life, and largely self-taught. He attended primary and high school, but mostly frequented the library, where he hand-transcribed volumes of poetry in addition to penning his own diaries and verse.

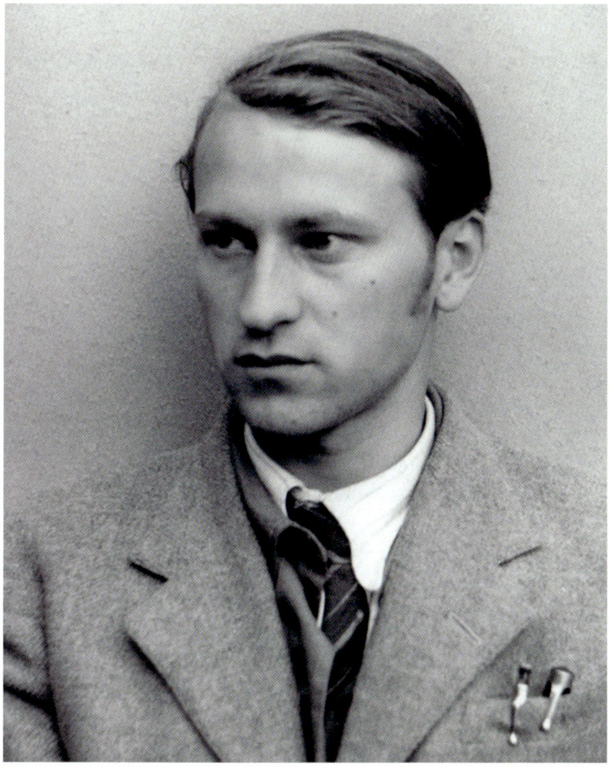

Jonas Mekas, ID photograph, Kassel, April 1946.

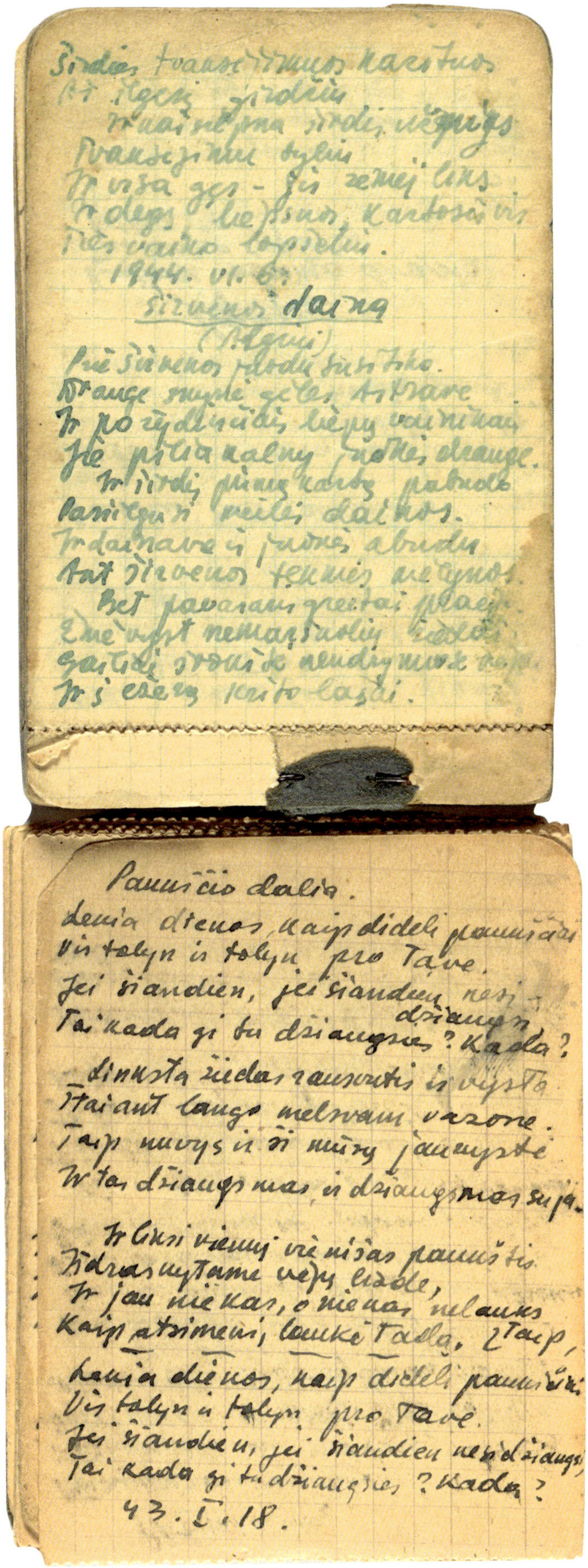

Poetry notebook of Jonas Mekas, c. 1943.

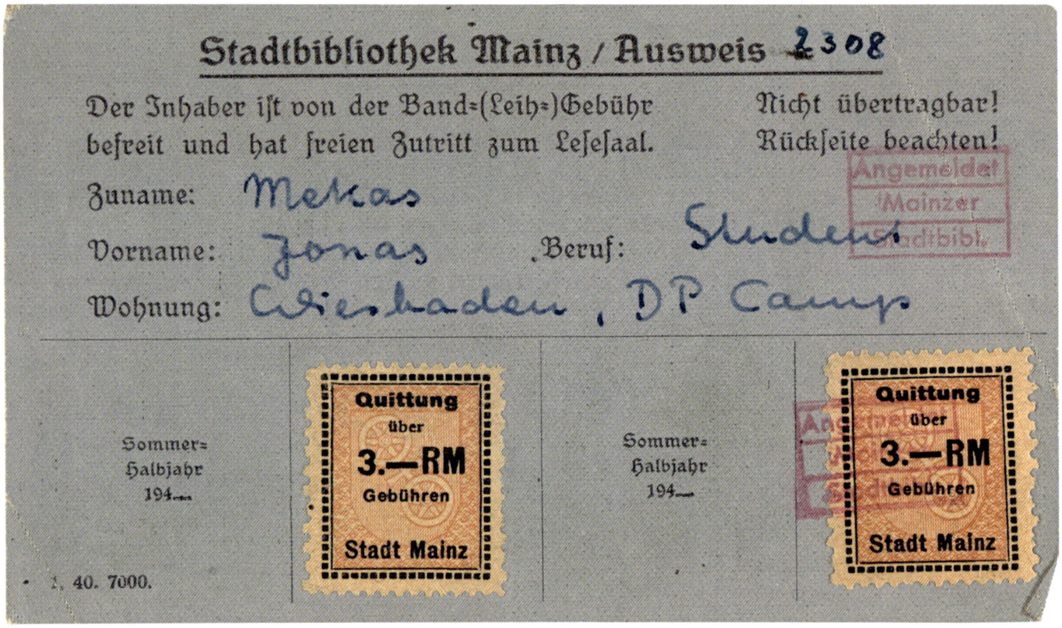
Stadtbibliothek Mainz / Ausweis 2308

Der Inhaber ist von der Band=(Leih=)Gebühr befreit und hat freien Zutritt zum Lesesaal.

Nicht übertragbar! Rückseite beachten!

Angemeldet Mainzer Stadtbibl.

Zuname: Mekas

Vorname: Jonas

Beruf: Student

Wohnung: Wiesbaden, DP Camp

Sommer=Halbjahr 194..

Quittung über 3.—RM Gebühren Stadt Mainz

Sommer=Halbjahr 194..

Quittung über 3.—RM Gebühren Stadt Mainz

1. 40. 7000.

Jonas Mekas's pass to the Mainz city library, listing his profession as student and his address as the D.P. camp in Wiesbaden, c. 1945.

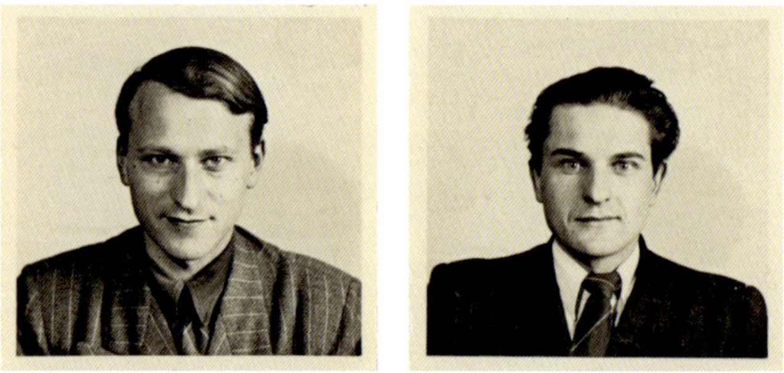

ID photographs of Jonas Mekas, 1948, and Adolfas Mekas, 1949.

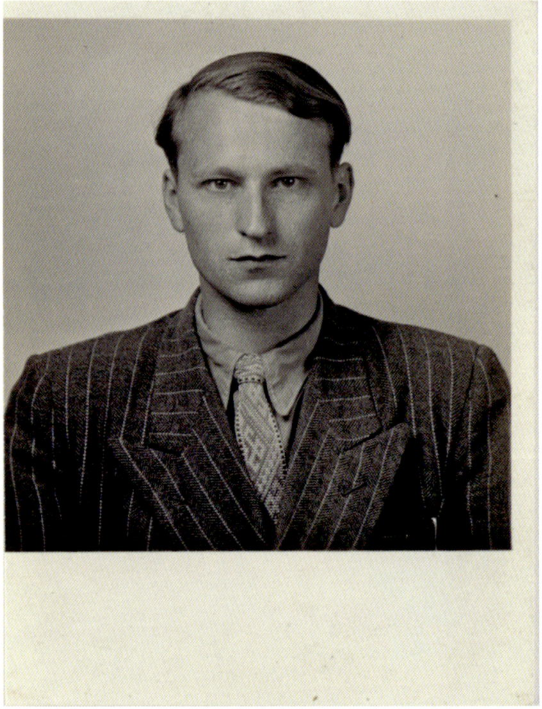

Jonas Mekas, 1949.

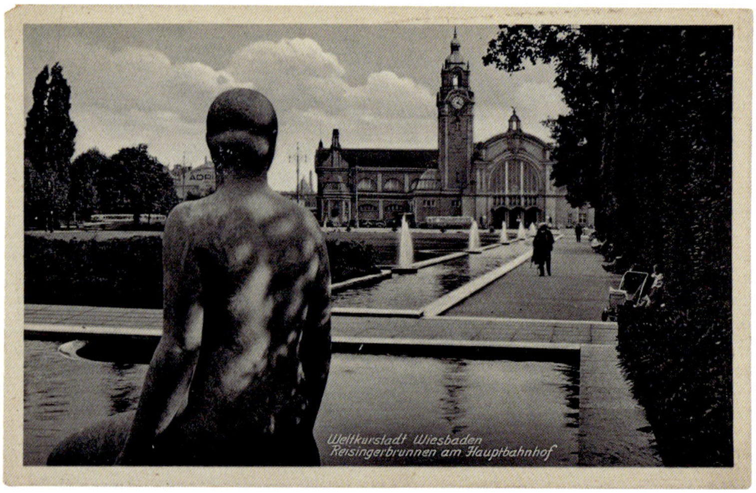

Postcard of Wiesbaden, Germany, site of a D.P. camp, undated.

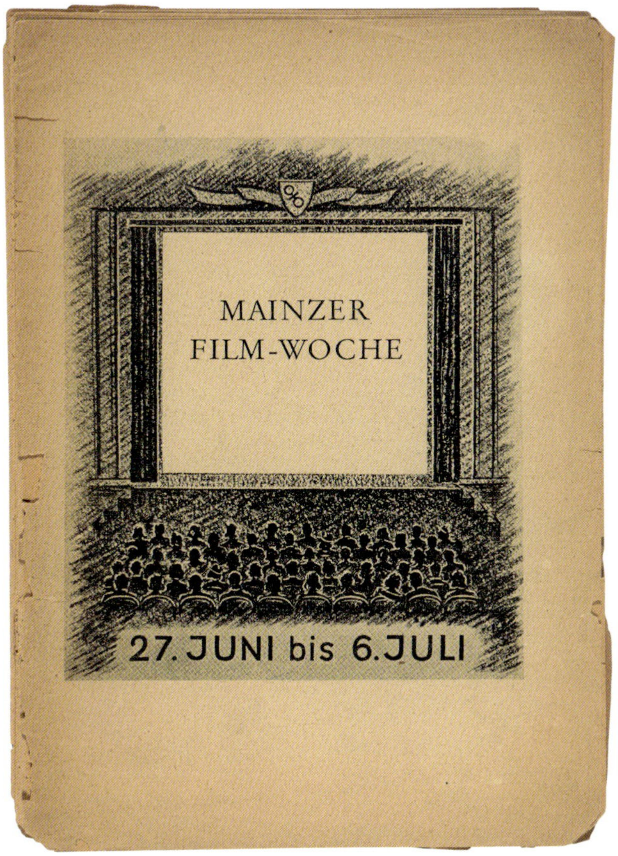

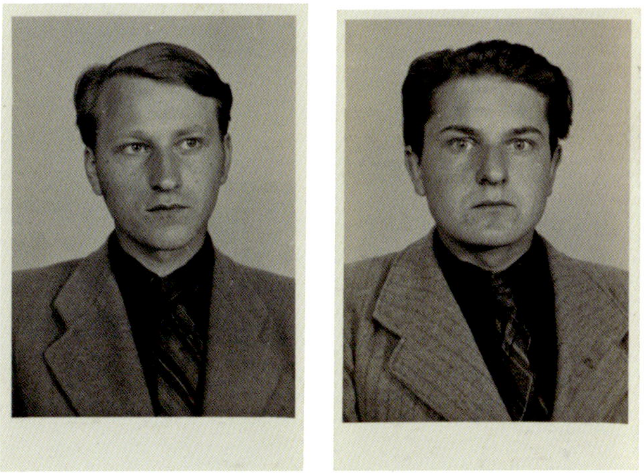

Jonas Mekas and Adolfas Mekas, Flensburg, 1945.

Jonas and Adolfas Mekas's migratory life between 1944 and 1949 is evidenced by their numerous ID photographs. In spite of his rootlessness, Jonas continued to pursue his academic and cultural education by attending the University of Mainz and frequenting film screenings near the camps.

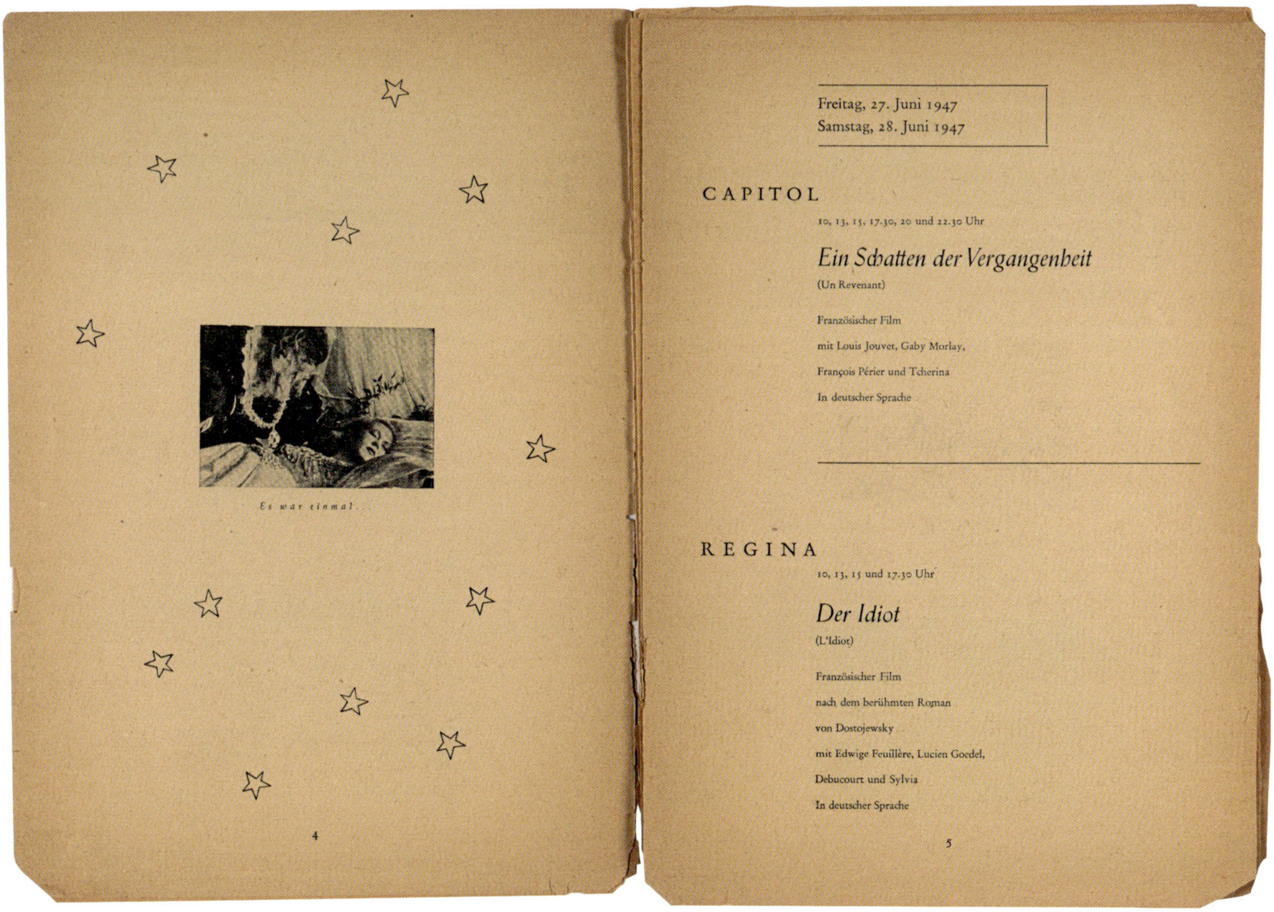

Cover and interior of program for the Mainz film festival, June 27 to July 6, 1947. Mekas called the event his "earliest introductory course into the art of cinema."

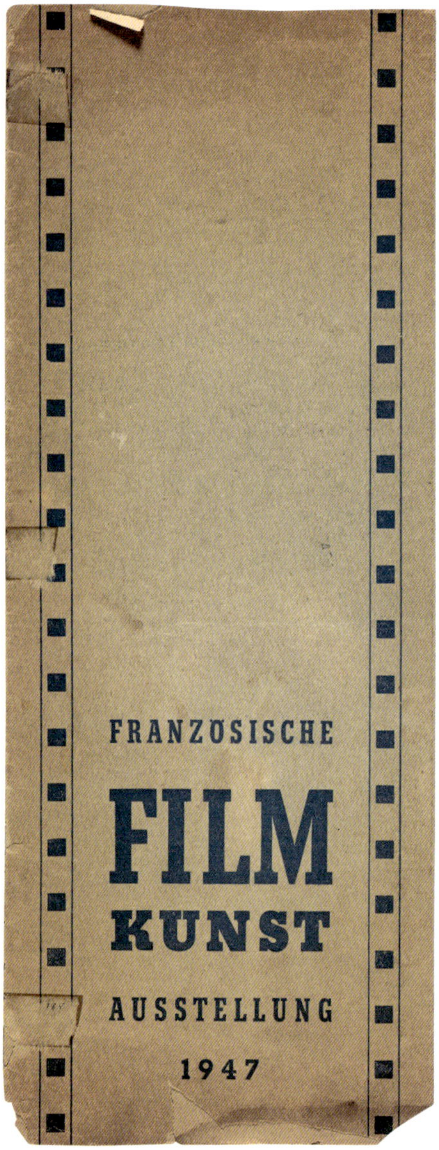

Program for an exhibition of French film, 1947. Jonas Mekas went to as many film screenings as possible while in the camps.

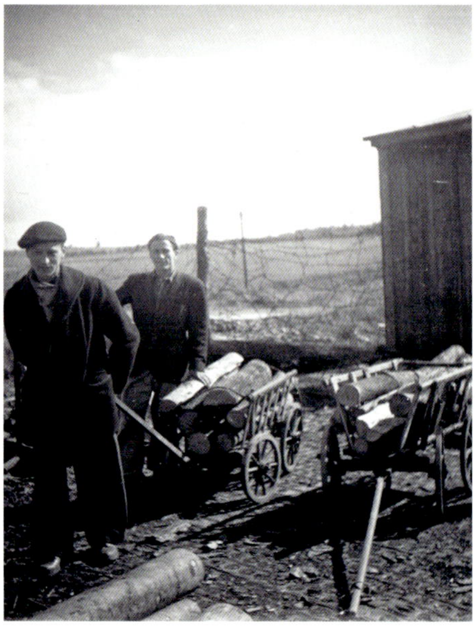

Jonas's caption: "Picking up the weekly firewood ration, Kassel/ Mattenberg Displaced Persons Camp, 1948," photograph.

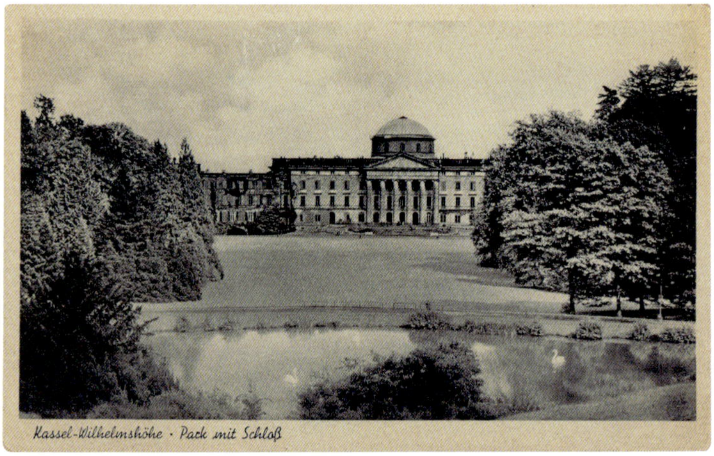

Postcard of Kassel, Germany, site of a D.P. camp, undated.

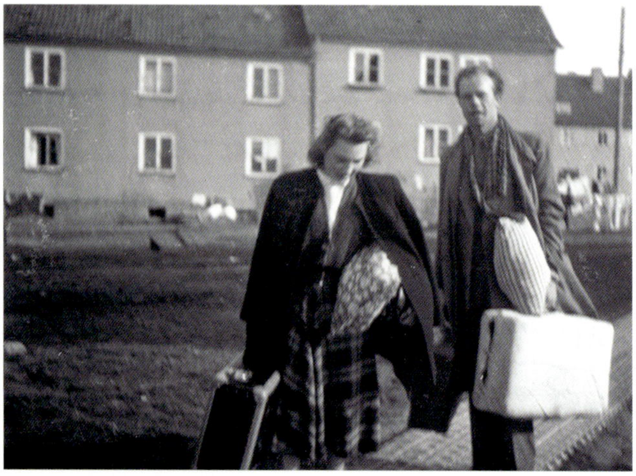

A couple with their luggage in a D.P. camp, 1945–49.

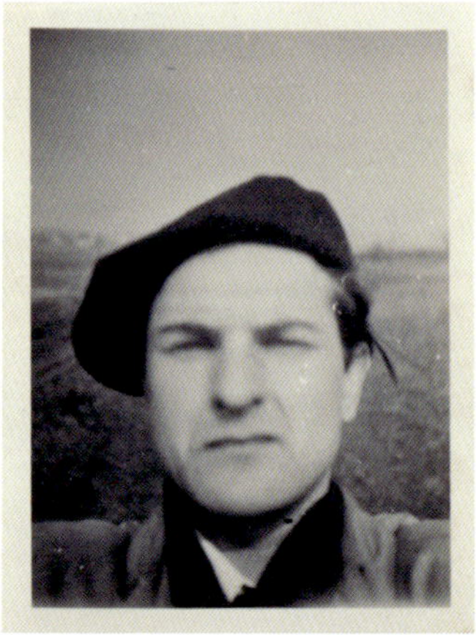

Adolfas Mekas, Germany, 1948.

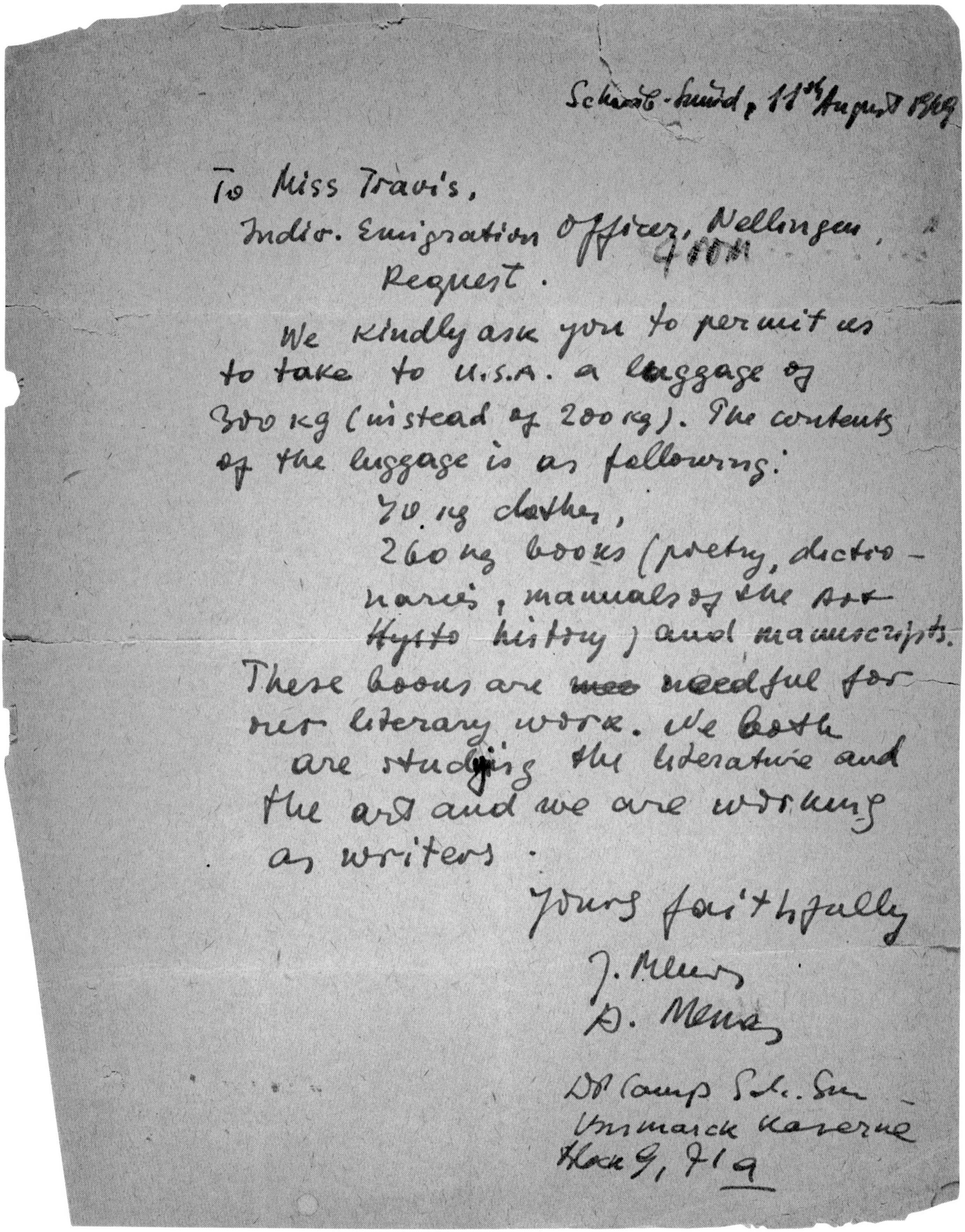

Schwäb.-Gmünd, 11th August 1949

To Miss Travis,
Indiv. Emigration Officer, Nellingen.
from
Request.

We kindly ask you to permit us to take to U.S.A. a luggage of 300 kg (instead of 200 kg). The contents of the luggage is as following:

70 kg clothes,
260 kg books (poetry, dictionaries, manuals of the art ~~Hysto~~ history) and manuscripts.

These books are ~~nee~~ needful for our literary work. We both are studying the literature and the art and we are working as writers.

Yours faithfully
J. Mekas
A. Mekas

DP Camp Sch. Gm
Bismarck Kaserne
Block 9, 71a

Letter from Jonas and Adolfas Mekas regarding their shipment of books to the United States, written in the Kassel D.P. camp, August 1949.

THE CAMERA WAS ALWAYS RUNNING

NOTES

0 Epigraph: Jonas Mekas, *I Had Nowhere to Go*, diary 1944–55 (Leipzig: Spector Books, 2017), 21.

1 Mekas made a distinction between being a filmmaker and a filmer; for him, a film camera was no different from a video camera or digital camera. He was committed to the act of filming, not the tools he used. Mekas remembered "22 families and 98 heads" living in his village. See ibid., 1.

The Camera Was Always Running: Exile and the Artist Jonas Mekas

Kelly Taxter

> You are welcome to read all this as fragments, from someone's life. Or as a letter from a homesick stranger. Or as a novel, pure fiction. Yes, you are welcome to read this as fiction. The subject, the plot that ties up these bits is my life, my growing up. The villain? The villain is the twentieth century.
>
> Jonas Mekas, diary entry, January 10, 1948

The poet, filmer, and institution-builder Jonas Mekas was born on December 24, 1922, in Semeniškiai, Lithuania, a farming village of fewer than one hundred people.[1] He died on January 23, 2019, in the Clinton Hill neighborhood of Brooklyn. Between his humble beginnings and his death, Mekas became a protagonist in the cultural history of the twentieth century. And as he tells the reader in his post–World War II diary *I Had Nowhere to Go*, that century—with its succession of wars and humanitarian crises—is the antagonist in his story.

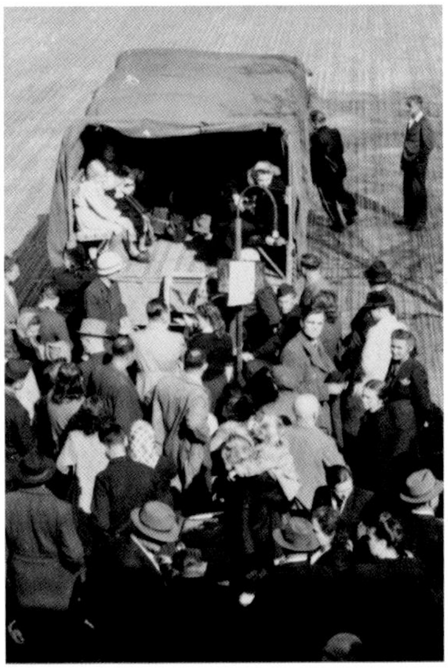

Jonas's caption: "We are being transported to another camp. Mattenberg, Kassel, 1949," photograph.

In his seminal essay *Reflections on Exile*, written at the turn of the third millennium, Edward Said defined the twentieth century, "with its modern warfare, imperialism, and the quasi-theological ambition of totalitarian rulers," as the age of the "refugee, the displaced person, mass immigration." In her essay *We Refugees*, written in the midst of World War II, Hannah Arendt argued that Jews displaced by forced flights across Europe were the "vanguard of their people," finally free to determine their own futures. More recently, Giorgio Agamben acknowledged the continued relevance of Arendt's essay and defined the refugee as "the sole category in which it is possible today to perceive the forms and limits of a political community to come." While Said—born in Palestine, raised in Egypt—supported the modern Palestinian struggle for independence, he was, like Mekas, firmly antinationalist, believing that true culture was pluralistic and diverse. In his essay, he aligns himself with generations of exiles and refugees who have shaped academic, intellectual, and aesthetic thought in the United States. But he also asserts that those achievements will never eclipse the "essential sadness" of exile, the "unhealable rift forced between a human being and a native place, between the self and its true home."[2]

Mekas, too, stressed how exile reverberated throughout his work.[3] When he first arrived in New York, with the pains of his recent past still fresh, he was driven to create. He fought the pangs of longing with recording, the voids of displacement by forging new networks and unorthodox definitions of home. As a young man, he wrote voluminous diaries and pastoral poetry, founded *Film Culture*—the first journal for American avant-garde cinema—and penned the unabashedly subjective and polemical "Movie Journal" column for the *Village Voice*.[4] Writing gave way to filmmaking, in forms influenced by poetry, literature, and diary writing, a practice he began as a young man and which defined the "diary film" genre that he brought to prominence. By the end of his life he had made more than 100 films and videos, as well as numerous photographic series, and published over 20 volumes of diaries and poetry.

Alongside his creative work, he was a tireless organizer and administrator: he built the foundations on which to present and stabilize the marginalized, experimental film community by establishing the New American Cinema Group; creating a new distribution channel in the Film-Makers' Cooperative; organizing screenings throughout the city under the auspices of the Film-Makers' Cinematheque; and finally, founding Anthology Film Archives.[5] Mekas traces his transformation from lonely émigré to New York artist in the film *Lost, Lost, Lost* (1976). During a series of scenes that mark a turning point between those two stages of his life, he explains his unquenchable need to film: "I have lost too much. So now I have these bits. That I have passed through."

Mekas arrived in the United States with the clothes on his back and nine crates of books.[6] He had fled Lithuania in 1944, accompanied by his younger brother, Adolfas. The family was not Jewish, but Jonas feared arrest by the occupying Nazis or the advancing Soviets—his artistic and clandestine resistance activities made him an enemy of both regimes. A well-connected uncle procured false papers for the brothers to attend university in Vienna, whence they planned to travel on to Switzerland. According to Mekas, their train was hitched to cars carrying Polish and Russian prisoners, and in consequence they were interned along with them in a Nazi forced-labor camp near Hamburg, Germany. In March 1945 they escaped and waited out the last weeks of the war on a nearby farm.

After the war, the brothers lived in displaced-persons (D.P.) camps in Elmshorn, Flensburg, Wiesbaden, and Kassel until 1949, when the International Refugee Organization found them jobs and housing in Chicago. They arrived in the United States on October 29. Landing at Manhattan's 23rd Street pier, they were struck by the city's vertical exuberance, its glistening skyscrapers a sharp counterpoint to postwar Germany's rubble-strewn landscapes.

2 Edward Said, "Notes on Exile," in *Reflections on Exile and Other Essays* (Cambridge, MA: Harvard University Press, 2000), 173; Hannah Arendt, "We Refugees," in *The Jewish Writings* (New York: Schocken Books, 2007), 274; and Giorgio Agamben, "We Refugees," *Symposium* 49, no. 2 (1995): 114. During his first years living in New York City, Mekas began to define his relationship to his Lithuanian roots. On July 20, 1952, he wrote, "No, I don't think I've ever been a good patriot. Neither is [my brother] Adolfas, in the way my Lithuanian friends are. Others, they love their country, their patria. But we two are attached only to Semeniškiai, to our little village, to the countryside and the people and the objects there. It has nothing to do with nationalism. We are regionalists." See Jonas Mekas, *I Seem to Live: The New York Diaries*, vol. 1, *1950–1969* (Leipzig: Spector Books, 2019), 50, 333.

3 Mekas was awarded a gold medal for his "devotion, passion, and selfless dedication to the rediscovery of the newest art" from the Philadelphia College of Art in 1966. He also delivered that year's commencement address, during which he described how his youthful idealism was "shook to the foundations" after witnessing the horrors of war. He told the audience, "It's really from this, and because of this, that I did what I did. I felt I had to start from the very beginning. I had no faith, no hope left. I had to collect myself again, bit by bit." "A Commencement Address by Jonas Mekas, Philadelphia College of Art 1966," https://docnomads.wordpress.com/2014/05/05/a-commencement-address-by-jonas-mekas-philadelphia-college-of-art-1966/.

4 Jonas and Adolfas Mekas cofounded *Film Culture* in 1954. Its contributors included P. Adams Sitney, Andrew Sarris, Annette Michelson, Stan Brakhage, Gregory Markopoulos, and others. In 1962, Mekas coined the term "New American Cinema" in the magazine to describe the emergence of a new, nonnarrative film genre opening up an entirely original direction, a "definite break with the traditional cinema in techniques and forms, in content and feeling." See Gerald R. Barnett, "Jonas Mekas Interview," *Literature / Film Quarterly* 1, no. 2 (Spring 1973): 103. Mekas wrote "Movie Journal" for the *Village Voice* from 1958 to the mid-1970s.

5 Mekas cofounded the New American Cinema Group (NACG) on July 14, 1961, with twenty-two New York artists, including Shirley Clarke, Ken and Flo Jacobs, Andy Warhol, and Jack Smith. The Film-Makers' Cooperative, a division of the NACG, was formed in early 1962 and is still in operation. The first iteration of Anthology Film Archives opened on November 30, 1970, at Joseph Papp's Public Theater. The institution, whose permanent home is a repurposed courthouse at 32 Second Avenue, was conceived by Mekas, Jerome Hill, P. Adams Sitney, Peter Kubelka, and Stan Brakhage as a museum dedicated to the art of cinema, guided by the sensibility of the avant-garde.

6 Mekas, *I Had Nowhere to Go*, 283. Mekas was primarily self-taught but took classes toward a degree at the University of Mainz while living in the D.P. camps.

Temporary foreign passport of Jonas Mekas, issued by the German Third Reich, listing his profession as worker and his address as Elmshorn, c. 1944.

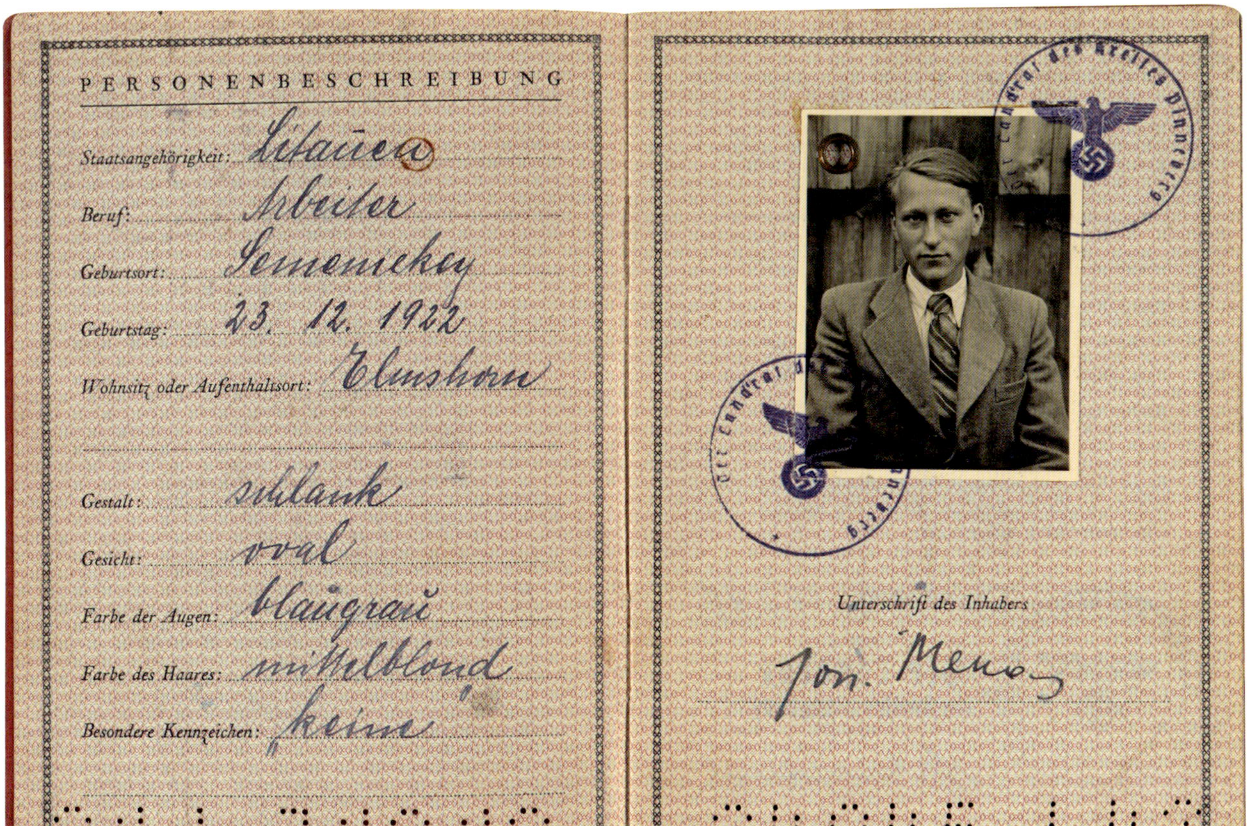

7 Drawing on his own experience, Mekas endeavored to capture the realities of immigrants, which he felt had been totally ignored in art. See Scott MacDonald, *A Critical Cinema 2: Interviews with Independent Filmmakers* (Berkeley: University of California Press, 1992), 92.

The palpable energy compelled the Mekases to stay in New York, and they settled in south Williamsburg, Brooklyn, among other Lithuanian refugees.

A few months later Jonas acquired his first 16mm film camera, a Bolex. The opening scenes of *Lost, Lost, Lost* show his wonder-filled encounters with it: he and Adolfas performatively goof around in their spare apartment, stare into its lens as though inspecting an alien. While these playful scenes unfold, Mekas narrates in a slow, melancholic voice: "O sing Ulysses. Sing your travels. Tell where you have been. Tell what you have seen. And tell the story of a man who never wanted to leave his home, who was happy and lived among the people he knew, and spoke the language. Sing how then, he was thrown out into the world." The film is made up of footage shot between 1949 and 1963, years that bookend Mekas's two arrivals—as an exile and an artist. Its first reel shows his initial attempts as a filmmaker, documenting the daily lives of his countrymen in Brooklyn, using a "fly on the wall" style.[7] He recorded their birthday parties and weddings, family dinners, and political meetings, but his disinterested camerawork suggests he was an onlooker, not a participant.

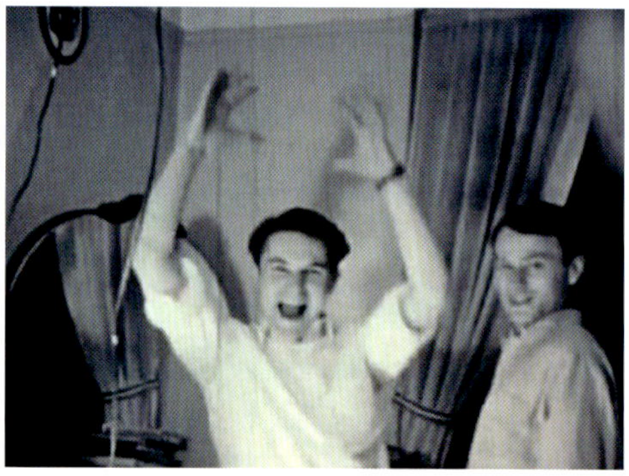

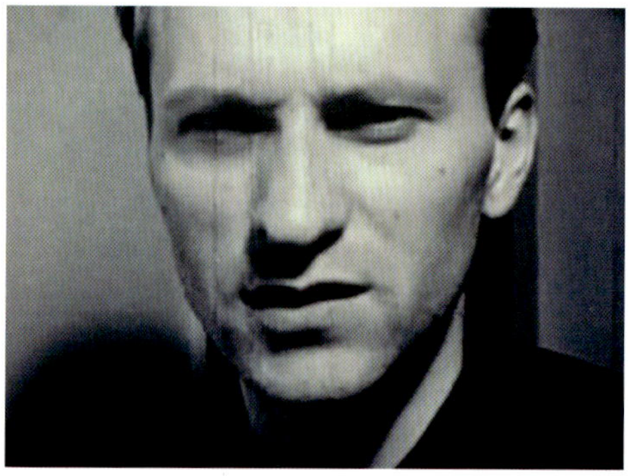

Two stills from *Lost, Lost, Lost*, 1976.

Lost, Lost, Lost was a retrospective project; with this work, Mekas was looking back on his earliest years in New York and his struggle to keep Lithuanian ties while breaking into New York's cultural scene. He comes to realize that the loss he feels most acutely is not of Lithuania as a nation but as a time, of his childhood and his intellectual awakening. These revelations came when his career was in full bloom. Seven years prior to releasing *Lost, Lost, Lost* he premiered *Walden (Diaries, Notes, and Sketches)* (1969), which introduced his diaristic style (see pages 91–101). Autobiographical yet lyrical, Mekas's diary films combine visuals, voice-over narration, and intertitles with the aim of invoking emotional and psychological states rather than straightforwardly documenting events. He captured scenes from his daily life in a style he referred to as "glimpses," a term expressing essence, momentariness, and incompleteness. He employed handheld camerawork and rapid-fire, often single-frame takes, and made frequent use of superimposition and so-called imperfections: soft focus, over- or underexposure, and lens flares. The diary films unfold in an improvisational, collagelike fashion, and juxtapose disparate times, places, and subjects. Intertitles help to orient the viewer, descriptively or poetically setting and summarizing scenes, while the voice-over narration adds a final historicizing and contextualizing layer, creating a dialogue between past and present, objective reality and subjective interpretation, artist and audience.

The emotional intensity of the diary films stands in sharp contrast to the neutrality of *Lost, Lost, Lost*, in which the camera

8 In addition to his trouble identifying with the exiled Lithuanian community, Mekas felt increasingly distanced from Europe—and its artistic legacies. He repeatedly blames his difficult working relationship with Édouard de Laurot (with whom he made *Guns of the Trees*, 1961) on the French filmmaker's "stubborn Europeanism." Mekas screened *Pull My Daisy* (1959) by the American Robert Frank for Laurot and explained, "I was postponing the screening. I knew that the film will mean nothing to Edouard. It was like showing a book to a horse. He is as stubborn in his Europeanism, and as smart, as a horse. The film went in through one end and came out through another, without having anything or doing anything, that's what he said. Only a bad taste in the mouth. That's what all America does to him, he said. Comes in and goes out. He gets ulcers from it." Furthermore, Mekas saw his embrace of the American avant-garde as the morally correct stance: "I tell you, that the dance, the music, the cinema which continue the perpetuation of old forms perpetuate also the old ideas, moralities of yesterday, forms and ideas which sustain the capitalism and wars—that these are immoral, poisonous. So don't talk to me about art without morality. The only art without morality is the art of yesterday: the art to which you devoted your lives and 99.99% of your magazines. You are part of the wax museum of horrors of the XX century." (Mekas, *I Seem to Live*, 247, 333.)

imposes a felt distance between the filmmaker and his subjects. Indeed, Mekas acknowledges his outsiderness halfway through the film: "I began to feel that I had been turning on one spot around my memories. I began to feel that if anything can be done for Lithuania, it can be done only by the people who live there. That the only way I may be useful to Lithuania is by building myself from scratch, from the beginning, and then giving myself back to it, back to Lithuania for whatever I am." The filmmaker then pivots from the Lithuanian community to New York City's burgeoning counterculture and his gradual immersion within it. He presents the beginnings of *Film Culture*, the Film-Makers' Cooperative, and his ever-increasing artistic circle, which included such luminaries as the Beat poets Allen Ginsberg and LeRoi Jones, and the filmmaker Shirley Clarke (see page 164). Still, Mekas conveys a wistful sorrow alongside this journey of discovery, a tension that entwines his achievements with loss. But a second, subtler paradox also pulses through this film: If Ulysses—whose story frames *Lost, Lost, Lost*—journeyed to heroically return home, Mekas left home so that he could triumphantly thrive elsewhere and "build himself from scratch." His life—like his film—may be understood in two parts.[8]

In her landmark study *Unclaimed Experience: Trauma, Narrative, and History*, Cathy Caruth defines traumatic experience as "not fully assimilated as it occurs." Mekas's obsessive recording, revisiting, and refashioning of the stuff of his life might have been a means to reconstitute and recapture something intangible, without which he felt fractured and incomplete. It might also have served another, more complicated function. Hamid Naficy, who has examined the work of filmmakers living in exile, including Mekas, proposes that the exile's most important journey is not finding a new "home" but fashioning a new identity. Following this idea, Mekas's trauma may be understood as both a crisis of returning *and* a process of becoming. After all, he championed and kept close company with Andy Warhol, who also arrived in New York City in 1949 and so significantly understood the power of persona. Mekas was a storyteller who put forward written and visual narratives about his life.

Still from Andy Warhol, *Screen Test: Jonas Mekas*, 16mm, black and white, silent, c. 4 min., 1966.

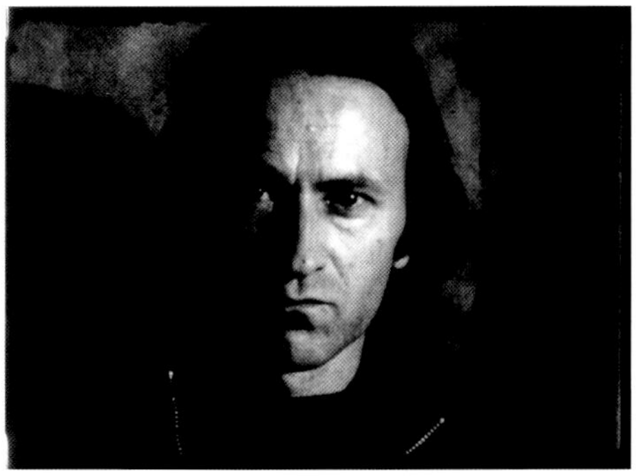

9 Cathy Caruth, *Unclaimed Experience: Trauma, Narrative, and History* (Baltimore: Johns Hopkins University Press, 1996), 5. Hamid Naficy, proposing a different relationship to exilic filmmakers' autobiographical work in *An Accented Cinema*, writes, "although their films are authorial and autobiographical, I problematize both authorship and autobiography by positing that the filmmakers' relationship to their films and to the authoring agency within them is not solely one of parentage but also one of performance. . . . In the best of the accented films, identity is not a fixed essence but a process of becoming, even a performance of identity. Indeed, each accented film may be thought of as a performance of its author's identity." See Naficy, *An Accented Cinema* (Princeton: Princeton University Press, 2001), 4, 6.

10 Michael Casper, "I Was There," *New York Review of Books*, June 7, 2018. While Casper's project of unearthing the long-repressed history of Lithuanian Jews is crucially important work, leveraging Mekas and his autobiography as a foil was misguided. For example, Casper reveals that the Soviet- and then Nazi-controlled newspapers in which Mekas published his poetry contained antisemitic propaganda. While Jonas's writing includes no trace of antisemitism, it nonetheless appeared in its proximity. Regardless, there had not been a free press since 1939, when the Soviets seized the country under the Molotov–Ribbentrop Pact. Mekas fled in 1944, well into the war and on the cusp of the Soviet invasion; Casper deduces that he feared the Soviets, attempting to diminish Mekas's role in the resistance to the Nazis while at the same time failing to acknowledge that the Soviet practice of mass executions was to be equally feared. Two million Lithuanians lingered for years in D.P. camps precisely because of their fear of Soviet retribution.

His diaristic forms rested on memory: the comingling of facts (the world he saw) and perceptions (how the world felt). That potent mix of seeing and feeling is not only a hallmark of Mekas's work but is precisely why it is so poignant. Thus, reinterpreting his autobiographical oeuvre as "a kind of fiction," which he allows the reader in *I Had Nowhere to Go*, may reveal other truths.[9]

In June 2018 the historian Michael Casper publicly challenged Jonas's autobiography in the *New York Review of Books*. Casper's focus is the history of the Holocaust in the Lithuanian provinces, places like Biržai, a small city where Mekas intermittently studied during the war. In his article, Casper accuses him of glossing over his proximity to the grim details of wartime Lithuania.[10] In August of 1941, in the forest that ringed Biržai, Nazis murdered 2,400 Jewish men, women, and children by gunfire. Many Lithuanians were willing collaborators in this brutal mass extermination; under the Soviet occupation they deeply resented Jews, who were able to open businesses and hold public office with the support of the oppressor. Nazi propaganda inflamed their anger into widespread, deadly animosity. Mekas welcomed Casper's many requests for interviews, but the article's title, "I Was There"—a refrain borrowed from *Lost, Lost, Lost*—implies a truth not told. Perhaps there are two versions of Mekas's story; however, borrowing from Caruth, they are not as Casper suggests, one shared and another concealed, but rather the story he was able to tell and the other that he *could not know*. In the wake of trauma, bifurcation is possible, a schism that, following Naficy's claim, may speculatively be understood as a gap in Mekas's life before and after his arrival in New York, between the first Mekas and the second one.

Jonas suggested such a break to Ina Navazelskis, with whom he spoke six months before his death. Their conversation is now part of the United States Holocaust Memorial Museum's oral history archive. Mekas explained to Navazelskis that he felt that the chaos

11 Jonas Mekas and Ina Navazelskis, "Oral History Interview with Jonas Mekas," filmed June 29 to July 1, 2018, Brooklyn, New York, United States Holocaust Memorial Museum, video, 4:16, https://collections.ushmm.org/search/catalog/irn619022. In the interview, Mekas said that his flight and subsequent displacement had forced him to jump from "a child to twenty-seven." Lithuania was annexed by the Soviets between 1939 and 1940, when Mekas was seventeen years old. He finally arrived in New York City when he was twenty-seven. In *I Had Nowhere to Go*, he explains how beginning school late because he was needed on his family's farm, and scrambling to catch up, was another kind of dislocation: "I have to work so much harder than my friends, Leo or Algis. They received a good, regular education, they grew up in the cities. My education was fragmentary, always in a hurry. My language—we didn't even speak the written dialect, we spoke a local dialect." Mekas, *I Had Nowhere to Go*, 142.

12 Ibid., 21. Then as always, Mekas clung fast to his identification as a poet and artist whose politics were bound up with everyday life. In his art, he proclaimed the power of beauty, creativity, friends, family, and conviviality. In his life, he demonstrated his anticapitalist ideology through a fierce commitment to art, artists, misfits, and the nonprofit institutions he nurtured—often to his own financial detriment. During an interview with Joseph Jon Lanthier on October 31, 2009, published in *Bright Lights Film Journal*, Mekas stated, "To me, real politics are those that have nothing to do with political systems or parties. . . . My politics are like those of the Beat Generation, or even hippies, the Woodstock Generation, or artists like Buckminster Fuller, John Cage. They changed society without politics, in a completely different way. They changed the style of living—the way people lived and behaved—with no violence, and no political parties." https://brightlightsfilm.com/film-and-film-and-film-an-interview-with-jonas-mekas/#.YDfxqy9h1VQ.

of war and his flight from home had forcibly ended his childhood. It was not the first time that he had articulated this interruption, which even during peacetime is a critical and complicated stage of development. Languishing in a displaced-persons camp on Christmas Eve (his birthday), 1947, Mekas wrote in his diary, "I am 25 years old so it would seem it's time to begin to walk more firmly, to live. But it all looks like first steps."[11] In his conversation with Navazelskis and in *I Had Nowhere to Go*, Mekas describes having an already split sense of self as a young adult. With a mix of confusion and regret, he explains that throughout his youth he paid little to no attention to his immediate surroundings or his family, but lived entirely immersed in books. Following this account, the loss and longing Mekas later suffered was not simply a casualty of war but was, in part, born of his own neglect. Even during wartime, when he actively took part in resistance activities, he struggled to understand the ramifications of his detachment. A day before he was apprehended, on July 19, 1944, he wrote, "I am a poet. . . . Let the big countries fight. Lithuania is small. . . . The only thing we can do, we, the small ones, is try to survive. . . . If you want to criticize me for my lack of 'patriotism' or 'courage'—you can go to hell! You created this civilization, these boundaries, and these wars, and I neither care nor want to understand you and your wars." Once arrested, he lamented, "Oh, how naïve we were! Even after all these years of war, we haven't really understood yet that THIS IS REALLY WAR."[12]

On the morning of September 11, 2001, Mekas went up to the roof of his loft in lower Manhattan with his video camera. He gathered there with his neighbors to see what was happening just a few blocks south, where the World Trade Center towers had been struck by two commercial airplanes. With his lens fixed on the smoking buildings, a woman off camera quips that the calamity will spark "a run" on the nearby high-end food market Gourmet Garage.

13 Mekas and Navazelskis, "Oral History Interview with Jonas Mekas."
14 This method was a form of in-camera editing, an economic as much as a formal decision. Mekas slowly captured a protracted amount of time on 100 feet of film, which was equivalent to roughly 3 minutes if recorded at the standard 24 frames per second. Not incidentally, the slowly rhythmic clackity-clack sound of this style of filmmaking is reminiscent of a typewriter, Jonas's other most important creative and administrative tool at the time.
15 Mekas, *I Had Nowhere to Go*, 125.

At that same moment, the south tower crumbles and her blithe comment transforms into piercing wails of distress as Mekas whispers, "I hope they managed to get some people out."

He recounted how he felt at that time to Navazelskis, confessing, "I did not react to the 9/11 event until I met some people who just managed to escape, or the firemen from SoHo where I live, then it became real." He spoke of his personal response as a way to explain why Lithuanians were slow to accept the murderous realities of the Second World War. Mekas felt that "Human beings are not made up personally to react to abominable events." Navazelskis asked, "Does it mean that when you had no real emotional response that you didn't care?" and he responded, "No, that you are not made physically—it's too big, too abstract, too big . . . it has to become more personal."[13] As Mekas suggests in his testimony, he may have struggled to close the gap between seeing/filming and understanding. In 2010 he made *WTC Haikus*, an atemporal collage of the iconic buildings culled from footage he had shot between 1975 and 1995. His World Trade Center material, like all his footage, was fundamentally a working archive. He never ceased to return to it, reorganize it, and historicize it; above all, he sought to understand his life through the moving images he captured.

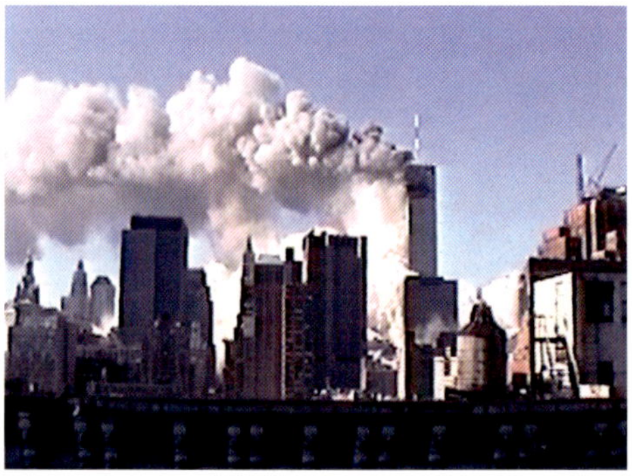

Still from *My 9/11 Footage*, video, color, sound, 40 min., 37 sec., 2001.

Whether labeled haiku or diary, Mekas's films are intentionally fragmentary and impressionistic; as he tells the viewer in *Walden*, "cinema is what happens between the frames." Caruth finds a parallel between traumatic experience and the style of literature it generates, which, she observes, is composed in "a language that defies, even as it claims, our understanding." Mekas often used his Bolex like a snapshot camera, capturing images in single frames to create staccato passages that quake with the gestural movements of the artist's hand and jump between subjects, places, and times, leaving the viewer to fill in the gaps.[14] These visual reshufflings, disconnections, and lacunae are only fortified by Mekas's voice-overs—the time between his recording of the footage on view and of the narration might be a few days or decades. Mekas's films are as rife with details as they are with cracks and fissures. His porous, open-ended construction allows his very personal material to skew toward the universal.

Mekas always presumed an audience for his work. He addressed the reader of his diary, assuming it would be published. In its pages he identifies himself as a poet, eschewing the call to sign up for placement in Canada, where "they are looking for tailors, shoemakers, professions like that . . . no requests for poets yet."[15] He spent days in the D.P. camp reading, writing, and discussing

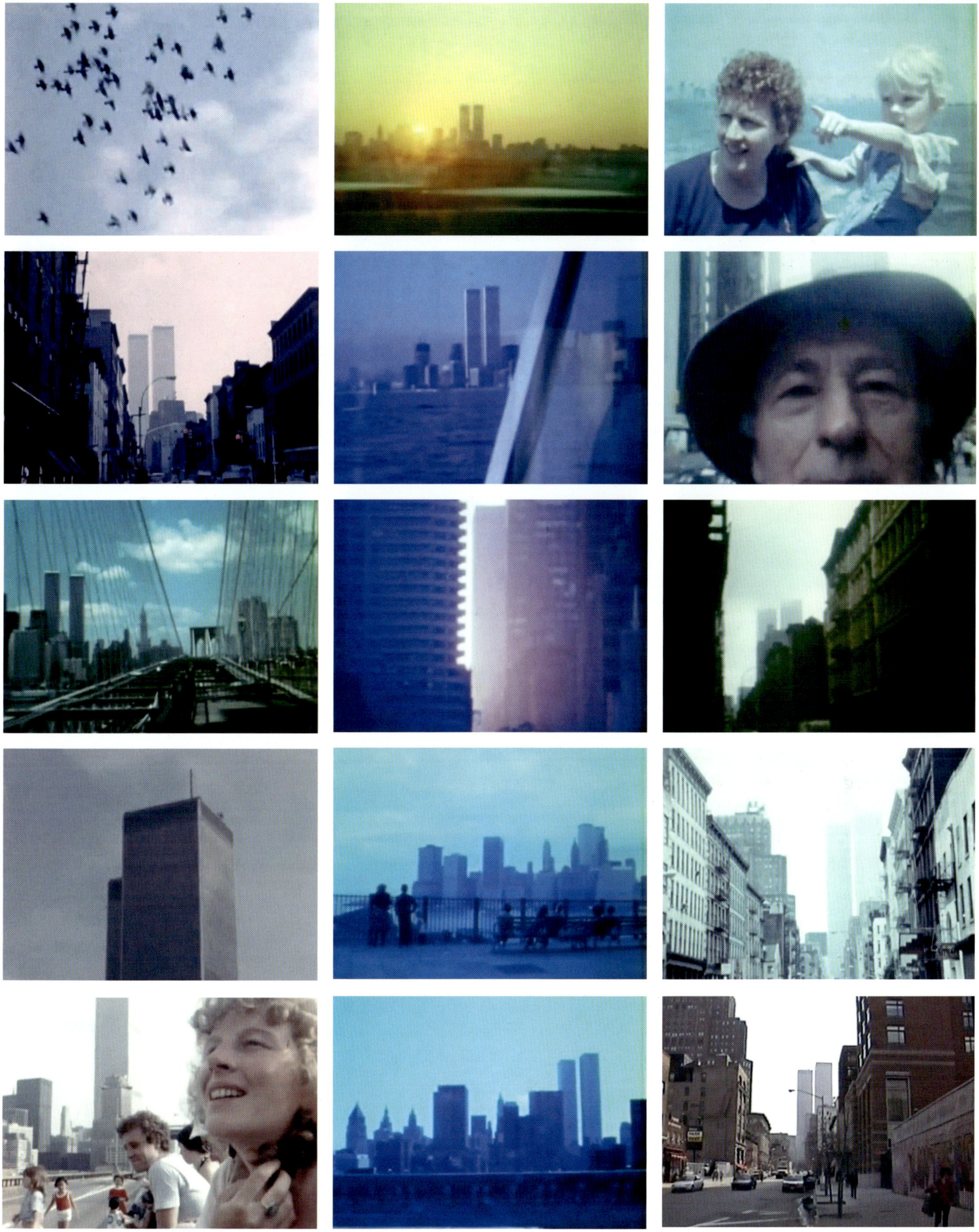

Stills from *WTC Haikus*, 16mm film transferred to video, color, sound, 14 min., 2010.

Still from *Walden (Diaries, Notes, and Sketches)*, 1969.

literature, seeing films, even publishing a literary journal that he called *Žvilgsniai* (Glimpses).

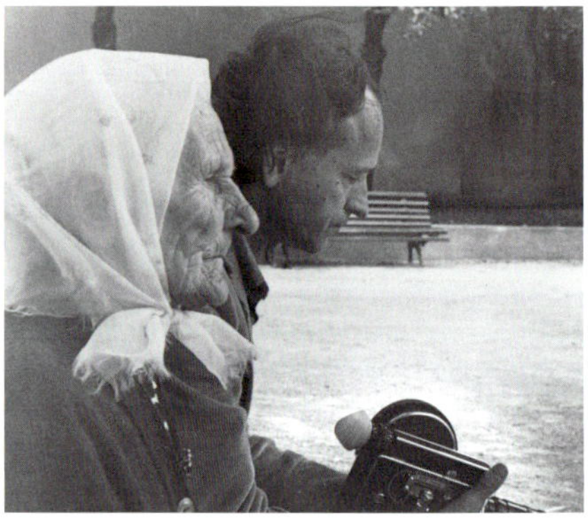

Jonas Mekas and his mother in Semeniškiai, Lithuania, 1971.

Years before Mekas arrived in New York, he was already moving away from his agrarian roots. He composed his first poem at age six, an oral improvisation about life on the farm that he ecstatically recited to his amazed father. His parents supported their young poet's creative pursuits. They always knew that he was destined to leave their small, rural life behind.[16] The demands of farming delayed Mekas's formal education, which he began at age nine. To catch up with his peers, he completed the equivalent of four years in one winter.[17] While in high school, he began distributing pamphlets that contained transcripts of BBC broadcasts—during the Soviet and Nazi occupations, there was no free press. The pamphlets were passed among intellectuals and played an essential role in organizing the resistance. Given Mekas's reticence and distaste for politics, it seems likely that the chance to associate with the intellectuals and artists who spearheaded those activities played a role in his involvement. The film curator and critic Jan-Christopher Horak probed this idea through a rereading of *Reminiscences of a Journey to Lithuania* (1972), which documents the artist's long-awaited return to Semeniškiai in 1971, twenty-seven years after he fled the country. Horak believes that Mekas survived nearly a decade of displacement between the D.P. camps and his first years in New York by clinging to his one stable identity—artist.

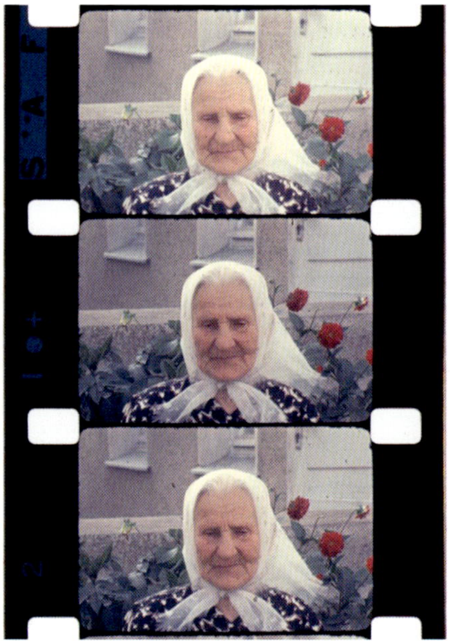

Three frames from *Reminiscences of a Journey to Lithuania*, 1972.

The opening scenes of *Reminiscences* picture Mekas, his brother, and other friends on a walk in the woods. Mekas is seen from the back, climbing a snowy path. He tells the viewer that the footage dates from 1957 or 1958, and reveals that he finally felt connected to the people he was with and the woods they walked through, that for the first time "he did not feel alone in America." During those years he was film critic for the *Village Voice* and the brothers were planning the production of their first feature, *Guns of the Trees*. Where other critics have understood his comment—coupled with his pleasurable, pastoral stroll—as a metaphorical "homecoming," Horak saw a different kind of arrival. The dates of the footage coincide with Mekas's entrée into the avant-garde film world—he had finally become the artist he imagined.[18]

On the evening of Saturday, July 24, 1964, Mekas, Warhol, Gerard Malanga, Henry Geldzahler, and John Palmer recorded Warhol's now legendary *Empire*. The 485-minute film of the skyscraper was captured on 16mm in black and white, between 8:00 PM and 4:00 AM, using one stationary shot; Mekas was the cinematographer.[19] Warhol and Mekas had met in 1962 while Warhol was regularly attending screenings at Mekas's loft at 414 Park Avenue South, which was also the headquarters of the Film-Makers' Cooperative.[20] The Happening-like evenings attracted a cross section of New York's underground filmmakers, artists, actors, and poets, several of whom

16 "In Conversation with Jonas Mekas," *Brooklyn Rail*, November 2010, https://brooklynrail.org/2010/11/art/in-conversation-with-jonas-mekas.

17 Mekas and Navazelskis, "Oral History Interview with Jonas Mekas."

18 Jan-Christopher Horak, "Regarding Mekas: Avant-Garde Film and Audience Subjectivity," *Millennium Film Journal* 53 (2010–11): 60, 62.

19 The group filmed the skyscraper from an office in the Time & Life Building in Midtown Manhattan.

20 According to Mekas, the two were formally introduced at a birthday party for the actor and filmmaker Naomi Levine.

Pages of the art and literary journal *Žvilgsniai* (Glimpses), published in the Kassel D.P. camp, 1948.

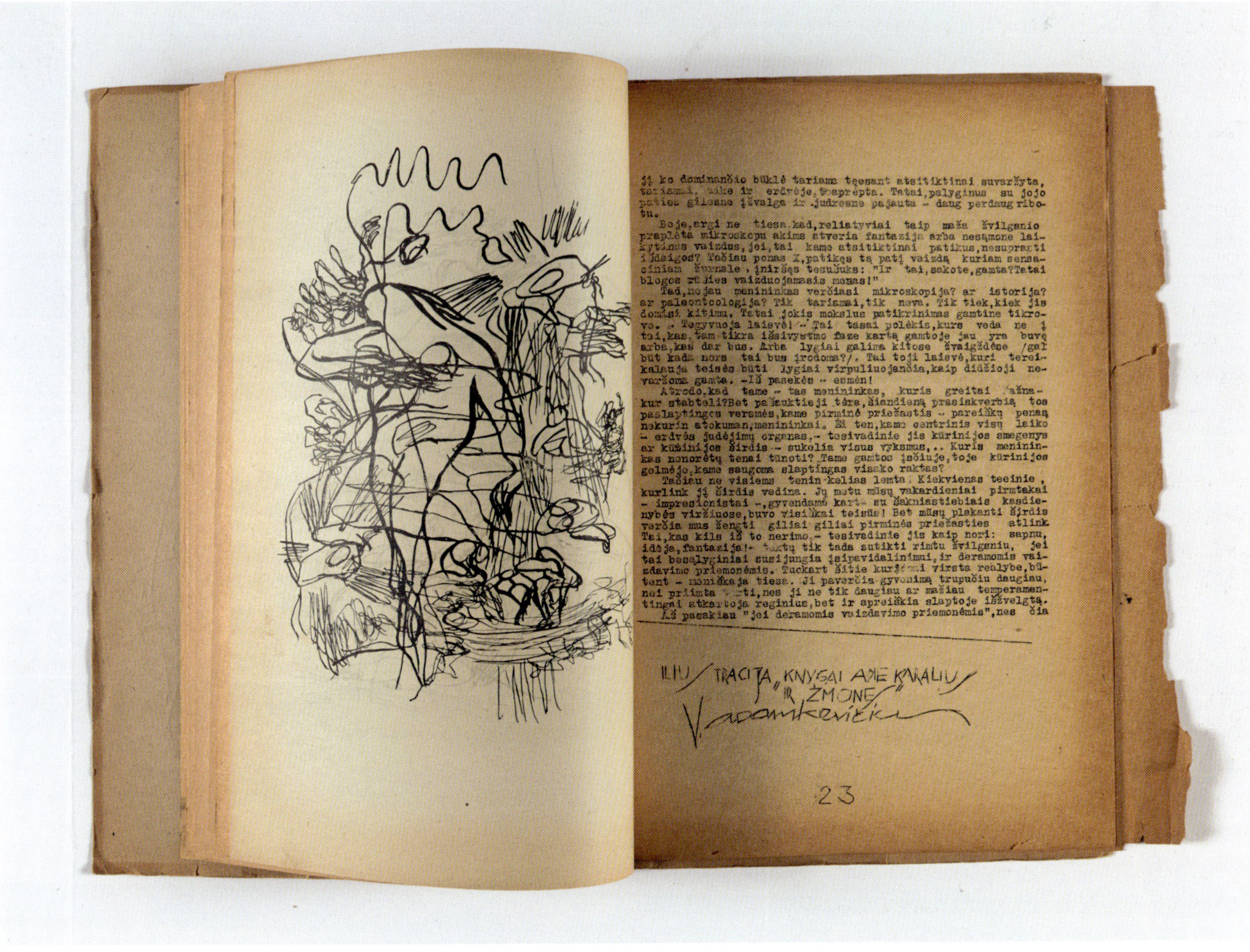
jį ko dominančio būklė tariama tęsant atsitiktinai suvaržyta,
tariamai laike ir erdvėje apprėpta. Tatai,palyginus su jojo
paties gilesne įžvalga ir .judresne pajauta – daug perdaug ribo-
tu.
Beje,ergi ne tiesa,kad,reliatyviai taip maža žvilgsnio
praplėta mikroskopu akims atveria fantazija arba nesąmone lai-
kytinus vaizdus,jei,tai kame atsitiktinai patikus,nesuprasti
įdaigos? Tačiau ponas X,patikęs tą patį vaizdą kuriam sensa-
ciniam žurnale, įniršęs tesušuks: "Ir tai,sakote,gamta?Tatai
blogos rūšies vaizduojamasis menas!"
Tad,nejau menininkas verčiasi mikroskopija? ar istorija?
ar paleontologija? Tik tariamai,tik neva. Tik tiek,kiek jis
domisi kitimu. Tatai jokis mokslus patikrinimas gamtine tikro-
ve. – Tegyvuoja laisvė! – Tai tasai polėkis,kurs veda ne į
tai,kas tam tikra išsivystymo faze kartą gamtoje jau yra buvę
arba,kas dar bus. Arba lygiai galima kitose žvaigždėse /gal
būt kada nors tai bus įrodoma?/. Tai toji laisvė,kuri terei-
kalauja teisės būti lygiai virpuliuojančia,kaip didžioji ne-
varžoma gamta. –Iš pasekės – esmėn!
Atrodo,kad tame – tas menininkas, kuris greitai kažna-
kur stabteli?Bet pašauktieji tėra,šiandieną prasiskverbią tos
paslaptingos versmės,kame pirminė priežastis – pareiškų penas
nekurin atokuman,menininkai. Iš ten,kame centrinis visų laiko
– erdvės judėjimų organas,– tesivadinie jis kūrinijos smegenys
ar kūrinijos širdis – sukelia visus vyksmus,.. Kuris meninin-
kas nenorėtų tenai tūnoti? Tame gamtos įsčiuje,toje kūrinijos
gelmėje,kame saugoma slaptingas visako raktas?
Tačiau ne visiems tenin kelias lemta. Kiekvienas teeinie,
kurlink jį širdis vedina. Jų metu mūsų vakardieniai pirmtakai
– impresionistai –,gyvendamė karta su šakniastiebiais kasdie-
nybės viržiuose,buvo visiškai teisūs! Bet mūsų plakanti širdis
verčia mus žengti giliai giliai pirminės priežasties atlink.
Tai,kas kils iš to nerimo,– tesivadinie jis kaip nori: sapnu,
idėja,fantazija!– tektų tik tada sutikti rimtu žvilgsniu, jei
tai besąlyginiai susijungia įsipavidalinimui,ir deramomis vai-
zdavimo priemonėmis. Tuokart šitie kurįiniai virsta realybe,bū-
tent – meniškąja tiesa. Ji paverčia gyvenimą trupučiu daugiau,
nei priimta ... ti,nes ji ne tik daugiau ar mažiau temperamen-
tingai atkartoja reginius,bet ir apreiškia slaptoje išžvelgtą.
Aš pasakiau "jei deramomis vaizdavimo priemonėmis",nes čia

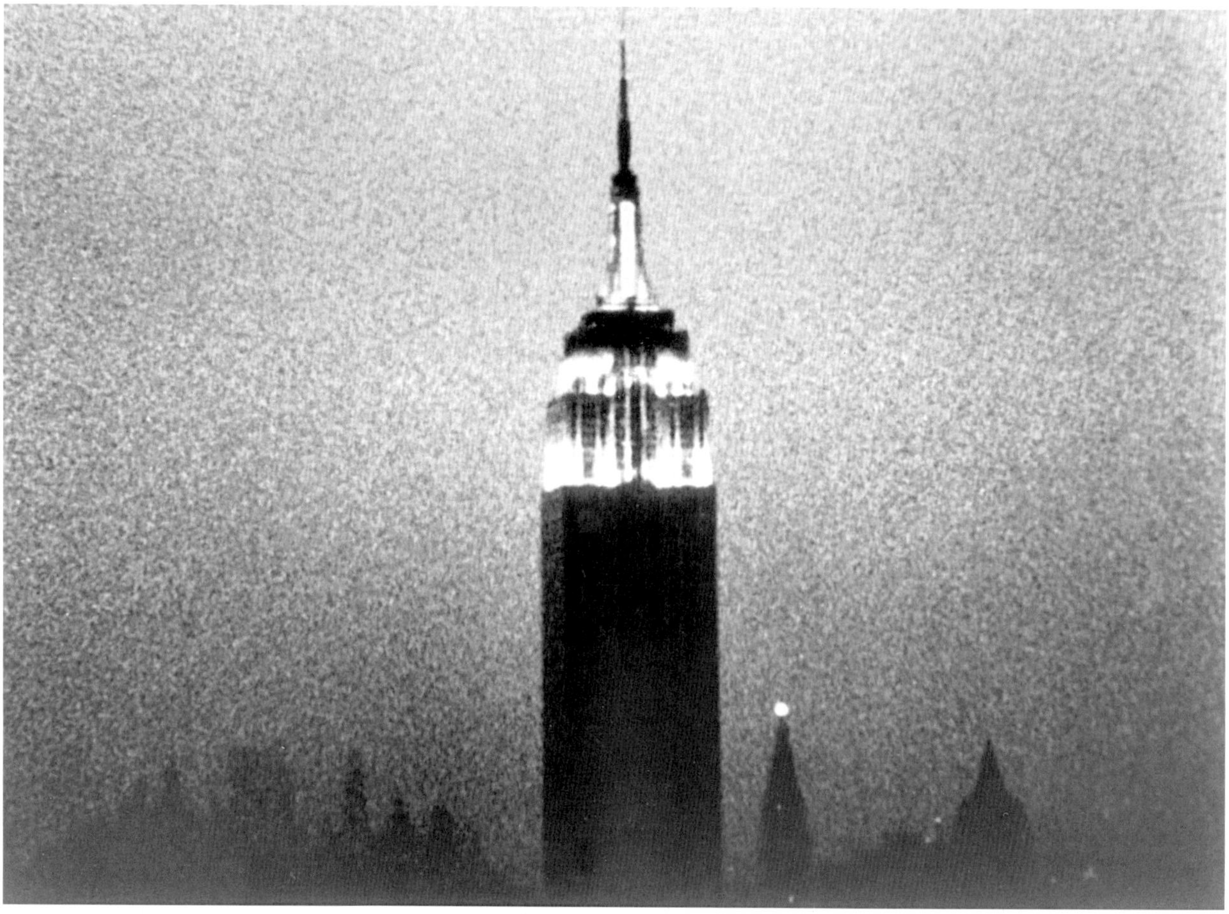

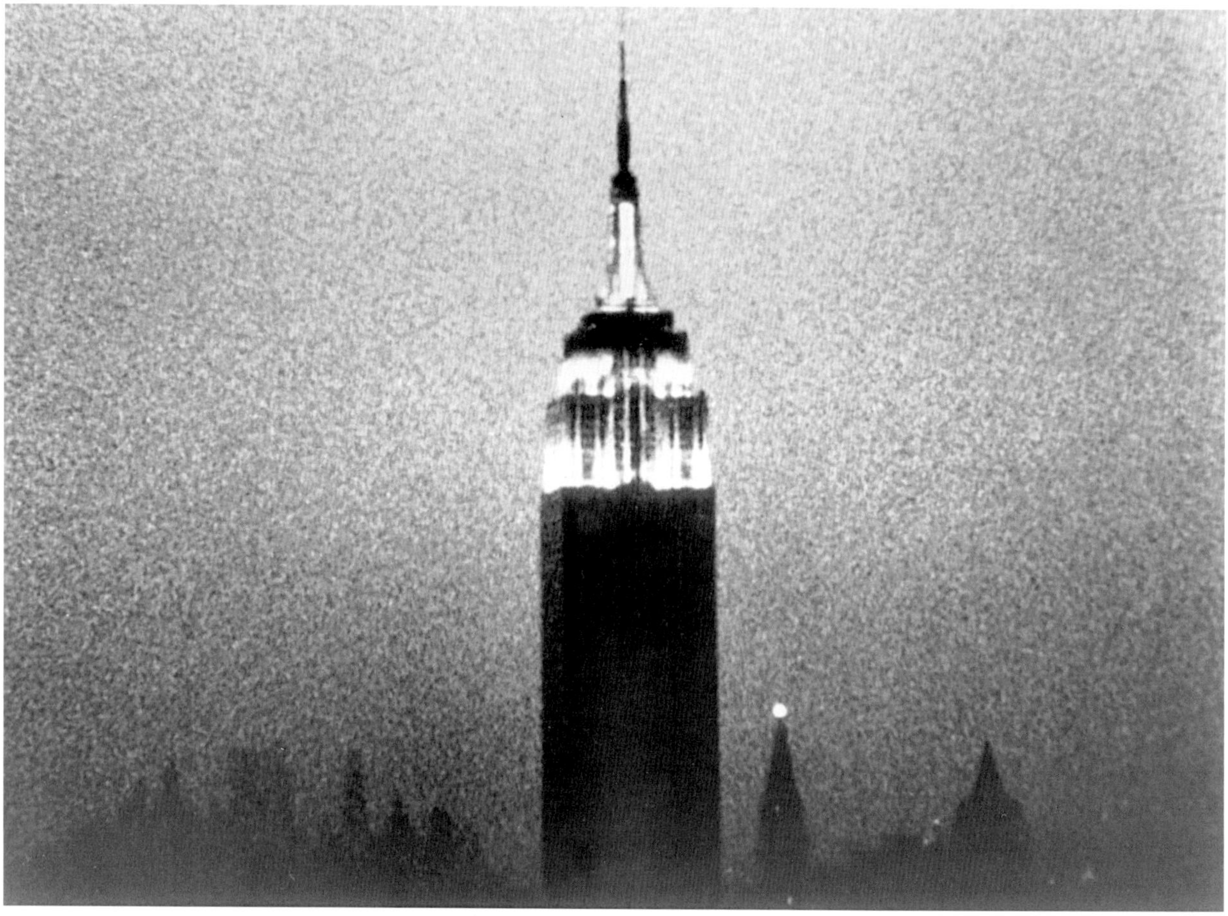

Stills from Andy Warhol and John Palmer, *Empire*, 16mm, black and white, silent, 485 min., 1964.

21 Jonas Mekas, *Movie Journal: The Rise of the New American Cinema, 1959–1971* (New York: Columbia University Press, 2016), 103, 157, 161, 311.

would become superstars of Warhol's Factory or subjects of his films, including Taylor Mead, Naomi Levine, and Mario Montez. Mekas was an early and ardent supporter of Warhol's filmmaking, proclaiming that his first film, *Sleep* (1963), had pushed the underground genre "farther than we were before. As simple as it is, it is a movement forward that carries others with it." After *Empire* he anointed Warhol the "most productive filmmaker in the world today" and the most "revolutionary filmmaker working today," who opened "a completely new and inexhaustible field of cinema reality." Mekas later clarified these bombastic statements, explaining in 1968 that Warhol's contribution to the history of cinema was not to recreate life as fiction but to make fiction out of real life.[21]

His observation was concurrent with the making of *Walden*, a film composed of scenes from Mekas's "real life" shot between 1964 and 1968 that poignantly narrates fragments of the social, cultural, and above all communal life he had created in his adopted hometown of New York City. *Walden* solidified Mekas's reputation as an avant-garde filmmaker; it established the diaristic aesthetic while it also positioned him as a central figure in New York's exploding interdisciplinary art scene. Mekas's daily routines—surrounded by friends or working at the Coop—collide with watershed cultural and political events, artists, and public figures. His painterly, gestural style unifies the disparate and disjunctive footage, which is awash in overexposure or flickering dimness, and is unleashed in frantic, atomized bits or slowly drifts by in languid passages. The rumbling subway, rushing wind, and John Cale's droning music bathe the film in urban noise. Titles display names—some well known, others obscure—dates, and places. Mekas rarely appears or speaks in this film; rather, he is visible through absence—a shadow in the grass, a reflection in a window, or a voice off camera. Toward the end of the film, trembling imagery of a red setting sun dances across black water. A woman off camera says, "I'm on, Mr. Mekas, really on!" The same landscape, shot through the window of a moving train, now appears pale pink and violet. Mekas replies, "Fantastic! See the Empire State Building in the blue evening light! Blue? Blue?" he asks her, as though unsure. She responds, "No, I don't think it's blue, I think it's kind of . . . white." As she speaks, sun and water dissolve into abstract magenta and black lines. Viewers watch the landscape morph into nothingness while Mekas allows them to conjure an image of the iconic skyscraper in their mind's eye.

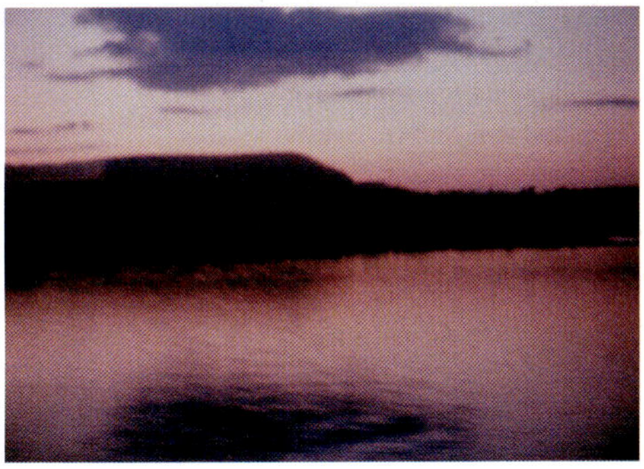

Two stills from *Walden*, 1969.

Warhol, too, understood the power of projection; his art presented celebrities, advertising logos, and even his own image as mirrors of desire. Mekas maintained a lifelong friendship with Warhol (see page 163). Whenever he discussed the artist and his studio, the Factory, it was as though he saw a paradigm for himself and the Film-Makers' Cooperative. Both men created centers for

22 Jonas Mekas, *A Dance with Fred Astaire* (New York: Anthology Editions, 2017), 385.
23 Gretchen Berg, "Andy Warhol, My True Story," *East Village Other* 23, November 1, 1966.
24 Bess Winakor, "Andy Warhol's Life, Loves, Art and Wavemaking," *Chicago Sun-Times*, Sunday, September 28, 1975.

artistic production and mythmaking; Mekas described Warhol as an accepting father figure who provided an unorthodox home for the "sad and confused souls" who flocked to him.[22] Mekas's own Coop was a home for all filmmakers—true to its name, all were invited to submit their films for screening and distribution. Its nightly events ushered in a radical genre of filmmaking that reflected the social politics erupting throughout the city. Warhol and others, including Jack Smith and Barbara Rubin, made films that examined questions of sexuality, gender, and countercultural labor. The Coop's most successful release was Warhol's 1966 film *Chelsea Girls*; its run was so popular that for a brief moment (prior to Warhol's withdrawing from the Coop and self-distributing) the fledgling nonprofit operated with a financial surplus.

In an interview that year, Warhol is clearly cultivating the enigmatic persona that would make him as famous as his subjects: "If you want to know all about Andy Warhol just look at the surface of my paintings and films and me, and there I am. There's nothing behind it."[23] *Scenes from the Life of Andy Warhol* (1990) shows the artist at his summer retreat in Montauk, which he shared with friends, including Mekas, Lee Radziwill (to whom the film is dedicated), her two children and their cousins Caroline and John F. Kennedy Jr., Peter Beard, Mick Jagger, and others. Warhol's remote cottages at the end of Long Island provided refuge, a quiet place for family celebrations, shared meals, and solitary moments. Mekas's film brings the inscrutable Warhol into close focus, presenting the infamously superficial artist unguardedly enjoying life's small pleasures; but like its filmmaker, Warhol is always with a camera. For both artists, the camera allowed engagement attended by a physical—even psychological—remove. In this way, it facilitated documentation while it fostered critical distance. Warhol never specified what his work was all about or offered any substantive statements on human nature. At one point during those Montauk summers, Warhol was asked in an interview, "What does life mean to you?" And he replied, "I don't know. I wish I knew."[24]

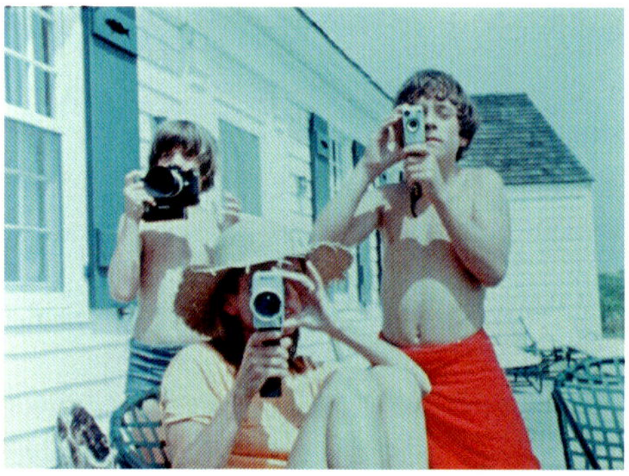

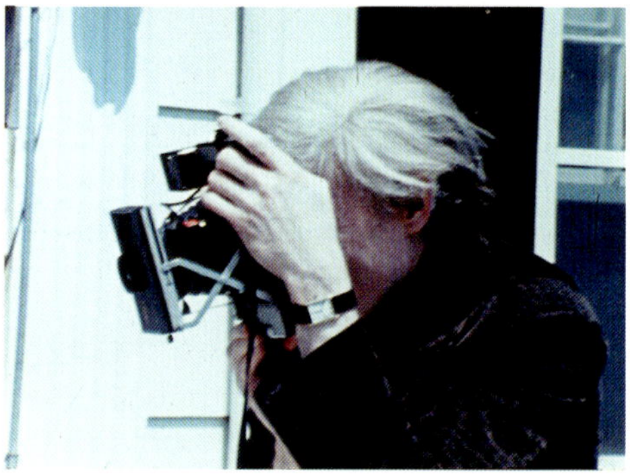

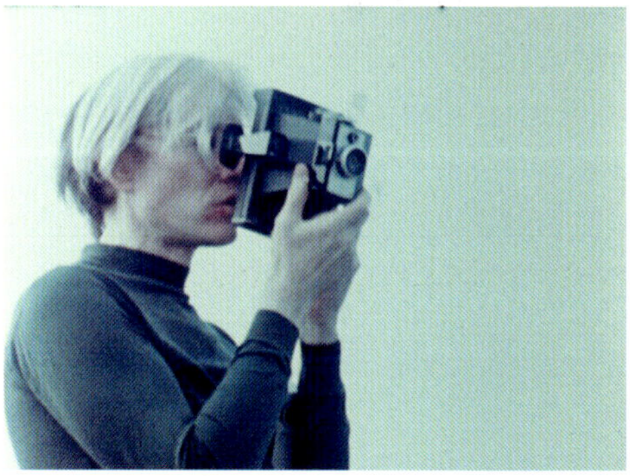

Three stills from *Scenes from the Life of Andy Warhol*, 1990.

"I have never been able really to figure out where my life begins and where it ends. I have never, never been able to figure it all out. What it's all about. What it all means." This is what Mekas tells the viewer at the beginning of *As I Was Moving Ahead Occasionally I Saw Brief Glimpses of Beauty* (2000), the last work he made entirely on 16mm film (see pages 186–94). The 288-minute piece focuses on Mekas's personal life: his relationship with his wife, Hollis, and his experience as a father to their two children, Oona and Sebastian. He employed a logic of chance operations reminiscent of the work

25 Mekas, "Commencement Address." Caruth, *Unclaimed Experience*, 7. Mekas speaking in *Jonas in the Desert*, Peter Sempel's 1994 documentary on him. Violence in his own work caused Mekas much anxiety, as he recounted on April 21, 1966, describing an incident after a screening of his film *The Brig* (1964) for a group of students. This was the first film Mekas made on his own. (*Guns of the Trees* had been a collaborative effort with his brother Adolfas and Édouard de Laurot.) He conceived *The Brig* as a real-time document of the Living Theatre's performance of Kenneth H. Brown's play of the same name, which portrays the aggressively dehumanizing realities of a military prison. It is anomalous in Mekas's oeuvre, both in content and form. The students were full of praise and inspired by the film's political charge. Their enthusiasm distressed him. "No! No!," he wrote later. "I don't want to make films on violence, on brutality any longer, even if brutality exists and will always exist. I don't want to see that reality even on film. I want to make films that would fill you with a good feeling—the feeling of happiness instead of thoughts of terror and violence: not an empty happiness but a blissful happiness—that's what I want now and anything less than that makes my heart sick, makes me suffer. So much ugliness around, so much ugliness—why should I contribute still more to it, even if it's through art, even if it's art!" Mekas, *I Seem to Live*, 559.

26 From an unpublished document in "Jonas' Writings: Small Pieces." Also in that collection is a piece on *Empire*, in which Mekas argues that it is not passively watched but actively experienced.

of John Cage to organize the nonlinear narrative into twelve chapters. Working from footage that spanned three decades, he randomly selected reels and strung together bits and pieces of film. The result is a wild swing through time, evoking the functions of memory: the children are at one moment newborns and in another preteens; the filmmaker is in the office of the Coop and suddenly at the kitchen table of his SoHo loft; winter collides with summer, which dissolves into spring and cuts to fall. Mekas's formal devices are inextricable from his sense of self. As a cat plays with a mouse in the dim blue light, he connects the seemingly arbitrary editing process with his own sense of precariousness, saying, "I don't really know, where any piece of my life really belongs. . . . There is some kind of order in it, order of its own that I do not really understand."

According to Mekas, the fragmentation that pervades his work took root when he fled in 1944, when he was "shook to the foundations—all my idealism, and my faith in goodness of man and progress of man; all was shattered." Like the piles of rubble that littered Germany after the war, he was no longer one person but "one thousand painful pieces." Caruth proposes that a traumatic experience is not singular but multiple, encapsulating the crisis of death and the ongoing experience of having survived it. Mekas seems to bolster this idea, both by his avoidance of overtly political or painful subject matter and his commitment to filming as an end in itself, which he maintained resisted the crushing bleakness that surrounded him. "I shot all my diaries out of self-defense," he explained, "in order not to be crushed by the blackness of the city, in order to withstand the attacks on all my senses, on my whole being. Yes, out of self-defense. . . . That is why the stress is on celebration, because that's lacking here today."[25]

For Mekas, the nearly five-hour running time of *As I Was Moving Ahead* forced him to "submerge into it to really begin to feel what it's all about, my life." In turn, he invites viewers on an epic journey through his life, to the extent that he hoped to conjure an immersive, meditative cinematic experience.[26] Roughly midway

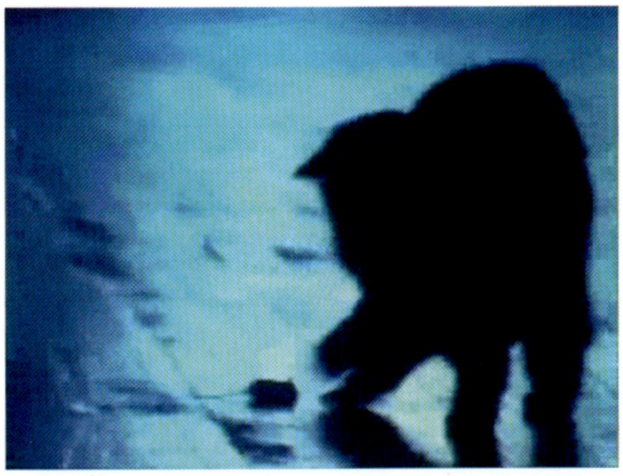

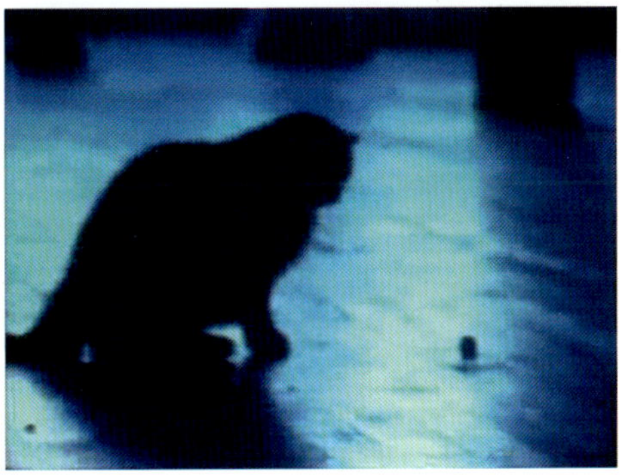

Two stills from *As I Was Moving Ahead Occasionally I Saw Brief Glimpses of Beauty*, 2000.

27 Mekas edited this film in late 1999, including on New Year's Eve. At the beginning of chapter ten he tells the viewer, "It's about twenty minutes till the end of this millennium, as I sit here in my editing room, and making splices, splicing things, bits of my own past, my own millennium. Each of us, each and every one of us has our own millennium."

28 Interestingly, Mekas's last work, *Requiem* (2019), evidences a return to the frenetic editing of the film works.

through, Mekas pauses to address viewers: echoing Warhol, he asks them to "please read these images and you'll be able to tell everything about me." By the film's end one would naturally deduce that Mekas's beautiful, revelatory, celebratory footage tells the story of a profoundly happy man whose life has been a progression of blissful moments. This is surely true—in part. But it is also true that Mekas's fragmentary aesthetic reveals as much as it conceals; much happens between the frames. During the final minutes, a title like something from a fairy tale appears: "A film about people who have never any arguments and no fights and who love each other." Mekas breaks the enchanted spell with a subtle, ironic gesture; as the experience ends, viewers realize that they have watched a story about the best of times, and have been spared the worst.

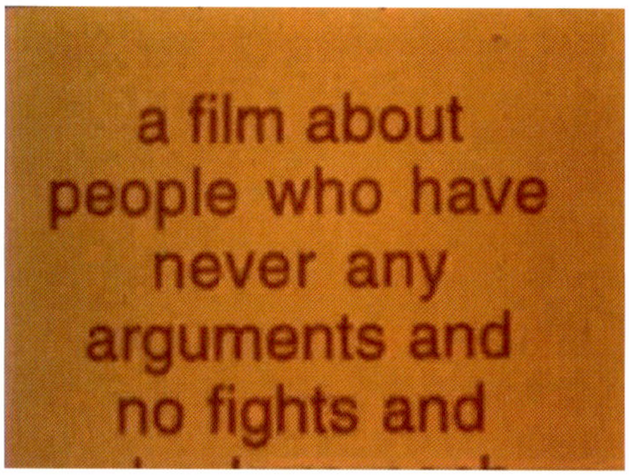

Still from *As I Was Moving Ahead Occasionally I Saw Brief Glimpses of Beauty*, 2000.

There is one rare moment of high-society glamour in *As I Was Moving Ahead*. Chapter eight begins on a boat. Warhol and the famed architect Philip Johnson mix with an elegant crowd, cruising around the southern tip of Manhattan at sunset. The Statue of Liberty comes into view, covered in scaffolding. Mekas toggles back and forth between the icon undergoing rehabilitation and the then newly erected World Trade Center towers as he narrates, "I do not know how I reached this point in my life. But I continue moving ahead, slowly. Moving ahead and some glimpses of happiness and beauty come my way." Now inside the boat, Johnson stands at a window and points to the skyline outside. The camera follows his hand and fixes again on the towers as Mekas says, "So I keep moving ahead, I keep moving ahead, my friends." Following the boat scene, a title reminiscent of those in *Lost, Lost, Lost* appears: "I envy the others. They seem to be in the very center of gravity, but I seem to live in a permanent flight, longing for rest." For Mekas, pushing ahead was a fact of life. But that notion is continually undercut by the film's vintage footage, spliced together as the sun was setting on the twentieth century.[27]

This film also marks a more personal turning point for the artist and a radical shift in his approach: he employed videotape, digital, and online technologies for the remainder of his life. In Mekas's video work, he pressed play and let the camera run as long as he liked, offering a less mediated, more real-time experience. With video, Mekas exchanged the poetic intensity of the glimpse for the lingering long take.[28] Just ten months after the premiere of *As I Was Moving Ahead*, he recorded the attacks of September 11, unedited and as they unfolded, from where he stood. The proximity of these two consequential moments lends an unexpected pathos to the

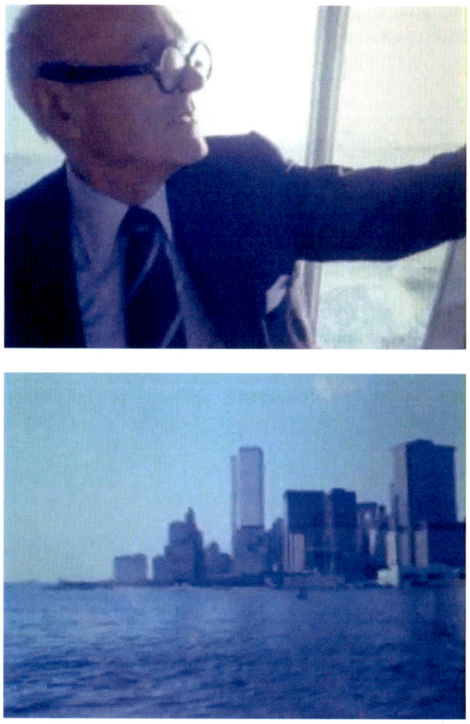

Two stills from *As I Was Moving Ahead Occasionally I Saw Brief Glimpses of Beauty*, 2000.

29 Mekas and Navazelskis, "Oral History Interview with Jonas Mekas."
30 Miriam Rosen, "Review: Jonas Mekas, Galerie du Jour," *Artforum* (September 1996): 118.

many appearances of the towers in the earlier film. Skyscrapers can be read as a touchstone for Mekas, woven through his story from the very beginning: from his first view of the glistening Manhattan skyline, which convinced him to stay in New York rather than carry on to Chicago; to an unusual film about the Empire State Building that helped to shape his filmmaking philosophy; and then, when the World Trade Center towers crumbled into millions of pieces, Mekas finally found the words to describe something that had always eluded him.

During his interview with Navazelskis, Mekas talked—as explicitly as he could—about what life was like during war. The camera shows him seated at his circular worktable in his Clinton Hill loft. The stacks of books and papers, boxes and binders, that filled his home and now constitute his vast archive are piled high behind him. Navazelskis asks Mekas to begin at the beginning. He relays as many details as he can remember about his family, their farm, the smallness of rural culture, the sociopolitical complexities of interwar Lithuania, the piecemeal nature of his education, and how he worked with the resistance. He tells of a pivotal encounter with a Miss Kelber, a Soviet Jewish political officer stationed at his high school. His classmates feared and hated Kelber because she worked for the Soviets, but more than that, they hated her because she was a Jew. Kelber stopped Mekas one day and lifted up his hat. Hidden there was a small, folded BBC transcript that he was covertly transporting. He tells Navazelskis that the officer looked at him sternly and warned, "Never do that again," and that he still cannot understand why she spared him. His crime could easily have led to his death and endangered his family. He speculates that she may have been a double agent and wonders what happened to her. He knows that she retreated with the other Soviets when the Nazis marched into Biržai and assumes that she, too, was killed in the woods. His eyes become glassy with tears as he says softly, "She saved my life."[29] We will never fully know what Mekas saw or what he endured during those years in Lithuania. He chose to tell other stories that he thought easier to understand, or more beautiful, or more hopeful as he witnessed the world becoming increasingly violent, isolationist, and fractured. Perhaps if he had had a Bolex in Lithuania we would have glimpses of Miss Kelber and the many others who disappeared. As soon as he was able, our protagonist began "making corrections" with his artwork and his community-driven projects.[30] He undertook a lifelong commitment to make the villainous twentieth century better.

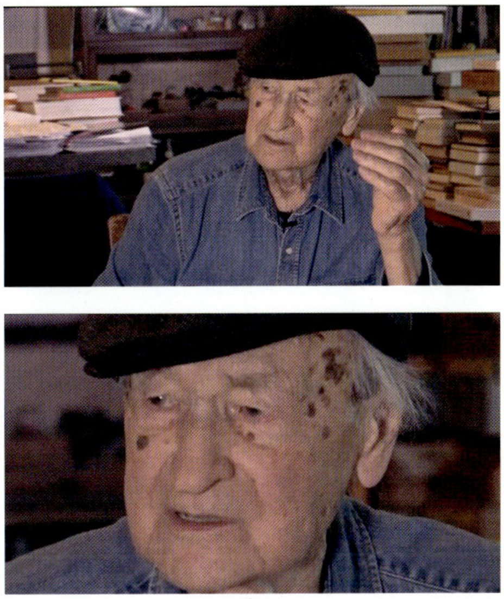

Two stills from oral history interview of Jonas Mekas, conducted by Ina Navazelskis, United States Holocaust Memorial Museum, June 2018.

New York welcomed the penniless, war-weary Mekas, who, in spite of all that he had seen, was still young and able to "build himself from scratch." This volume details the vastness of his contributions, not just to the development of avant-garde film but to the evolution of what is now defined as interdisciplinary art, born in downtown Manhattan. It is difficult to imagine what would have happened if the International Refugee Organization had not aided the Mekas brothers. As of early 2021, the United Nations High Commissioner for Refugees calculated that eighty million people around the world were living in forced displacement. At the same time, the United States, the United Kingdom, and Europe are accepting fewer refugees than ever before in modern history. Even in his youth Mekas sensed that he would someday leave Lithuania, and while his route was not one he would have chosen, his new home allowed him the anonymity and freedom to forge the identity he was destined to inhabit. New York forever changed a shy young poet into a full-fledged, multidimensional artist; in turn, Jonas Mekas forever changed New York.

GUNS OF THE TREES, 1961

FILMS

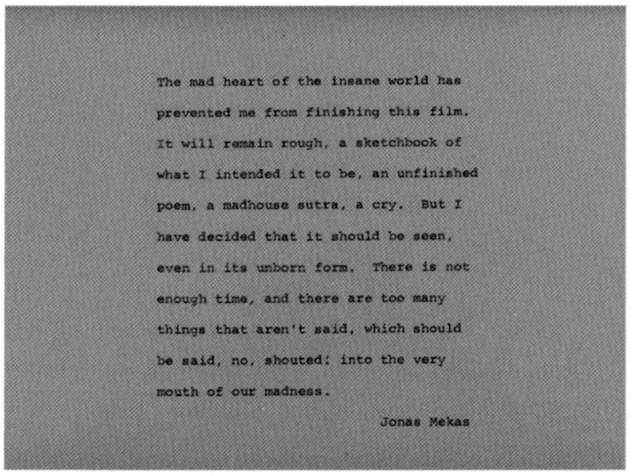

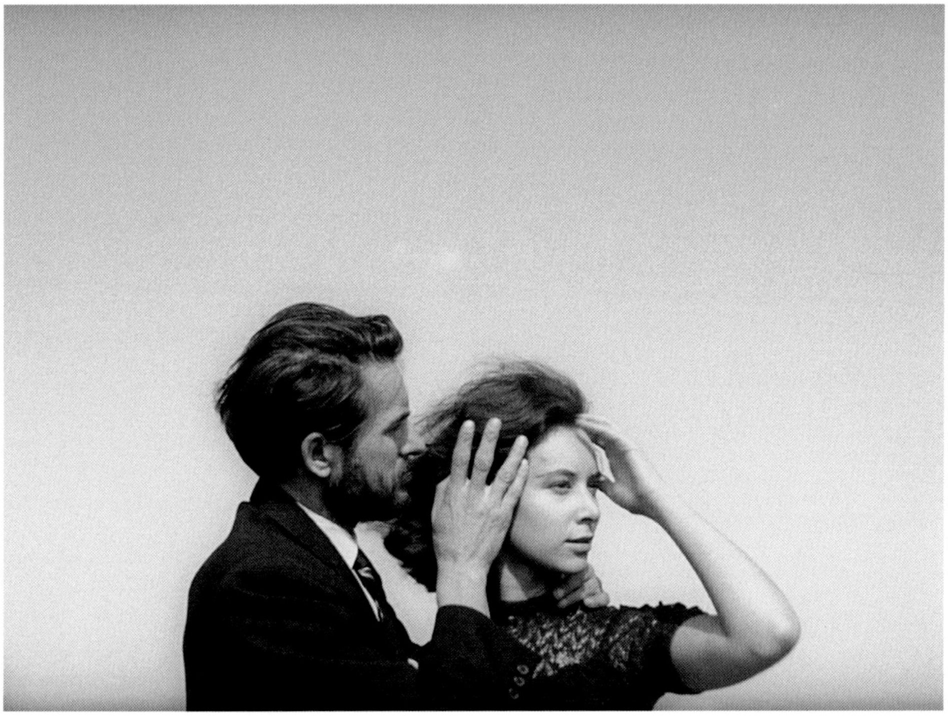

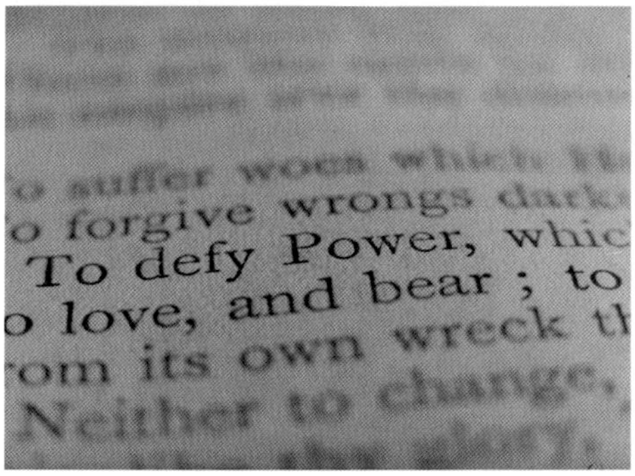

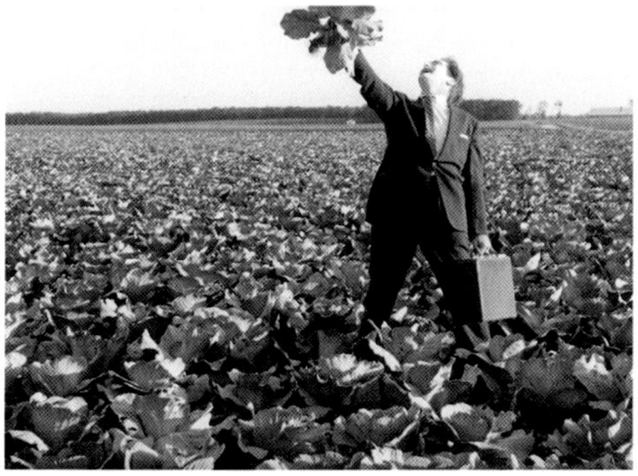

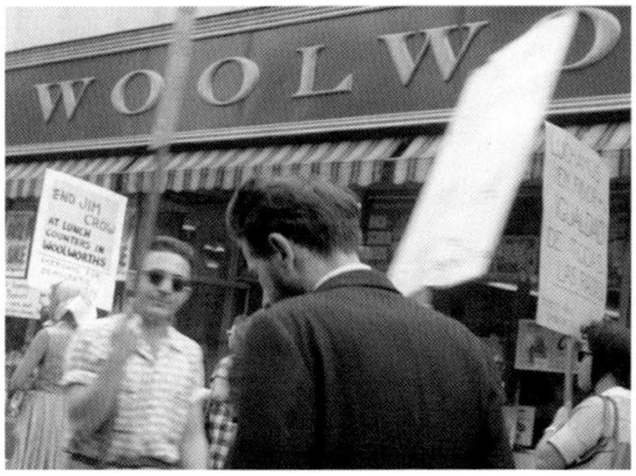

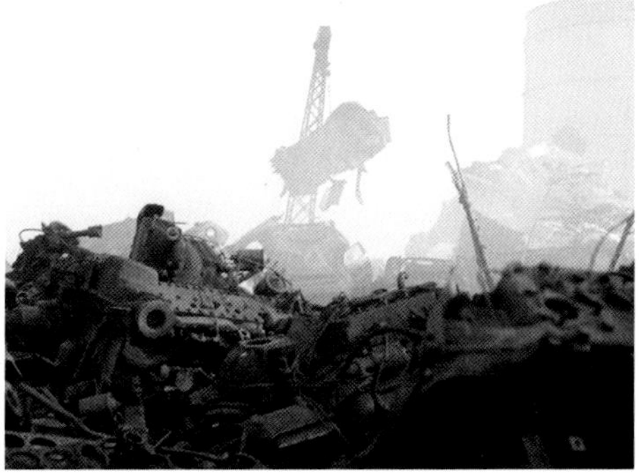

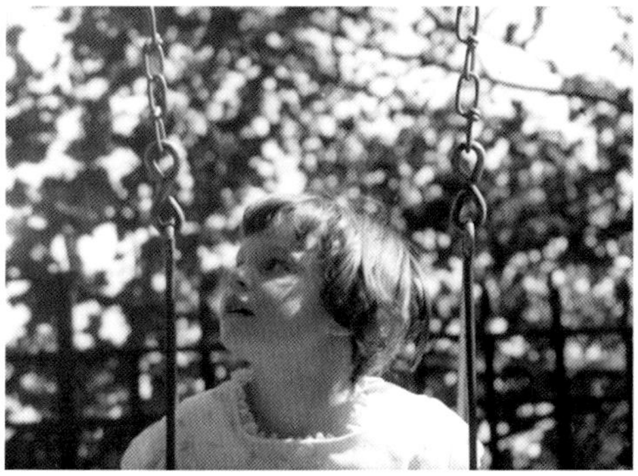

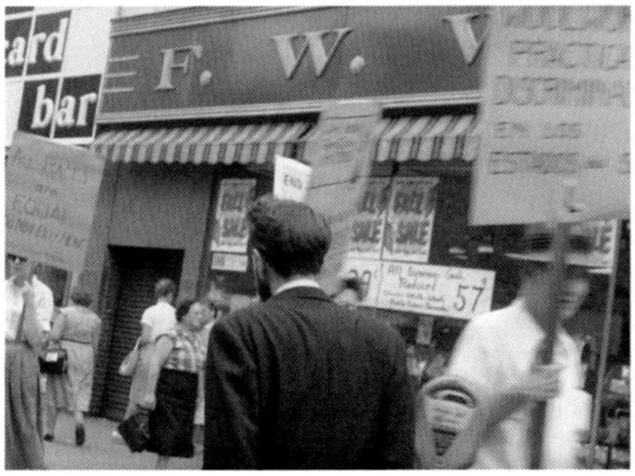

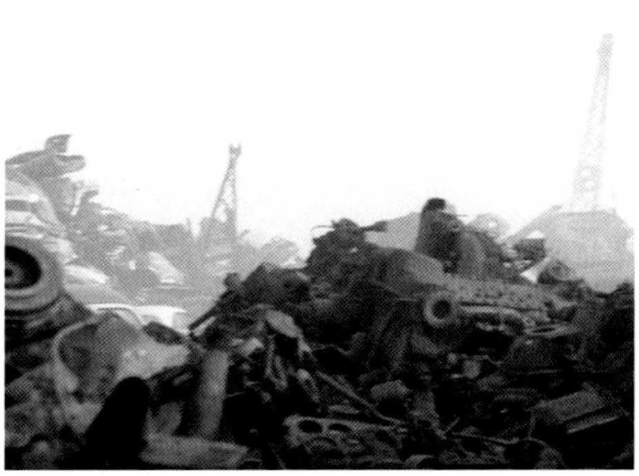

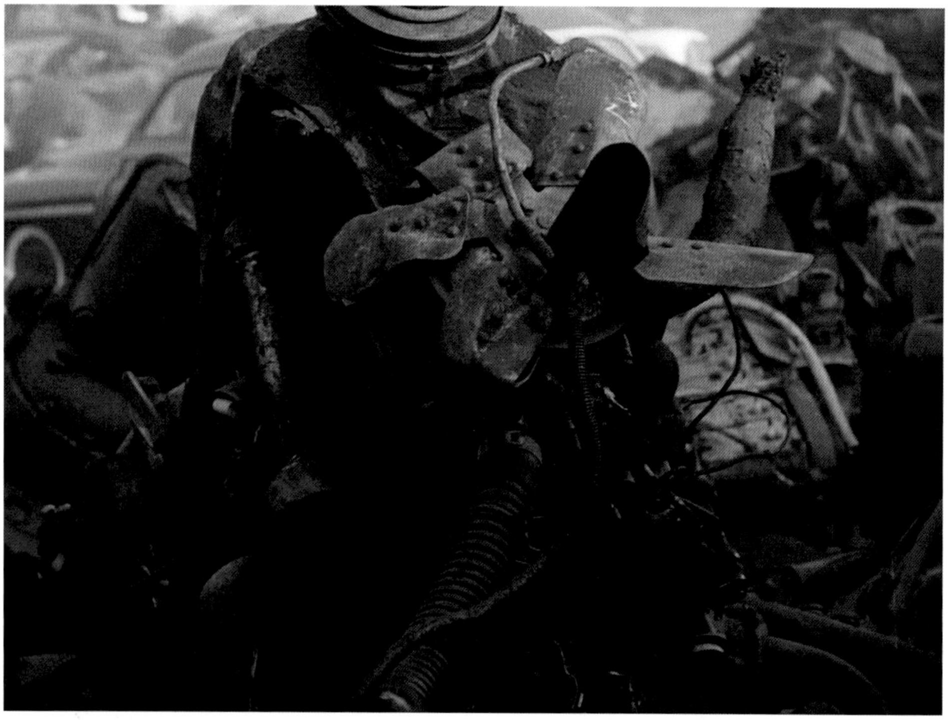
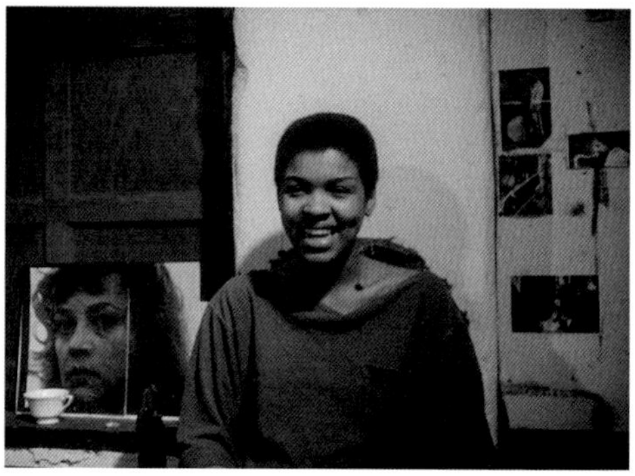
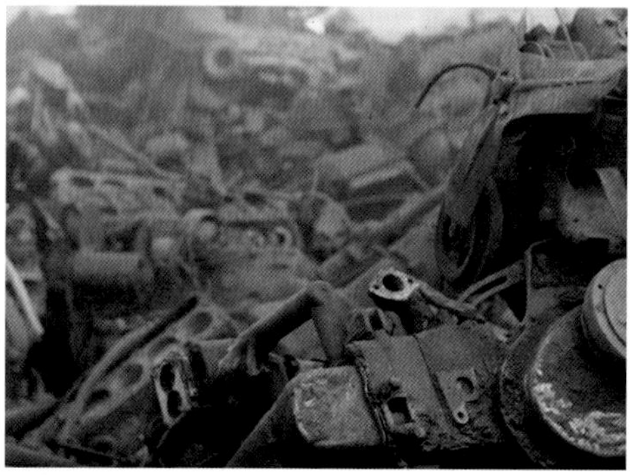
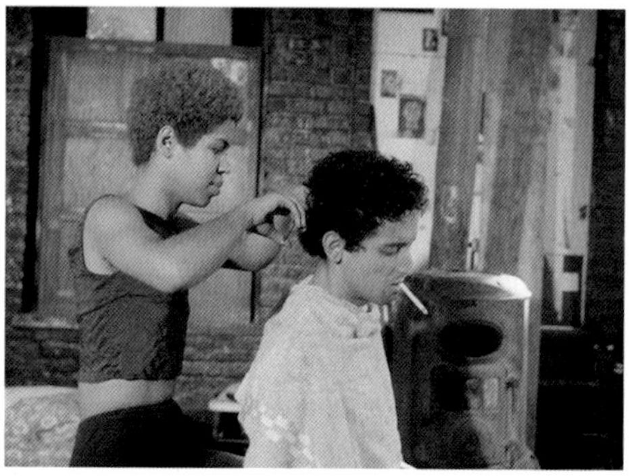
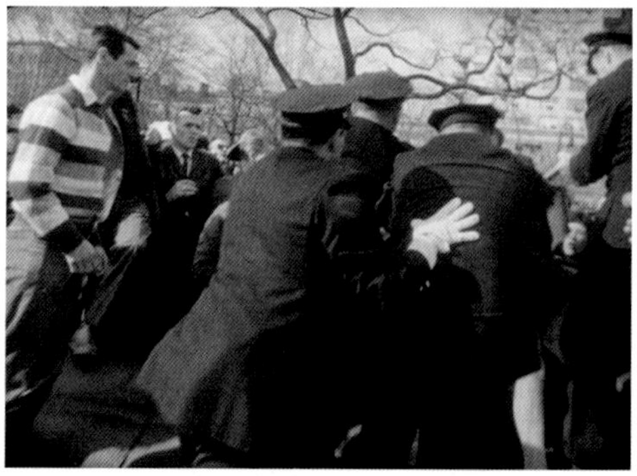
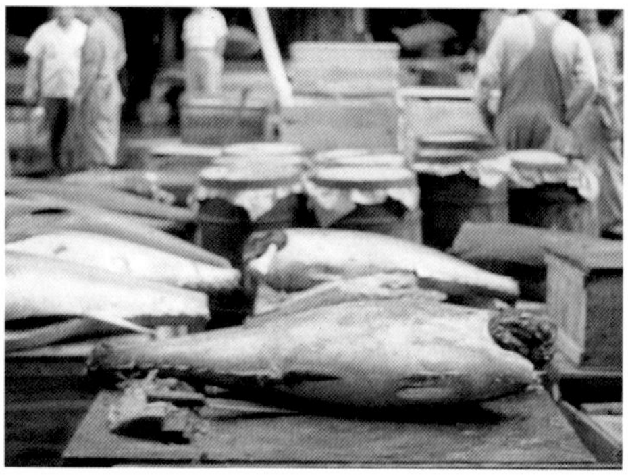
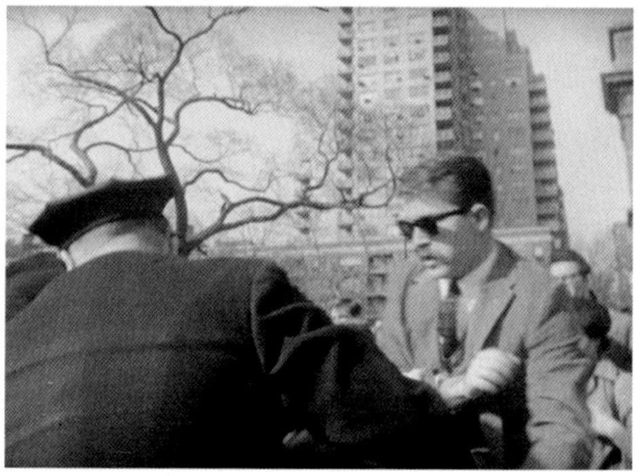
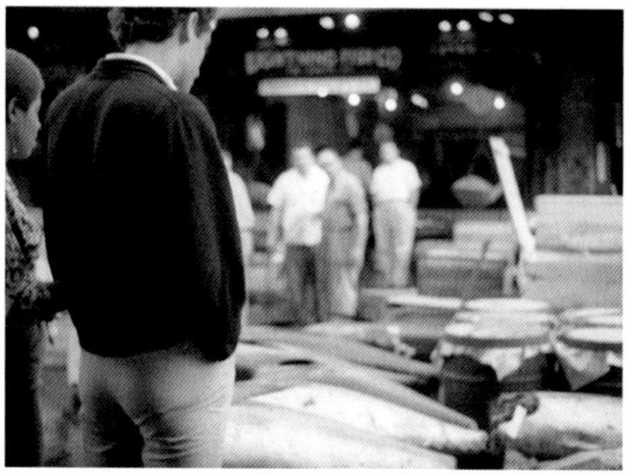
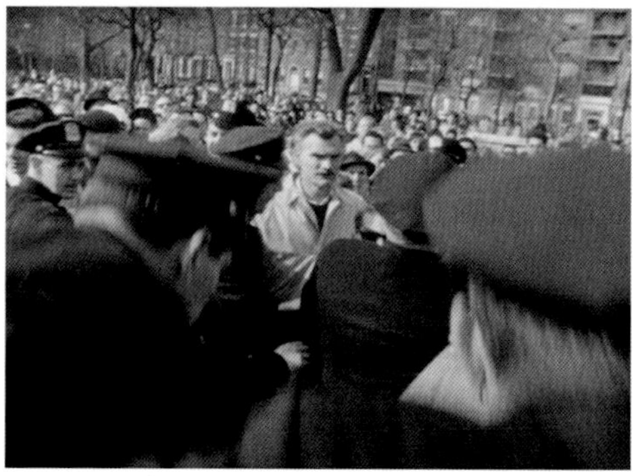

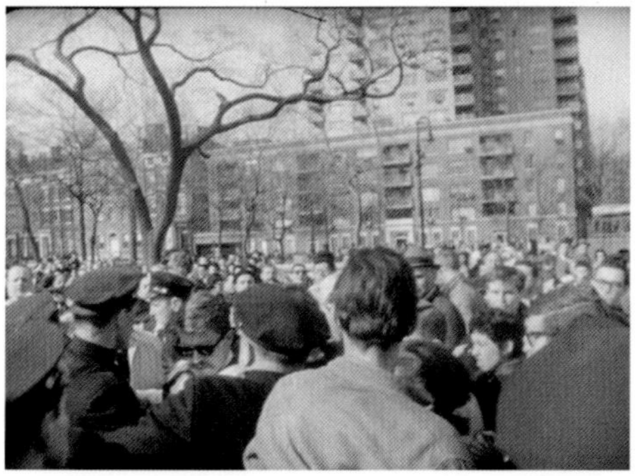

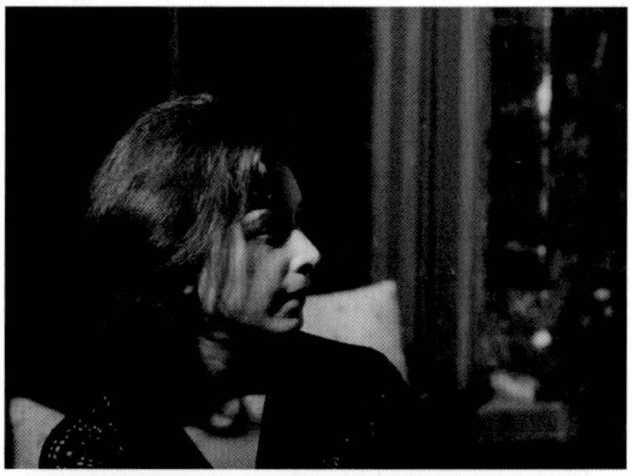

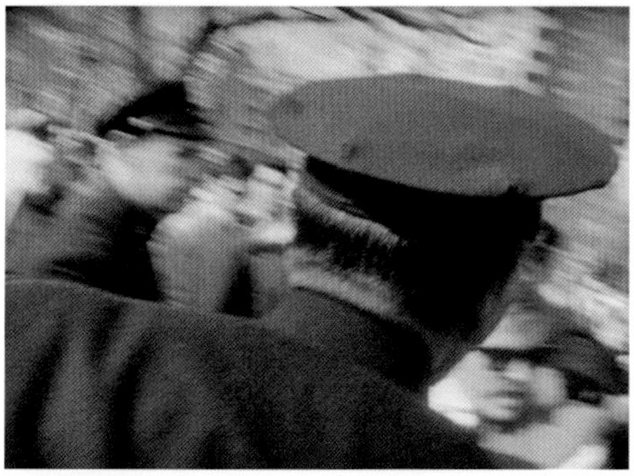

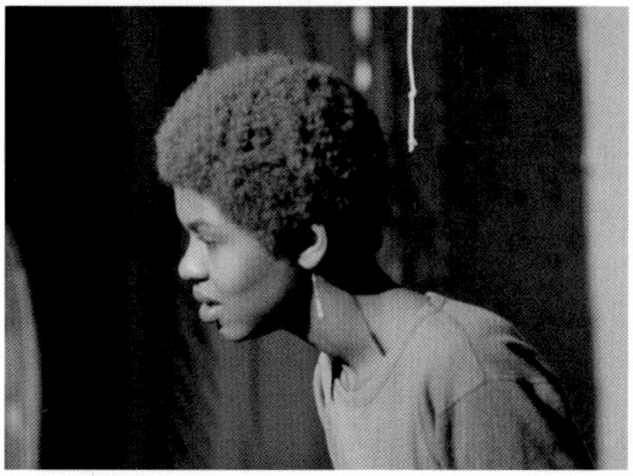

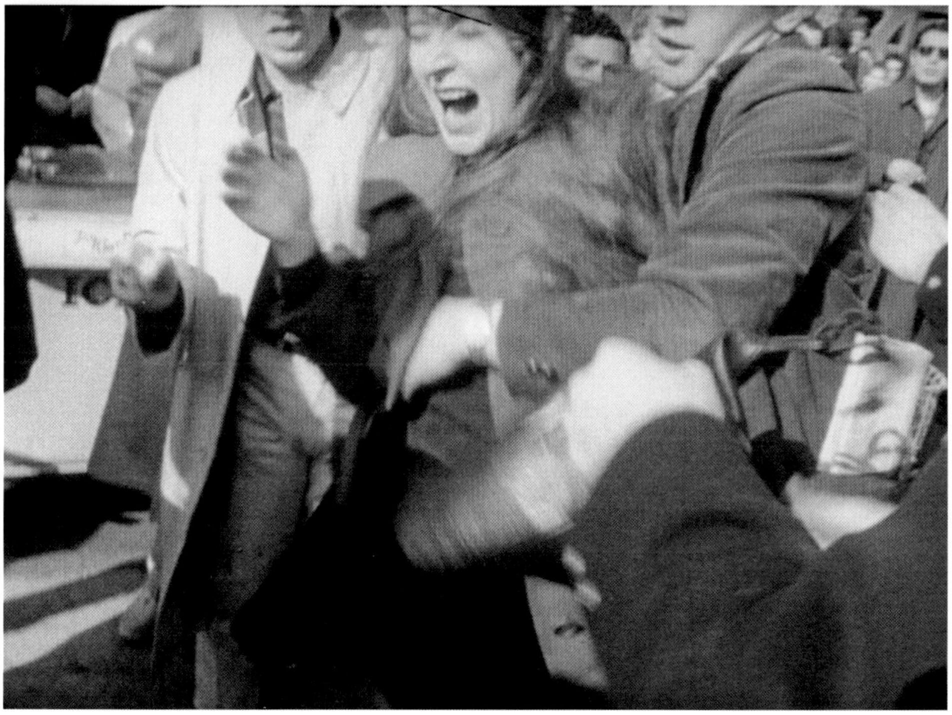

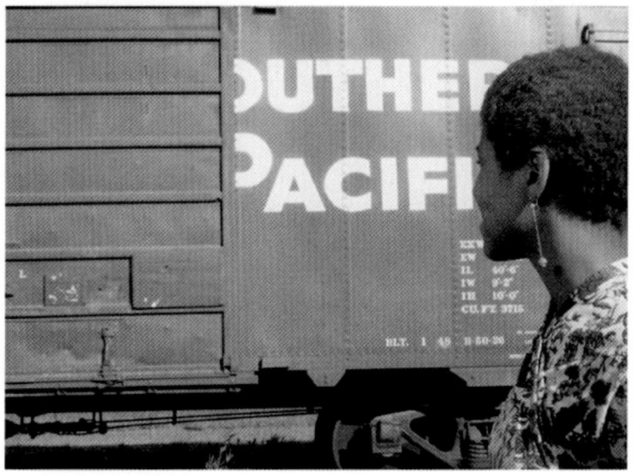
OUTHE
ACIF

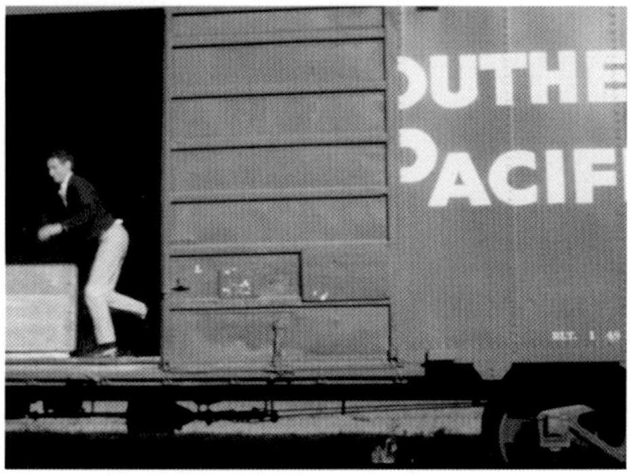
OUTHE
ACIF

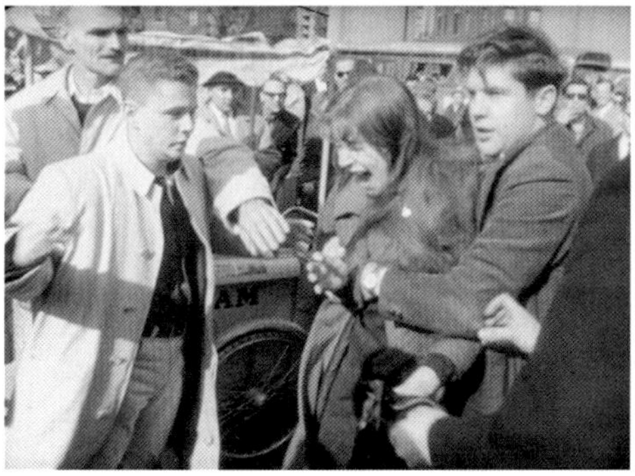

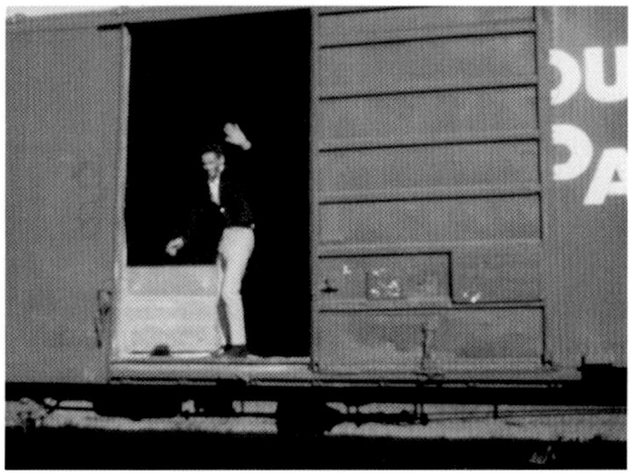

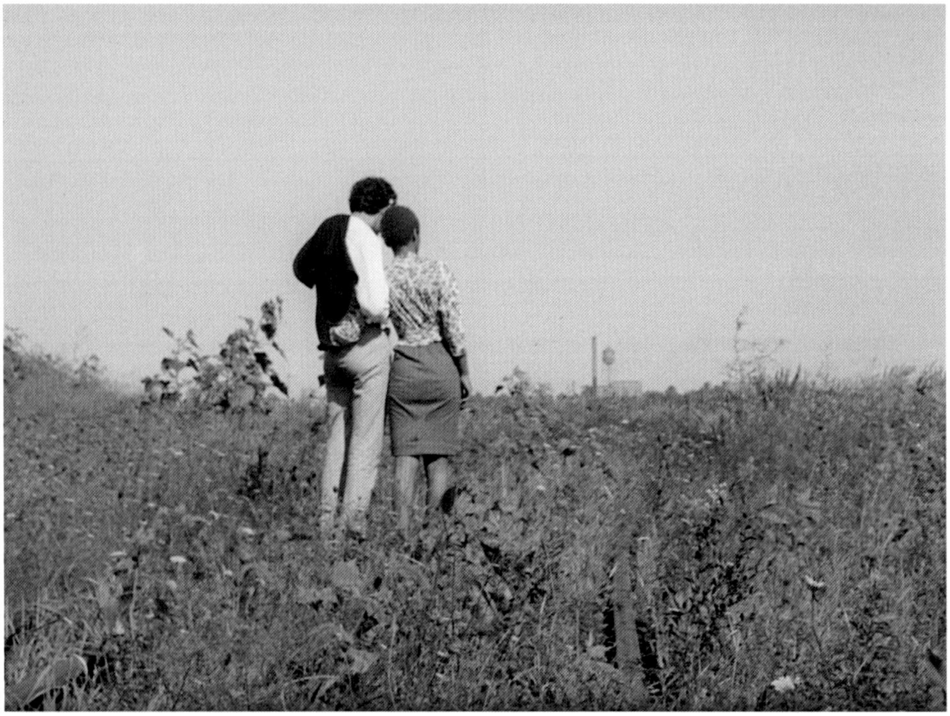
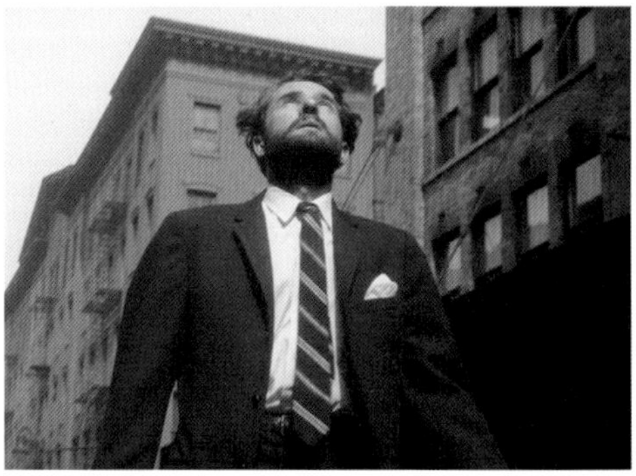
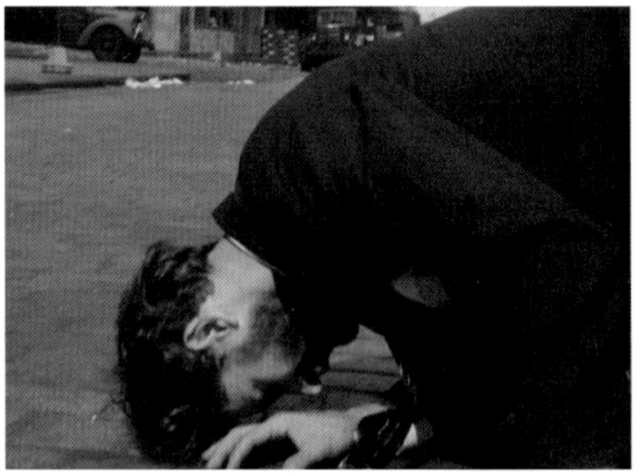
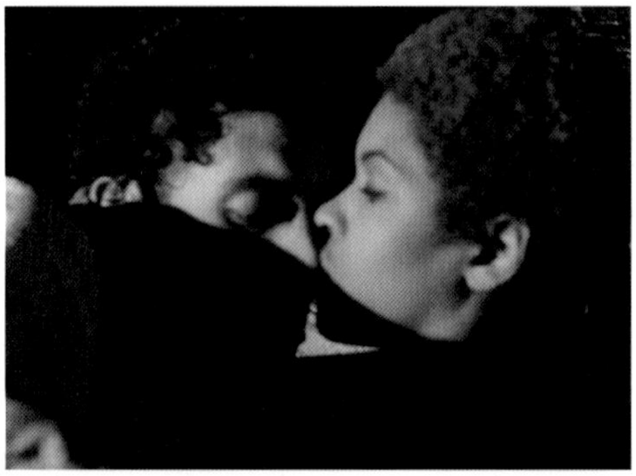
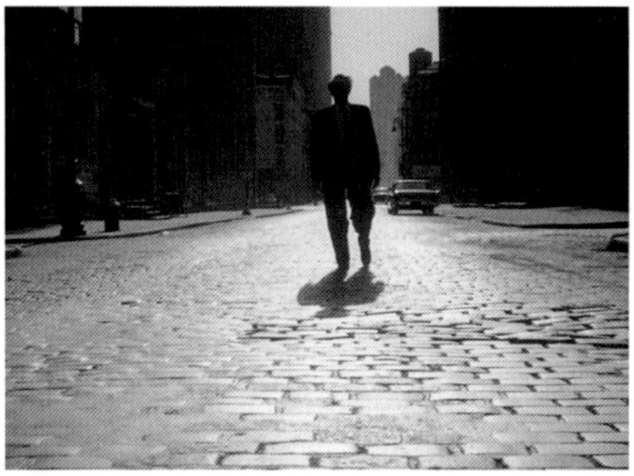
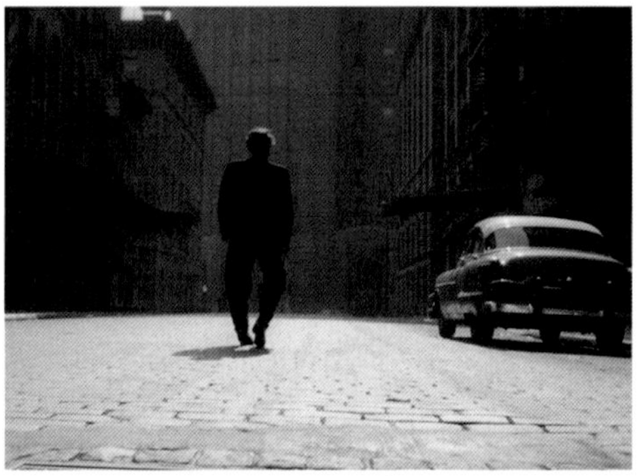
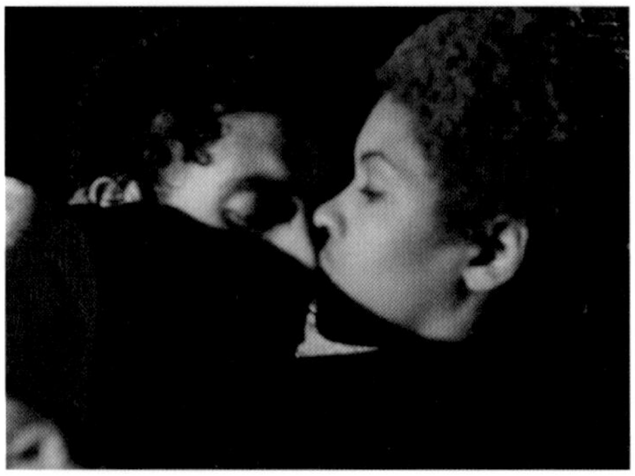
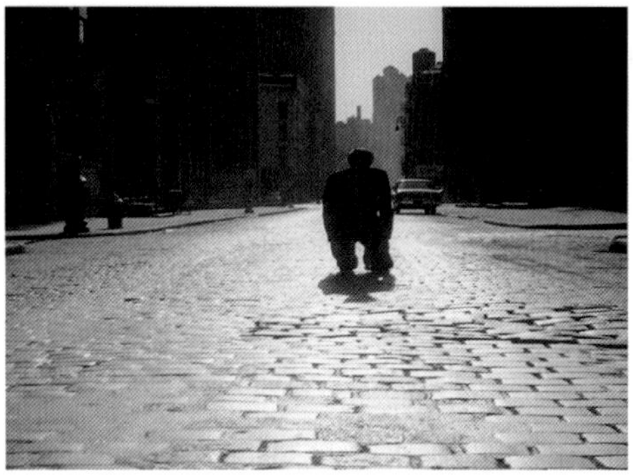
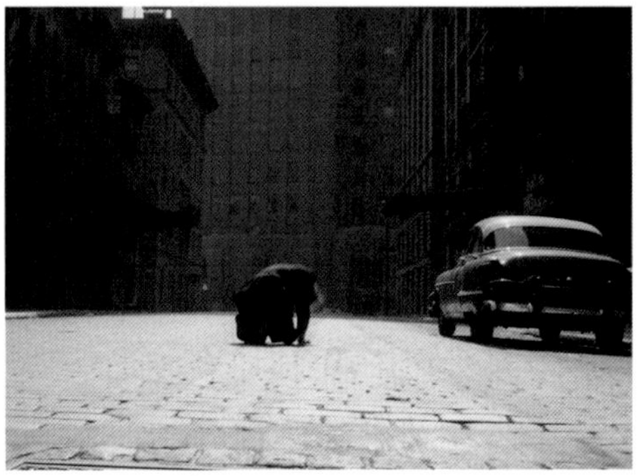
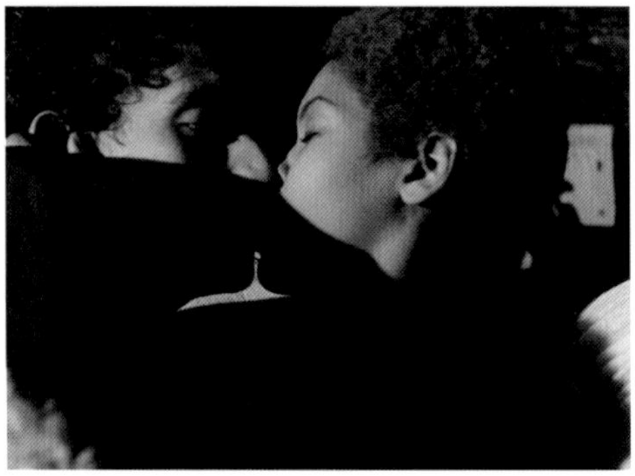
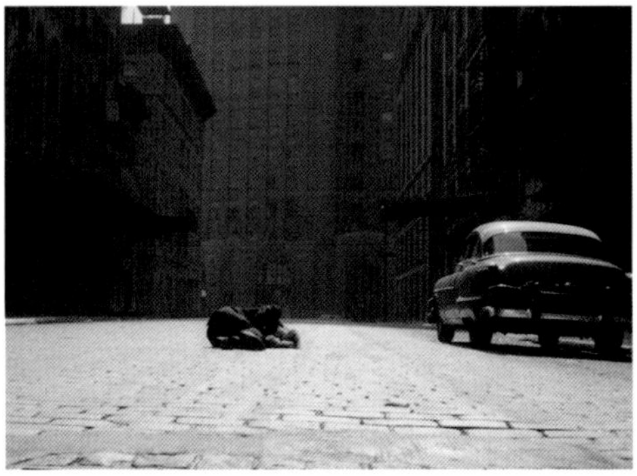

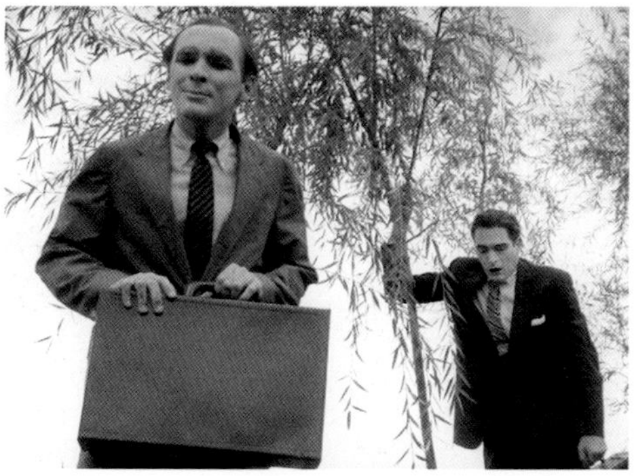
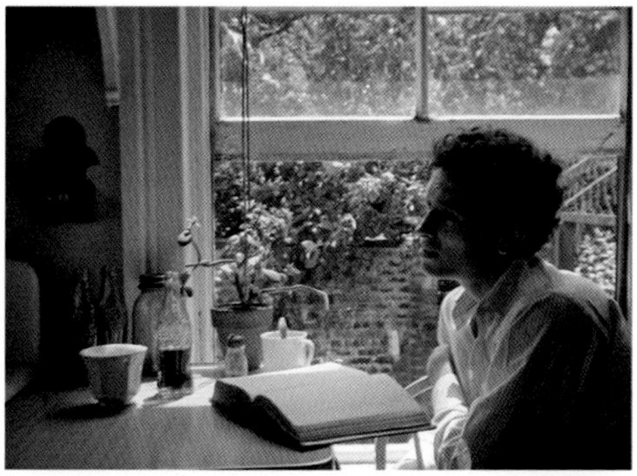
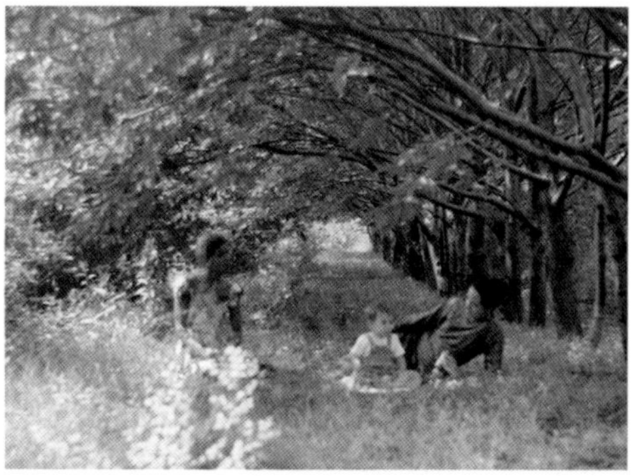
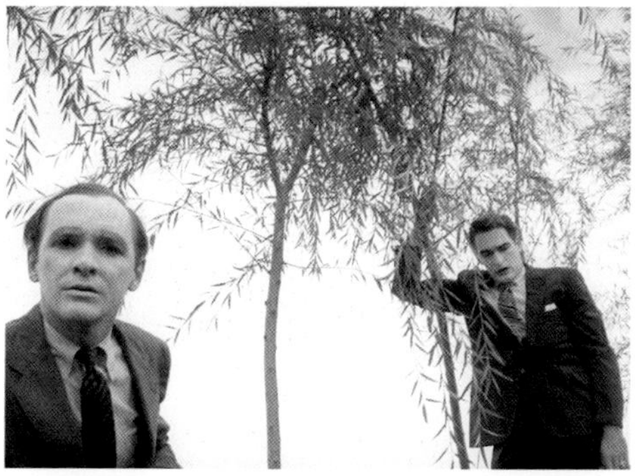
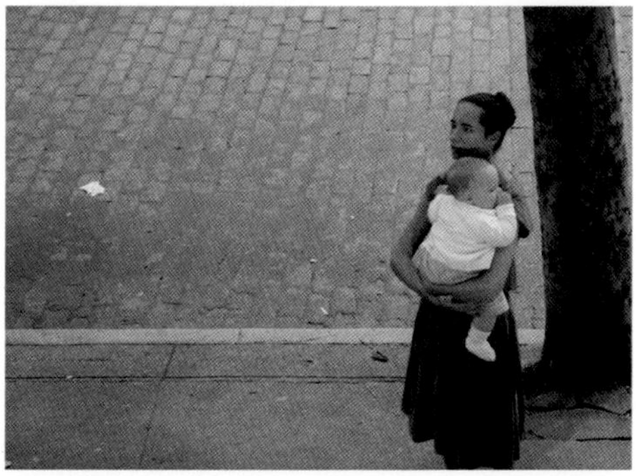
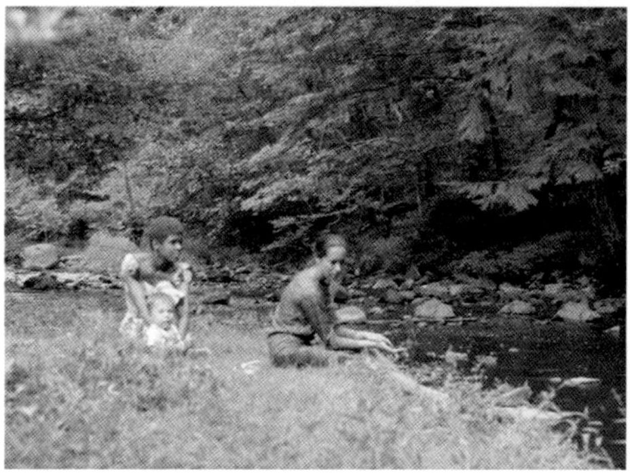
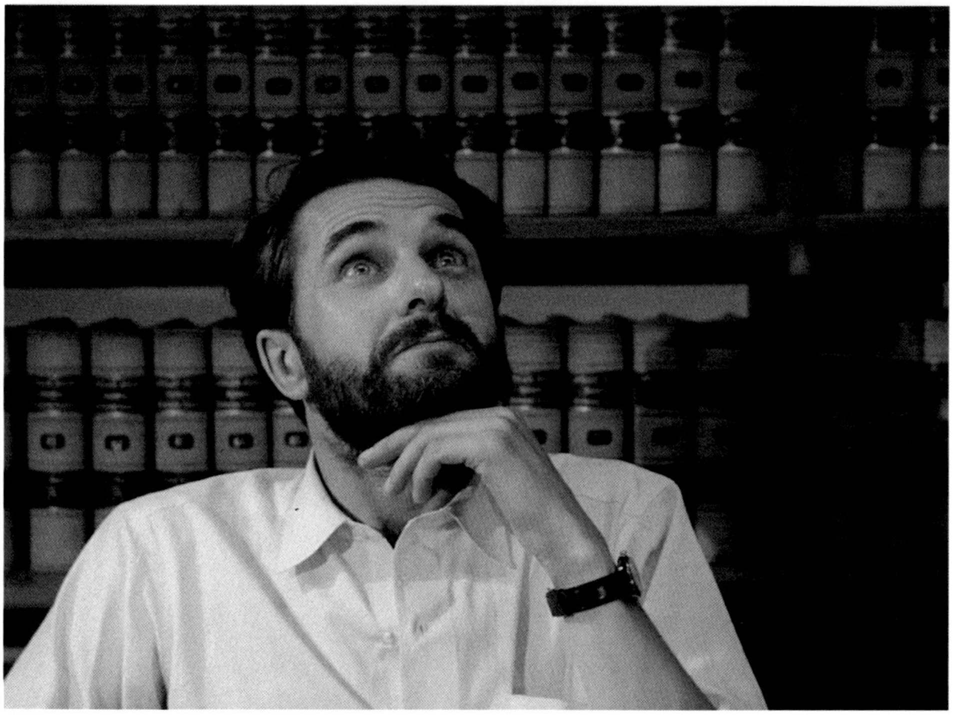
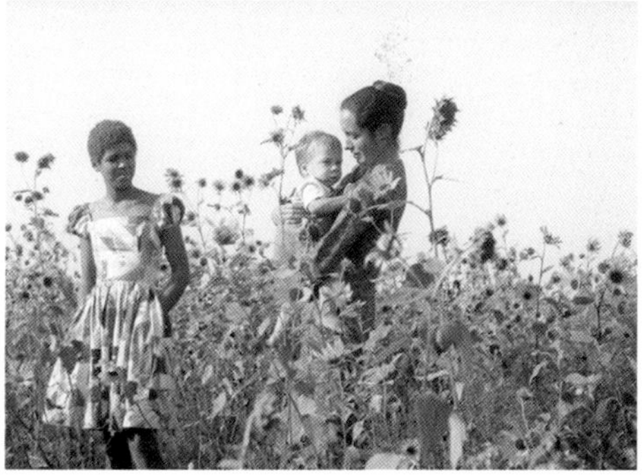
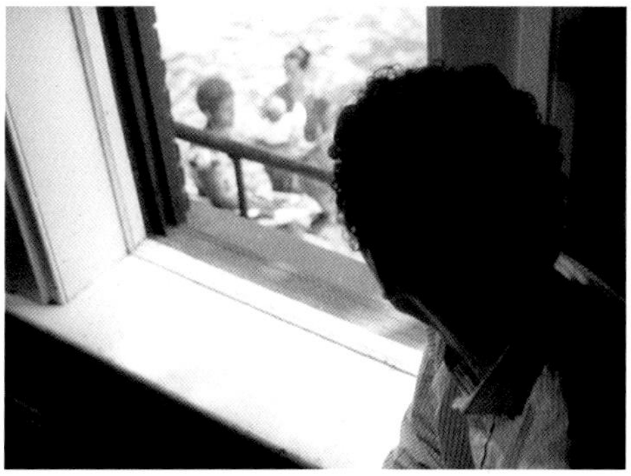

FILMS BLACK AND WHITE SOUND 87 MIN

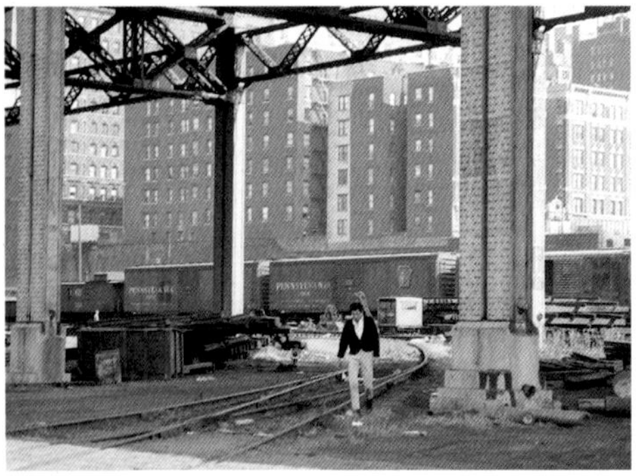

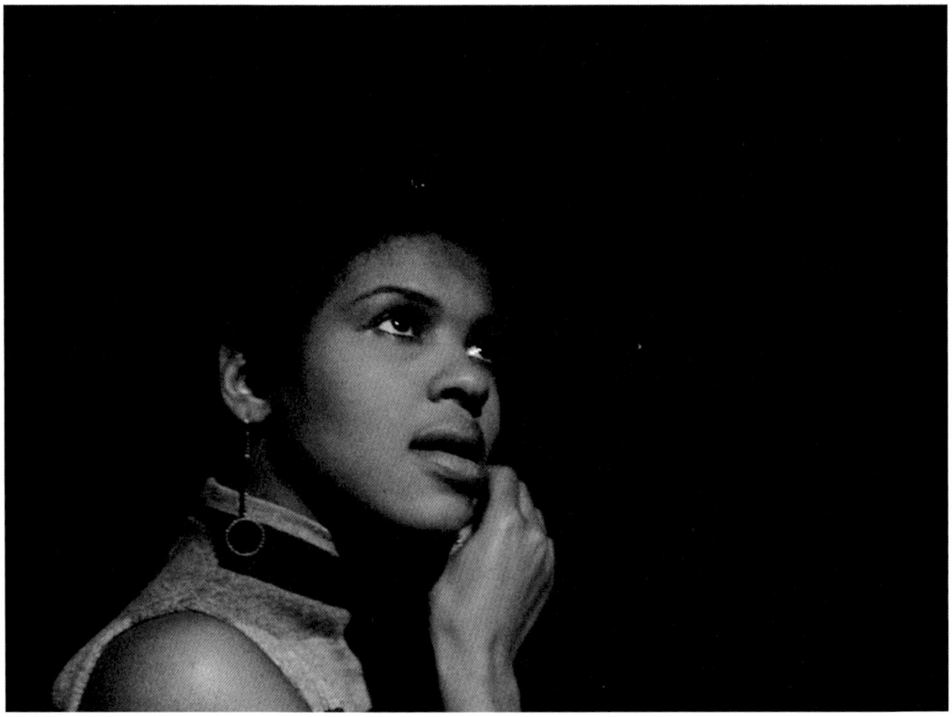

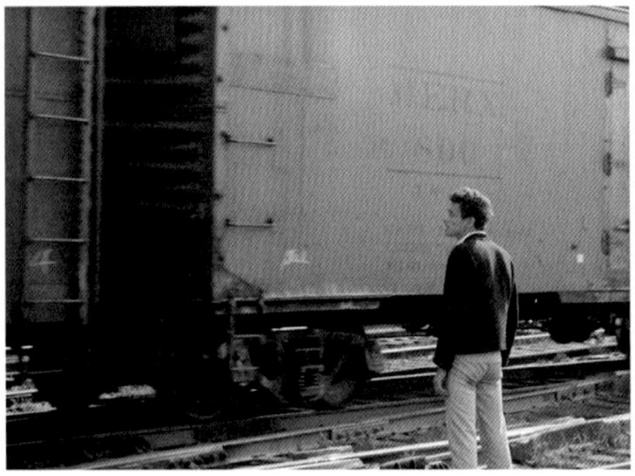

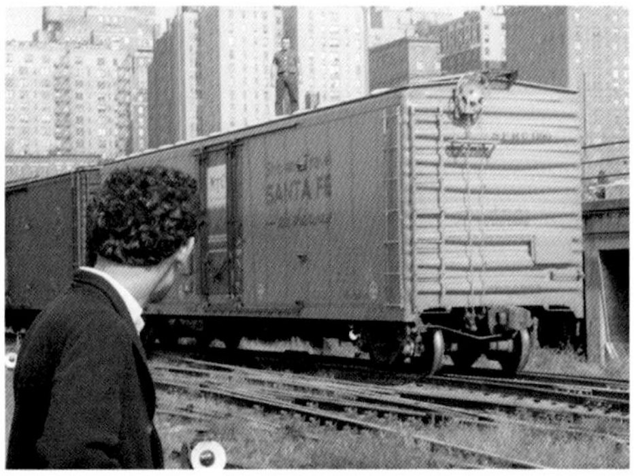
SANTA FE

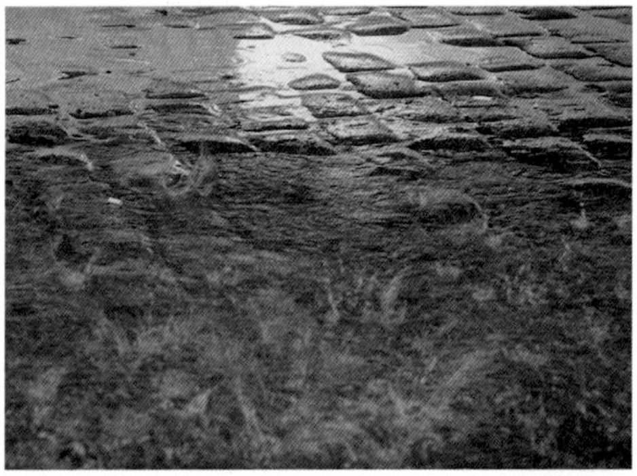

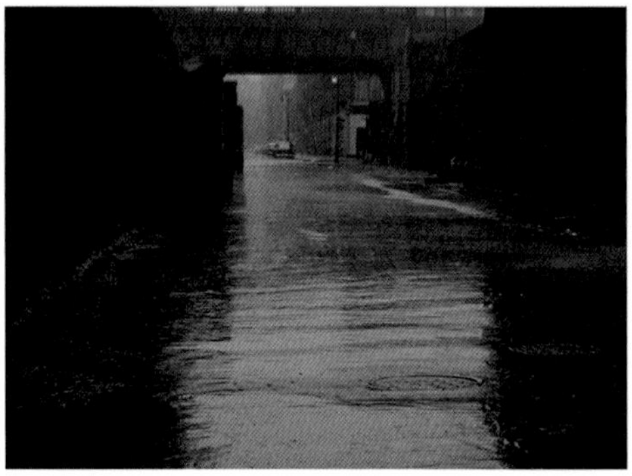

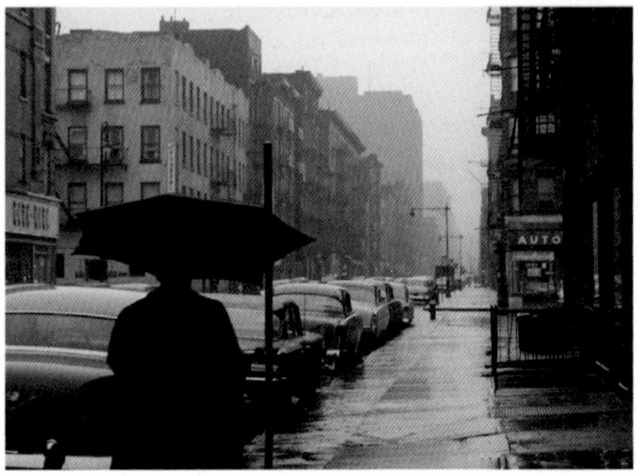
AUTO

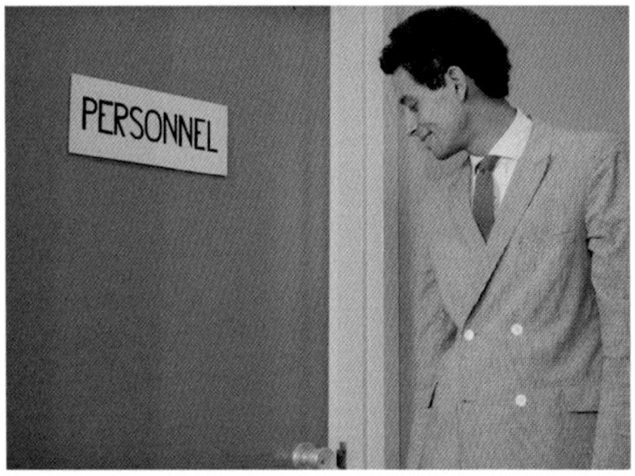
PERSONNEL

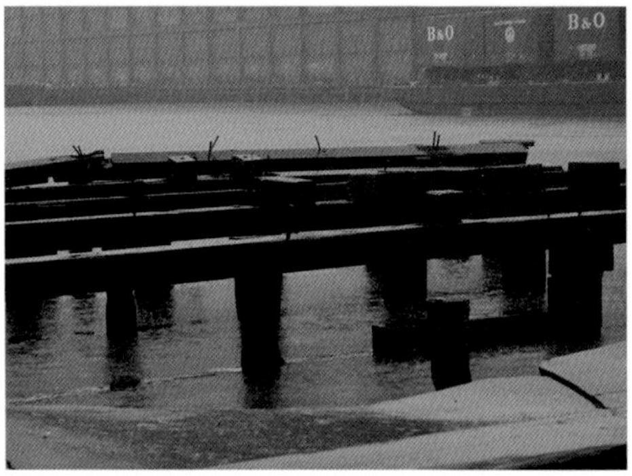
B&O
B&O

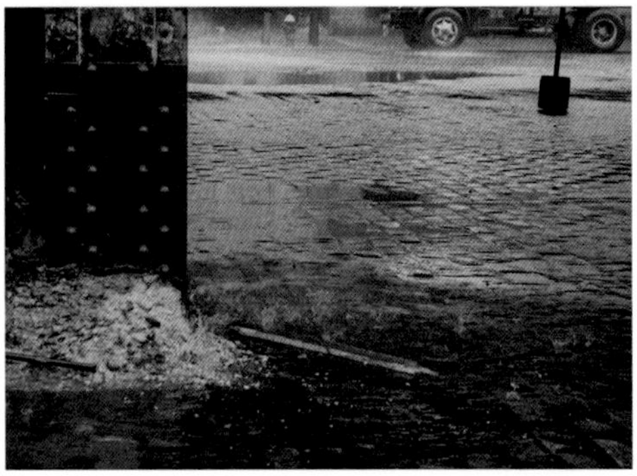

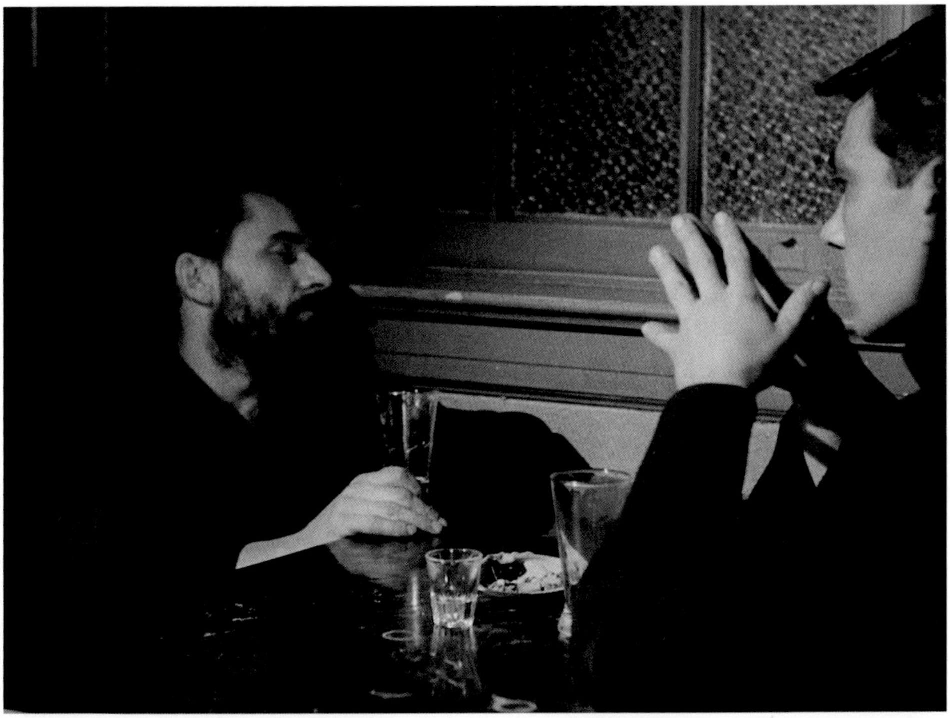
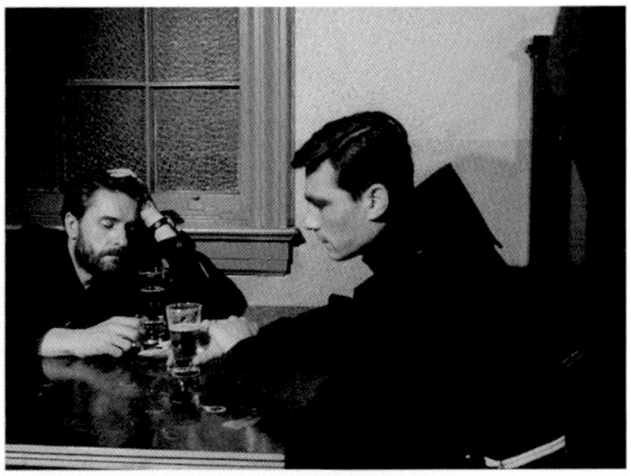
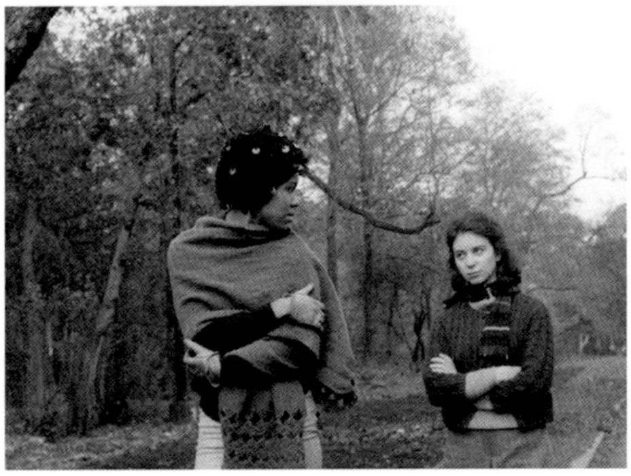
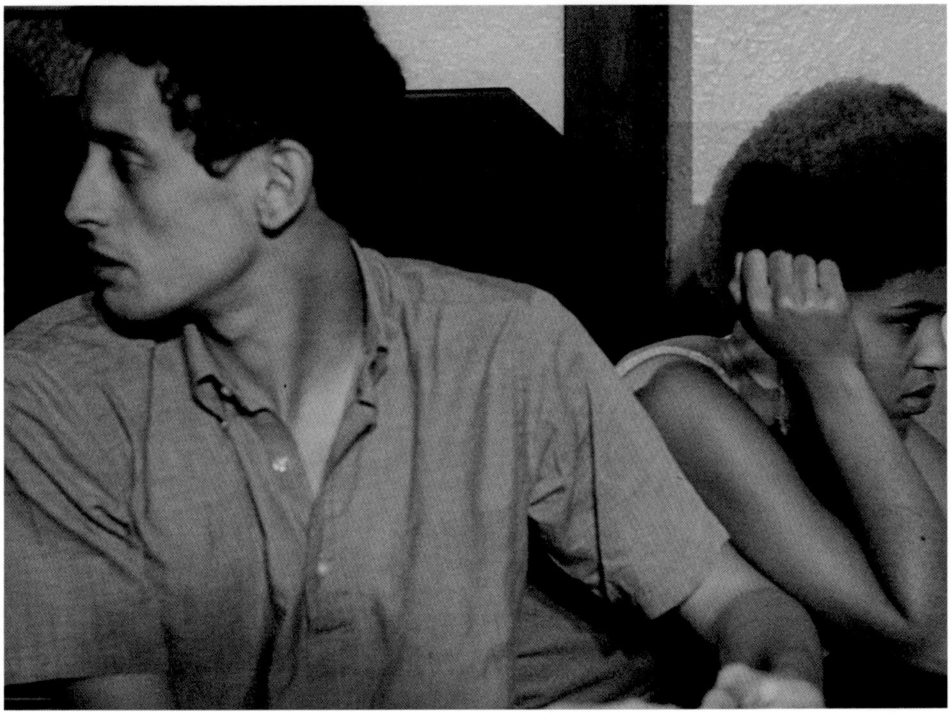
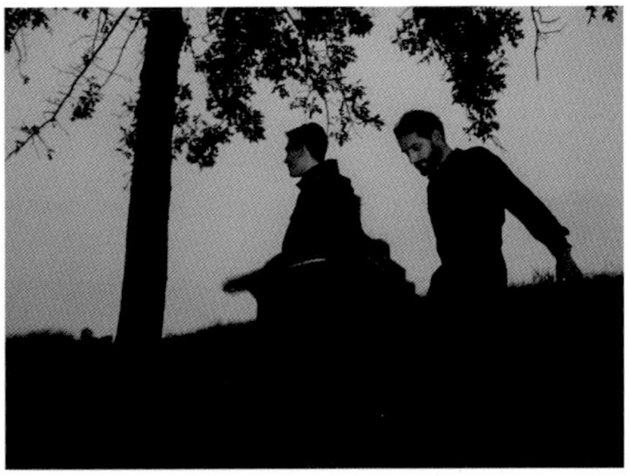
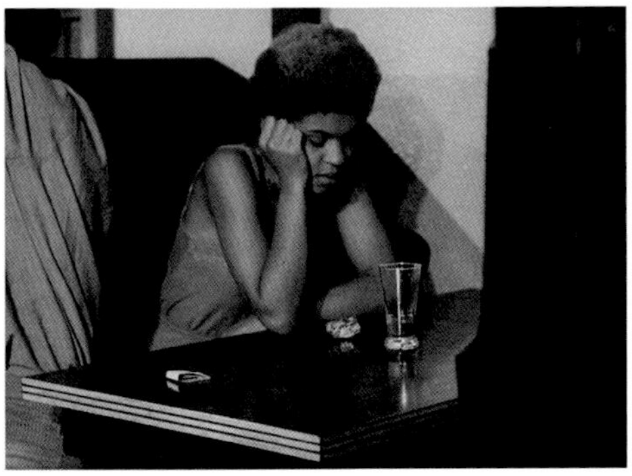
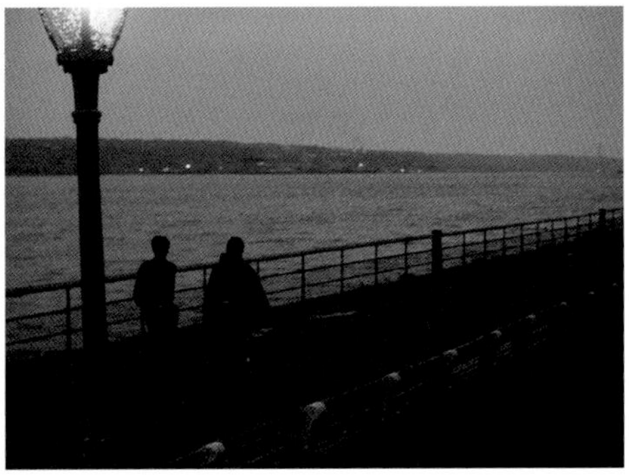

FILM MAGAZINE OF THE ARTS, 1963

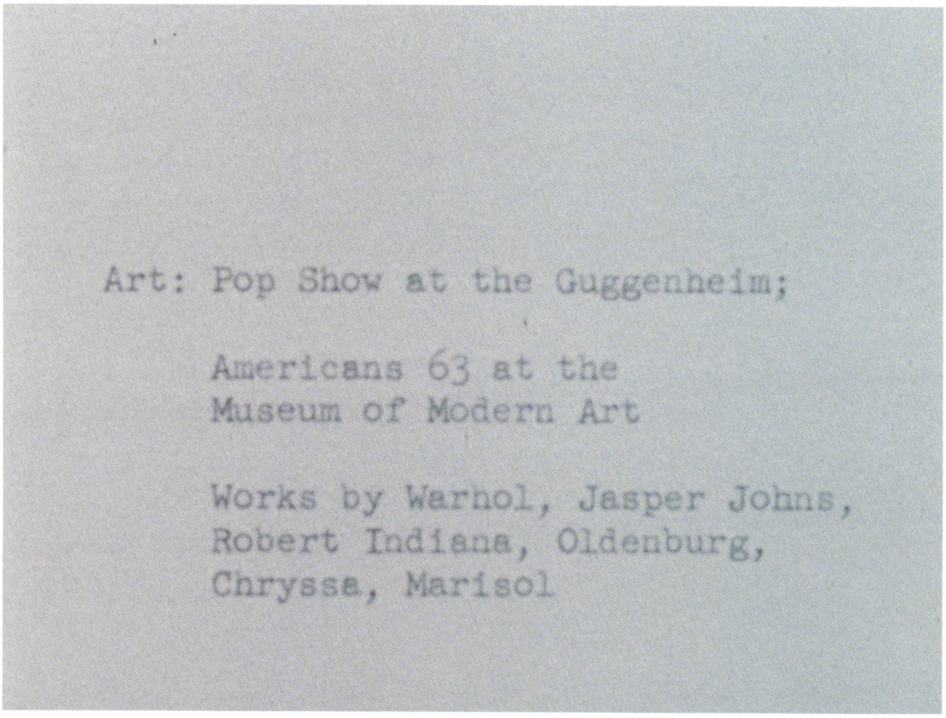

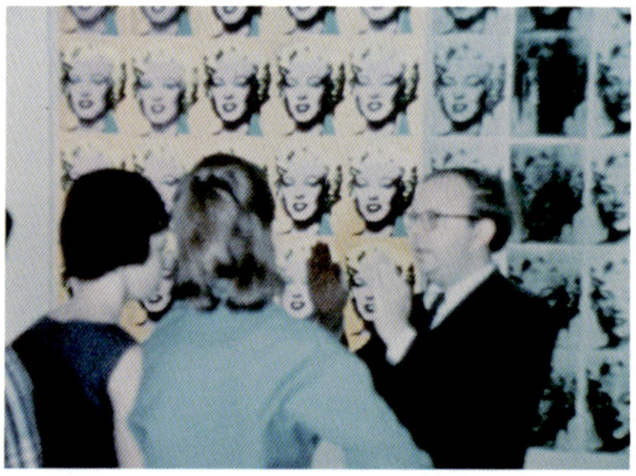

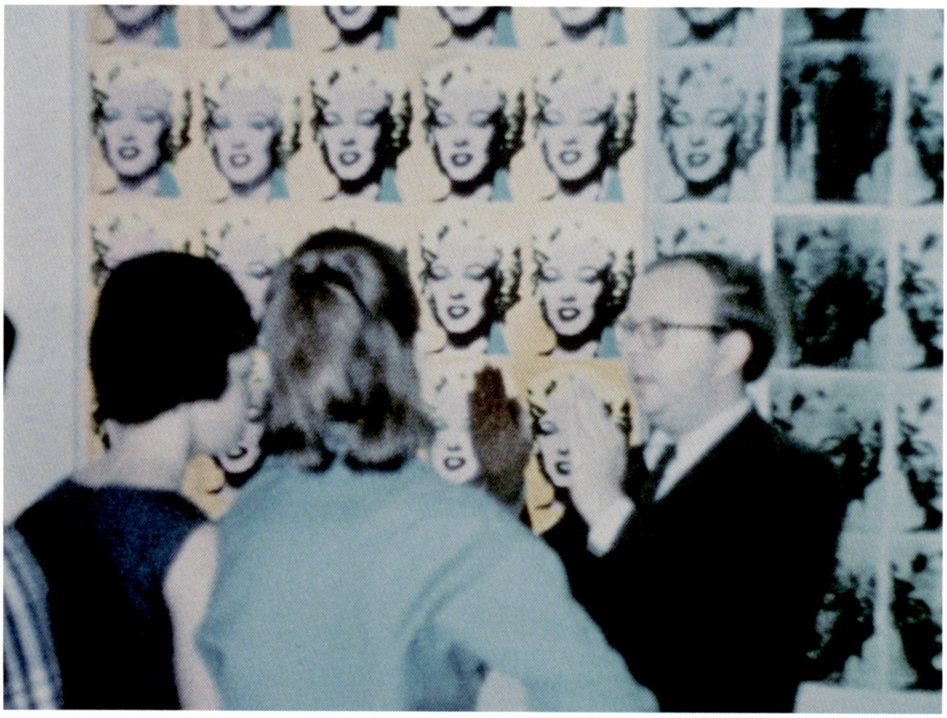

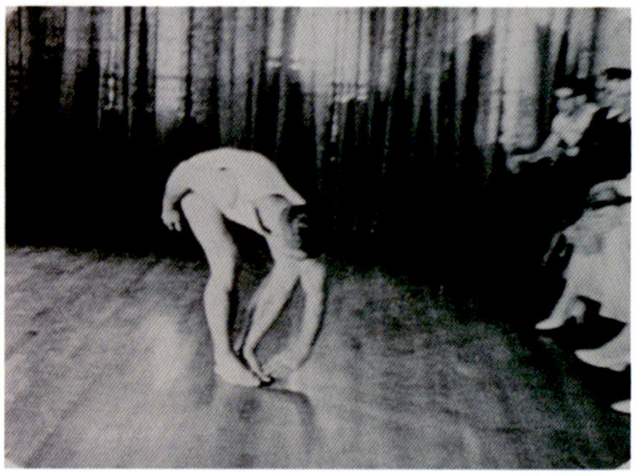

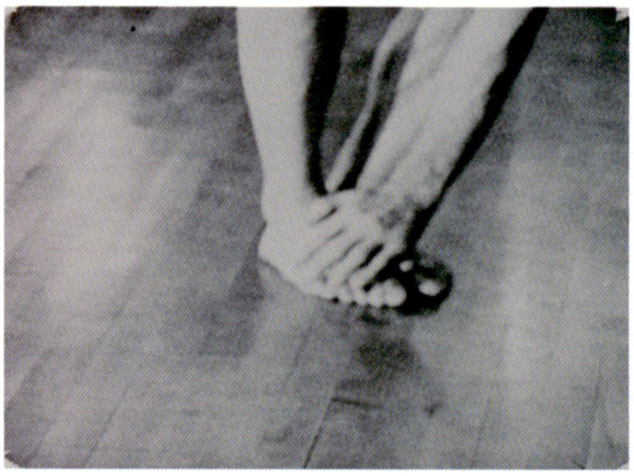

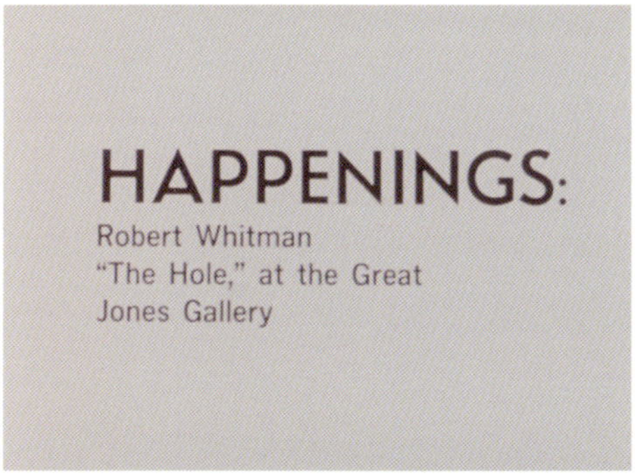

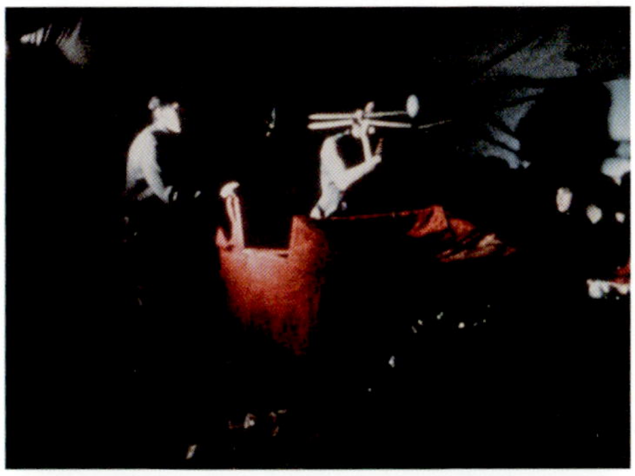

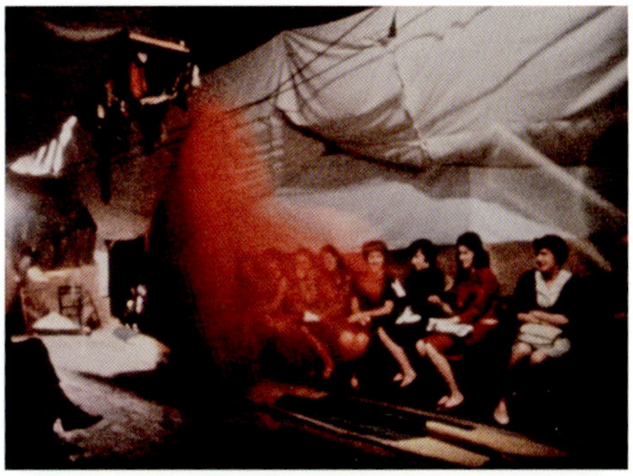

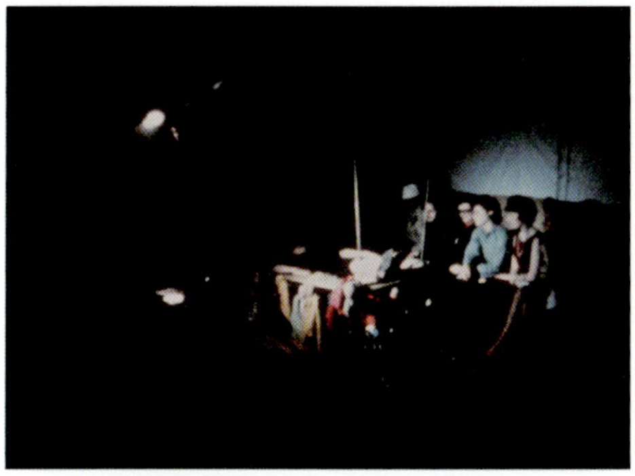

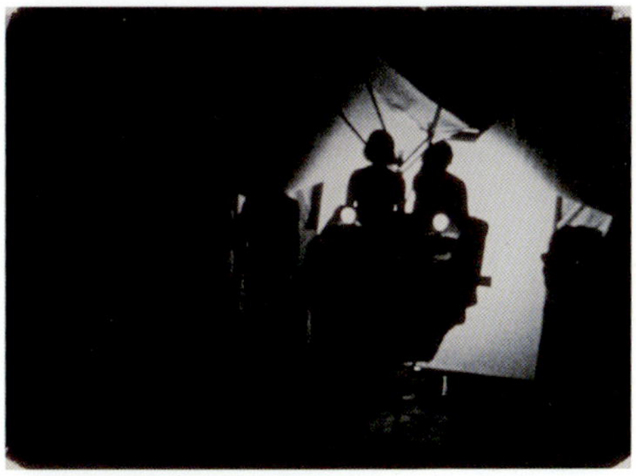

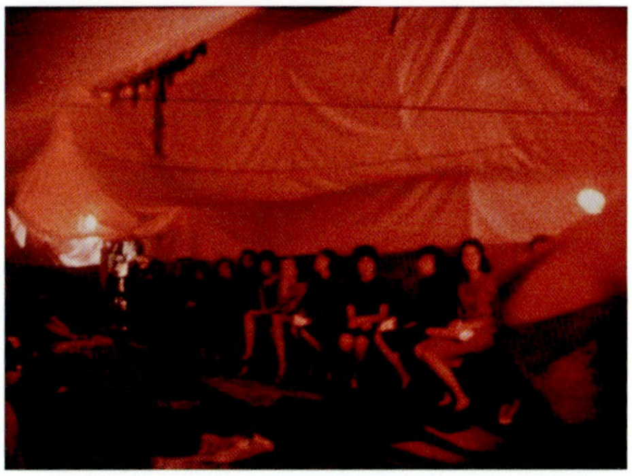

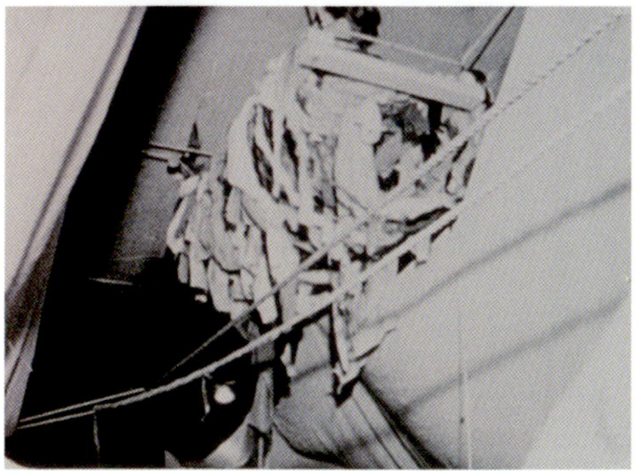

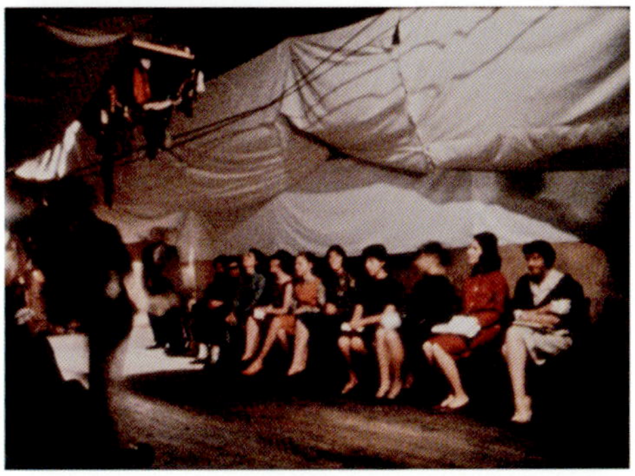

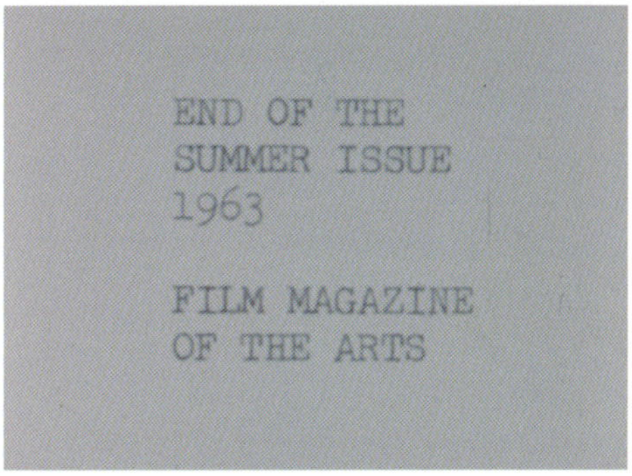

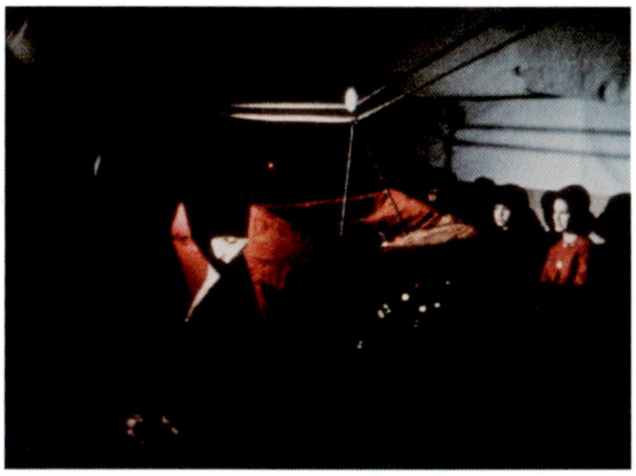

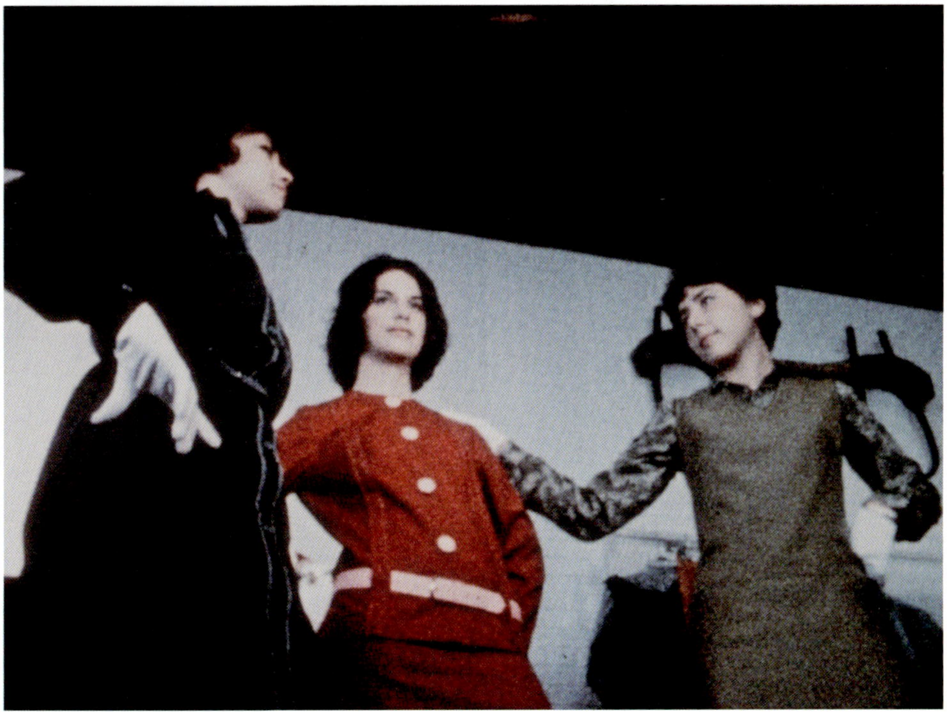

FILMS | COLOR, BLACK AND WHITE | SOUND | 20 MIN

AWARD PRESENTATION TO ANDY WARHOL, 1964

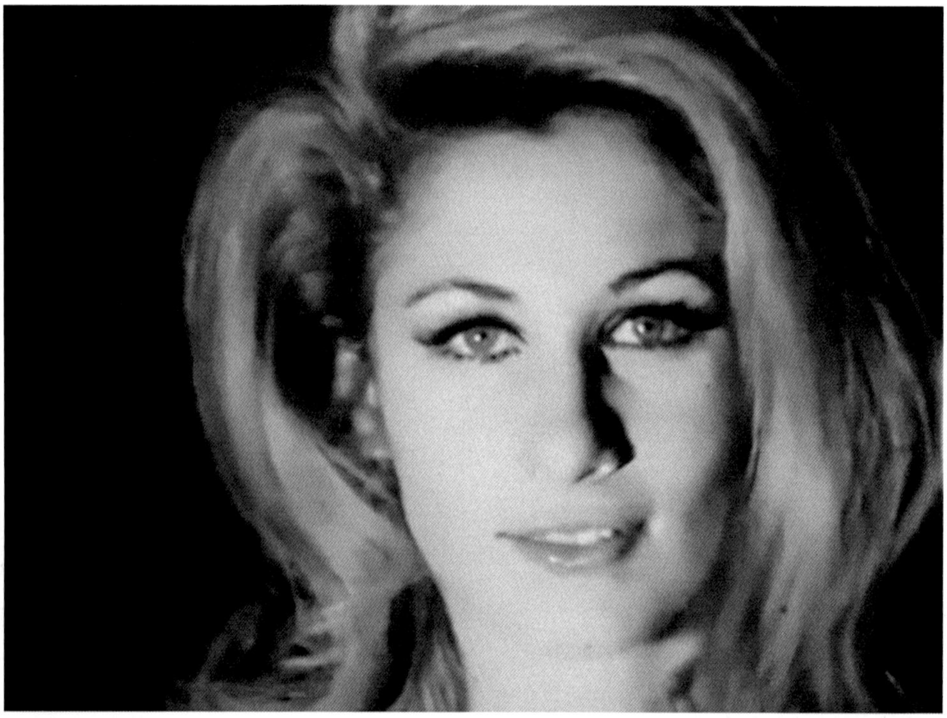

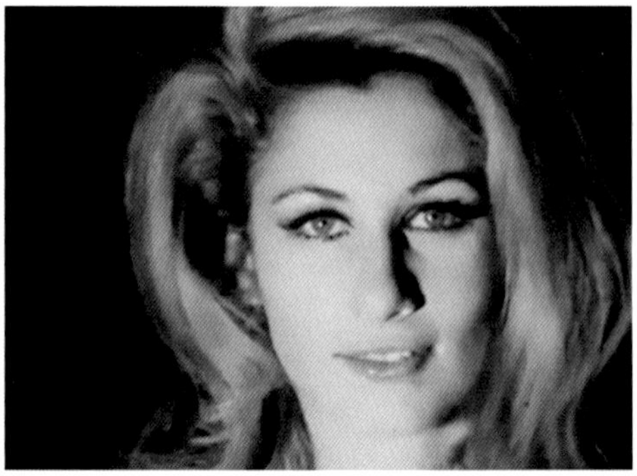

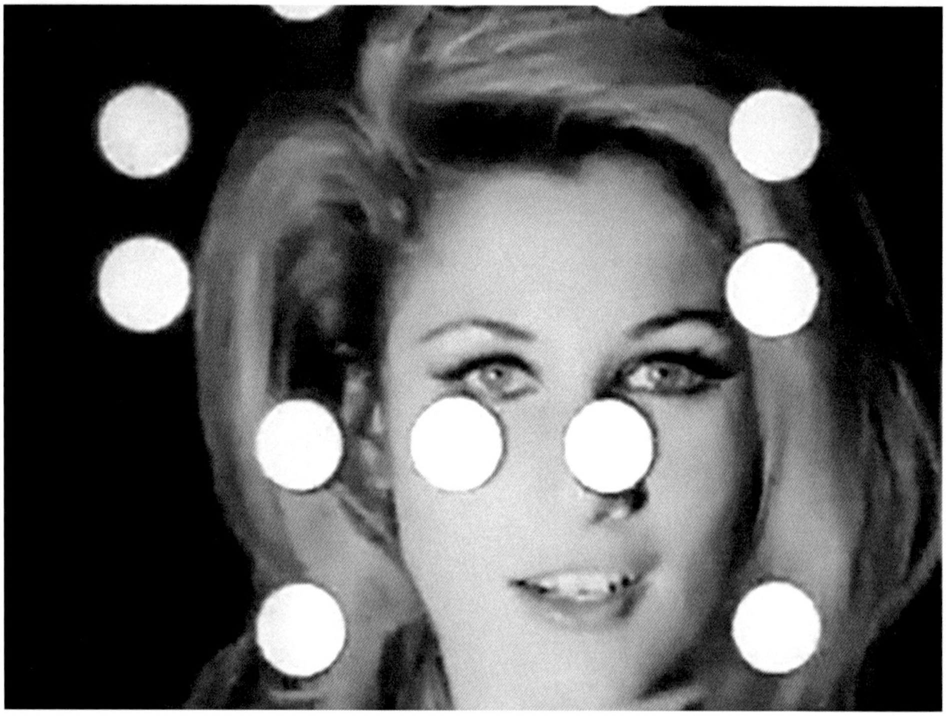

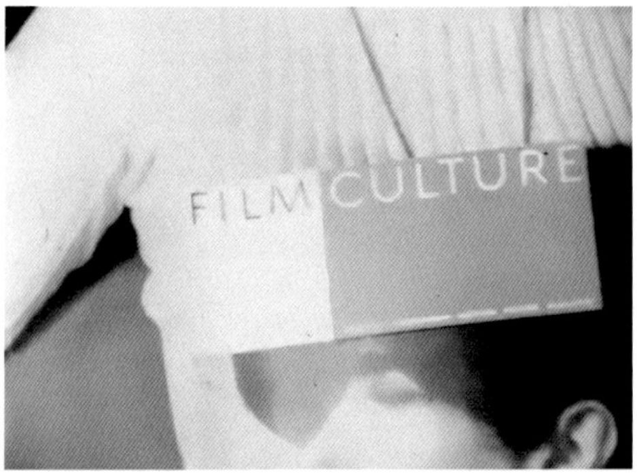

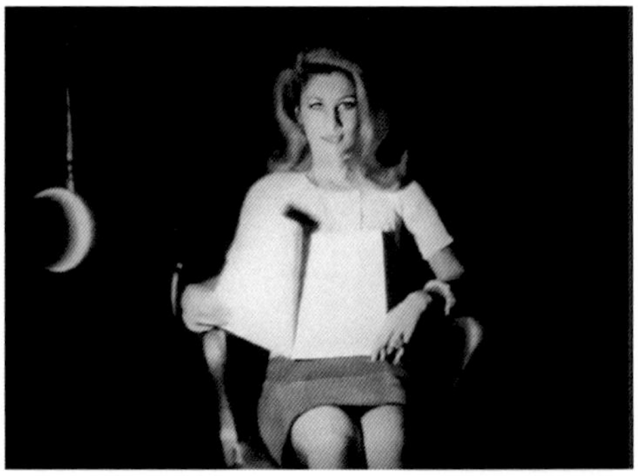

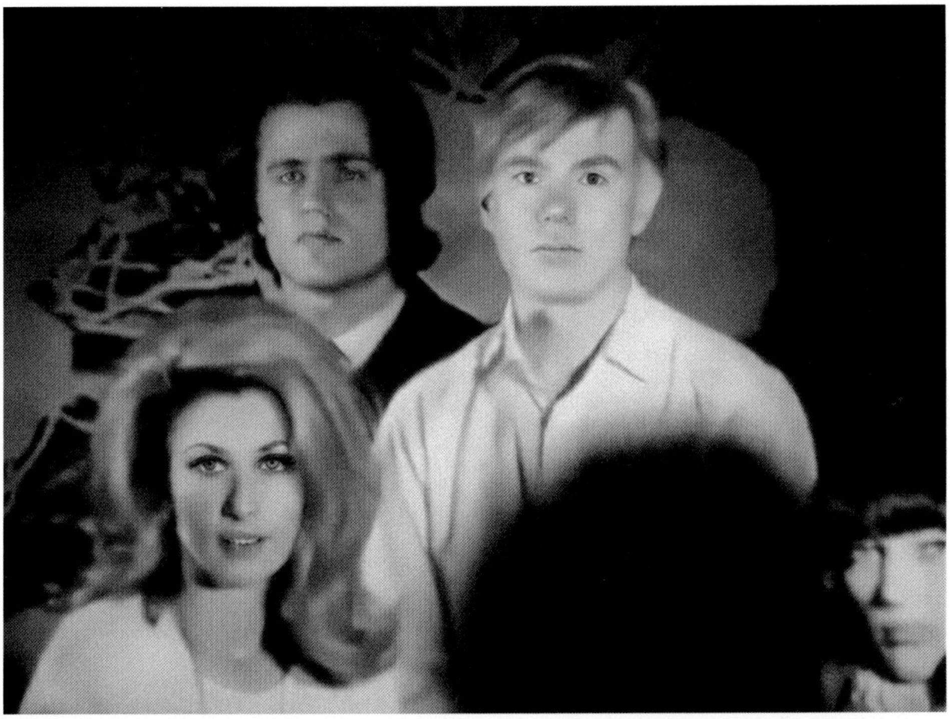
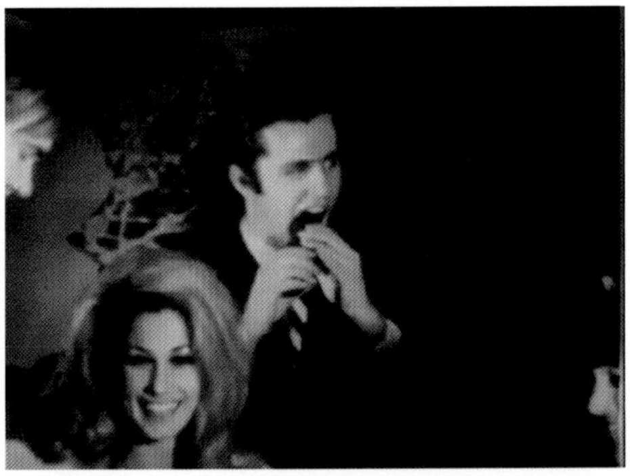
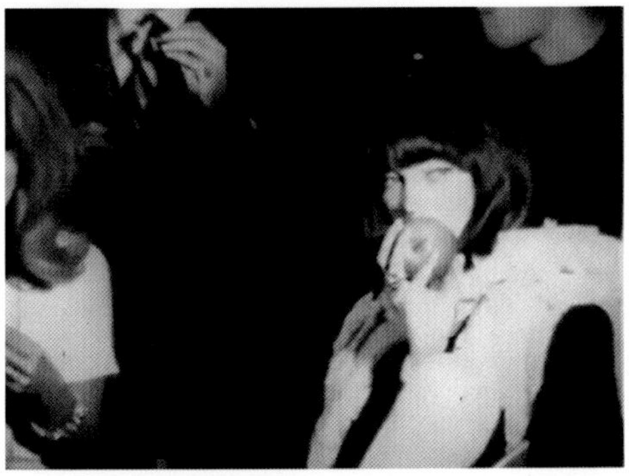
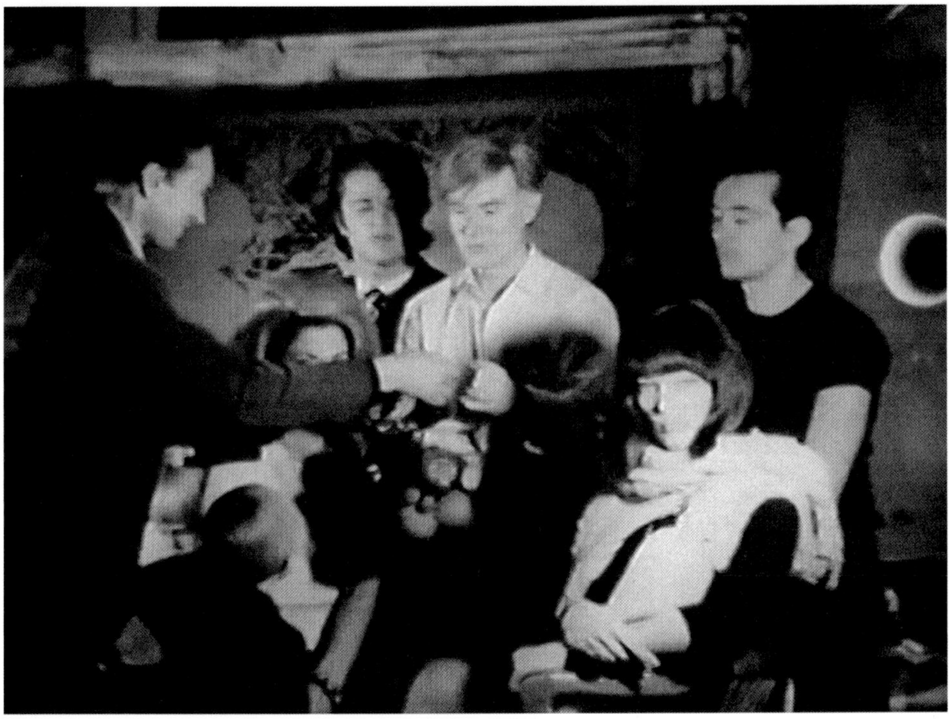
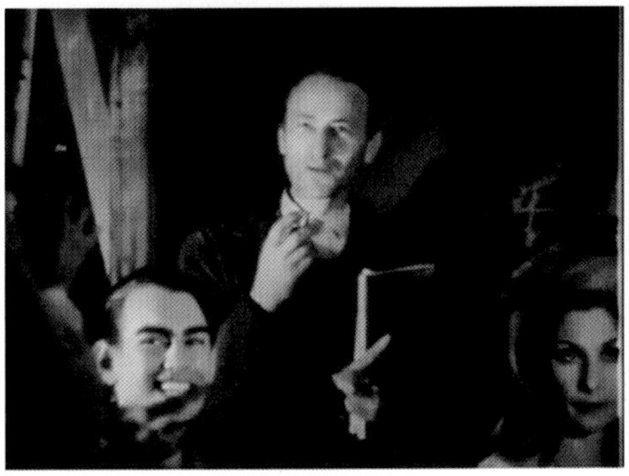
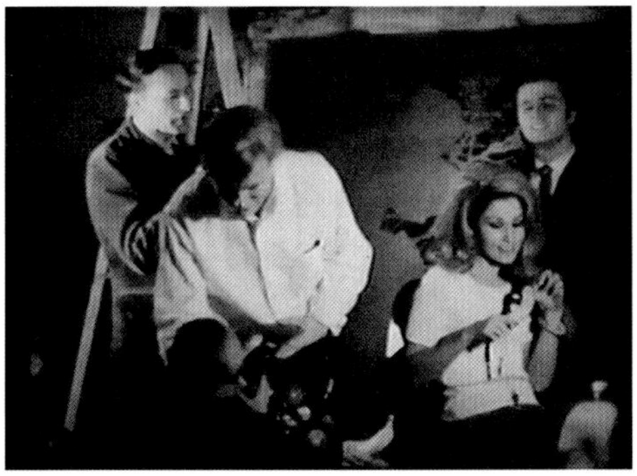
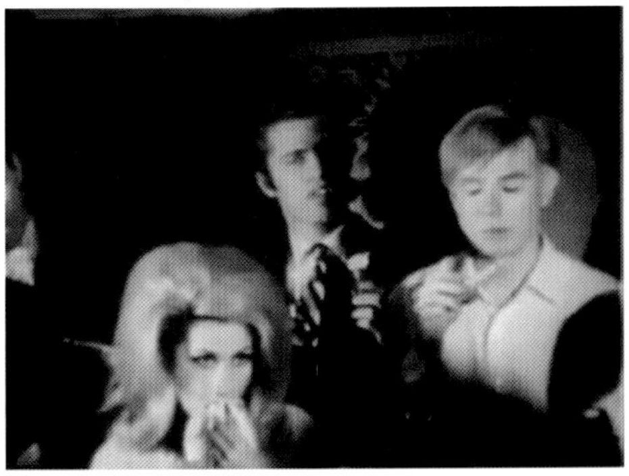

 FILMS BLACK AND WHITE SOUND 12 MIN

THE BRIG, 1964

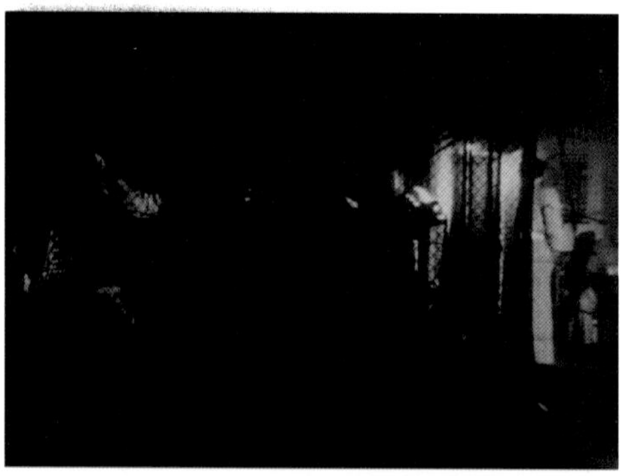

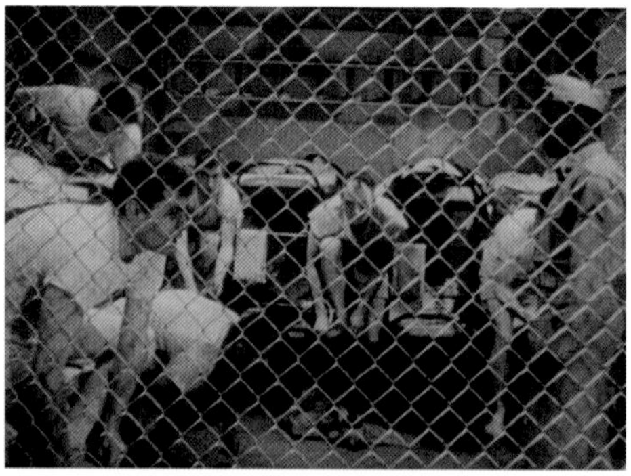

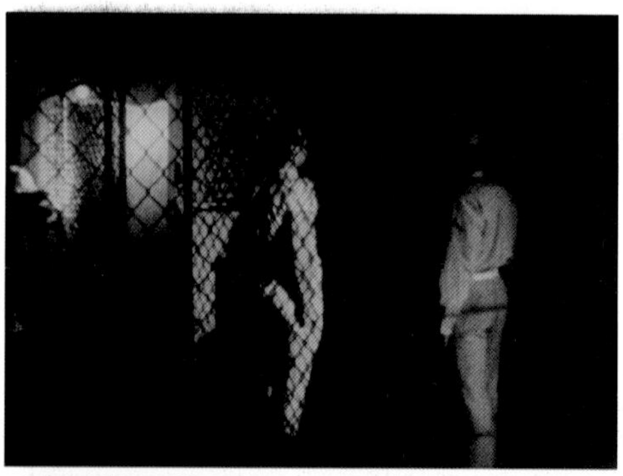

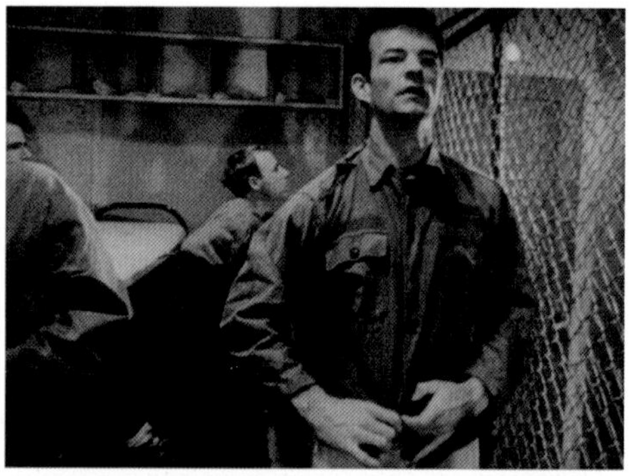

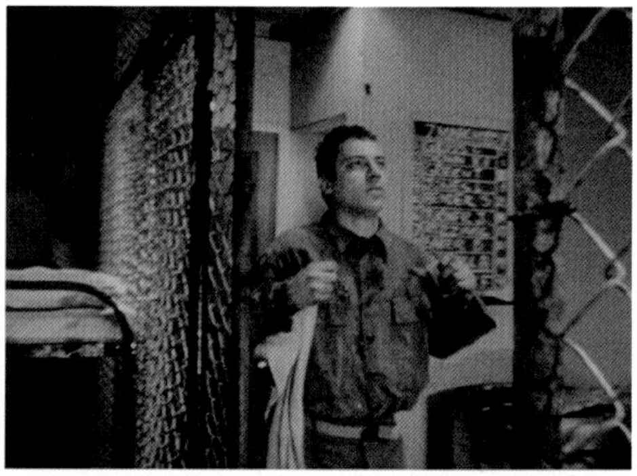

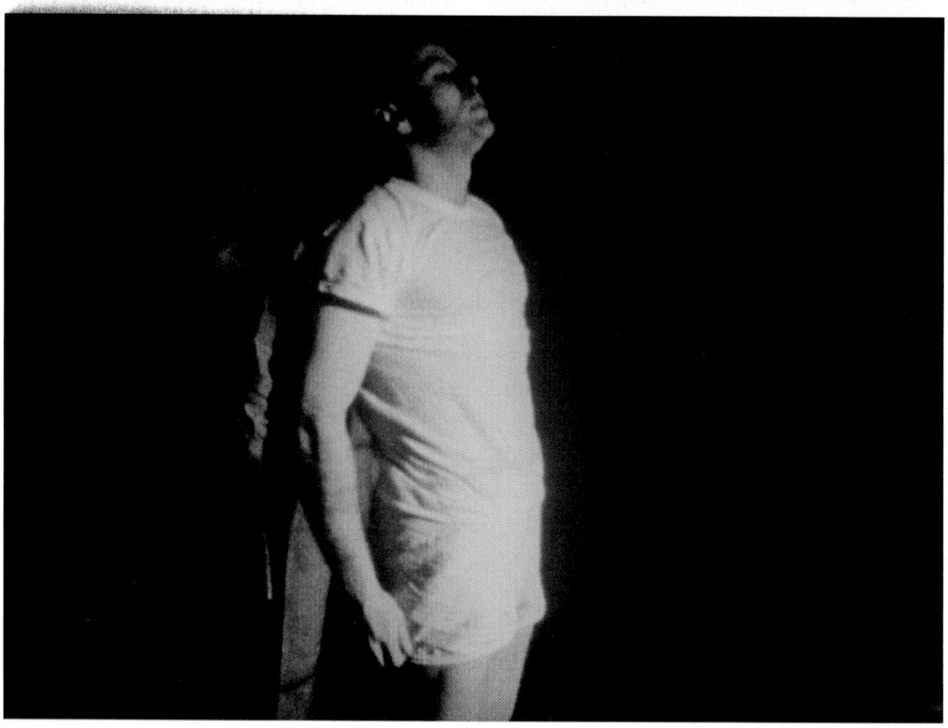

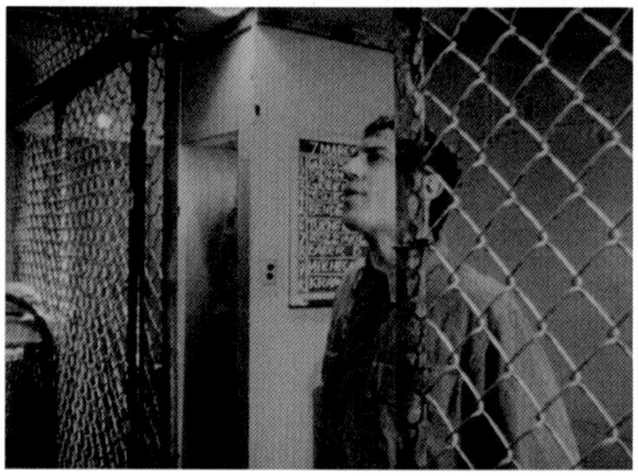

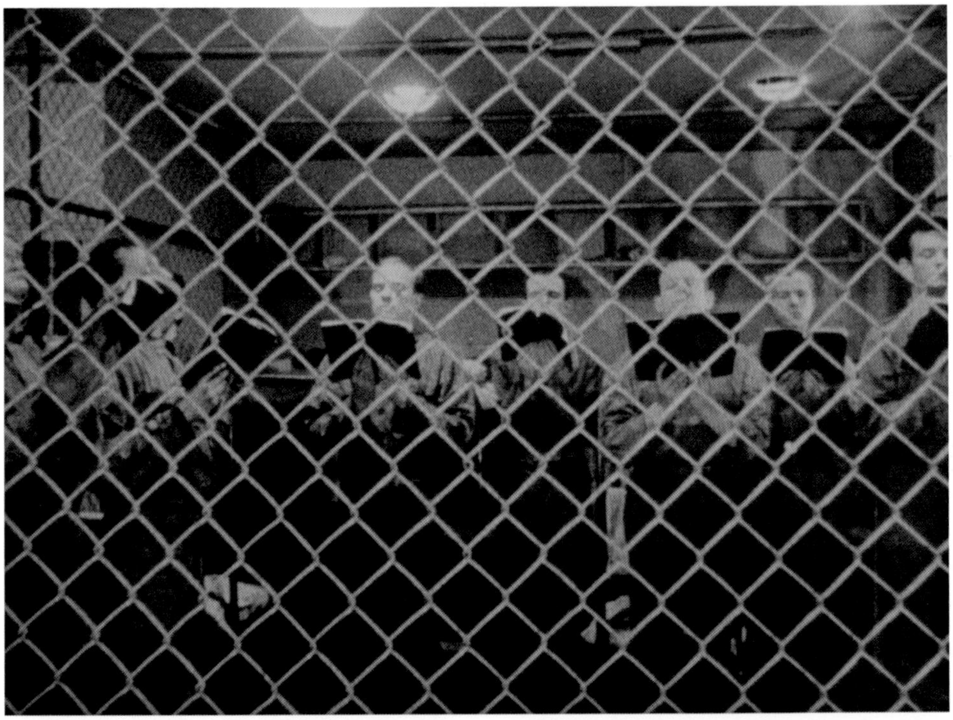

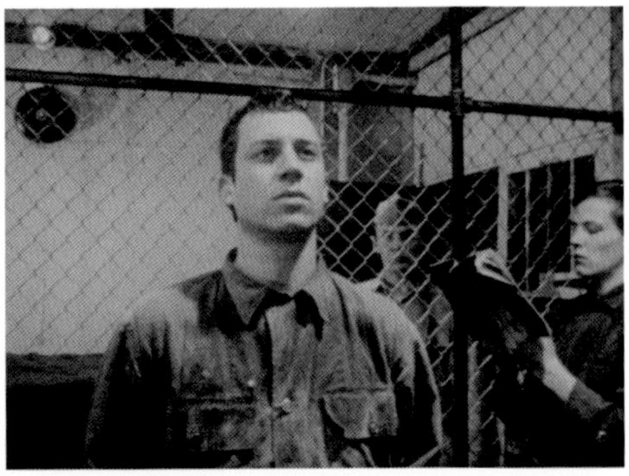

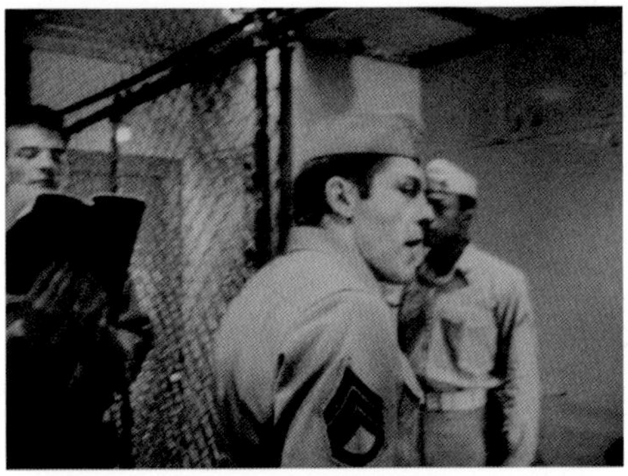

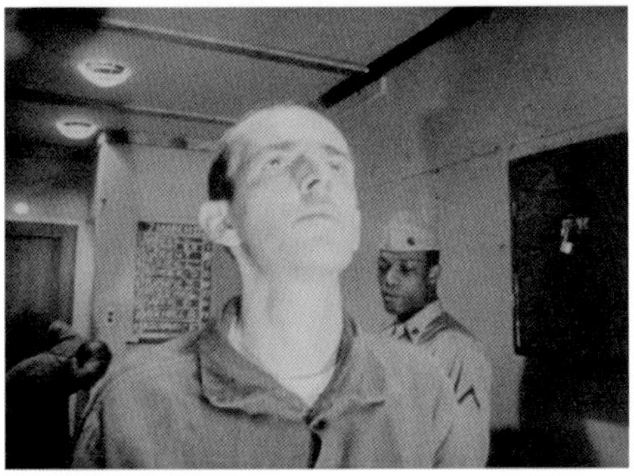

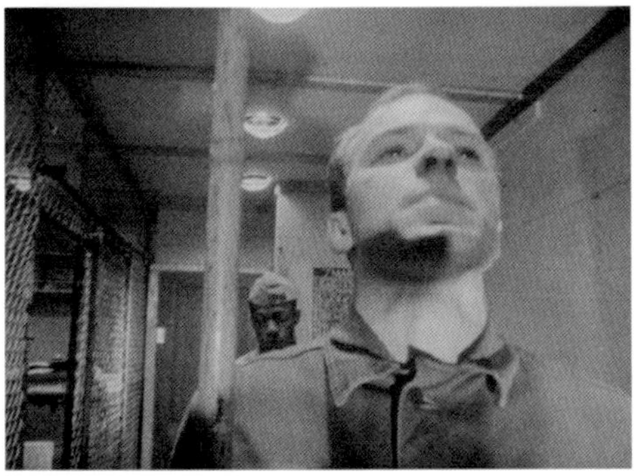

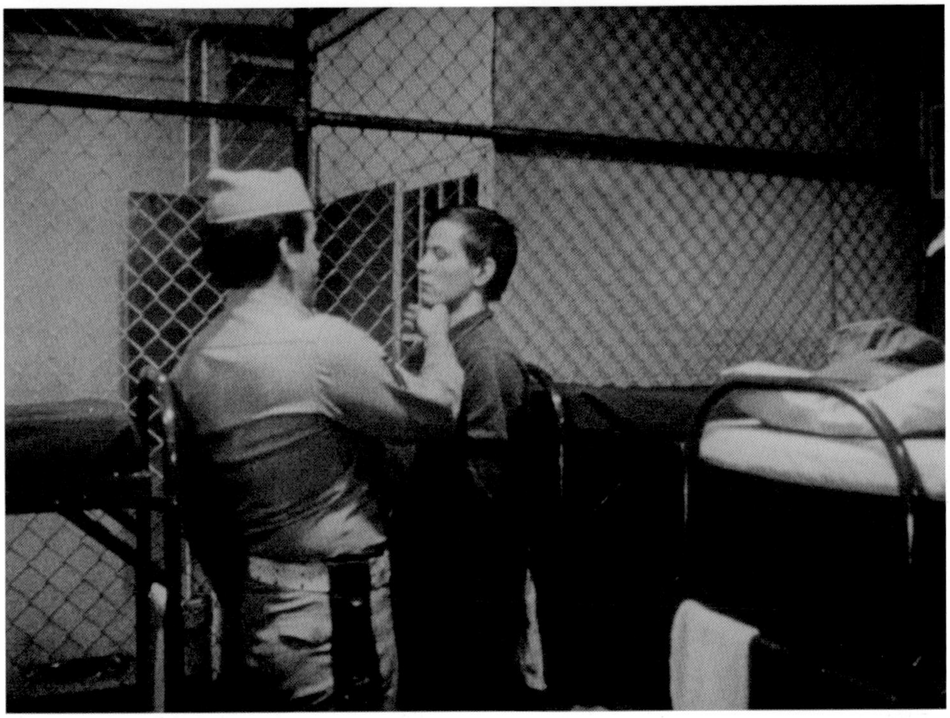

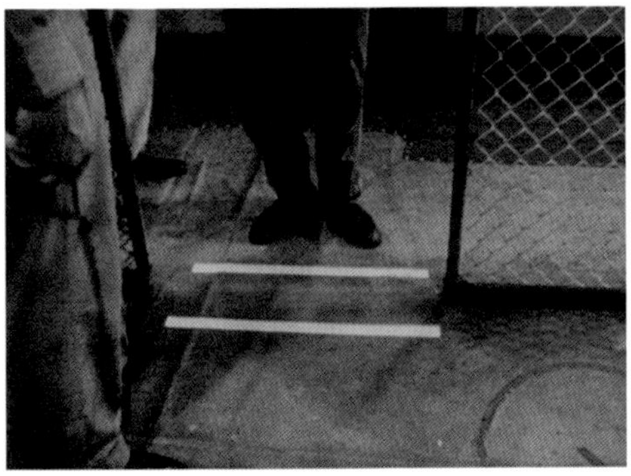

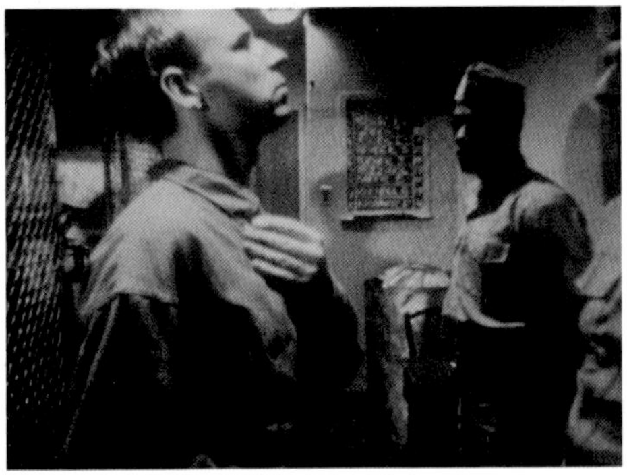

FILMS BLACK AND WHITE SOUND 68 MIN

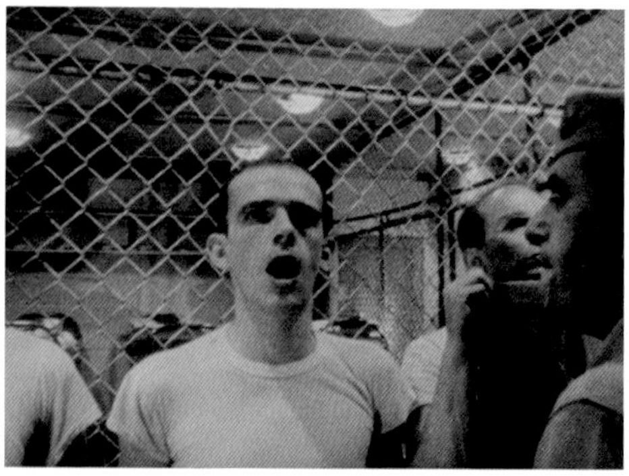
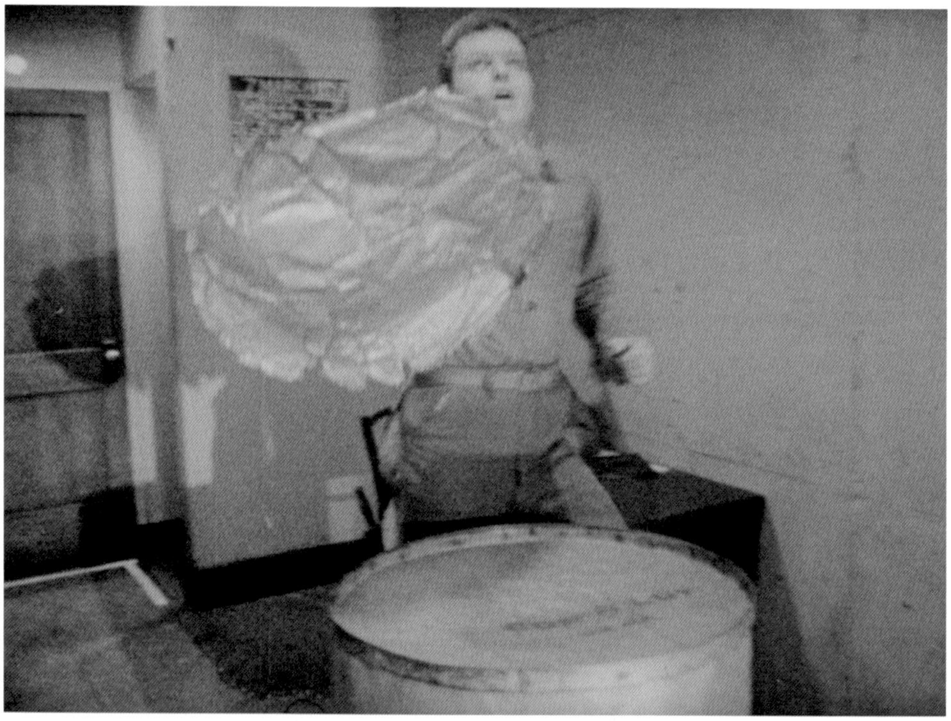
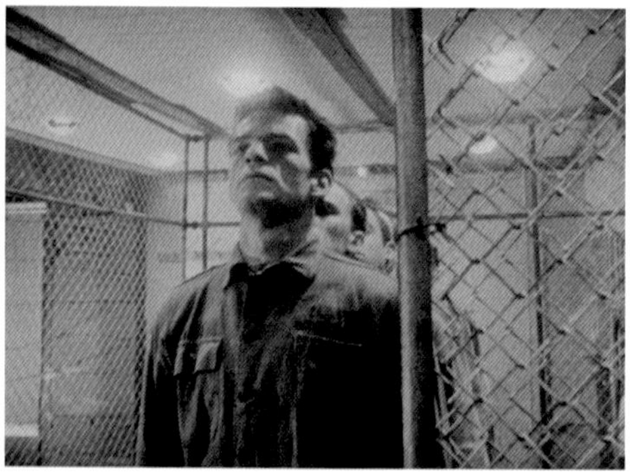
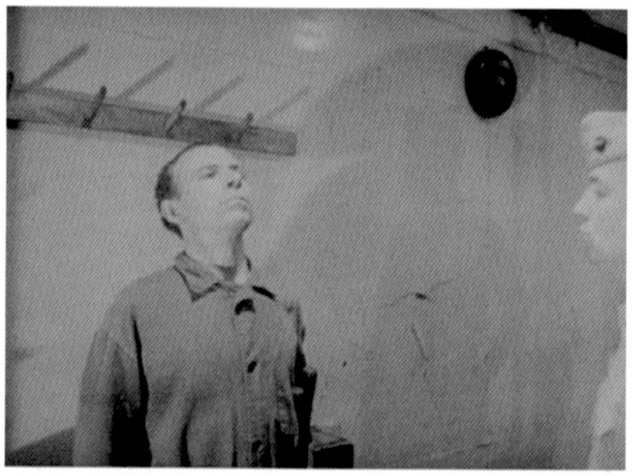
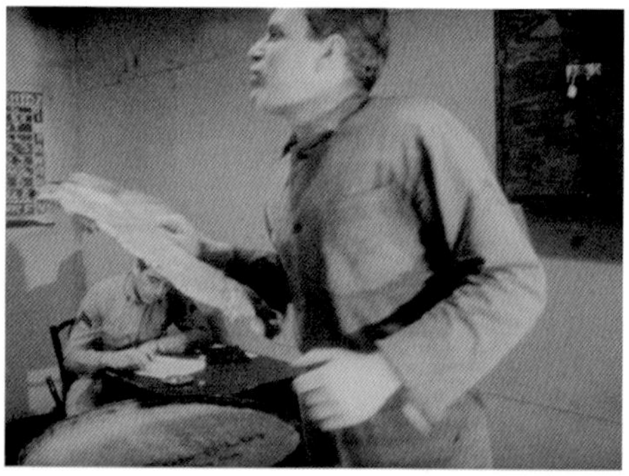
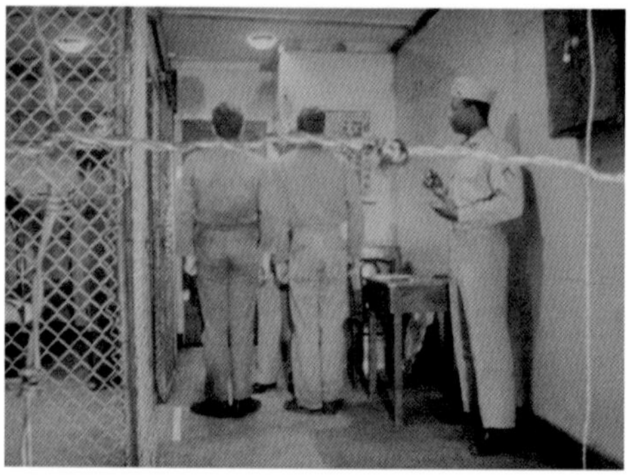
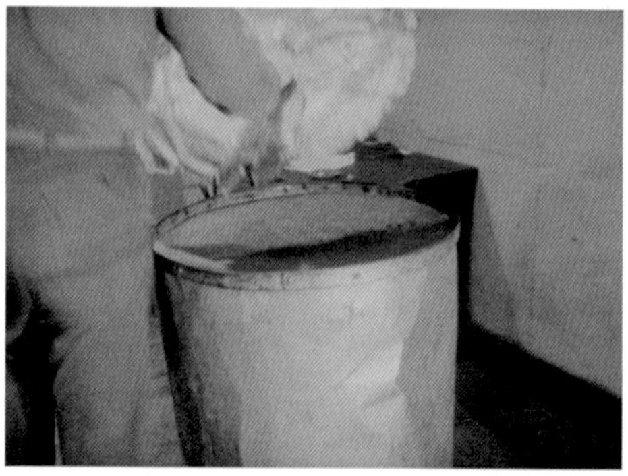
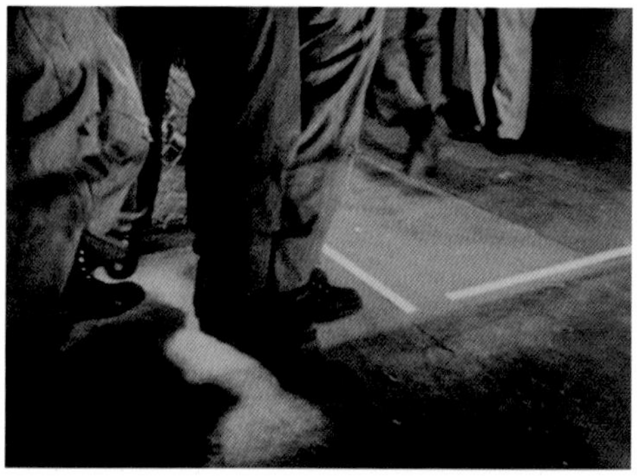
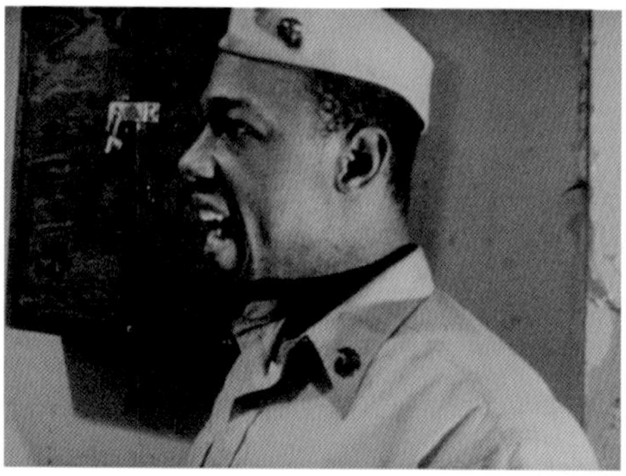
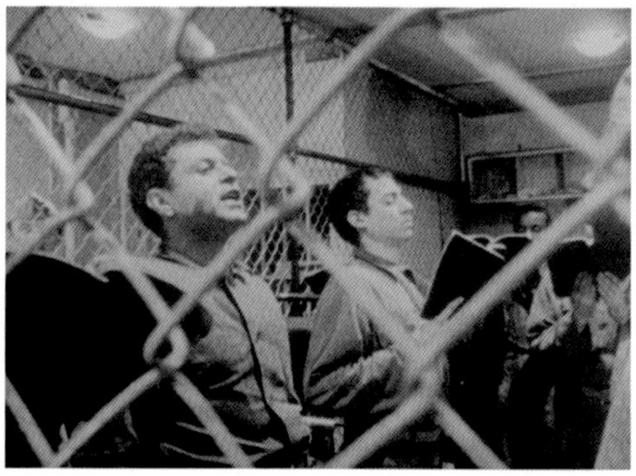

THE BRIG 16MM 1964

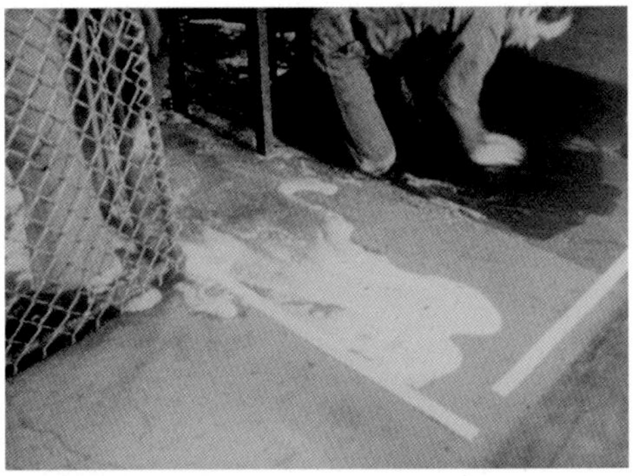
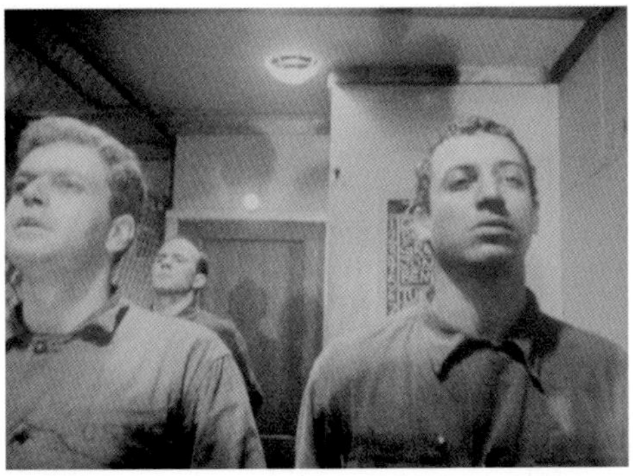
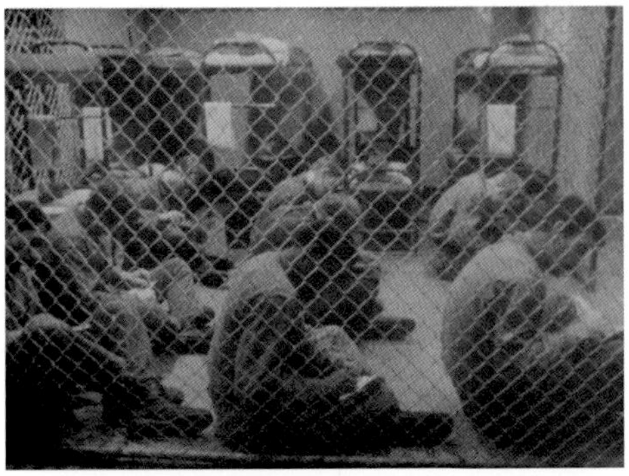
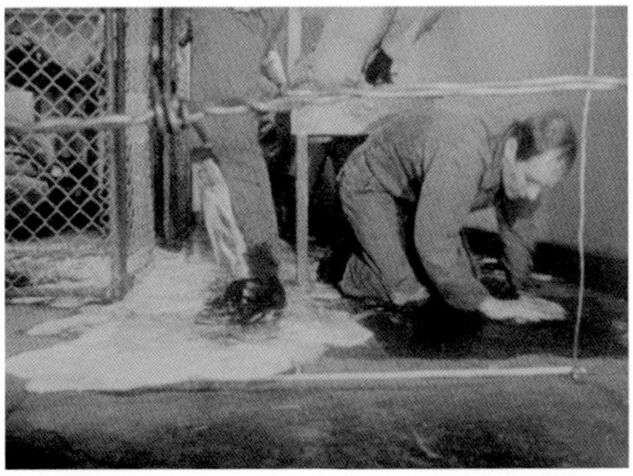
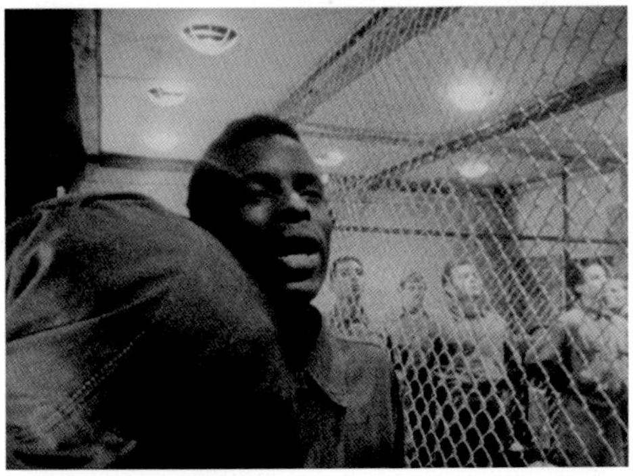
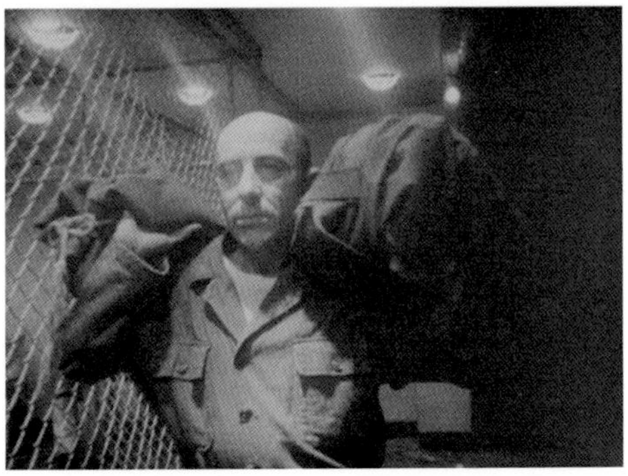
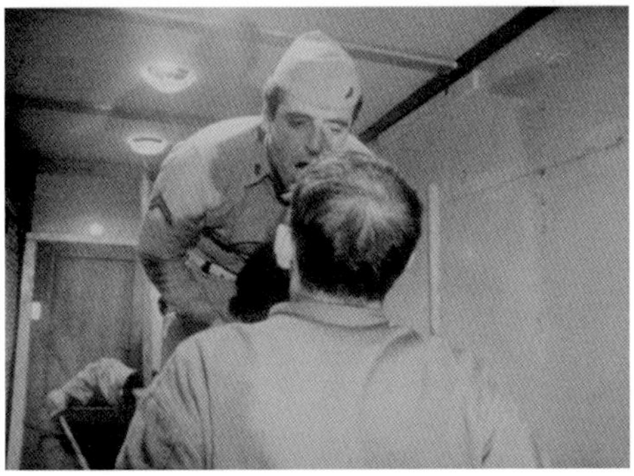
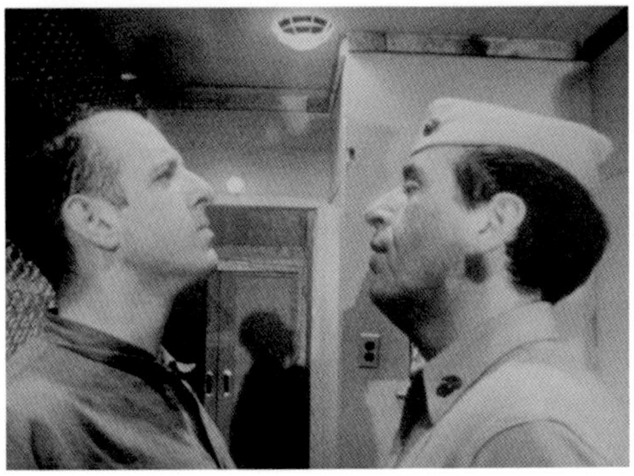
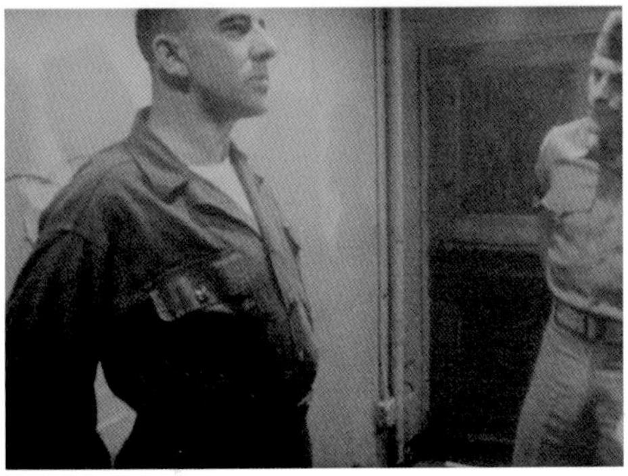
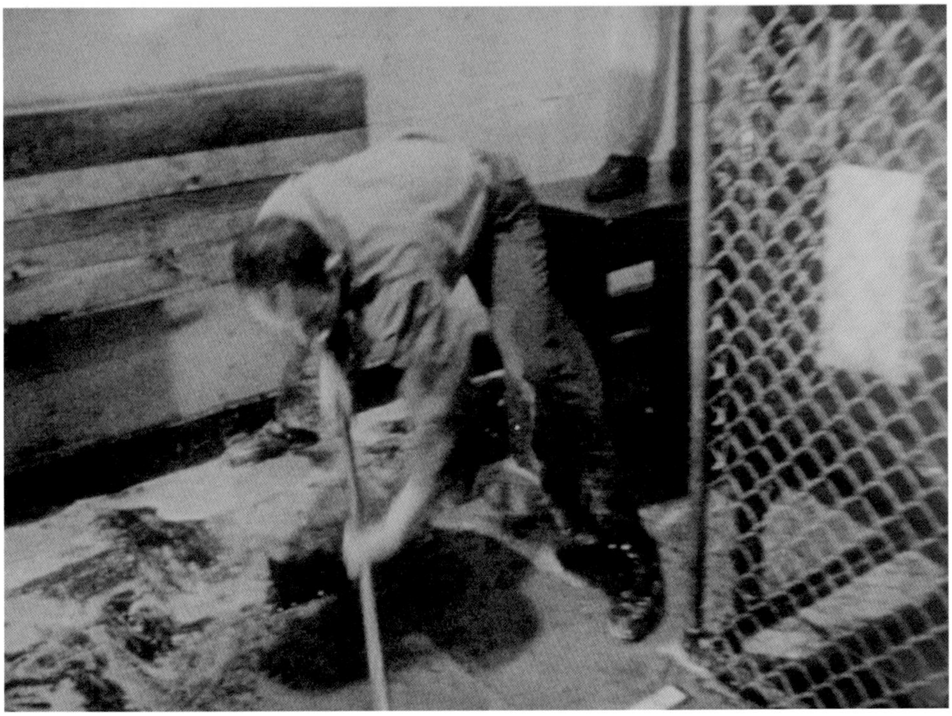
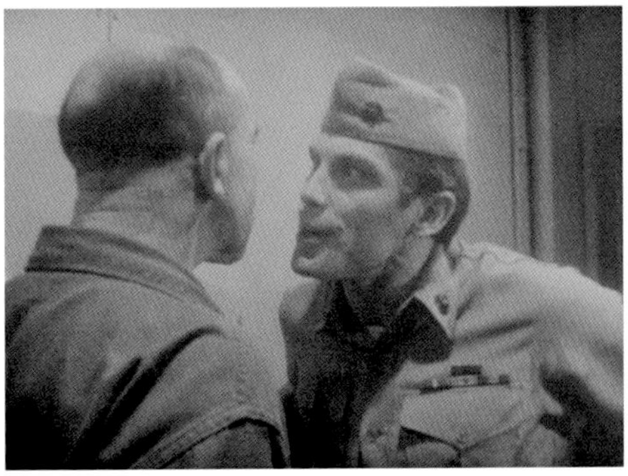

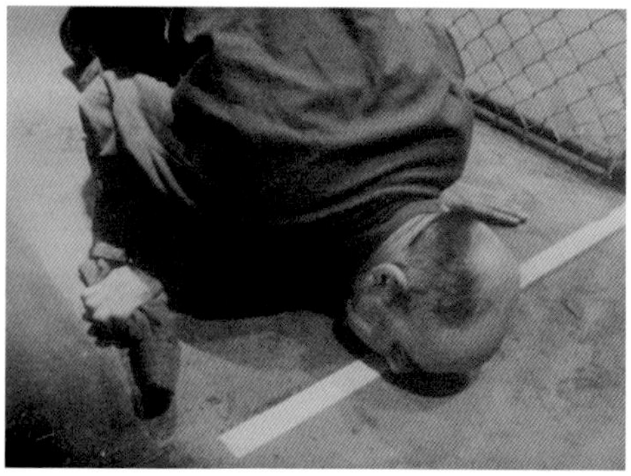
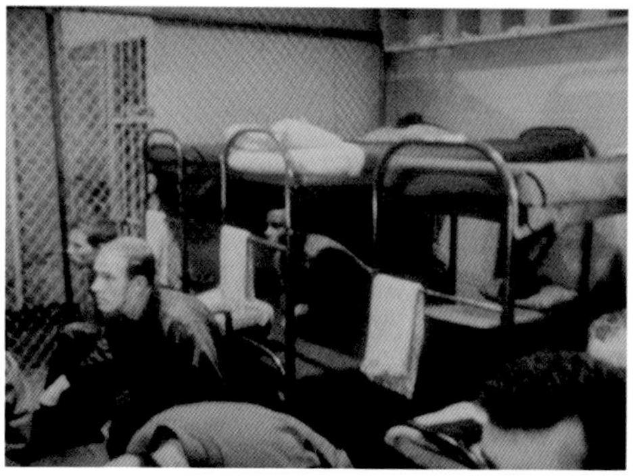
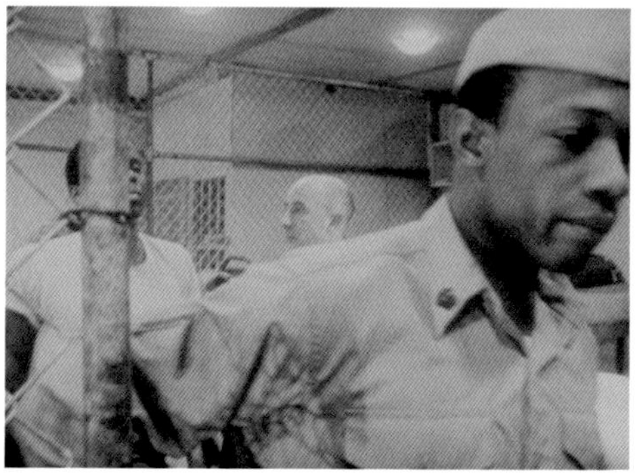
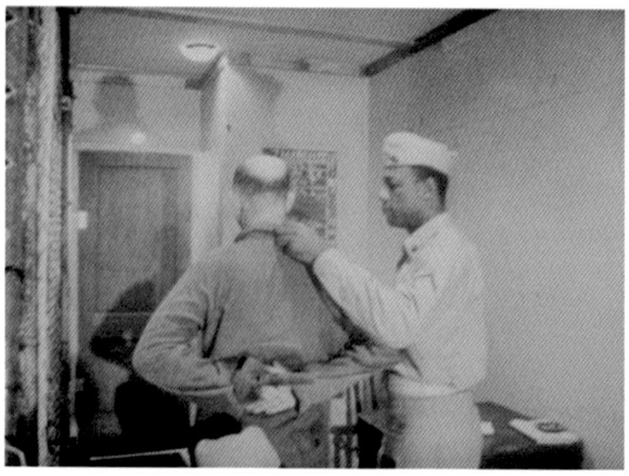
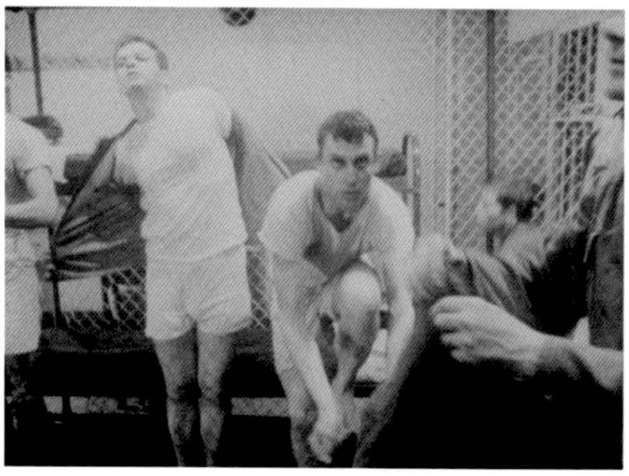
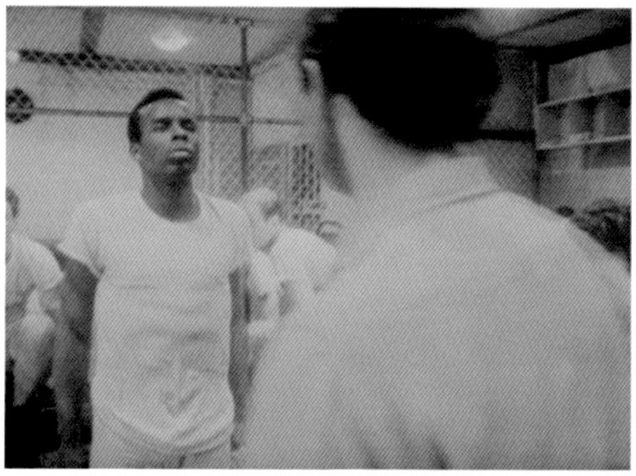
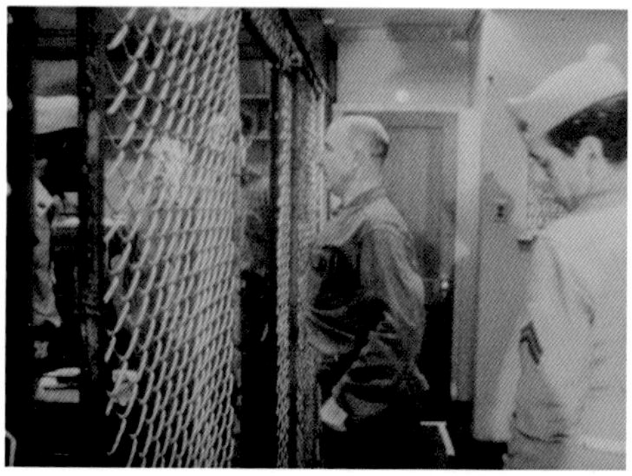
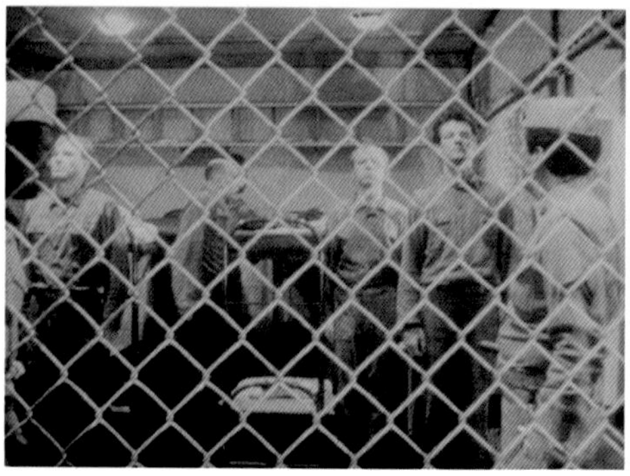
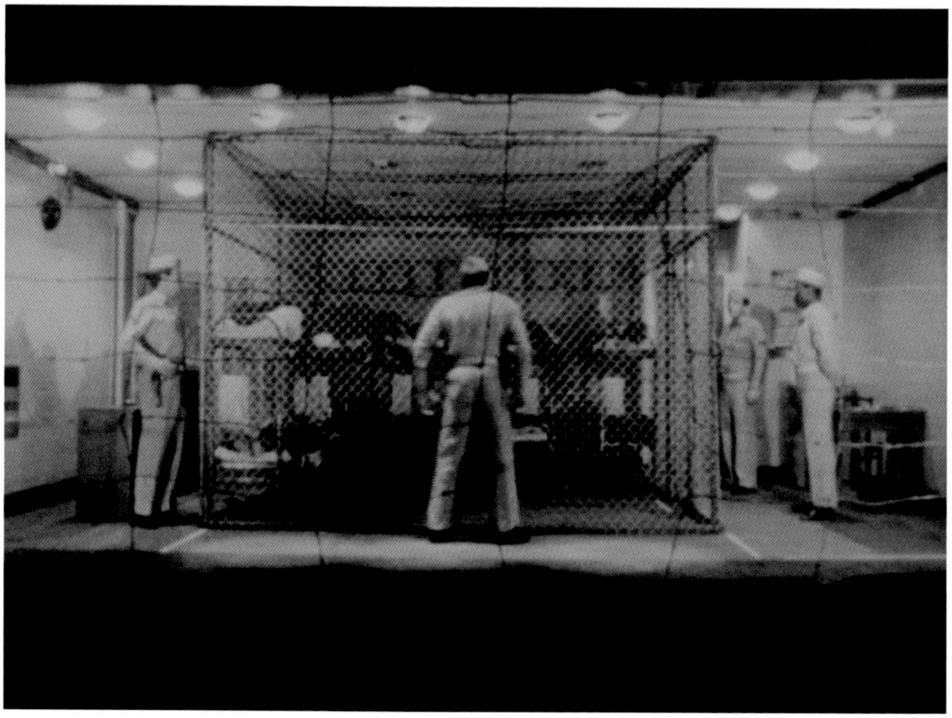

EPHEMERA

F I L M O S   L A P A S   1 9 5 1 M.

No.	Title by with		Country
S a u s i o men.			
1.	The Thief of Bagdad by Raoul Walsh,& Douglas Fairbanks		Amer. '24
2.	Devil's Doorway		Amer. '50
3.	Two Weeks with the Love		Amer. '50
4.	The Land by R.Flaherty		Amer. '42
5.	Industrial Britain by R.Flaherty		Amer. '32
6.	Moana by R.Flaherty		Amer. '25
7.	Manon by		Frac. '50
8.	~~Long Voyage Home~~ by Distant Journey by		Chec. '48
9.	Under the Sun of Rome by		Ital. '49
10.	David Copperfield by Zuckor		Amer. '35
11.	Mr. Trull Finds Out by Joseph Krumgold		Amer. '40
12.	I Walked With a Zombie by Jacques Tourneur		Amer. '43
13.	King's Soloman Mines by Zymbalist		Amer. '50
14.	He's a Hocheyed Wonder		Amer. '50
15.	The Invisible Man by James Whale		Brit. '33
16.	Your Children Sleep by Brian Smith and Jane Massy	C16	Brit. '47
17.	Flugten by Albert Mertz and Jørgen Roos	C16	Denm. '42
18.	Legato by Henning Bendtsen	C16	Denm. '4
19.	Aybervilliers by Eli Lotar	C16	Frnc. '49
20.	The World of Paul Delvaux by Henri Storck	C16	Belg. '4
21.	Waverley Steps by John Eldridge	C16	Brit. '4
22.	Carmen by Lotte Reininger		Germ. '33
23.	The Band Concert by Walt Disney		Amer. '35
24.	Mickey's Grand Opera by Walt Disney		Amer. '36
25.	The Old Mill by Walt Disney		Amer. '37
26.	Water,Friend or Anemy by Walt Disney		Amer. '43
27.	Swooner Crooner by Leon Schlesinger		Amer. '44
28.	Musical Poster #1 by Len Lye		Amer. '
V a s a r i o men.			
29.	Passion of Joan of Arc by Carl-Theodor Dreyer &Falconetti		Frnc. '28
30.	Mutiny in Odessa by Zecca,Ferdinand		Frnc. '07
31.	Patemkin by Sergei Eisenstein		Russ. '25
32.	The March of Wooden Soldiers		Amer. '34
33.	Mr. Music		Amer. '50
34.	Born Yesterday by Cukor		Amer. '50

Filmos Lapas (movie page), listing the films that the Mekas brothers saw in January and February 1951.

FILMS BY I. F. A. MEMBERS:

STAN BRAKHAGE:
Interim
Desistfilm
In Between
The Way To Shadow Garden
Reflections on Black

RICHARD SERLY BRUMMER:
First Fear (with Allan de Forest)
The Drum (with Allan de Forest)
Jazz Dance (with Roger Tilton and Robert M. Campbell)
Theodore At Midnight (with Robert M. Campbell and "Theodore")
One Every Second

RUDOLPH BURCKHARDT:
The Climate of New York
See Naples and the Island of Ischia
Mounting Tension
The Dogwood Maiden
Crime Makes A Down Payment
A Day in the Life of a Cleaning Woman
The Automotive Story

ROBERT M. CAMPBELL:
Arrangement in Grey and Black
The Ladies from Dry Gulch
Degas
Jazz Dance (photographer)
Tommy and Julie

SHIRLEY CLARKE:
Dance in the Sun
In Paris Parks
Bullfight

DOUGLAS CROCKWELL:
Glen Falls Sequence
Long Bodies

KIT DAVIDSON:
Third Avenue El (with Helena Sands)
Auntie's Inferno (with Helena Sands)

ALLAN deFOREST:
First Fear (with Richard Brummer)
The Drum (with Richard Brummer)

MAYA DEREN:
Meshes of the Afternoon
Study in Choreography for Camera
At Land
Ritual in Transfigured Time
Meditations on Violence
The Very Eye of Night

WHEATEN GALENTINE:
Treadle and Bobbin (with Noel Sokoloff)

HILARY T. HARRIS:
Longhorns

ROBERT HARRISON:
Les Taudis
Le Lac
Profiles of Paris '45
Horra Nor Giren
La Fete des Vieux
Colonie d'ete
Suicide in G-Flat Minor

IAN HUGO:
Ai-Ye (Mankind)
Bells of Atlantis (with Len Lye and Louis and Bebe Barron)
Jazz of Lights (with Louis and Bebe Barron)
Tropical Noah's Ark

LEWIS JACOBS:
Brady, Photographer of an Era
The Raven
Ode on a Grecian Urn

PETER HOLLANDER:
One Is One
The Lion, The Griffin and the Kangaroo
Alfabeto Notturno
Dimitri Works in Black Wax
Sometimes a Newspaper
Selinunte

SAM KANER:
Between Two Worlds (with Vladimir Telberg)

MARIA KORWIN:
Lantern Love
Cherry Blossoms

FRANCIS LEE:
1944
Le Bijou
Idyll
Creation

WALTER LEWISOHN:
Miramagic
The Blue People
Trail Without End
The Serpent God
The Constant Geisha
Passage to Nirvana
Eternal Pageant
The Palio of Siena
The Saga of the Erie Canal
Mystic Figureheads (with Miriam Arsham)
Not So Long Ago
Dancing Through Wonderland

WILLARD MAAS:
Image in the Snow
Geography of the Body
The Mechanics of Love (with Ben Moore)
Narcissus (with Ben Moore)

BEN MOORE:
Narcissus (with Willard Maas)
Four American Artists
The Mechanics of Love (with Willard Maas)
Visual Variations on Noguchi

HELENA SANDS:
Third Avenue El (with Kit Davidson)
Auntie's Inferno (with Kit Davidson)

JOHN D. SCHIFF:
Lantern Love (with Marian Korwin)
Cherry Blossoms (with Marian Korwin)

RUTH SCHONTHAL:
Lantern Love (produced by Marian Korwin)

JOE SLEVIN:
Summer Sequence

NOEL SOKOLOFF:
Treadle and Bobbin (with Wheaten Galentine)

JOHN STRANG:
A Poem of Life
The Bridge

VLADIMIR TELBERG:
Between Two Worlds (with Sam Kaner)
Lepra Blanca
Mexican Ruins

ROGER TILTON:
Jazz Dance
New Ways of Seeing (Contemporary Films)

ROBERT VICKERY:
Card Sharks
The Texture of Decay
Appointment with Darkness
Oedipus
Carnival

DAVID ANDERSON
The Slaughter of the Germanic Horsemen
I Giuoco
Horray for Homer

List of films by members of the Independent Filmakers Association, c. 1955.

Independent
Filmakers
Association

Logo of the Independent Filmakers Association, 1955.

FILM FORUM

PROGRAM NO. 3 JUNE 19, 1954, at 8 PM

The Poetical Documentary

TWO OF THE GREATEST DOCUMENTARY FILMS OF THE BRITISH AND AMERICAN SCHOOLS

The River

PARE LORENTZ

Night Mail

BASIL WRIGHT AND HARRY WATT

ANALYSIS AND COMMENTS BY GEORGE CAPSIS

The forums are held at the auditorium of the Food Trades School, 208 W. 13th St., NYC, every Saturday at 8 PM.

Persons wishing to attend film forums become members with their first attendance. Admission $ 1.00. Attendance is limited to 200. Reservations are not required, but recommended.

For information and reservations call or write corresponding secretary: Adolfas Mekas, 95 Orchard St., New York 2, N.Y. Tel.: CAnal 6-2245.

Flyer for the Film Forum screening of "The Poetical Documentary," June 19, 1954.

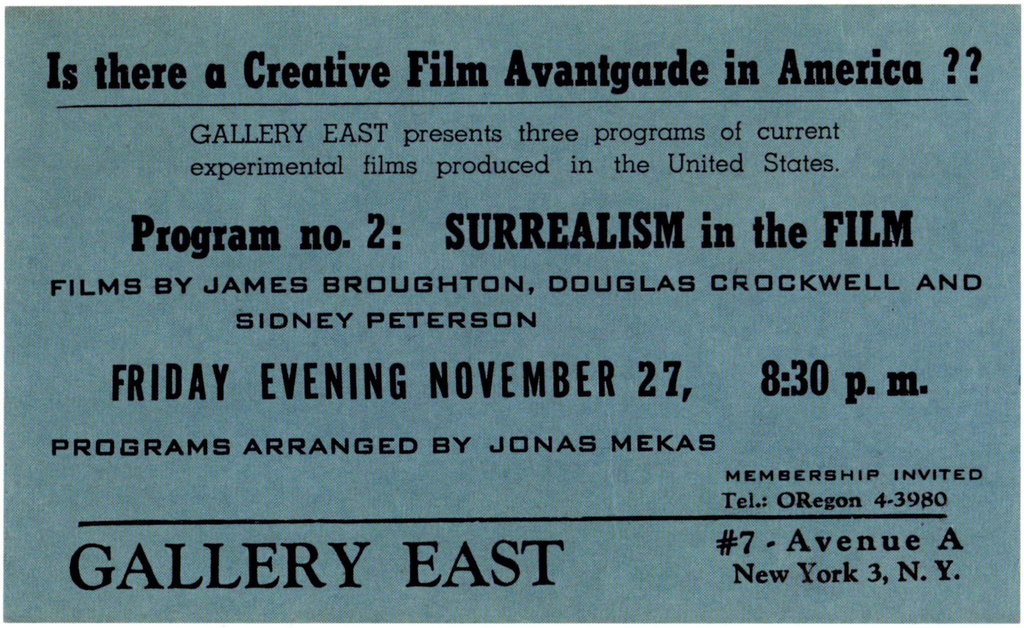

Is there a Creative Film Avantgarde in America ??

GALLERY EAST presents three programs of current experimental films produced in the United States.

Program no. 2: SURREALISM in the FILM

FILMS BY JAMES BROUGHTON, DOUGLAS CROCKWELL AND SIDNEY PETERSON

FRIDAY EVENING NOVEMBER 27, 8:30 p. m.

PROGRAMS ARRANGED BY JONAS MEKAS

MEMBERSHIP INVITED
Tel.: ORegon 4-3980

GALLERY EAST

#7 - Avenue A
New York 3, N. Y.

Flyer for a film series organized by Jonas Mekas at Gallery East, November 27, 1953.

Before Jonas and Adolfas Mekas established *Film Culture*—the first of many resources and organizations for American avant-garde cinema that Jonas created—the brothers were students of New York's burgeoning avant-garde art and film scene. They tracked every film they saw (still in their native Lithuanian), organized screenings at downtown arts clubs and theaters such as Gallery East and Film Forum, and Jonas attended meetings of the Independent Filmakers Association, a cooperative organization formed by the visionary filmmaker Maya Deren, who inspired him to spearhead the New American Cinema Group.

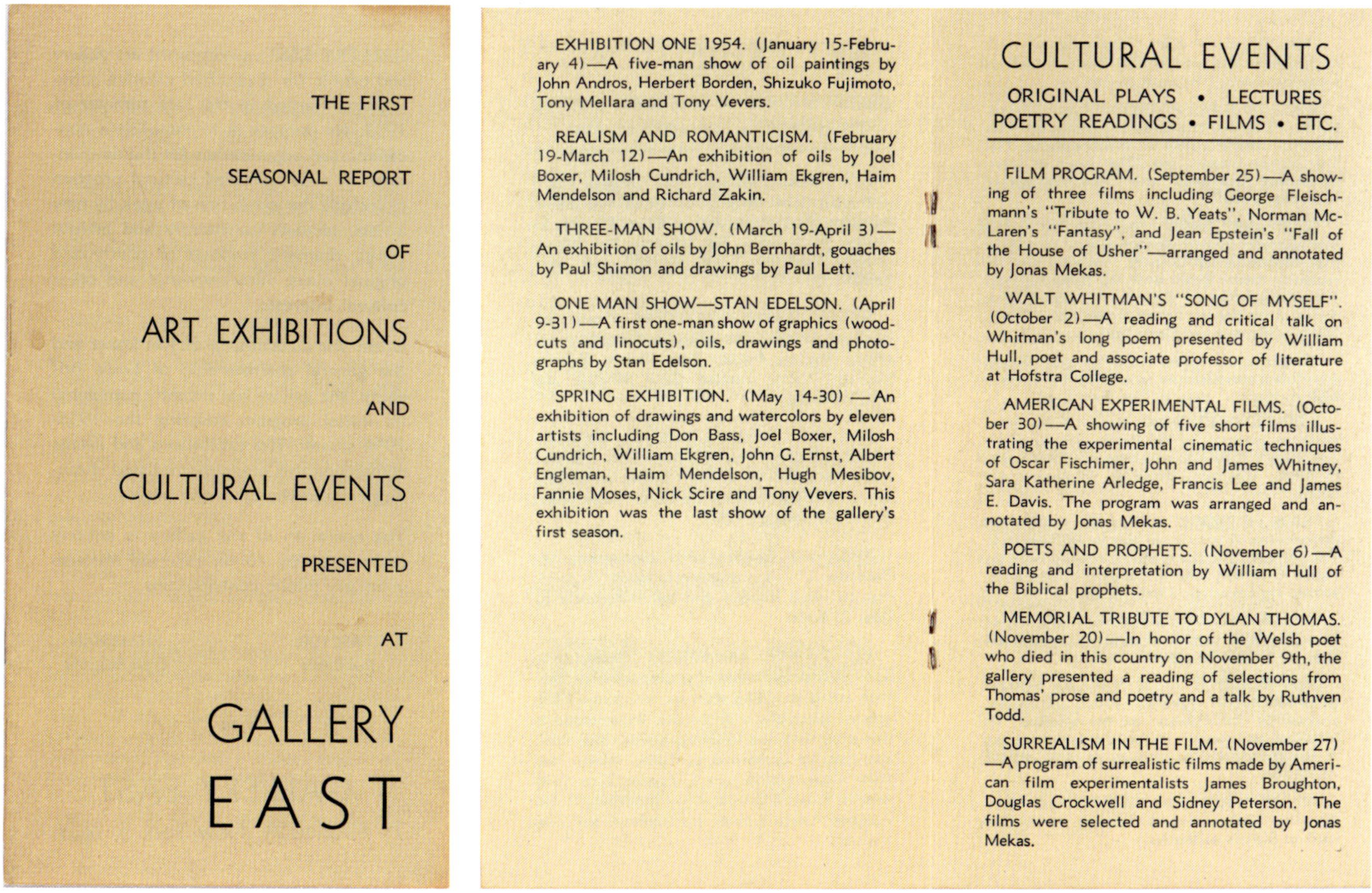

THE FIRST SEASONAL REPORT OF ART EXHIBITIONS AND CULTURAL EVENTS PRESENTED AT GALLERY EAST

EXHIBITION ONE 1954. (January 15-February 4)—A five-man show of oil paintings by John Andros, Herbert Borden, Shizuko Fujimoto, Tony Mellara and Tony Vevers.

REALISM AND ROMANTICISM. (February 19-March 12)—An exhibition of oils by Joel Boxer, Milosh Cundrich, William Ekgren, Haim Mendelson and Richard Zakin.

THREE-MAN SHOW. (March 19-April 3)—An exhibition of oils by John Bernhardt, gouaches by Paul Shimon and drawings by Paul Lett.

ONE MAN SHOW—STAN EDELSON. (April 9-31)—A first one-man show of graphics (woodcuts and linocuts), oils, drawings and photographs by Stan Edelson.

SPRING EXHIBITION. (May 14-30)—An exhibition of drawings and watercolors by eleven artists including Don Bass, Joel Boxer, Milosh Cundrich, William Ekgren, John G. Ernst, Albert Engleman, Haim Mendelson, Hugh Mesibov, Fannie Moses, Nick Scire and Tony Vevers. This exhibition was the last show of the gallery's first season.

CULTURAL EVENTS

ORIGINAL PLAYS • LECTURES
POETRY READINGS • FILMS • ETC.

FILM PROGRAM. (September 25)—A showing of three films including George Fleischmann's "Tribute to W. B. Yeats", Norman McLaren's "Fantasy", and Jean Epstein's "Fall of the House of Usher"—arranged and annotated by Jonas Mekas.

WALT WHITMAN'S "SONG OF MYSELF". (October 2)—A reading and critical talk on Whitman's long poem presented by William Hull, poet and associate professor of literature at Hofstra College.

AMERICAN EXPERIMENTAL FILMS. (October 30)—A showing of five short films illustrating the experimental cinematic techniques of Oscar Fischimer, John and James Whitney, Sara Katherine Arledge, Francis Lee and James E. Davis. The program was arranged and annotated by Jonas Mekas.

POETS AND PROPHETS. (November 6)—A reading and interpretation by William Hull of the Biblical prophets.

MEMORIAL TRIBUTE TO DYLAN THOMAS. (November 20)—In honor of the Welsh poet who died in this country on November 9th, the gallery presented a reading of selections from Thomas' prose and poetry and a talk by Ruthven Todd.

SURREALISM IN THE FILM. (November 27)—A program of surrealistic films made by American film experimentalists James Broughton, Douglas Crockwell and Sidney Peterson. The films were selected and annotated by Jonas Mekas.

"The First Seasonal Report of Art Exhibitions and Cultural Events Presented at Gallery East," c. 1954.

THE CHARLES THEATRE
12th St. and Ave. B
GR 3-6170

FILMMAKERS FESTIVAL PROGRAM
June 29, 1962

1. George Manupelli: THE HOUSE
2. George Zabriskie: THE WORLD OF LINDSAY DECKER
3. Herb. Krosney: EARLY BIRDS
4. Lincoln Diamant: YANKEE DOODLE
5. George Manupelli: ABSTRACT FILM (Untitled)
6. Don Dunaway: TRANSIT TO BLACK
7. Don Volkman: SIGNS
8. Don Volkman: NEW YORK NOISES

Intermission of 15 minutes

9. Herman Kroll: I'M NOT AFRAID
10. Virginia Carteaux: UNTITLED ABSTRACT
11. Arthur Tress: GARDENS OF TIVOLI
12. Philip and Michael Burton: JOURNEY ALONE
13. Bill Powers: THE FIGHT GAME
14. Stanley Vanderbeek: WHEEEELS #2
15. Lincoln Diamant: FALLING OUT

Program for the Filmmakers Festival at the Charles Theatre, June 29, 1962.

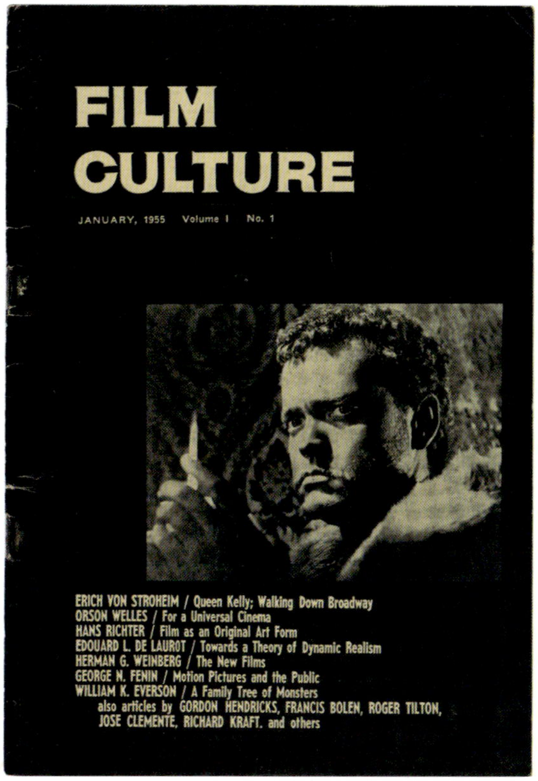

Cover of *Film Culture* 1, January 1955.

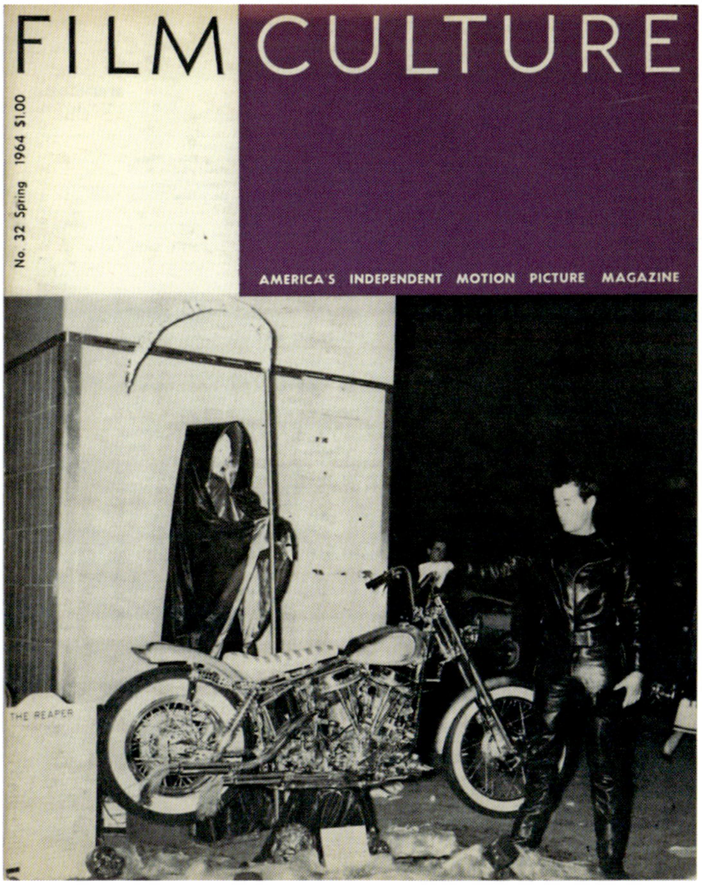

Cover of *Film Culture* 32, Spring 1964.

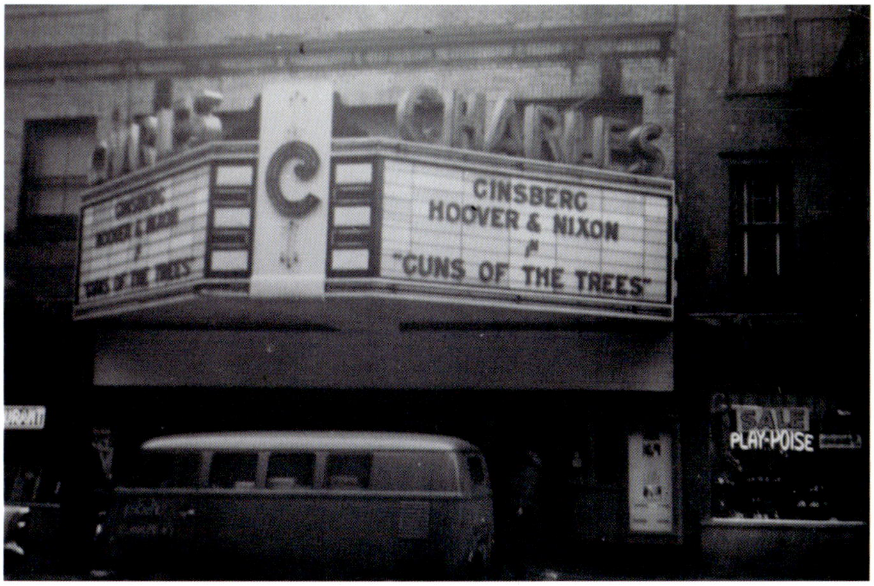

Marquee of the Charles Theatre, 12th Street and Avenue B, undated photograph.

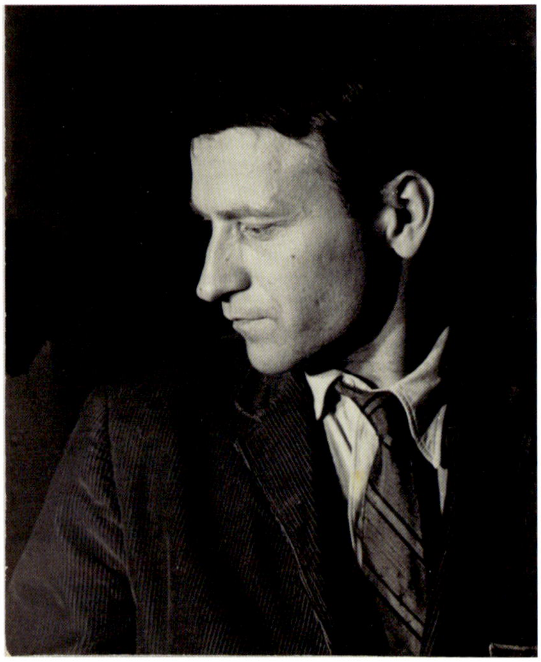

Portrait of Jonas Mekas, 1958.

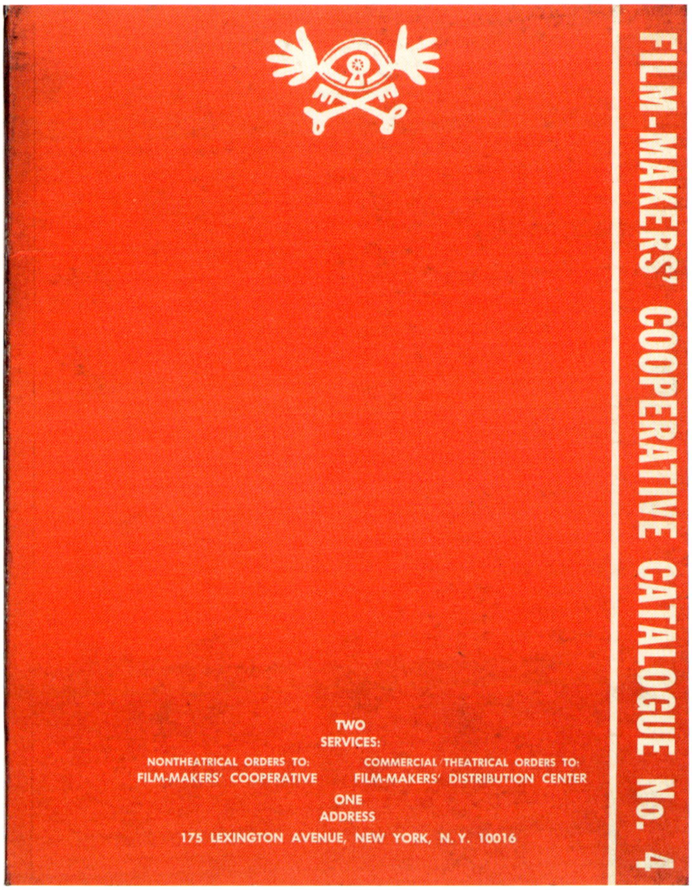

Cover of *Film-Makers' Cooperative Catalogue*, no. 4, 1967.

FILM-MAKERS' COOPERATIVE
414 Park Avenue South
New York 16, New York

Logo of the Film-Makers' Cooperative.

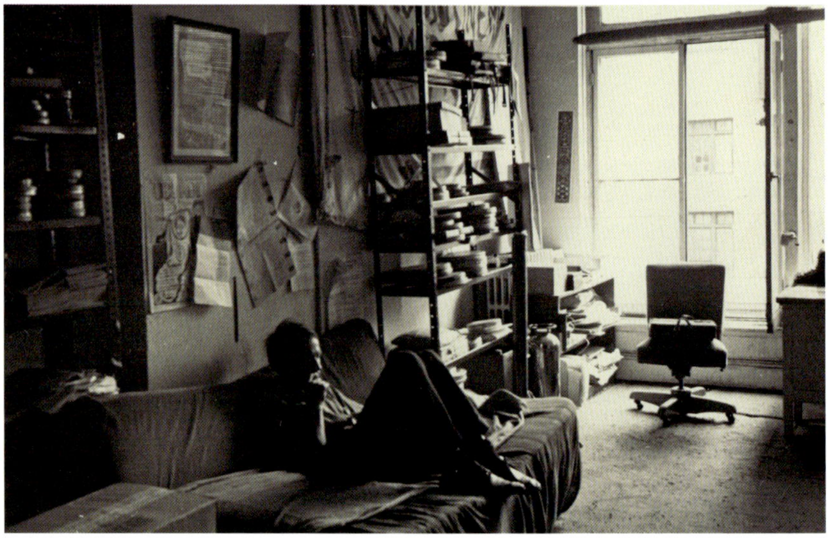

Jonas at the Film-Makers' Cooperative, 414 Park Avenue South, 1964.

FILM-MAKER'S COOPERATIVE
414 Park Avenue South
New York 16, New York

WHAT IS THE FILM-MAKER'S COOPERATIVE?

The Film-Maker's Cooperative is a division of the new American Cinema Group, Inc., a free organization of independent Filmmakers. The Cooperative was set up as a non-profit organization operated by filmmakers, to distribute their work; all income from film rentals and sales go to the filmmakers.

FILMS LISTED IN THE CATALOGUE are available to theatres, schools, universities, film societies, and other film users. Rental prices indicated in the catalogue apply to average-sized audiences. For larger theatrical and other showings the prices will increase. Prints of these films are available for sale for non-commercial purposes only.

WE WISH TO MAKE ONE SUGGESTION concerning the bookings of films. Whenever it is possible, you should prepare programs devoted to one particular filmmaker, instead of booking, as it is usually done, potpourri programs. Films of a particular director can be properly understood and enjoyed only in the larger context of his work. A discussion of his films by the filmmaker is another means of enhancing the program. Arrangements for this can be made through the Film-Maker's Cooperative.

YOU ARE HELPING THE INDEPENDENT FILMMAKER TO CONTINUE HIS WORK!

Film-Maker's Cooperative

Information from the Film-Makers' Cooperative about its activities, with suggestions to the renters of its films.

JONAS MEKAS, THE LIVING THEATRE, AND THE PLACE OF PERFORMANCE

NOTES

1 This story has been repeatedly mischaracterized throughout the literature, from the earliest newspaper reviews to the catalogue of the Judson Dance Theater published by the Museum of Modern Art in 2018. Even the late Sally Banes, in her invaluably detailed study *Greenwich Village 1963: Avant-Garde Performance and the Effervescent Body* (Durham, NC: Duke University Press, 1993), writes: "On October 17, 1963, the IRS shut down the Living Theatre . . . that night, too, Jonas Mekas filmed *The Brig*" (182), and elsewhere, "it was Mekas who crossed police lines . . . to make a documentary film of *The Brig* at its fateful last performance when the Living Theatre had been closed down and sealed shut by the IRS; it was Mekas who realized the weight that a permanent record—especially of *that* night's performance—could have" (76–77). Two completely separate events are being conflated in these accounts. In his "Movie Journal" column, Mekas clearly states that he shot the film in late February 1964, almost four months after the initial incident with the IRS and the "street theater" it inspired. For an account of this earlier episode, which Mekas most certainly did not film, see John Tytell, *The Living Theatre: Art, Exile, Outrage* (New York: Grove Press, 1995), 187–91. Perhaps adopting something of Mekas's own penchant for self-mythologization, authors have opted to create a more streamlined and dramatic version, or simply to repeat a story they had read without question.

2 Jonas Mekas, *Scrapbook of the Sixties: Writings 1954–2010* (Leipzig: Spector Books, 2005), 58.

3 Ibid., 54. The final phrase of this quotation, "not knowing what will come next, like real life," is a retrospective clarification by Mekas for the 2005 collection. These final words do not appear in his original 1965 column in the *Village Voice* or in its republication for his 1972 *Movie Journal* anthology, where he instead concludes simply by emphasizing his sense of compulsion: "I *had* to film it." Jonas Mekas, *Movie Journal: The Rise of a New American Cinema, 1959–1971* (New York: Macmillan, 1972), 190.

Jonas Mekas, the Living Theatre, and the Place of Performance in the Emergence of a New American Cinema

Andrew V. Uroskie

On a cold night in late February 1964—through a basement coal chute, under cover of darkness—Jonas Mekas broke into the Midway Theatre off Times Square accompanied by Judith Malina, Julian Beck, and the cast of the Living Theatre.[1] They had all been there the night before for what was supposed to have been the final performance of Kenneth H. Brown's *The Brig*. The company had been served with an eviction notice, and that evening's performance was to mark the end of its fifteen-year residency in New York. But Mekas had been overwhelmed—by the work as well as the occasion. After a few minutes, he stormed out of the crowded theater to wait alone outside, possessed by an idea: out of the ephemeral experience of a live performance, he would craft an unscripted documentary record on film.

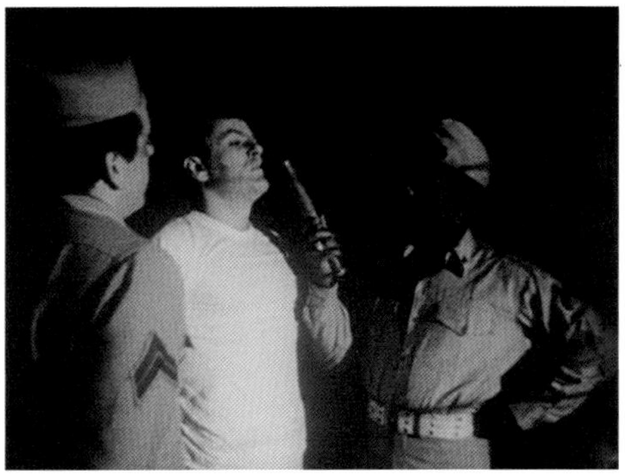

Still from *The Brig*, 1964.

Three years earlier, Shirley Clarke's cinematic adaptation of *The Connection*, the Living Theatre's prior effort, had become one of the breakthrough successes of the fledgling New American Cinema. Yet Mekas did not wish to follow Clarke's path: "I am not interested in adapting plays, I always said so." He would produce "not an adaptation of a play" but "a record of my eye and my temperament lost in the play."[2] This was what had necessitated his sudden departure: "I didn't want to know anything about what would happen next in the play," he later wrote in his "Movie Journal" column for the *Village Voice*. "I wanted to see it with my camera. I had to film it, not knowing what will come next, like real life."[3] Outside the theater, the cast and crew agreed that they would return the following evening to reprise the performance one last time for Mekas and his camera. But when they arrived, the eviction had already gone into effect; the doors were padlocked by the theater's owner. By urging them all to break in that evening, Mekas effectively insisted on reprising not simply the play but the very street theater for which the company had become infamous.

Just four months previously, the IRS had closed the Living Theatre's long-standing home on 14th Street and Avenue A—ostensibly for its failure to pay back taxes.[4] After Beck and Malina refused to leave, the police locked them inside and erected a barricade. A crowd gathered on the street to offer support and encouragement. The next day, addressing the assembled crowd from his window, Beck announced a final, illegal performance. That evening, followers, along with several members of the press, were secretly admitted to the theater by way of a fire escape and an upper-story window. The police allowed the performance to go on, but afterward Beck and Malina were arrested, bail was set, and the two were released pending trial. By then *The Brig* had attracted significant attention, and perhaps sensing an opportunity, Irving Maidman—the wealthy owner of several New York theaters—came to the rescue by offering his Midway Theatre rent-free so the production could continue. At least, he did so until February 1964, when he abruptly changed his mind and began demanding a Midtown rent the Living Theatre could not possibly afford. And so once again the police were called, the doors padlocked, and another break-in ensued. But this time Mekas did not merely read about it in the papers—he resolved to be an active participant. His participation serves to index a vital, historically neglected exchange between postwar radical theater and the emergence of American independent cinema.

Since their origins in the 1970s, the academic disciplines of film and performance studies have tended to be carefully demarcated from that of art history. Yet the actual history of experimental film, performance, and what now sometimes goes by the facile and restrictive rubric of "visual art" were thoroughly imbricated, both socially and aesthetically, in the New York of the 1950s and 1960s.[5] The model of Beck and Malina's Living Theatre provided a framework for understanding both the social and aesthetic importance of the New American Cinema to Mekas in the early 1960s. These two dimensions—the social and the aesthetic—were becoming ineluctably intertwined through new models of "realism" and the disintegration of boundaries between "art" and "life" across both performance and film. Mekas's experimental documentary *The Brig* (1964) functioned as a culmination and a break, both the summing up of a certain period of investigation and commitment he had shared with the Living Theatre and, following its departure, the beginning of a new path (see pages 58–62).

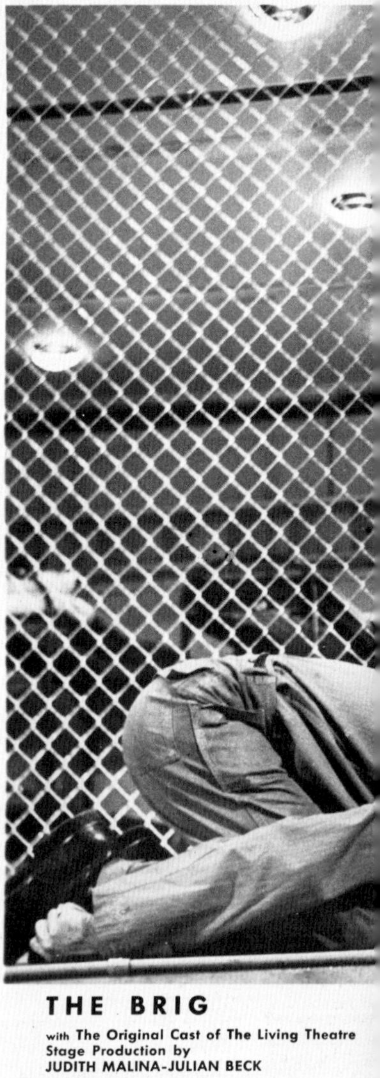

Production still of *The Brig*, 1964.

4 The Living Theatre had a habit of not enforcing admission charges, and they did not bring in enough money to pay the actors a regular salary. According to Tytell, the company had not paid its full taxes in years and the IRS had always been content to look the other way. It is unclear what finally tipped the balance. One possibility may have been the New York World's Fair, which had caused a citywide crackdown on a wide range of cultural institutions deemed by the mayor's office to present an "unhealthy" image of the city. Rising rents may have been another problem: this is what Amos Vogel describes as forcing the closure of his legendary film society Cinema 16 after fifteen successful years.

5 See, for example, Alan Licht's tribute to Mekas in the pages of the music publication *The Wire*, where he describes Mekas's profound influence on the growth of an intermedia arts scene in New York that comprised several generations of practitioners across postwar avant-garde music, film, and performance: https://www.thewire.co.uk/in-writing/essays/jonas-mekas-alan-licht.

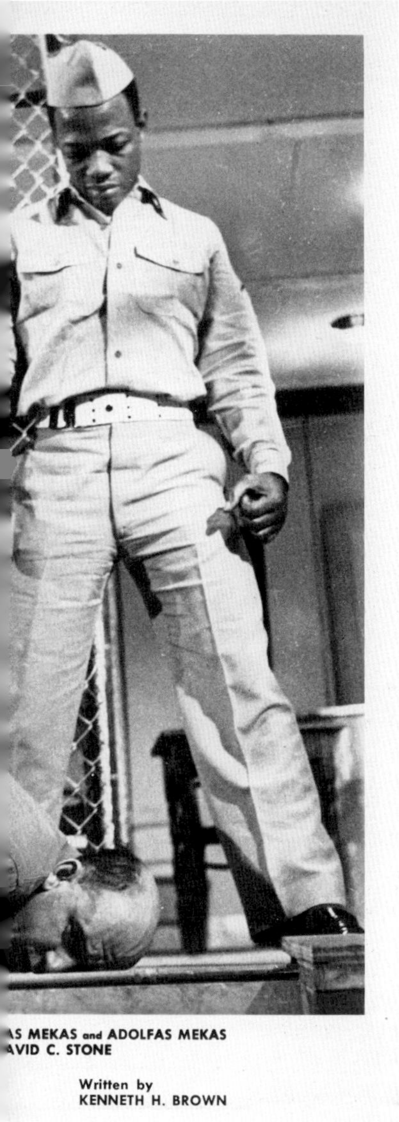

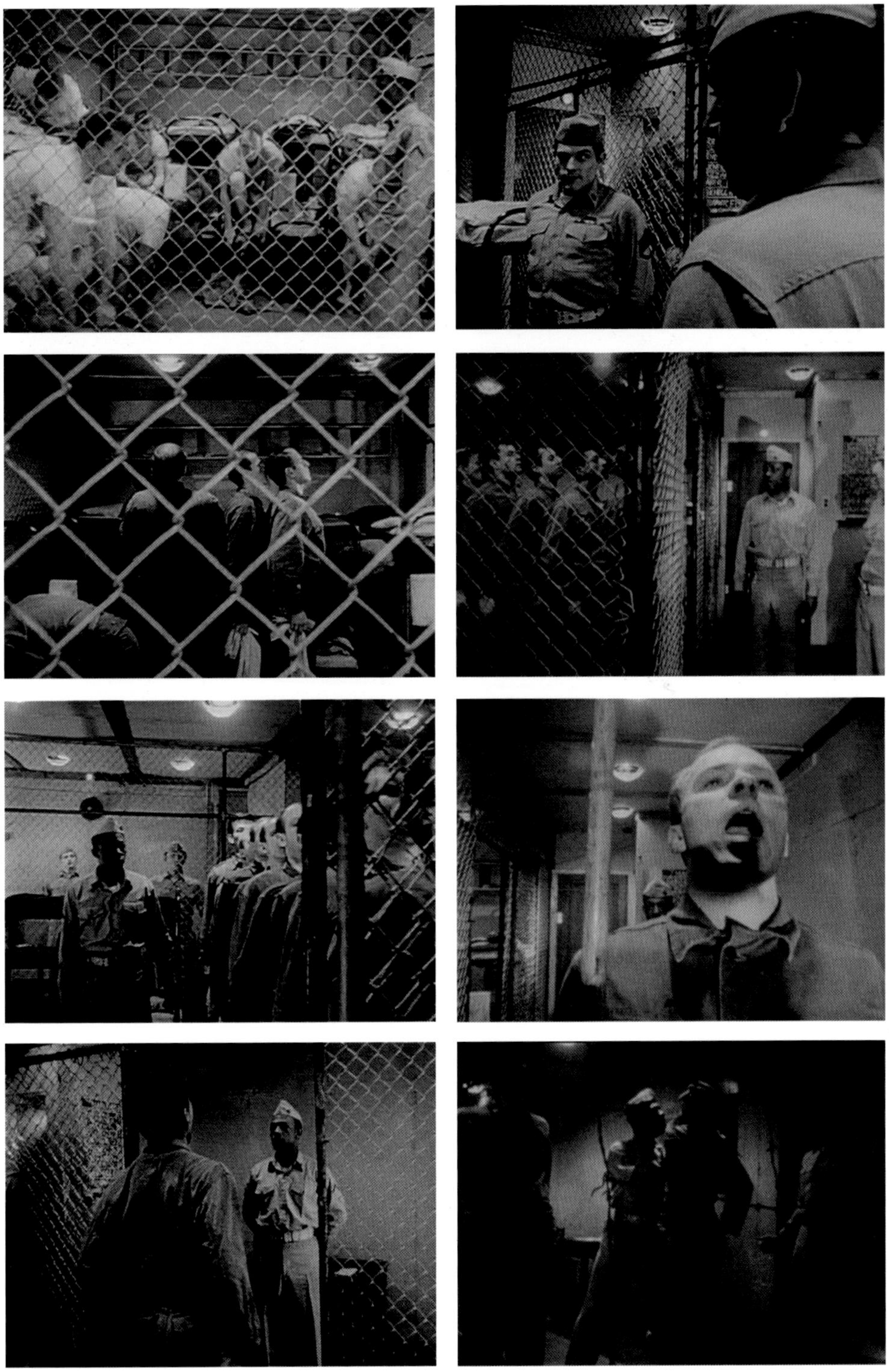

Eight stills from *The Brig*, 1964.

6 Mekas claims to have attended "absolutely every screening . . . of the so-called experimental films in Cinema 16's whole existence. It became my Sunday Church, my university." Scott MacDonald, *A Critical Cinema 2: Interviews with Independent Filmmakers* (Berkeley: University of California Press, 1992), 82. The "so-called experimental films" actually constituted but a small fraction of the diverse, wide-ranging exhibitions Vogel assembled from documentary, scientific, and educational films from around the world—one of the many differences that distinguished Mekas's Film-Makers' Cinematheque from Vogel's Cinema 16.

7 Haidee Wasson, *Museum Movies: The Museum of Modern Art and the Birth of Art Cinema* (Berkeley: University of California Press, 2005).

8 David E. James, *To Free the Cinema: Jonas Mekas and the New York Underground* (Princeton: Princeton University Press, 1992), 9.

9 Scott MacDonald, *Cinema 16: Documents Toward a History of the Film Society* (Philadelphia: Temple University Press, 2002), 18–19.

The history of postwar avant-garde cinema in New York quite literally begins in the world of independent theater, when Maya Deren rents the Provincetown Playhouse in Greenwich Village to screen and discuss her own works outside the highly regulated system of commercial cinema. Inspired by Deren's audacity (and intrigued by her capacity audiences), Amos Vogel used that same theater to inaugurate his independent film society Cinema 16 the next year. Cinema 16 quickly grew to become the largest independent film exhibitor of the 1950s, as well as an indispensable source of information and inspiration.[6] As the film historian Haidee Wasson has written, the independent cinema theater in America was explicitly modeled on the independent theatrical playhouse.[7] Promising an art free of both commercialism and censorship—the rhetoric Mekas would employ in the founding of the New American Cinema Group in 1961—was stirring and dramatic for the time, but it had been employed in countless independent stage programs in lower Manhattan going back to the 1920s. And postwar experimental film and experimental theater shared not only audiences but also numerous physical spaces. Mekas's own Cinematheque alternatively occupied, shared space with, or gave ground to a number of theatrical venues over the brief course of its peripatetic existence.

From the founding of the New American Cinema Group in 1961, the Film-Makers' Cooperative in 1962, and the Film-Makers' Cinematheque in 1964, Mekas's insistence on building an infrastructure for experimental film was not merely an effort to showcase a certain kind of film but to foster institutions through which a new generation of artistic experimentation could develop.[8] Far more than providing a venue for accessing a common experience, he was creating a novel community. For many years, the Coop was physically located in Mekas's apartment, and meetings, screenings, and discussions took place there throughout the day and night. The intimacy of this community, and the lack of separation it implied, marked a decisive shift from the detached professionalism of Vogel's Cinema 16. Indeed, Vogel castigated Mekas for his lack of critical distance from the filmmakers he quite straightforwardly promoted.[9] The Coop, known for its intimacy and intensity, was modeled on Mekas's experience of Beck and Malina's Living Theatre rather than Cinema 16.

10 Mekas, *Movie Journal*, 2–3.

11 Stan VanDerBeek's first use of the term "underground" to refer to experimental film is from "The Cinema Delimina: Films from the Underground," *Film Quarterly* 14, no. 4 (1961): 5–15. His reference to the Living Theatre is from *Jonas Mekas, Conversations with Film-Makers* (Leipzig: Spector Books, 2018), 177–78.

In the second-earliest review selected for his anthology *Movie Journal*, Mekas describes the extraordinary atmosphere that attended the 1959 retrospective of Maya Deren's films, including the long-awaited New York premiere of *The Very Eye of Night* (1952–55; released 1958). The place was "bursting with people—sitting everywhere on the floor, standing by the walls, on the stairway." He underscores the aesthetic and social importance of the event in almost existential terms: "a most unusual and exultant moment for a film poet to experience in this sober world."[10] The scene is reminiscent not of an ordinary movie audience but specifically the intense, crowded, participatory audiences for which the Living Theatre had become known. It also speaks to the vitality and the importance of the Living Theatre as a venue for the New York experimental film community in the 1950s, in the years prior to the founding of the New American Cinema Group and the Film-Makers' Cooperative. Mekas himself had originally helped to implement a lecture series Deren had held at the Living Theatre since the mid-1950s. Stan Brakhage, whose experimental films would become almost synonymous with the New American Cinema, had traveled from Colorado to show and speak about his films at a Living Theatre event in 1958. Mekas would later recall that as the moment when he first came to appreciate Brakhage's importance—a recognition that proved pivotal for his own shift toward the American experimental film by the end of the 1950s. When Stan VanDerBeek coined the term "underground cinema" in 1959, he was showing his earliest experimental films at the Living Theatre simply because "there was *no* place to show them" otherwise.[11]

Cinema 16 and the Living Theatre were both founded in 1947, the year Jackson Pollock began using the drip technique that came to be seen as emblematic of a newly immersive and highly performative model of "action painting." And over the course of the 1950s, the popularity of Cinema 16, the Living Theatre, and the collaboration of Robert Rauschenberg, John Cage, and Merce Cunningham would form the foundation of a major turn toward performance by the late 1950s. Together, they laid the seeds for Happenings, Fluxus, and the Judson Dance Theater of the early 1960s, which would, in turn, spur the rise of video and performance art by the end of that decade. These groups were all intertwined not simply at the level of aesthetic form but also of institutional structure, in terms of establishing new norms of exhibition and spectatorship, and, ultimately, of the critical discourse surrounding late modernist art. It was from within this richly interdisciplinary nexus that Mekas began to exhibit and champion the New American Cinema.

12 Judith Rodenbeck, *Radical Prototypes: Allan Kaprow and the Invention of Happenings* (Cambridge, MA: MIT Press, 2011), 153. See, in particular, Rodenbeck's chapter "Madness and Method," one of the rare critical elucidations of the links between experimental theater and early performance art in this period.

13 Michael Kirby first introduces his idea of "non-matrixed performance" in "The New Theatre," *The Tulane Drama Review* 10, no. 2 (1965): 23–43. He would subsequently elaborate a continuum of stages between "complex acting" and "non-matrixed performance" in "On Acting and Not-Acting," *The Drama Review: TDR* 16, no. 1 (1972): 3–15.

14 Mekas, *Movie Journal*, 5.

Malina and Beck had become accustomed to a peripatetic existence for their Living Theatre, staging their avant-garde works in "spaces as scavenged—and often as ephemeral—as the junk materials Beck used for his collaged sets."[12] When nothing else was available, they had employed their own apartment as a makeshift theater. Mekas adopted their model in establishing the Film-Makers' Cooperative—which he ran out of his own apartment—and his Film-Makers' Cinematheque, which he was forced to relocate more than a dozen times over the course of the 1960s. But the Living Theatre also proved a model for Mekas in terms of its concrete elaboration of a space for an alternative community. In addition to presenting plays that spoke to the social and political questions of community, Beck and Malina also used their theater as a space for the articulation of community—hosting poetry readings and dance concerts, film screenings, and political organizing for their General Strike for Peace activities.

Mekas had known Beck and Malina practically since arriving in America but especially since moving to Greenwich Village in the mid-fifties, when he founded the journal *Film Culture*. They were fellow poets, as well as friends and neighbors. Beck wanted to establish an independent "poet's theater"—just as Mekas, after Deren, sought to establish an independent "poet's cinema." Both Mekas and the Living Theatre spent most of the 1950s looking to Europe for inspiration. But by the end of the decade, both shifted simultaneously in the direction of a new model of realism, one grounded in the manner in which American artists—in painting and sculpture, performance and film—sought to challenge the aesthetic demarcation between art and life. In Robert Frank and Alfred Leslie's Beat film *Pull My Daisy* (1959), as in Jack Gelber's play *The Connection* (1959), contemporaneous with Allan Kaprow's *18 Happenings in 6 Parts* (1959) and George Brecht's *Toward Events: An Arrangement* (1959), traditional demarcations between art and life, between acting and nonacting, were being radically transformed by the introduction of what Michael Kirby termed "non-matrixed performance."[13]

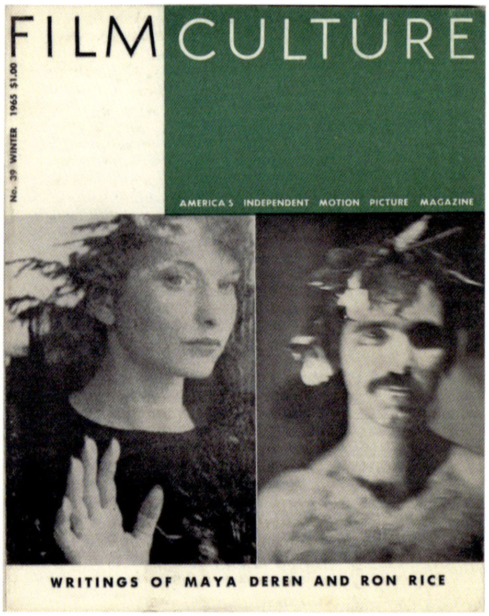

Cover of *Film Culture* 39, Winter 1965.

In his "Movie Journal" column, Mekas specifically references the Living Theatre in his spirited defense of Robert Frank's critically maligned *Pull My Daisy*, finding it "as much a signpost in cinema as *The Connection* is in modern theatre."[14] Mekas saw both as pointing toward "a new sensibility" in the arts that would prove vital to his critical elaboration of the New American Cinema in the years to come. One aspect of this shared sensibility lay in the rejection of

15 David James, *Allegories of Cinema: American Film in the Sixties* (Princeton: Princeton University Press, 1992), 92.
16 Mekas, "On the Baudelairean Cinema," May 2, 1963, *Movie Journal*, 85–86.
17 Mel Gussow, "Jack Gelber," *New York Times*, May 10, 2003.
18 Mekas, *Movie Journal*, 69–70.

traditional narrative structure through what David James called a "profligacy" or "careless expenditure" of action: "De-centered and only loosely structured, it distributes the authorship of its action casually among the participants rather than constraining them to the singleness of pre-extant narrative necessity."[15] This loose, distributed structure emerged as a hallmark of what Mekas called the "Baudelairean cinema" of Jack Smith, Ken Jacobs, Ron Rice, and Bob Fleischner.[16]

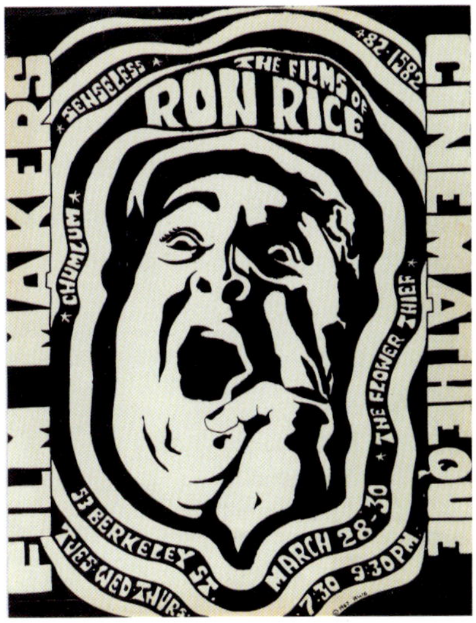

Film-Makers' Cinematheque flyer for a program featuring Ron Rice, 53 Berkeley Street, Boston, March 28–30, 1967.

But an equally important dimension of this new sensibility was the transformation of the idea of "acting" and the "actor" by means of a confusion, even elimination, of what is traditionally understood as "character." Frank and Leslie's *Pull My Daisy* was ostensibly a film about the Beat lifestyle, but it was based on Jack Kerouac's play *Beat Generation*, in which Kerouac himself provided voice-over narration, and the poets Allen Ginsberg and Gregory Corso were "cast" in the role of Beat poets. While some reviews praised the work for the authenticity of its depiction, we might just as easily describe a confusing mise en abyme, wherein neither the audience nor perhaps the actors themselves could tell where their "acting" stopped and their real-life "character" began. Similarly, *The Connection* is oriented by a Pirandellian play-within-a-play structure that frequently left the audience confused as to what was scripted and what was improvised, what was being simulated and what was not. The play begins unusually with a message from the director, who informs the audience that they will be witnessing the making of an underground film in which heroin addicts onstage will improvise scenes from his script loosely related to their real lives. Two cameramen are indeed seen to be filming; there are stumbling and awkward silences, live jazz by musicians of obvious talent, and a director who frequently stops the production when he deems that things have gotten "out of hand." The audience is panhandled during an intermission, after which real heroin is circulated. In at least one performance, an actual overdose occurred onstage. Spectators reportedly fainted at regular intervals over the course of the performance.

The playwright Edward Albee claims to have been thoroughly "affected and energized" by the play, finding it "exciting, dangerous, instructive and terrifying."[17] But for Mekas, it was the deliberate *lack* of drama that pointed to a refreshingly new aesthetic of realism: "Nothing happens. . . . They talk, they goof, they play jazz. No ideas arise, no dramatic climaxes occur—or, if they do occur, they are of little importance, they don't change anything. . . . It shows something of the essence of our life today only because it is about nothing. It doesn't point at truth—it sets truth in motion."[18] Beck understood

Gelber's elongated temporalities as crucial to a newly realist aesthetic: "What had been passing for realism was not real. There had to be pauses. Directors had to learn to let actors sit still for a long time in one place as in life, and actors had to learn to adapt to this new idea. . . . we had to risk embarrassment, we had to risk boring the audience, but it had to be done."[19] A new realism based upon deliberate withdrawal of dramatic action, the inclusion of lengthy encounters with silence and stillness, even at the risk of boring the audience, and the portrayal of socially ostracized individuals then deemed outside the pale of commercial representation—all marked elements Mekas embraced. When Andy Warhol turned to filmmaking in the years to come, Mekas both personally encouraged and publicly celebrated these qualities in his work. *The Connection* was a watershed for the Living Theatre and the off-Broadway theater movement more generally, garnering considerable attention and favorable reviews, especially for a work considered shocking by so many. But *The Connection* quickly became a watershed for the New American Cinema as well—consequential not simply for its aesthetic innovations but because of the material social and political consequences that it engendered.

Shirley Clarke employed virtually all its original cast members to create a film adaptation that premiered at the Cannes Film Festival in 1961, but she was subsequently denied an exhibition license in New York due to the work's extensive use of profanity. Technically, film licensing was required only for public, commercial screenings; private film societies such as Cinema 16 could circumvent government censorship so long as none of their members filed an official complaint. But Lewis Allen, the film's producer—with help from Clarke, Mekas, and others from the New American Cinema Group—turned *The Connection* into a vehicle to force a legal challenge to the city's licensing laws and de facto censorship.[20] Publicly announcing an unlicensed exhibition at the D. W. Griffith Theatre in Manhattan on 45th Street in the heart of Broadway's theater district, they effectively forced the police to intervene.[21] When they arrived, they found the projection booth locked from the inside and had to forcibly break in to stop the screening. The filmmakers had invited notable critics to attend and the resulting media debacle created a public-interest story about censorship that proved wildly successful: the legal case advanced quickly, and the resulting decision established that the First Amendment prohibited censorship of art based on vulgarity, a decisive victory for the 1960s counterculture against the 1950s establishment.[22]

Salacious or prurient content, however, remained outside First Amendment protection, which is why the screenings of Jack Smith's *Flaming Creatures*, beginning in April 1963, were repeatedly met with police harassment, arrests, and theater closures. Mekas initially tried to skirt the law, technically presenting Smith's films "free of charge" so as to adhere to the noncommercial rule governing

19 Julian Beck, "Storming the Barricades," in Kenneth H. Brown, *The Brig* (New York: Hill and Wang, 1965), 26–27.

20 Together with Mekas, Lewis Allen, the film's producer, had called the original meeting of what would become the New American Cinema Group, and had helped draft the group's first public statement explicitly demanding the elimination of all film censorship and licensing requirements. See "The New American Cinema Group" and "First Statement of the Group" in *Film Culture* 22–23 (Summer 1961): 130–33; MacDonald, *Cinema 16*, 18–19.

21 Bosley Crowther, "Screen: 'Connection' Here and Gone: Adaptation of Gelber's Play at the Griffith: Controversial Movie Is Shown Only Twice," *New York Times*, October 4, 1962.

22 Film censorship declined sharply in the later 1950s when the U.S. Supreme Court overturned a ban on Marc Allégret's 1955 film *Lady Chatterley's Lover*, arguing that absent any visibly prurient content, the First Amendment prohibited censorship on the basis of an immoral "idea" alone. "Obscenity" thus remained the only valid criterion for censorship, and in the case of *The Connection*, the use of the colloquial slang "shit" for heroin was judged to be vulgar but not obscene. See Laura Wittern-Keller, *Freedom of the Screen: Legal Challenges to State Film Censorship, 1915–1981* (Lexington: University Press of Kentucky, 2008). John Gruen chronicled the rapid transformation of language in Greenwich Village publications like *Fuck You: A Magazine of the Arts*, and in his "The Four-Letter Word and How It Grew," in *The New Bohemia: The Combine Generation* (New York: Grosset and Dunlap, 1966), chapter 5.

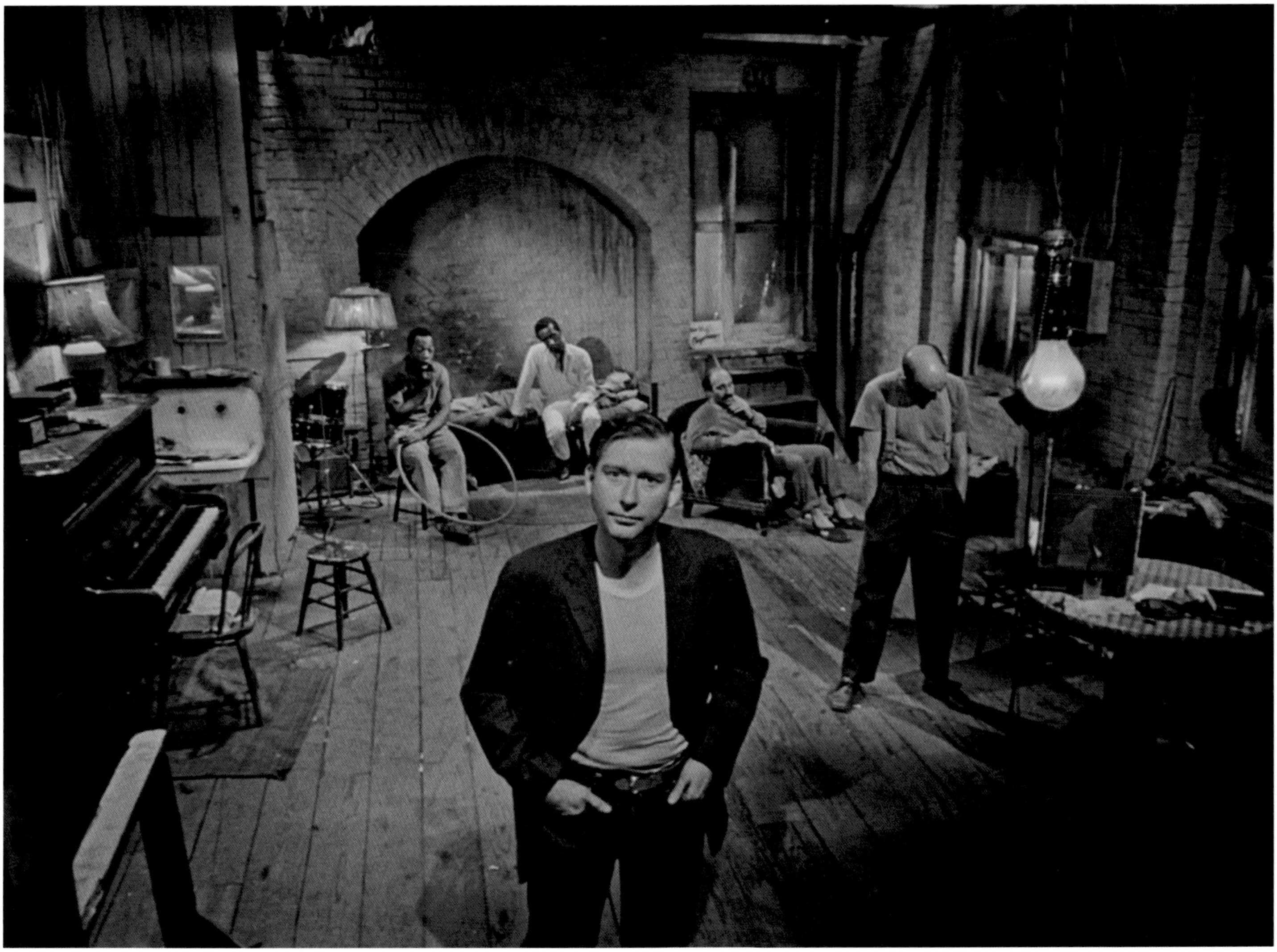

Still of William Redfield in Shirley Clarke's *The Connection* (1961).

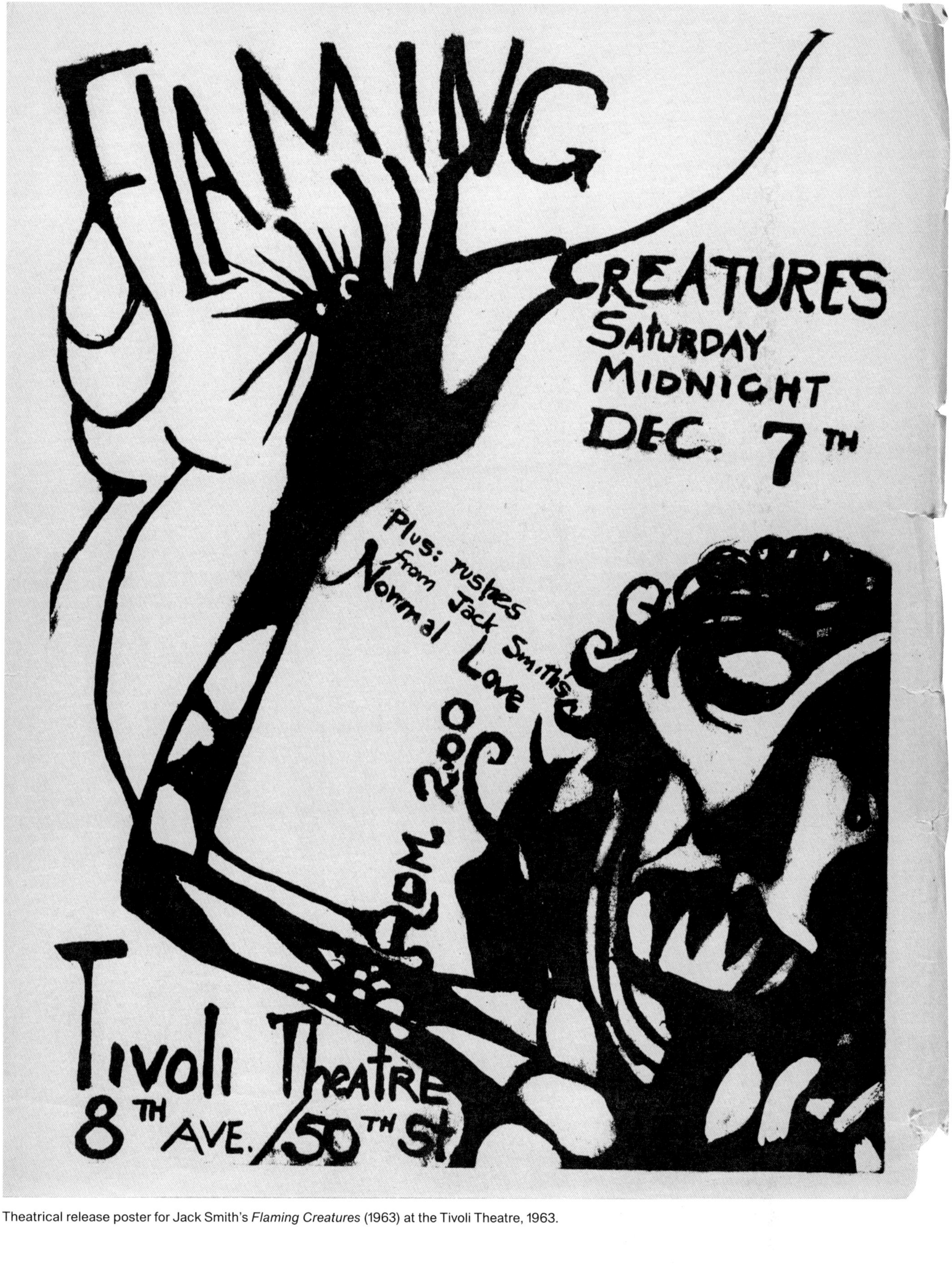

Theatrical release poster for Jack Smith's *Flaming Creatures* (1963) at the Tivoli Theatre, 1963.

23 J. Hoberman, *On Jack Smith's Flaming Creatures (and Other Secret-Flix of Cinemaroc)* (New York: Granary Books/Hips Road, 2001), 39.

24 VanDerBeek, "Cinema Delimina," 8. Smith later came to resent Mekas for the way he felt he had been, in the words of Callie Angell, "put on display as a kind of poster child for the promotion of freedom of speech in the arts," with Mekas exploiting the scandal "to get publicity for himself and his organizations." Callie Angell, "Batman and Dracula: the Collaborations of Jack Smith and Andy Warhol," *Criticism* 56, no. 2 (2014): 164–65.

25 While censorship was diminishing overall in this period, *Flaming Creatures* was still judged obscene. *Roth v. United States*, 354 U.S. 476 (1957), held that an expression is obscene (and thus unprotected by the First Amendment) if "the dominant theme of the material taken as a whole appeals to prurient interest." Art, by definition, does not fit this category, but rather than the status of "art" being an affirmative defense against obscenity, a work's prurient appeal was understood to undermine any potential claim to the status of "art." Thus, in the case of *Flaming Creatures*, the defense attempted to call eleven witnesses (including Allen Ginsberg, Susan Sontag, and more than a half dozen university professors and filmmakers) to testify that the film was a work of art and thus not obscene, but the presiding judge would not allow any of them to testify to this effect—ostensibly because its salacious nature was already established. An appeal eventually made it to the Supreme Court, but their guilty verdict was affirmed in June 1967 (and by the supposedly liberal stalwarts Justices Earl Warren and William J. Brennan Jr., no less). See Brian L. Frye, "The Dialectic of Obscenity," *Hamline Law Review* 35, no. 229 (2012): 232. *Roth* was not reversed until 1973.

unlicensed films while soliciting donations for the "Love and Kisses to Censors Film Society."[23] Yet, throughout his "Movie Journal" columns of the period, one finds Mekas becoming increasingly radicalized by the harassment. Less and less willing to allow his fledgling artists to remain "secret members of the underground"—as VanDerBeek had described them in 1961—Mekas sought an increasingly confrontational strategy of forcing *Flaming Creatures* into the public eye. As with *The Connection*, Mekas imagined that it might become the vehicle through which to incite a more general legal and social transformation.[24] That December, he rented the Tivoli Theatre in the heart of the Manhattan theater district to present Smith with *Film Culture*'s annual Independent Film Award, yet the theater management refused to allow the screening to proceed when it realized the film was unlicensed. The result was a performance of street theater that saw Mekas delivering the award outside on the roof of a parked car in front of hundreds of supporters. Weeks later, Mekas would be physically wrestling with authorities at a film festival at Knokke-le-Zoute, Belgium, attempting to show *Flaming Creatures* after the film jury informed him that its screening was impossible under Belgian law. Finally, two months later, he would be in police custody, the film impounded, and *Flaming Creatures* would get the trial he had wanted, even if the resulting verdict would not be what he had hoped for.[25]

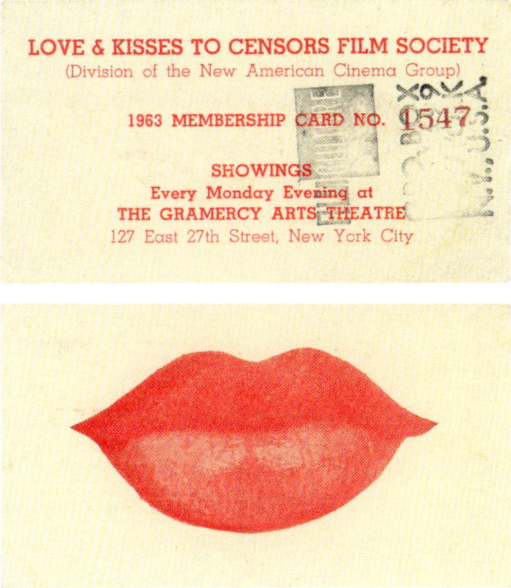

Membership card for Love & Kisses to Censors Film Society, front and back, 1963.

This link between art and social change was something that had characterized the Living Theatre since the beginning. Mekas had not previously been arrested, and was shocked and horrified by the experience, but Beck and Malina already had a long history on that score. Declared anarcho-pacifists, they had held antiwar film screenings and benefits for various pacifist organizations at the Living Theatre since the early 1950s, and Malina had first been arrested in a War Resisters League opposition to the Operation Alert civil defense drill in 1955. As Dee Garrison has described, the civil defense drills of the 1950s and early 1960s were an organization of biopower on a massive scale, with eight million New Yorkers legally required to go underground each year when citywide sirens signaled a mock attack.[26] Perpetuating conditions of fear and servility through the inculcation of a permanent state of war, it was an effort at mass regimentation, a disciplining of the civilian population to the vicissitudes of an uncontestable extra-civilian authority. A 1955 pamphlet distributed by the war resister Dorothy Day stated, "We will not obey this order to pretend, to evacuate, to hide. . . . We know this drill to be a military act in a cold war to instill fear, to prepare the collective mind for war."[27] At Malina's trial, the judge labeled her a murderer, held her responsible for the (mock) deaths of three million New Yorkers, and was so outraged by her lack of deference to his authority that he had her involuntarily committed to Bellevue psychiatric hospital.[28] She and Beck were further radicalized after they were both arrested at a similar demonstration in 1957. Mekas may not have been arrested, but he was definitely involved. A short sequence from *Lost, Lost, Lost* (1976) places him at one of the later demonstrations from 1960 or 1961, where he captures what was surely the demonstration's most conspicuous and powerful image: a woman holds a large placard—"THERE IS NO SHELTER IN NUCLEAR WAR"—while nursing an infant. Garrison claims that the unusually large number of women at these demonstrations had an effect on both the media coverage and the police response, but that the specific imagery of young mothers holding their infant children was what turned the tide within media coverage and led to the public's rejection of civil defense drills, which the government would abandon in 1962.

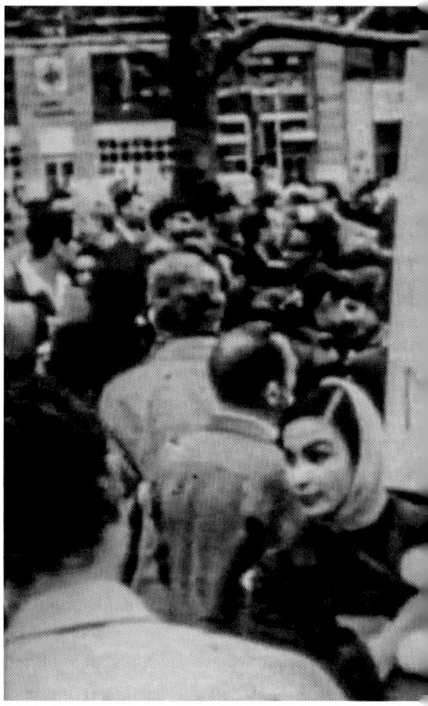

Still from *Lost, Lost, Lost* (1976).

Yet despite the resurgence of the peace movement, by the spring of 1963 the Cold War was heating up. After a brief moratorium, the Soviet Union had resumed nuclear testing, the Cuban Missile Crisis had brought America to the brink of nuclear war, and an ever-increasing number of young men were being deployed to a local insurgency in Vietnam. Soon, the government accelerated the draft as American involvement in the war grew. While Mekas was preparing the premiere of *Flaming Creatures*, the Living Theatre was involved in organizing the New York General Strike for Peace. Simultaneously, they were preparing a new production that aligned their political action in the streets with a correlative ambition for the theater. The ruthless regimentation and disciplining of soldiers' bodies within *The Brig* represented the flip side of the polymorphous sexuality of Jack Smith's anarchically liberated *Flaming Creatures*. The controversies surrounding both spoke to the power of the body in this moment—conceptualized as a site of production and reproduction, discipline and resistance at the intersection of art and life.

Kenneth H. Brown, who wrote *The Brig*, served from 1954 to 1957 in the US Marines, stationed in Japan. After returning

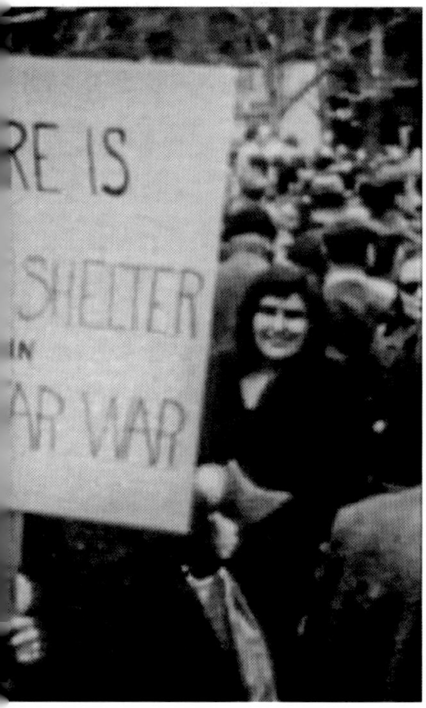

26 "8,000,000 in City Go to Shelters," *New York Times*, May 4, 1960.
27 Dee Garrison, *Bracing for Armageddon: Why Civil Defense Never Worked* (New York: Oxford University Press, 2006), 76. On the typically unacknowledged significance of women's protests against the civil defense drills, also see Garrison's "Our Skirts Gave Them Courage: The Civil Defense Protests in New York City, 1955–1961," in *Not June Cleaver: Women and Gender in Postwar America, 1945–1960*, ed. June Meyerowitz (Philadelphia: Temple University Press, 1994), 201–26.
28 Garrison, *Bracing for Armageddon*, 91.
29 Judith Malina, "Directing *The Brig*," in Brown, *The Brig*, 83.

late to base one night, he was punished by thirty days of physical assault, psychological humiliation, and emotional degradation in the Fujiyama brig. A fellow prisoner he knew there left in a strait-jacket from the experience. *The Brig* was Brown's attempt to document, as precisely as possible, the meticulous rituals of the prison. For Malina, this precision was key to sustaining the more general idea of the brig as ritual structure—a model for the coercive power of a carceral state so vividly exemplified by her experience with the civil defense drills. In language that presages Michel Foucault's analysis of biopower in his famous study *Discipline and Punish* a decade later, Malina described *The Brig* using terms specifically intended to deflate and subvert the soaring rhetoric of President John F. Kennedy's 1961 inaugural address. Where Kennedy had demanded, "ask not what your country can do for you—ask what you can do for your country," Malina responded, "whether that structure calls itself a prison or a school or a factory or a family or a government, that structure asks each man what he can do for it, not what it can do for him, and for those who do not do for it, there is the pain of death or imprisonment, or social degradation, or the loss of animal rights."[29]

Two stills from *The Brig*, 1964.

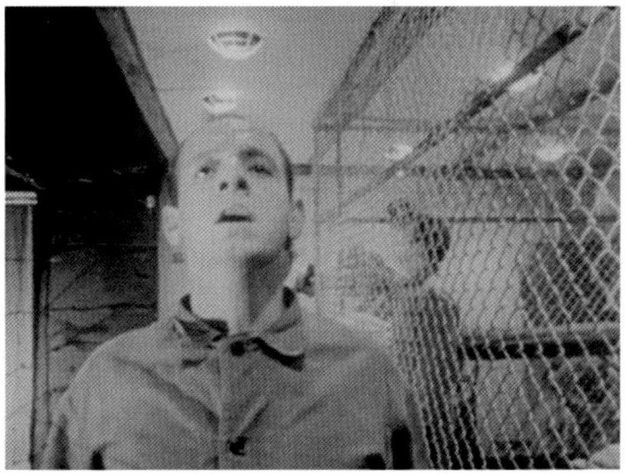

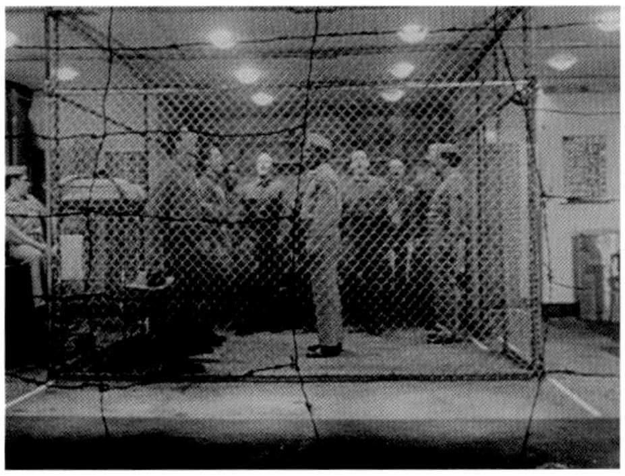

Mary Caroline Richards's 1958 translation of Antonin Artaud's *Theater and Its Double* had become an instant sensation throughout the downtown performance community years before, but *The Brig* offered the company its first opportunity to engage with the radical "theater of cruelty" Artaud had proposed. Less script than score, Brown's instructions articulated a strict disciplinary structure, blocking out bodily movements in space that deliberately throttled all vestiges of improvisational freedom. The action takes place within and around the circumscribed space of a literal cage.

30 Banes, *Greenwich Village*, 178.

The cast's preparation did not consist of learning lines or even "getting into character" so much as absorbing the grueling bodily rituals of basic training—internalizing the prescriptive manner in which every spontaneous action would be circumscribed:

> Every action, even every step they take is hedged about with requests and rules. . . . Every action must be done efficiently, in the proper posture, with the proper gestures, according to the rules—or punishment ensues. Every action is also an occasion for the guards to humiliate the inmates by reminding them of their completely debased status. . . . They must constantly show their deference to the prison authorities, and they are relentlessly beaten or given other sorts of cruel punishments for the smallest infractions of what seem like utterly arbitrary rules.[30]

In the early 1960s, after the victory of the "Greatest Generation" in World War II but before the national trauma of the Vietnam War, Americans still tended to venerate the military, associating it with the virtues of honor and sacrifice, duty and respect. It was into this cultural atmosphere that *The Brig* dropped like a bomb: the casual brutality and systematic dehumanization of men in uniform toward those who were ostensibly their peers was shocking, disorienting. Critics uniformly described the work's grim power, even if most felt it was too excessive to endure: "A fist in the guts, a mad ritual of degradation." "A nightmare." "Throbbing, claustrophobic." "Terrifying, devastating, shattering, relentless." "An act of conscience, decency, and moral revolt." These were the words and phrases they used to describe their experience—not so much of watching a play but of inhabiting the almost incomprehensible situation to which the play gave rise.

Three stills from *The Brig*, 1964.

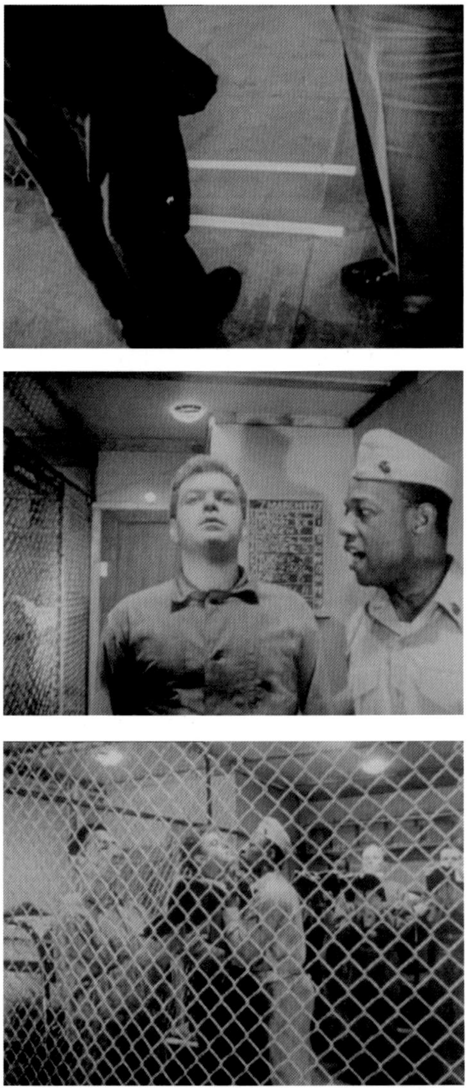

Mekas attended the performance only on its closing night. Why had he waited so long? He regularly writes of viewing works multiple times, and especially after Malina and Beck's arrest and eviction in October 1963, he would have known the precarity of their situation. Still, he had waited until the last possible moment. Perhaps he was building up the intensity of the experience, knowing that it would mark the end of an era: the final closing of the Living Theatre in America. Having been so influential in fostering the downtown performance scene—one that had nurtured him, provided him with a model of community that tightly integrated art and life—they were now leaving to seek freedom in the Europe he had long left behind. They were leaving him behind, too, with the responsibility he had only just assumed in founding the Coop and trying to secure a viable cinema screening space after the loss of Vogel's long-standing Cinema 16.

31 Mekas, *Movie Journal*, 194.
32 Ibid., 190.

Why was Mekas so adamant about wanting to film *The Brig*? It might seem obvious: not only had he long respected the Living Theatre, but Clarke's adaptation of *The Connection* had proven quite successful, bringing attention to the New American Cinema at a crucial phase, and even helping to initiate a transformation of the censorship laws against which Mekas had inveighed. Nevertheless, it is clear that Mekas had no interest in doing something similar, or he would have approached Malina and Beck long before that final night. "I am not interested in adapting plays," he wrote in his column, "I always said so."[31] And yet there he was, waiting outside the theater on the closing night—having had to leave because he was consumed by the idea that he simply *had* to film the performance. "I wanted to see it with my camera." Without prejudice, without forethought, without expectation or anticipation. Not adaptation but documentary—or, more precisely, a kind of performance documentation.

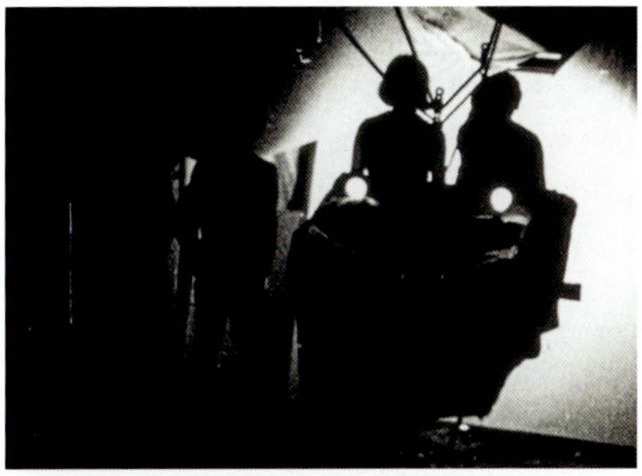

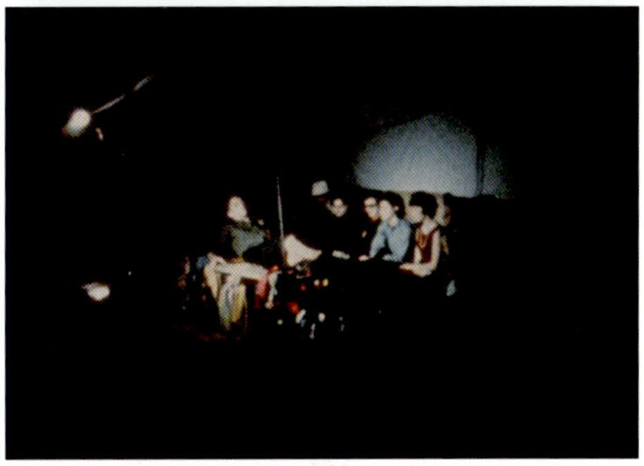

Two stills from *Film Magazine of the Arts*, 1963.

Months before, Mekas had been hired by *Show* magazine to create a prototype *Film Magazine of the Arts*, intended to be a regular report in film form, covering New York dance and theater, music, and Happenings. Mekas collaborated with Ed Emshwiller and David Brooks on photography, and Barbara Rubin on editing, but the finished film was rejected by *Show* and destroyed. (According to Mekas, it was deemed insufficiently commercial.) The work print, which Mekas fortunately retained, provides an extraordinary glimpse into a world of performance from this period that has largely been forgotten, and only survives—poorly served—by still photography and textual descriptions.

The Living Theatre's new production provided Mekas with the occasion to continue this kind of performance documentation, yet he initially harbored no plans to do so. But on that closing night of *The Brig*, something about the intimacy and intensity of his encounter—both the piece itself and the significance of its occasion—led him back to performance documentation from a radically different angle. "Suppose this was a real brig; suppose I was a newsreel reporter," Mekas wrote, unable to dislodge the thought.[32] Yet this "suppose" was not about manufacturing a cheap hoax, an attempt to hoodwink the audience into thinking that he had somehow managed to surreptitiously infiltrate an actual military jail. His "suppose" is that of an actor striving to inhabit the role, or, in the case of *The Brig*, the place within what Malina called the brig's overdetermining "structure."

Mekas called his film "an essay in film criticism" intended to "undermine some of the myths and mystifications of cinema verité." But he makes clear that this was not about cinema verité as such, but specifically an application of "cinema verité (direct cinema) techniques to a stage event." The work is an "essay" in film criticism (original meaning of the term: a testing, trial, or experiment); an essay concerning the possibilities of performance documentation. "I threw myself into it, and I used it as raw material, as it happened, *as if it were a real event—which, in truth, it was*."[33] To treat the action of *The Brig* as a "real event" is precisely to treat it as a performance and to acknowledge its reality as such, rather than seeking to adapt it to a more "cinematic" form.

And the reality of *this* performance—the way in which the actors were not simply taking on roles but had allowed themselves to be molded and manipulated by the structure of the brig—seemed to necessitate that Mekas no longer afford himself the typical distance required of a neutral documentation. Rather than remaining at a remove, he felt compelled to throw himself *into* the performance, even at the cost of interrupting it:

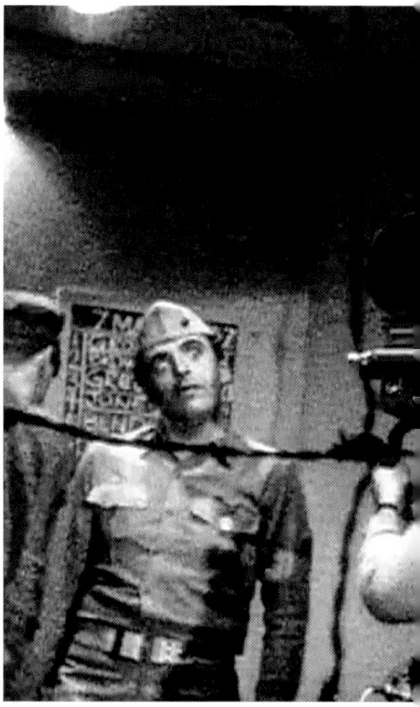

Two stills from Storm de Hirsch, *Newsreel: Jonas Mekas Shooting the Brig*, 1964.

> I remained inside the brig, among the players, constantly stepping in their way, disrupting their usual movements and *mise-en-scènes* . . . this kind of shooting required an exhausting concentration of body and eye. I had to operate the camera; I had to keep out of the cast's way; I had to look for what was going on and listen for what was said; I had to make instantaneous decisions about my movements and the camera movements, knowing that there was no time for thinking or reflecting; there was no time for reshooting, no time for mistakes: I was a circus man on a tightrope high in the air. All my senses were stretched to the point of breaking.[34]

This breathless description is the diary of a performer, a description of filming as a kind of performance. Mekas doesn't just place himself inside the cage among the performers, he describes how arduous it was for him: lugging multiple heavy cameras and backup recorders, stopping and starting while trying to maintain continuity. In describing his action in and among the ensemble, he seems caught between the roles of active participant and neutral observer, with the thrust of his "essay" lying in how he navigates this duality. Must he "keep out of the cast's way," as an observer, or must he keep "stepping in their way, disrupting their usual movements," like a fellow participant? His description reflects the ambivalence of the situation within which he has placed himself, where he aspires to document, simultaneously, both those actions taking place all around him, *as well as his own reactions to those actions*. His solution is doubled attention, a layered recording of recording, in which he situates himself within the very performance he is seeking to document.

Even before the recording commenced, Mekas seems to have been caught up in a kind of guerrilla theater. He had felt compelled to film the work, even—or was it *especially*?—if it required that the

33 Ibid., 192.
34 Ibid., 191.

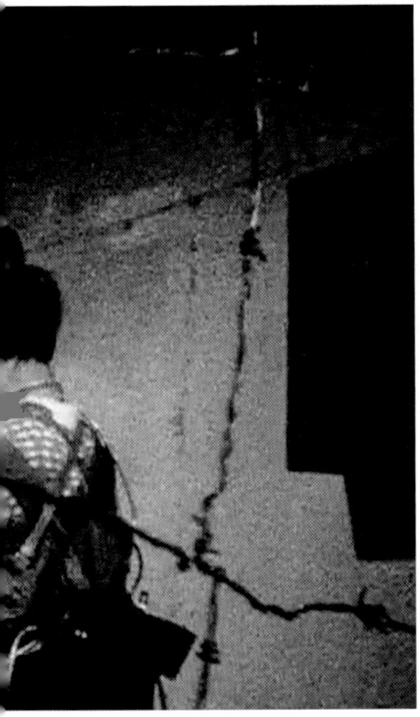

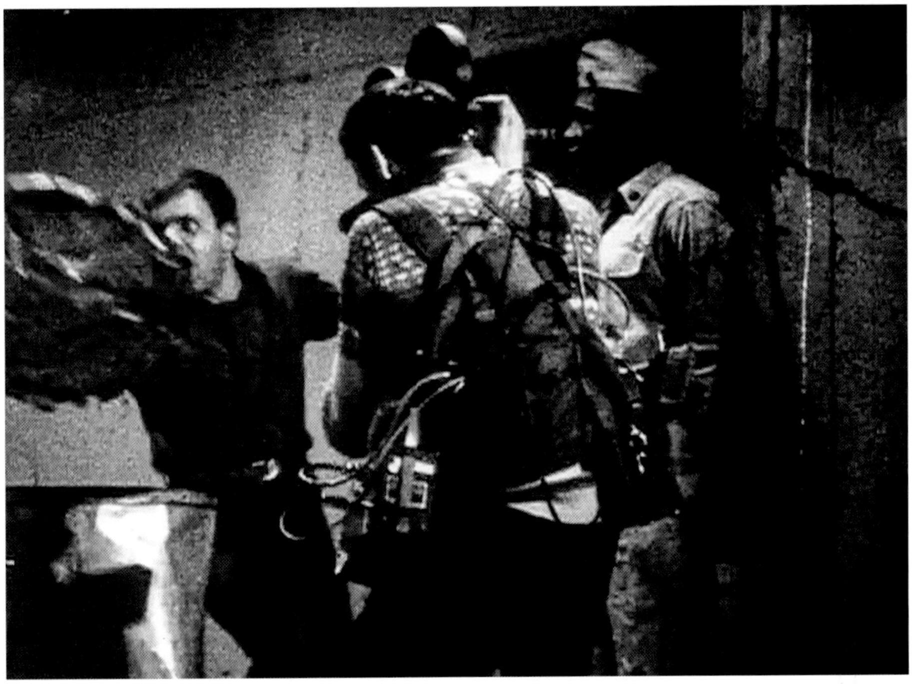

cast restage the play one last time, *for him*—thus effectively including him among the participants—and additionally required that they all, together, break into a locked venue, engaging in a trespass that mimicked the conditions of that now notorious performance four months prior, when the Living Theatre was evicted from its long-standing home in Greenwich Village and could no longer afford to remain in New York. Whether or not it had been his explicit intention, Mekas managed to make himself an indelible part of the performance that final night—part of that which he had set out to record. Storm de Hirsch was fully conscious of the way in which Mekas had stepped over the line from distanced observer to engaged performer when she opted to film Mekas's own act of recording that night in her *Newsreel: Jonas Mekas Shooting the Brig* (1964).

As might be expected, the resulting film was quite distinct from the theatrical work it documented. For the original production, there was no proscenium stage. Audiences were seated behind a chain-link fence; they remained a moderate distance from the actors, and the entirety of the space and the action within it were always visible. By contrast, even Mekas's widest shots afford only a partial view of the space, and most of the time his camera is so close to the actors that only an individual or part of an individual is visible. And once we move within the cage, everything happens so close to the lens that it is impossible to see anything but fragments. Our perspective is constantly in motion, often vertiginous.

Clarke's adaptation of *The Connection* had been painstakingly shot on a professional soundstage, with 35mm film, in clear, even lighting. While technically proficient, it had the perverse effect of draining much of the gritty realism from the environment, making the flophouse set look like a Hollywood simulation. Mekas's documentation of *The Brig*, by contrast, was a professional cinematographer's nightmare. The harsh, undiffused lighting made the shadows dark to the point of invisibility and the scorching intensity of the lights frequently flared out into blur. We are never given a proper establishing shot with which to set our bearings but are thrown into the middle of the action, which confronts us on all sides. We turn and turn, but almost nothing in the film is seen at a remove. It is impossible for us ever to place ourselves at an intellectual or emotional distance from what is taking place.

Similarly, Mekas's audio recordings of the performance are explosively "hot." If microphones are placed too close to the source, the voices are driven far beyond the safe limits of the recorder. The natural curvature of the recorded waveform becomes clipped and angular, resulting in harsh cacophony of inhuman timbres. Voices dissolve into squeals and fuzzed-out noise—an effect not unlike the distortion postwar electric guitarists were achieving by intentionally overcranking or otherwise mistreating their amplifiers. Mekas had been especially attracted to the sounds of *The Brig*, its incessant "stamping and running and shouting," and the tortured soundtrack he produced accentuated the play's chaotic soundscape into an incessant clamor of half-human noise.[35] As in Warhol's early films, the result derives not from something planned but from a decision not to correct an accidental artifact of the recording process. Mekas had simultaneously recorded both optical and magnetic soundtracks as insurance against failure, and could have cut among them to select the cleanest version for each section. Instead, he did the opposite: *combining* the optical and magnetic soundtracks to deliberately accentuate the distortion he had discovered on the "hottest" recordings.

With only ten-minute film reels, Mekas had been forced to repeatedly stop the play to avoid missing any of the action. On every changeup, he had asked the cast to redo their last sequence so as to ensure continuity of action. In typical documentary filmmaking, these overlaps would obviously be edited out to ensure seamless continuity, but Mekas decided to include the entirety of the uncut reels—not unlike what Andy Warhol (who himself had learned filmmaking from Mekas and Marie Menken) was then doing in his "portrait" films of 1964.[36] In this original version, short sequences would have thus repeated from a slightly different perspective at regular ten-minute intervals: a self-reflexive gesture that would have conspicuously foregrounded the work *as* an act of performance documentation.[37]

Both Malina and Brown, discovering that certain scenes had not been captured, implored Mekas to reshoot them, and out of respect, he agreed to do so. But he ultimately refused to incorporate any of that new footage, arguing that it lacked the spontaneity of the

35 MacDonald, *Critical Cinema 2*, 93.

36 Mekas was the one who gave Warhol the idea of filming the Empire State Building and, after Menken got them all access to a nearby building from which to shoot, Mekas did the actual filming of *Empire* (1964) while Warhol and others sat around talking. Mekas did not mention his involvement when the film was screened at his Film-Makers' Cinematheque. See the interview: https://henitalks.com/talks/making-of-andy-warhols-empire/.

37 These repetitions were still present during the original screening, and Mekas describes Beck and Malina agreeing with him to leave them in. Nevertheless, once David and Barbara Stone agreed to distribute the film, they decided to eliminate all of the overlaps "for distribution's sake," and the original version appears to have been destroyed. See MacDonald, *Critical Cinema 2*, 93. The footage was given to his brother Adolfas to trim down but not otherwise manipulate: "Now I have seen the play, I said to myself; now I have ideas about it; now I can't edit this footage without dragging in my post-thoughts and post-considerations." See Mekas, *Movie Journal*, 192.

38 Ibid., 192, 194.

39 Sheldon Renan, *An Introduction to the American Underground Film* (New York: E. P. Dutton, 1967), 167.

original: "I already knew the action, I knew the movements, and even against my will, I began anticipating the action. It turned out lifeless, so I threw the footage out." They also objected to the soundtrack, in which the dialogue was often distorted to the point of incomprehension. But again, Mekas held his ground. *The Brig* was his "gift" to Malina and Beck, "those two beautiful human beings . . . as mad as I was; their devotion to their art . . . fantastic and beyond reason." But for that very reason, it could only be something deeply personal: "a record," yes, but not of the play alone, rather one "of my eye and my temperament lost in the play."[38]

So what had Mekas actually created, in the end? Not a cinematic adaptation of the play, in any accepted sense of the term. But also not a straightforward documentation, such that future scholars or performers might reconstruct the precise reality of the historical performance. *The Brig* won the grand prize for Best Documentary in the 1964 Venice Film Festival, which says something about the instability of this category in the wake of Neorealism, with the rise of cinema verité, the resurgence of the newsreel, and a proliferation of performative models among the arts that seemed to demand new forms of time-based documentation.

As late as 1967, Sheldon Renan could describe *The Brig* as Mekas's most frequently seen film.[39] Today, looking back at Mekas's total oeuvre, it can seem like an incongruous anomaly. But if Mekas eventually came to be known for his complex film diaries—art wrested out of the mundane circumstances of his everyday life—the fact remains that the "mundane" circumstances of Mekas's life were inseparable from an extraordinary artistic community within which he always situated himself. And that rather than seeking to elevate the mundane into the mythopoetic, Mekas's films poetically document the lived communities that undergird the poetry of creation and the life of art.

It seems no accident that it was only in 1964 that Mekas began to shoot the material that would come to constitute *Walden* (1969), the first of his major film diary compilations that would come to define his mature style. And his statement for the 1975 catalogue

40 *Film-Makers' Cooperative Catalogue*, 1975, 178, as cited in James, *To Free the Cinema*, 109.

41 For an overview of Mekas's early film criticism and his wavering commitment to cinematic realism, see John Pruitt, "Jonas Mekas: A European Critic in America," in James, *To Free the Cinema*, 51–61.

for the Film-Makers' Coop might even be read as a belated rejoinder to Malina and Beck—explaining his refusal to incorporate any of the later footage of *The Brig* regardless of what was missing or how it might affect the result:

> To keep a film (camera) diary, is to react (with your camera) immediately, now, this instant: either you get it now, or you don't get it at all. To go back and shoot it later, it would be restaging, be it events or feelings . . . it has to register the reality to which I react and also it has to register my state of feeling (and all the memories) as I react. Which also means, that I had to do all the structuring (editing) right there, during the shooting, in the camera.[40]

Up until 1964, Mekas had been torn between his ethical commitment to documentary realism, on the one hand, and his celebration of the absolute idiosyncrasy of individual creativity, on the other. In more than a decade of film criticism, he had wavered between the two, and in his own nascent practice of filmmaking, he had not yet landed on a suitable form for his aesthetic ambitions.[41] The singularity of feeling Mekas discovered in his experience of filming *The Brig*—the necessity he had felt to capture the immanent intensity of an aesthetic and personal experience—seems to have solidified for him the model of a film diary as a spontaneous and performative practice, a mode of preservation and creation that might prove equal to the task of bridging art and life.

FILMS

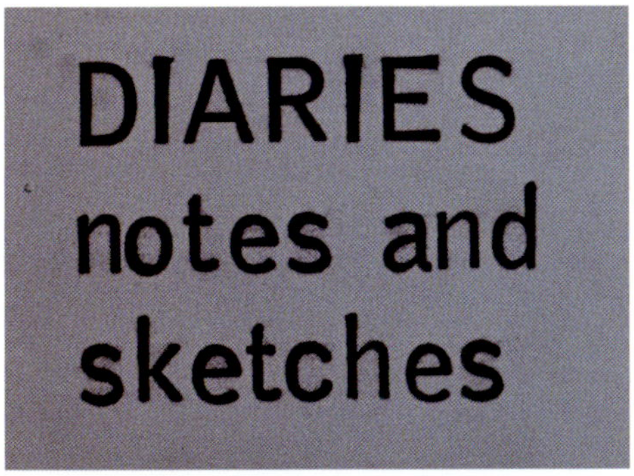
DIARIES
notes and
sketches

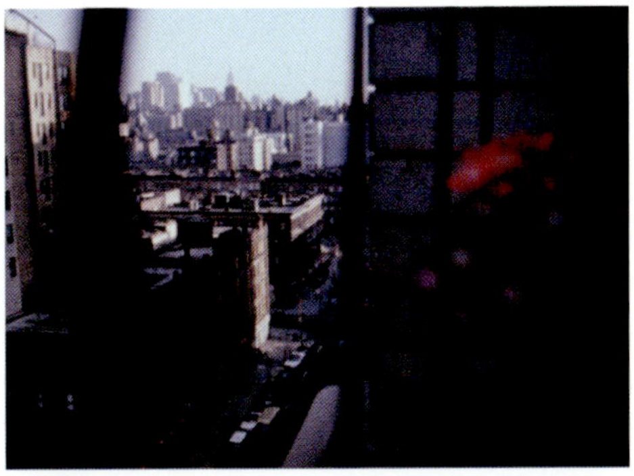

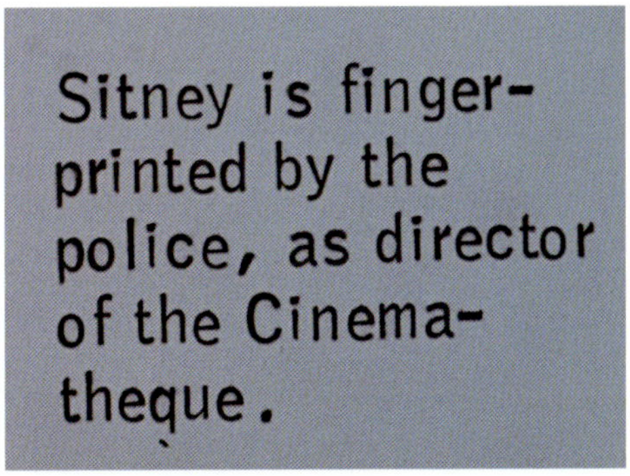
Sitney is finger-
printed by the
police, as director
of the Cinema-
theque.

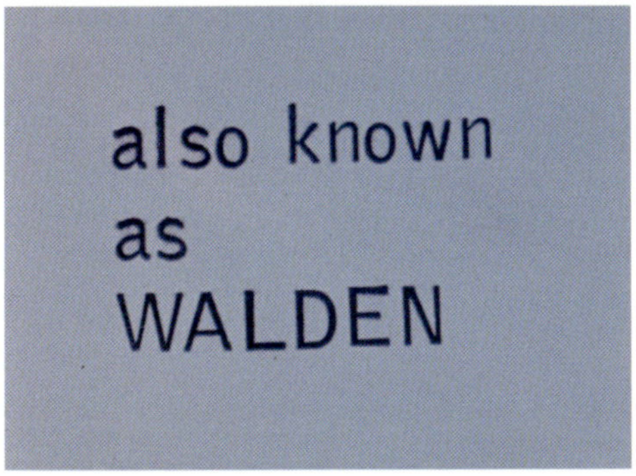
also known
as
WALDEN

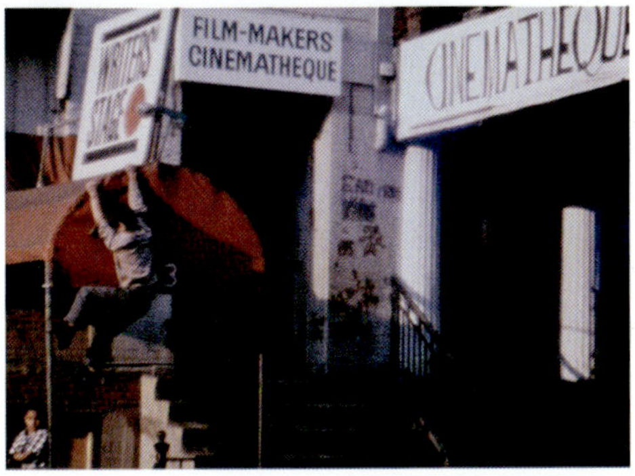
FILM-MAKERS
CINEMATHEQUE

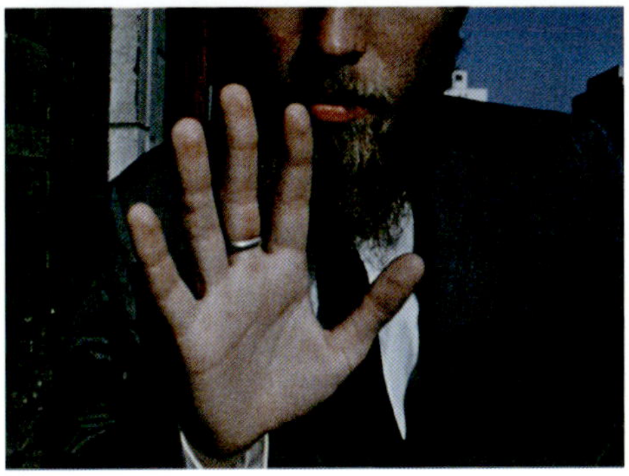

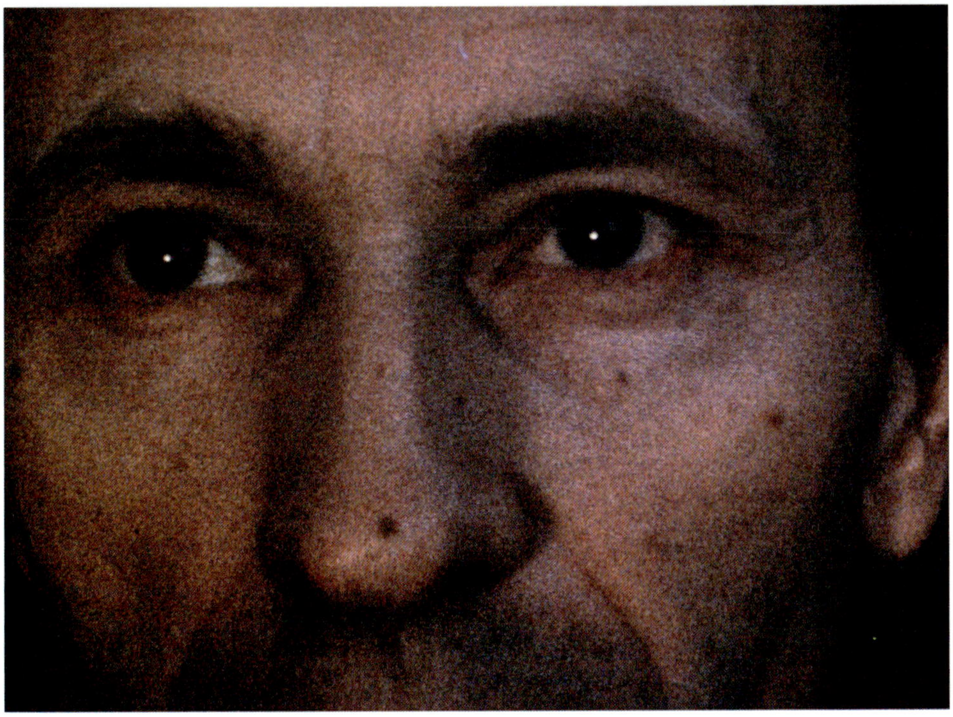

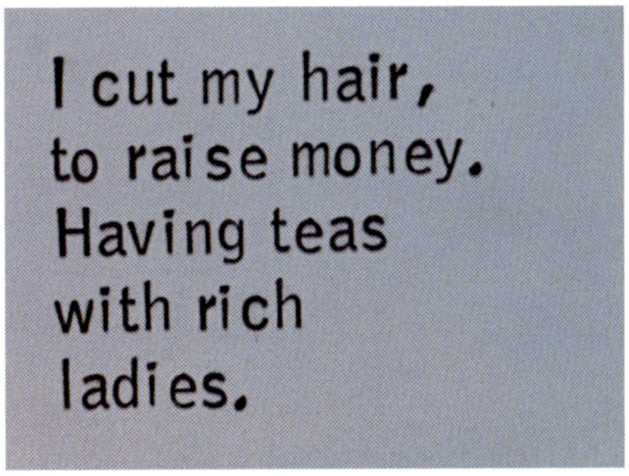
I cut my hair,
to raise money.
Having teas
with rich
ladies.

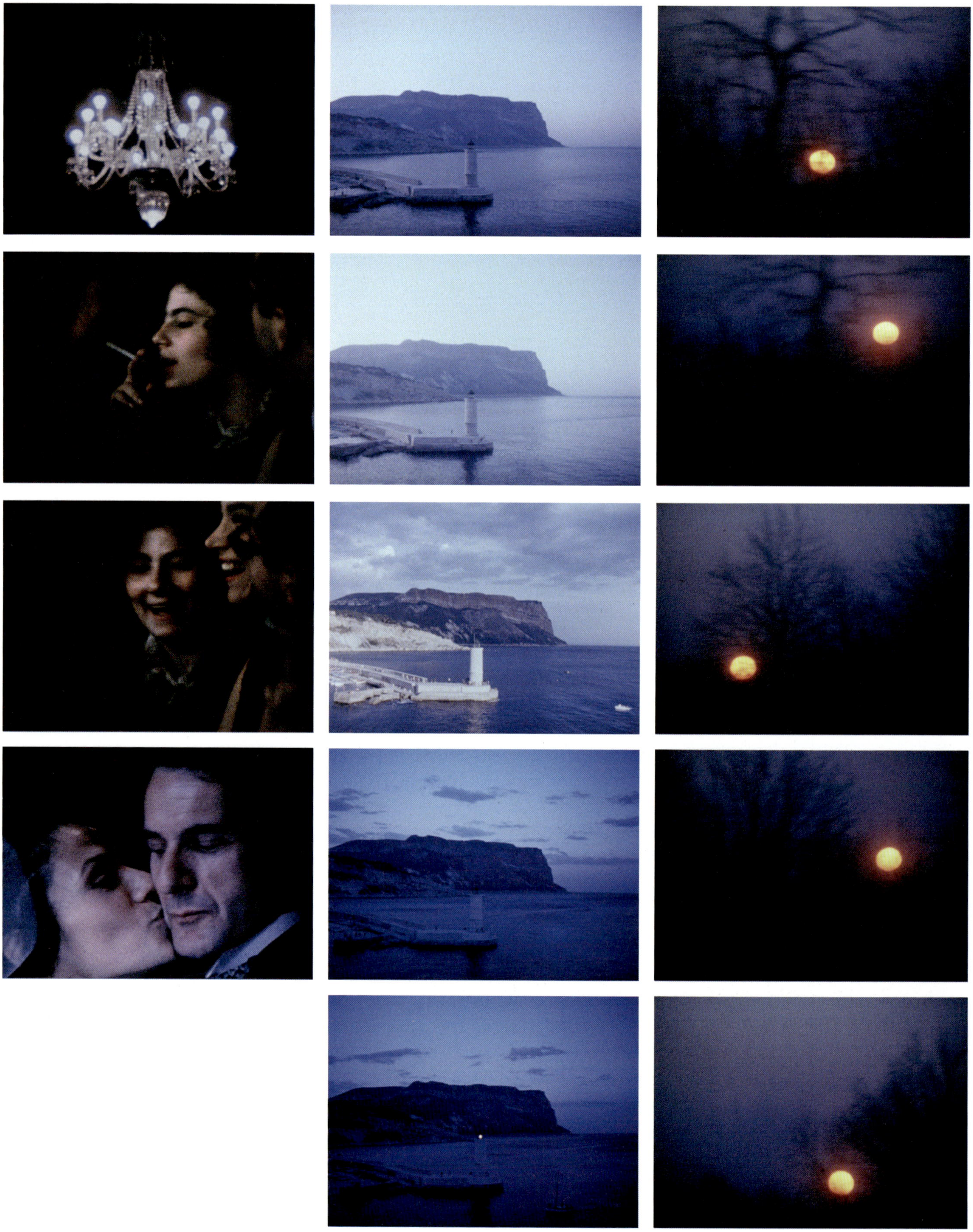

WALDEN (DIARIES, NOTES, AND SKETCHES) 16MM 1969

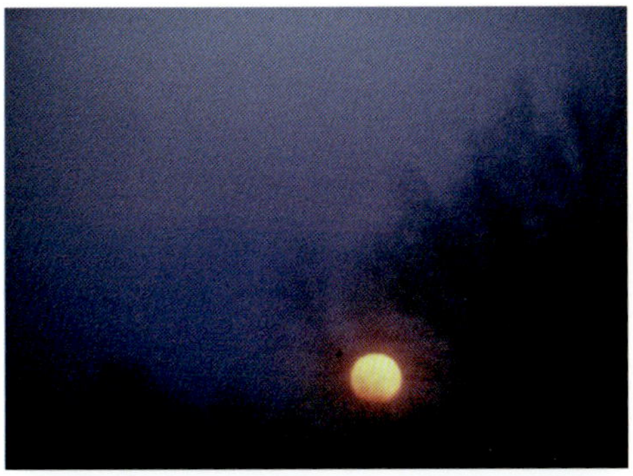
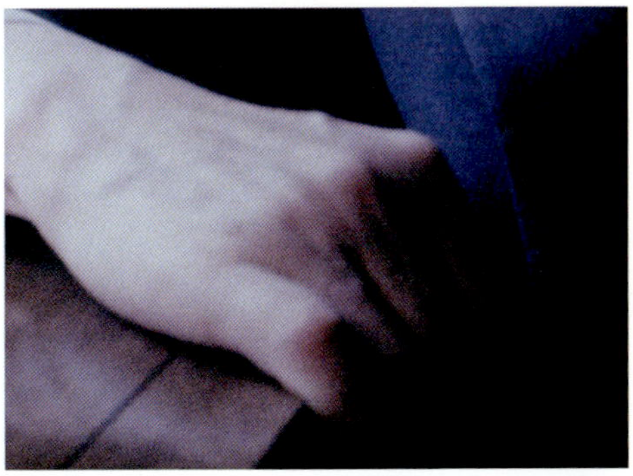
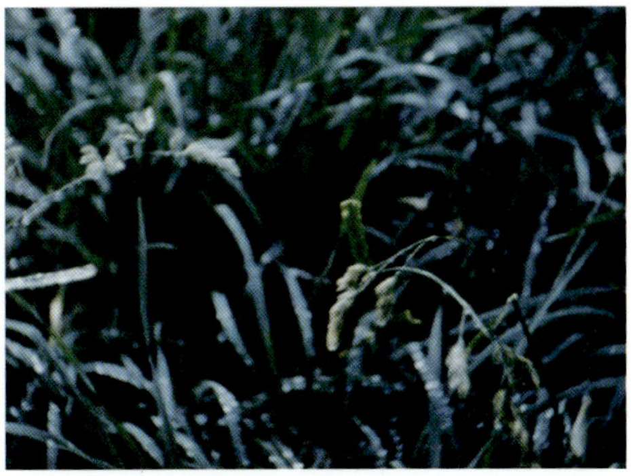
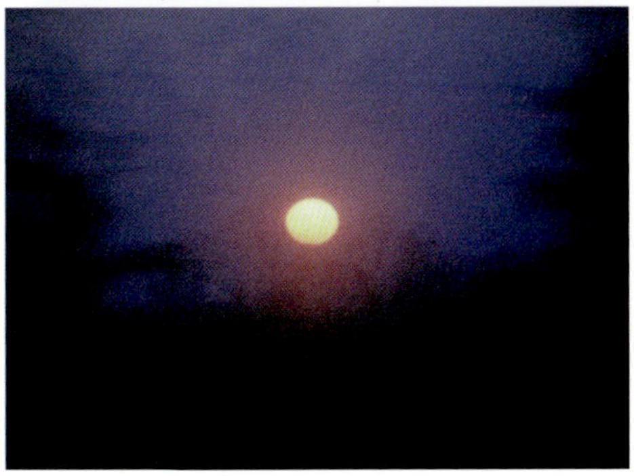
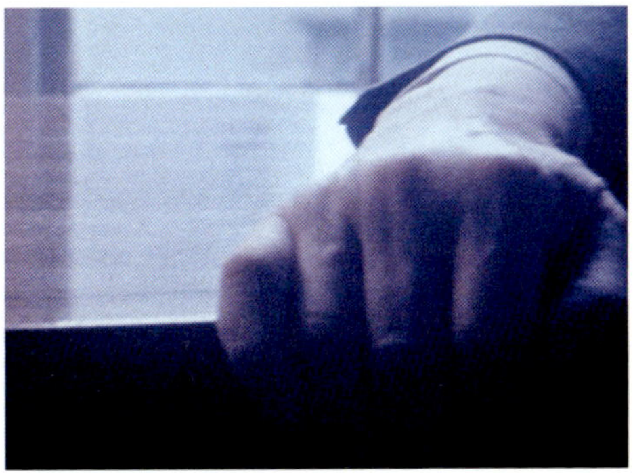
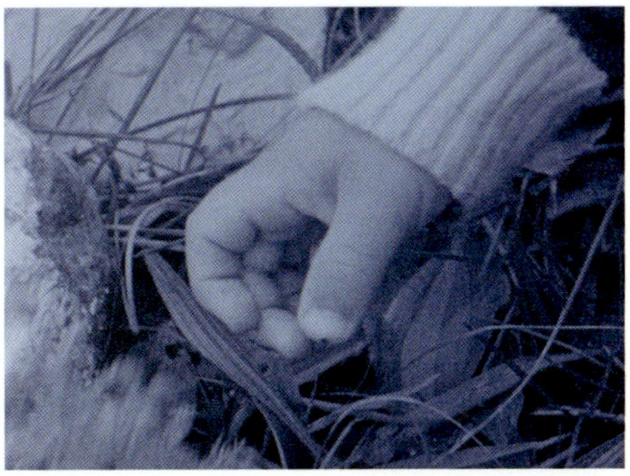
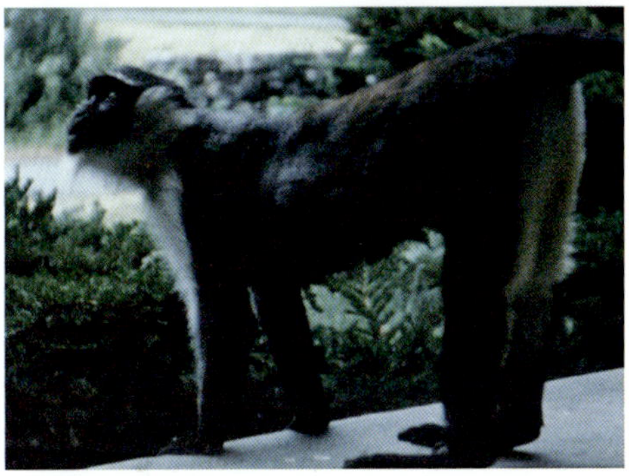
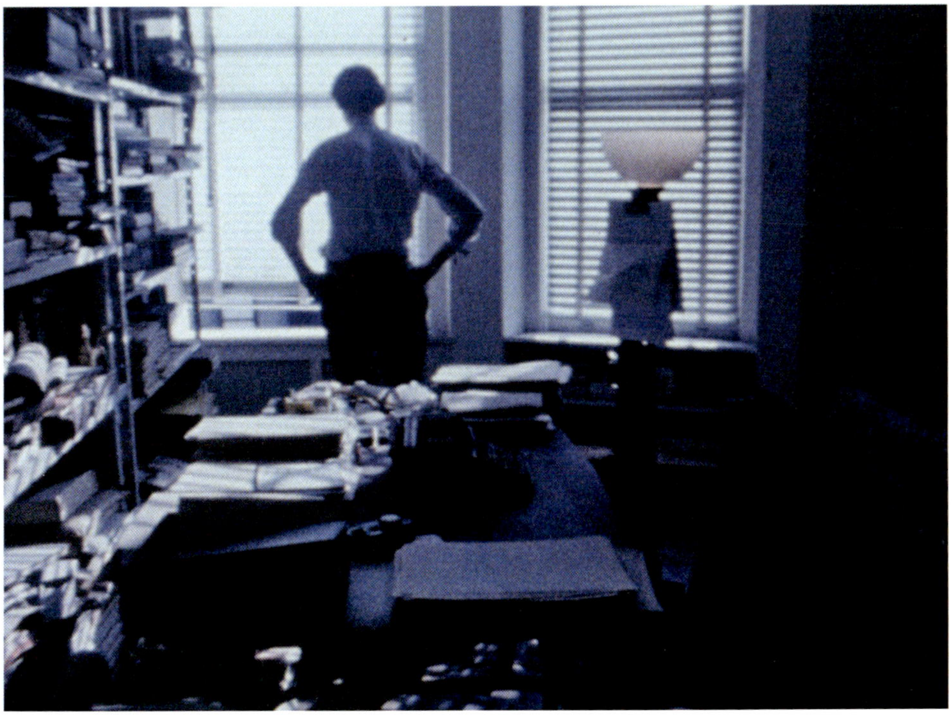
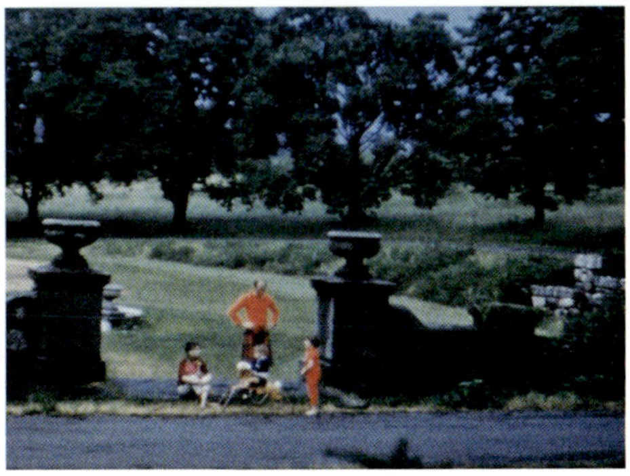

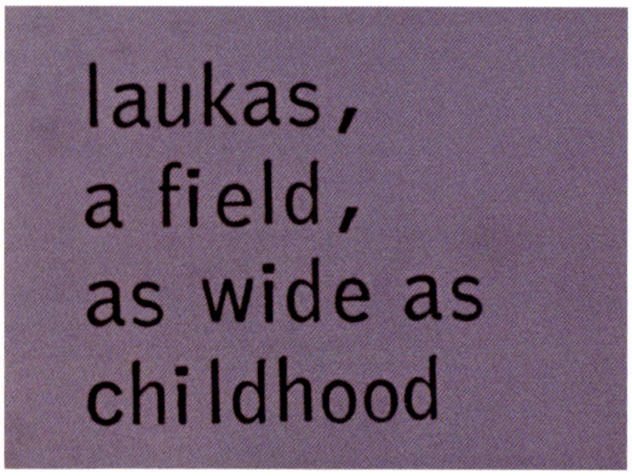
laukas,
a field,
as wide as
childhood

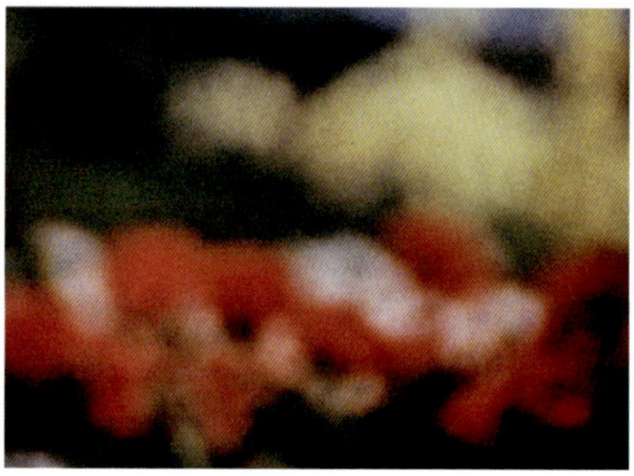

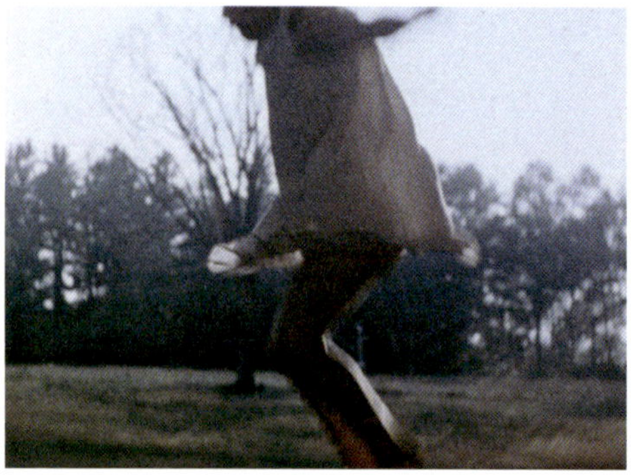

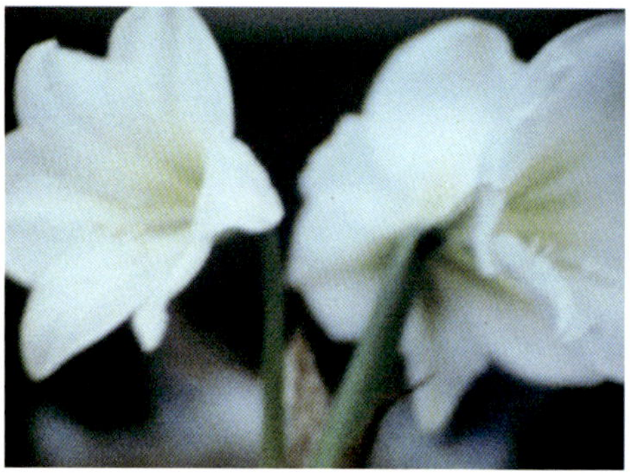

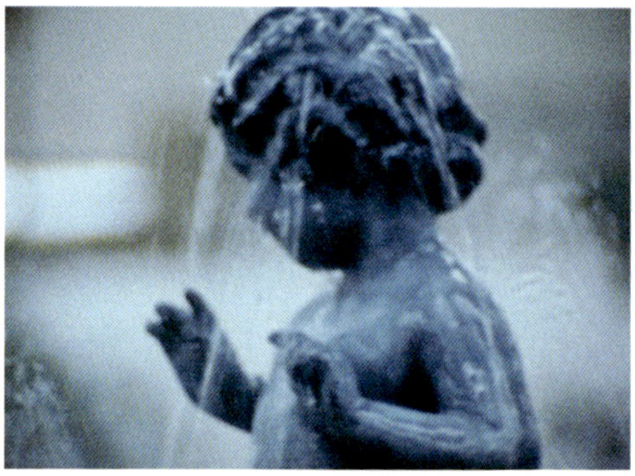

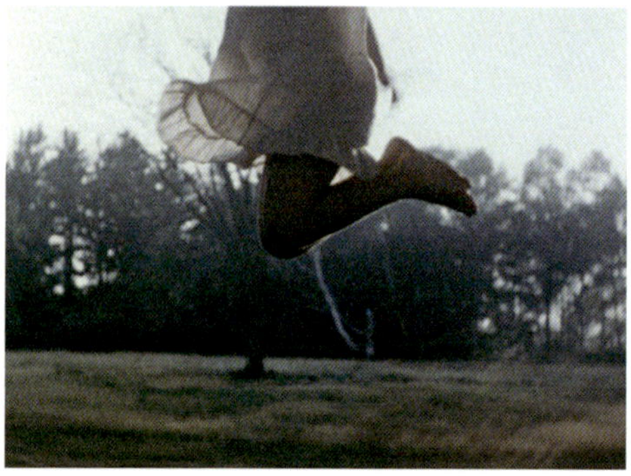

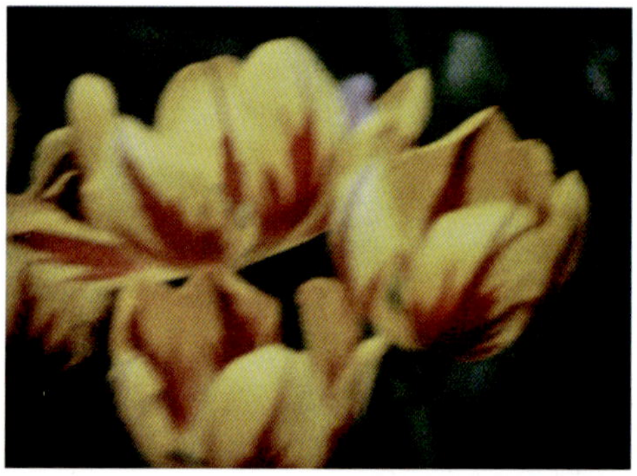

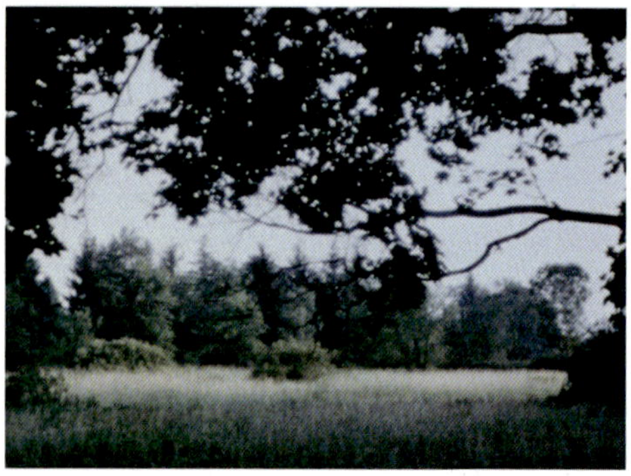

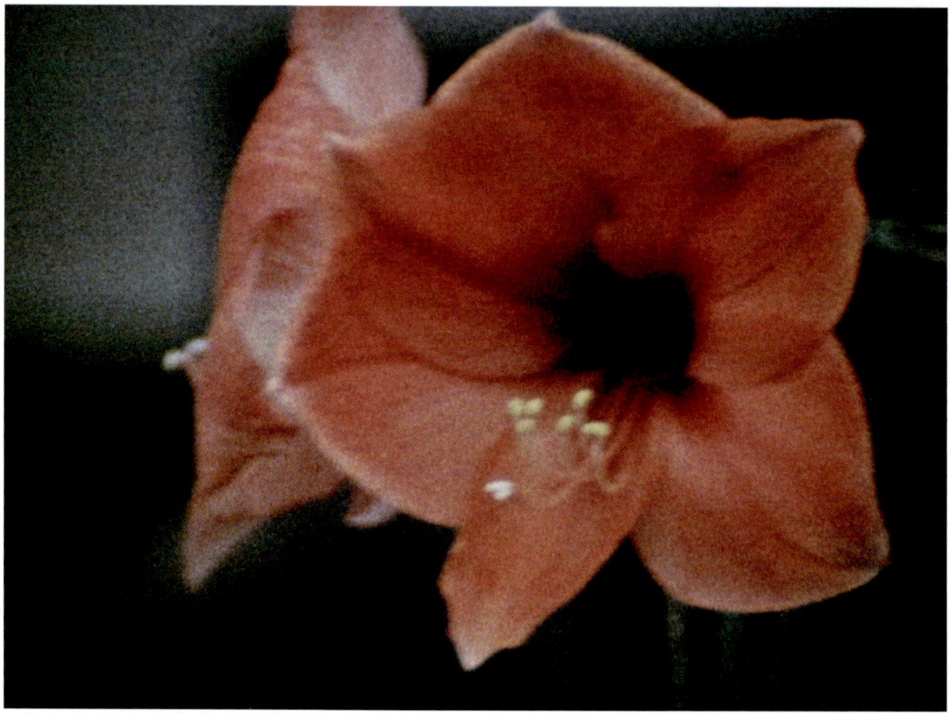

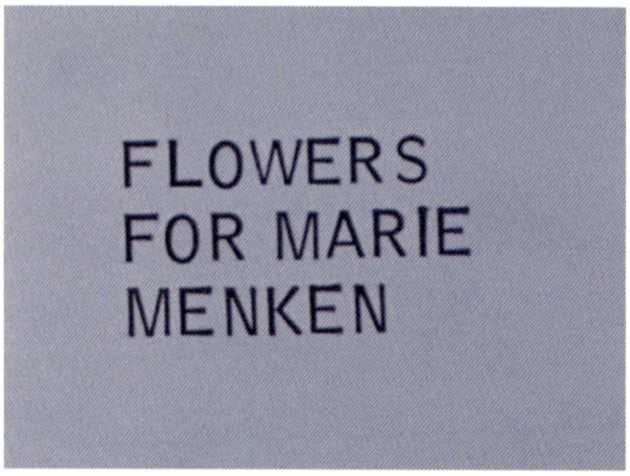
FLOWERS
FOR MARIE
MENKEN

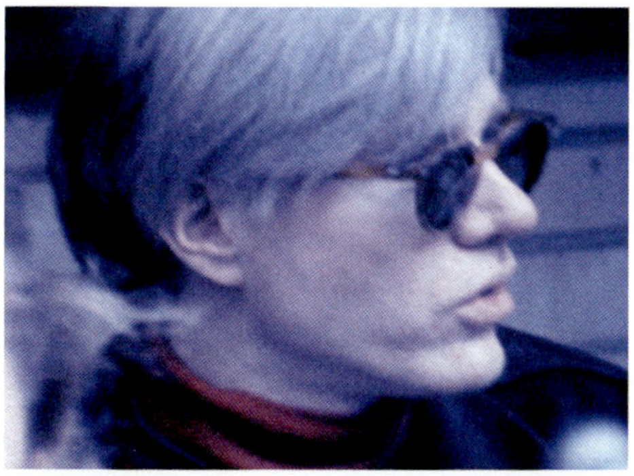
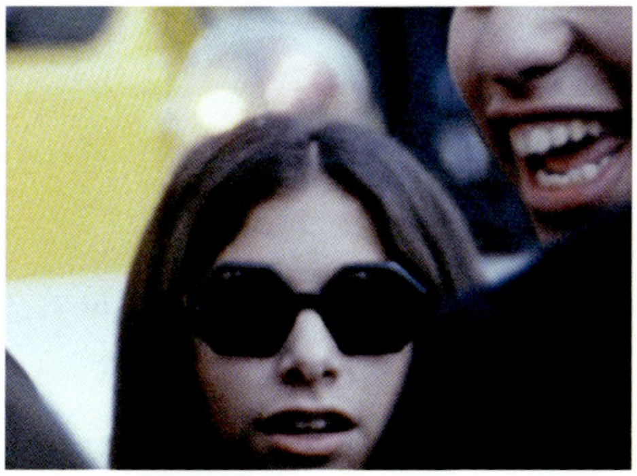
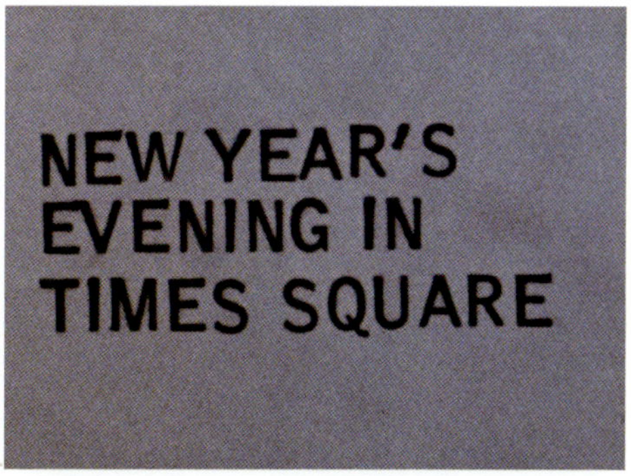

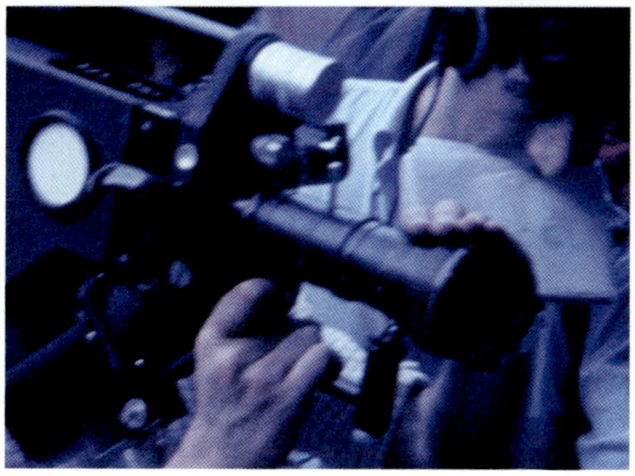
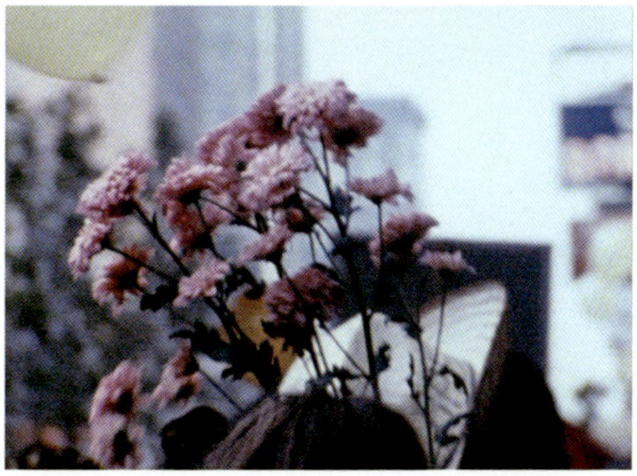
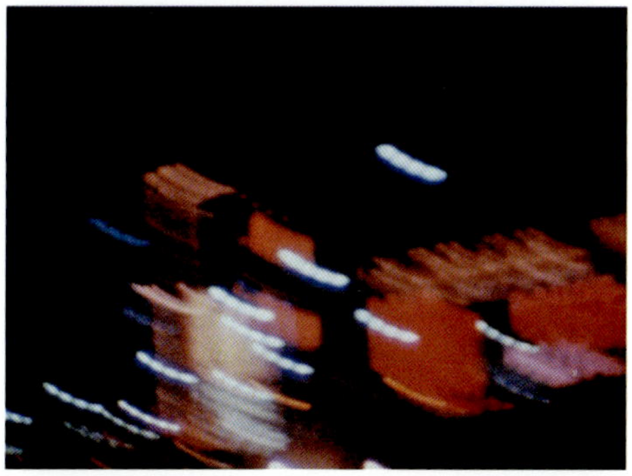
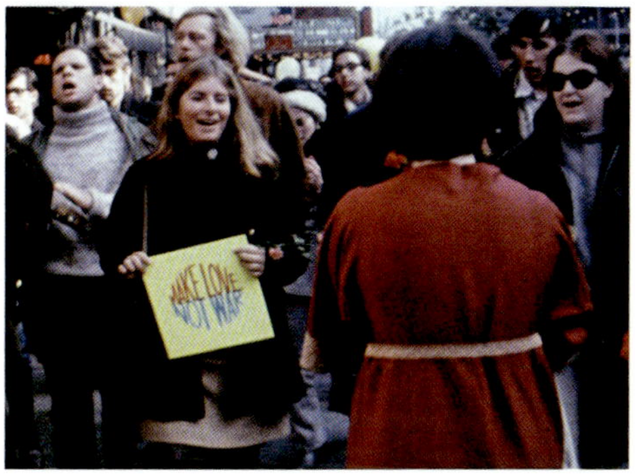

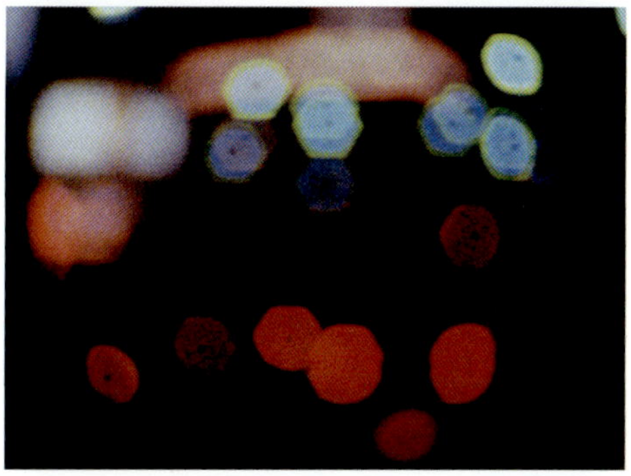
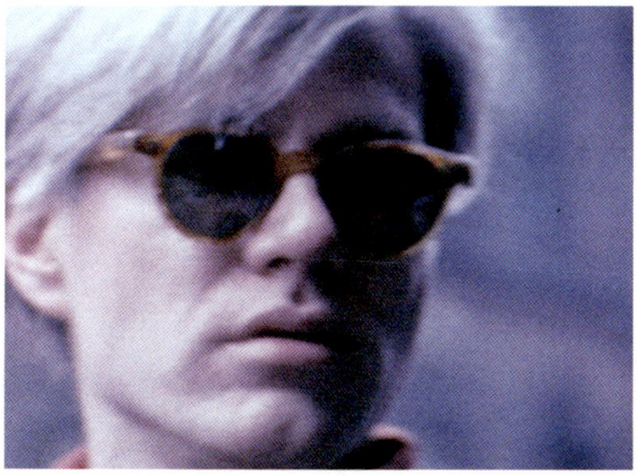
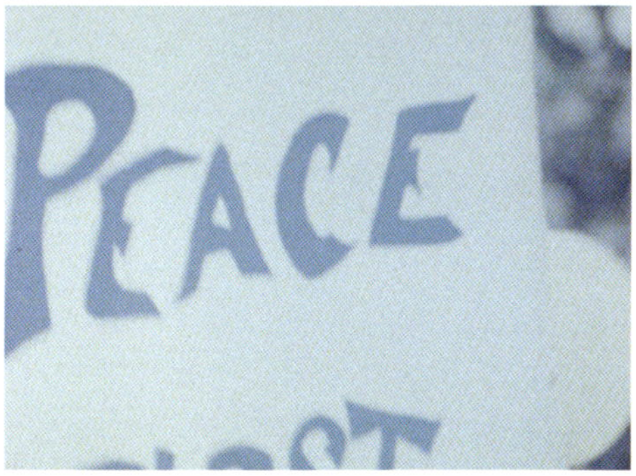

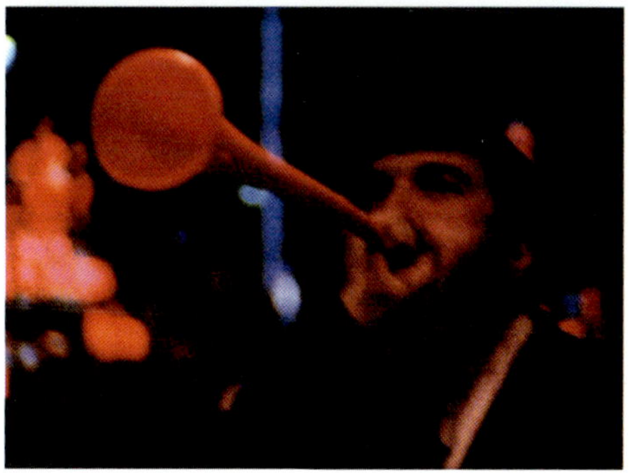
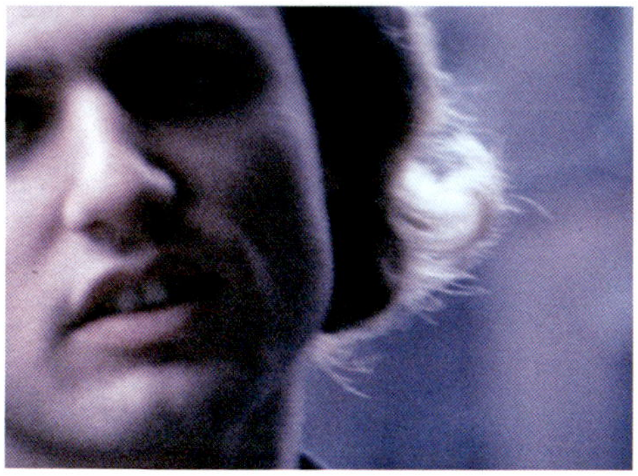
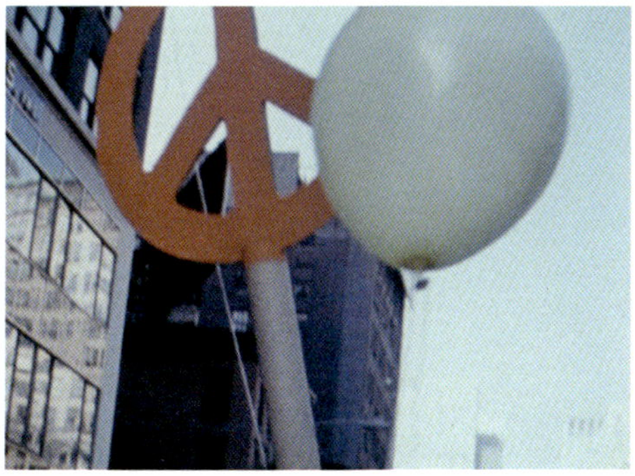

 FILMS COLOR, BLACK AND WHITE SOUND 180 MIN

UPTOWN
PARTY

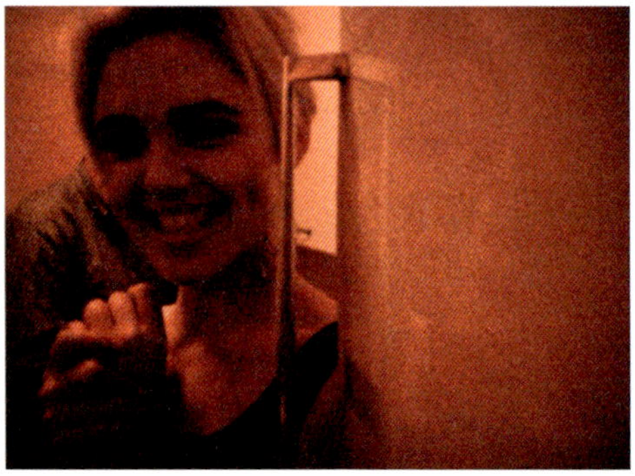

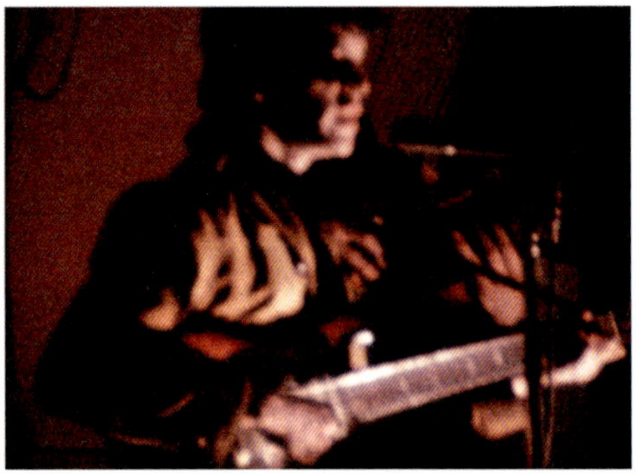

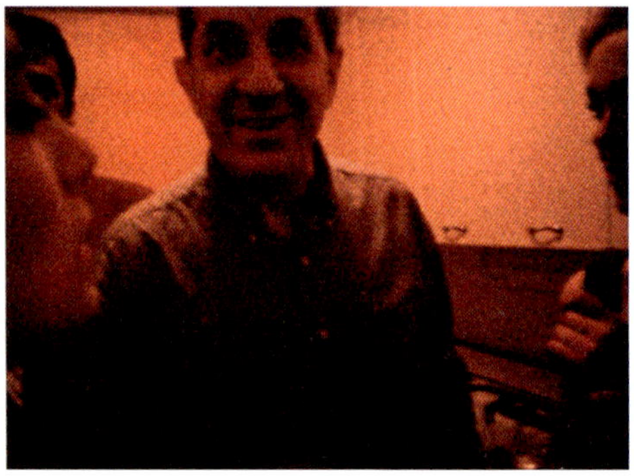

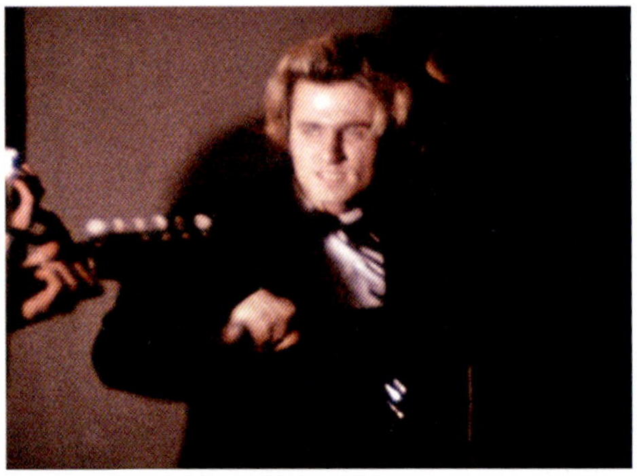

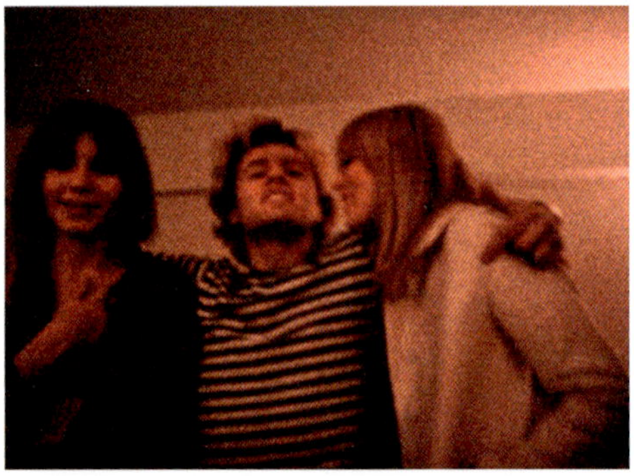

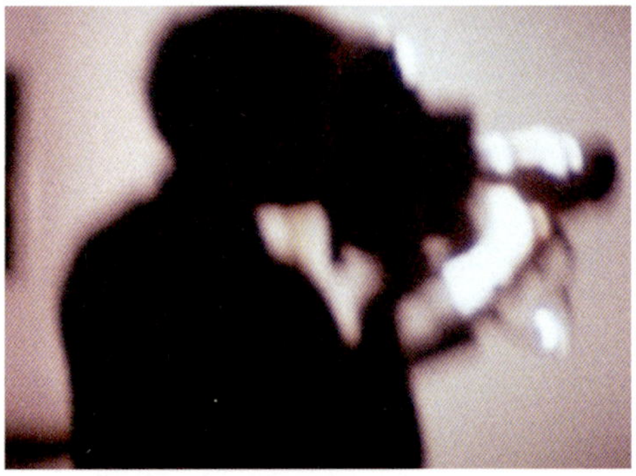

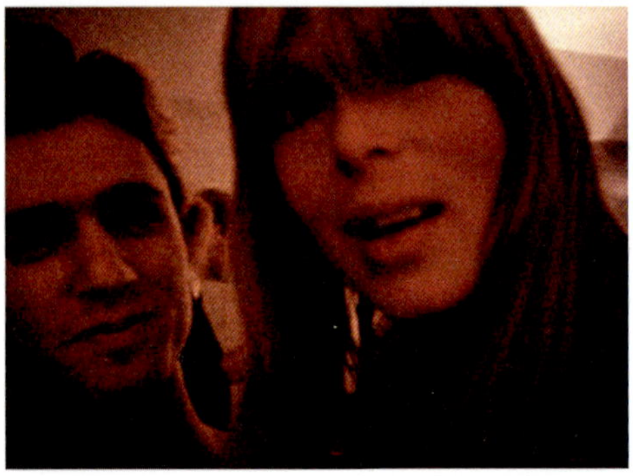

VELVET
UNDERGROUND'S
FIRST
APPEARANCE

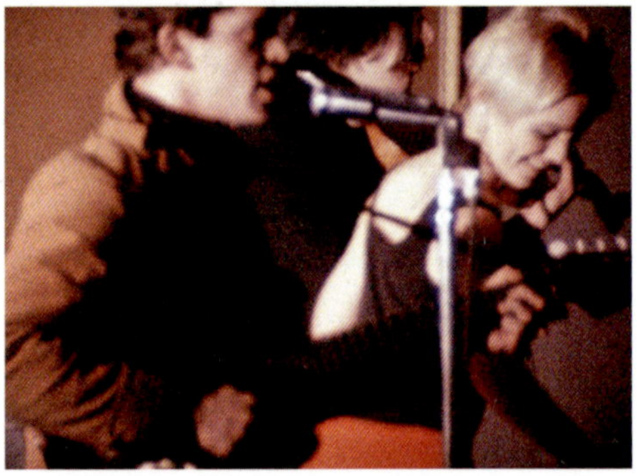

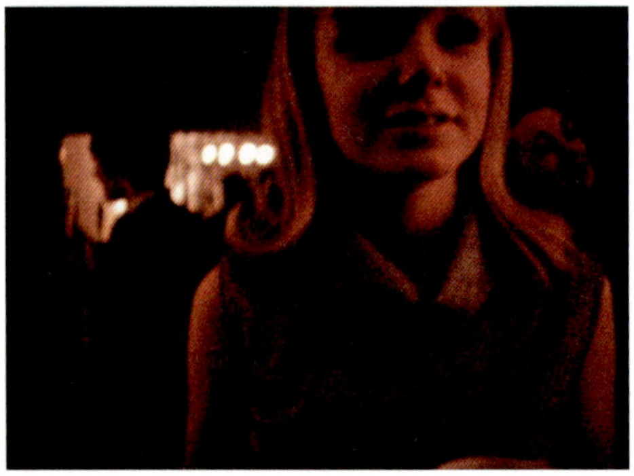

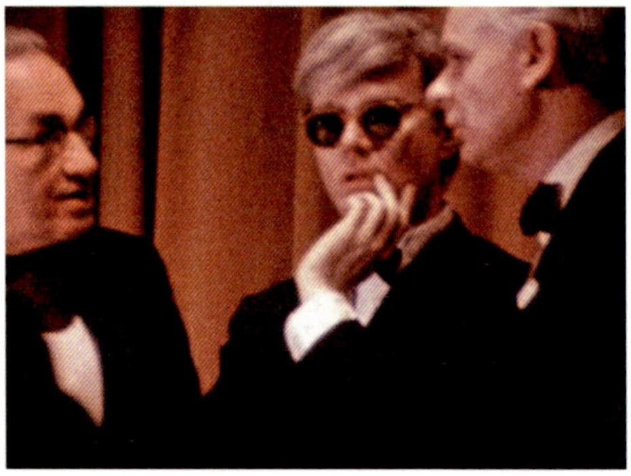

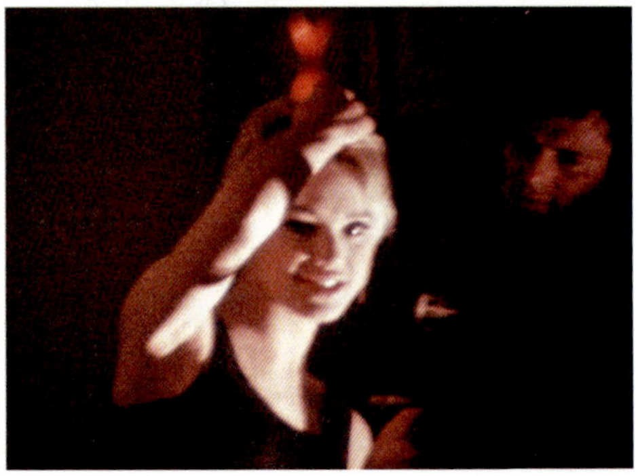

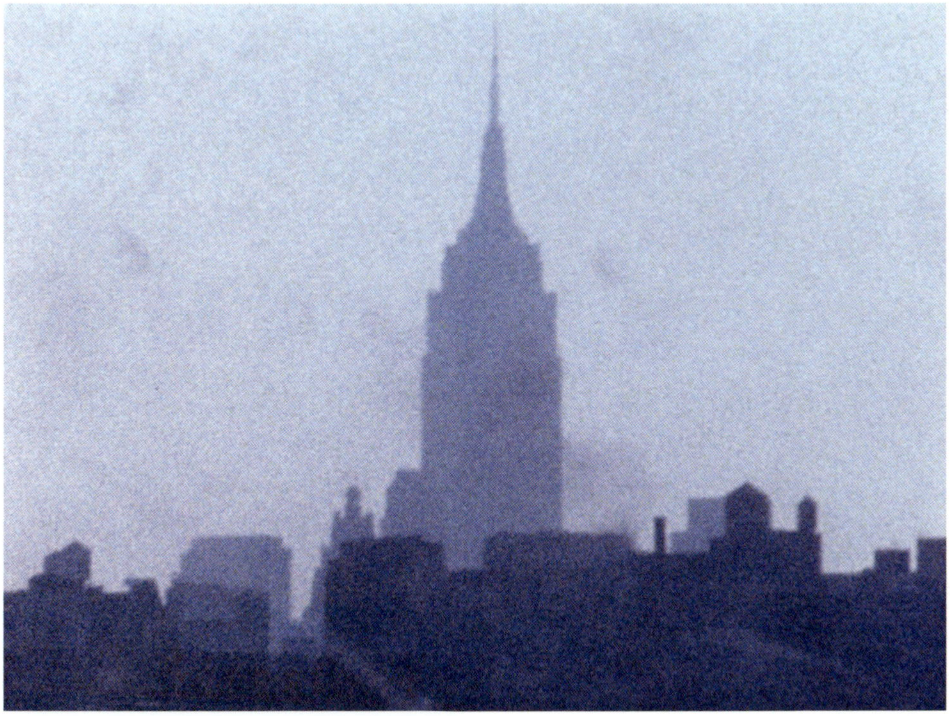

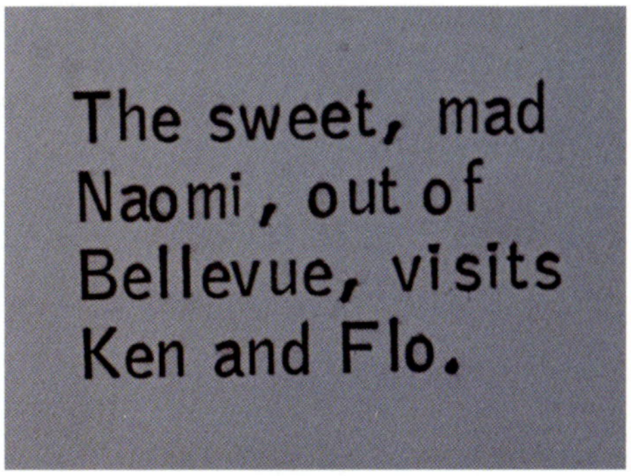

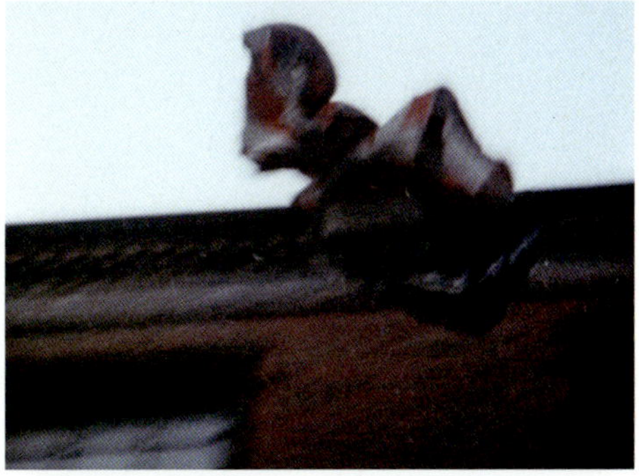

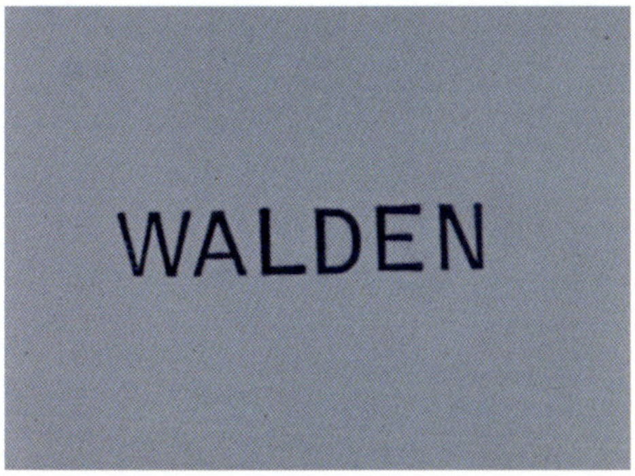

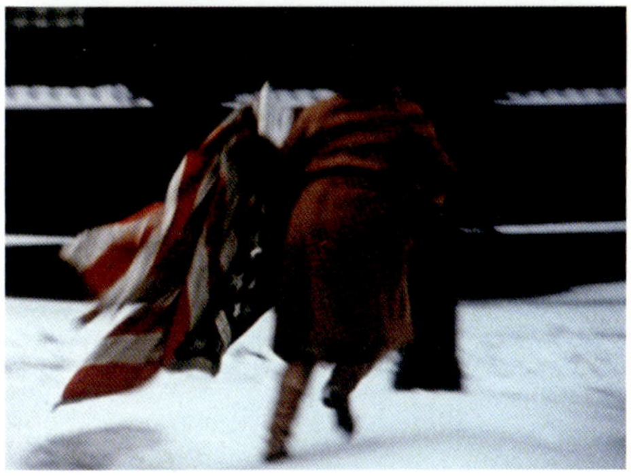

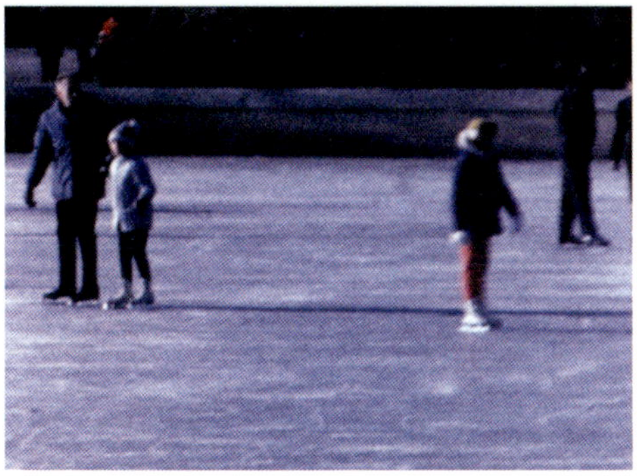

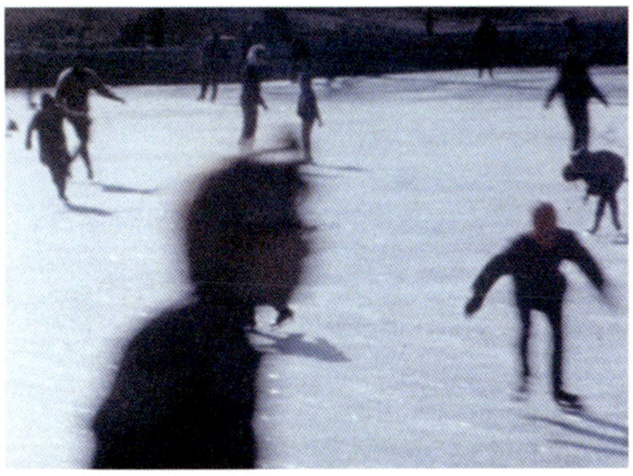

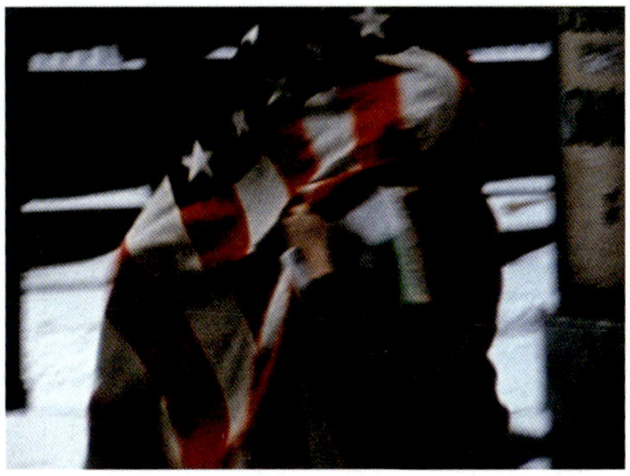

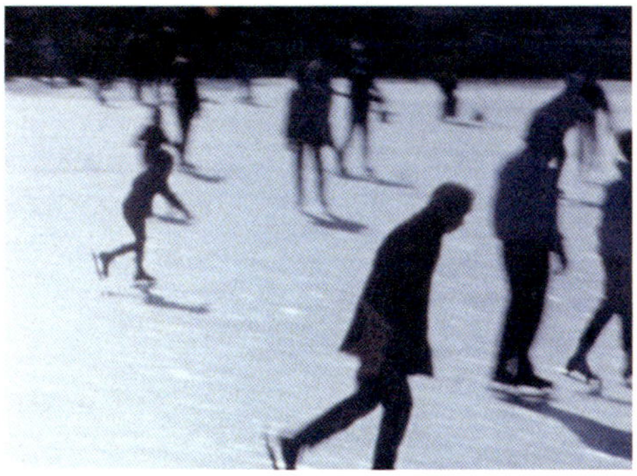

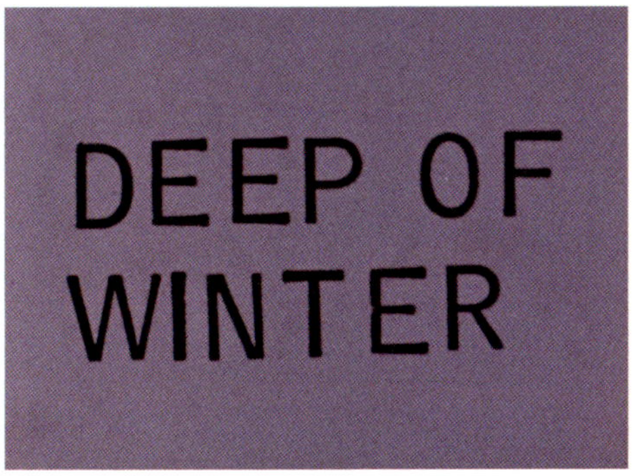

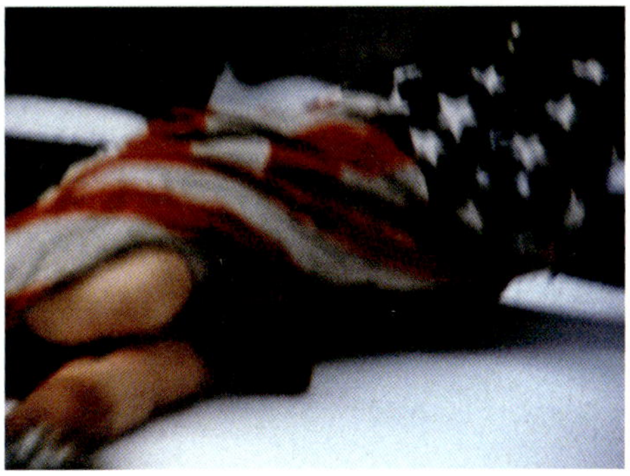

COLOR, BLACK AND WHITE SOUND 180 MIN

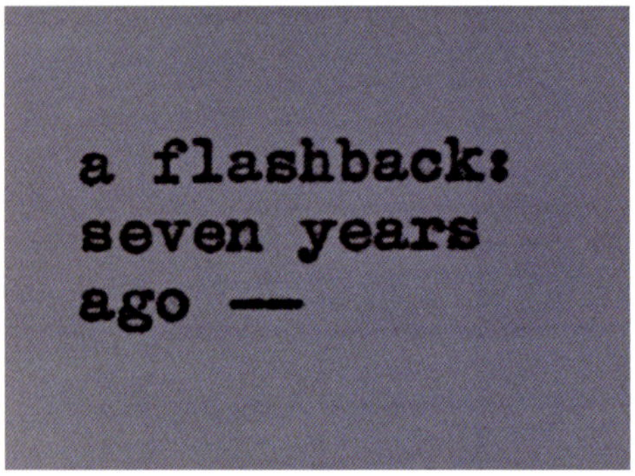
a flashback:
seven years
ago —

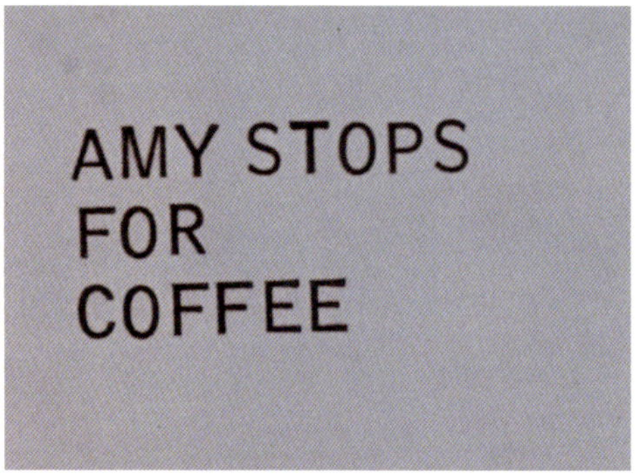
AMY STOPS
FOR
COFFEE

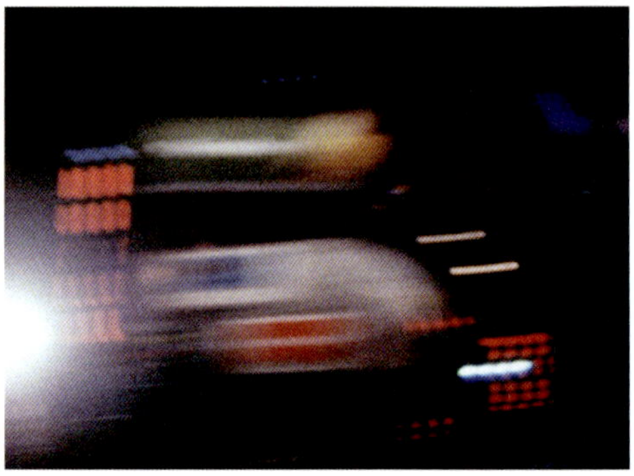

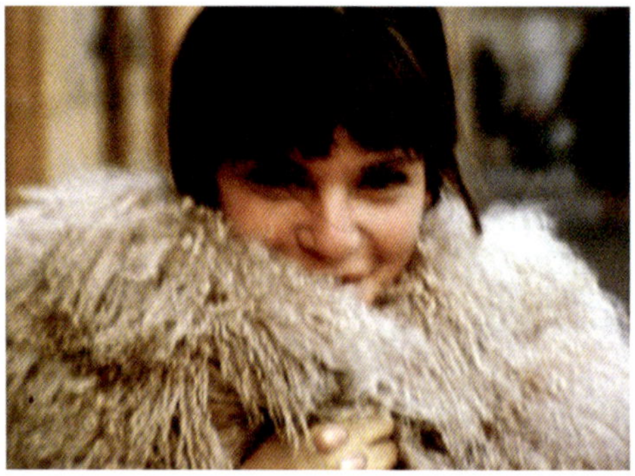

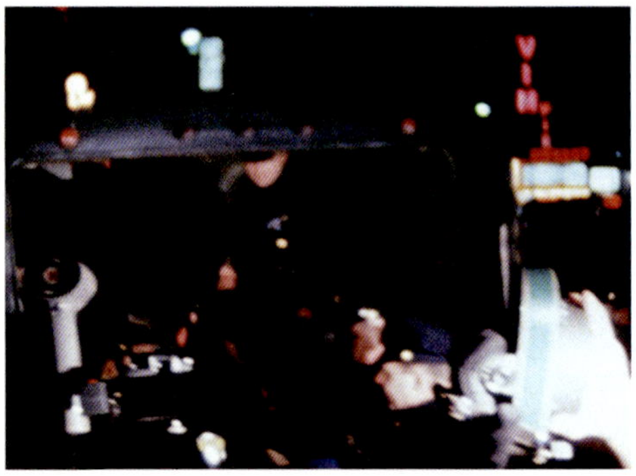

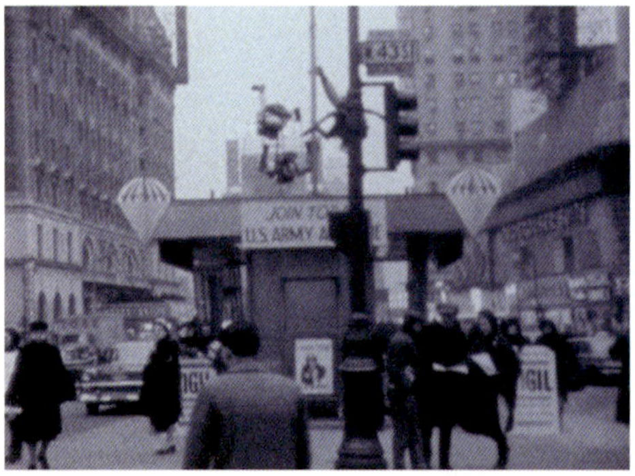

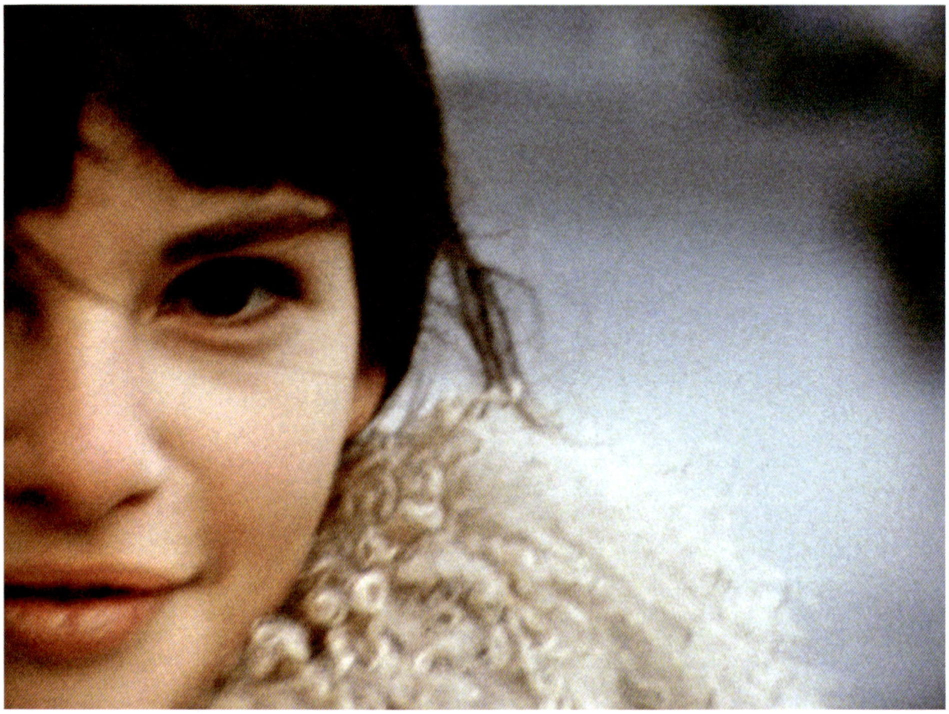

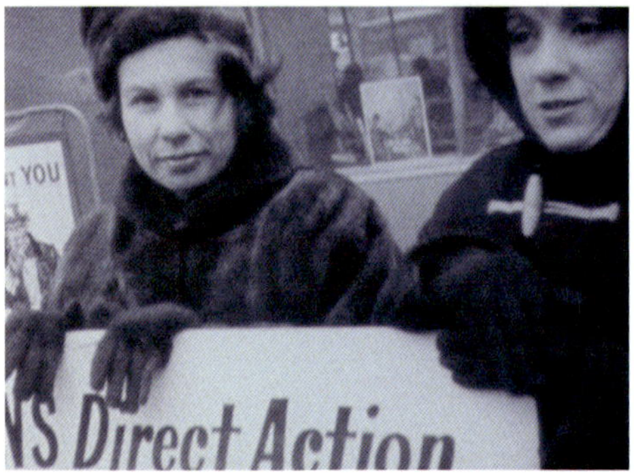
Direct Action

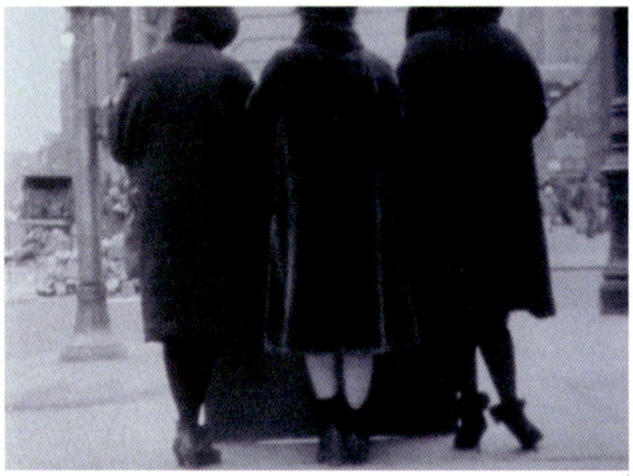

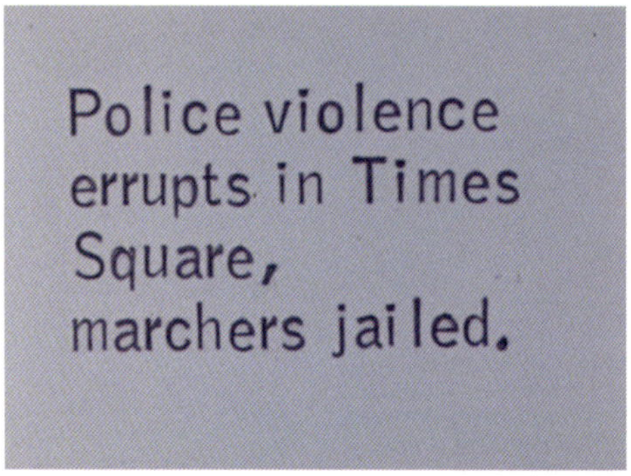
Police violence
errupts in Times
Square,
marchers jailed.

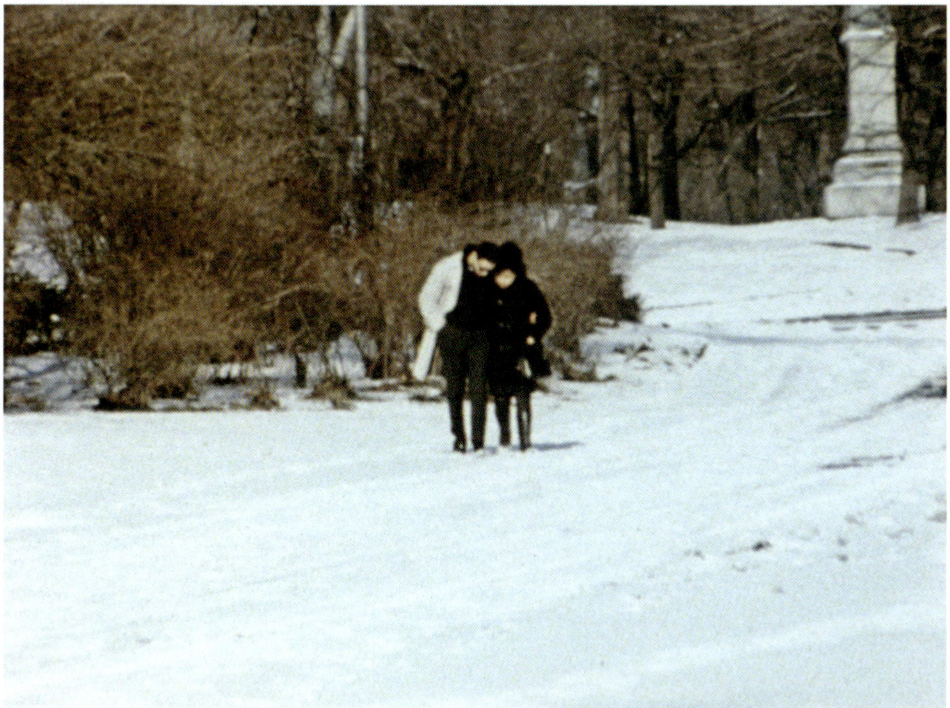
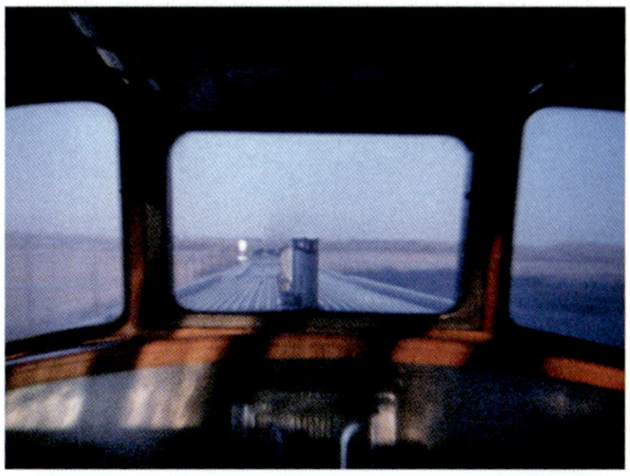
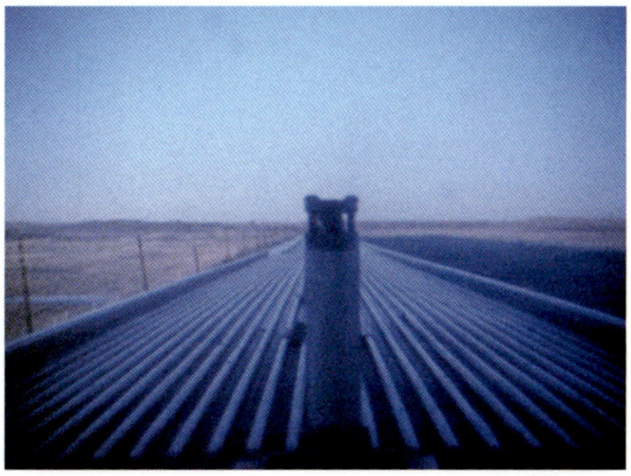
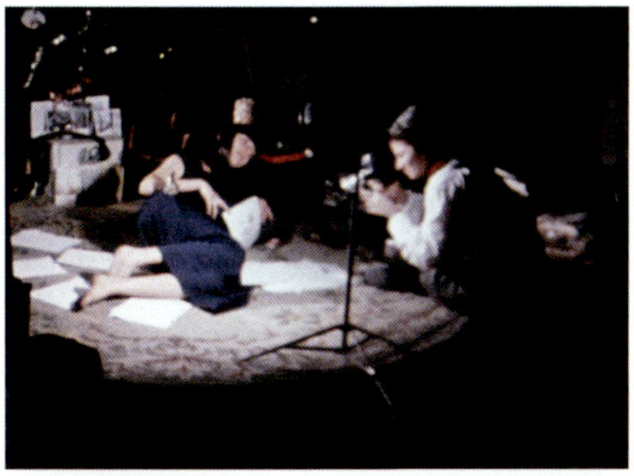
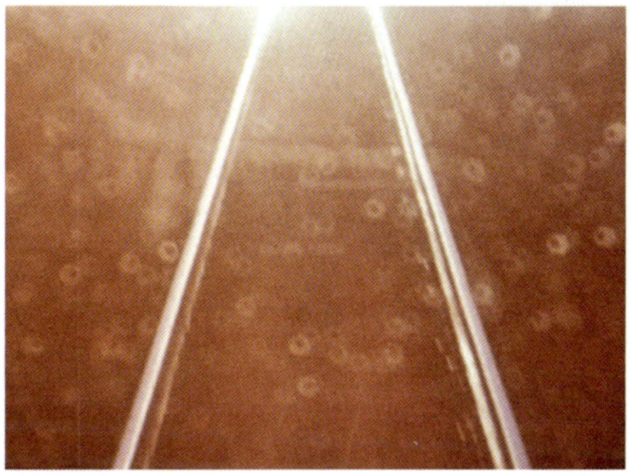
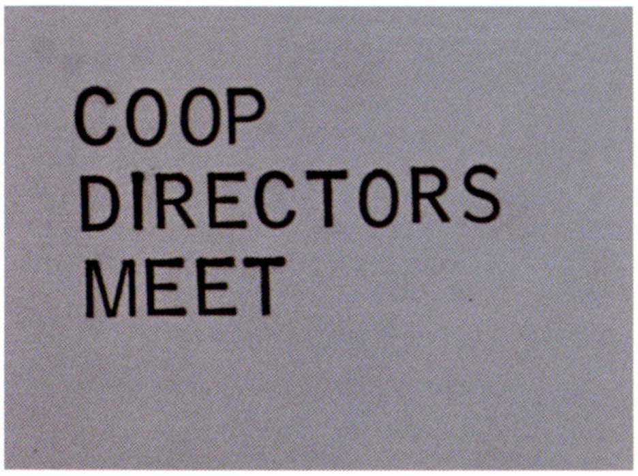
COOP
DIRECTORS
MEET
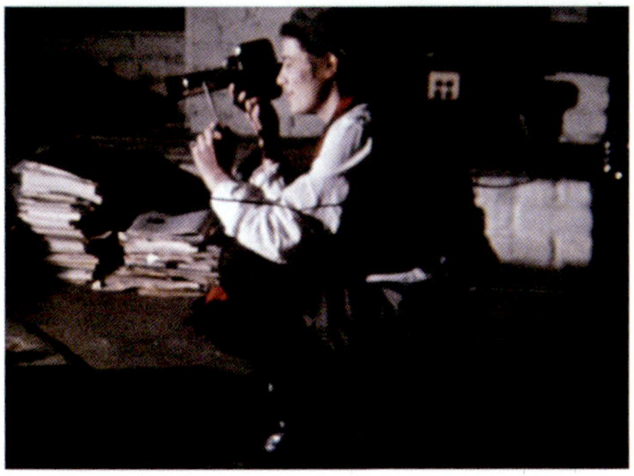
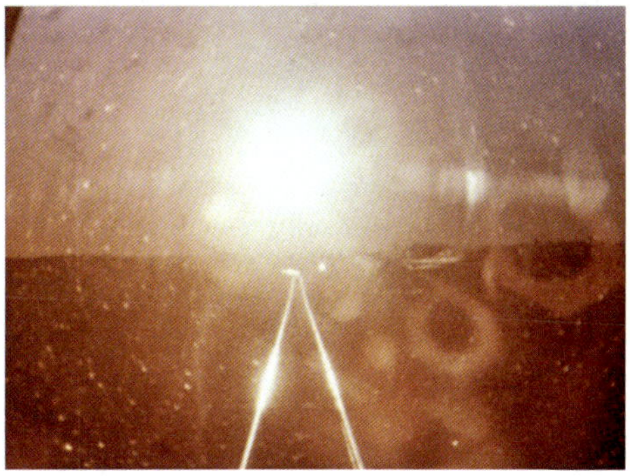
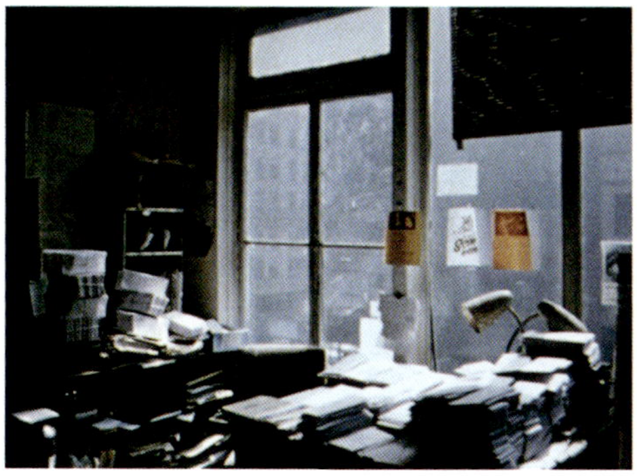
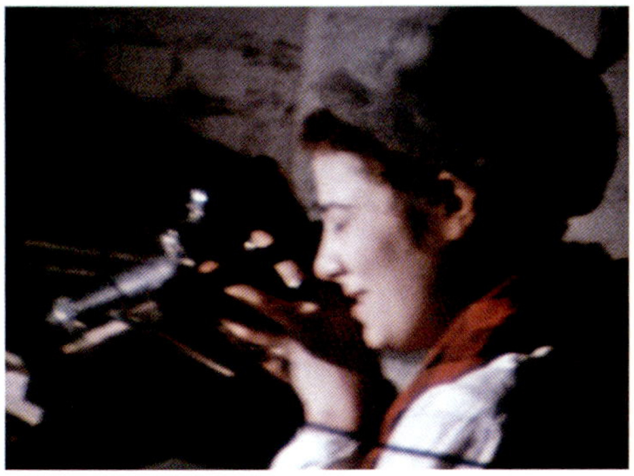
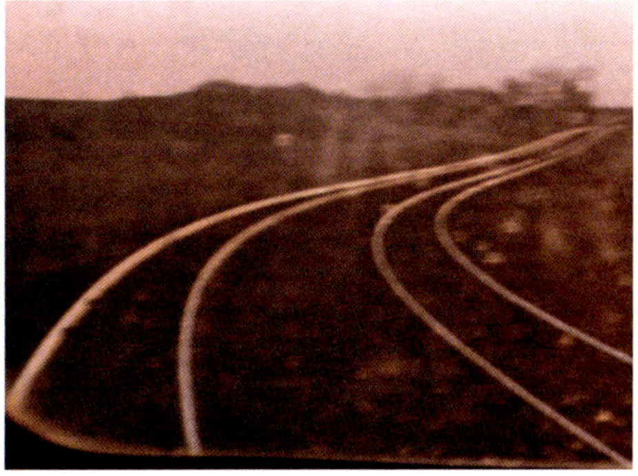

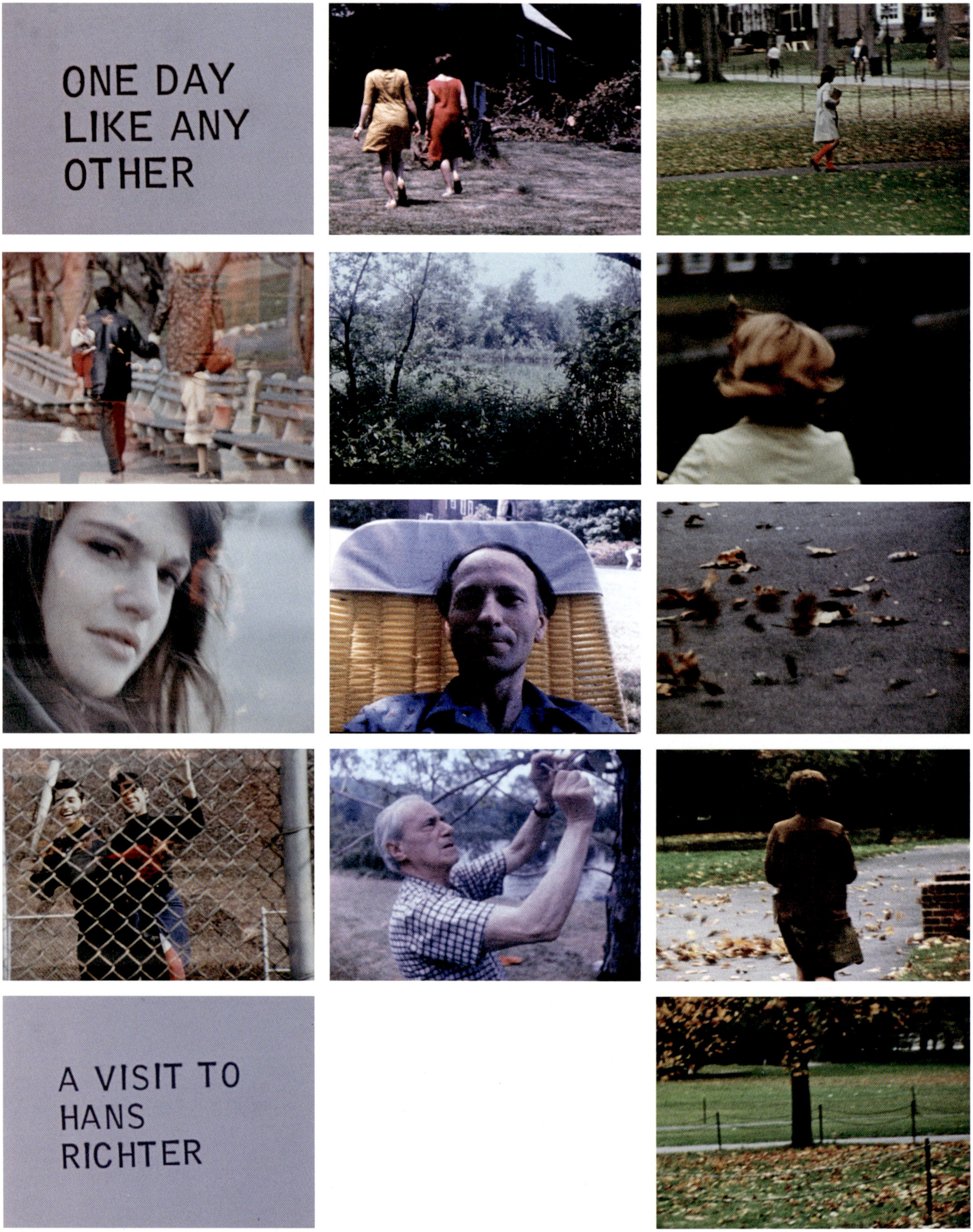
ONE DAY
LIKE ANY
OTHER
A VISIT TO
HANS
RICHTER

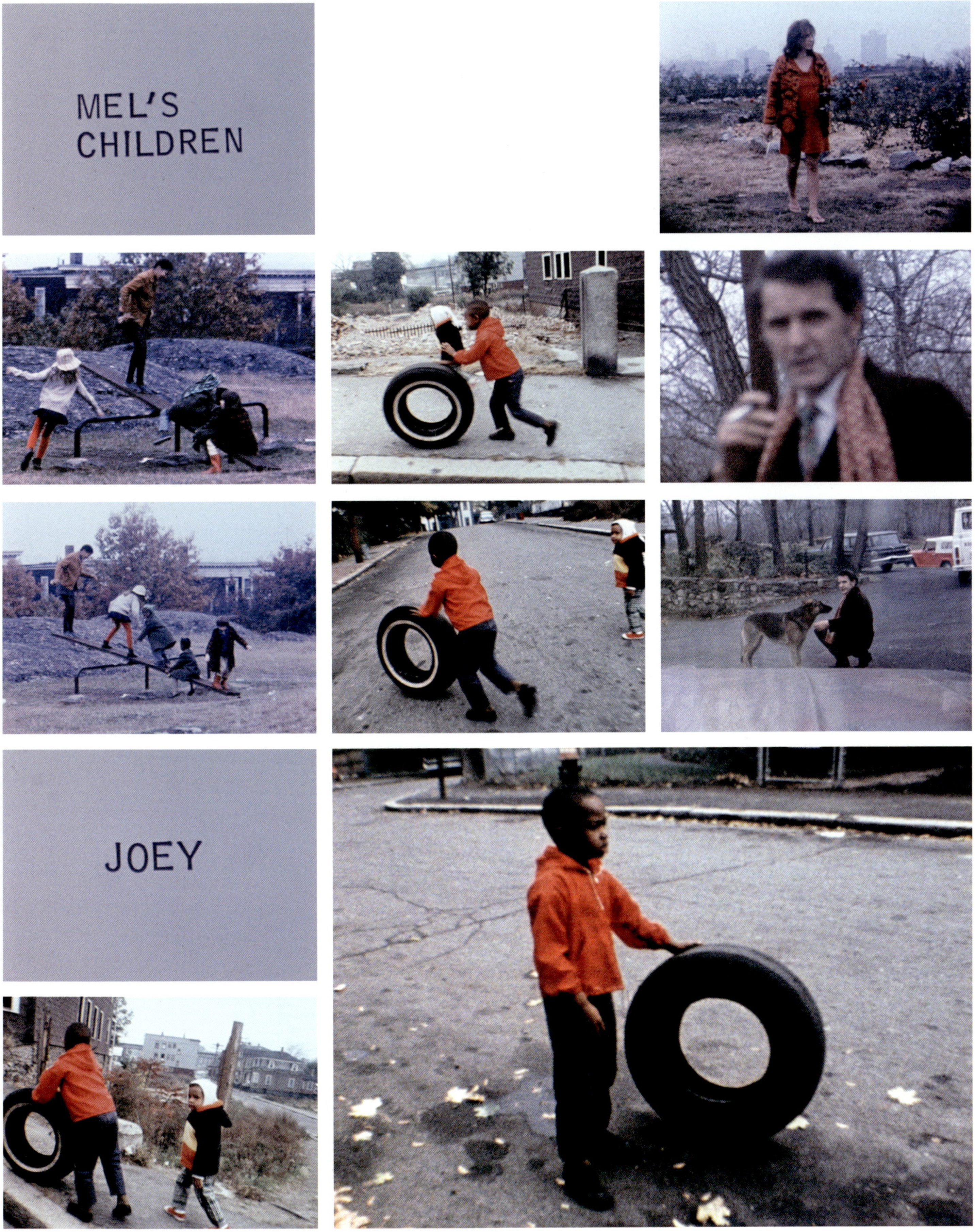

 FILMS COLOR, BLACK AND WHITE SOUND 180 MIN

REMINISCENCES OF A JOURNEY TO LITHUANIA, 1972

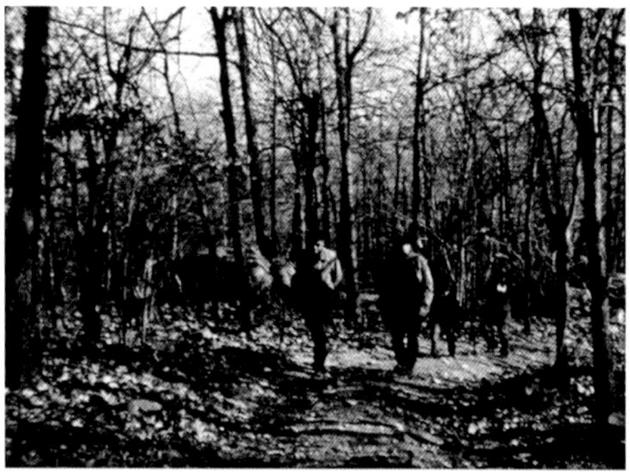

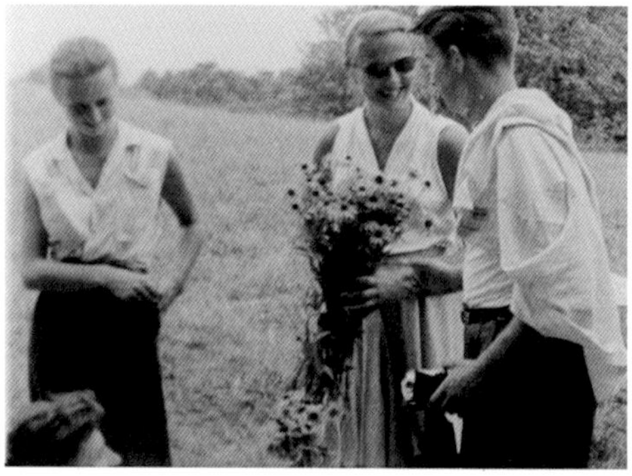

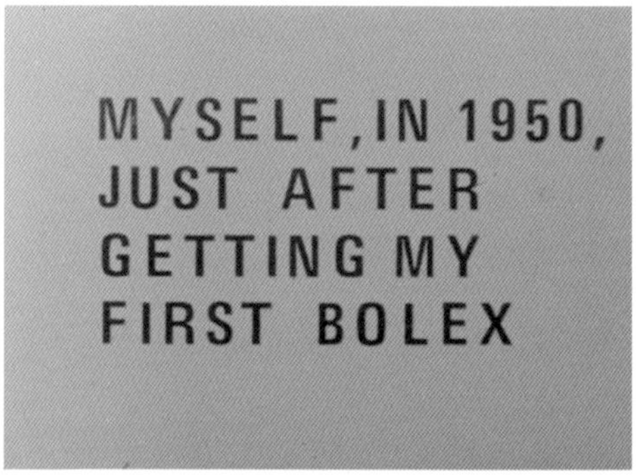

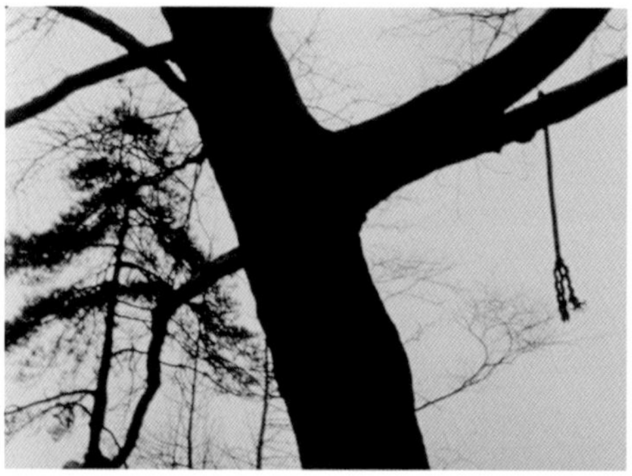

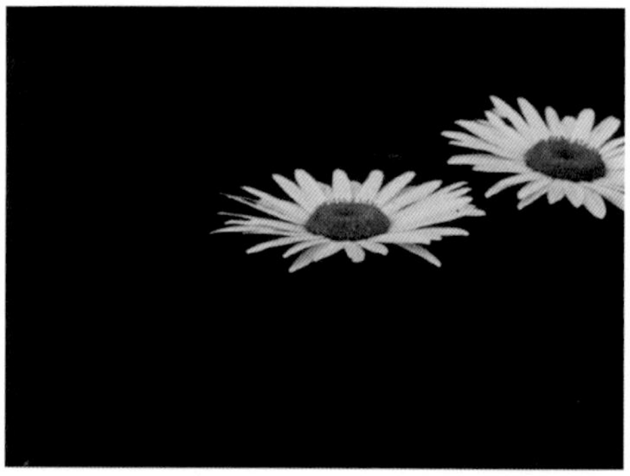

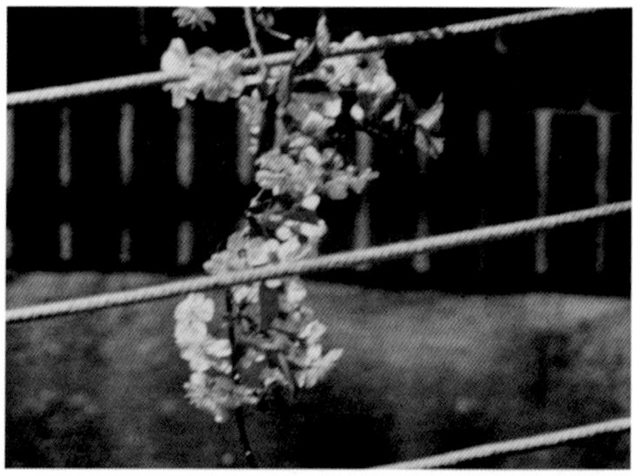

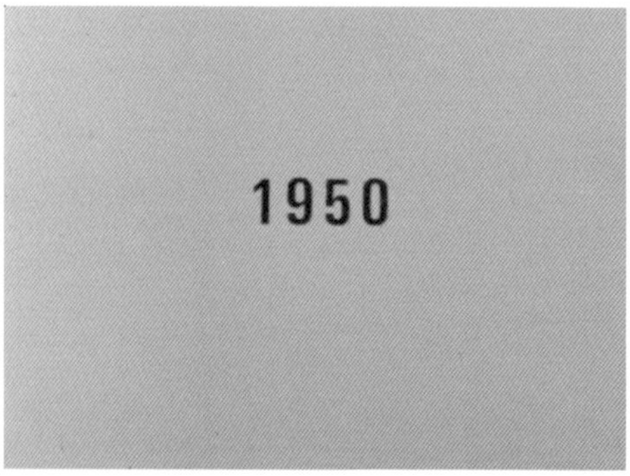

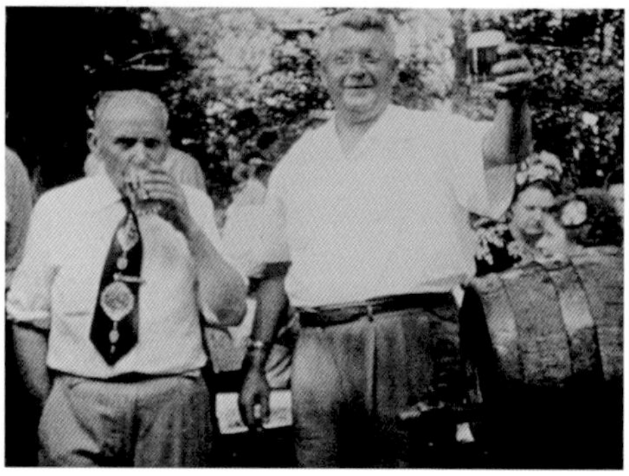

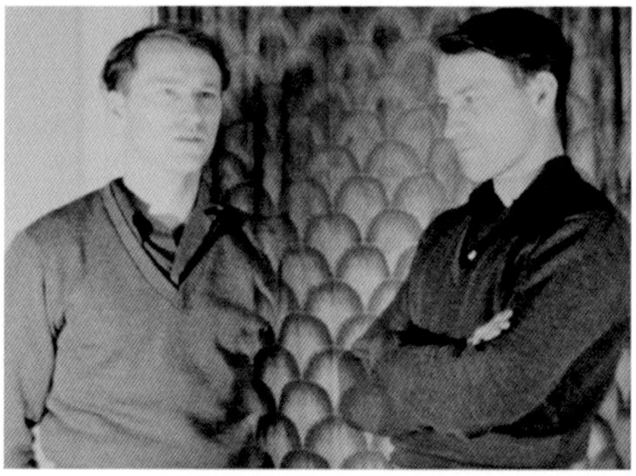

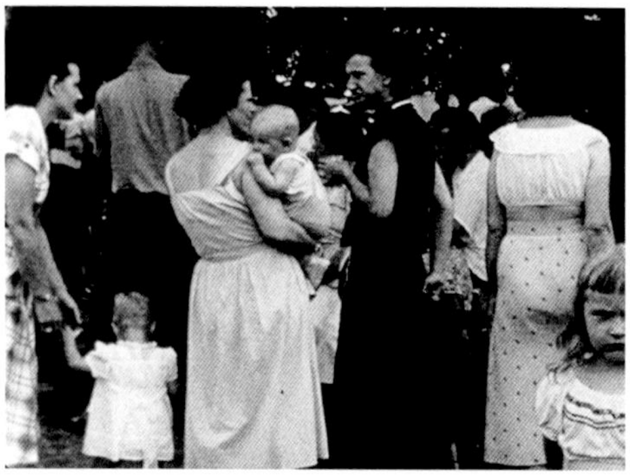

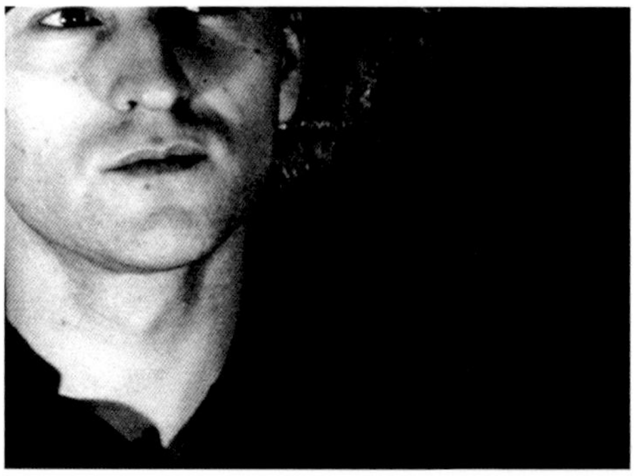

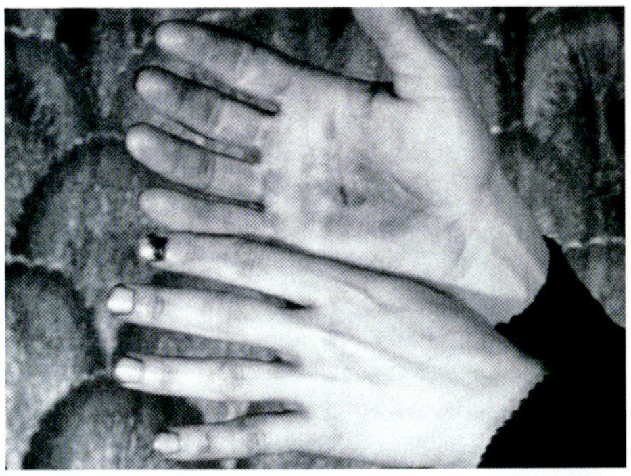

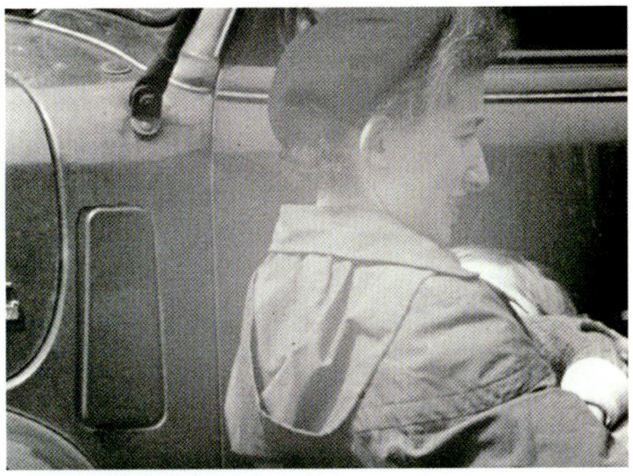

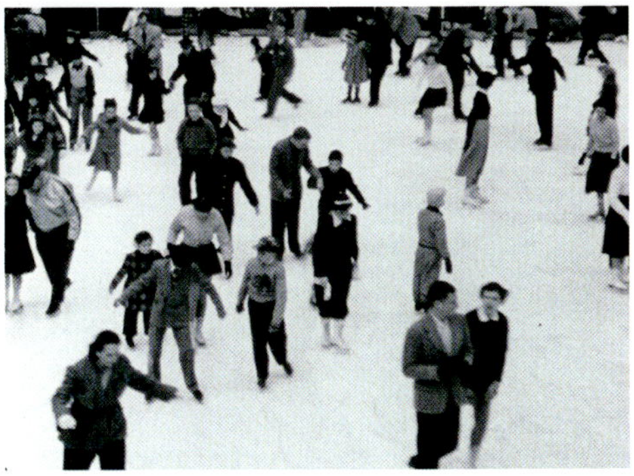

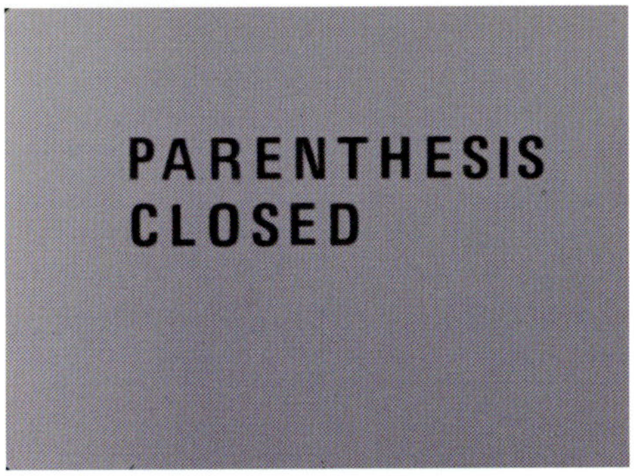

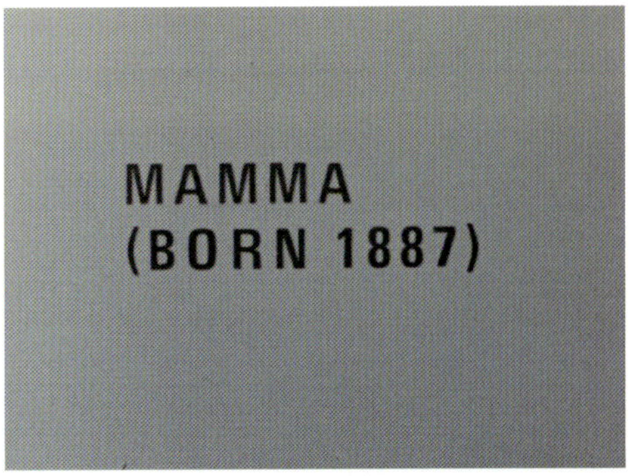

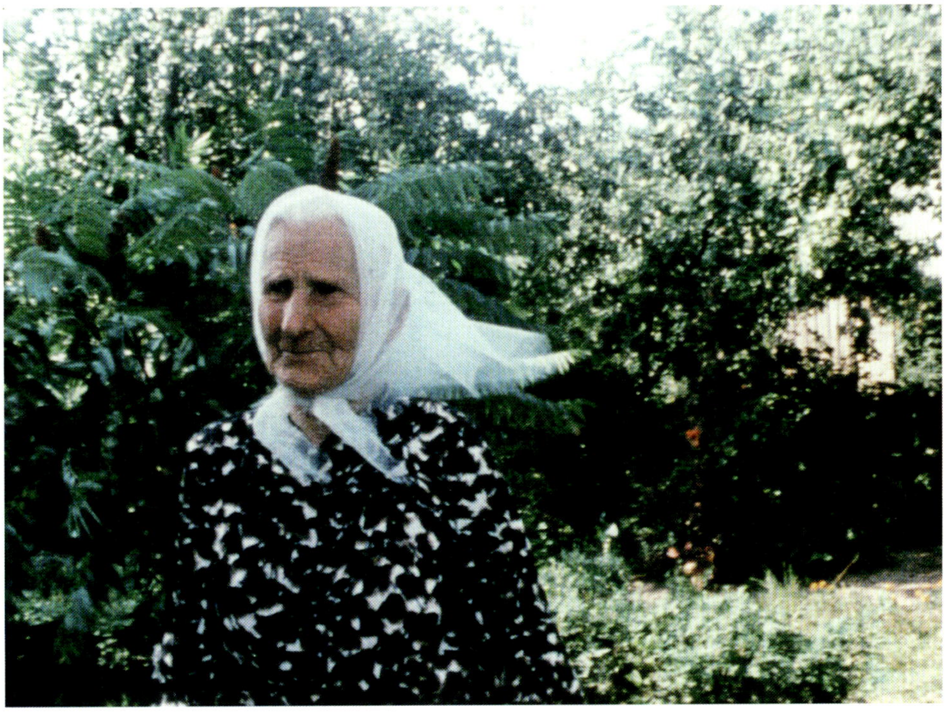

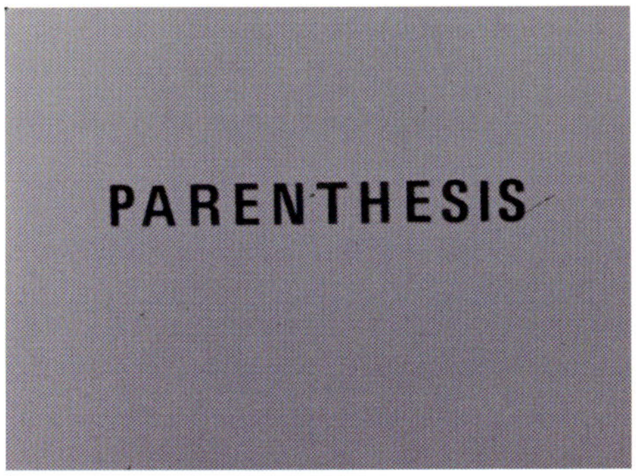

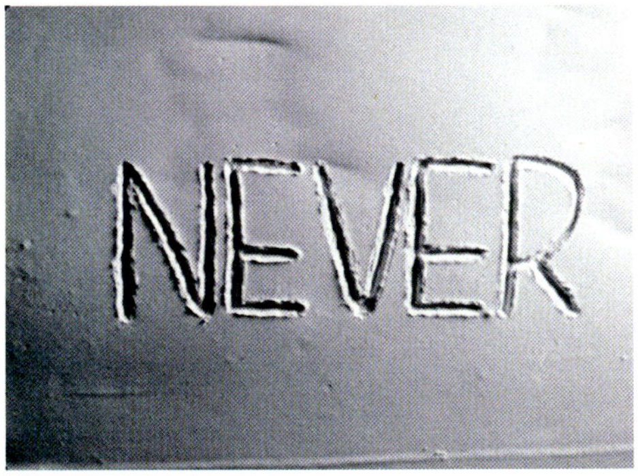

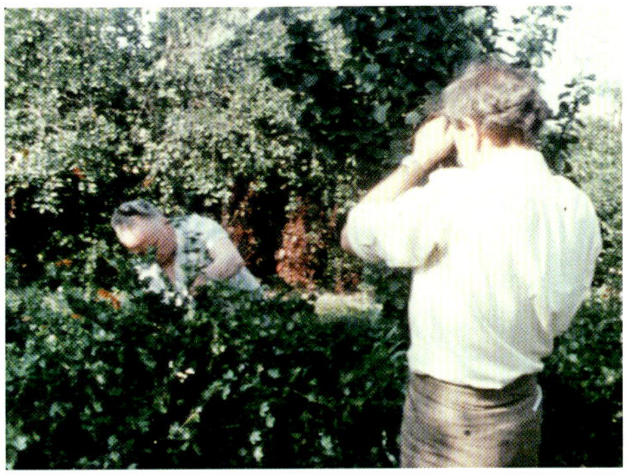

103 FILMS COLOR SOUND 82 MIN

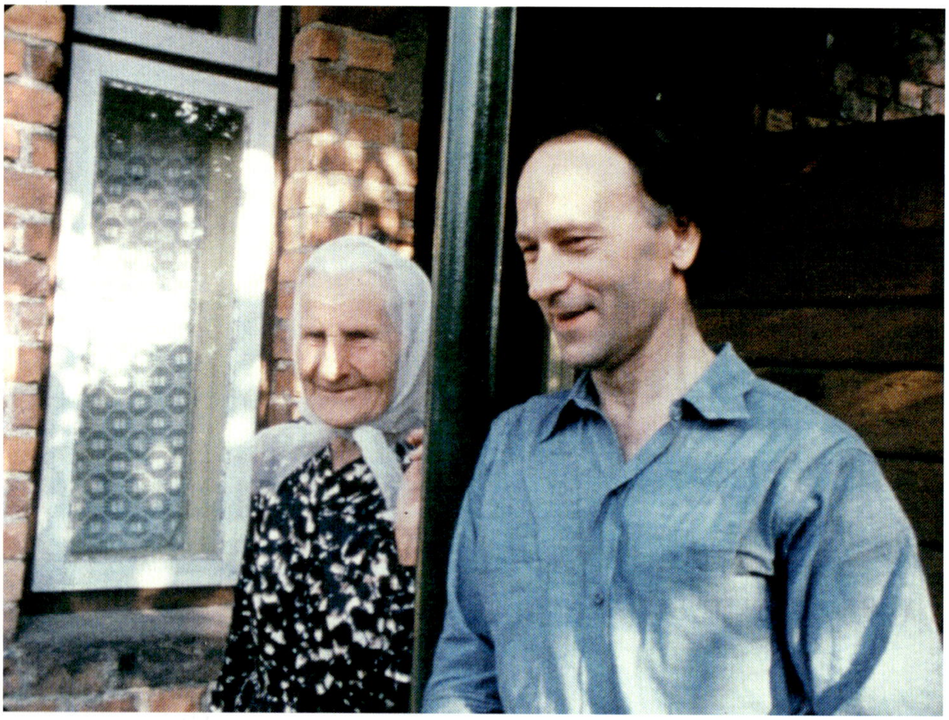

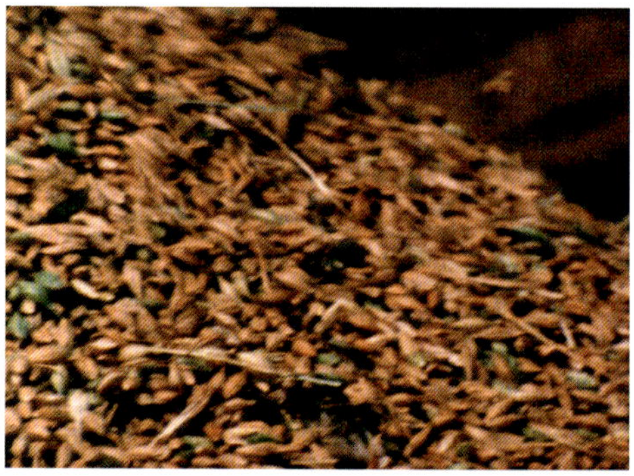

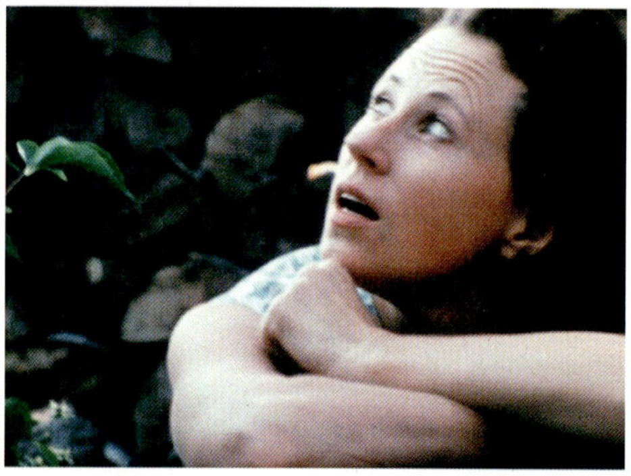

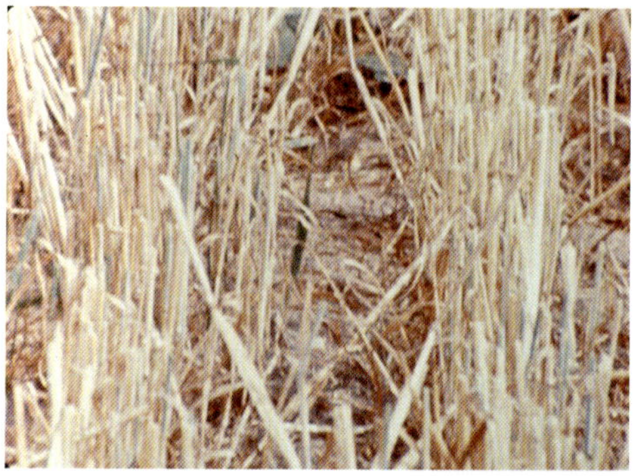

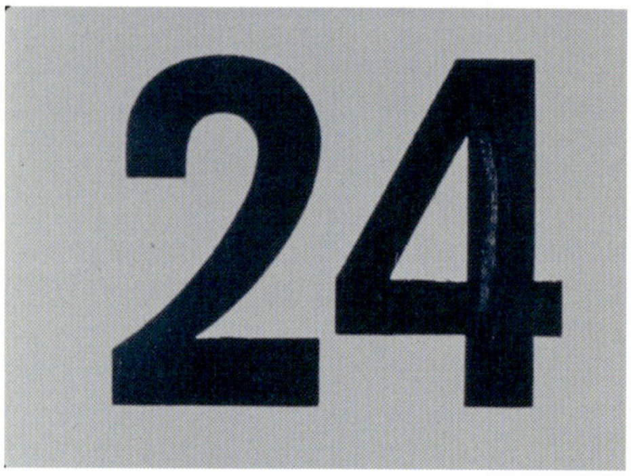
24

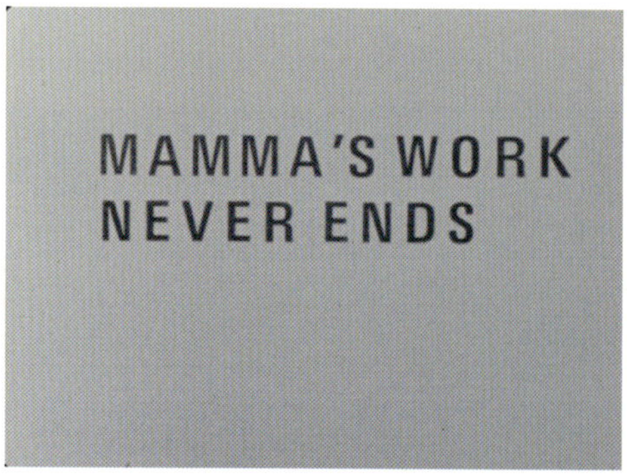
MAMMA'S WORK
NEVER ENDS

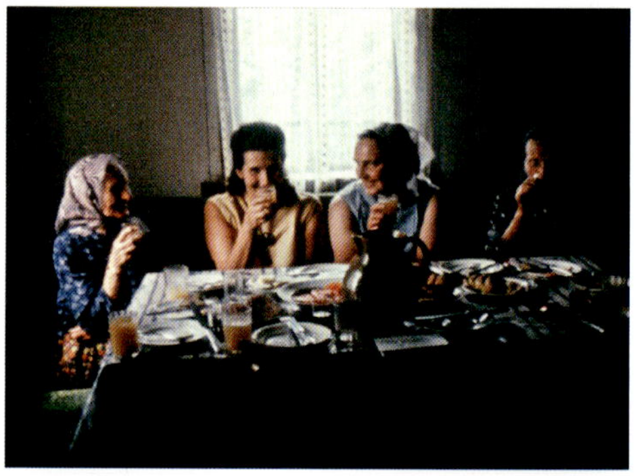

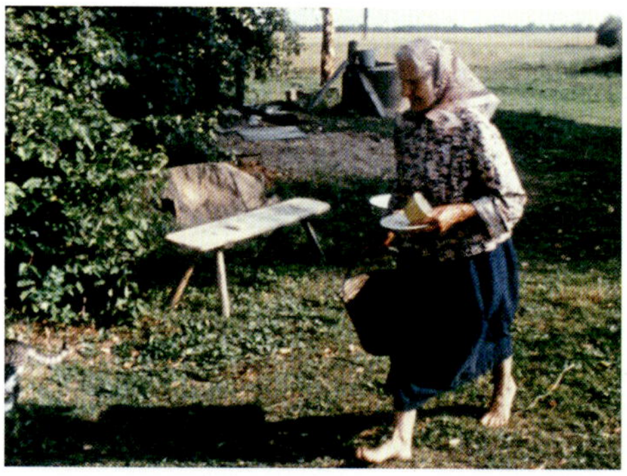

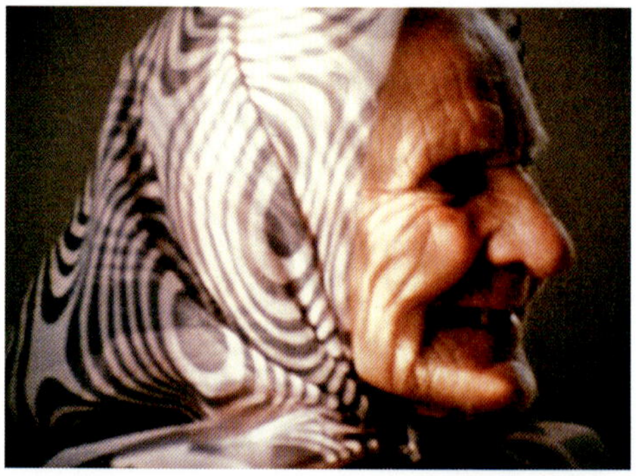

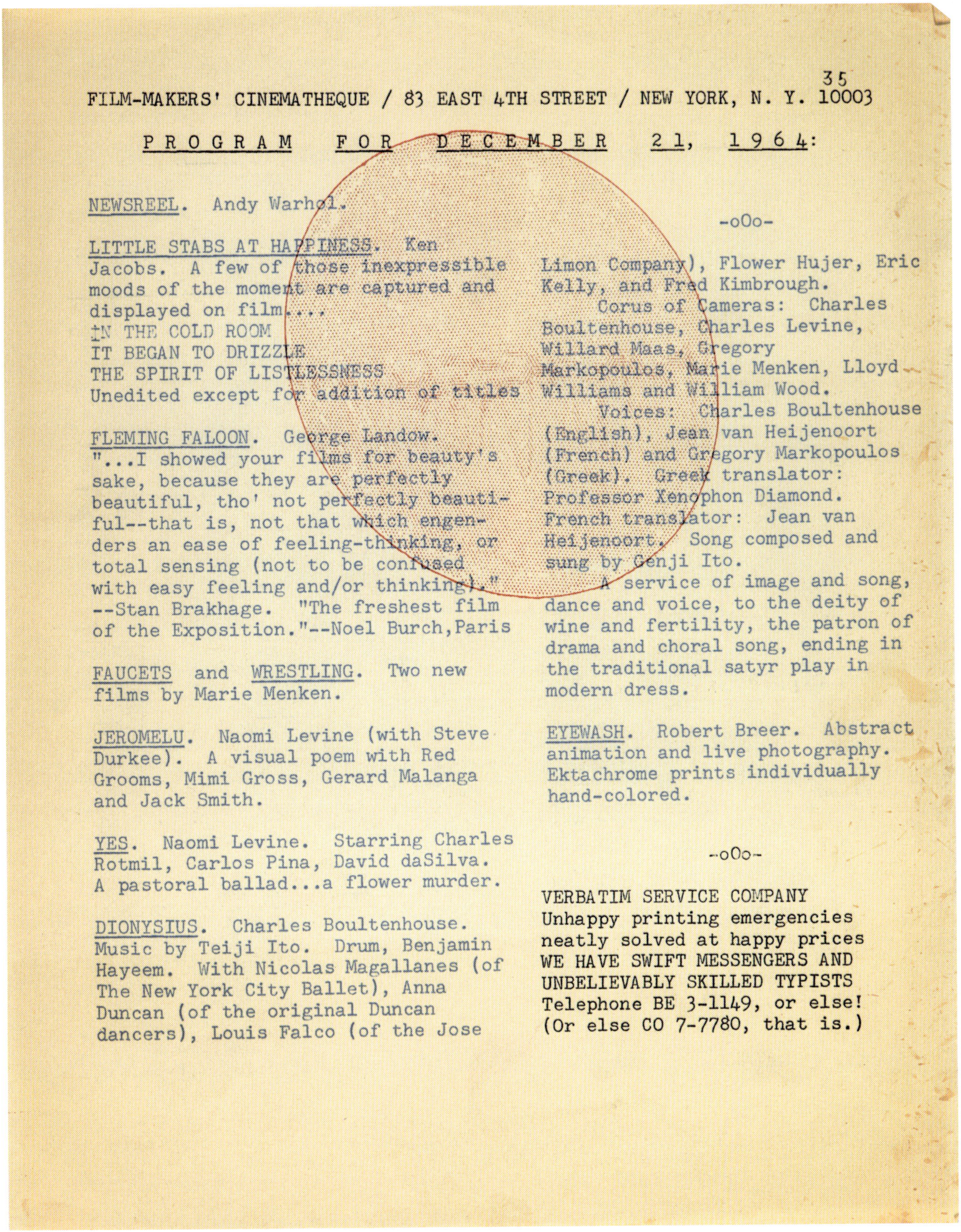

35

FILM-MAKERS' CINEMATHEQUE / 83 EAST 4TH STREET / NEW YORK, N. Y. 10003

P R O G R A M   F O R   D E C E M B E R   2 1,   1 9 6 4:

NEWSREEL. Andy Warhol.

LITTLE STABS AT HAPPINESS. Ken Jacobs. A few of those inexpressible moods of the moment are captured and displayed on film....
IN THE COLD ROOM
IT BEGAN TO DRIZZLE
THE SPIRIT OF LISTLESSNESS
Unedited except for addition of titles

FLEMING FALOON. George Landow. "...I showed your films for beauty's sake, because they are perfectly beautiful, tho' not perfectly beautiful--that is, not that which engenders an ease of feeling-thinking, or total sensing (not to be confused with easy feeling and/or thinking)." --Stan Brakhage. "The freshest film of the Exposition."--Noel Burch,Paris

FAUCETS and WRESTLING. Two new films by Marie Menken.

JEROMELU. Naomi Levine (with Steve Durkee). A visual poem with Red Grooms, Mimi Gross, Gerard Malanga and Jack Smith.

YES. Naomi Levine. Starring Charles Rotmil, Carlos Pina, David daSilva. A pastoral ballad...a flower murder.

DIONYSIUS. Charles Boultenhouse. Music by Teiji Ito. Drum, Benjamin Hayeem. With Nicolas Magallanes (of The New York City Ballet), Anna Duncan (of the original Duncan dancers), Louis Falco (of the Jose

-oOo-

Limon Company), Flower Hujer, Eric Kelly, and Fred Kimbrough.
Corus of Cameras: Charles Boultenhouse, Charles Levine, Willard Maas, Gregory Markopoulos, Marie Menken, Lloyd Williams and William Wood.
Voices: Charles Boultenhouse (English), Jean van Heijenoort (French) and Gregory Markopoulos (Greek). Greek translator: Professor Xenophon Diamond. French translator: Jean van Heijenoort. Song composed and sung by Genji Ito.
A service of image and song, dance and voice, to the deity of wine and fertility, the patron of drama and choral song, ending in the traditional satyr play in modern dress.

EYEWASH. Robert Breer. Abstract animation and live photography. Ektachrome prints individually hand-colored.

-oOo-

VERBATIM SERVICE COMPANY
Unhappy printing emergencies
neatly solved at happy prices
WE HAVE SWIFT MESSENGERS AND
UNBELIEVABLY SKILLED TYPISTS
Telephone BE 3-1149, or else!
(Or else CO 7-7780, that is.)

Program for December 21, 1964, at the New Yorker Theater, Manhattan. The Film-Makers' Cinematheque organized film screenings and Happenings across New York City, beginning in 1961 at the Charles Theatre and ending in 1970 with the founding of Anthology Film Archives. Jonas and members of the "Tek" (as well as George Maciunas, a fellow Lithuanian émigré) designed flyers to advertise their many events.

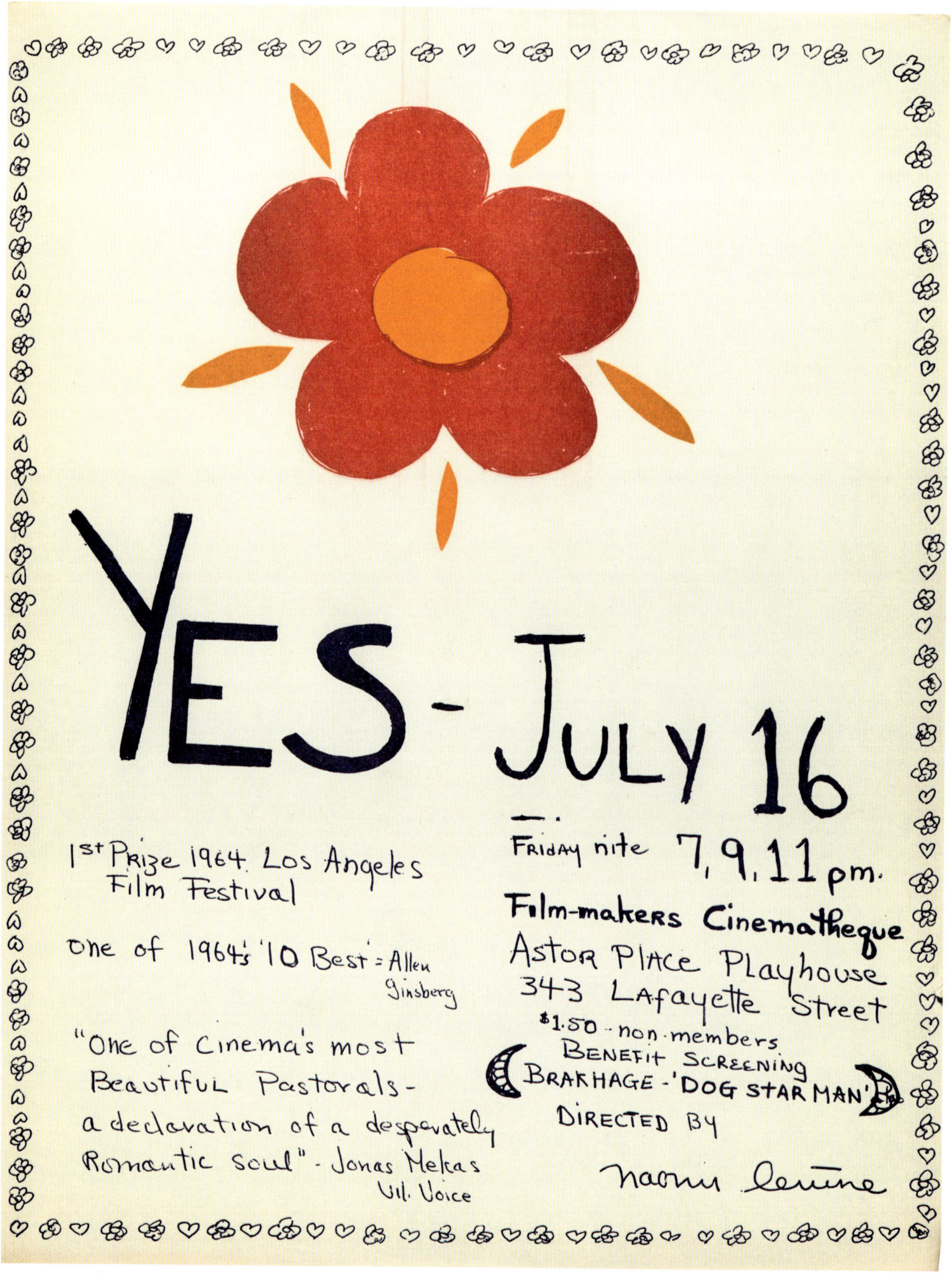

Flyer for Naomi Levine's *Yes* (1963) at Astor Place Playhouse, July 16, 1965.

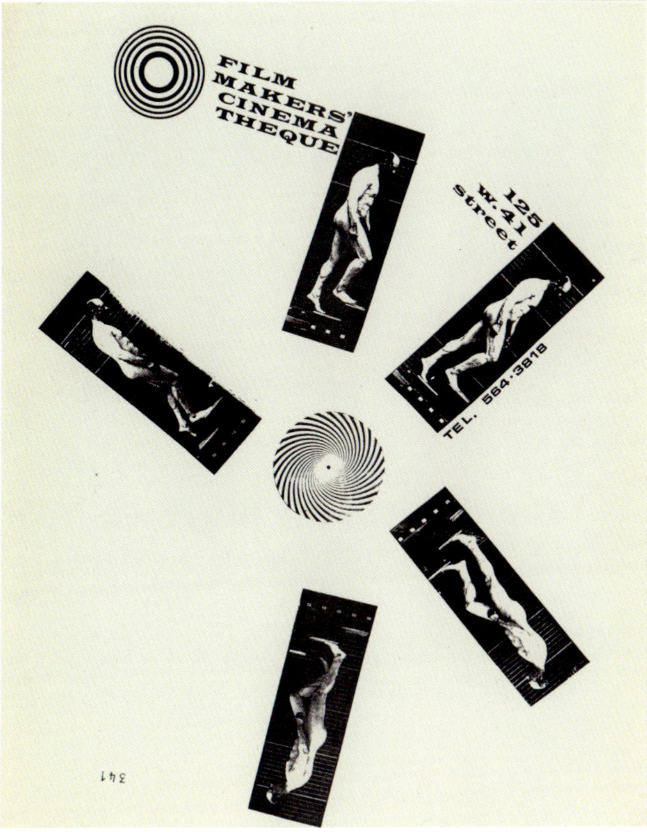

Advertisement for the Film-Makers' Cinematheque at 125 w. 41st Street, 1965 or 1967.

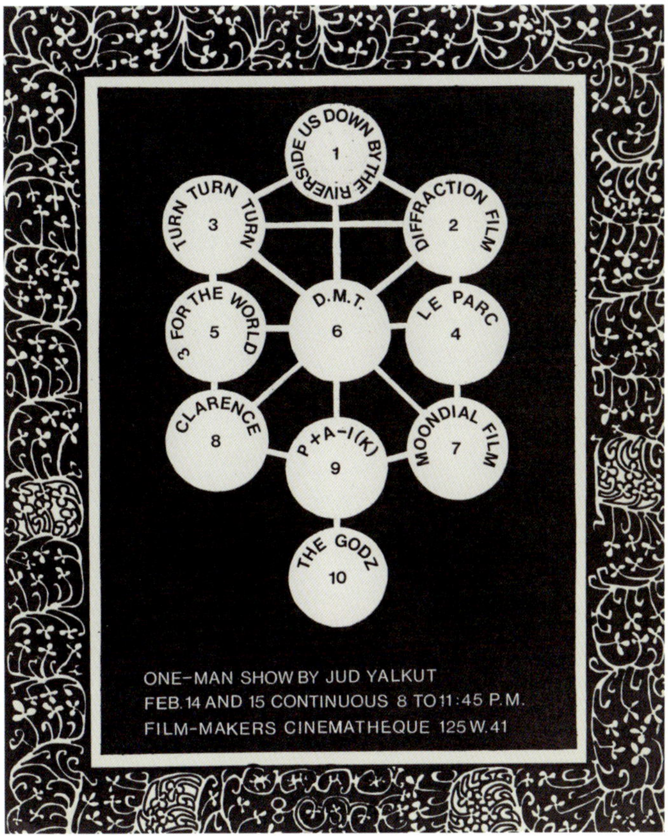

Flyer for a one-man show by Jud Yalkut at 125 w. 41st Street, February 14–15, 1967.

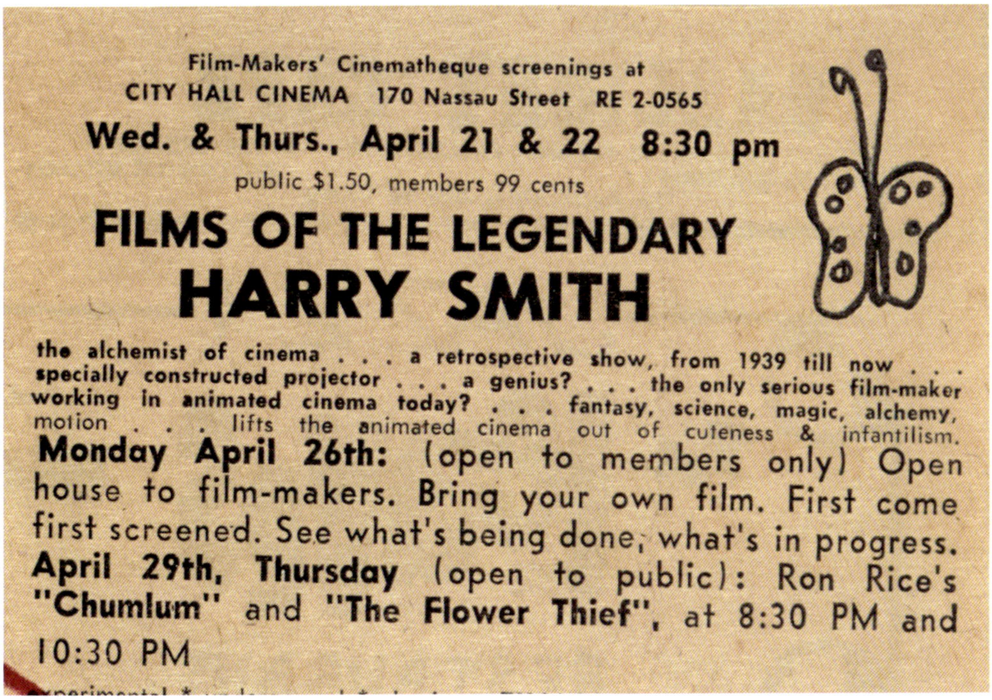

Film-Makers' Cinematheque screenings at
CITY HALL CINEMA 170 Nassau Street RE 2-0565
Wed. & Thurs., April 21 & 22 8:30 pm
public $1.50, members 99 cents

FILMS OF THE LEGENDARY
HARRY SMITH

the alchemist of cinema . . . a retrospective show, from 1939 till now . . . specially constructed projector . . . a genius? . . . the only serious film-maker working in animated cinema today? . . . fantasy, science, magic, alchemy, motion . . . lifts the animated cinema out of cuteness & infantilism.

Monday April 26th: (open to members only) Open house to film-makers. Bring your own film. First come first screened. See what's being done, what's in progress.
April 29th, Thursday (open to public): Ron Rice's **"Chumlum"** and **"The Flower Thief"**, at 8:30 PM and 10:30 PM

Clipping from the *Village Voice* announcing screening of Harry Smith films and other programs at City Hall Cinema, April 1965.

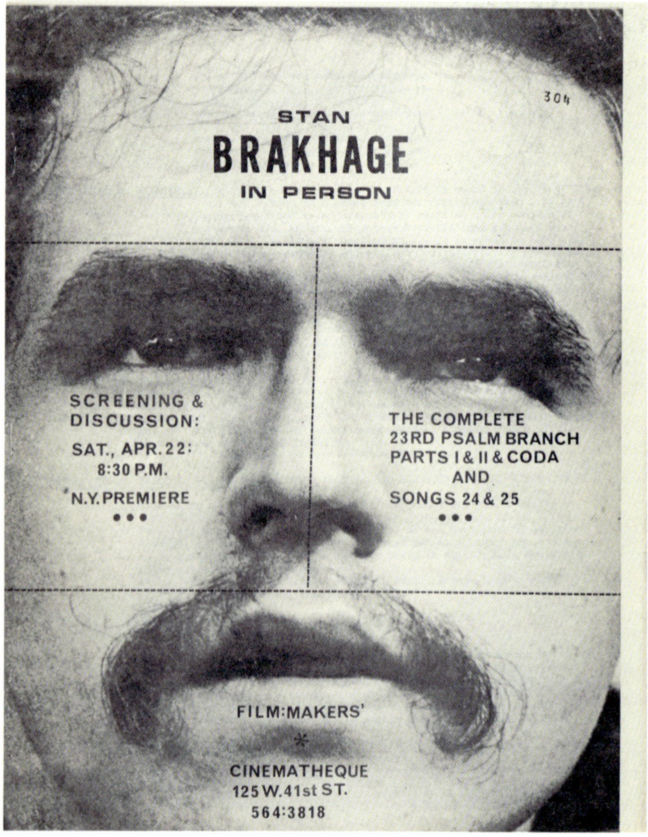

Flyer for a program featuring Stan Brakhage at the Film-Makers' Cinematheque, 125 w. 41st Street, April 22, 1967.

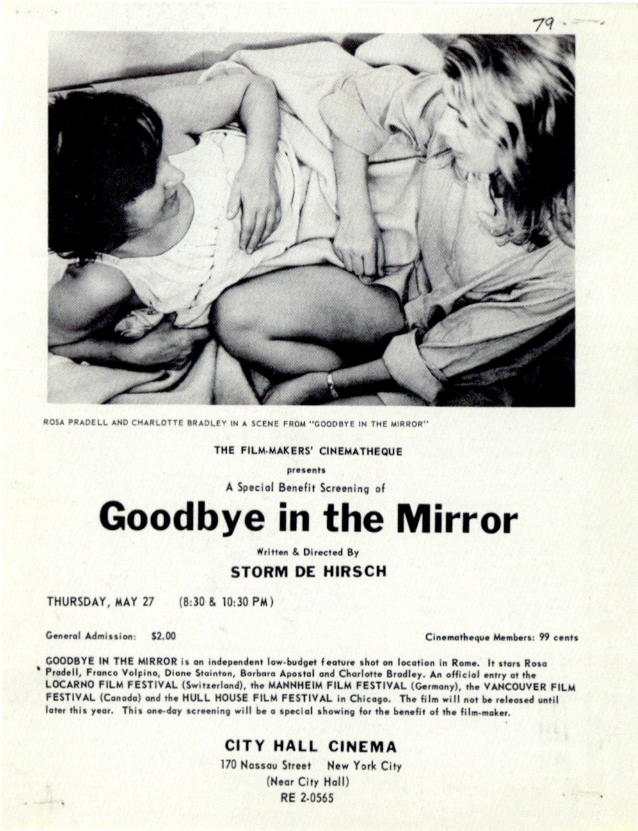

Flyer for Storm de Hirsch's *Goodbye in the Mirror* (1964) at City Hall Cinema, May 27, 1965.

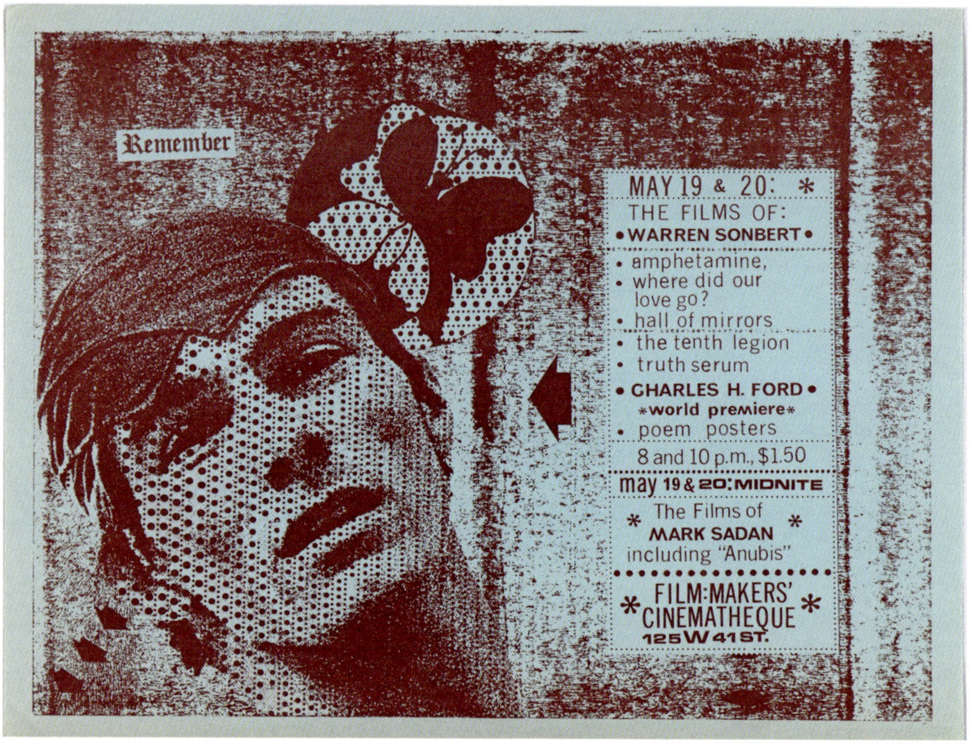

Flyer for the films of Warren Sonbert, Charles H. Ford, and Mark Sadan at the Film-Makers' Cinematheque, 125 w. 41st Street, May 19 and 20, 1967.

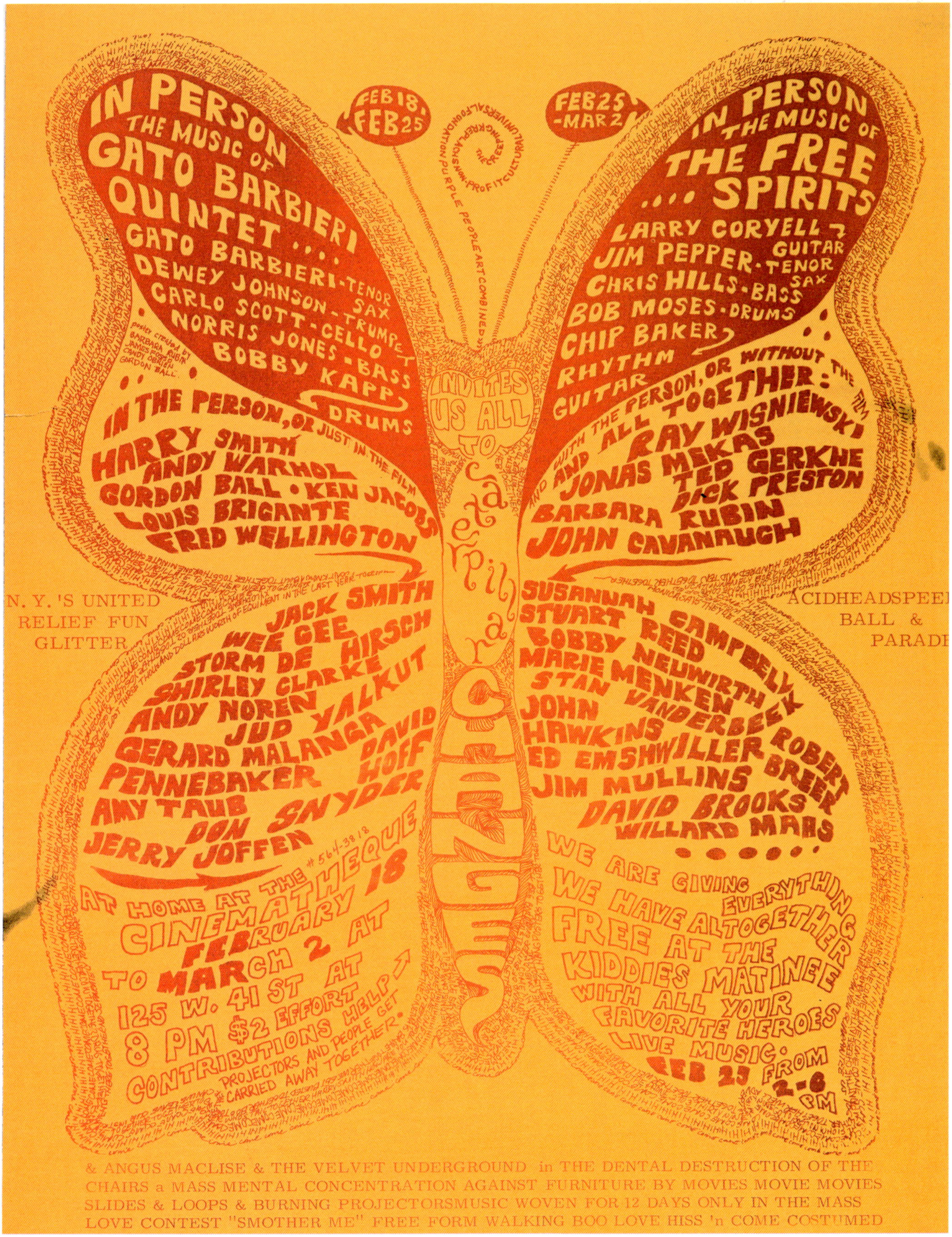

Poster for Caterpillar Changes, a multimedia festival organized by Barbara Rubin and held at the Film-Makers' Cinematheque, February 18–March 2, 1967.

JONAS MEKAS, LIFE ITSELF

NOTES

1 P. Adams Sitney, "Introduction," *The Essential Cinema: Essays on the Films in the Collection of Anthology Film Archives*, ed. P. Adams Sitney (New York: Anthology, 1975), vi.

2 See Sky Sitney, "The Search for the Invisible Cinema," *Grey Room* 19 (2005): 102–13, for a definitive account of its design and construction.

Jonas Mekas, Life Itself

Ed Halter

In *Letter to John from Jonas*, shot on March 7, 1999, Jonas Mekas sits in the offices of Anthology Film Archives, looking toward the lens of a camcorder placed on the wooden table in front of him. He is seventy-six years old in the video, and wears a dark brown jacket and rumpled, flat-brimmed fedora—an everyday outfit for him in his later decades. "When I have my hat on, I'm official," he says, with a faint, boyish smirk, in *Letter*'s opening moments. Over the twenty-four minutes of the tape, Mekas uses video to speak directly to John Hanhardt, then a curator at the Solomon R. Guggenheim Museum, addressing the camera as if it were Hanhardt himself. Mekas relates how Hanhardt had discussed with him the possibility of the Guggenheim taking over Anthology Film Archives, much in the way that, earlier that year, the nonprofit contemporary arts center PS1 in Queens had announced it would become an affiliate institution of the Museum of Modern Art. The occasion for Mekas's video letter is his refusal of Hanhardt's offer. He addresses Hanhardt warmly, as a longtime compatriot of the dispersed nation of cinema, yet ultimately remains firm in his denial, without ambiguity.

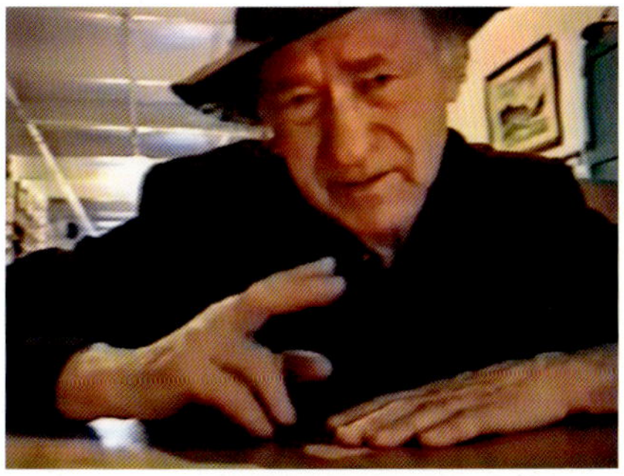

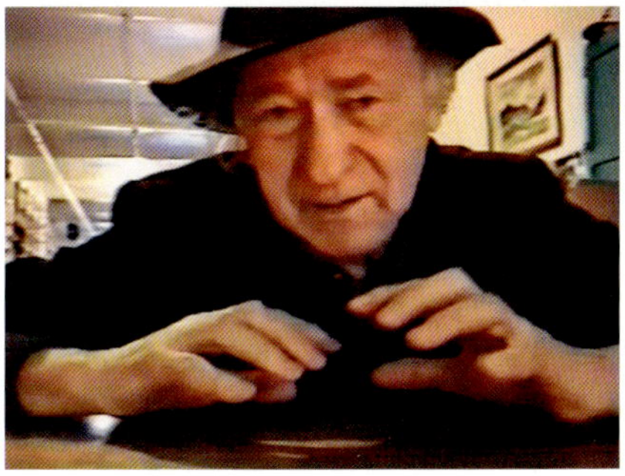

Two stills from *Letter to John from Jonas*, March 7, 1999.

In 1999, the Guggenheim Museum was in a moment of expansion after opening the Guggenheim Museum Bilbao in 1997; Anthology Film Archives, by contrast, had been one of the more financially strapped arts organizations in New York for years. Anthology had begun in 1970, attempting to create what its founders called "the first film museum exclusively devoted to *the film as an art*" in a manifesto issued at their initial screening at Joseph Papp's Public Theater.[1] This venue, near Astor Place in downtown Manhattan, held Peter Kubelka's legendary blinkered-seat architectural experiment, the Invisible Cinema, but Anthology had to relocate to a different space for the second half of the 1970s.[2] By the end of that decade, the organization had, after a bit of a struggle between competing bidders, successfully purchased the defunct Lower Manhattan Magistrates Courthouse from the city. Located at the corner of Second Avenue and Second Street in the East Village, this squat brick fortress of a building did not open its doors to the public until 1988, after nearly a decade of costly renovations.

In the late 1990s, as Mekas relates in *Letter to John*, Anthology still struggled under its bank debt and could not fulfill some of its most basic functions as an archive. "We had no archivist, and we had no librarian. The films were falling to pieces. We had no funds for preservation of any kind," Mekas confesses to Hanhardt through the camera. "We were at maybe the lowest point in the entire history of Anthology Film Archives." Nevertheless, Mekas continues, after word got out that Anthology could become part of the Guggenheim, the community of younger filmmakers who worked in and around Anthology—the "second and third generation of the sixties," Mekas calls them on the tape—rallied around the cause and brought new energy to the organization, promoting successful new screening series and holding fundraisers. Galleries around the world also hosted benefits. This push from a local and international community of film lovers gave Mekas new hope for Anthology's future and helped clarify his position. In the end, Mekas relates, Anthology's founder and staff collectively agreed to reject Hanhardt's invitation, despite the obvious benefits the museum's investment would bring in the short term:

> To all of us, [it] became clearer and clearer that Anthology has to remain totally independent from any other established international or national institution. That we need one such showcase, workshop, experimental maybe and anarchic a little bit, but open to all the possibilities, where money does not dictate, the boards do not dictate, and even the directors do not dictate, but the filmmaking, video-making community—the things that happen very naturally and develop—life itself will dictate the policies of Anthology Film Archives.

Jonas gave VHS copies of this to me and others who were around Anthology at the time; looking back, I realize it might have been only a few days after he had made the video. Though I never worked there in a formal sense, from 1998 to 2006 I hosted a showcase in their theaters each March called the New York Underground Film Festival; the event was put on by a separate organization whose members became increasingly intertwined with Anthology's crew as time went on. My copy of *Letter to John* bears a plain paper sleeve over the unmarked tape; Jonas's signature scratched into the sleeve with a ballpoint pen is the only indication of its contents. I remember him handing it to me, without explanation, in Anthology's lobby, and I watched it, a few blocks away, in my East Village apartment on a secondhand television nearly as old as Anthology itself. Mekas's insistence on the necessity of Anthology's independence has echoed in me ever since. "Anthology is one of the last places that is truly independent," he tells the camera. "We are like the last island left. I spent my life building it, when nobody believed that it can be built. I cannot permit, now, this cathedral of the free spirit to become part of the establishment."

In the decade prior to his death, the descriptor used most frequently to refer to Mekas in the press and scholarship was probably *filmmaker*, followed secondarily by terms like *writer*, *diarist*, or *critic*. Yet the Mekas we encounter in *Letter to John*—a seemingly improvised video, constructed with an artlessness that emphasizes the use of the medium as a mere conveyance—occupies none of these roles primarily. He instead speaks as founder and artistic director of Anthology and, ex cathedra, as a vocal representative of what he calls the "independent, avant-garde" filmmaking community as a whole. This version of Mekas would have been best known in New York, where he had remained well known from the early 1960s through the early 2000s as a promoter and exhibitor of films. It was this version of Mekas, in his showman-*cum*-spokesperson mode, that allowed him to act as a living metonym of American avant-garde cinema in the public eye.

Mekas sustained a high level of media visibility as a prolific founder of organizations, movements, and publications during his time in America before the establishment of Anthology. After moving to New York following World War II, Mekas started the journal *Film Culture* in the mid-1950s, along with his brother Adolfas and others, and later became the first film critic for the *Village Voice* in 1958. His column "Movie Journal," which he published through the mid-seventies, related the activities of the avant-garde to thousands of weekly readers in the city and beyond. After this, a long list of organizations pop up over the span of just a few years. The New American Cinema Group, which gave a name to the nascent movement of American independent film, began in 1960 with an assembly of twenty-two filmmakers invited by Mekas and Lewis Allen, the producer of Shirley Clarke's *The Connection*. In 1962, Mekas and the New American Cinema Group created the Film-Makers' Cooperative, a collective, nondiscriminatory distribution system for independent filmmakers, and perhaps more importantly, a gesture toward countercultural autarky.

Mekas's awareness of the need for something like Anthology began to emerge in this period. A statement written by him in 1964, after he, Ken Jacobs, and two theater staff were jailed and charged with obscenity for screening Jack Smith's *Flaming Creatures*, comes surprisingly close to what would be built decades later—though at this juncture, Mekas imagines that it would be run with the city government, rather than independently:

> THE CITY SHOULD GIVE THE FILM-MAKERS
> A BUILDING FOR A THEATER
>
> The Group now feels that the best solution to all our exhibition problems would be to have an auditorium of our own, a small theater where the independent film-maker could show his work to the interested audiences and exhibitors, stir interest, and generate more creativity in the low budget cinema. It is clear from past experiences that a commercial theater, even if we leave the legal problems out, even one

420

UNCHAINING LETTER
TO ALL FRIENDS OF THE AVANTGARDE CINEMA

As you may know, the showcase of the avantgarde cinema in New York, the Film-Makers' Cinematheque, has been closed for the last three months. Our midtown theater was too expensive to keep. We got another place downtown, 80 Wooster Street, much cheaper. For the last three months we have been trying to raise money to fix up the new place (plumbing, heating, seats, projectors) but we have been turned down by all money-giving "cultural" institutions. As our last attempt to save the Cinematheque we are appealing now to our audience, to you. Please make two or more copies of this letter and mail them to those of your friends who may be interested in the fate of the avantgarde cinema in this country. Each receiver of this letter is being asked to send one dollar to the Film-Makers' Cinematheque, G.P.O. Box 1601, New York, N.Y. 10001. Larger contributions will be accepted. For each dollar the sender will receive one ticket to the Cinematheque's screenings, open any date. Cinematheque is a tax-deductible foundation. If you have no time to do the typing, Film-Makers' Cooperative (175 Lexington Ave., N.Y.C.) will xerox free as many copies of this letter as you need and will help with the mailing. Be with us. Support the avantgarde film-maker in his quite lonely work.

Jonas Mekas
Film-Makers' Cinematheque
November 7, 1967

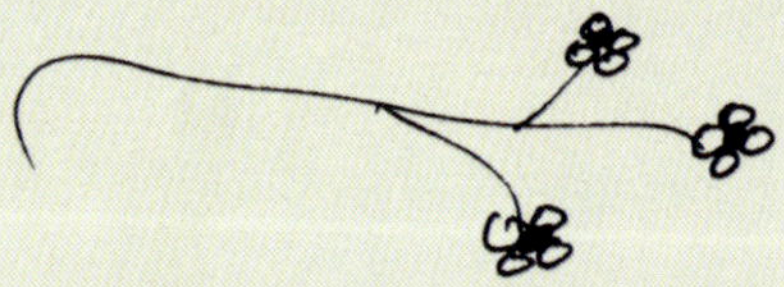

Letter from Jonas Mekas to "all friends of the avantgarde cinema," soliciting support for the Film-Makers' Cinematheque, November 7, 1967.

3 Jonas Mekas, *I Seem to Live: The New York Diaries*, vol. 1, *1950–1969* (Leipzig: Spector Books, 2019), 428.

4 Paul Arthur, "Routines of Emancipation," in *To Free the Cinema: Jonas Mekas and the New York Underground*, ed. David E. James (Princeton: Princeton University Press, 1992), 24, 38.

> with the best intentions, cannot give the film-maker the necessary freedom he needs.
>
> This city should give the film-makers one of its old or unused buildings for this purpose. Rental expenses being free, [a] film-maker could afford to show his films free, and thus avoid all the complications involved with the paid and public screenings. Ideally, such a showcase should have 100–200 seats and be equipped with 8mm, 16mm and 35mm projectors. It would serve as a workshop-showcase for independent film-makers. In England, this work is done by the British Film Institute; in France by the Cinémathèque Française. Both institutions are sponsored by the city municipalities.[3]

Mekas began screening films by fellow artists at the Charles Theatre in Greenwich Village. He put on regular series and festivals of new films at various movie theaters and art venues in Manhattan throughout the decade, first calling these events the Film-Makers' Showcase, in 1963, while presenting them under the aegis of the Film-Makers' Cooperative. The following year he changed the name to the Film-Makers' Cinematheque and programming continued under this banner until 1969. A plethora of other entities existed under various names: one-off charities like the Love and Kisses to Censors Film Society and the Anti-Censorship Fund, both set up by Mekas in cheeky attempts to evade police action; exploratory offshoots of the New American Cinema Group/Film-Makers' Coop collective core like the Film-Makers' Workshop, the Film-Makers' Lecture Bureau, and the Friends of the New American Cinema, all spun off in 1964; and a short-lived attempt at a commercial feature-film booking agency called the Film-Makers' Distribution Center, begun two years later.

Logo of the Charles Theatre, designed by George Maciunas, 1961.

Reassessing Mekas's history, the critic Paul Arthur writes that these endeavors and others should be understood as partaking of the logic of the New Left activism of the 1960s, stating that this long litany of invented organizations is "testament to the common political tactic by which simply naming a group or event validated its existence while disguising its actual clout in numbers or funds." Arthur argues that although Mekas gave vocal support to various American political movements and, more materially, lent his guidance and supplies to the radical documentary collective Newsreel in New York, his deployment of protest rhetoric was largely aesthetic, "adopting similar slogans and methods of polarization" but focusing on the promotion of the American independent film in its numerous emergent varieties rather than any greater social issues.[4]

Arthur notes that the New Left, in turn, had little time for American avant-garde filmmakers, partly due to "a sub rosa admiration for the instrumentality of commercial cinema."[5] The antiwar activist Abbie Hoffman's 1971 *Steal This Book* confirms a preference for mass media as communication over artistic experiment; the underground how-to manual includes sections on underground newspapers, print shops, switchboards, television and radio, but not filmmaking—"Guerrilla TV is the vanguard of the communications revolution, rather than the avant-garde cellophane light shows."[6] His only mention of cinema comes in a chapter on how to sneak into theaters for free. For Arthur, the "ideological crosscurrents" at play in Mekas's public life speak to difficulties of promoting "advanced art in the juggernaut of rebellion" and "point to a wider uneasiness within sixties counterculture."[7]

This "uneasiness" for Arthur seems to be the slippage between what he sees as legitimately engaged protest and radical chic, and this blurring was indeed part of sixties counterculture. Note, for instance, how the term "underground film" gained its force through allusion to World War II–era resistance movements but ultimately came to connote, as J. Hoberman puts it, "movies that erupt out of individual libidos." The term described an oppositional cinema not so much concerned with political revolution but, rather, one that expressed sentiments more broadly "anti-bourgeois, anti-patriotic, and anti-religious, as well as anti-Hollywood."[8] Indeed, the central artistic works of the period, as discussed in P. Adams Sitney's comprehensive survey *Visionary Film* or noted in Anthology's Essential Cinema list, display a great deal of emphasis on the advancement of formal, technical, and personal expression—of sexuality, especially.[9] Yet they contain fewer overtly political statements of the kind found in the work of European filmmakers like Jean-Luc Godard, Chris Marker, or Guy Debord during the same decade, not to mention contemporaneous developments from the insurgent Third Cinema being produced in Cuba, Brazil, and elsewhere in Latin America.[10]

Protest for Mekas intertwined with his promotion of cinema, most notably his time spent in jail for screening *Flaming Creatures*—an event which, given that he was initially not charged by police and "asked to be arrested as the one responsible for the screening," was partially staged but spontaneous.[11] Although Mekas functioned solely as an advocate for a specific artistic community rather than promoter of a broader political movement, what he certainly shared with figures like Abbie Hoffman and Jerry Rubin, cofounder of the radical media prankster group known as the Yippies, was a great skill in leveraging the power of the press. This is not only in the sense of propagating ideas through forms of mass media operated directly by the counterculture—guerrilla television, the Newsreel collectives, the underground newspapers like the early *Village Voice*—but also

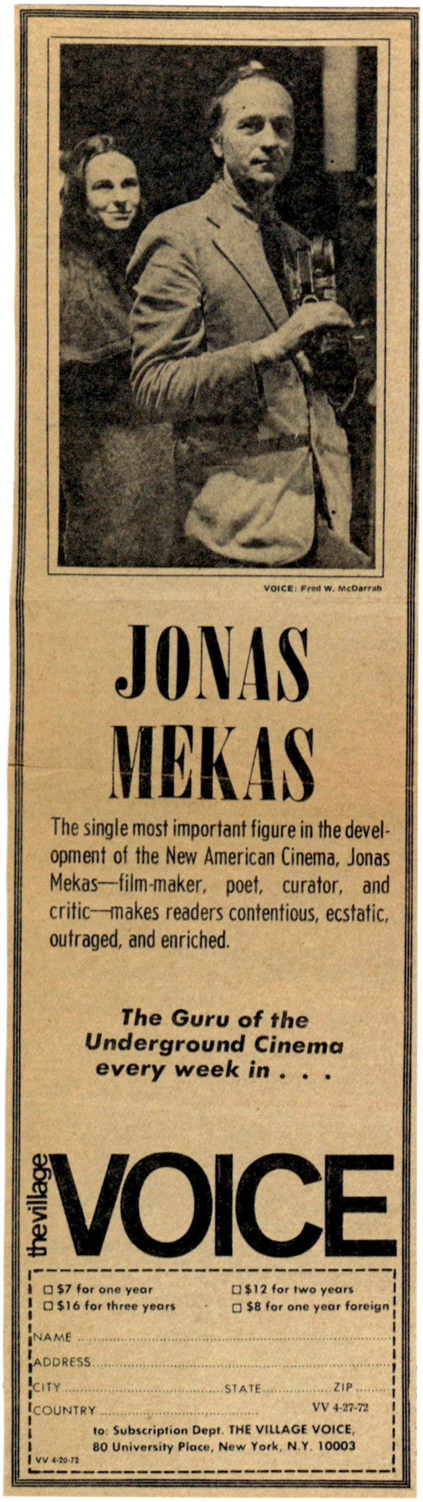

Subscription advertisement in the *Village Voice* featuring Jonas Mekas, October 12, 1972.

5 Arthur, "Routines of Emancipation," 39.

6 Abbie Hoffman, *Steal This Book* (New York: Pirate Editions, 1971), 144.

7 Arthur, "Routines of Emancipation," 41. A profile of the New American Cinema in *Commentary*, published prior to the rise of the New Left when the magazine spoke for the anti-Soviet liberal elite, seems prescient of Arthur's point, if articulated from a different position. "For all the general liberal or radical orientation of the New American Cinema, few of the pictures concern themselves with politics directly," its writer declares. "The politics of *Guns of the Trees*, as of the New American Cinema in general, represents the politics of the nonpolitical. Its 'argument' amounts to little more than anti-*them* and pro-*us*, the 'us' being people and the 'them' being everything else." Harris Dienstfrey, "The New American Cinema," *Commentary* (June 1, 1962): 498, 499.

8 J. Hoberman, introduction to Parker Tyler, *Underground Film* (New York: Da Capo Press, 1995).

9 P. Adams Sitney, *Visionary Film: The American Avant-Garde* (New York: Oxford University Press, 1974). The Essential Cinema was a project of Mekas's to establish a list, to be screened regularly, of the key films that define the art of cinema.

10 Carolee Schneemann's *Viet-Flakes* (1965), Robert Kramer's *The Edge* (1967) and *Ice* (1969), Andy Warhol's *Nude Restaurant* (1967), José Rodriguez-Soltero's *Dialogue with Che* (1968), and Joyce Wieland's *Rat Life and Diet in North America* (1968) are a handful of divergences from this general tendency, all trafficking in explicit antiwar sentiment or leftist characters—though in Warhol's case, sexual expression remains at the forefront. Mekas's *The Brig* (1964) could fit in this category as well.

11 Mekas, *I Seem to Live*, 431.

12 Thank you to Drew Adler for this research.

13 Tom Wolfe, "Pariah Styles: The New Chic," *Harper's Bazaar* (April 1965): 233; Sara Davidson, "New Type of Marathon? It Takes Intrepid Fan to View Film Festival," *Boston Globe*, September 28, 1965, 18; Lee Langley, "Metro Goldman," *The Guardian*, November 29, 1966, 7; "On Film: A Critic and a Festival," *Wall Street Journal*, September 23, 1969, 22; Bob Thomas, "Low-Cost Films Draw Well," *The Austin Statesman*, January 8, 1968, 22; "'Film Underground' Would Air Wares in 100 Outlets; Only 12 in U.S. Now," *Variety*, April 27, 1966, 17; "Show of Concern," *Newsweek*, September 4, 1967, 74; Jack Kroll, "Up from Underground," *Newsweek*, February 13, 1966, 118; Vincent Canby, "Burgeoning Underground Adds 2 Cinemas," *New York Times*, August 25, 1967, 28; and Gregory McDonald, "The Underground Film Makers," *Boston Globe*, May 5, 1968, G38.

the cultivation of more mainstream press attention that would sustain their message over time and, hopefully, spread word of their mission beyond the confines of their personal networks.

Mekas's tireless efforts to engage the press bore copious fruit. Searching the archives for mentions of his name in newspapers and magazines of the 1960s reveals more than a hundred individual instances, with a wide and deep reach: nationals and trades like *Variety*, *Town & Country*, *Cosmopolitan*, and *Womens' Wear Daily*; journals such as the *New Reader*, *Evergreen Review*, and *Commentary*; New York outlets from *Newsday* to the *New Yorker* to the *Wall Street Journal*; and metropolitan papers in Chicago, Los Angeles, Philadelphia, Austin, and beyond.[12]

When choosing words to describe Mekas, the press at first turned to spiritual or even magical terminology, describing his role variously as pastoral or mystical. In a 1967 essay in *Harper's Bazaar*, Tom Wolfe referred to Mekas as a "priest of Underground movies," prone to "incredible hydrocephalic preaching." The *Boston Globe*'s Sara Davidson envisioned Mekas as an elfin creature "wearing green corduroy jacket and slacks," dubbing him "the Pied Piper of the New York film underground." Other journalists employed monikers like "arch-priest," "high priest," "conscience and sage," and "guru." *Newsweek* limned Mekas as a "priest and prophet" and "frail, mystical spirit," Vincent Canby in the *New York Times* called him "shaggy-haired and ascetic-looking," and a fellow journalist made note of Mekas's "prophet-of-Lebanon haircut."[13]

job description

if you think you are working here for
salary;
if you are looking for justice or fairness
or any personal -- psychological or material
profit;
or love or respect;
or normal, "real" job, career;
"expect a raise"

this is a Cathedral of Cinema where a p rfect selfless
devotion is required from all monks and nuns of
cinema working here
and everything is everybody's job /"this is not my
area" "this is not my job" is not accepted/

Typescript of a job description for Anthology Film Archives employees by Jonas Mekas, undated.

14 Mekas, *I Seem to Live*, 357; Dienstfrey, "New American Cinema," 500; Parker Tyler, *The Three Faces of the Film* (New York: Thomas Yoseloff [1960]), 105; and Tyler, "Orson Welles and the Big Experimental Film Cult," in *Film Culture Reader*, ed. P. Adams Sitney (New York: Praeger, 1970), 376.

15 "Cinematheque Lights Anew for Clarke Pic," *Variety*, September 27, 1967, 7.

As his reference to Anthology as a "cathedral of the free spirit" in *Letter to John* shows, Mekas himself never shied from taking on a (perhaps) mock-godly tone from time to time; his diaries and columns show a propensity for terms like "heaven," "paradise," "spirit," and "Zen" in his discussions of new film art. Above the doors of the Coop, Mekas once placed a sign reading, "THIS IS THE MONASTERY & CONVENT of the ORDER OF FOOLS." Such transposition of the religious onto the cinematic was not unique to Mekas. As early as 1962, *Commentary* noted that the films of the New American Cinema frequently displayed "an interest in religion and personal salvation," in part "a carry-over from beat writers like Ginsberg, Kerouac, Corso, and Snyder." In the context of Mekas, particularly, such rhetoric calls to mind the critic Parker Tyler's evocation of Hollywood as a "Universal Church," opposed by both the "Big Cult" of art cinema and the "little cult" of the avant-garde, a set of metaphors grounded in obvious similarities between a cinema's audience of devotees and a temple's congregation of the devout. When the press searched for ways to describe succinctly what role Mekas played vis-à-vis the New American Cinema, such colorful terminology clearly proved useful.[14]

By 1967, however, *Variety* hit upon a new descriptor for Mekas that bears further analysis. In an item about the Film-Makers' Cinematheque, the broadsheet reported on Mekas moving his venue from the Forty-First Street Theatre to new locations downtown, one on Wooster Street and the other on Greene Street. Only part of this venture was to succeed. The Cinematheque ran at 80 Wooster Street for the first half of 1968 as part of a venture by a number of arts groups but never opened its doors on Greene Street. Mekas's stated plans, however, show him still working toward the dream of a permanent home. "The Greene St. address will also house a film workshop, archives, lecture rooms and screening rooms," the paper reported. "As in the past, these larger operations will all be spoken for by underground impresario Jonas Mekas."[15] This same appositive phrase—"underground impresario"—appears in *Variety*'s follow-up reports published in November and December, which chronicle Mekas's difficulties in fundraising for the move, and again in February 1969, in a piece about Mekas demanding that the Ann Arbor Film Festival pay rental fees to filmmakers, among other reforms.

A telling variation on this label appears in an article reporting that Mekas, "spokesperson for the N.Y. underground," launched criticism of the Third International Festival of New Cinema, held in Pesaro, Italy, at a press conference in Rome; *Variety* titled the piece

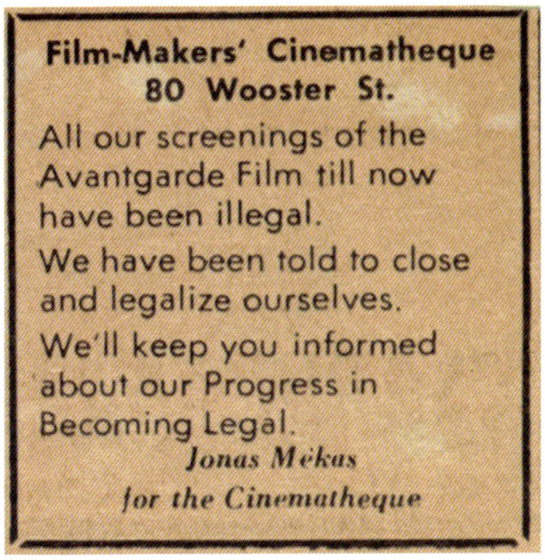

Film-Makers' Cinematheque
80 Wooster St.
All our screenings of the Avantgarde Film till now have been illegal.
We have been told to close and legalize ourselves.
We'll keep you informed about our Progress in Becoming Legal.
Jonas Mekas
for the Cinematheque

Announcement in the *Village Voice* that the Film-Makers' Cinematheque, 80 Wooster Street, is closed to "legalize ourselves," August 1, 1968.

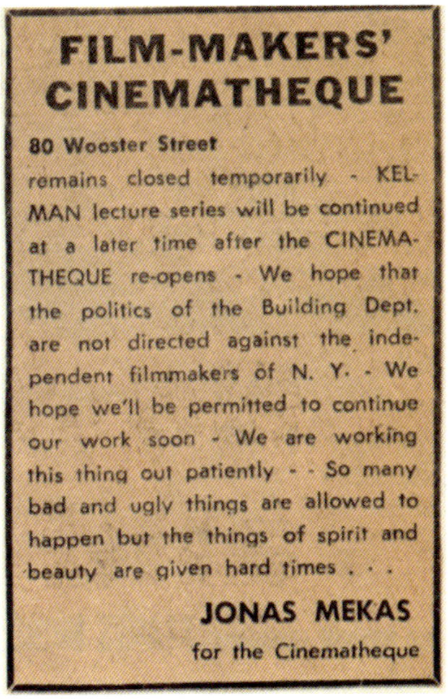

FILM-MAKERS' CINEMATHEQUE
80 Wooster Street
remains closed temporarily - KELMAN lecture series will be continued at a later time after the CINEMATHEQUE re-opens - We hope that the politics of the Building Dept. are not directed against the independent filmmakers of N. Y. - We hope we'll be permitted to continue our work soon - We are working this thing out patiently - - So many bad and ugly things are allowed to happen but the things of spirit and beauty are given hard times . . .
JONAS MEKAS
for the Cinematheque

Announcement in the *Village Voice* that the Film-Makers' Cinematheque, 80 Wooster Street, "remains closed temporarily," August 15, 1968.

1969

TO THE PEOPLE OF NEW YORK

from the Film-Makers' Cinematheque

You may have ~~mmmmmm~~ or you may have not noticed it, but the Film-Makers' Cinematheque is — at the moment — running the following showcases dedicated to the independent, Underground, Avantgarde film-maker:

Elgin Series

Jewish Museum Series

Gotham Art Theater Series

Gallery of Modern Att Series (beginning March 1st)

We are surrounding the City from all sides. Our aim is to surround, to infiltrate the city with the Young Cinema untill the City capitulates.

In a sense, we are at War.

The New against Old.

We dind't choose this war. The Mayor's office chose it, by closing the Cinematheque (80 Wooster St), by keeping it closed thru phony excuses with outdated BD regulations.

We have been forced to devide ourselves, to look for other places to screen our work, any place, anywhere, in a guerilla way.

That's what our tactics will be, from now on. We'll instigate, we'll cause other showcases to open, whoever feels like opening one. In a sense you did us a favor: we'll abandon the Centralized (Tek) screening era.

Draft letter from the Film-Makers' Cinematheque to the "people of New York" soliciting support, 1969.

People tell us: why dodn't you bribe THEM, like everybody else does: you could have your 80 Wooster place that way.

But we chose the fool's way: we do not believe in neither in bribing nor in the police & BD maffia.

So we are destined to run from place to place.

Which is tiring, wasted energy and wasted money.

But we have no other choice.

The Mayor has stated on a number of occasions that he im wants to make New York into a movie town. But WE ARE the Moviemakers of this town and we are getting a foot into your mouth, your foot, stinking foot.

Ask anybody anywhere whom do they mean when they speak about the New York cinema, the NY school of cinema, and they'll tell you: it's the Underground film-maker. We are holding the flag of Cinema in this town. But our Mayor is dealing with the commercial renegates, with the miserable film businessmen.

So here we are. Appealing to the people of New York.

As you can see: we are sticking with you. Despite the most difficult conditions into which we have been put by the Mayor by depriving us of our own home -- despite all that, we are sticking with you, we are not betraying cinema in New York: we are providing you with showcases of the new cinema. We are giving you a chance and a choice to see other kinds of cinema so that the commerce wouldn't take completely over this City.

The press doesn't review our movies. The newspapers think that only the Hollywood and European Art cinema is Cinema. Despite of that: we are not letting you down, we are not going to leave this city to the commercial cinema alone. We are sticking to our principles.

So, be with us. We are with you.

We need your help. Help us with your coming and help us with money. It is true that we need money badly, that our bills make a mountain, our debts make another mountain: but please do not misunderstand us: we are going to continue, by hooks or crooks, even if nobody comes to our help. Those days when the apathy & ignorance of people closed the Cinema 16, those days are over.

We beleive in what we are doing, we know what we are doing, and we know the meaning of what we are doing; and we are going to continue it and we'll give it up only when our lives will give up. So you should know it, We are a bunch of fanatics, get it?

16 *The Life of P. T. Barnum* (1855) and *Struggles and Triumphs: or, Forty Years' Recollections of P. T. Barnum* (1869). Discussing Mekas, it is difficult to disentangle his "mythic self" from what might be called his behind-the-scenes life of intimate personal relationships and everyday minutiae. The best portrait of this "backstage" Mekas is found in the video diaries of the artist Andrew Lampert, captured while Lampert was working as Anthology's first in-house archivist. The full project, *Question a Day with Jonas Mekas*, was shot in 2003, and excerpted and distributed as Lampert's 2008 video *Question a Day*.

"Mekas, N.Y. Underground Barnum, Raps Critics' Cool Stand on Pesaro." While the name could connote a mere bamboozler, P. T. Barnum was nevertheless nineteenth-century America's most successful and famous showman, and is remembered as one of the key architects of the modern entertainment industry. Given *Variety*'s allegiances, a comparison of Mekas to Barnum could be viewed as highly complimentary (if somewhat backhanded), praising Mekas's ingenuity for drumming up interest in unusual fare. Somewhat paradoxically, in this scrappy East Coast exhibitor, Hollywood saw glimmers of its own ancestor.

Moreover, the evocation of Barnum allows for a vivid rendering of American showmanship, an image of its tactics and styles. And the notion of Mekas as impresario may in some ways prove just as useful as ideas about political insurgency in trying to understand his activities in the 1960s. The term *impresario*, meaning an organizer of popular exhibitions and events, can more generally refer to an entrepreneur in its original Italian usage; the word began to appear regularly in English in the eighteenth century, initially as part of the terminology of opera. When applied to a figure like Barnum, the impresario might produce any number of theatrical forms or invent new ones. Barnum oversaw freak shows, museums, musical concerts, and circuses. Rather than underwriting a fixed company of performers, Barnum gathered around him a loose constellation of figures who changed over time (for example, the Feejee Mermaid, Tom Thumb, and the operatic soprano Jenny Lind). The acts and venues might change, but Barnum remains the constant figure, a symbol of the whole, a central node in an unfixed and shifting interpersonal network. Notably, in addition to the day-to-day management behind the scenes, Barnum functioned as a performer, one whose medium was marketing and publicity and whose stage was the press. And for Barnum, the promotion of his shows involved the ongoing creation of a mythic self, articulated through live appearances, interactions with reporters, and his own best-selling autobiographical writings.[16]

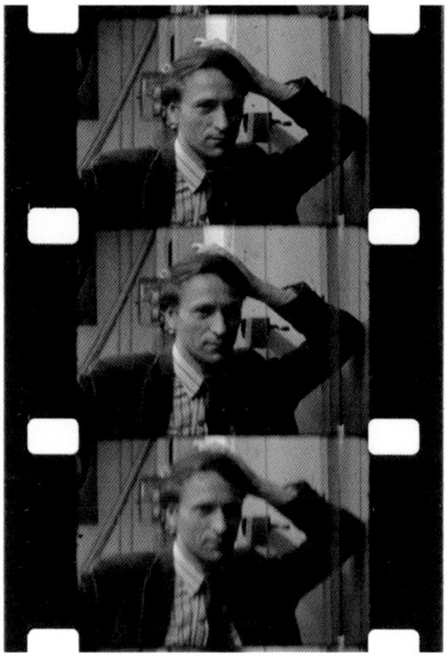

Three frames showing Jonas Mekas, unidentified film, c. 1965.

Related patterns can be traced through figures in twentieth-century American cinema, ranging from early road-show types like Oscar Micheaux and Kroger Babb to Hollywood producers like David O. Selznick and Roger Corman. Their names and, in some cases, visages became part of their marketing, a way of framing expectations about the films they offered. In a recollection of past times with Mekas, the artist and filmmaker George Kuchar alludes to Mekas's success at self-promotion and notes its potency. "In those old days, Jonas Mekas's columns in the *Village Voice* popped off the page with passion and that weird little line drawing of his profile," Kuchar writes, "a visual logo that was completely the opposite of the one associated with Alfred Hitchcock and yet somehow just as menacing. He was one of the very few people writing about underground films in that period and so he had a lot of power and was feared, respected, and hated."[17]

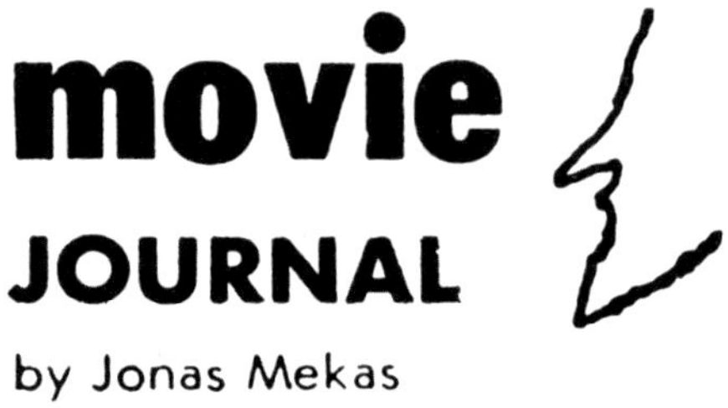

Profile of Jonas Mekas accompanying his "Movie Journal" byline in the *Village Voice*, undated.

Kuchar's point is important: while Mekas might have spoken of his role as one filmmaker among equals, not everyone saw it that way. Yet Mekas's activities, including his column, also had the ability to bring a collection of people together, whether by gathering filmmakers to form the New American Cinema Group, name-checking and profiling people in the *Village Voice*, or compiling footage of their meetings in his diary films. Mekas's organization-building, filmmaking, and journalism cannot be extricated from one another as discrete activities: "movie journal," after all, is a synonym for "film diary." These various configurations reshuffled many of the same artists, a number of whom ended up on the Essential Cinema list—which, perhaps significantly, was organized around the names of individual filmmakers rather than the titles of their films.

Homologies between Mekas's underground activities and the machinations of Barnum or Hollywood producers have certain limits. Barnum has long been viewed as exploitive of his performers and manipulative of his audiences, operating primarily in the service of making money. Mekas, in stark contrast, believed deeply in the importance not only of the films he championed but also the independent filmmaking community as a whole, and he only expressed interest in money insofar as it could help him support this community and make more films. This mendicant quality is something that, perhaps, religious metaphors of the period are attempting to capture. Nonetheless, at least one observer, unsympathetic to the cause of advanced cinema and uncomfortable with the sexuality on display, painted Mekas as akin to a carnival barker or panderer. In 1966, after the box-office success of Andy Warhol's *Chelsea Girls* had brought mainstream attention to the New York underground, an editorial in *Back Stage* offered this lurid picture:

> Few people attend a viewing of an Underground film for any reason other than to observe the freaks. Andy Warhol, Jack Smith, Mario Montez (who plays all his parts in high drag), Taylor Mead—they are big draws in just the same way that the geek was in the old circus side show. They dance around, they make curious sounds, someone feeds them a pound of raw chicken gizzards; they nictate, micturate, fornicate and the crowd squeals. Despite the sweet sentiments and garbled rhetoric of Jonas Mekas, his boys are nothing more than manifestations of a curious and ghastly exhibition. . . . Mekas labors under the delusion that he has created

17 George Kuchar, "The Old Days," in James, *To Free the Cinema*, 49.
18 David Milton, "The Film World," *Back Stage*, August 26, 1966, 5, 13.

> a movement; he labors under the misapprehension that he is fighting the tide of our modern society. No, my friend, modern America has created you.[18]

Notably, during the same period, charges of unethically Barnum-like behavior were more often leveled at Warhol than Mekas. Warhol, whose productions moved from art to film to rock music to theater to television, aimed for a greater and less countercultural audience than Mekas. Some of Warhol's superstars famously accused him of cheating them out of pay, while his least perceptive critics claimed that Warhol trafficked in fraudulent art. Even within the underground, Warhol could be divisive, and particularly once he started producing increasingly commercial features after *Chelsea Girls*. Mekas retained a friendship with him until Warhol's death in 1987; Warhol, the son of Slavic immigrants, grew up in a neighborhood in Pittsburgh that housed many Lithuanians, and one wonders if this served as something of a bond between the two men. In any case, both were known for their skills at self-promotion and moving through rarefied social circles. Mekas's memorial film *Scenes from the Life of Andy Warhol* (1990) compiles footage ranging from the artist's early multimedia events in the Village to his later vacationing with the Kennedys. The title, like those of a few other Mekas films, echoes a convention for picturing the life of a saint, but it can also be taken as an acknowledgment of the many social "scenes" through which Warhol moved. The film is primarily a chronicle of Warhol, but it is also testament to the fact that Mekas too was circulating through these worlds.

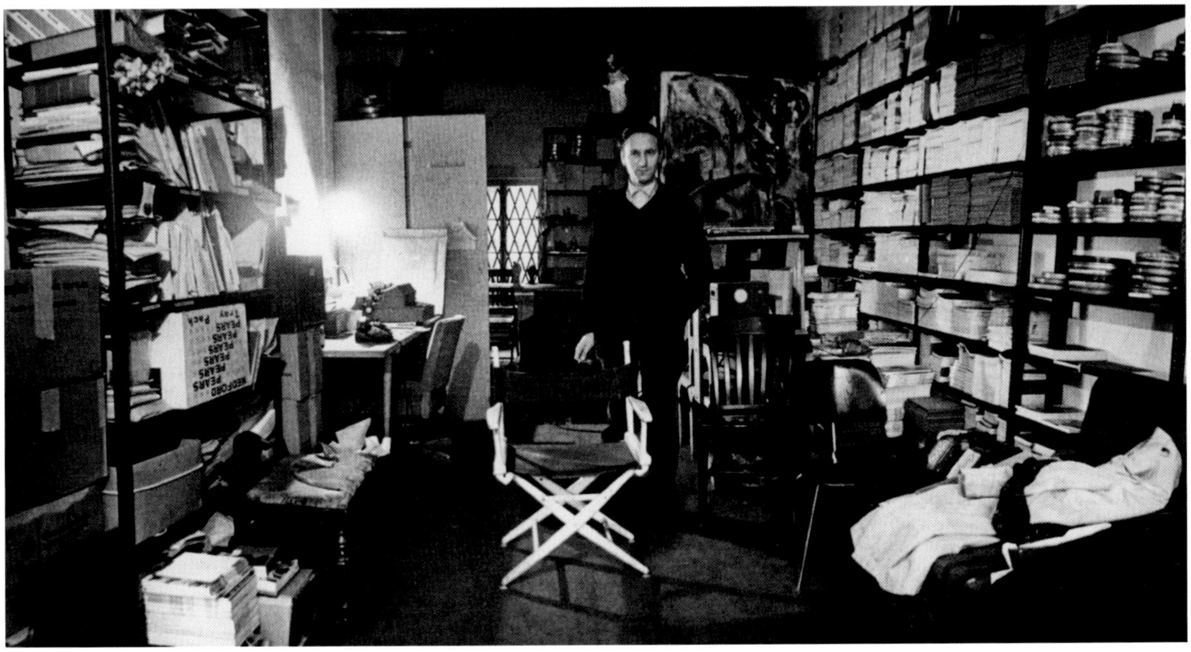

Jonas Mekas in the Film-Makers' Cooperative, 414 Park Avenue South, undated photograph.

19 Jonas Mekas, *A Dance with Fred Astaire* (New York: Anthology Editions, 2017), 145.

20 Sheldon Renan, *An Introduction to the American Underground Film* (New York: E. P. Dutton, 1967), 22.

21 Jem Cohen, notes for a talk given on June 23, 2019, at Anthology Film Archives, New York, on the occasion of the series "Jonas Mekas Tribute Screenings, Part 1," 31.

22 P. Adams Sitney, interview with author, June 8, 2020.

23 In New York City, police and fire departments can cause trouble for film theaters in terms of enforcing rules about noise levels, the physical capacity, the placement of proper exits, illegal drug use, and other concerns; perhaps due to the high number of movie theaters in New York City, the projectionists' union has been able to enforce labor standards that can potentially be an impediment to more nontraditional forms of exhibition if their services are required by their contract with the theater operator.

For Mekas, the maintenance of such relations with various constituencies, particularly wealthy or connected individuals who might aid his work, was a constant from the 1960s through the twenty-first century. The price of independence, evidently, was maintaining a never-ending hustle: in *Lost, Lost, Lost*, Mekas includes a shot of himself in a suit, adding an intertitle that reads: "I cut my hair, to raise money, having teas with rich ladies." For a while, the filmmaker Jerome Hill, grandson of a railroad magnate, assisted the scene financially, but this support was interrupted by Hill's death in 1972, just when it was crucially needed. As time went on, Mekas became publicly affiliated with a range of famous names—John Lennon and Yoko Ono, the clothier agnès b., and hip young filmmakers like Harmony Korine.

One of Mekas's later publications, *A Dance with Fred Astaire*, plays with the humor inherent in the collision of an avant-garde figure with well-known celebrities. It collects anecdotes not only about filmmakers close to him, such as Gregory Markopoulos and Barbara Rubin, but also his interactions with outsized media personalities like Salvador Dalí, Weegee, and Al Pacino. The tales include an account of Mekas's "brief career as a music agent" for the singer Tiny Tim and a surprise run-in with Arnold Schwarzenegger at a Hollywood Christmas party, where the future governor of California arrives in a Santa suit bearing gifts. In the same book, Mekas makes sure to highlight the more unglamorous side of his life, including a diary entry from 1975 that indicates Harry Smith, Markopoulos, and Jack Smith all contacted him within the span of one day, each desperate for money. "I say, yes, yes, I'll see if there's any money. I have only $12 in my bank."[19]

This long-term, ongoing desperation makes it all the more astonishing that Mekas would reject the Guggenheim's offer in the late 1990s. In *Letter to John*, the core ideal that Mekas reiterates is that of independence. When applied to film, the term "independent" long ago became hollow; this was true even in 1967, according to Sheldon Renan, who claimed that its use by "Hollywood-type films outside the system" had already led avant-gardists "to disassociate themselves from the word."[20] But what Mekas means by independence can be linked to a much deeper set of ideas about art's relation to politics that he seems to have carried with him throughout his life.

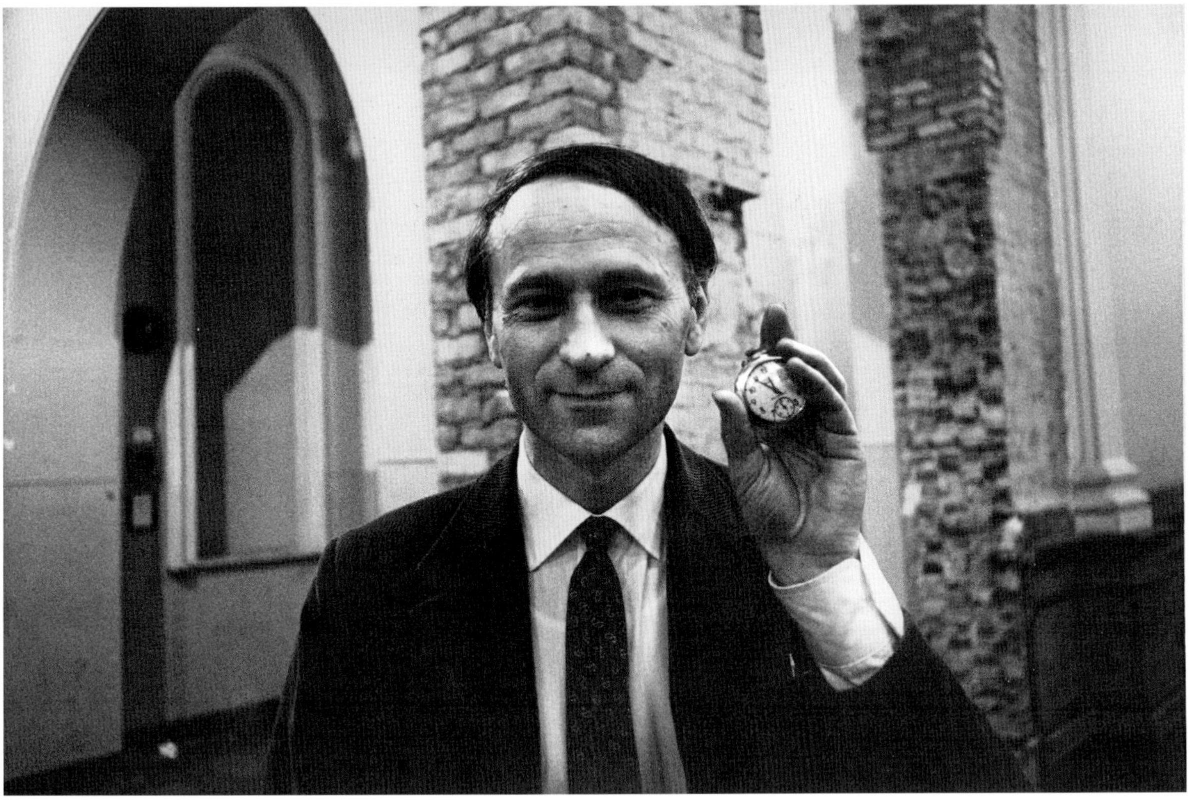

Jonas Mekas at the opening of Anthology Film Archives at the Public Theater, photographed by Gretchen Berg, c. 1970.

Though generally on the left, Mekas had no particularly consistent politics in any conventional sense. In remarks written for Mekas's memorial, Jem Cohen, a filmmaker a few generations younger, raised the question of whether Mekas was "apolitical or just non-judgmental." Cohen had difficulties understanding why the clearly "antiestablishment" Mekas would, for instance, celebrate his wealthy friend Peter Beard's lavish wedding in *Walden*. "He embraced simplicity, but was surely full of complex contradictions," Cohen writes. "Filmmaker Ken Jacobs, who likely knew him as well as anyone, said Jonas couldn't be pinned down and referred to him, in both love and frustration I'd guess, as a 'greased pig.' "[21] Despite organizing for the rights of filmmakers, Mekas was often at loggerheads with unions, particularly those for projectionists; according to Sitney, this attitude led to personal clashes with Annette Michelson when she was in the midst of unionizing professors at New York University.[22] Mekas had no love for police, as chronicled by innumerable mentions in his column and diaries; Sitney remarked that Mekas even bore enmity toward the fire department. Probably not coincidentally, the projectionists' unions, police, and fire departments are all organizations he would have to struggle against to screen experimental films theatrically.[23]

In a journal entry from August 1960, Mekas laments a recent police breakup of eleven gangs in East Harlem: "Gangs! They still uphold some independent spirit, some disrespect for the officialdom, parenthood. And how could one consider the abandoning

XERO COPY XERO COPY XERO COPY XERO COPY

FILM CULTURE NON PROFIT CORPORATION

a non profit membership corporation with charitable foundation status

Members: Jonas Mekas, Adolfas Mekas, David C. Stone, Barbara Stone, Herman G. Weinberg

Directors: Barbara Stone, P. Adams Sitney, David C. Stone, Jack M. Perlman, Herman G. Weinberg

Officers: P. Adams Sitney (president)
Jack M. Perlman (secretary)
Herman G. Weinberg (treasurer)

FILM CULTURE DIVISION | CINEMATHEQUE DIVISION

* *

THE NEW AMERICAN CINEMA GROUP, INC.

a non profit membership corporation

Members: approximately 250 film-makers

Directors: Jonas Mekas, Ed Emshwiller, Stan Vanderbeek, Robert Breer, Shirley Clarke, Ken Jacobs, Peter Kubelka, Charles Levine (honorary director), Carl Linder (west coast liaison)

Officers: Jonas Mekas (president)
Jack M. Perlman (secretary-treasurer)

FILM-MAKER'S CO-OP DIVISION | FILM-MAKER'S DISTRIBUTION CENTER DIV.

(The above is a typewritten clear copy of a handwritten organization chart ppovided by Jack M. Perlman: 1/4/68.)

Organizational chart for Jonas Mekas's many nonprofit ventures, including *FIlm Culture*, the New American Cinema Group, and Film-Makers' Coop, prepared by Jack M. Perlman on January 4, 1968.

24 Mekas, *I Seem to Live*, 243, 760.
25 Ibid., 793.
26 Sitney, interview.

of alliances a positive act, a virtue? It's a betrayal of friendships, it's a complete loss of honor, it's giving up independence." Independence, for Mekas, was tied to spontaneity, improvisation, artistic freedom, and above all, the rights of individuals to associate as they wish. Maintaining this independence meant the hard work of balancing the needs of individuals with that of the collective enterprise. Within the New American Cinema, this led to numerous squabbles and rivalries in which Mekas became enmeshed, all while he labored to promote their cause and, into the 1970s and 1980s, build Anthology while also raising a family with two young children. Reflecting on the past of the New American Cinema in 1968, he makes clear that fighting for autonomy holds a greater value than, as those on the New Left might argue, struggling to change the whole society:

> Our attitude, our spirit is TO BUILD, TO CREATE, not to destroy. We didn't waste energy on destroying Hollywood film industry: we directed our energies towards creating a new kind of cinema, a more personal cinema, towards the liberation of the camera; we didn't waste our time fighting the competitive, commercial film distribution set-ups and systems: we created our own . . . based on noncompetitive human relations.[24]

If there was any consistency to Mekas's stated politics, it was that he always placed himself on the side of the independent filmmaker. Even in the volatile late sixties, he still drew an unwavering line in the sand. "The Underground Film (the Avant-Garde Film) is the only revolutionary cinema today," he wrote in his diaries in 1969. "To call oneself a revolutionary or a radical and at the same time to pay money and support capitalist-imperialist cinema while ignoring revolutionary cinema, is an act of collaboration and an act of betrayal."[25] For Mekas, the independence of the individual filmmaker was a necessary precondition for art; if the auteur theory, as articulated by Andrew Sarris in the pages of *Film Culture* in 1962, argues that a film artist is one who is able to express an individual vision despite working under the impersonal structures of the Hollywood studio system, then Mekas's independent filmmaker dispenses with said system altogether, allowing in theory for a more direct and powerful access to the creative spirit. Staying small and independent might mean poverty, but this was a poverty that also served as a road to freedom.

Attempting to pin him down politically, Arthur describes Mekas as an anarchist. Sitney disagrees, adding that Mekas held a variety of political opinions that changed widely over time.[26] Mekas did present some antistatist views in a diary entry in 1960, though

27 Mekas, *I Seem to Live*, 228. The Essential Cinema roster takes the same stand for the autonomy of individual artistic vision against politics by including works of propaganda like D. W. Griffith's white supremacist *Birth of a Nation*, Marxist films by Sergei Eisenstein and Dziga Vertov, and Leni Riefenstahl's Nazi Party–commissioned *Triumph of the Will*. The valorization of these films partakes in a quasi-auteurism, in which the artist achieves excellence despite the political structures in which he or she works, rather than commercial ones.

28 Ibid., 181.

again couched in relation to filmmaking. "What I want to achieve—ideally—with my film: is to overthrow the government," he wrote. "All governments. So that we could begin from the beginning." Taking this tiny manifesto at face value, what was this "beginning"? Perhaps it is the same thing as "paradise," that lost state that Mekas so often invokes, lamenting his attempts to return.

Or the answer may be more personal for Mekas. Coming from Lithuania, a small country besieged by both Germany and the Soviet Union during World War II, Mekas expressed resistance to overarching ideologies and imperial ambitions; art provided access to a truth that neither required, nor desired, dogma and power. "You don't have to be a Communist to be an anti-capitalist," he opined in 1960. "It's enough to be a poet."[27] A few years earlier, he had recorded some stray thoughts on the nature of small countries versus big countries. "I am a regionalist," he began, "No abstract internationalism for me."

> Lithuanian songs are small and they are directed inwards because there is nowhere else to go, it's a very small place, so you sit by yourself, you know, and you sing to yourself, two, three friends, maybe—
>
> And then we have the big countries, and the big rivers, and big mountains and big histories and big armies and big wars, and they always get together, like at the United Nations, and they proclaim themselves the Big Three, or the Big Four, or the Big Five, and they always think they are the only ones, and others, you know, others should be only a part of them, or speak their language. . . .
>
> So you know why I am for small countries, and small rivers, and small mountains, and for a world in which there are languages which nobody understands outside the people who speak it.[28]

In Mekas's diary films, he constructed an imaginary Lithuania out of the trees in Central Park, out of the romps upstate with his American friends. In building the anti-institutional institutions of the American avant-garde, grown out of rich personal alliances with artists, he tried to recreate the best aspects of the small-scale intimacies of his old village existence, in defiance of the big structures that cinema had traditionally demanded. For Mekas, this was not only a way to create better art. It was meant to embrace life itself.

LOST, LOST, LOST, 1976

A WEEK AFTER
WE LANDED IN
AMERICA (B'KLYN)
WE BORROWED
MONEY & BOUGHT
OUR FIRST BOLEX

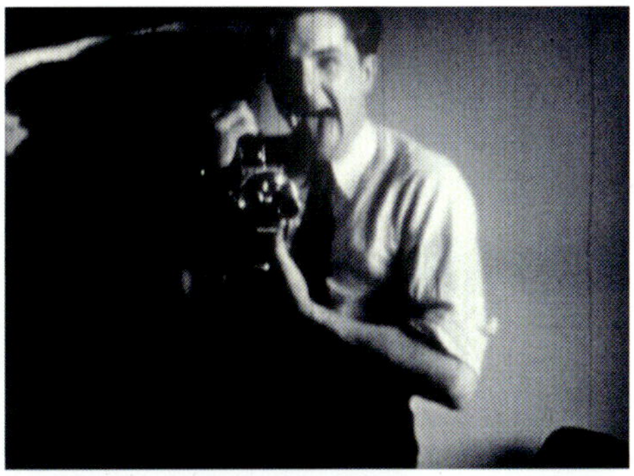

ON 23RD ST PIER
DP'S ARRIVE IN
AMERICA

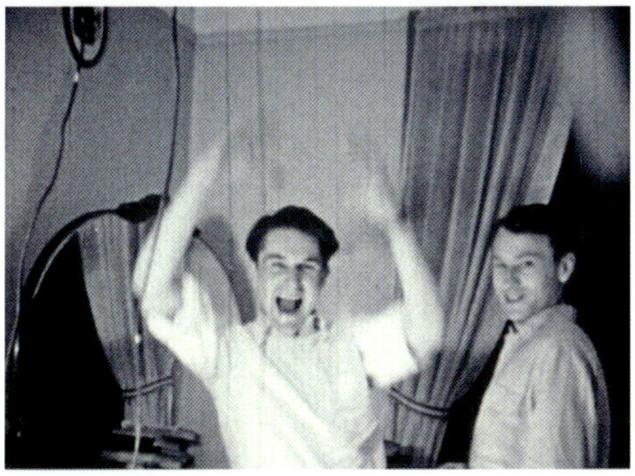

THE YEAR WAS
1949

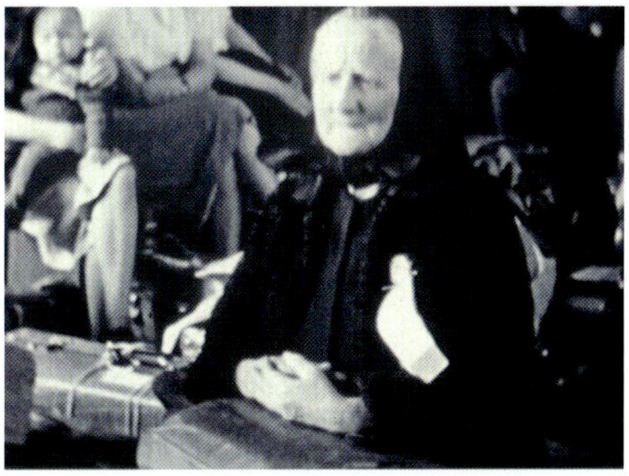

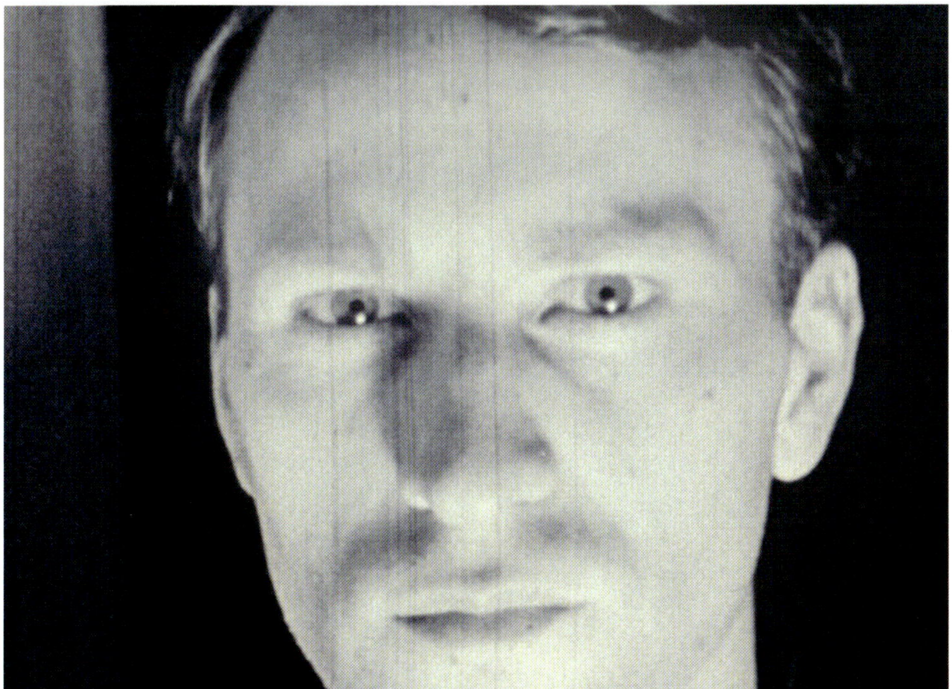

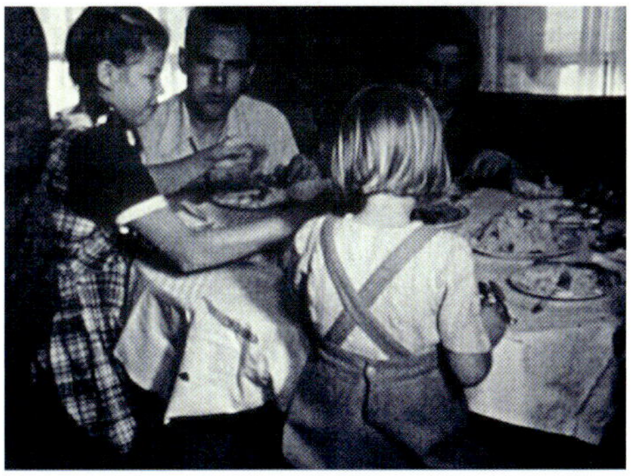

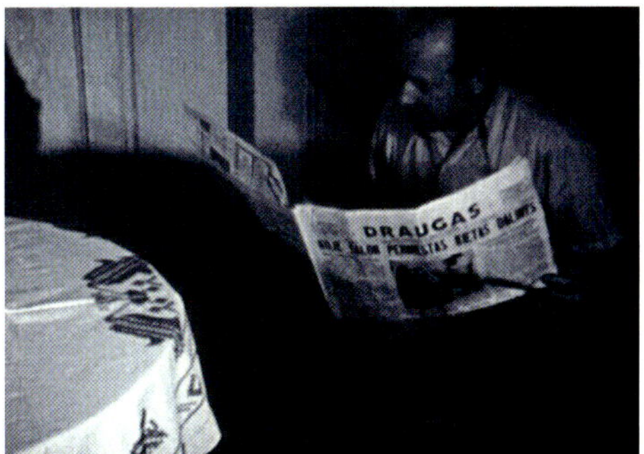

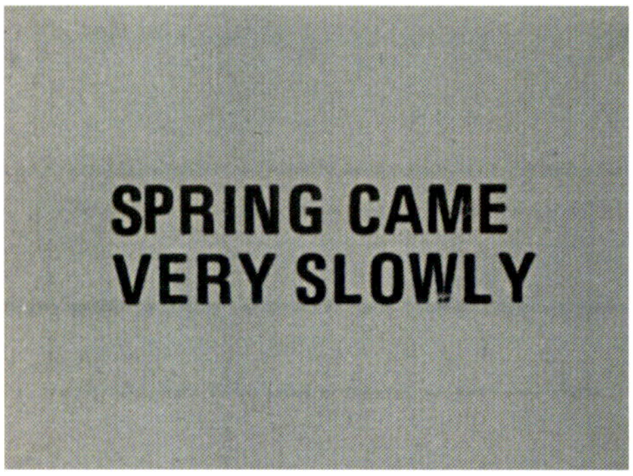
SPRING CAME
VERY SLOWLY

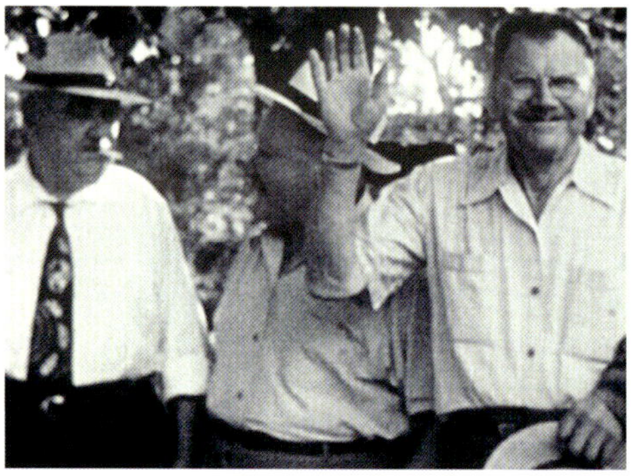

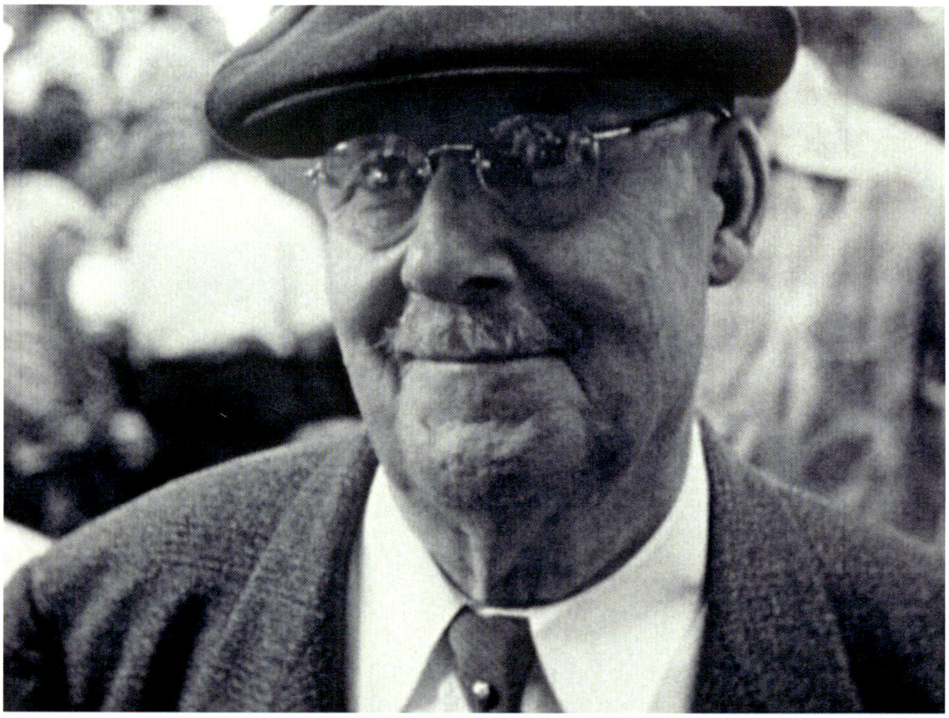

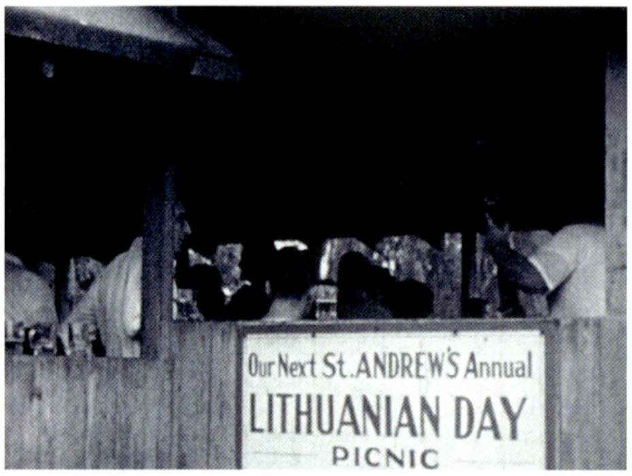
Our Next St. ANDREW'S Annual
LITHUANIAN DAY
PICNIC

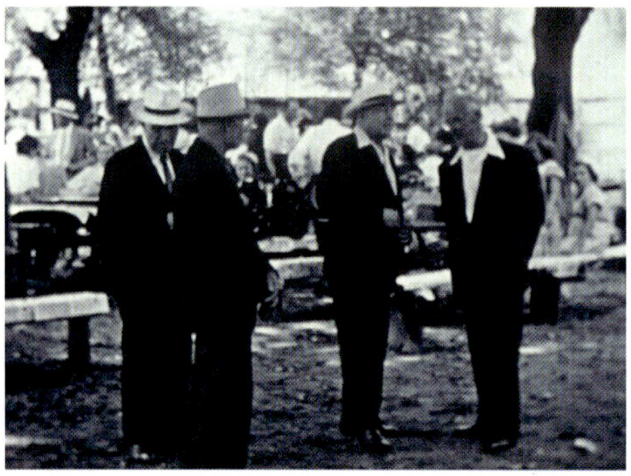

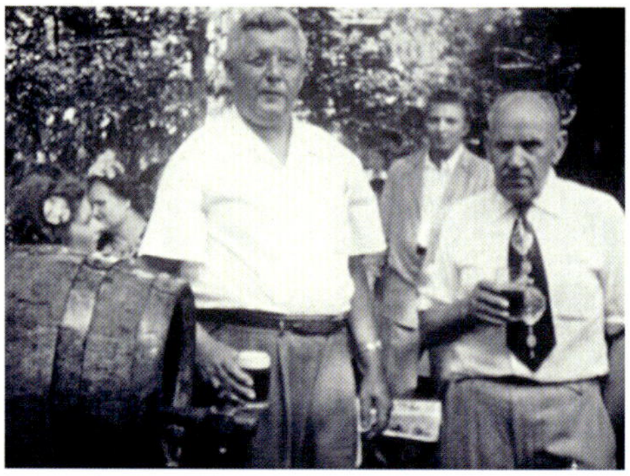

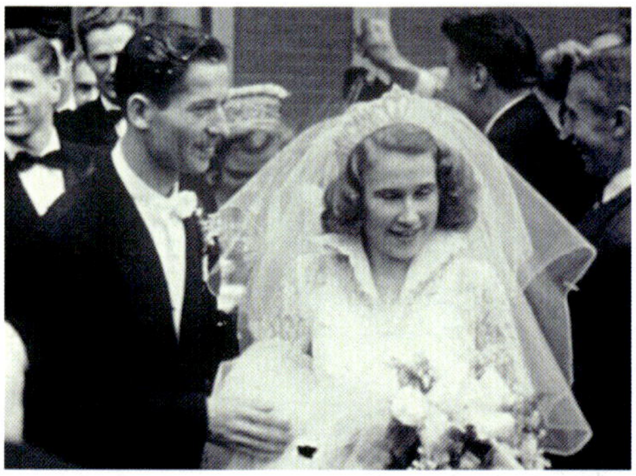

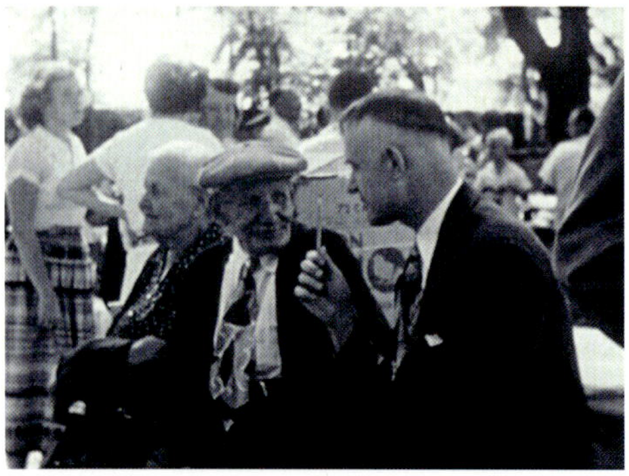

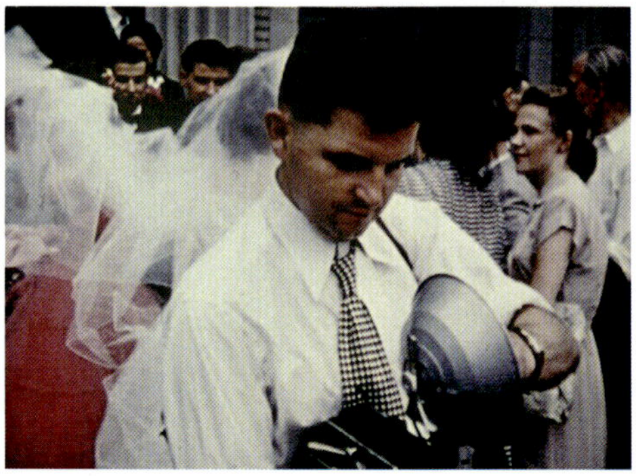

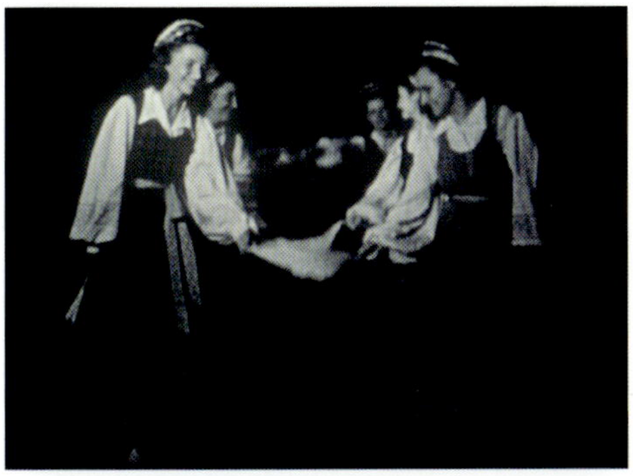

ON LIBERTY AVE
DP'S PICKET
LITHUANIAN
COMMUNIST
NEWSPAPER

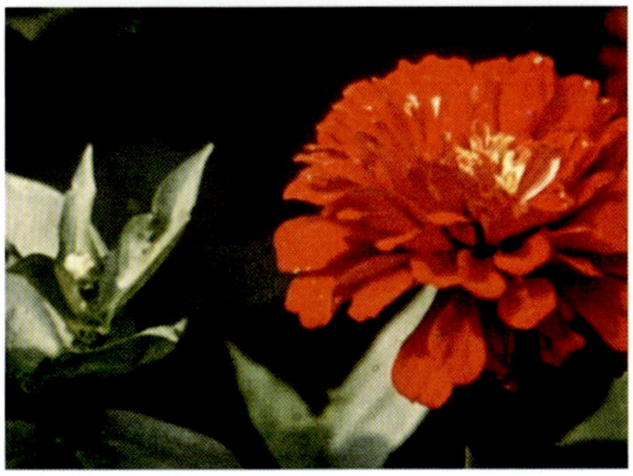

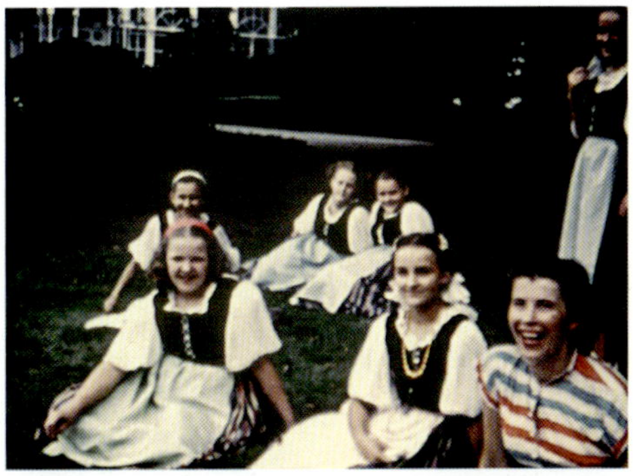

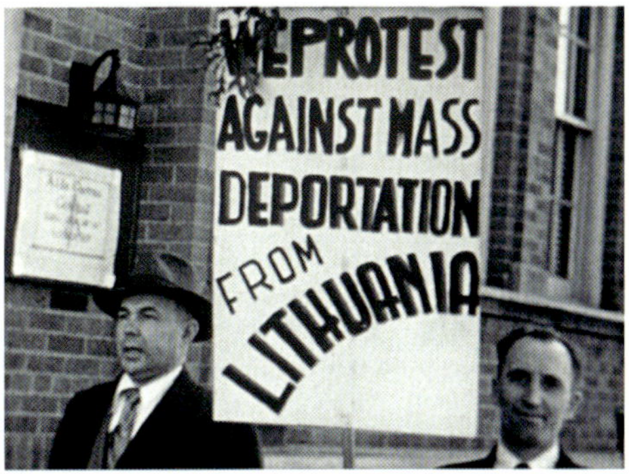
WE PROTEST
AGAINST MASS
DEPORTATION
FROM
LITHUANIA

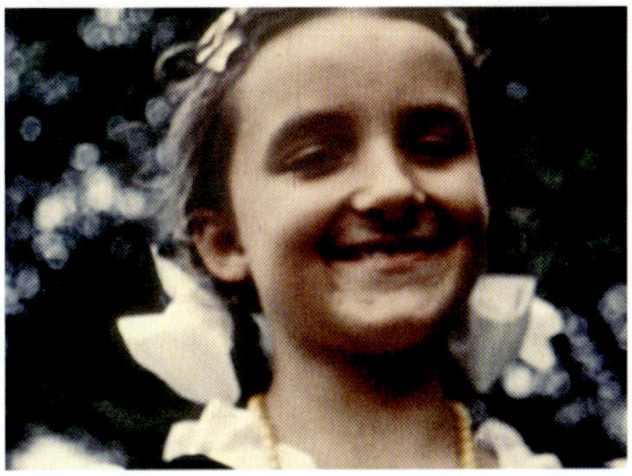

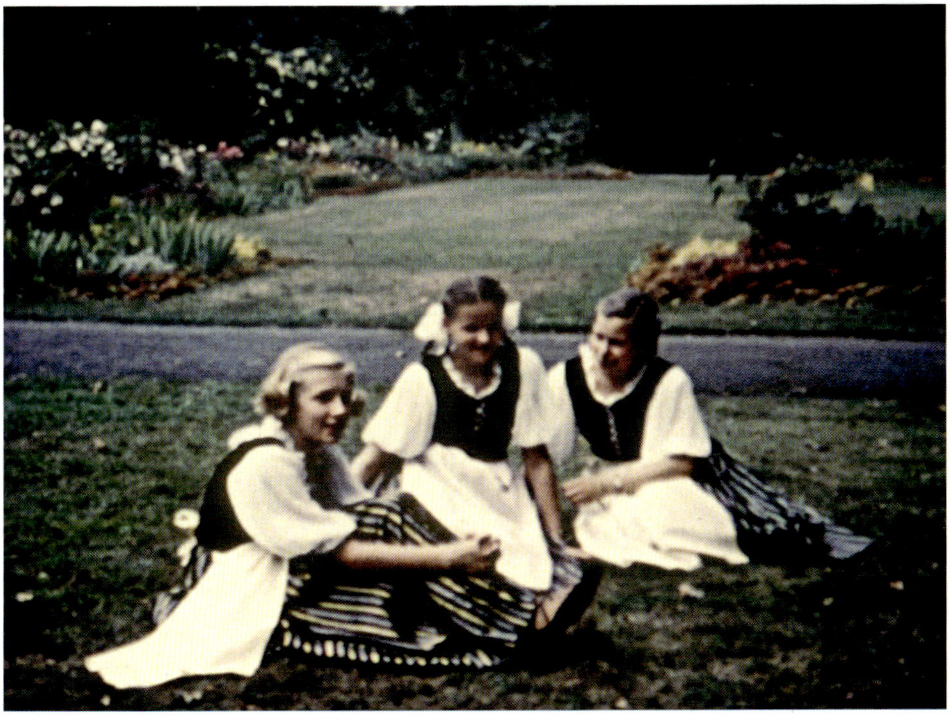

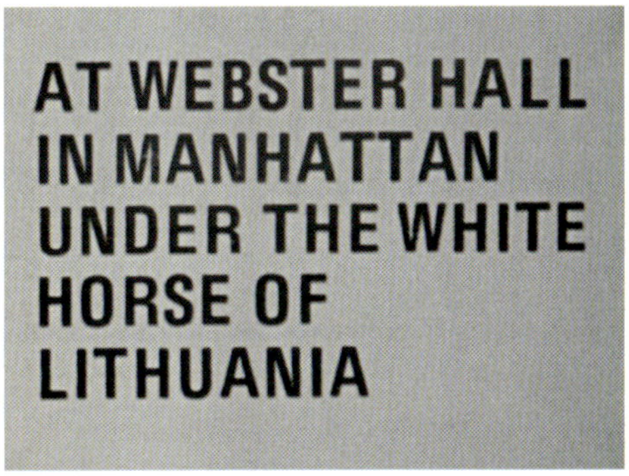
AT WEBSTER HALL
IN MANHATTAN
UNDER THE WHITE
HORSE OF
LITHUANIA

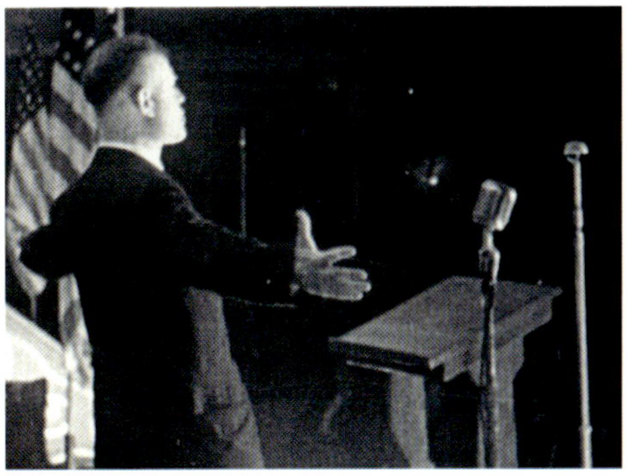

THE SPRING OF 1953
FOUND US ON
ORCHARD STREET

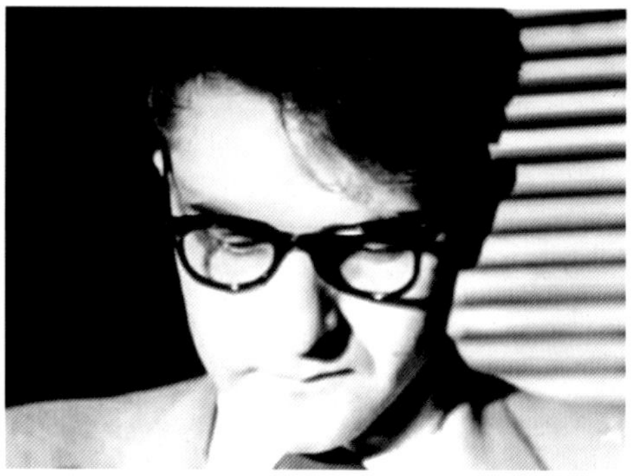

COLLECTING
MONEY FOR
FILM CULTURE

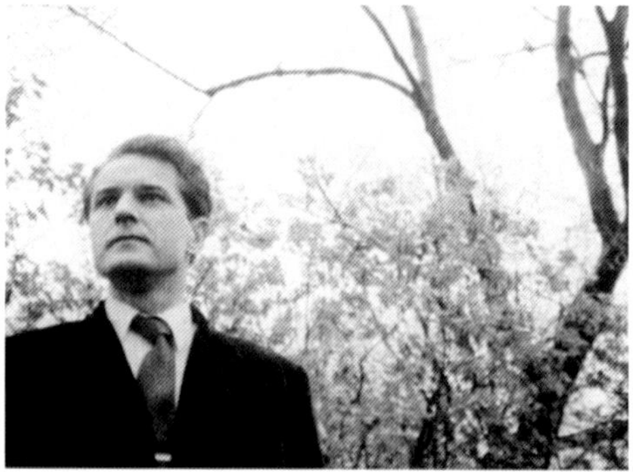

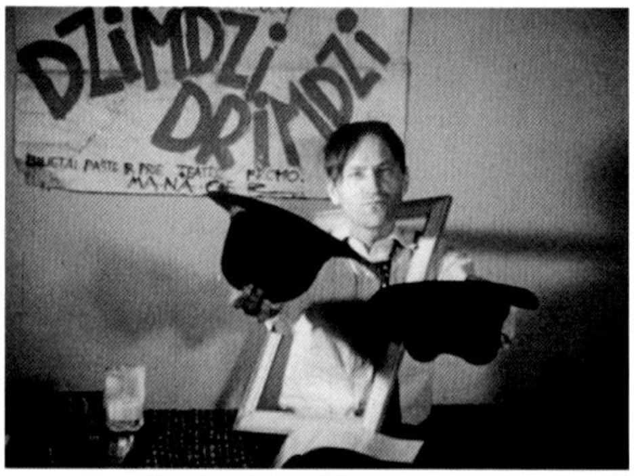

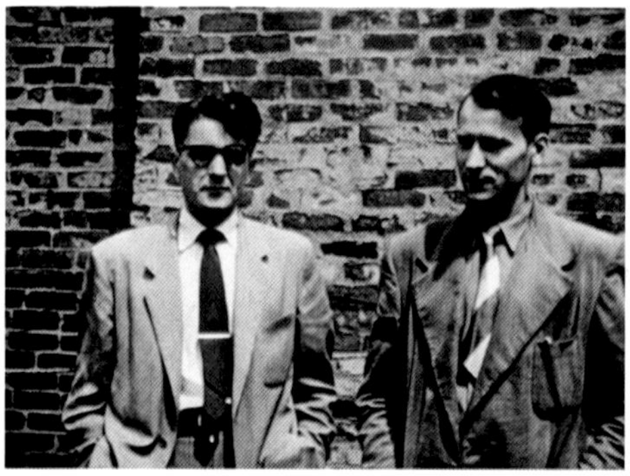

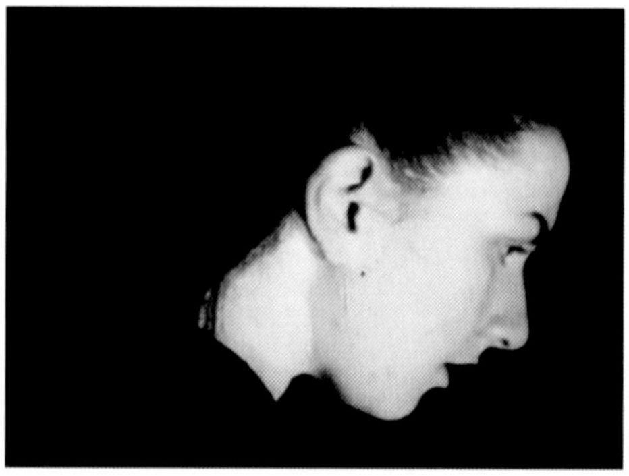

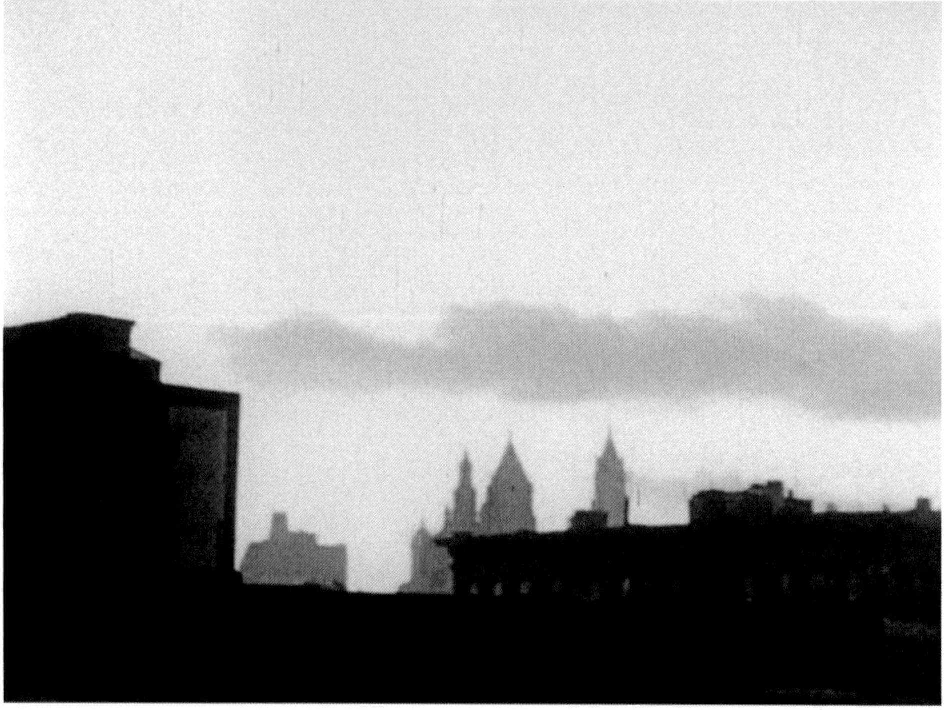

LIFE ON
13TH ST

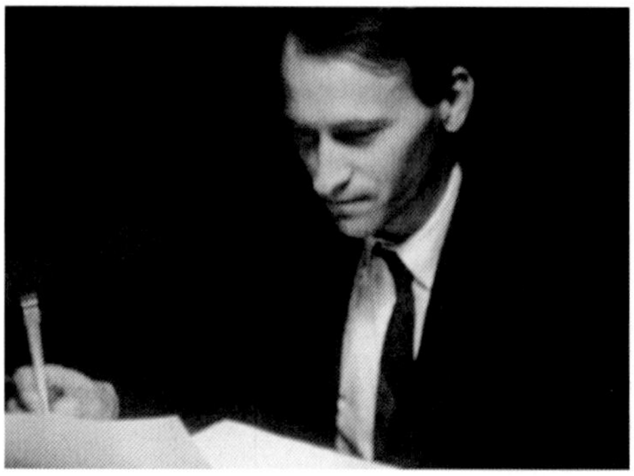

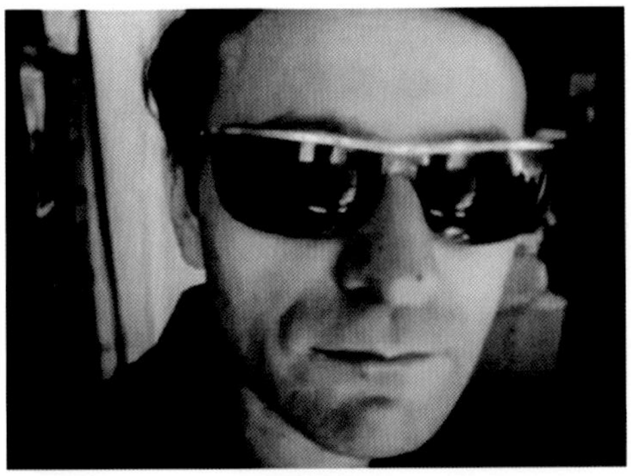
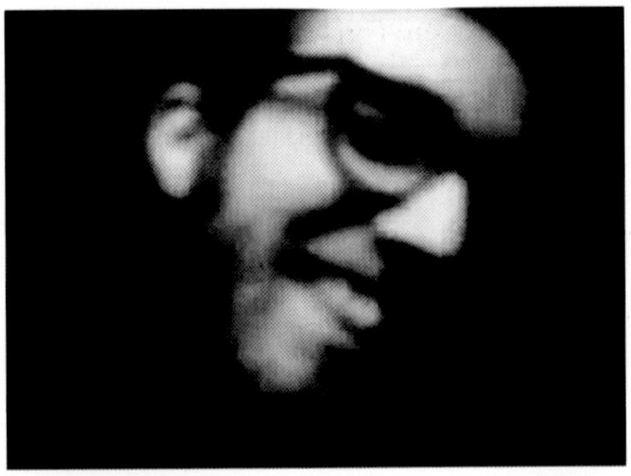
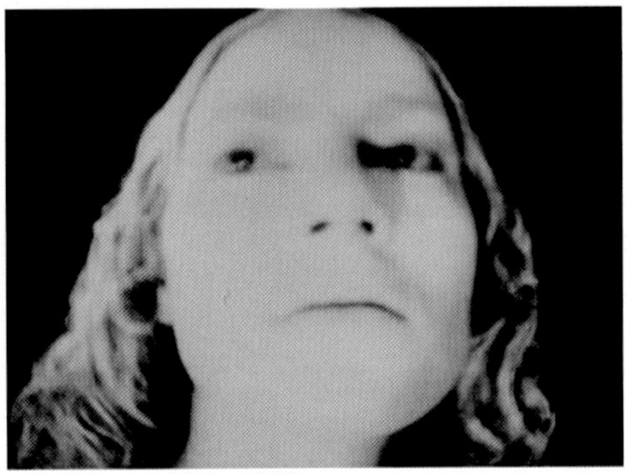
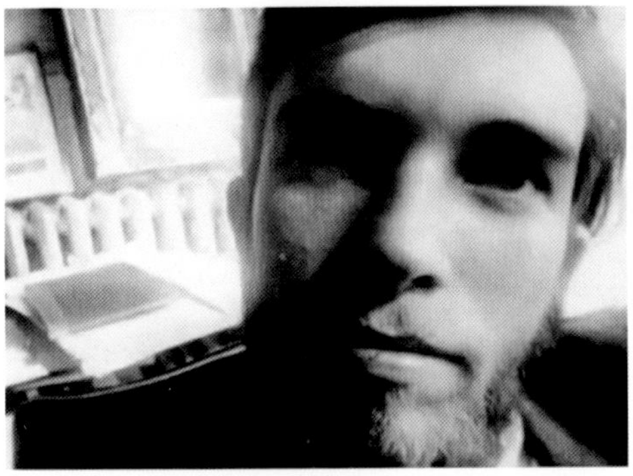
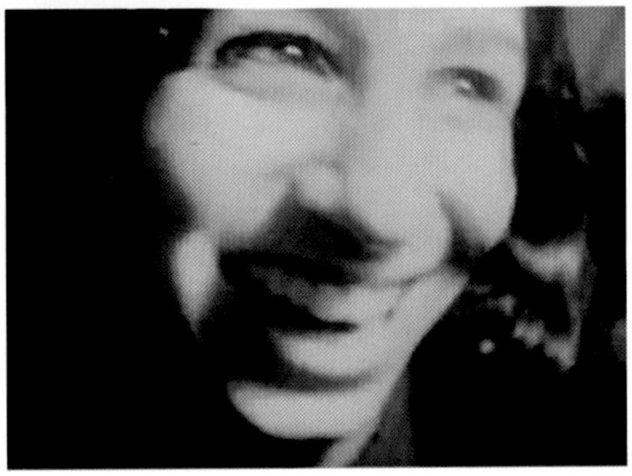
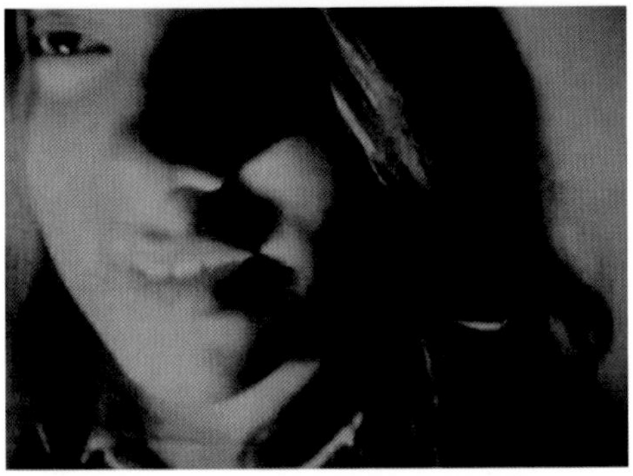
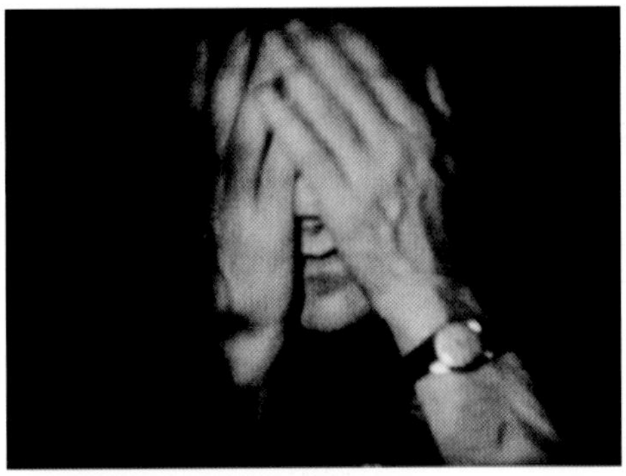
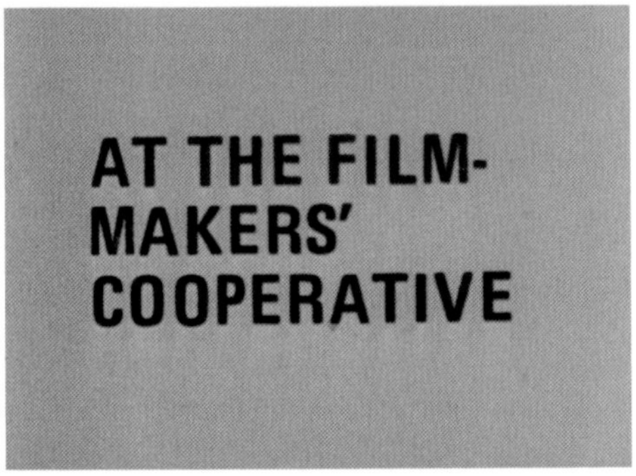

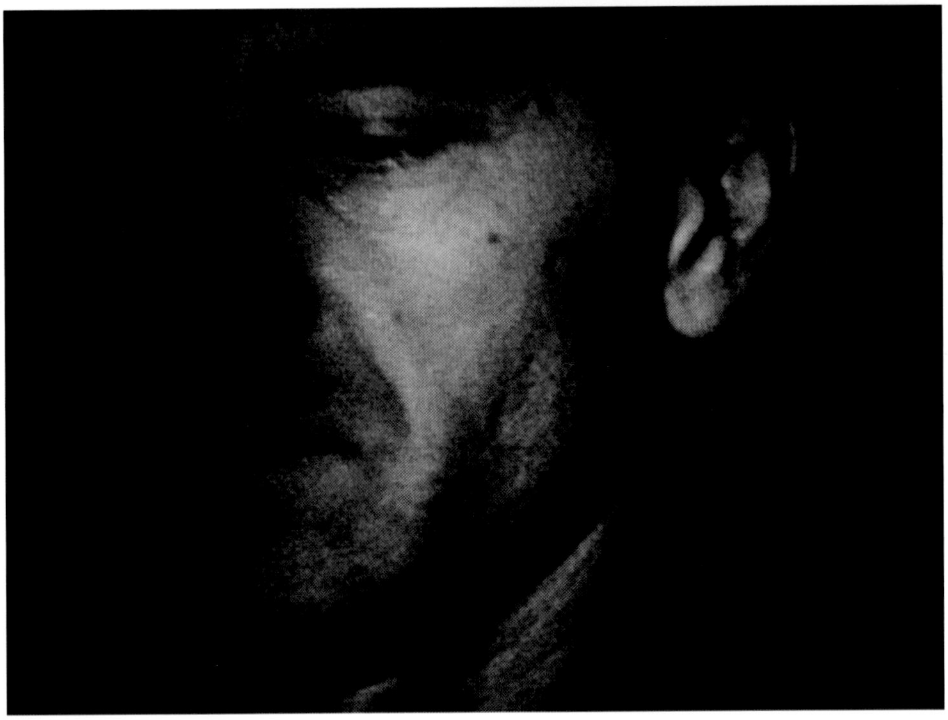
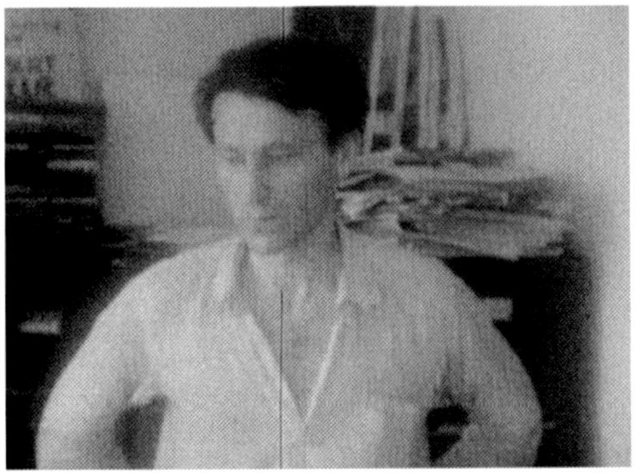

 FILMS COLOR, BLACK AND WHITE SOUND 180 MIN

NOTES FOR JEROME, 1978

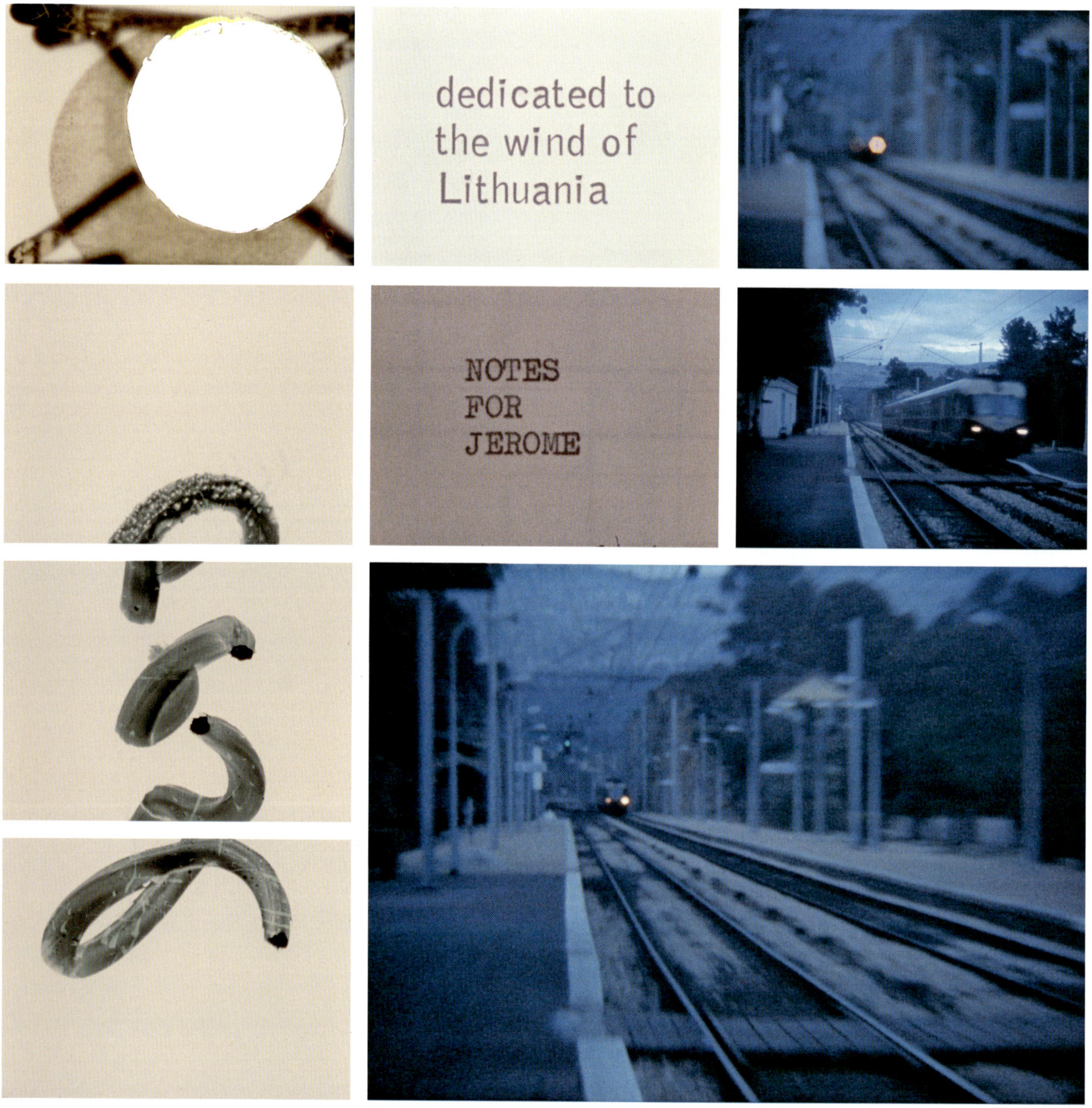

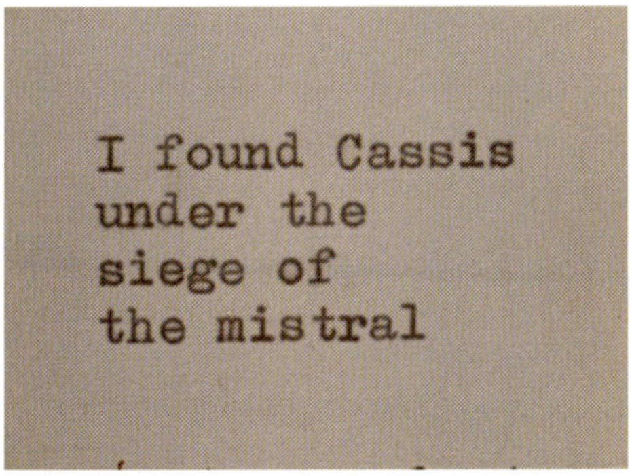
I found Cassis
under the
siege of
the mistral

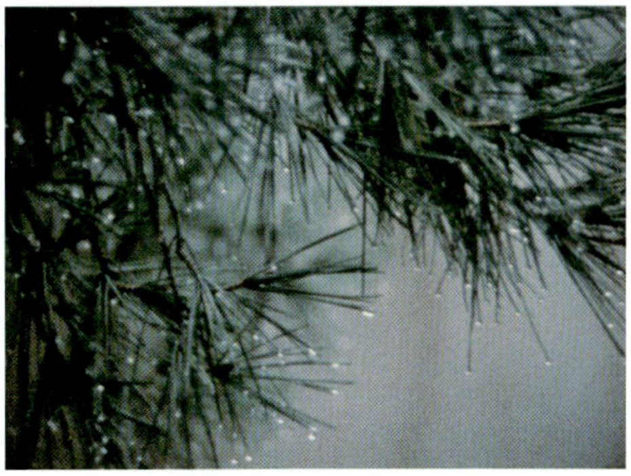

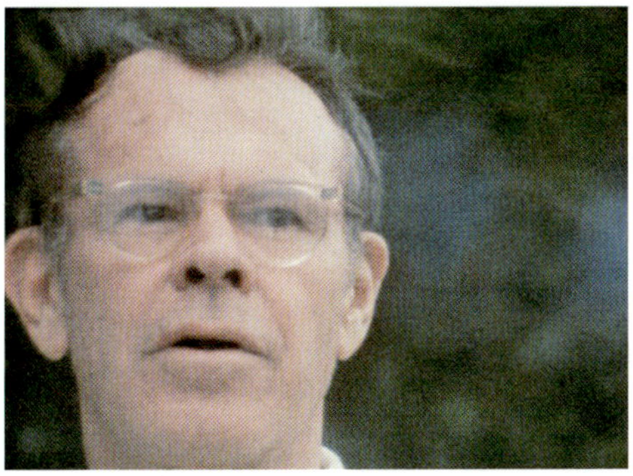

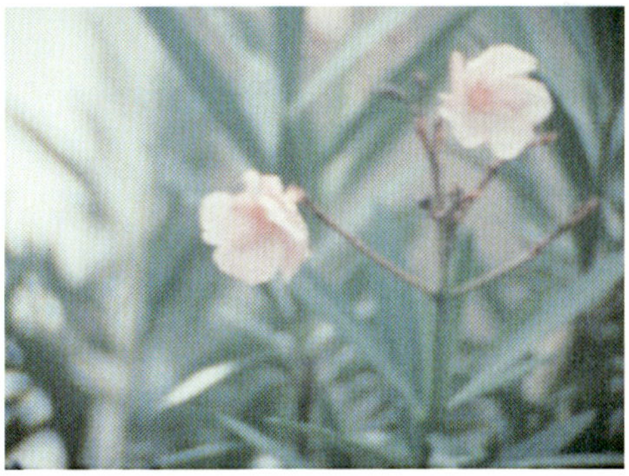

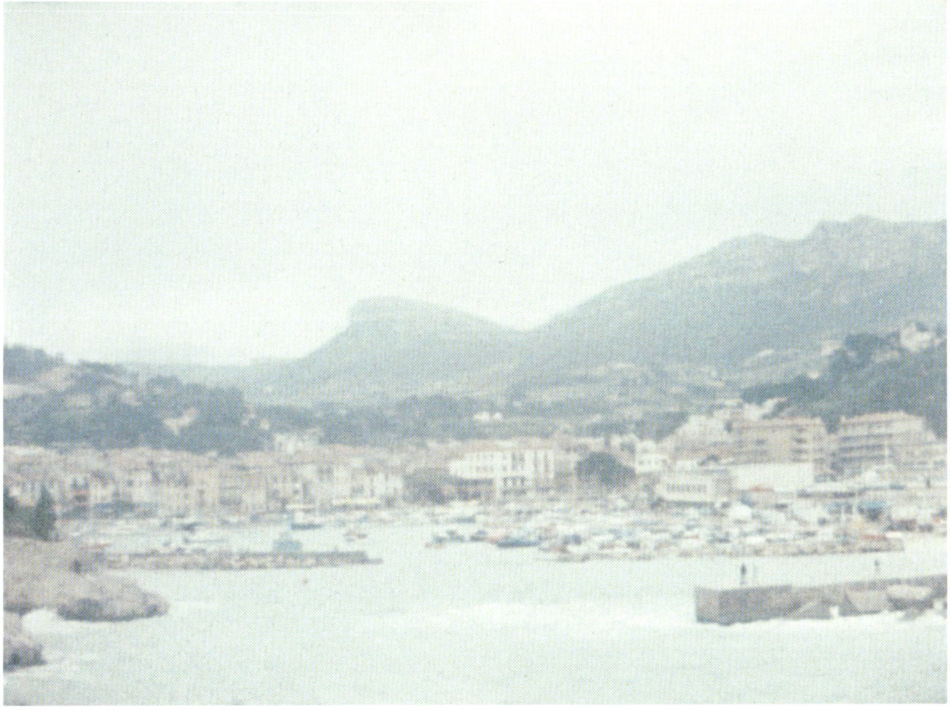

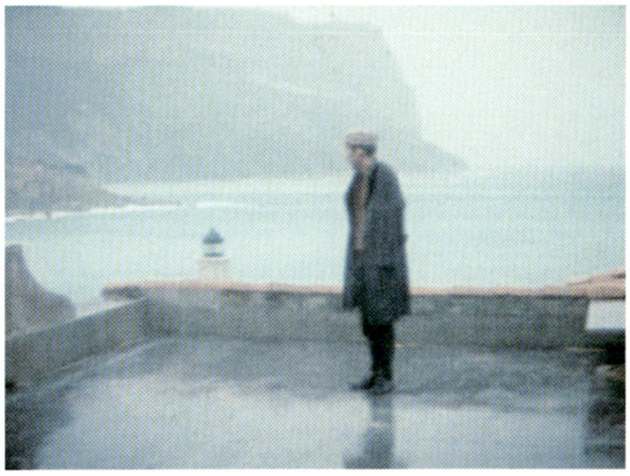

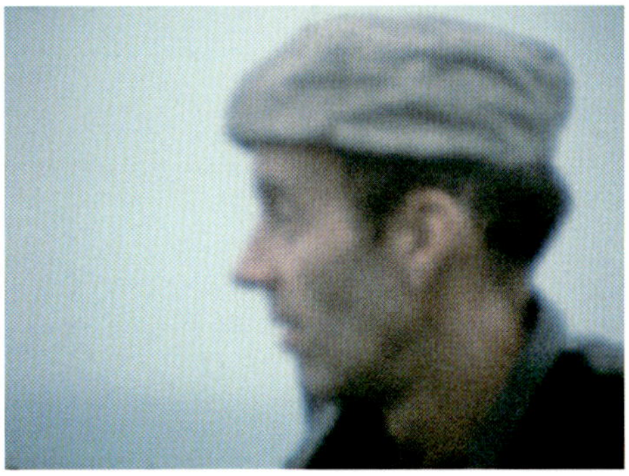

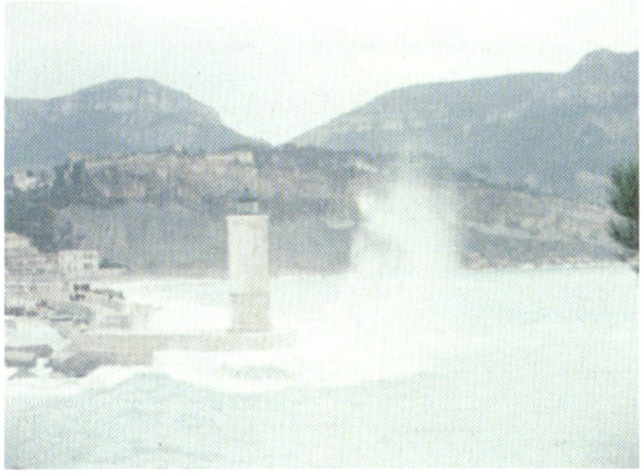

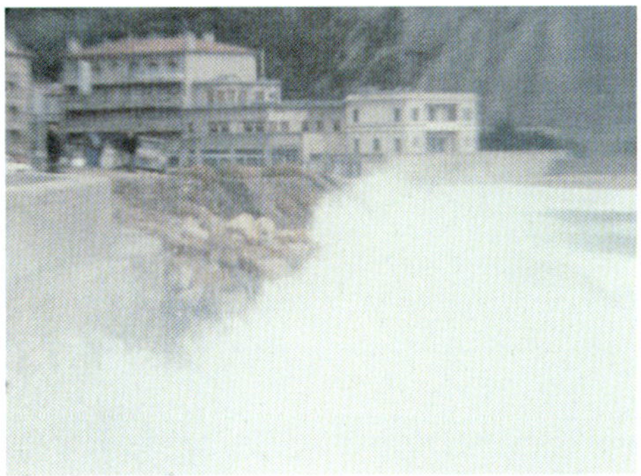

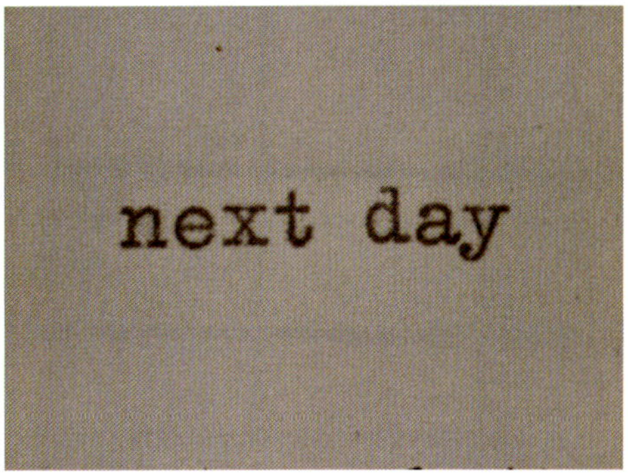
next day

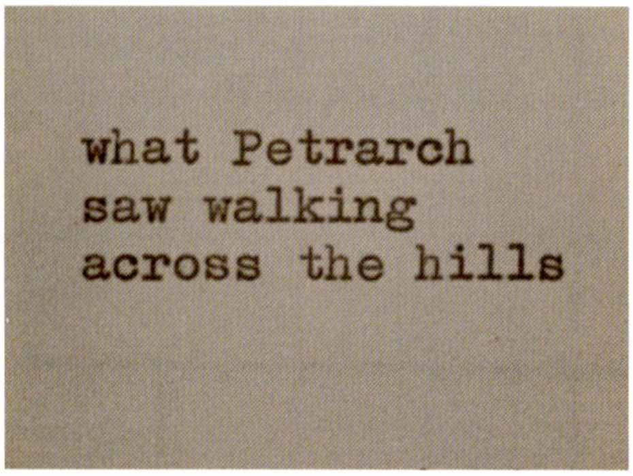
what Petrarch
saw walking
across the hills

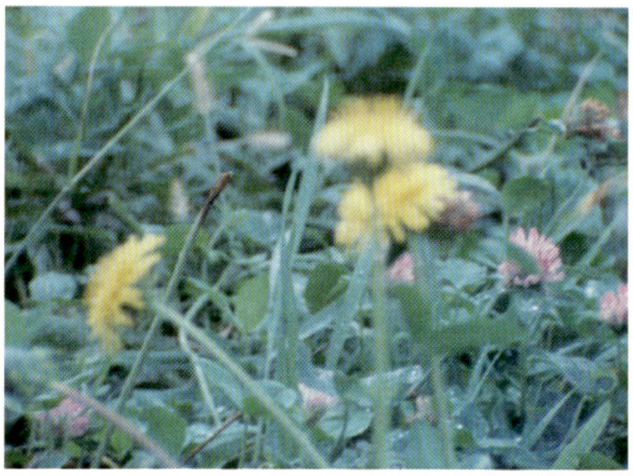

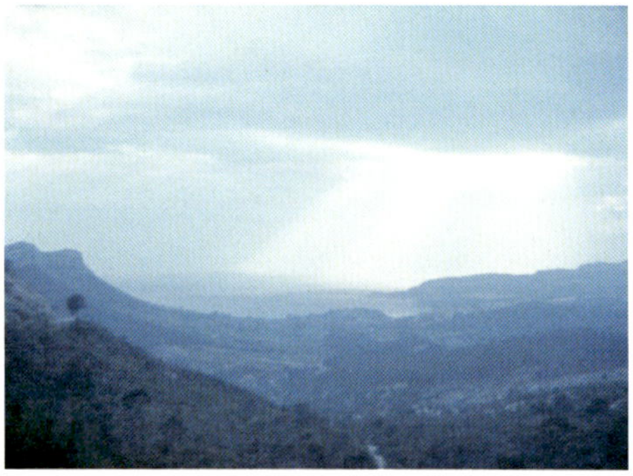

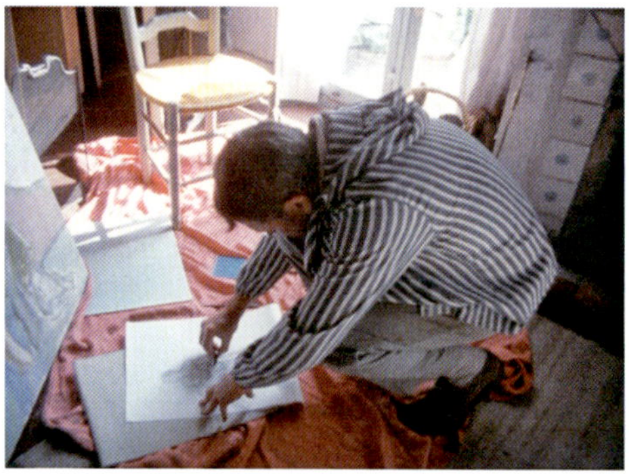

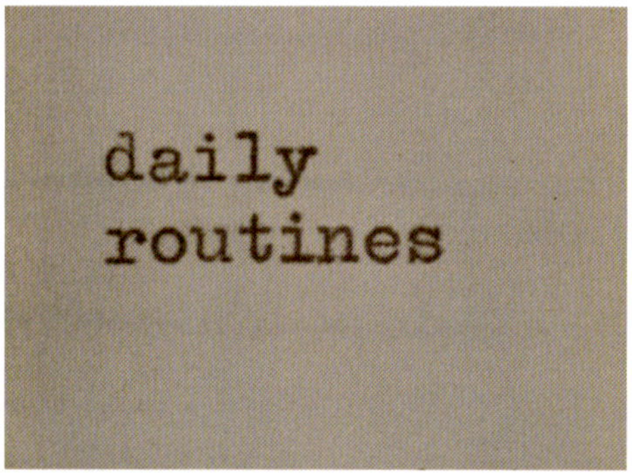
daily
routines

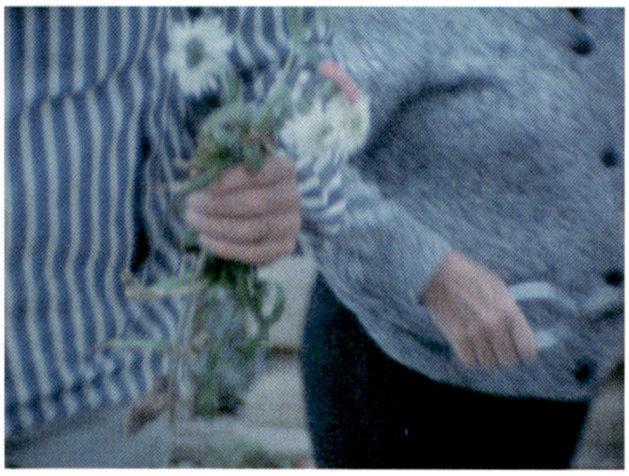

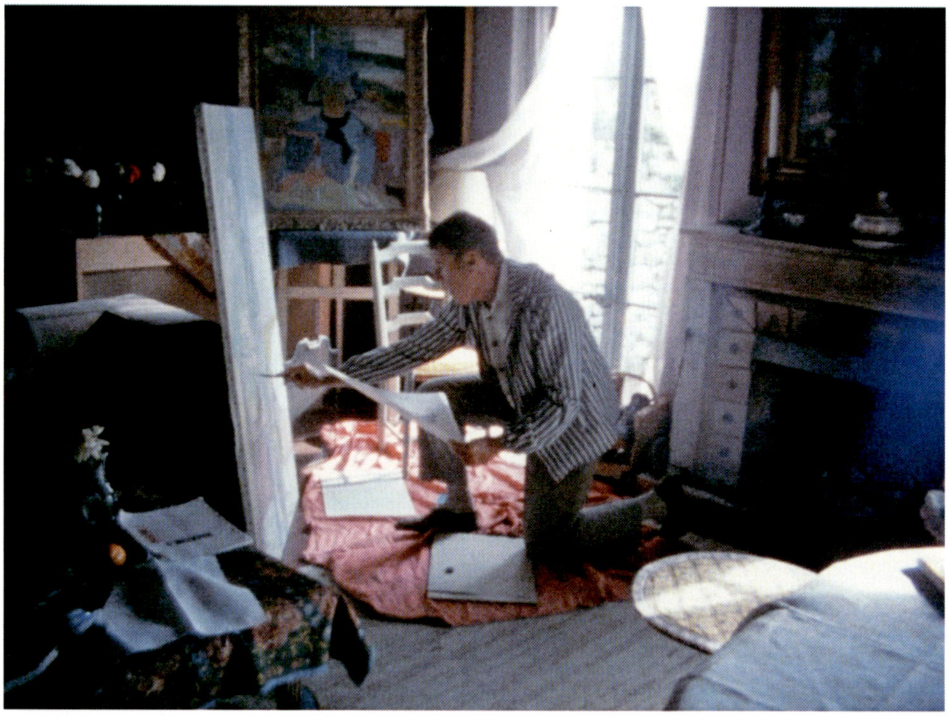

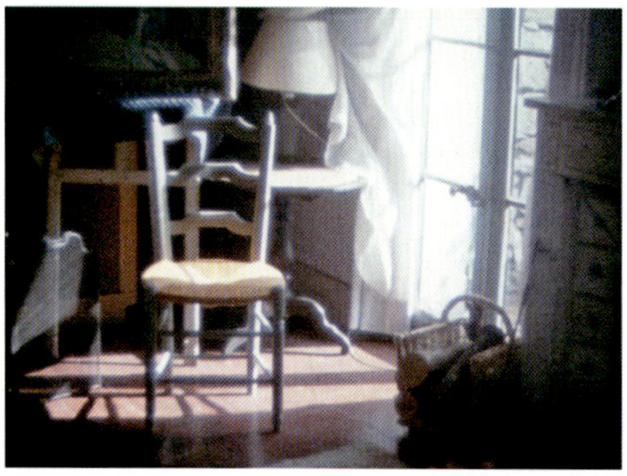

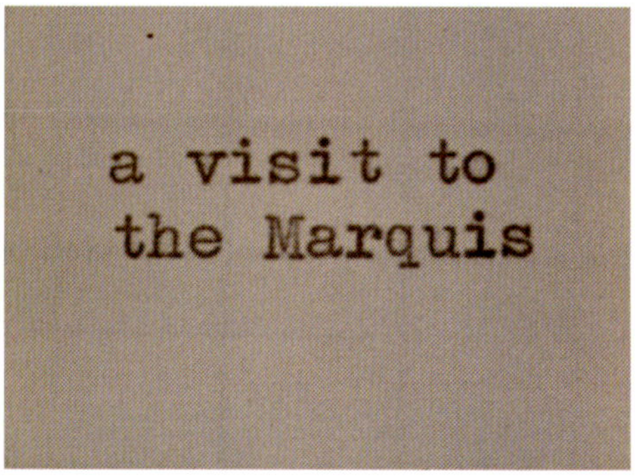
a visit to
the Marquis

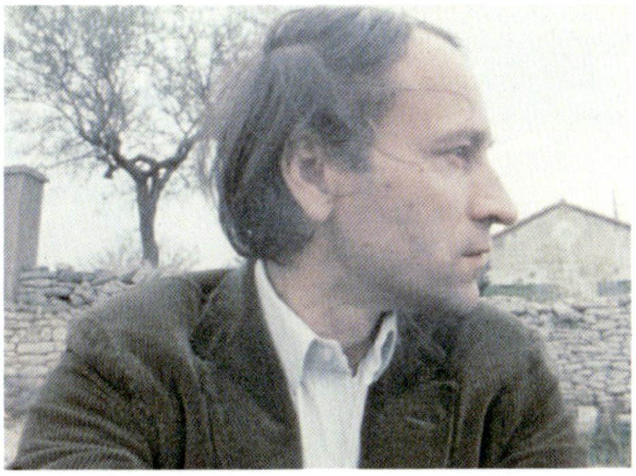
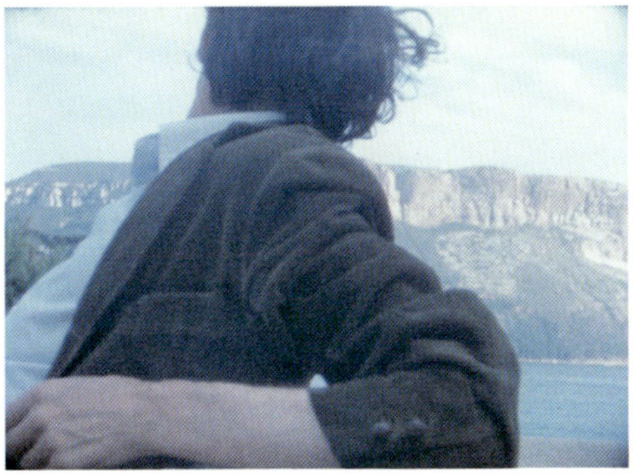
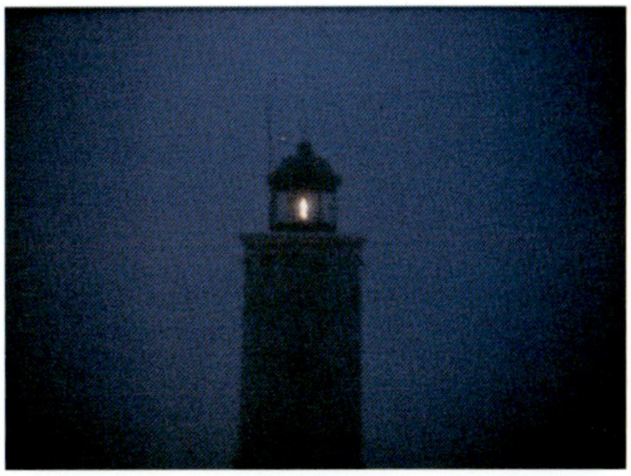
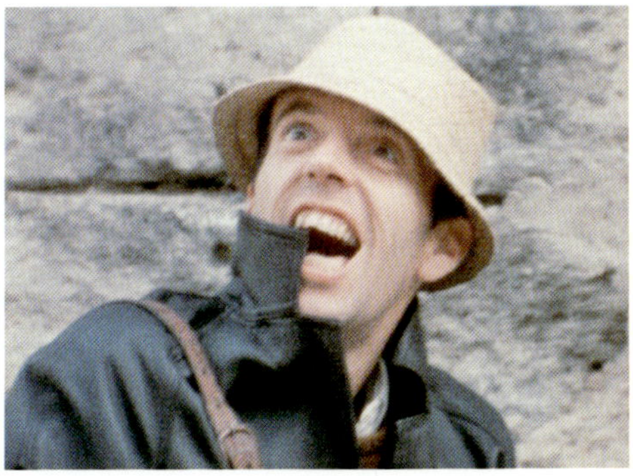
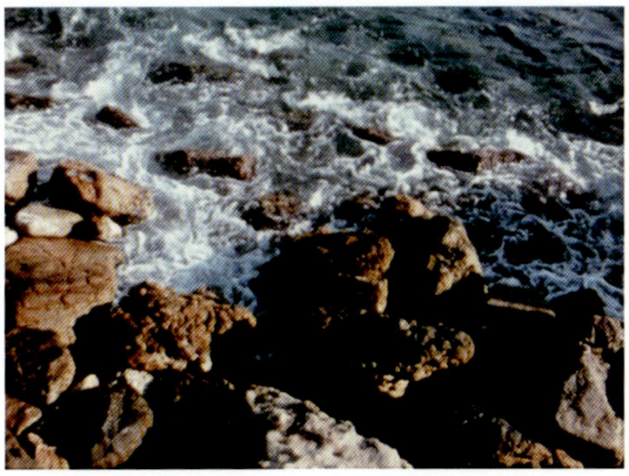
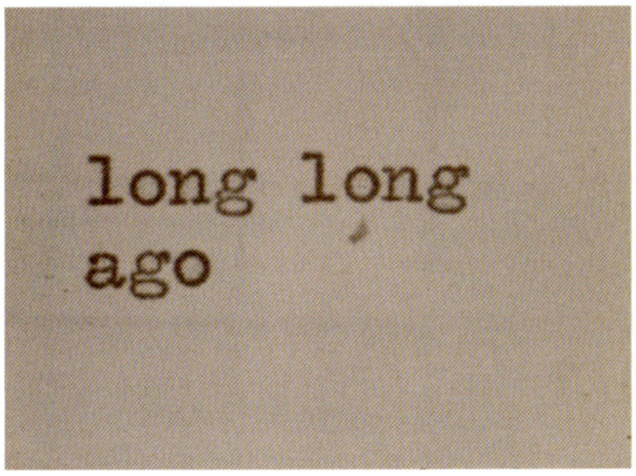
long long
ago
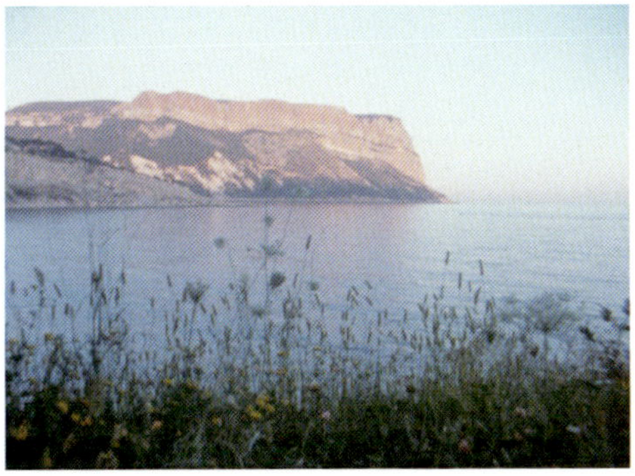
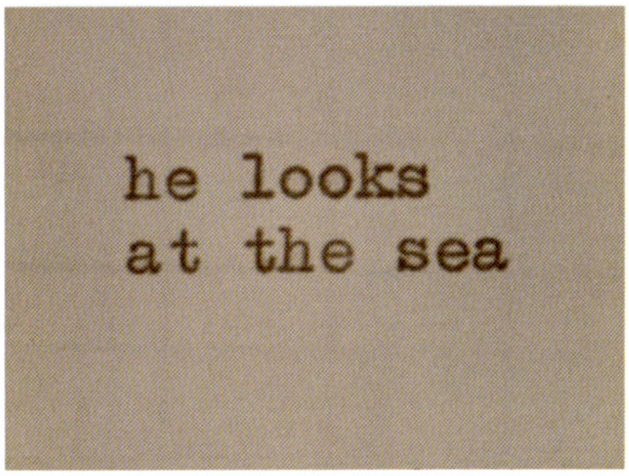
he looks
at the sea
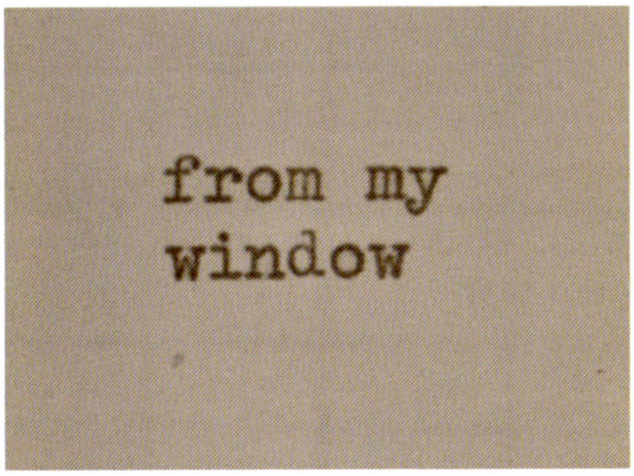
from my
window
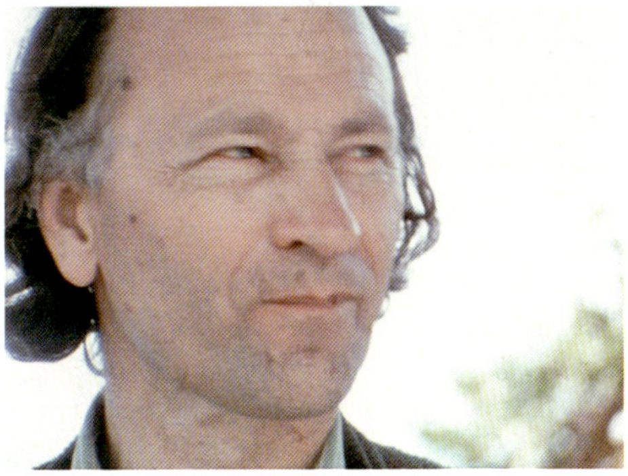
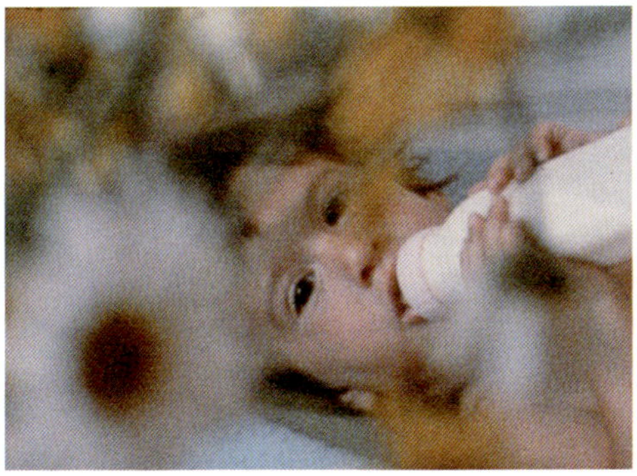
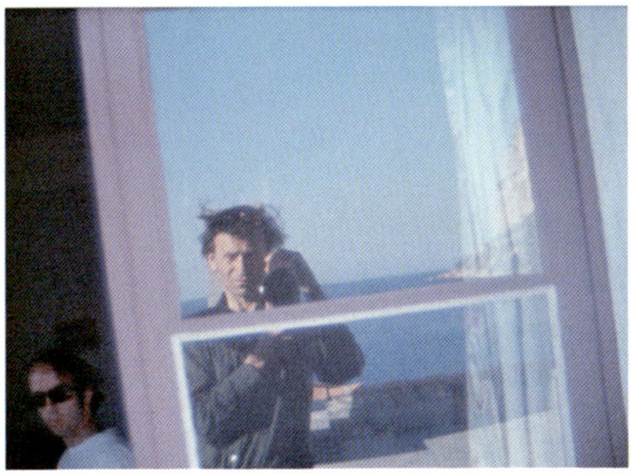
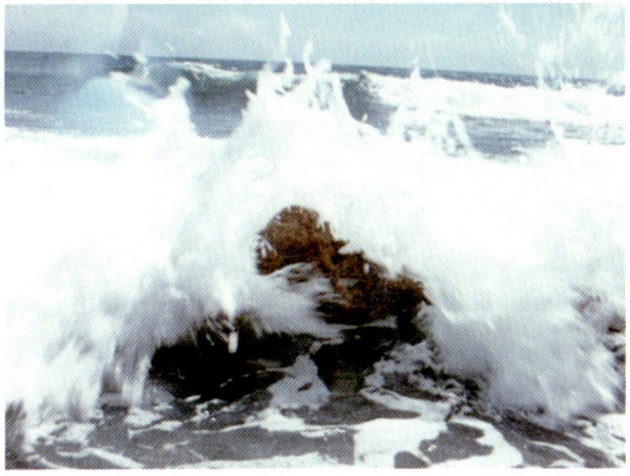

SELF PORTRAIT, 1980

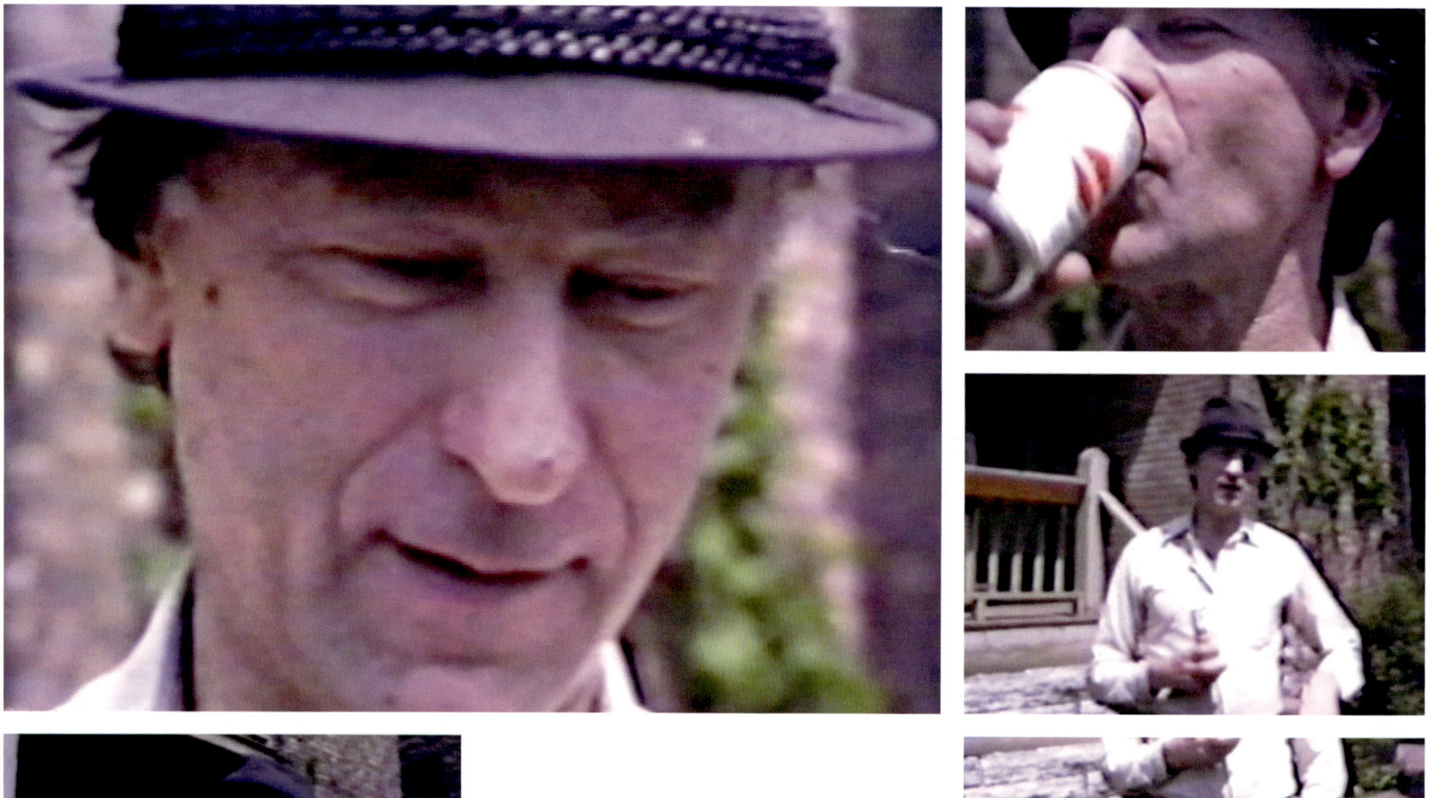

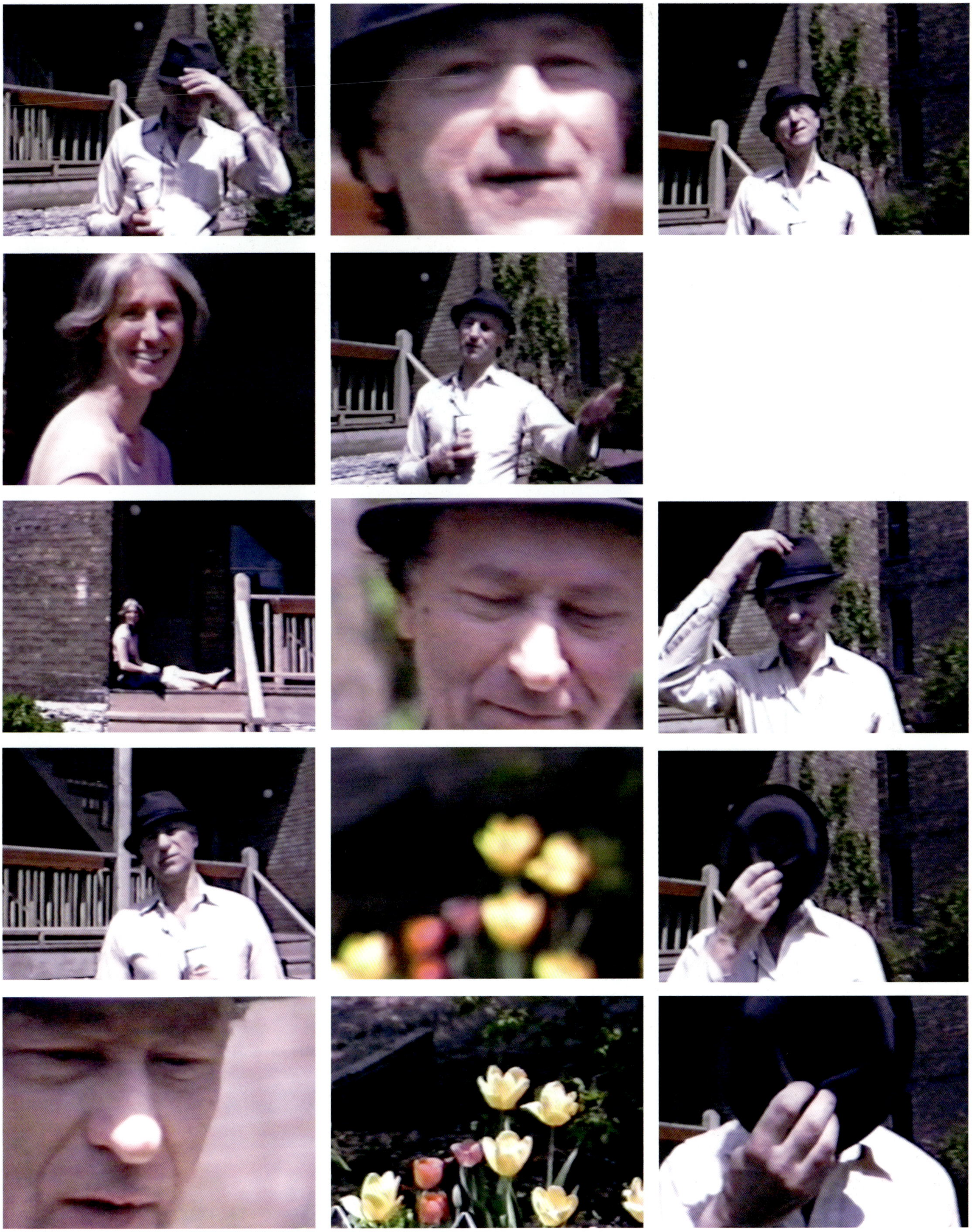

 FILMS COLOR SOUND 20 MIN

SCENES FROM THE LIFE OF ANDY WARHOL, 1990

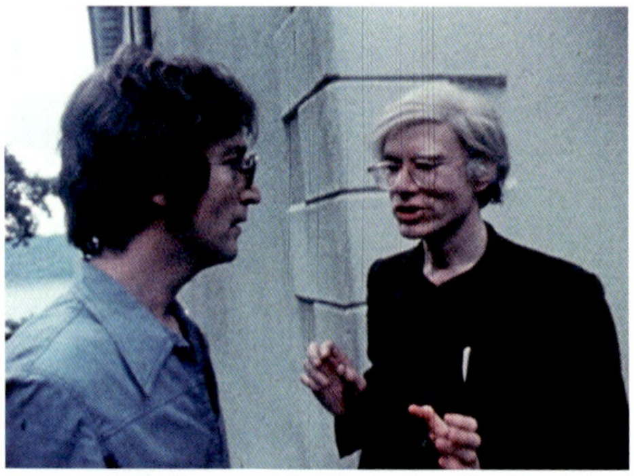

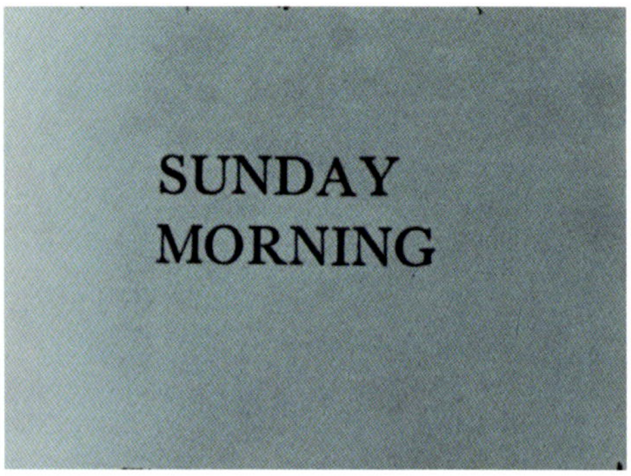

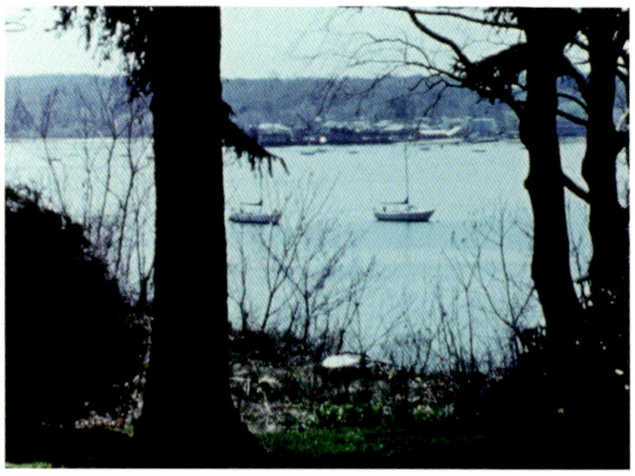

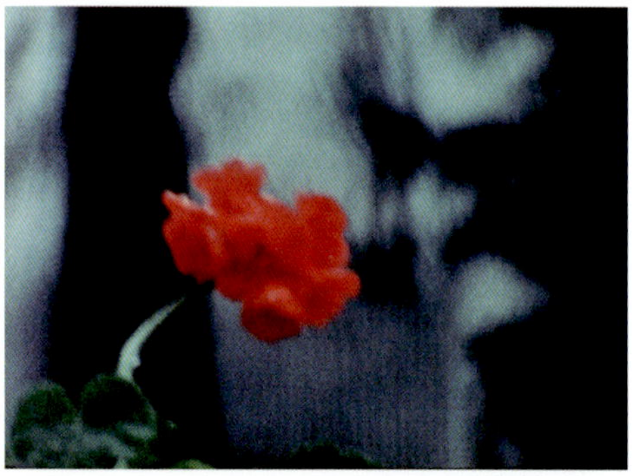

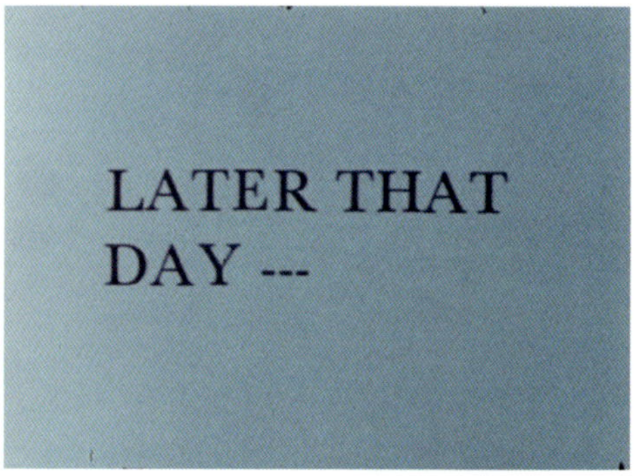

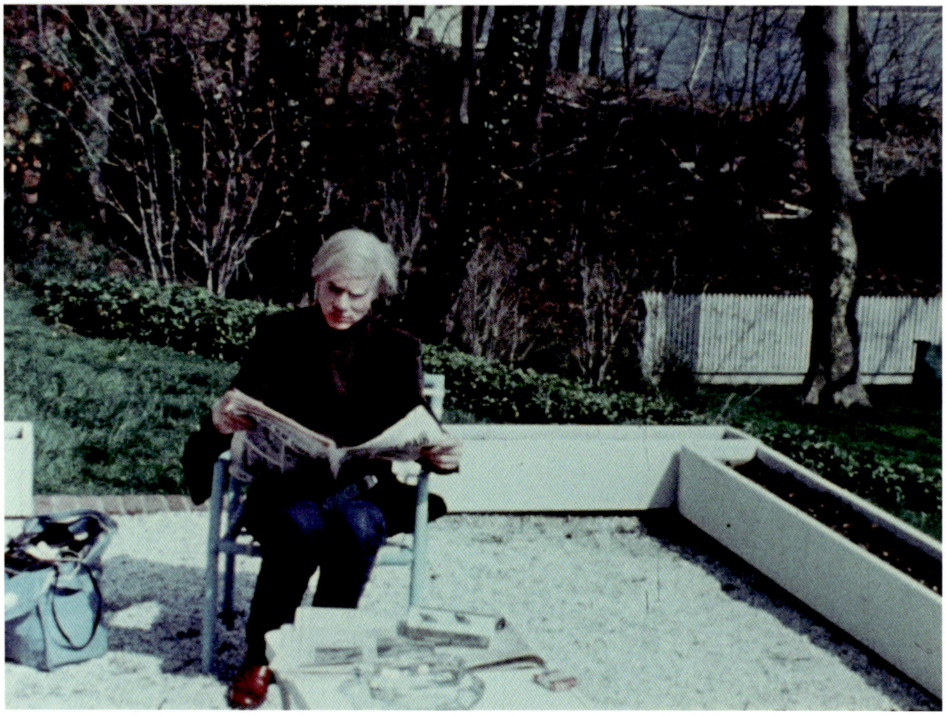

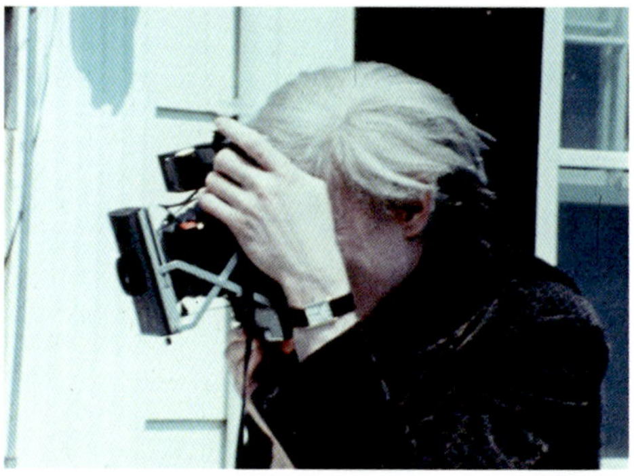

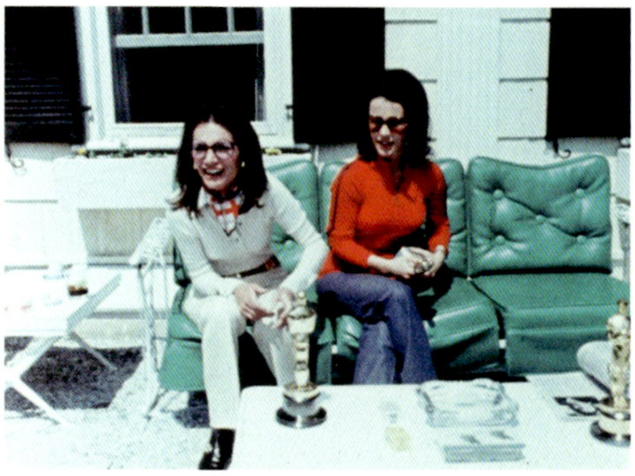

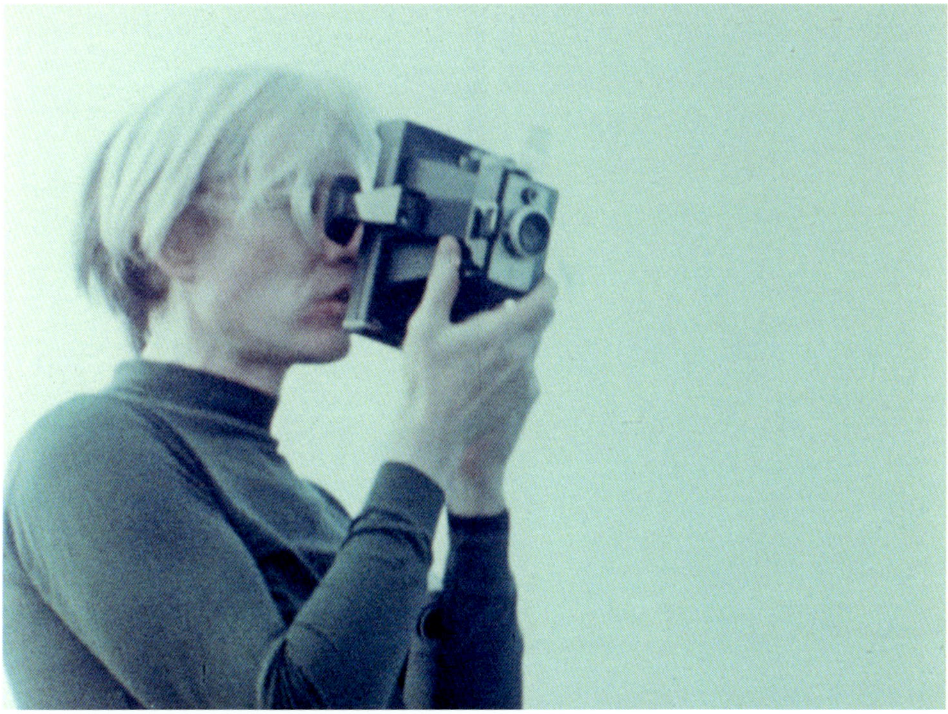

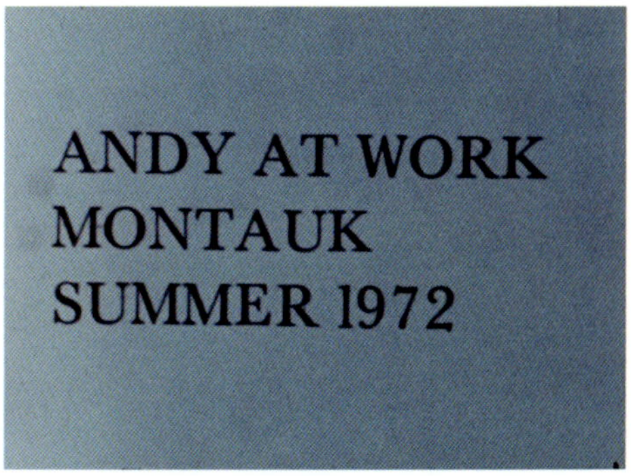

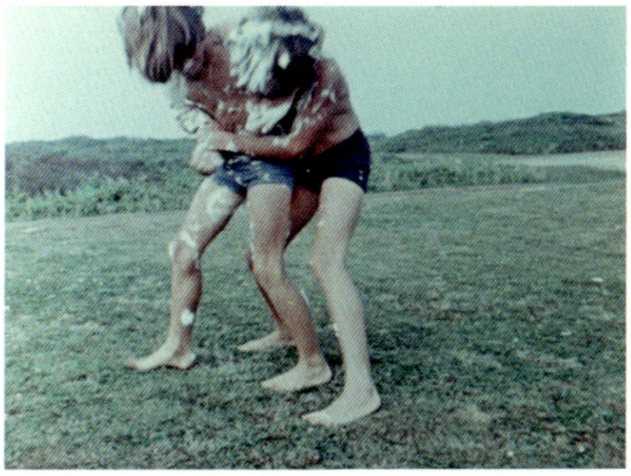

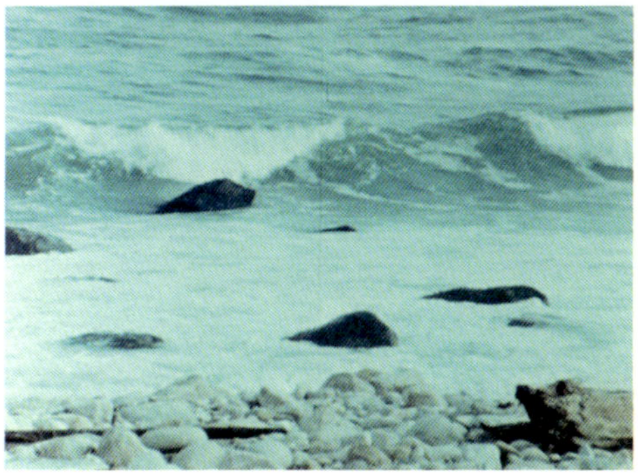

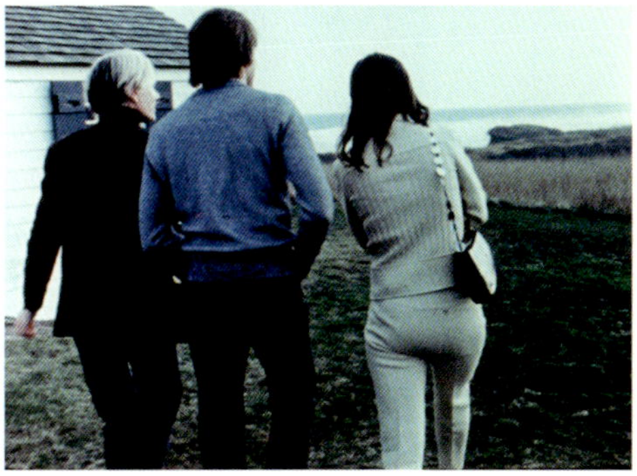

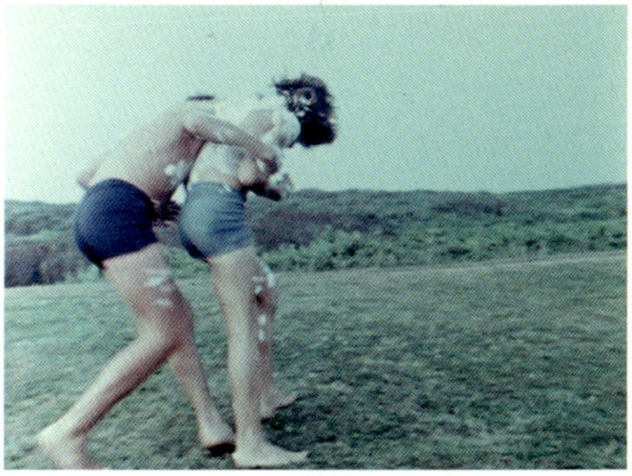

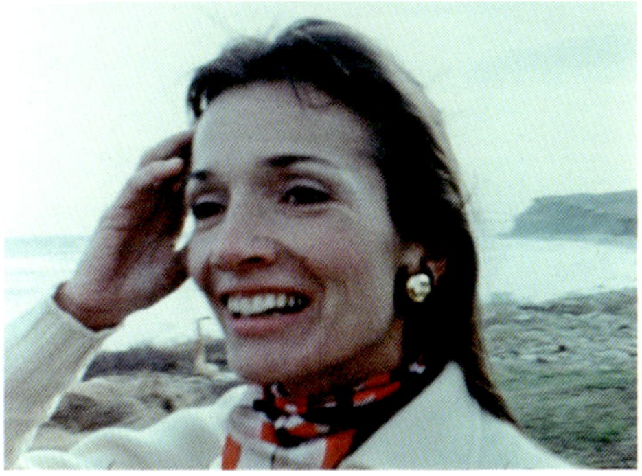

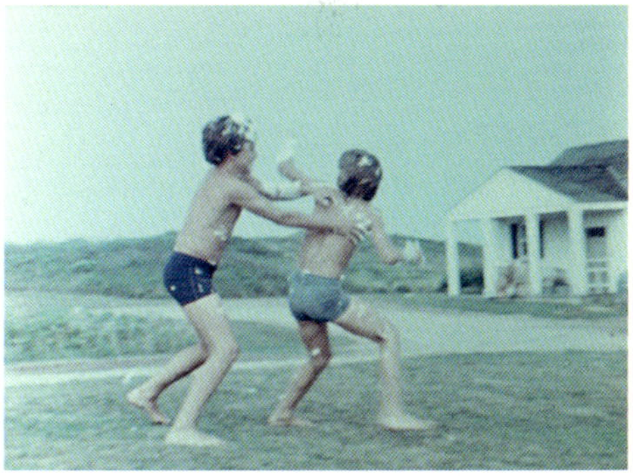

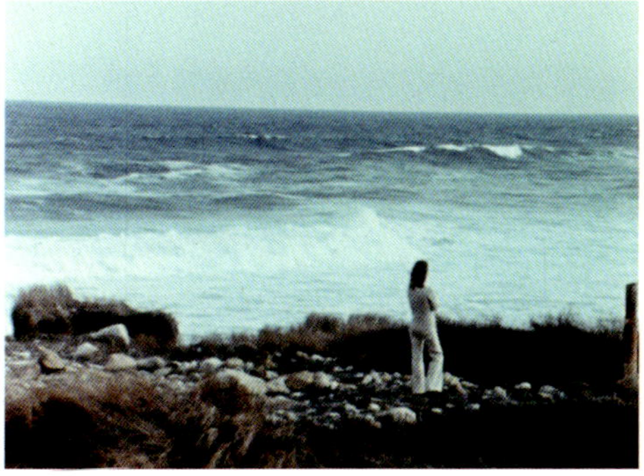

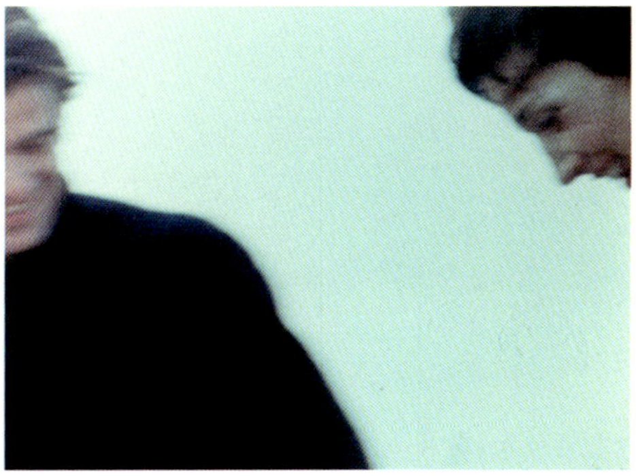

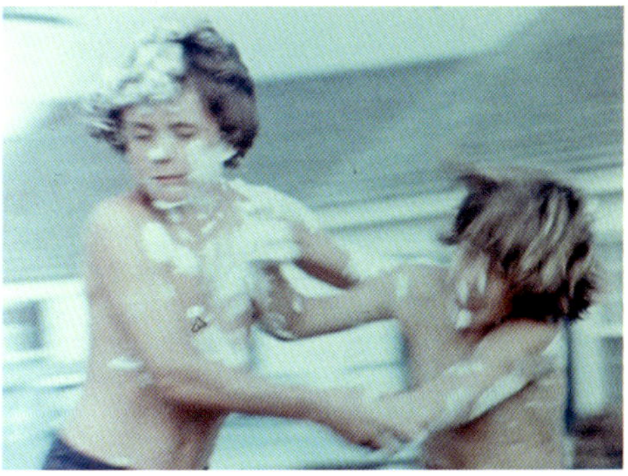

147 FILMS COLOR SOUND 35 MIN

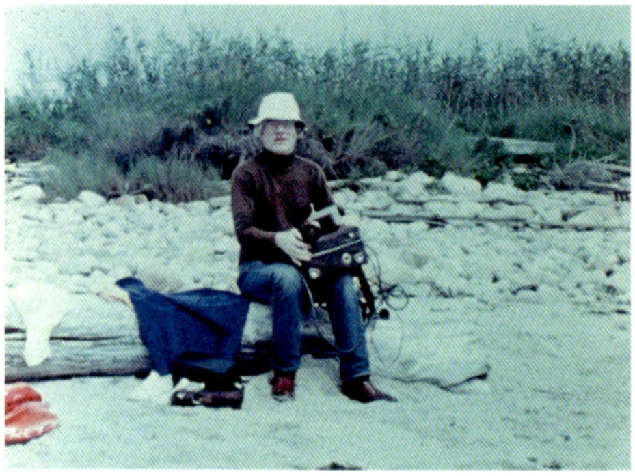

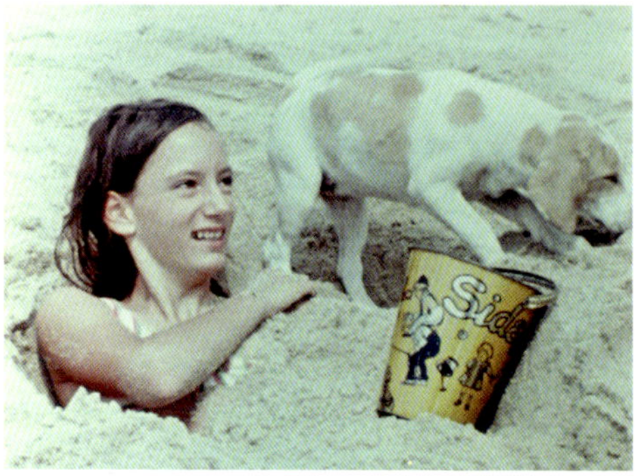

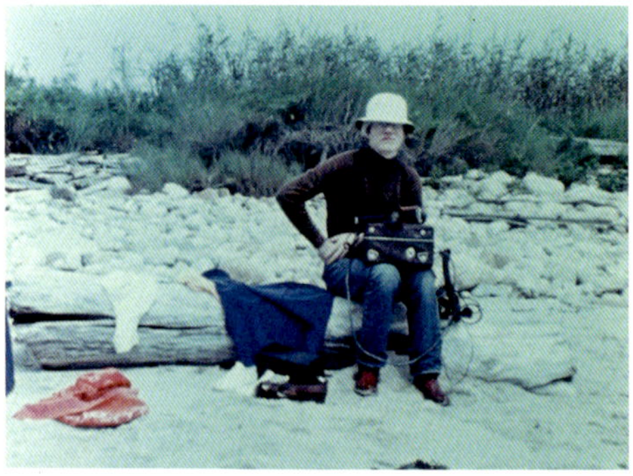

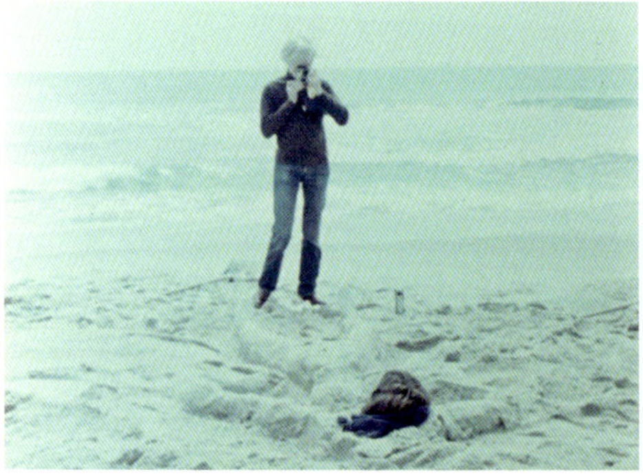

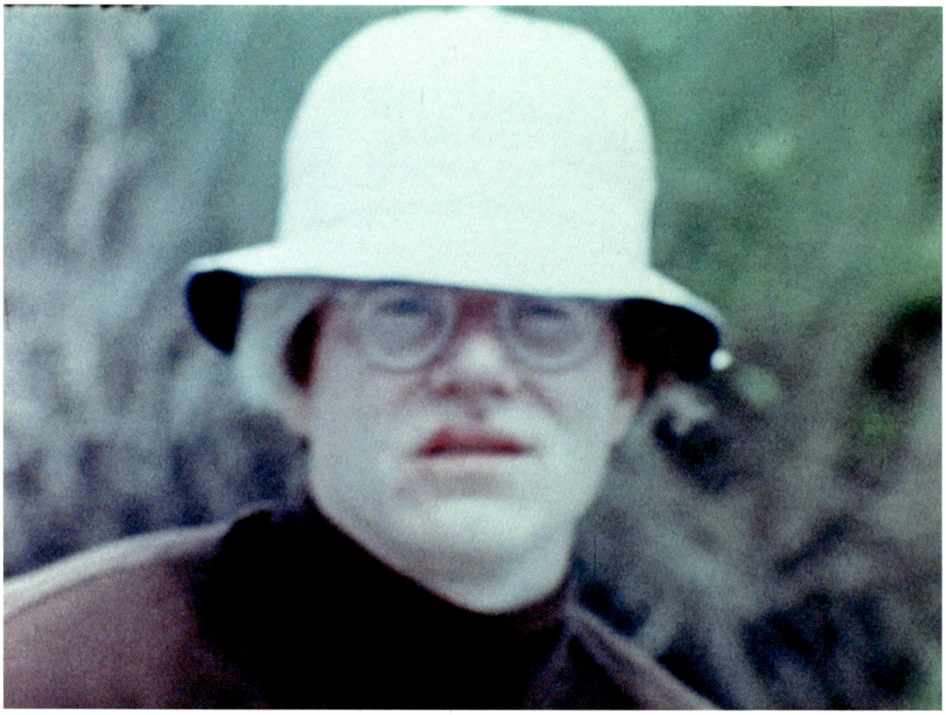

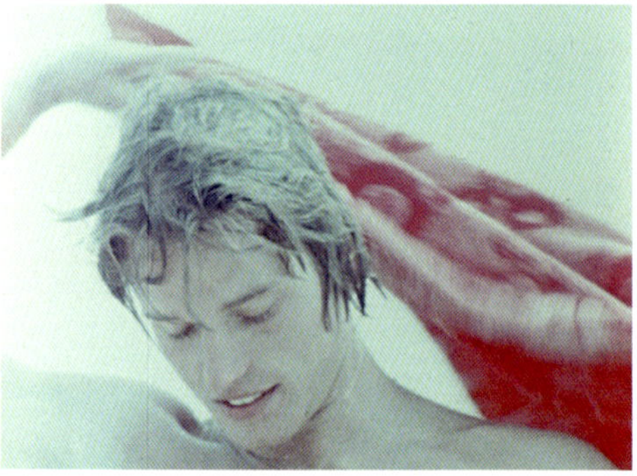

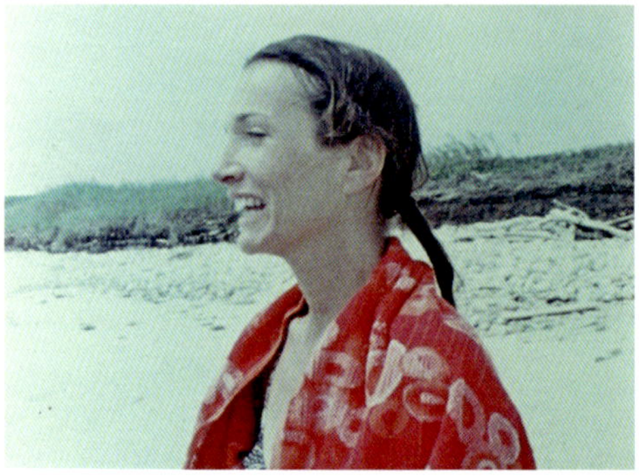

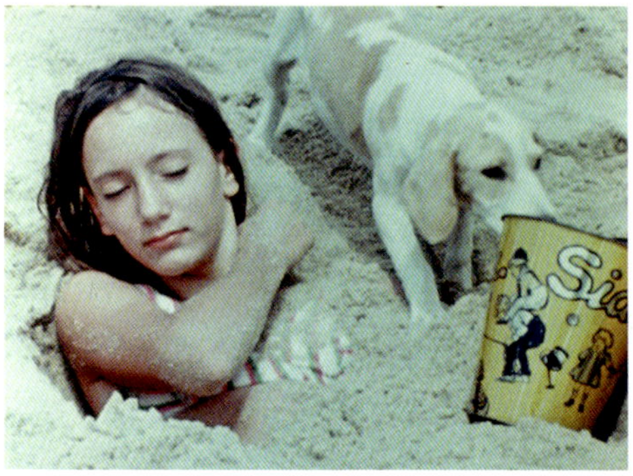

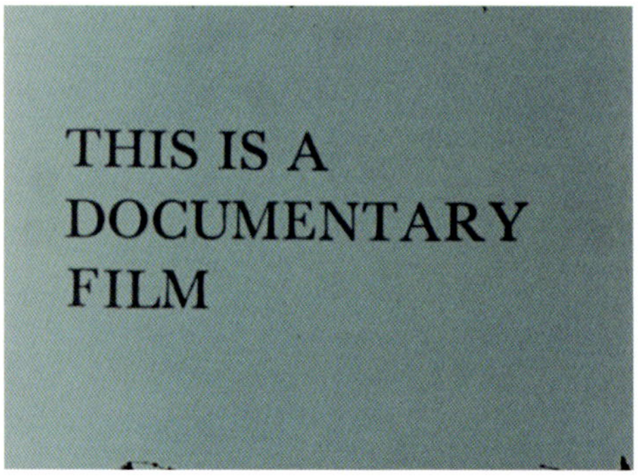

SCENES FROM THE LIFE OF ANDY WARHOL 16MM 1990

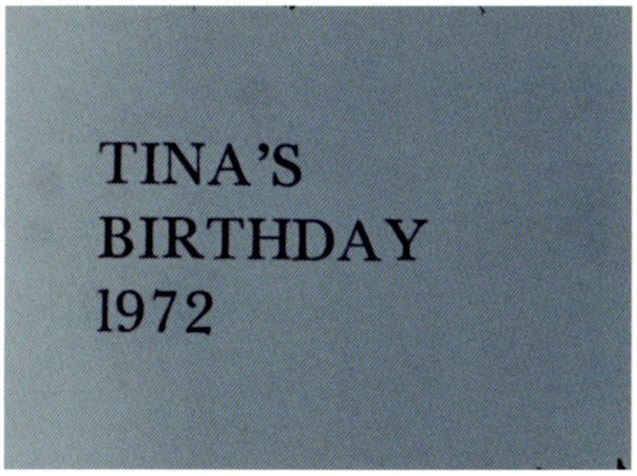

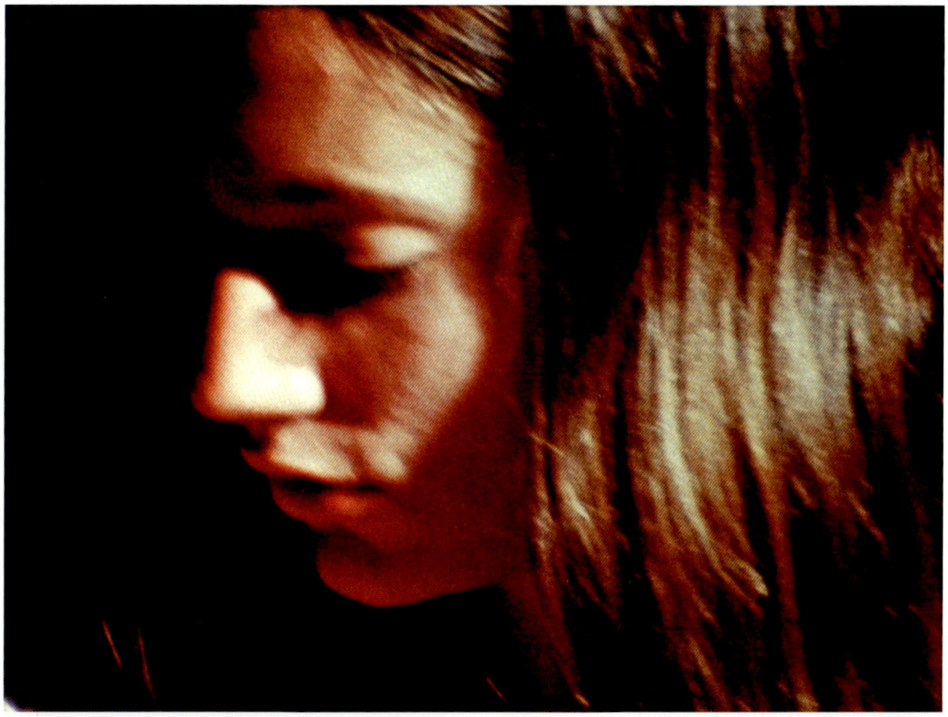

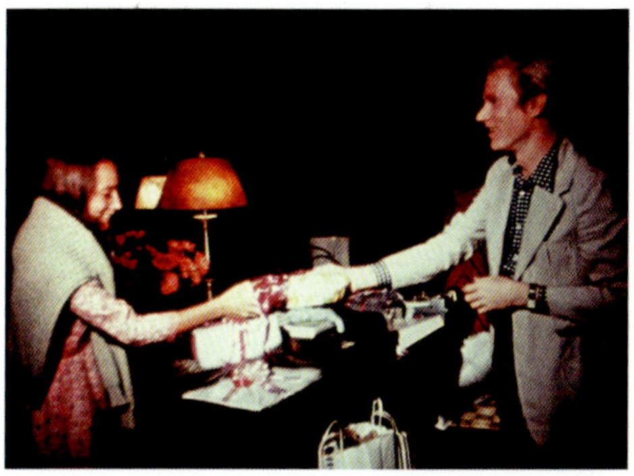

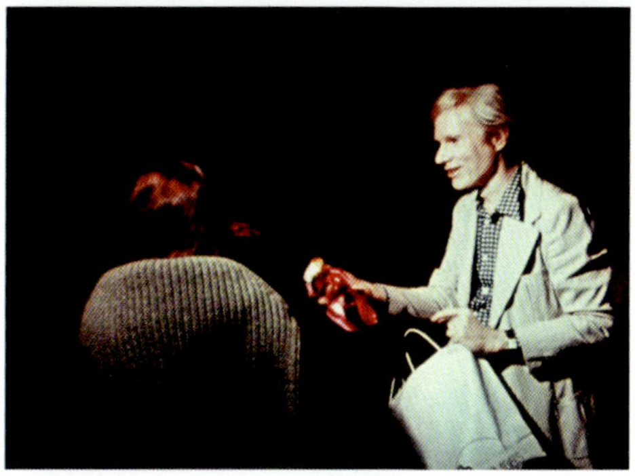

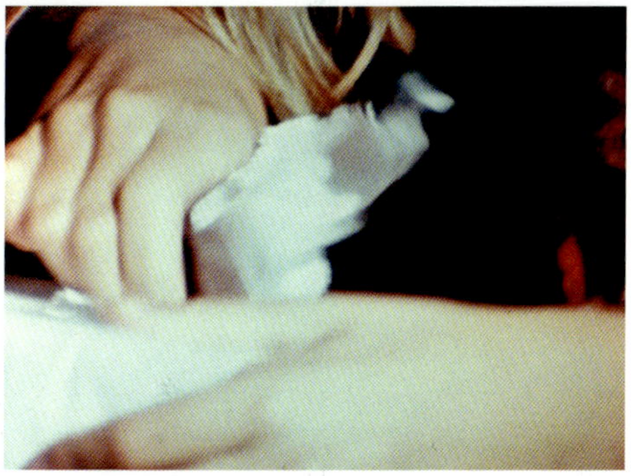

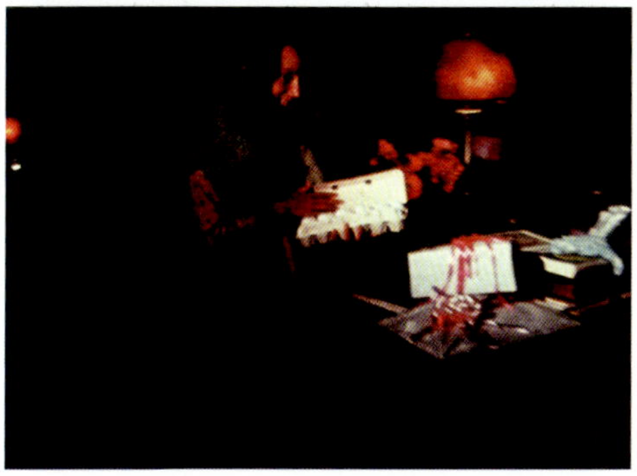

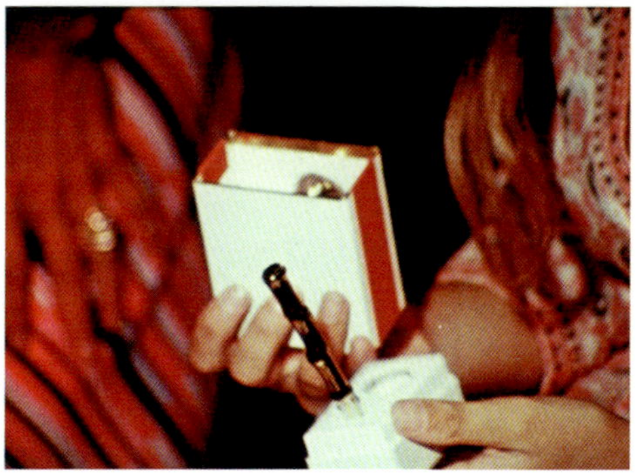

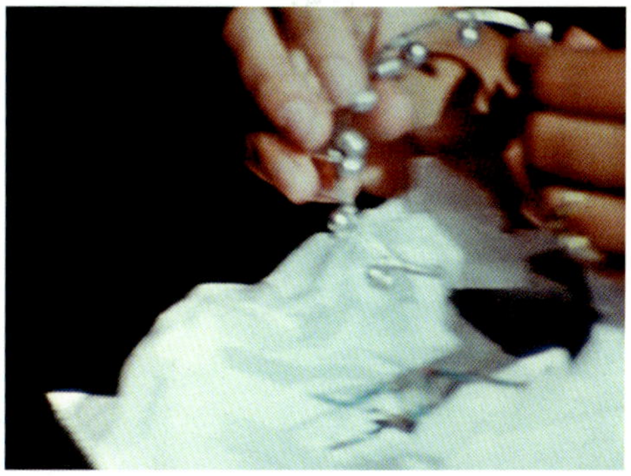

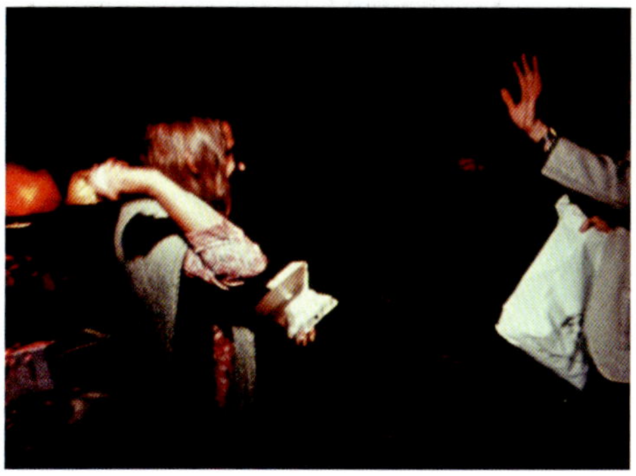

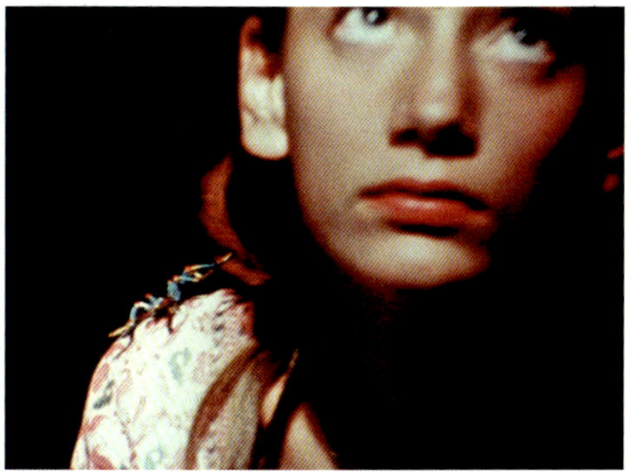

FILMS COLOR SOUND 35 MIN

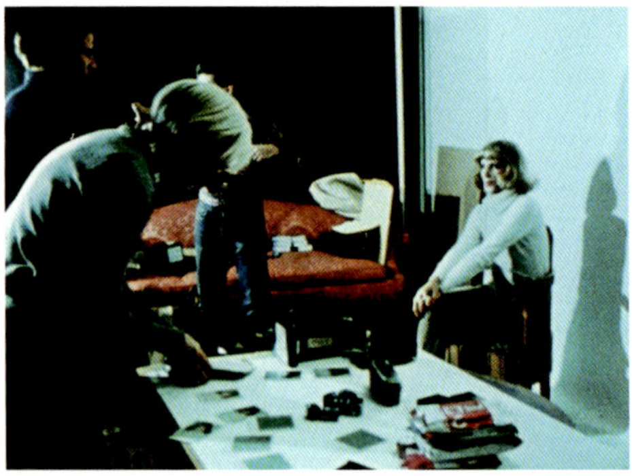

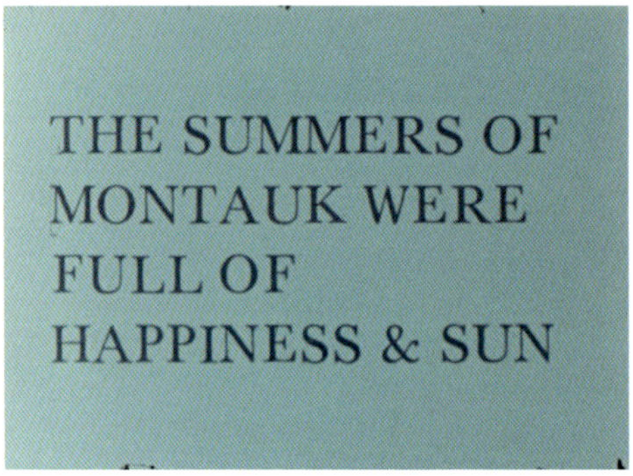
THE SUMMERS OF
MONTAUK WERE
FULL OF
HAPPINESS & SUN

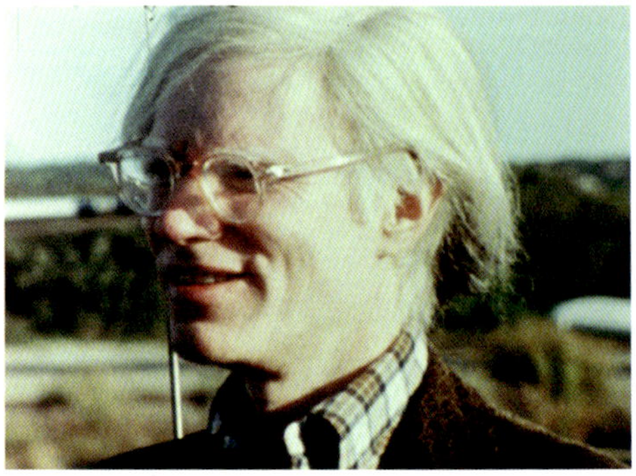

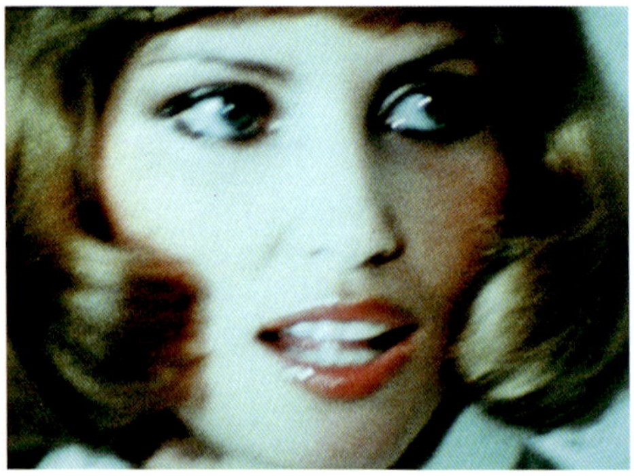

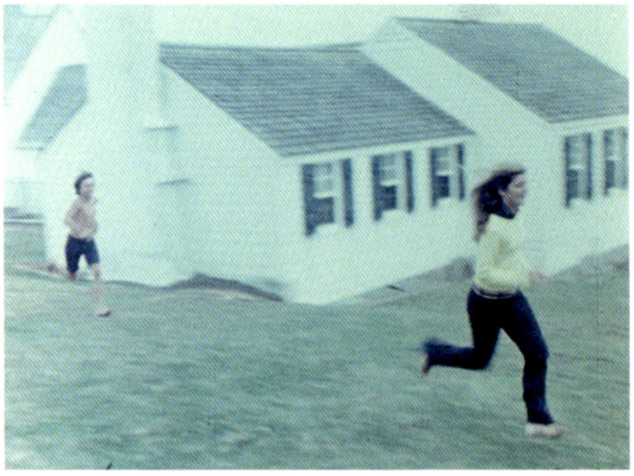

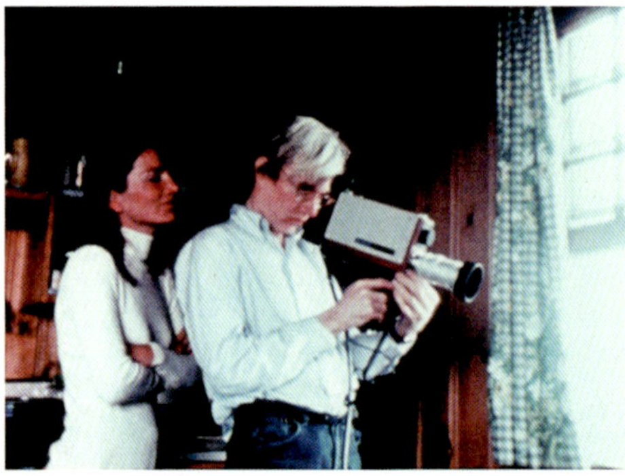

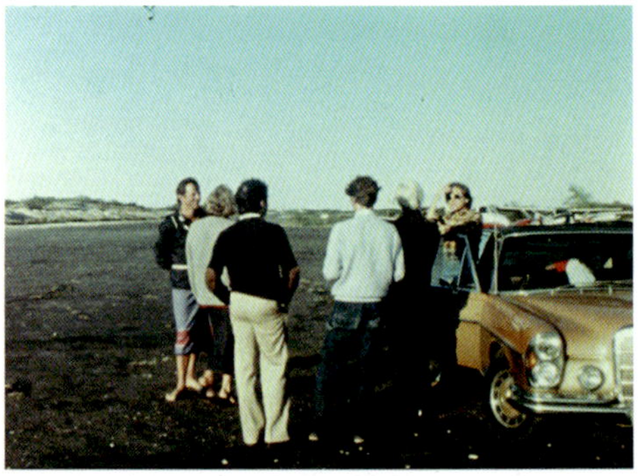

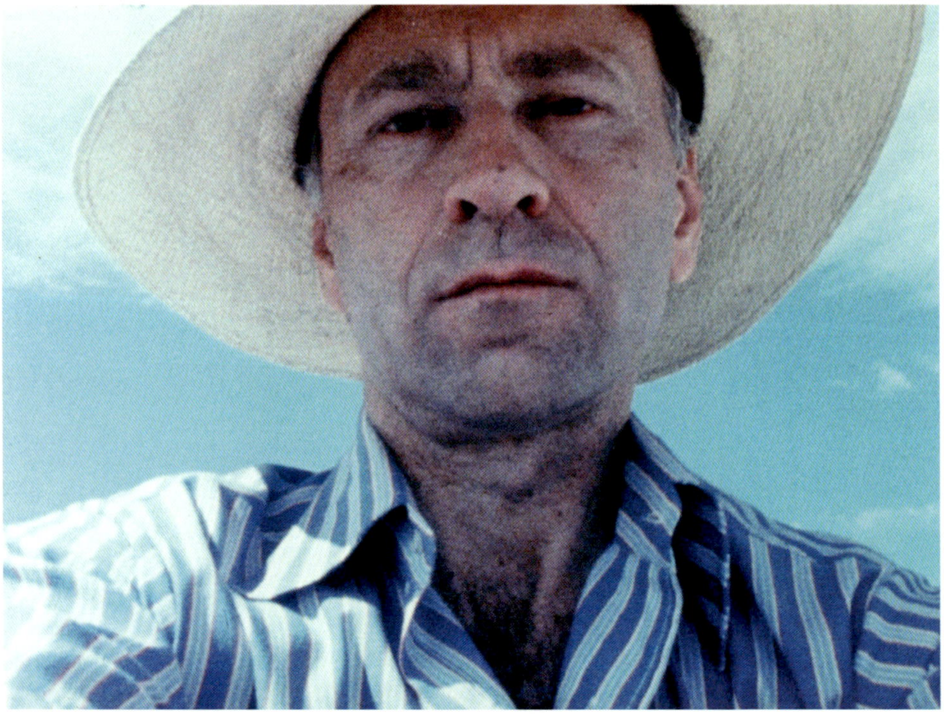

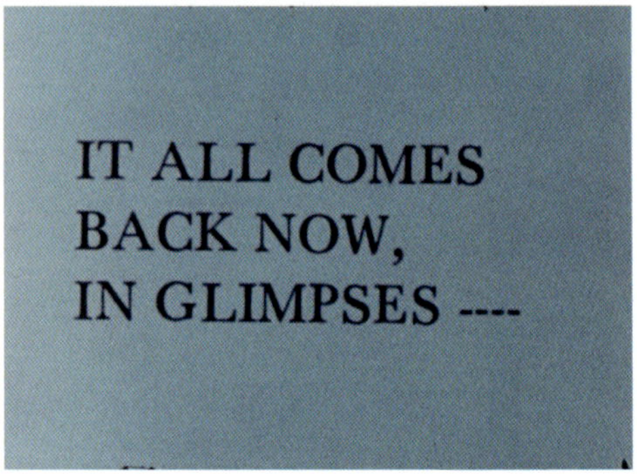
IT ALL COMES
BACK NOW,
IN GLIMPSES ----

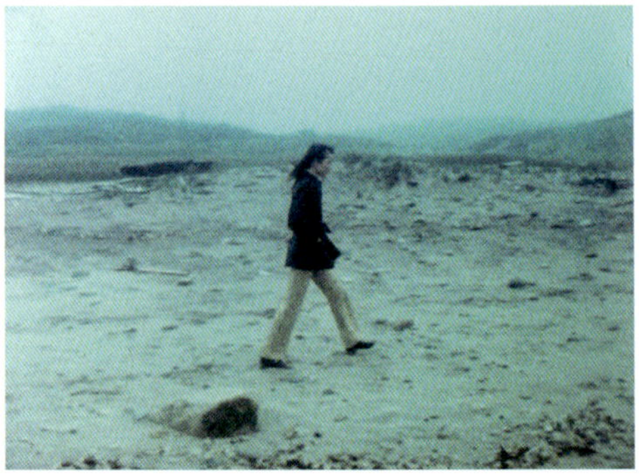

EPHEMERA

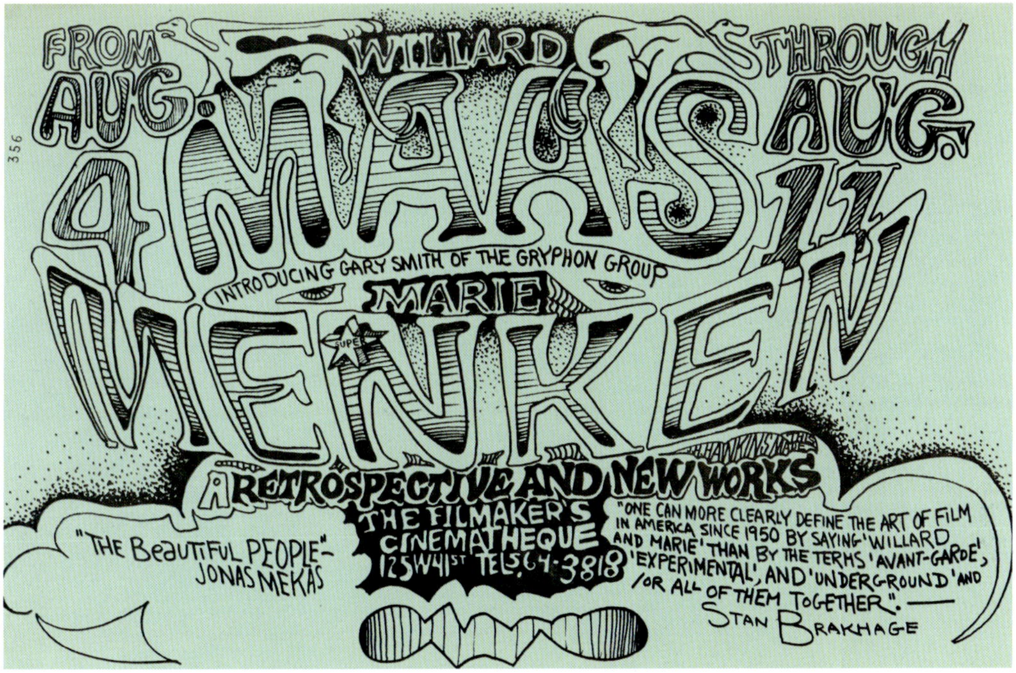

Flyer for a program featuring Willard Maas and Marie Menken at the Film-Makers' Cinematheque, 125 w. 41st Street, August 4–11, 1967.

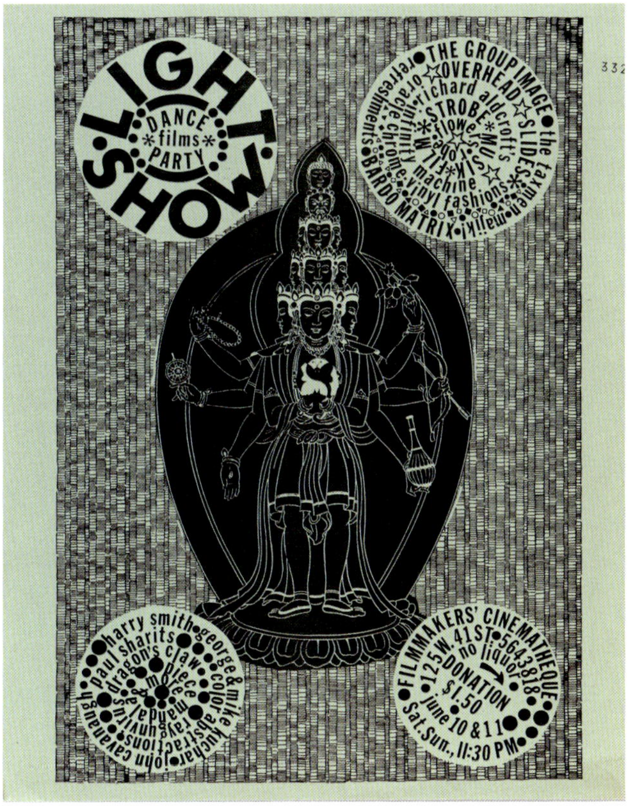

Flyer for a light show, dance party, and film screening at the Film-Makers' Cinematheque, 125 w. 41st Street, June 10–11, 1967.

Flyer for a "majik lite show," film screening, fashion show, and live music at the Film-Makers' Cinematheque, 125 w. 41st Street, June 23–24, 1967.

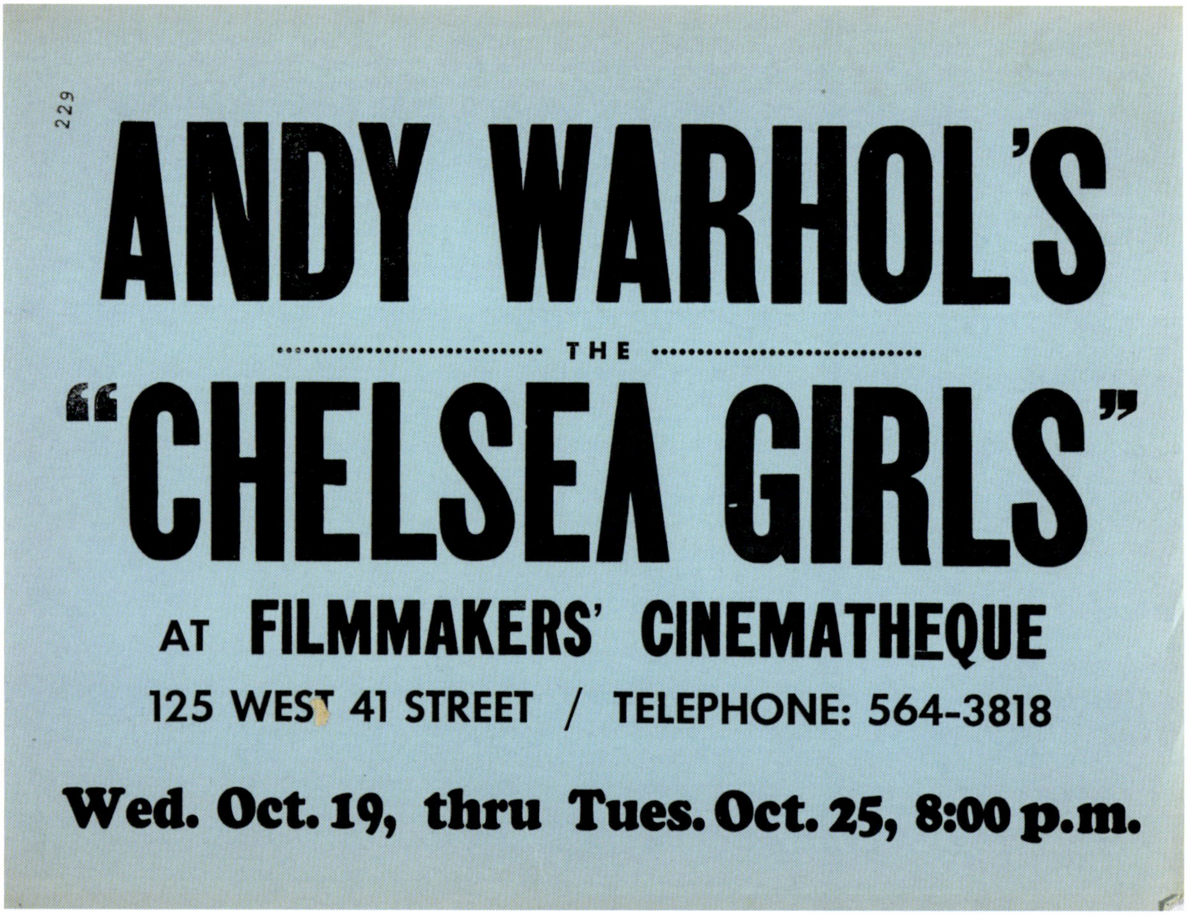

Poster for Andy Warhol's *Chelsea Girls* (1966) at the Film-Makers' Cinematheque, 125 w. 41st Street, October 19–25, 1966.

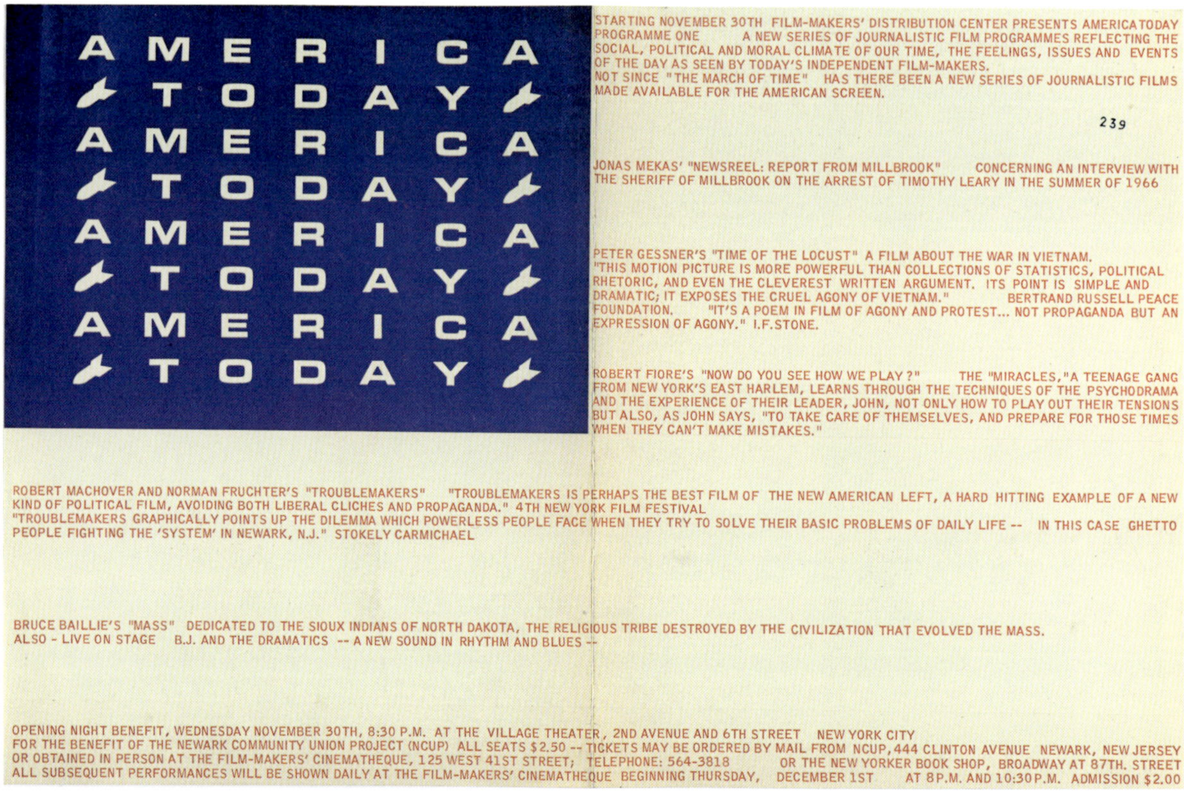

Flyer for the program "America Today" at 125 w. 41st Street, 1966. Described as "a new series of journalistic film programmes reflecting the social, political, and moral climate of our time," it featured Jonas Mekas's *Report from Millbrook* (1966).

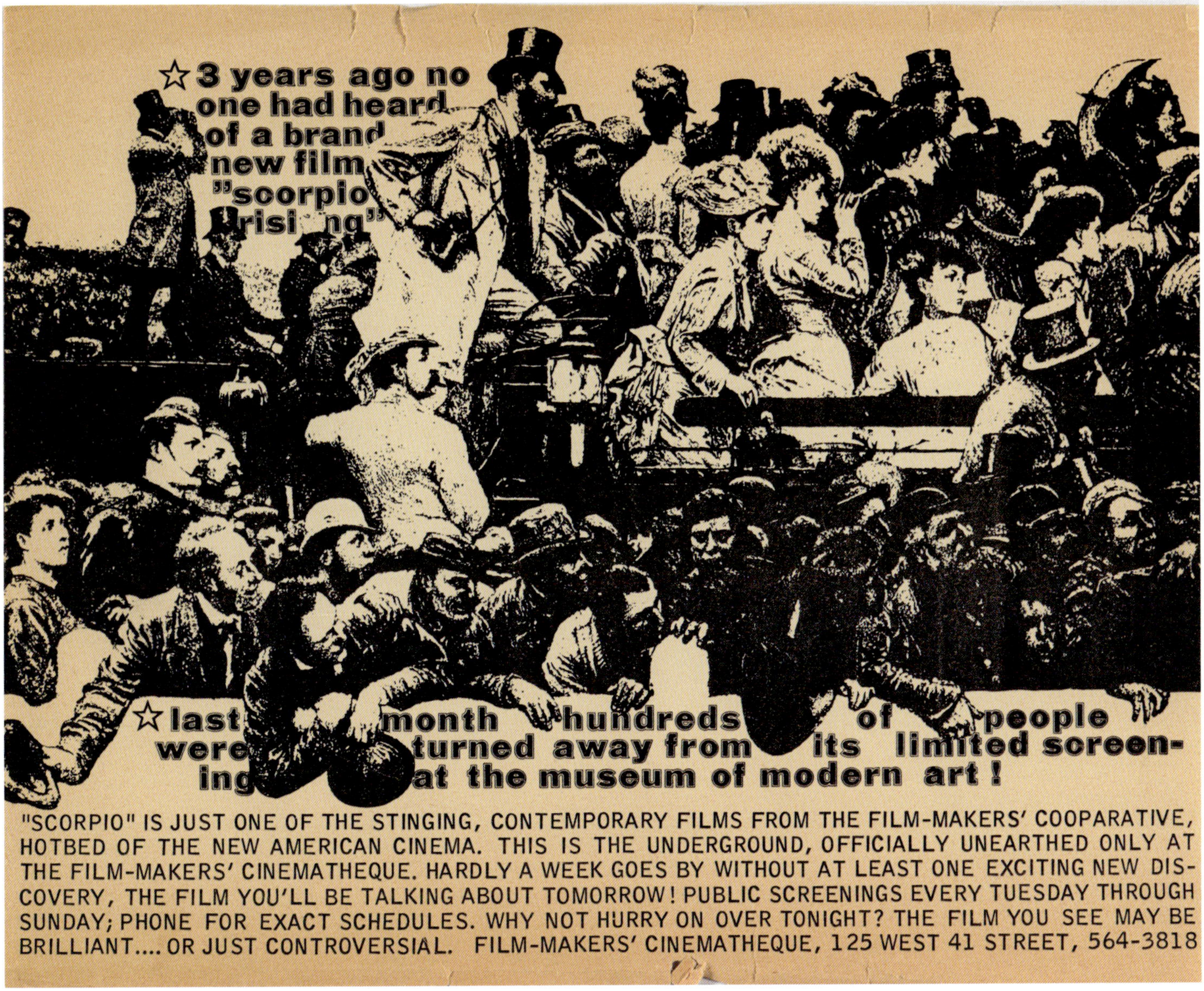

Flyer for a screening at the Film-Makers' Cinematheque, 125 w. 41st Street, featuring Kenneth Anger's *Scorpio Rising* (1963), 1966.

386

FILM•MAKERS'

FILM-MAKERS' CINEMATHEQUE, 80 WOOSTER ST. TEL: 925-7136. TICKET: $1.50; IF YOU CAN'T AFFORD IT - $1

APRIL 1, MON. 8 P.M. KEN KELMAN: EXERCISES IN FILM HISTORY, LECTURE 16. FILMS: PEOPLE ON SUNDAY BY SIODMAK - ULMER; RAIN BY IVENS; H20 BY STEINER. A LANDMARK IN IMPROVISATIONAL FILM, AND TWO APPROACHES TO WATER.

APR. 2, TUES. 8 P.M. EXPERIMENTAL FILMS BY THE STUDENTS OF THE FILM SCHOOL, SCHOOL OF VISUAL ARTS.

APRIL 3, WED. 8 P.M. WINNERS OF THE 4TH EXPERIMENTAL FILM COMPETITION (BELGIUM): GRATEFUL DEAD BY ROBERT NELSON, WAVELENGTH BY MICHAEL SNOW. ALSO: NEW YORK EYE AND EAR CONTROL BY MICHAEL SNOW.

APRIL 4, THURSDAY, 8 P.M. ... SAME AS APRIL 3 ... GRATEFUL DEAD, WAVELENGTH ... NEW YORK EYE AND EAR...

APR. 5, FRI. 8 P.M. ... SAME AS APR. 3 ... GRATEFUL DEAD, WAVELENGTH ... NEW YORK EYE AND EAR CONTROL ...

APR. 6, SAT. 8 P.M. ... SAME AS APR. 3 ... GRATEFUL DEAD, WAVELENGTH ... NEW YORK EYE AND EAR CONTROL ...
APR. 6, SAT. 10 P.M. THE GUERRILA NEWSREEL. ACTUALITY FILM.

APR. 7, SUN. 8 P.M. ... SAME AS APR. 3 ... GRATEFUL DEAD, WAVELENGTH ... NEW YORK EYE AND EAR CONTROL ...

APR. 8, MON. 8 P.M. KEN KELMAN: EXERCISES IN FILM HISTORY, LECTURE 17. FILMS: ENTRE'ACTE BY CLAIR; ANAEMIC CINEMA BY DUCHAMP, HGOSTS BEFORE BREAKFAST BY RICHTER, BALLET MECANIQUE BY LEGER, EMAK BAKIA, RETURN TO REASON, ETOILE DE MER - ALL THREE BY MAN RAY.

APR. 9, TUES. 8:30 P.M. ANGELFACE - ONTOLOGIC AND HYSTERIC THEATER (LIVE), BY RICHARD FOREMAN.

APR. 10, WEDNESDAY, 8:30 P.M. ANGELFACE - ONTOLOGIC AND HYSTERIC THEATER (LIVE), BY RICHARD FOREMAN

APR. 11, THURSDAY, 8:30 P.M. ANGELFACE - ONTOLOGIC AND HYSTERIC THEATER (LIVE), BY RICHARD FOREMAN.

APR. 13, SAT. 8 P.M. CLASSICS OF THE AVANTGARDE FILM: VENOM AND ETERNITY (1953), BY JEAN-ISADORE ISOU.
APR. 13, SATURDAY 10 P.M. THE GUERRILA NEWSREEL. ACTUALITY FILM.

APR. 14, SUN. 8:30 P.M. ANGELFACE - ONTOLOGIC AND HYSTERIC THEATER (LIVE), BY RICHARD FOREMAN.

APR. 15, MON. 8 P.M. KEN KELMAN: EXERCISES IN FILM HISTORY, LECTURE 18. FILMS: SMILING MADAME BEUDET BY DULAC; SEASHELL AND THE CLERGYMAN BY DULAC; MENILMONTANT BY KIRSANOV. TWO PSYCHOLOGICAL EXPERIMENTS, AND A PERFECTION OF NARRATIVE STYLE.

APRIL 16, TUESDAY 8 P.M. OPEN HOUSE. BRING YOUR OWN FILMS, COMPLETED OR IN PROGRESS

APR. 17, WED. 8 P.M. BENEFIT SCREENING FOR THE FILM-MAKERS' NEWSLETTER. FILMS BY BOB COWAN, ED EMSHWILLER, CHARLES LEVINE, CARL LINDER, JONAS MEKAS, PAUL MORRISSEY, WARREN SONBERT & OTHERS.

APRIL 18, THURSDAY 8 P.M. PREMIERE OF GREGORY MARKOPOULOS' ILLIAC PASSION. AN OCCASION TO REJOYCE FOR ALL FRIENDS AND LOVERS OF CINEMA.

APRIL 19, FRIDAY 8 P.M. AND 10 P.M. ILLIAC PASSION BY GREGORY MARKOPOULOS.

APRIL 20, SAT. 8 P.M. ILLIAC PASSION BY GREGORY MARKOPOULOS. 10 P.M. THE GUERRILA NEWSREEL.

APRIL 21, SUNDAY, EIGHT AND TEN P.M. ILLIAC PASSION BY GREGORY MARKOPOULOS.

APRIL 22, MON. 8 P.M. KEN KELMAN: EXERCISES IN FILM HISTORY, LECTURE 19. FILMS: THE FALL OF THE HOUSE OF USHER, A VERSION BY EPSTEIN, NAD ONE BY WEBBER AND WATSON; UN CHIEN ANDALOU BY BUNUEL AND DALI. TWO SYMBOLIC NARRATIVES, AND A CULTURE - SHAKING DENIAL OF SYMBOL AND NARRATIVE.

APRIL 23, 24, 25, TUESDAY, WEDNESDAY, THURSDAY, 8 P.M. ILLIAC PASSION BY GREGORY MARKOPOULOS.

APRIL 26, FRIDAY, 8 AND 10 P.M. ILLIAC PASSION BY GREGORY MARKOPOULOS.

APR. 27, SAT. 8 P.M. ILLIAC PASSION BY GREGORY MARKOPOULOS. 10 P.M. THE GUERRILA NEWSREEL.

APRIL 28, SUNDAY, 8 P.M. ILLIAC PASSION BY GREGORY MARKOPOULOS.

APR. 29, MON. 8 P.M. KEN KELMAN: EXERCISES IN FILM HISTORY, LECTURE 20. FILMS: ARSENAL BY DOVSHENKO. THE CULMINATON OF ONE EXTREME OF SOVIET SILENT FILM - A PLOTLESS MOVIE HELD TOGETHER ONLY BY THEME.

APRIL 30, TUESDAY, 8 P.M. ILLIAC PASSION BY GREGORY MARKOPOULOS.

COMING IN MAY: ONE MAN SHOWS BY WARREN SONBERT, STORM DE HIRSCH, LARRY JORDAN (COMPLETE RETROSPECTIVE), GEORGE LANDOW, AND NEW WORKS BY ANDREW NOREN.

CINEMATHEQUE

Program for the Film-Makers' Cinematheque at 80 Wooster Street, April 1968.

FILMS OF STORM DE HIRSCH

379

FILM-MAKERS' CINEMATHEQUE (80 Wooster Street—Where Wooster & Spring Streets meet—3 blocks South of Bleecker St. Cinema)
May 16, Thursday, 8PM May 17, Friday, 8PM May 18, Saturday, 8PM Students $1.50 Others $2.00

JOURNEY AROUND A ZERO (3 minutes)
A phallic invocation...an abstract occasion of image and sound.

CAYUGA RUN—Book I of HUDSON RIVER DIARY (20 minutes)
Film-maker's almanack. A train named Cayuga makes its run along the riverbank from New York City to Poughkeepsie via Marble Hill, Spuyten Duyvil, Yonkers, Dobbs Ferry, Irvington, Tarrytown, Ossining, Croton-Harmon, Oscawana, and Crugers Landing. Here the eye locks the lens, registers moments in time and fragmented contemplations in celebration of the seasons and the river Hudson.

TRAP DANCE (2 minutes)
Death-rattle for killers of the dream. An anti-war statement in abstraction.

JONAS IN THE BRIG (5 minutes)
Newsreel of Jonas Mekas shooting his filmed version of *The Brig* on the set of the Living Theatre's stage production.

THE COLOR OF RITUAL THE COLOR OF THOUGHT (Trilogy) (30 minutes)
This film trilogy, consisting of DIVINATIONS, SHAMAN and PEYOTE QUEEN, records a psychic event in color, shape and sound. Voyages into buried continents of the self, exploring out-of-bound areas of no-time, new space. A journey through the underworld of sensory derangement, of interior vision, where the inner eye reveals its powers and the Mysteries are enacted in the Theatre of the Soul. Dedicated to all the magic makers of the world, to those who enter the atlas of the soul, rummage through the refuse and flowers of time and weave a talisman for man's rebirth in his house of breath.
Johannus Keppler Award for Eccentricity of Orbit Around a Star, San Joaquin Delta College Film Festival, 1968.
"Delicately wrought fantasies combining photographed and brilliantly hand-painted objects and abstractions."—Ken Kelman, *The New American Cinema Anthology*
"Among my favorites....moments of beauty and excitement."—Jonas Mekas, *The Village Voice*
"The animated sequences in this film are unique and fascinating...like watching an illuminated scroll of magic calligraphy unfolding on the screen with blasts of color and the purity of light."—Alan Callahan, *Variety*
"A film of great beauty and imagination. The abstract images engraved directly on film are like the paintings of Miro."—Dominique Noquez, *La Nouvelle Revue Francaise*
"A truly aggressive attack on the eye. The first impression is that of an extremely bold and illuminating essay on film techniques which defy all the traditional laws of animation. A profound artistic attempt."—Giuliano Ranieri, *Gazzetta del Popolo (Torino)*

Premiere
THIRD EYE BUTTERFLY—Split-screen projection (10 minutes)

intermission

GOODBYE IN THE MIRROR (80 minutes)
A narrative feature filmed on location in Rome. The film is centered around the adventures and illusions of three girls living abroad. It explores the restlessness and uncertainty of their individual quests, their personal involvements in assuming the role of woman as hunter.
Cast: Rosa Pradell, Franco Volpino, Diane Stainton, Barbara Apostal, Charlotte Bradley. Cameraman: Giorgio Turi. Associate Director: Louis Brigante. Music: Norman Blagman and Jeffrey Menkes. Harpsichord: Stewart Robb. Italian songs arranged and sung by Pola Chapelle. "From beginning to end the film spectator's pleasure and understanding is enhanced on that same social filmic scale of that grand experimentalist Rossellini...the turning streetcar, the protagonists Maria and Marco, the sweeper, the scurrying nuns, the very amusing song: "I wish I was a Fascinating Bitch", the visual melodies as conceived in the walk episodes, which alternate between one character and another...that sense of existence in the tradition of Rene Clair's SOUS LES TOITS DE PARIS."—Gregory J. Markopoulos, *Film Culture*

Festivals: Cannes, Locarno, Mannheim, Vancouver, and Chicago.

Flyer for a program featuring the films of Storm de Hirsch at the Film-Makers' Cinematheque, 80 Wooster Street, May 16–18, 1968.

The Jewish Museum: December 1968

448

The Jewish Museum under the auspices of The Jewish Theological Seminary of America, 1109 Fifth Avenue, New York 10028, New York. Telephone: RI 9-3770

Programs of specific commitment, immediate concern, conscience, threshold, scholarship, and patronage.

NEW EXHIBITION

Up Against the Wall: Protest Posters/December 5 through January 19, 1969. (Galleries 10 and 15, Third Floor.) Posters of protest from France and Czechoslovakia created during the student uprisings of May and June in Paris, and in Prague during the crisis of August. These strong graphic statements will be placed in the context of photographs of the students, streets, and events, and supplemented by sound. There will be special screenings in the Auditorium of films of the events.

For information regarding the film schedule, please call RI 9-3770.

The Museum of Modern Art will display French protest posters during the same period.

CURRENT EXHIBITIONS

Ingathering: Ceremony and Tradition in New York Public Collections/October 18 through January 5, 1969. (First and Second Floors.) An exhibition of traditional arts from Biblical times through the 19th century, selected from the major public institutions of New York City.

Robert Whitman: Pond/October 18 through January 5, 1969. (Second Floor.) Described by Mr. Whitman as, "A nice quiet place to walk around—sit down take it easy—looking at the reflection in the mirror of yourself and people—different ways—surprise the mirror with your look—look at a word—on you—or a picture—get closer to yourself upside down—..."

Sculpture Court/October 18 through January 5, 1969. Three recent sculptures lent by New York City museums. Alexander Calder's *The Cock's Comb*, 1960, of sheet iron, from The Whitney Museum of American Art; Dimitri Hadzi's *Helmet V (Elmo)*, 1962, in bronze, from The Solomon R. Guggenheim Museum; and Eduardo Paolozzi's *Lotus*, 1964, of welded aluminum, from The Museum of Modern Art.

PERMANENT EXHIBITIONS

Traditional Ceremonial Objects From the Museum's Collections. (Third Floor.) The richest and most extensive collection of Jewish decorative arts in this country.

Samuel Friedenberg Collection of Coins and Medals. (Third Floor.) The history of Judaism traced through historic coins and an encyclopedia of portrait medals.

Contemporary Ceremonial Art. (Third Floor.) Ritual objects imaginatively reinterpreted by leading craftsmen, including Ludwig Wolpert and Moshe Zabari of the Museum's Tobe Pascher Workshop, in both familiar and experimental media reflecting current trends in design.

FORTHCOMING EXHIBITION

European Painters Today/Opens January 22, 1969. An exhibition of about a hundred works by fifty-three artists from ten countries representing current trends in European art, organized and shown in Paris, and sponsored by The Mead Corporation.

FILM PROGRAM

Avantgarde Film Series at The Jewish Museum/Tuesdays, 5:30 p.m., and 7:00 p.m. Two showings. (Warburg Auditorium.) A series of film programs on successive Tuesdays arranged and conducted by the Film-Makers' Cinematheque of New York under Program Director, Jonas Mekas. The emphasis of the series is on the American film of the last decade, the most fruitful period of the Avantgarde Film. For program and ticket information call the Film-Makers' Cinematheque, around noon hours, 925-2250. Tickets will be sold at the door. Admission: $1.50; Members, $1.00. The program for December is:

*Tuesday, December 3rd:
Peter Kubelka: *Adebar; Schwechater; Arnulf Rainer; Unsere Afrikareise*

*Tuesday, December 10th:
Ron Rice: *Senseless; Chumlum*

*Tuesday, December 17th:
Paul Sharits: *Seven Loops; Nothing*

*Tuesday, December 24th:
Stan Brakhage: *Cat's Cradle; The Wonder Ring; The Dead; Prelude*

*Tuesday, December 31st:
Bruce Baillie: *Castro Street; All My Life; Quixote*

*Program subject to change without prior notice.

ACTIVITY

On Sunday, December 22, 1968, 1-3 p.m., Members' children only, ages 8-13, admission free, are invited to an Ingather-In, a conducted tour of the galleries and a Turn-On in the *Pond*.

PUBLICATION

Ingathering: Ceremony and Tradition in New York Public Collections. An illustrated catalogue with an introduction by Karl Katz, and text by Irene Winter. Distributed to Contributing, Sustaining, Patron and Sponsor Members.
Price: $3.50; Members, $3.00

MEMBERSHIP

Privileges include free admission, invitations to major exhibition previews, free Museum publications, discounts on books and gifts sold at Museum, etc. Categories of membership are: Resident member, $18; Non-resident member, $15 (living beyond 50 mile radius); Contributing member, $50; Sustaining member, $100; Patron member, $250; Associate Sponsor member, $500; Sponsor member, $1000.

HOURS

Sunday	11:00 a.m. – 6:00 p.m.
Monday–Thursday	12:00 noon – 5:00 p.m.
Friday	11:00 a.m. – 3:00 p.m.
Saturday	Closed

Admission: Members free, adults 50 cents, children under 16, art students, organized groups 25 cents.
Guided tours for groups on written request, and special tours of *Ingathering* will be announced.

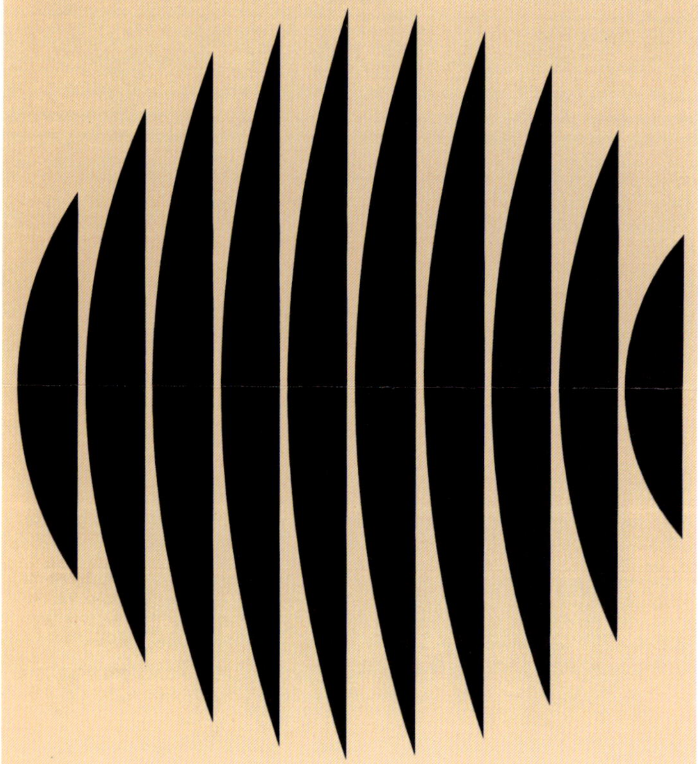

Arnold Saks

Jewish Museum newsletter, December 1968.

The Jewish Museum

under the auspices of The Jewish Theological Seminary of America / 1109 Fifth Avenue / New York 28 / Riverside 9-3770

OFFICE OF THE DIRECTOR

October 30, 1969

Mr. Jonas Mekas
Filmakers Cinemateque
80 Wooster Street
New York, N.Y. 10012

Choreography for Cam
Schwechater
KKK
Cassis (Gran)
Castro Street

Dear Jonas:

The next Board Meeting of the Jewish Museum's Board of Governors will be held on November 25 at 4:30 at LEASCO Data Processing Corporation, 280 Park Avenue, 35th floor in the office of Mr. Saul Steinberg.

At the last meeting of the Board a strong interest on the part of these distinguished members was directed towards finding out what Filmakers Cinemateque is doing at the Jewish Museum.

I suggested, and then spoke with you about, your putting together a film clip of 15-20 minutes, showing diversity and range, historical, chronological, subject, etc., of what kinds of movies have been shown at the Filmakers Cinemateque and that you would talk for a little bit.

May I ask you to please prepare this 15-20 minute movie and talk appearance for our next meeting?

Thank you.

Sincerely,

Karl Katz
Director

KK:cgw

Letter from Karl Katz, director of the Jewish Museum, to Jonas Mekas, requesting him to prepare a presentation for the museum's board about the Film-Makers' Cinematheque, October 30, 1969.

FILM-MAKERS' CINEMATHEQUE at

The Jewish Museum

under the auspices of The Jewish Theological Seminary of America / 1109 Fifth Avenue / New York 10028 / New York / 749-3770

427

THE AVANTGARDE FILM TUESDAY SERIES

Avantgarde Film Series at the Jewish Museum, Tuesdays, 5:30 p.m., and 7:00 p.m. Two showings. (Warburg Auditorium.) A series of programs on successive Tuesdays arranged and conducted by the Film-Makers' Cinematheque of New York under Program Director, Jonas Mekas. The Classical Avantgarde Film and selected contemporary authors.

PROGRAM FOR DECEMBER 1968:
Tuesday, December 10th:
RON RICE: SENSELESS; CHUMLUM

Tuesday, December 17th:
PAUL SHARITS: SEVEN LOOPS; N:O:T:H:I:N:G

Tuesday, December 24th:
STAN BRAKHAGE: CAT'S CRADLE; THE WONDER RING; THE DEAD; PRELUDE

Tuesday, December 31st:
BRUCE BAILLIE: CASTRO STREET; ALL MY LIFE; QUIXOTE

PROGRAM FOR JANUARY 1969:
Tuesday, January 7th:
LARRY JORDAN: GYMNOPEDIES; OLD HOUSE PASSING

Tuesday, January 14th:
MARIE MENKEN: VISUAL VARIATIONS ON NOGUCHI; EYE MUSIC IN RED MAJOR; BAGATELLE FOR WILLARD MAAS; NOTEBOOK; MOONPLAY; LIGHTS; EXCURSION

Tuesday, January 21st:
NO SCREENINGS

Tuesday, January 28th:
STAN VANDERBEEK: WHAT WHO HOW; SCIENCE FRICTION; WHEEEELS N.2; SNAPSHOTS OF THE CITY; BREATHDEATH; SEE, SAW, SEEMS

PROGRAM FOR FEBRUARY, 1969:
Tuesday, February 4th:
JAMES BROUGHTON: MOTHER'S DAY; ADVENTURES OF JIMMY; FOUR IN THE AFTERNOON; LOONY TOM

Tuesday, February 11th:
WARREN SONBERT: WHERE DID OUR LOVE GO; PREMIERE OF A NEW FILM

Tuesday, February 18th:
ED EMSHWILLER: DANCE CHROMATIC; TRANSFORMATION; LIFELINES; THANATOPSIS; TOTEM; GEORGE DUMPSON'S PLACE

Tuesday, February 25th:
KEN JACOBS: BAUDELAIRIAN CAPERS; WARNING SHADOWS; SKY SOCIALIST (exerpt)

Program for the Film-Makers' Cinematheque Avantgarde Film Tuesdays at the Jewish Museum, December 1968–February 1969. The series was held at the museum from 1968 to 1970.

SONIC MEKAS

NOTES

0 Epigraphs: Jonas Mekas, "I Seem to Live: The New York Diaries (1950–2008)," unpublished book manuscript, 593–94. Parts have now been published as *I Seem to Live: The New York Diaries*, vol. 1, *1950–1969* (Leipzig: Spector Books, 2019). First and foremost, I would like to thank Kelly Taxter, director, Parrish Art Museum (formerly, the Barnett and Annalee Curator of Contemporary Art at the Jewish Museum in New York) for inviting me to write about Jonas Mekas's inventive approaches to sound and her invaluable insights in response to earlier drafts of this essay. Infinite gratitude for the rigorous editing performed by Eve Sinaiko, director of publications at the Jewish Museum in New York. And, many thanks to the filmmaker Abigail Child for earlier critical readings of this essay; John Klacsmann, archivist at Anthology Film Archives, for fielding questions about Mekas's film work; MM Serra, executive director of Film-Makers' Cooperative in New York, for providing access to Mekas's films; and Elle Burchill, co-director of Microscope Gallery in Brooklyn and Mekas's long-time film editor, for generously sharing her knowledge of Mekas's filmmaking practices. And, finally, specially thanks to Mekas's brilliant son—cinematographer, actor, archivist—Sebastian Mekas, for his never-ending support of all levels of this project.

1 This list is culled from my conversations with Burchill, as well as names Mekas cited in "I Seem to Live."

Sonic Mekas

Melissa Ragona

> I never realized until this evening the purity of [John] Cage & how old fashioned and impure and melodramatic sounding [Karlheinz] Stockhausen is, when listening to Cage! I sat there in absolute suspense, completely caught by these sounds, on the edge of my seat, and I was myself like an instrument on which he seemed to work now, and things were happening inside, stirred & touched . . . my own life became clearer to me somehow, illuminated in a new way.
>
> Jonas Mekas, January 2, 1965

> I get high on music.
>
> Jonas Mekas, November 19, 1970

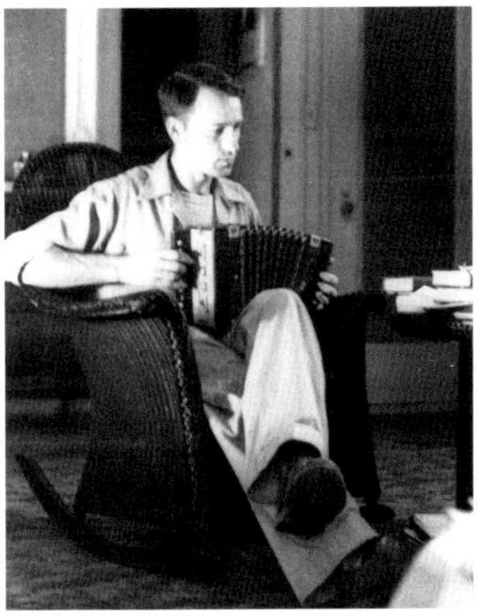

Jonas Mekas playing the accordion, c. 1952.

Sound saturated Jonas Mekas's life. In his childhood in Semeniškiai, Lithuania, he sang as well as played the mandolin, violin, trumpet, and accordion. As an adult in the New York art world he immersed himself in the post–World War II work of John Cage, La Monte Young, Philip Glass, Steve Reich, Tony Conrad, Maryanne Amacher, the Velvet Underground, Yoko Ono, and others. His musical tastes were eclectic: he listened to, and sometimes borrowed from, Nirvana, R.E.M., Madonna, John Zorn, Cecil Taylor, Björk, Johann Sebastian Bach, Anton Bruckner, Giuseppe Verdi, Claudio Monteverdi, Ornette Coleman, Charlie Parker, Patti Smith, Amy Winehouse, Sonic Youth, and Bright Eyes. And of course this is only a partial list.[1]

Many of the contemporary musicians and composers he admired, he also met and befriended, including Smith, Zorn, Glass, Laurie Anderson, Lou Reed, John Cale, Kim Gordon, and Thurston Moore, to name just a few. Moreover, Mekas was a member of an ever-changing group of musicians who gravitated around the Lithuanian musician and composer Dalius Naujokaitis-Naujo, affectionately known in downtown New York in the 1990s as the Anthology Gang or the Lithuanian Mafia.[2]

To understand Mekas's use of sound in his work, one has to understand the centrality of music—how it permeated his life—even before poetry, literature, and filmmaking became his obsessions. Some of his earliest memories are of song: "we sang / I grew up singing / we sang about everything and nothing / in moments of silence, we heard other people singing in other villages / songs were floating around the country / women sang while they were working in the fields."[3] The importance of the voice as a language, as a storytelling device, as a communal experience, as a form of survival was central for Mekas. Equally important were the more abstract sounds of objects around him—the silence of the forest, the high pitch of electricity through the countryside, or, as Mekas called it, "the singing of the wooden telephone poles" that he savored on the long walks between his grandmother's house and his own.[4]

Much scholarship on Mekas has focused on his personal, intimate forms of cinema: the diary film, the home movie, the film journal, the film poem.[5] Though these forms were central in terms of how he was framing his own work, their emphasis in the critical literature has eclipsed his broader interest in conceptual approaches to music, sound, and language. As early as 1961, Mekas identified a "new humor" in the film works of Ron Rice (*Flower Thief*, 1960), Robert Frank and Alfred Leslie (*Pull My Daisy*, 1959), Stan VanDerBeek (*Achoo Mr. Kerrichev*, 1960), and Robert Breer (*Blazes*, 1961); the literary works of William Burroughs (*Naked Lunch*, 1959) and Gregory Corso (*The American Express*, 1961); and La Monte Young's sound works (*Compositions 1960*, 1960). *Compositions 1960* was a series of conceptually based musical pieces infused with performative actions: building a fire or releasing a butterfly during the performance, providing a bale of hay and a bucket of water with which to feed the piano. Young's scores include instructions for these actions.[6] Mekas describes this work as emanating from a combination of Beat and Zen approaches. He points to a performativity (in terms of language) and detachment (in relation to its subject) in these works, and to a lighthearted reexamination of the self, using improvisation, animation, live action, collage, and duration or "time" as a medium.[7]

Four years later, in 1965, Mekas, along with John Brockman, managing director of the Film-Makers' Cinematheque, began organizing the New Cinema Festival I (also called the Festival of Expanded Cinema), which included a vast range of experiments in performance, film, music, dance, and writing by more than fifty artists over several months.[8] The centrality of sound to the development of various forms of spatialization in expanded cinema practices—multiple screens, immersive light projections, wandering audiences/

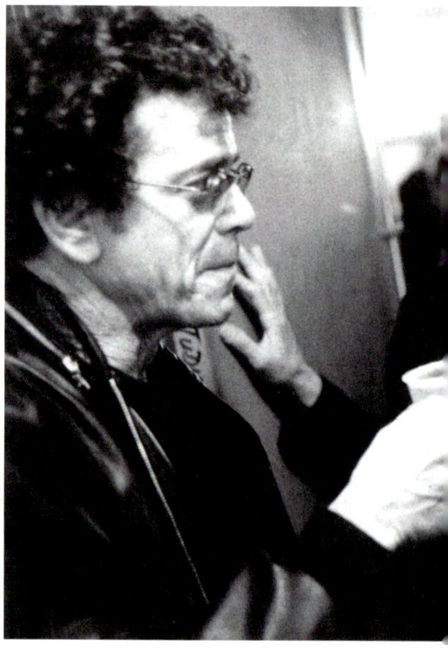

Lou Reed, Philip Glass, and Jonas Mekas at Anthology Film Archives, 1995.

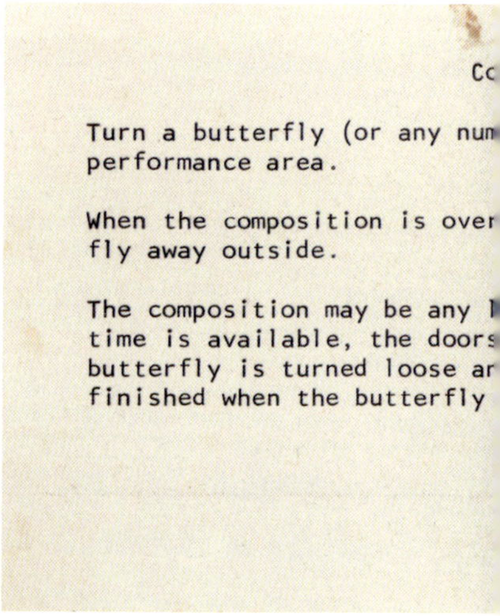

Cc

Turn a butterfly (or any num
performance area.

When the composition is over
fly away outside.

The composition may be any l
time is available, the doors
butterfly is turned loose ar
finished when the butterfly

La Monte Young's performance directions for *Composition 1960 #5*, June 1960.

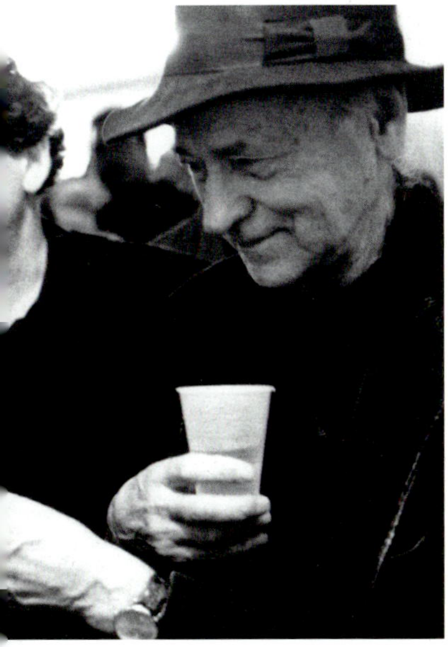

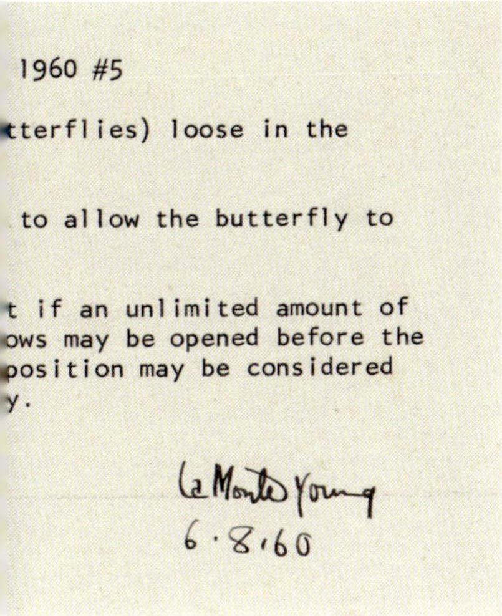
1960 #5

tterflies) loose in the

to allow the butterfly to

t if an unlimited amount of
ows may be opened before the
position may be considered
y.

La Monte Young
6.8.60

2 Edvardas Šumila, "New York Scenes and Echoes from Lithuania: Jonas Mekas' Musical Milieu," *World New Music Magazine* 18, https://www.mic.lt/en/discourses/lithuanian-music-link/no22-january-december-2019/edvardas-sumila-new-york-scenes-and-echoes-lithuania-jonas-mekas/?fbclid=IwAR134oA2aAuhYy0IXMV1cnbh4JTXUMrJ5spTI5EOQ6VI-iJPzy-.

3 Jonas Mekas, *I Had Nowhere to Go* (Leipzig: Spector Books, 2017), 21.

4 Ibid.

5 David E. James, "Film Diary/Diary Film: Practice and Product in *Walden*," in *To Free the Cinema: Jonas Mekas and the New York Underground*, ed. James (Princeton: Princeton University Press, 1992). Also in that volume, Maureen Turim ("Reminiscences, Subjectivities, and Truths," 193–212) examines the contradictions in Mekas's description of his work as diary films or "personal cinema." Her position is close to my own.

6 La Monte Young, "Compositions," *An Anthology of chance operations, concept art, anti-art, indeterminacy, plans of action, diagrams, music, dance constructions, improvisation, meaningless work, natural disasters, compositions, mathematics, essays, poetry*, ed. Young and Jackson Mac Low (Bronx, NY: Jackson Mac Low and La Monte Young, 1963).

7 In 1959, Mekas described the Beat and Zen influences at work in Robert Frank and Alfred Leslie's *Pull My Daisy*: "Here is the first truly 'beat' film, in the sense that beat is an expression of the young generation's unconscious rejection of the middle-class way, the business man's way; an outburst of spontaneity and improvisation as an unconscious opposition to the mechanization of life. It also expresses the very concrete influence of Zen Buddhism on the young American intellectuals. The film itself resembles a Zen koan: approached logically, it is meaningless and absurd. It is not a film of action or logical statements: it is a portrait of inner feelings. This is Zen on film, and it is a thoroughly serious film, despite its apparent robe of nonsense." Jonas Mekas, "New York Letter: Towards a Spontaneous Cinema," *Sight and Sound* 28, nos. 3–4 (1959): 120.

8 The Film-Makers' Cinematheque (1964–69), nicknamed the Tek, was conceived by Jonas Mekas in late 1964. Its first official program was presented at the New Yorker Theater on the Upper West Side of Manhattan and featured Naomi Levine's *Yes* (1963), Charles Boultenhouse's *Dionysus* (1963), and David Brooks's *Nightspring Daystar* (1964). See Jonas Mekas, *Movie Journal: The Rise of the New American Cinema, 1959–1971* (New York: Columbia University Press, 2016), 182.

Music and sound were central features of the programming throughout the Cinematheque's history. In 1965, works included La Monte Young's Theatre of Eternal Music and the Velvet Underground, performing with Angus MacLise. In 1966 the Tek staged a prototype performance of Warhol's multimedia event *Exploding Plastic Inevitable*, a few weeks after its debut at a formal dinner of the New York Society for Clinical Psychiatry, billed as *Andy Warhol, Uptight*, in which Mekas and Barbara Rubin also provoked and filmed. Other notable performances were Nam June Paik's *Opera Sextronique* (1967), in which Charlotte Moorman was arrested for indecency for her topless cello performance; Robert Nelson's film *Grateful Dead*, programmed together with the premiere of Michael Snow's film *Wavelength* (both 1967); and in 1968, Philip Glass's first public concert, "New Music—Philip Glass" (in which Steve Reich participated), and James Tenney's *Concrete and Computer Music*.

9 Mekas, *Movie Journal*, 217. Notable among the performers were Angus MacLise, Jerry Joffen, Jack Smith, and La Monte Young.

10 Mekas stood at the center of a set of astonishingly rich and complex artistic networks. In addition to being influenced by Cage's ideas of chance and indeterminacy, he also began to absorb the concepts of process and emergence, drawn from other sound artists he knew. For example, he befriended the young Philip Glass and staged the composer's "Piece in the Shape of a Square" at the Cinematheque in 1968. Glass was working at the time as studio assistant to the sculptor Richard Serra, who was producing his own early process-oriented splash/cast works. See Jeffrey Weiss, "Due Process: Richard Serra's Early Splash/Cast Works," *Artforum* 54, no. 3 (November 2015), https://www.artforum.com/print/201509/due-process-richard-serra-s-early-splash-cast-works-55532.

participants—was not lost on Mekas. Presciently, he recognized the programs of the festival as representing a "Period of Emergence," in which "the edges of where a specific work of art begins and where its ends are blurred out."[9] "Emergence" was a term that was already in the air, sometimes identified by other closely related terms such as "process" (for example, used selectively by Robert Morris, Richard Serra, Eva Hesse in sculpture; by Reich, Terry Riley, Glass, Pauline Oliveros, and others in music).[10] The theater director and theorist Richard Foreman, a prominent figure in the downtown avant-garde and a regular audience member at Mekas's Cinematheque in the mid-sixties, recalls that the two events that stood out for him were both sound-based: Angus MacLise's *Rites of the Dreamweapon* (with the Velvet Underground) and La Monte Young's *Dream Music:*

11 Richard Foreman, "During The Second Half of the Sixties," in *To Free the Cinema: Jonas Mekas and the New York Underground*, ed. David E. James (Princeton: Princeton University Press, 1992), 143.

12 Jonas Mekas, *Lost, Lost, Lost*, 16mm film, color and black and white, sound, 180 min., Film-Makers' Cooperative, New York, filmed 1949–63, edited 1976. The Film-Makers' Cooperative, still active today, came into existence in 1962 and was housed initially in Mekas's Manhattan loft. It was a division of the New American Cinema Group founded in 1961. Anthology Film Archives (cofounded by Mekas in 1970) is an outgrowth of the Film-Makers' Cinematheque (1964–69), which showcased avant-garde film, and was cofounded by Mekas, Jerome Hill, and George Maciunas.

A Light Sound Production (with the Theatre of Eternal Music). He was captivated by the way they both "used loud, repetitive, drone-like sound against slowly shifting onstage textures." More significantly, he was struck by what happened when they were juxtaposed with the work of other artists, especially Jack Smith's stage piece *Rehearsal for the Destruction of Atlantis*, presented within the projection work of the painter and filmmaker Jerry Joffen. Smith performed an extended, time-based reading of his "play" by waiting excruciatingly long periods of time, up to twenty minutes, between the delivery of each line of dialogue. For Foreman, the result was a profound altering—through sound—of space/time relations. Indeed, both Young and Smith radically toyed with the audience's aural and visual perception, "replacing the mythic level of narrative or thematic development with the microscopic level of moment-attending (implying that the seed of the moment held the energy of all possible future flow-into-form)."[11]

It is precisely these tensions between mythic narrative and abstract form, between content-infused music and indeterminate, emergent forms of sound that pulse throughout Mekas's filmic work. Holding close this historical moment, in which Mekas presents melodrama as a structural cinematic problem (through Smith) and the ever-expanding frequencies of the Dream Syndicate, let us turn to Mekas's voice. Let us view it as a kind of instructive urtext of these seemingly disparate worlds, curated and ingeniously synthesized by him and his contemporaries into new aesthetic worlds.

VOICE

> You sit in your own homes, but I speak with an accent and you don't even know where I come from. These are some images and some sounds recorded by someone in exile.
>
> Jonas Mekas, *Lost, Lost, Lost* (1976)[12]

Jonas Mekas's voice—as we still know it, as we still hear it—has the grit and pathos located in voices such as Leonard Cohen's or Patti Smith's. However, his voice is laced with an accent born far from New York. It is an insistent cantoring: one that addresses loneliness, money troubles, and ambition all in one breath. It careens from humble soliloquy about isolation, aimlessness, and insecurity to oratorical authority, articulating his central position within avant-garde film culture.

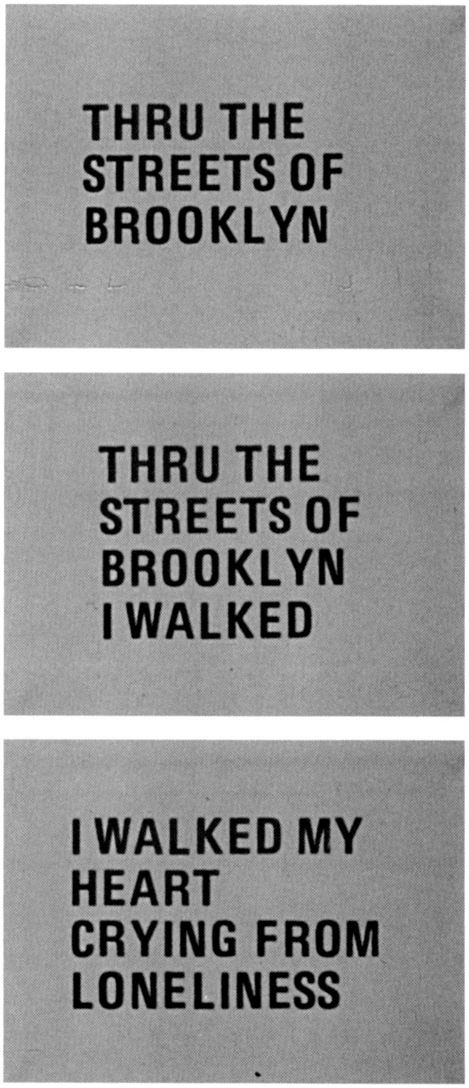

Three stills from *Lost, Lost, Lost*, 1976.

13 In 1979, Mekas described his complex, multilayered editing and sound-recording strategies: "One has attachments to certain things & one looks at footage of oneself or one's friends, immediately after the event, maybe just after a few weeks or days, & one's memory of the actual event or situation is still so strong & so vivid that it superimposes over the footage & one doesn't really see it for what it is. So that one really needs a perspective of time. I need usually several years of perspective. When I look back at my material years later, when the actual events are forgotten, then the footage itself becomes the event, the film, what you see, & you begin to work with that. I know myself, I know that in cases where I attempted to edit very recent material, I made very bad mistakes. I need perspective. . . . Here is my tape recorder [shows it], a cassette Sony. And I have a Nagra sitting in my room & I talk into it when I look at the footage & I feel like talking." Mekas, "I Seem to Live" manuscript, 1270–72.

14 "Yes, boy, work boys, if you want to see the new cinema grow. Run, boy run. It's all your idea, after all, who needs it! So I run. Because I am a sentimental midwife who doesn't want this newborn new art [to] die untimely or live on oatmeal, like myself, from day to day." Mekas, "I Seem to Live" manuscript, 1270–72, 596.

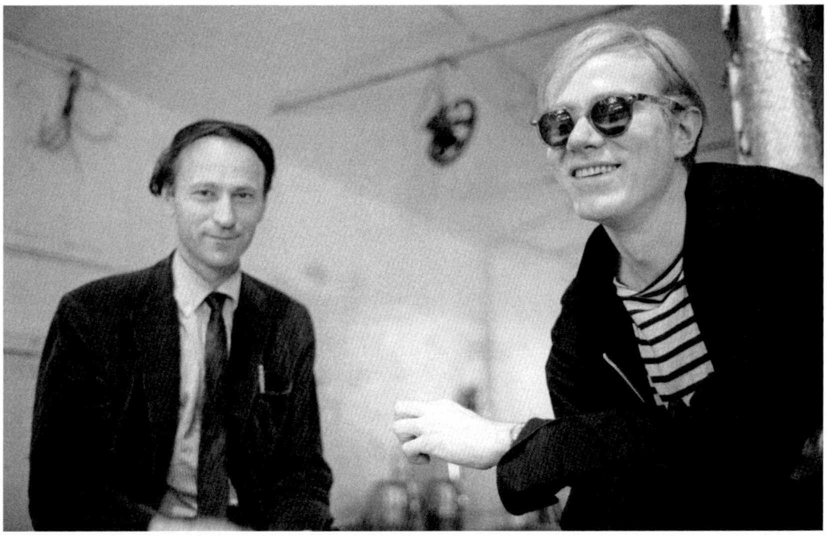

Jonas Mekas and Andy Warhol at the Factory, photographed by Stephen Shore, undated.

There is something at once authentic and performed in the cadence of his voice—especially in his films, since he almost always adds a layer of sound, of commentary, later as a way to process his memories.[13] It is often unabashedly sentimental, as Mekas proudly acknowledges: "I know I'm sentimental," he says in *Lost, Lost, Lost*, and "I am a sentimental midwife," he notes in his 1965 diary.[14] In the former, he defends the idea of presenting the trauma of exile in the form of an affective, experimental narrative, expressed through the voice, rather than as an abstraction: "You would like these images to be more abstract." On the one hand, his claim that he was an *outsider* was real: in the early 1950s, he felt ostracized, or exoticized and objectified, in any social circles that fell outside his small, New York–based Lithuanian community. But, by the late fifties and early sixties, he had wide-ranging connections with major figures from the worlds of avant-garde film, literature, and journalism, like Stan Brakhage, P. Adams Sitney, Annette Michelson, Norman Mailer, Jill Johnston, Andy Warhol, Ken Jacobs, and Shirley Clarke. Nevertheless, he continued to feel a profound sense of not fully belonging to American culture. Recording, in a sense, helped negotiate his sense of alienation. Mekas's inclination, like Warhol's, to record, to always have a camera, tape recorder, or any recording device in hand, served as both a link and a barrier to other people.

Like Warhol, Mekas had a nonstop recording process in which the voice, especially his own voice, takes on a preternatural, stylized tone or becomes what Mladen Dolar calls a voice-object, "a material element recalcitrant to meaning."[15] That is, for Mekas, the voice was not only a conveyor of meaning, but a sounding device. With a rigor comparable to Warhol's strategy of evacuation—presenting a voice that seems roboticized, programmed, emptied of any affect—Mekas's approach was one of excess, an overabundance of information, deeply personal as well as consciously public. If Warhol emptied himself of content, Mekas saturated himself with content. If Warhol stripped himself of his immigrant background, Mekas lavishly paraded his refugee status, making it the centerpiece of his work. Warhol's voice in his films is mechanistic, mimicking the recording process, whereas Mekas's voice takes on a knowing performativity—he is activating a complex relay between feeling, emotion, and affect.

Poetry is a model for the way Mekas structures affect in his films. He invokes the poet's voice, which carries with it a recognition of the rhythm, cadence, and materiality of language. His early autodidactic training as a young poet in Lithuania, as well as his immersion in the works of the Beat and New York School poets, prepared him well for the experimental film worlds that he would both encounter and help forge, in which the everyday was exalted as a central focus of the camera's eye and ear. These poets—Frank O'Hara, Allen Ginsberg, LeRoi Jones (later Amiri Baraka), Diane di Prima—were masters of the vernacular tone, the casual inflection, the sonic effect of everyday speech.

Throughout Mekas's film oeuvre, especially revealed in the auditory structures of his works, is an ongoing tension between private and public worlds, between documentation and melodrama, between sentiment and sentimentality.[16] His 1969 film *Walden*, his first large-scale diary film, employs the full panoply of Mekas's sound techniques and devices, and serves as an exemplar of their range and complexity. In the final reel, there is a section of lush single-framing—across Central Park, across its ice-skating rink, while Mekas asserts in voice-over: "And then I got tired and just started shooting for myself. That's what cinema is, single frames. Cinema is between the frames. Cinema is light, movement, sun, light, heartbeating, breathing life. And, in the background, those are the steps of the filmmaker, as he walks the city day and night, day and night."[17] His self-image as a sole artist doggedly roaming the city is a conscious citation of Dziga Vertov's *Man with a Movie Camera* (1929), the heroic "everyday *kino*-worker," filming a city symphony almost single-handedly—a lonely, harrowing task that must be done, driven by the demands of posterity as well as by the film artist's own inner, burning desire to capture it all.[18]

Minutes later, the tone in *Walden* shifts and we hear the throbbing beat of the Beatles' protest song "Give Peace a Chance"

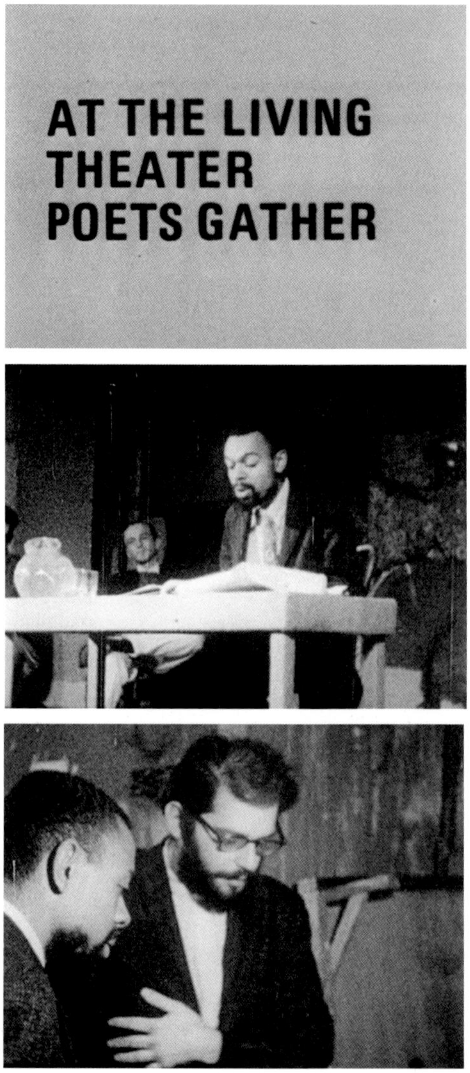

Three stills from *Lost, Lost, Lost*, 1976, showing the poets LeRoi Jones and Allen Ginsberg.

15 Mladen Dolar, *A Voice and Nothing More* (Cambridge, MA: MIT Press, 2006), 15. For Dolar, the voice-object is elusive and non- or extralinguistic. The voice "is the material element recalcitrant to meaning, and if we speak in order to say something, then the voice is precisely that which cannot be said. It is there, in the very act of saying, but it eludes any pinning down, to the point where we could maintain that it is the non-linguistic, the extra-linguistic element which enables speech phenomena, but cannot itself be discerned by linguistics."

16 Throughout his writing, Mekas makes a repeated effort to refine the distinction between "sentiment" and "sentimentality." For example, he remarks that his film *As I Was Moving Ahead Occasionally I Saw Brief Glimpses of Beauty* (2000) is "about 'family,' 'children,' etc. . . . And I think I dealt with it with the minimum of sentimentality. Sentiment, feeling—yes. Those are realities. But, not sentimentality." Jonas Mekas, letter to P. Adams Sitney (2002), in *I Seem to Live*, 1002. As early as 1961, writing about the films of Howard Hawks, he observed, "There is no triviality or sentimentality in a bad sense, no melodramatics in Hawks. He is almost documentary. Direct relationships, no fussing." Jonas Mekas, *I Seem to Live*, 370.

17 *Walden (Diaries, Notes, and Sketches)* (1969), 16mm, color and black and white, sound, 180 min., the Film-Makers' Cooperative, filmed 1964–68, edited 1968–69.

18 Mekas invoked Dziga Vertov, a forerunner of New American Cinema, frequently. Mekas considered Vertov's work "Essential Cinema," a term he later used as the name of a regular, rotating repertoire of film screenings at Anthology Film Archives. In 1969, Mekas even referred to himself as a Dziga Vertov: "Yes, yes, this Dziga Vertov is a sick man, a man without a home, busying himself with everything and anything, but deep inside always longing for home." Mekas, "I Seem to Live" manuscript, 955.

19 I diverge from David James's position here: "Mekas's decision to reserve from this film [*Walden*] both the 'personal' and the 'abstract' material from its period is especially unfortunate and, as well as ensuring the discomforting obsession with the famous [especially John Lennon and the Kennedys], it reinstates the separation of public and private whose subversion otherwise marks his work's importance." James, "Film Diary/Diary Film," 168n28.

20 See Mladen Dolar, *A Voice and Nothing More*, 60.

blaring over images of John Lennon and Yoko Ono staging one of their Bed-Ins for Peace. Intimate moments abound: John and Yoko hug, kiss, eat, smoke, make telephone calls. Kyoko, Ono's five-year-old daughter, snuggles with them, twirling a lollipop. A gaggle of reporters and journalists film, record, and ask questions. Mekas captures several of them swinging their enormous, invasive cameras right over the bed.

This is a quintessential Mekas sequence: at one moment, we are basking in the idyll of the film poet's inner eye and voice. Then in a flash we are ripped away, thrown into a confusing morass of staged and unstaged private and glaringly public and political situations. It is this constant shuttling between incongruent affective worlds that gives the performativity of Mekas's voice its complexity. He undermines the concept of an urban *Walden* as much as he promotes it, especially in his soliloquy-like voice-overs, which address idylls of inner-city nature (Central Park, balcony gardens), interruptions of protest (sometimes with celebrity appearances), spectacles of displacement (exile, poverty, isolation), and communities of intellect (shared literature, film, music).[19]

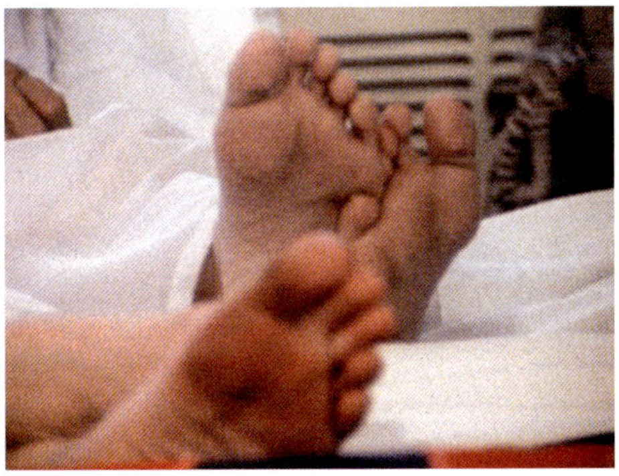

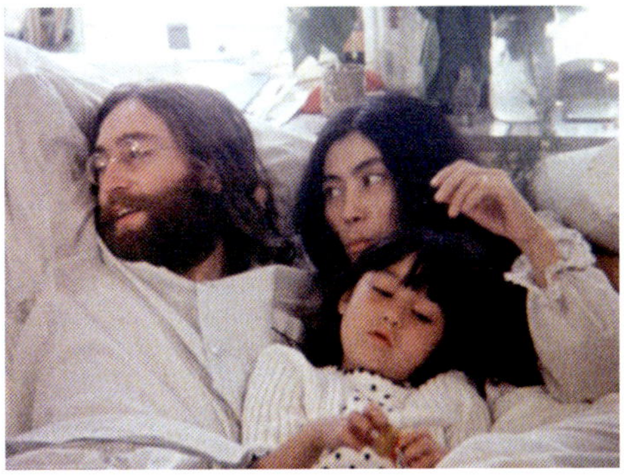

Two stills from *Walden (Diaries, Notes, and Sketches)*, 1969: John Lennon and Yoko Ono's feet; John, Yoko, and Yoko's daughter Kyoko at a Bed-in for Peace.

The performativity of sentiment in Mekas's work is tied to the resonant, sometimes dramatic quality of his voice. It enacts an overwhelming signification of his presence within his films, as an entity, *Jonas Mekas*, distinct from the person we have come to know as Jonas Mekas. The voice has the uncanny effect of seeming to exist simultaneously inside and outside the body—and it is precisely the difficulty of locating it that makes its dislocation significant.[20] The voice in many of his films, especially *Walden* and *Lost,*

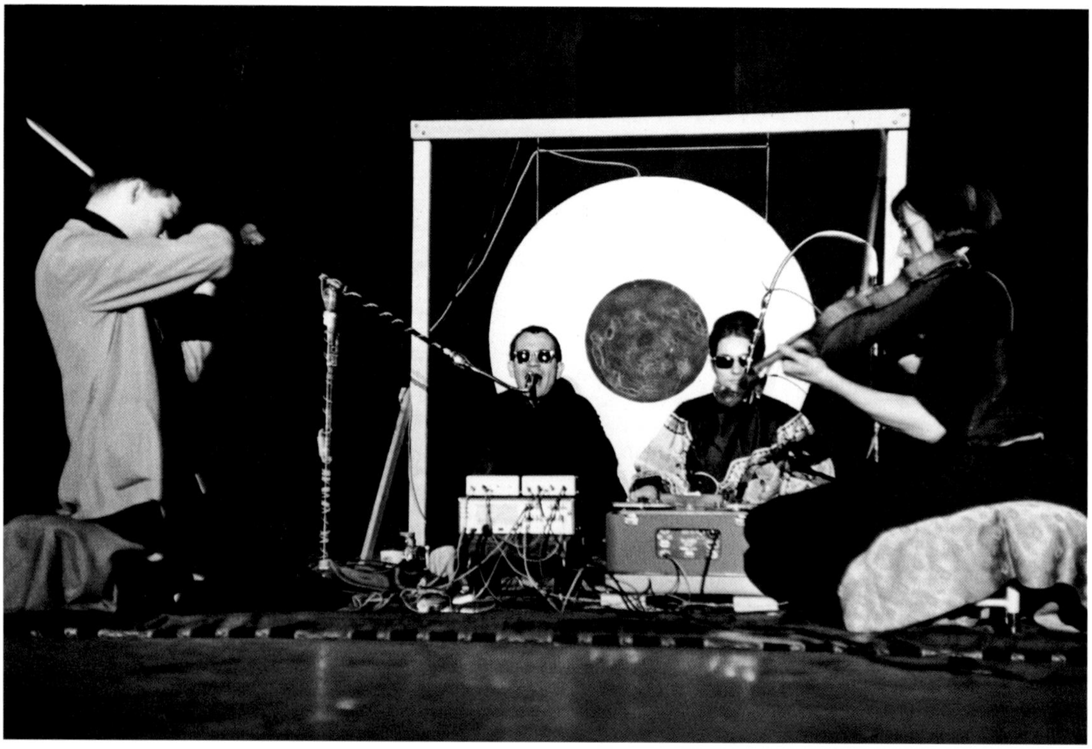

Performance of the Theatre of Eternal Music at the New York Film-Makers' Cinematheque, photographed by Fred McDarrah, 1965. Left to right: Tony Conrad, La Monte Young, Marian Zazeela, and John Cale.

Lost, Lost, embodies the slippage that is so central to Mekas's complex use of audition throughout his work. He recorded his disjunctively, speaking in first and third person—intimate and impersonal, diaristic and documentary—over the course of many years.

EMERGENCE

Interrelated with the performativity of Mekas's voice are the durational, generative structures of various forms of music, film, and language experiments (across poetry, diary, and audio recording) that informed his use of sound. He had been attracted to durational sound since his youth; now, important models for him were the sustained drones of the Velvet Underground, produced by Warhol, and of La Monte Young's Theatre of Eternal Music.[21] Especially interesting to Mekas was the concept of the overtone, which produced the sensation of hearing other frequencies that floated above a basic, fundamental sound. Mekas's interest in sustained drones found formal expression in his own filmic transmutations of these ideas. The composer Steve Reich argued that the drone as used by Young and the Velvet Underground was not a pure example of what he termed a "gradual process," in which the "compositional process and [the] sounding music are one and the same thing."[22] Nevertheless, Mekas recognized in them an emergent form important to his own process: "La Monte Young goes beyond all melody until his music becomes one uninterrupted sound, until all sounds fade into one, and then you listen to its surface and you begin to discover the most fantastic

21 The Theatre of Eternal Music (also called the Dream Syndicate) included La Monte Young, Marian Zazeela, Tony Conrad, and John Cale. Cale was also a member of the Velvet Underground, together with Lou Reed, Sterling Morrison, Angus MacLise, and later Moe Tucker.

22 Steve Reich, "Music as a Gradual Process" (1968), in *Writings on Music 1965–2000*, ed. Paul Hillier (New York: Oxford University Press), 34.

23 Mekas makes this comment about Young's music in his diary in March 1965 as part of a larger list of artists whom he believes explore the concept of "surface" as opposed to the more conservative idea of "essence" in art. Along with Young, he includes Carolee Schneemann (*Meat Joy*, 1964) under the category of The Happening Theatre. Under Cinema, he names Jack Smith, Andy Warhol, Stan Brakhage, Gregory Markopoulos, Barbara Rubin, and Ken Jacobs. Mekas, "I Seem to Live" manuscript, 602–3.

24 Justin Colannino, Francisco Gomez, and Godfried T. Toussaint, "Analysis of Emergent Beat-Class Sets in Steve Reich's 'Clapping Music' and the Yoruba Bell Timeline," *Perspectives of New Music* 47, no. 1 (Winter 2009): 112.

25 Mekas, "I Seem to Live" manuscript, 1269.

26 Jonas Mekas and Scott MacDonald, "Interview with Jonas Mekas," *October* 29 (Summer 1984): 107.

27 MacDonald suggests to Mekas that the subway noise that accompanies the opening segment of *Walden*—because it goes on for "a very long time"—perhaps signals the passage of time from winter to spring. Mekas does not affirm this interpretation, and simply responds, "I like that [subway] noise. It has continued through all the volumes of my film diaries."

melodies, the greatest music of the Century."[23] Minimalist composers like Young, Reich, Riley, and Glass shared several concerns that also interested Mekas, namely, "non-functional tonality and reiteration of musical phrases, often small motifs or cells, which evolve gradually."[24] Emergence becomes a major strategy in Mekas's construction of his diary films, as well as in his writing and his non-filmic musical practices. Many of his films are characterized visually by the extremely brief and staccato form of his single-framing and camera bursts, often repeating variations of one image. The technique inspires, like Minimalist musical forms, a microscopic attention to gradual changes in tone, color, and texture. For Mekas, editing is not about "cutting"; rather, it is related to a gradual process of becoming—in which the "footage itself becomes the event."[25]

The same approach is found in his construction of sound, and here Mekas's use of it also owes something to the moment-attending, ever-expanding frequencies of Young's work. In *Walden*, Mekas used many hours of recorded noise from New York subways and streets to organize a kind of emergent score. As he describes it, the subway sound acted as "a general background in which all other sounds are planted."[26] The opening subway sound assaults the viewer/listener from the get-go: film countdown, reel number, dedication, title, opening close-up shot of Mekas's eyes, intertitle "In New York was still Winter," a family sledding in Central Park, intertitle "But the Wind was Full of Spring," naked branches swaying, Mekas playing his accordion.[27] Through its loud, repetitive, driving pulse, it introduces all visual and sound events on an equal footing: close-up of filmmaker, text, long shot of a family, location, seasons changing, accordion music. Its effect is cumulative, rather than narrative. Something is building, but it is not measured in dramatic time.

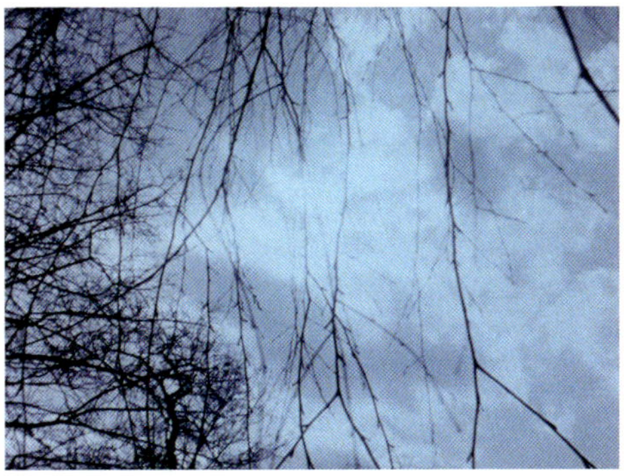

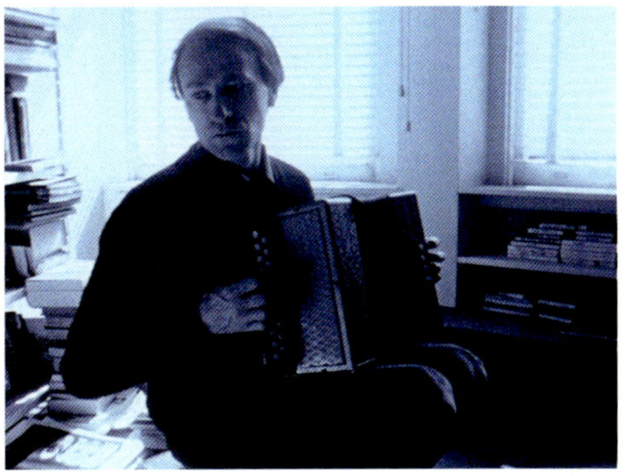

Two stills from *Walden (Diaries, Notes, and Sketches)*, 1969.

John Cale recorded sound for several segments in *Walden*. Mekas originally, in *Walden*'s 1969 program notes, called these the "Velvet Underground (rearranged)," but later renamed them, more

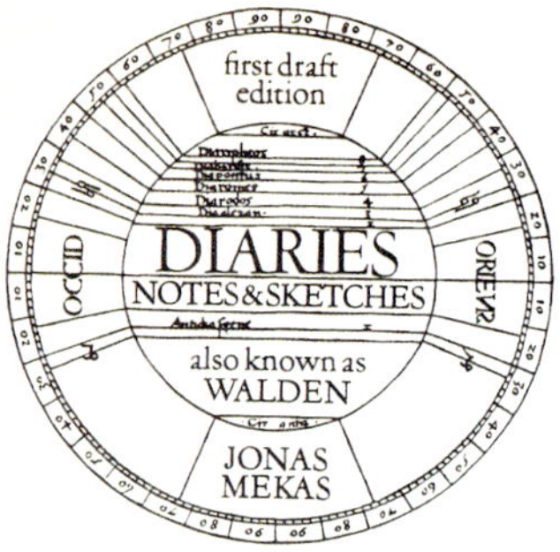

This film being what it is, i.e. a series of personal notes on events, people (friends) and Nature (Seasons) – the Author won't mind (he is almost encouraging it) if the Viewer will choose to watch only certain parts of the *work (film)*, according to the time available to him, according to his preferences, or any other good reason. To assist the Viewer in this matter, particularly in cases of repeated viewings (forgive the Author this presumption), the following Contents, a list of scenes and their time tables, reel by reel, have been prepared.

A note in the begining says, that this is the First Draft of the Diaries. Why should the Author permit then, one may ask, the unpolished or half-polished edition to come out? His answer is, he thought that despite the roughness of sound and some parts of the images, there is still enough in them – he felt – to make them of some interest to some of his friends and a few strangers. In order to go to the next stage of polishing, he felt, he had to look at the footage as it is, many many more times, and gain more perspective to it – that's why this edition. There is another reason. A few months ago, suddenly he saw his room filling up with smoke – he couldn't even see the film cans – and only a very lucky coincidence stopped the fire next door which would have consumed five years of his work. So he gave himself word to bring out as soon as he can this First Draft version, and there he stands, and hopes that some of you will find some enjoyment in what you'll see.

December, 1969 The Author

Jonas Mekas

1

Chopin street & subway noise

DEDICATED TO LUMIERE
DIARIES NOTES AND SKETCHES
ALSO KNOWN AS WALDEN
Close up of the Author
IN NEW YORK WAS STILL WINTER
Central Park, scattered snow
BUT THE WIND WAS FULL OF SPRING
naked branches in wind
the Author playing accordion
BARBARA'S FLOWER GARDEN
Barbara planting flower seeds on the window sill
Film-Makers' Cinematheque, 4th St.
SITNEY IS FINGERPRINTED BY THE POLICE, AS DIRECTOR OF THE CINEMATHEQUE

1 min. Sitney, CU of his hand
I CUT MY HAIR, TO RAISE MONEY, HAVING TEAS WITH RICH LADIES
the Author, showing his haircut, turning around
daily expense notes
SUNDAY AT STONES
the Author, eating; also, David & Barbara Stone

street & subway noise

2 min. I WALKED ACROSS THE PARK. THERE WAS A PHANTASTIC FEELING OF SPRING IN THE AIR.
apple blossoms
a group of boys, in sport shirts, jumping up and down, in Central Park
TONY CONRAD AND BEVERLY GRANT AT THEIR SECOND AVENUE HOME
we see Tony Conrad and Beverly Grant in the doorway
they look at the yard, at the trees

3 min. PHOTOGRAPH THE DUST FALLING ON THE CITY, ON THE WINDOWS, ON THE BOOKS, EVERYWHERE
the Author, in bed, can't sleep, turns around
I THOUGHT OF HOME
Central Park lake
WALDEN
Bibbe Hansen, in Central Park, with books in her arms
she studies a tiny flower in her fingers
the ground, grass, Bibbe, clower blossom
a sunlit tree

madrigal

Bibbe runs across the road and sits on a bench
she watches a yogi type, standing on his head
WALDEN
THE GIRL WITH THE BICYCLE & BLUE SHIRT
the girl with the bike
the Author (shadow from a bridge in Central Park)

6 min. a letter from Naomi
Diane, in Central Park, touching grass with her foot

dialogue about dreams

MORBID DAYS OF NEW YORK & GLOOM
the Author, eating in dingy luncheonette, self-filmed (in the mirror wall)
Central Park

7 min. BURNED, HOT GRASS
WALDEN
Central Park, John Brockman with guitar
the girl in blue, in Central Park, in the grass
General Post Office

Barbara combs Alexandra by the window
David Brooks, John Palmer, Harry Smith
Stone's baby sitters having good time

organ music

8 min. A WEDDING
wedding images; church lights; people outside
comes the bride (Pola)

wedding ceremonies (Adolfas) (Gantt)

IN FRONT OF THE CHURCH
Emshwiller; Frank Kuenstler; Leo Adams; the street
Algirdas Landsbergis and the Author, walking along the street

10 min. THE WEDDING PARTY
the wedding party; Gretchen Weinberg; Barbara Rubin; Stones

Author sings and plays accordion

SITNEY CATCHES THE GARTER, WILL HAVE TO MARRY NEXT
Sitney, the garter
Povilas Mekas (father)
Elžbieta Mekas (Mekienė) (mother)

12 min. AL MOVES OUT
empty room, the bed, bedsheets in loundry bags
BREAKFAST IN MARSEILLES
the Author, between trains, eating breakfast; a cat joins in

13 min. CASSIS

Cassis from sunrise to sunset, the lighthouse

ocean waves

14 min. Cassis from sunrise to sunset

16 min. SITNEY DECIDES TO LEAVE NEW HAVEN, GOES TO NEW YORK
Sitney in New Haven, in front of his old house, looking at the trees, at the street

subway noise

17 min. FIRE ON 87TH STREET
fire images
BRAKHAGE CROSSES CENTRAL PARK
Brakhage, the park, the trees, grass
COMING HOME FROM ST. VINCENT COLLEGE

Author singing

18 min. sunrise on way home; the smoke stacks of Newark
BREAKFAST AT STONES
Jordan; David on phone; Alexandra, finger in mouth, teeth are growing
the Author, at home, on 89th St., standing by the window, looking out

subway noise

19 min. CARL TH. DREYER
a few Central Park images, then Carl Th. Dreyer, in New York Hotel (Fifth Ave & 62nd St.), Sept. 18, 1965
WALDEN

Chopin

CU of the Author
Central Park lake & Amy Taubin

subway noise

27 min. WALDEN text
lake images; Author's shadow on the grass

A TRIP TO MILLBROOK
the Author, on the train

22 min. TIM'S PLACE
Timothy Leary's place, just after the rain,
a glimpse of Tim in red shirt
grass, and the dog, as he runs through wet grass,
Hm, it's nice, says dog
the dog in the wet grass field
the porch, close up of a boy, the road

Baghavagita

the porch, the road, grass, trees
on the porch, Dr. Alpert walks back and forth
the dog in the fields, in far distance; the dog is inspecting the fields after the rain
the dog on the porch, the girl with cat;
dog tries to get the cat, as he should
a girl on the trampoline, jumping up and down

a monkey jumping around the porch; Miss Leary
the Author, jumping up and down, on the trampoline
Shep Sherbell, the girl in red dress, the *mansion*

24 min. *LAUKAS,* A FIELD, AS WIDE AS CHILDHOOD
the girl, jumping up and down

a quiet field just before sunset
Shep, with the dog, on the porch
the bell on the porch, the field
Dr. Alpert, on the porch
the girl, jumping up and down

the evening, the porch; Dr. Alpert and the girl, walking into the misty distance of evening
red evening skyline, from the roof, all quiet
a small animal in the dark branches of night
yellow flowers in the garden (the flower of St. John)
Dr. Metzner & wife
a little boy holding a puffy grass in front of lens

on dreams

26 min. Tim's studio, the monkey, books, painting
green, dark green grass, the ground
the pool, Shep

27 min. FLOWERS FOR MARIE MENKEN
flowers

28 min. GREGORY MARKOPOULOS SHOOTS BACKGROUNDS FOR *GALAXIE*
Gregory setting up the tripod, winding up the camera, shooting

Lionel Rogosin and Louis Brigante on Bleecker Street
Mike Jacobson and Sitney, by the table
APRIL

madrigal

sparrows in naked branches
boys and girls sitting on Central Park fence, waiting for Spring
flower gardener on Sixth Avenue

Jim Kweskin's jug band

29 min. MAY 16TH 1966
NOTES ON THE CIRCUS
Circus images

42½ min. *END OF REEL ONE*

2

Kreplach voices

1 min. KREEPING KREPLACHS MEET TO DISCUSS WORLD PROBLEMS
Kreeping Kreplachs – at the Village Gate – Jun

Tuli Kupferberg, Ed Sanders, Al G. Aronowitz,
Rubin, Allen Ginsberg, Peter & Julius Orlovsky
Warhol,

2 min. Storm De Hirsch, Gerard Malanga, Ronna, Walte

the Capitalist Press, etc.

Ginsberg & Orlovsky sing

3 min. SEPTEMBER
Hare Krishna group singing and dancing in Thor Park

29 min. NOVEMBER
a crowd of people, singing and dancing, as they
uptown (Nov. 6, 1966) singing Hare Krishna all

Hare Krishna

4 min. Philip Corner beating the gong, Marty Greenbau

harmonica; Barbara dancing
as they move along the street, uptown

7 min. AUTUMN CAME WITH WIND & COLD
trees, leaves, N.Y. skyline
autumn park, children playing with leaves
two girls in red dresses, Central Park
children, loads of leaves

subway noise

8 min. STREET WORKS
street workers digging on Fifth Avenue
JEROME, TRYING TO PEEK INTO LARRY RIVERS' SHOW
Jerome Hill, peeking thru the window into the Jewish Museum
Walden text, from the book
Stones, crossing the park, looking at autumn trees & wind

Chopin

9 min. ALEXANDRA AND JORDAN
Alexandra, sitting on the window sill, laughing at Jordan on the floor
the cat in window, washing face

organ music

10 min. SITNEY'S WEDDING
Wedding (just before the wedding) party – Barbara Rubin, Brakhage, Kelman, the Author, Sitney (Dec. 19, 1965)

a glimpse of Julie and Sitney, leaving the churc
NEW YEAR'S EVENING IN TIME SQUARE
Times Square images, at night, lights
Sitney blows a trumpet, Julie joins in
on subway

subway noise

11 min. BARBET SCHROEDER
Barbet Schroeder having breakfast at Stones
Jordan; Alexandra, all dressed up, ready to go c
Jordan playing with his foot

camera clicks

12 min. Walden text, from the book
New York skyline, looking from Central Park, e
GOOFING ON 42ND STREET

42nd Street, at Grant's – Kelman, Bob Cowan,
Hiler, John Cavanaugh, Nick Dorsky, Gretchen Weinberg, eating frankfurters, goofing
COAL DELIVERER
a black worker unloading a coal truck, 41st Str

14 min. AN UPTOWN PARTY
Gerard Malanga dancing, Jack Smith & Mario M
on the floor, Nico, Eddie Sedgwick, etc,
at Steve Shore's place

Velvet Underground (rearranged)

15 min. VELVET UNDERGROUND'S FIRST APPEA
psychiatrists' convention; Andy Warhol; Velvet Underground plays, Gerard & Eddie dance

ALEXANDRA AND JORDAN
Jordan on the floor; Alexandra pressing a doll
breast; Barbara by the window; David, Chaplin
West River Drive
WALDEN
people skating in Central Park, the pond

17 min. DEEP OF WINTER
fire lights, the cat washing face, the mime
THE SWEET, MAD NAOMI, OUT OF BELLE
VISITS KEN AND FLO
Naomi in a cold winter street
Ferry Street
Ken Jacobs throws a flag out the window, Nao
in snow & flag

19 min. Ken, by the window, showing us the city; he is
at Brooklyn Bridge, no doubt
FLO WAS SICK AND IN BED, AND WAS LO
AT THE WINDOW, KEN'S NECKTIE, AND H
FRIEND CAT
the window, the necktie, the cat

more guests arrive; shots down, from the wind
by the table, eating, Naomi, and friends
Naomi and Ken in the street, dancing in snow

20 min. WALKING NAOMI BACK TO BELLEVUE, ON MY WAY TO THE TEK, IN SNOWSTORM
snowstorm, Times Square

text on Becks

A FLASHBACK: SEVEN YEARS AGO

Judith Malina with friends, in Times Square, s
VIGIL; snowing, cold

22 min. WINTER SCENE
children by the river, with sleigh; city streets in
WINTER SCENE
street workers, in cold and snow; flowers in wi
Central Park

Walden text, from the book
Central Park, a squirrel, and a bird
Tek's secretary, lights

in. MAILING FILM CULTURE
mailing Film Culture; winter streets
AMY STOPS FOR COFFEE
Amy in the street; Amy in a drugstore, having coffee
frankfurter man; a black man with his horse; the hoof

in. STREET WORKS
street workers in yellow raincoats, in snow,
keeping fires burning in barrels
PEACE MARCH AT NIGHT
marchers, on 42nd Street, at night

in. POLICE VIOLENCE ERRUPTS IN TIMES SQUARE, MARCHERS JAILED
violent commotion, police, marchers dragged, lights

BLACK POWER
demolition workers, blacks, tearing down
a building on 88th Street

in. WHAT LESLIE SAW THRU THE COOP WINDOW
city streets
Walden text, from the book
Alexandra in the window, playing with Venetian blinds

CHINESE NEW YEAR
Fire crackers exploding in the streets; in a restaurant
(Kelman, Hiler, Dorsky, Cavanaugh)

in. COOP DIRECTORS MEET
the Coop; Christopher Rice (age six months); Amy Rice, the Author, Ken Jacobs, David Brooks, Gregory Markopoulos, Storm De Hirsch
WEINBERGS IN WIND & SLUSH
Weinbergs, H.G. & Gretchen, in a windy slush street, Broadway & 86th Street

in. SPARROWS FOR FLO WHO IS STILL SICK
sparrows in cold branches
WINTER SCENE
children with sleigh, by the Hudson

wet city streets, lights, at night
daytime snow scenes, in the park; window cleaner on Columbus Ave;
demolition workers

in. DREAMS OF JEAN COCTEAU
snow fight in Central Park
the *lovers;* the *poet;* snow fight continues

IN CENTRAL PARK
Sitney, in the Park, looking at trees; tracks in snow of some animal; Author's shadow
LATE WINTER SLUSH

wet snow streets
Tina & Hannelore, on their way to Olmsted

min. OLMSTED HIKE
groups of people moving across the cold woods
towards Olmsted (Lindsay, Hoving, Javits)

in. windy hilltop

people moving across the woods, blown by wind

min. at Holmsted, end station, coffee, warming up,
bee hive, Tina & Hannelore, a brief glimpse of the Author, CU

min. *END OF REEL TWO*

3

ON THIRD AVENUE
the Author, by his working table, drinking coffee;
Barbara editing

the Author, reading a book, in bed

in. Barbara & Ronna, shooting, under a Christmas tree

Ronna and friends singing Christmas songs
driving thru the snowing street, from the car
CHRISTMAS EVE

in. Alexandra under a Christmas tree, opening gifts,
blowing soap bubbles

OPENING CHRISTMAS GIFTS
Al & Pola & Mother, opening Christmas packages

in. A VISIT TO BRAKHAGES

on way to Colorado, from the train

on way to Colorado; Author, in a mirror

in. ONE DAY LIKE ANY OTHER
at Brakhages; children in snow; Stan in front of his house

in. PONIES
children & ponies

in. ROSCOE
Roscoe, the donkey

STAN GOES TO TOWN
Stan driving to town;

min. STAN LISTENS TO LILI BOULANGER
the dog; Stan on bed, listening to music, looking out into the woods;
Jane goes to Post Office

IN THE WOODS
the Author, and Jane, in the woods; the Author running around, jumping, like crazy; the dog

voices of Brakhages; Author plays accordion

13min. NEOWYN AND CRYSTAL RETURN FROM SCHOOL
Neowyn and Crystal, returning from school
DOG STEALS BIRD'S FOOD, RUNS AWAY, AS WE SHOUT THRU THE WINDOW,
SHAME ON YOU, SHAME ON YOU!
dog steals bird's food, runs away; children watch thru the window

14min. ON THE MELTING PORCH
Stan watching the melting mountains; full view of the house
JANE CLEANS THE ROOF
Jane on the roof

SUDDENLY IT LOOKED LIKE SPRING
melting porch, Stan, children, animals, the sun

15min. JANE & JONAS DECIDE TO RIDE THE DONKEY
Jane and the Author riding the donkey, which isn't that easy to do; children film the event

STAN & THE CHILDREN
Stan on the porch, children, with 8mm cameras

17min. JANE
Jane with the horse
NEOWYN: *I'M NOT AFRAID, I'M NOT AFRAID*
Neowyn on the donkey (or pony?), very very proud & daring

18min. EVENING
evening shots at Brakhages, table
THE BREAKFAST
morning at Brakhages, huge amounts of pancakes consumed, children around the table, or helping at the sink

Boulanger

19min. A VISIT TO THE BEAVERLAND
Jane and the Author wade thru the snow & woods;
stumps of trees, cut down by beavers
AN UNSUCCESSFUL ATTEMPT TO GET DOWN A TREE CUT DOWN BY BEAVERS BUT STUCK IN THE WOODS
the Author, trying to get the tree, with little success

20min. I FIND RABBIT SHIT!
shots of rabbit shit in snow

Author's voice

NEXT MORNING
last shots at Brakhages; on way to Denver; sunset shots from train

a Lithuanian folk song

22min. AT TABOR FARM LITHUANIANS DANCED TILL SUNRISE
dancing; dawning sky
at Monroe, the girl with flowers, at the railroad station
GULF COAST UNDERGROUND IN SPRING FEVER
Austin film-makers, shooting in the park, fooling around

subway noise

23min. sunrise on way back to New York
New Jersey skyline, smoke stacks, chimneys

Chopin

apple trees in blossoms, Central Park
24min. Amy and Richard by the Hudson
the Author, his shadow

Amy & the kids of Amsterdam Avenue

26min. Author, in a boat

jazz

POLA & MOTHER IN THE COUNTRY
Pola & mother gathering blooming branches, walking down the road, Leo's house

Richter's voice, etc.

27min. A VISIT TO HANS RICHTER
Hans Richter's place; the meal; Al & Pola walk into the distance; the road; water lillies; Hans's working room; Author's feet;

28min. Author shoots the fly; Standish Lawder with his arri;
the bug; Hans's studio; Hans leaves his room;
the Author, changing tape

on Nagra; the pond, the road, the bucolic scenes...
with everybody standing, gazing very romantically...
Herman G. Weinberg, standing

alone by himself, gazing into distance, thinking about Renoir;

31min. Pola & Al walk down the road; Hans, pruning the dead branches, everybody joins in; Hans resting in his studio room; *8x8* tree.

Author's voice

32min. IN CENTRAL PARK
Tina on stilts. Hannelore's stilt party.

Ray Johnson, Paul Krasner, the park

Viennese Music

34min. PETER'S WEDDING
Newport, Peter, Minnie, Cushings
areal shots of Newport & Cushing's place
in the church
Wedding feast, in the tent
departure of Peter & Minie by helicopter
at the neighbor's house, next morning

48min. *END OF REEL THREE*

4

leaves in wind

00 SOON AFTER THAT CAME AUTUMN
leaves, autumn trees & park at the University of Delaware, branches in wind, University grounds, wind
a brook in autumn woods

1min. MEL'S CHILDREN
children on a swing board, Roxbury

Chopin

2min. JOEY
Joey and children in the autumn street, playing with tires, leaves all around; Mel looks from behind the window; Jessie picks roses

3min. A TRIP TO NEW JERSEY
Willard Van Dyke, Adolfas, Gideon Bachmann, Hella Hammid go to New Jersey *hunting*

Author's voice

4min. Al makes friends with the dog;
at the cafeteria; Al is having a conference outside, with Willard; more coffee

5min. driving again; stoping at the *hunting* grounds; the *hunter* in red jacket; Al in a tree; Al *directs* a film *(HTH)*, for Gideon's TV crew; Al cleaning his shoes, fooling around in a dug-out; the German crew moves in..

Chopin

8min. Hella, Willard; the autumn ground

Group Image, rearranged

9min. WENDY'S WEDDING
Wendy's wedding images, by the church
wedding party, 80 Wooster Street
AND MUSIC PLAYED AND PLAYED
wedding party cont.

16min. COMING BACK TO NEW YORK FROM BUFFALO
sunrise over Manhattan, over Harlem

Author's voice & camera clicks

17min. Shirley Clarke, Jud Yalkut, Gideon, on 12th Street,
Sunday breakfast
Shirley eating bagels

fooling around in Central Park

20min. skating ring

shots from Chelsea Hotel; the window, the street

22min. newspaper man on 23rd St. & 7th Avenue corner

WINTER SCENE
New York streets in winter
Walden text, from the book
winter streets in heavy snow

Louis and Shirley in a downtown street
Amy, putting make-up
at the Coop, Ernie Gehr
Sitneys, in the street

subway noise

24min. MARIE MENKEN & SISTER
Marie Menken, sunset, from Brooklyn Heights
DEEP OF WINTER
winter streets

25min. SIXTH AVENUE & BLEECKER
Sixth Avenue, empty, only pigeons and snow
SNOW FIGHT ON BLEECKER STREET
boys fighting, throwing snow at the Author

26min. THE VILLAGE VOICE
Voice offices; Fancher; Stoller

Author on Becks

A FLASHBACK: SEVEN YEARS AGO

27min. Becks & friends, at UN, picketing, in snow and cold, heavy with rucksacks and things
Walden text, from the book

subway noise

28min. windy streets, people hurrying, with their coats flying
SUNDAY MORNING
SNOW STORM ON EIGTH AVENUE
a heavy snow falling on Eigth Avenue

Buxtehude

29min. MARTHA WHOM I HADN'T SEEN FOR SOME TIME
Martha Menujin; the Author, rolling in the street & snow, with camera running
NEXT DAY

30min. Central Park scenes, after the storm
WOOSTER STREET
Wooster Street, workers keeping fires

subway noise

31min. ANTHOLOGY CINEMA MEETS
Kubelka, Brakhage, Kelman, Broughton, Sitney, Stones, on Broadway, uptown
A GIRL WAITING FOR SPRING, AT RUTGERS
Walden text, from the book
a few shots in Central Park; Michael Snow, Richard Foreman, Joyce Wieland
Richard on Wooster Street; a poor cat with rat's tail joins him

32min. students at Marlboro College

Author's voice

Howard Schulman (Rasputin) on 8th Street
sunset
scenes at Cranbrook Academy; strawberries

"Give Peace a Chance"

clouds

35min. TO YOKO & JOHN, WITH LOVE
clouds
SING TOGETHER
John and Yoko, bed-in in Montreal
(also: Tim Leary, Al Cap, Nat Hentoff)

39min. sunrise
Eigth Avenue, from a bus

41min. BLAKE SITNEY IS BORN
Blake Sitney in a crib; New Yorker Theater seen across the street, *Andalousian Dog* is playing

Sitney with Melville (dog) in Central Park

subway noise

JULIE WITH BLAKE
42min. the Author, in bed, reading

I THOUGHT OF HOME
a hand holding a clover blossom; gypsy poster
Walden text, from the book
red flowers; the girl in red sweater

Chopin

43min. SEPTEMBER
the girl in red, cont. Central Park. She looks at the tree, the leaves are getting brown already

44min. she caresses the grass, with her foot;

subway noise

camera runs thru the grass
Walden text, from the book
the girl in red, cont. Now she sits down, and looks at the park, lights a cigarette
she smiles, sort of; in her fingers she has a tiny flower, or just a stem of grass, she studies it
WALDEN

45min. END OF FIRST DRAFT OF THE DIARIES

This film may be rented from the Film-Makers' Cooperative, 175 Lexington Avenue, New York, N.Y.

Program notes for the premiere of *Walden (Diaries, Notes, and Sketches)*, 1969. In these notes, Mekas suggests to his viewers that they may wander in and out of the screening. To aid them, he provides a detailed, timed breakdown of every scene—who appears and what sounds are playing—for each of the film's four reels.

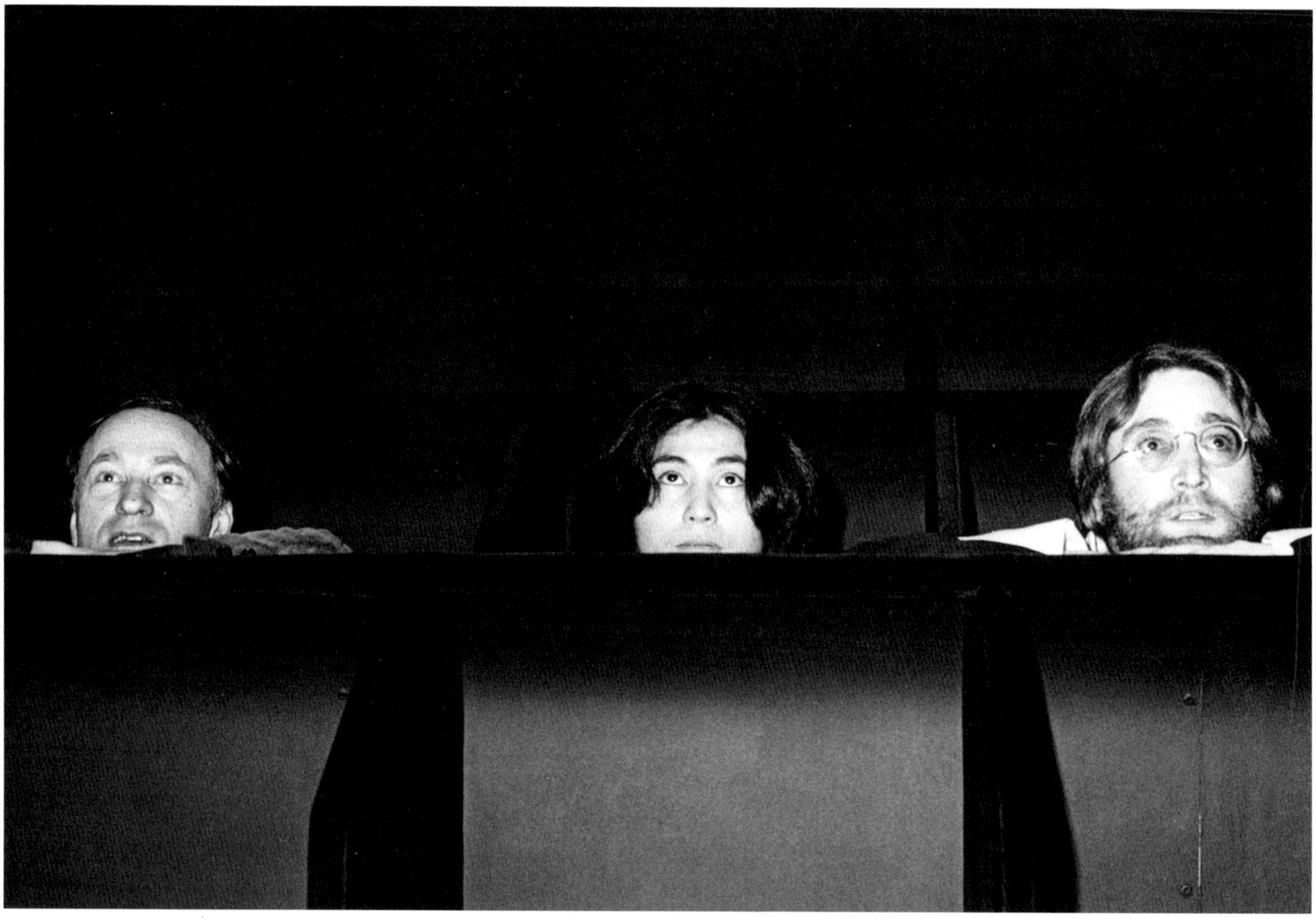

Jonas Mekas, Yoko Ono, and John Lennon at the Invisible Cinema, photographed by Gretchen Berg, 1970.

28 Jonas Mekas, program notes for *Diaries, Notes, and Sketches, aka Walden*, first draft, Anthology Film Archives, December 1969.

29 Mekas and MacDonald, "Interview," 107.

30 Jonas Mekas, final version of program notes for *Walden*, https://film-makerscoop.com/catalogue/jonas-mekas-walden.

31 For a fuller discussion of the use of affect in Chopin, see Paulo C. Chagas, *Unsayable Music: Six Reflections on Musical Semiotics, Electroacoustic, and Digital Music* (Leuven, Belgium: Leuven University Press, 2014), 46.

32 "The first tone of a scale, the tonic, is a point of rest and is considered to be the most stable. Other tones lead toward or away from it, creating varying degrees of tension or relaxation." Bruce Benwards and Marilyn Nadine Saker, *Music in Theory and Practice*, vol. 1 (Boston: McGraw-Hill, 2009), 28.

accurately, as "the John Cale sound."[28] Only in 1984 did he mention that he had tinkered with Cale's work: "I should add or rather reveal a secret: that *John Cale sound* is tampered with . . . I doubled the speed. . . . It didn't work as it was."[29] The increased speed draws parallels between Cale's drone and the subway's sound structure. Mekas uses this adroitly—equalizing, in tense, unexpected ways, the litany of single-frame images that are paired with, and thus accentuated by, Cale's intense pulse—from a series of fleeting shots of the young, stunning Amy Taubin drinking a cup of coffee to frenetic, disturbing scenes of police officers violently dismantling a peaceful protest against the Vietnam War.

Even the recurring use of Frédéric Chopin's *Études* in several of his films, especially in *Walden*, is related to Mekas's interest in and use of emergent forms. Often, during his in-person introductions to his films as well as in the program notes for *Walden*, he would confess that he was a romantic, pointing to his use of Chopin: "For the soundtrack I used some of the sounds that I collected during the same period: voices, subways, much street noise, bits of Chopin (I am a romantic) and other significant and insignificant sounds."[30] In *Walden* he uses Chopin primarily to accompany conventionally romantic images: Barbara Rubin planting flowers, a montage of spring flowers for Marie Menken, Amy Taubin frolicking near the lake in Central Park, P. Adams Sitney's wedding, couples walking along the Hudson River. On the level of image, Mekas falls victim to the "sound poetics of affects" that Chopin elicits in his listeners, intentionally presenting commonplace sound-objects, such as simple melodies—easily consumed by a mass audience.[31] At the level of sound composition for *Walden*, however, Mekas tucks very short segments of Chopin in between larger segments of ongoing subway sound or Cale's electric barrage. In this way, Chopin's roving polyphony is highlighted—tonally inductive, almost imperceptibly moving in on (and away from) a tonic—every time it has a moment to shine in the film.[32]

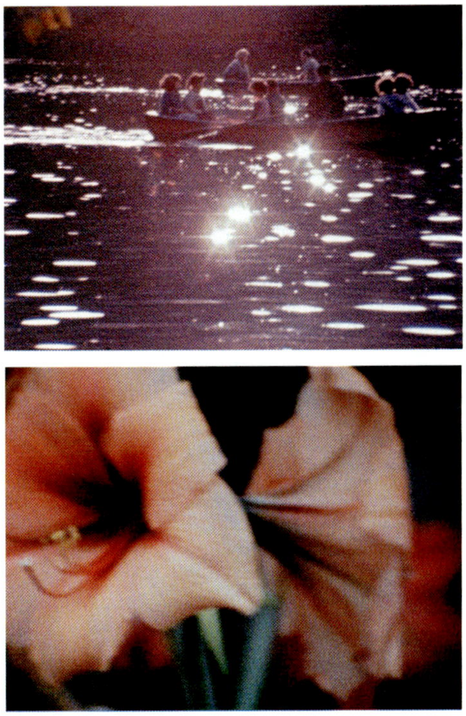

Two stills from *Walden (Diaries, Notes, and Sketches)*, 1969.

CHANCE

Hand in hand with theories of emergence, John Cage's ideas about chance operations, indeterminacy, and silence influenced Mekas's way of thinking about image and sound constructions. In his film *As I*

33 Jonas Mekas, *As I Was Moving Ahead Occasionally I Saw Brief Glimpses of Beauty* (2000), 16mm, color and black and white, sound, 288 min.

34 John Cage, *Silence: Lectures and Writings* (Hanover, NH: University Press of New England, 2000), 63.

35 Jonas Mekas, "I Seem to Live" manuscript, 593.

36 Cage, *Silence*, 10–11.

Was Moving Ahead Occasionally I Saw Brief Glimpses of Beauty (2000), culled from thirty years of his diary footage, he proclaims: "So, when I began, now, to put all these rolls of film together, to string them together, the first idea was to keep them chronologic. But then I gave up, and I just began splicing them together—by chance, the way that I found them on the shelf."[33] The durational element in his epic-length films—this one is almost five hours long—is closely tied to Cage's rethinking of sound and silence in temporal terms. Cage recognized that of all the characteristics that define sound—pitch, timbre, loudness, and duration—only the last could be shared equally by silence.[34] Mekas was already familiar with Cage's theories of music before he made *Walden*. In 1965, after hearing a concert that included Stockhausen's *Kontakte* (1958–60) and Cage's *Atlas Eclipticalis* (1961) and *Winter Music* (1957), Mekas wrote in his diary:

> After the first few moments of Cage everything became immediately clear. What a difference [compared to Stockhausen's work]: here I heard sounds, or almost pure [sounds] (execution sometimes seemed to dramatize them, particularly piano, but not enough to destroy the purity or nakedness of the sounds)—the beauty of sounds left by themselves is enough to keep you in suspense, yes, almost in suspense, because of the tremendous tension and dynamics created by silences, because of the tensions between the sounds.[35]

The idea of "sounds left by themselves," both intentional and unintentional (those made during the supposed moments of *silence*), was a dictum that Mekas used to create the soundtracks in many of his film and video works. He welcomed the unorthodox mix of classical and experimental chance structures in Cage's work. In 1957, Cage wrote: "Those involved with the composition of experimental music find ways and means to remove themselves from the activities of the sounds they make. Some employ chance operations, derived from the source as ancient as the Chinese *Book of Changes* [aka the *I Ching*], or as modern as the tables of random numbers used also by physicists in research. . . . It goes without saying that dissonances and noises are welcome in this new music. But, so is the dominant seventh if it happens to put in an appearance."[36]

In his wide-ranging choice of sound and music for his films and videos, Mekas embraced the dominant seventh, a chord popular in classical and Romantic music, as well as rock 'n' roll and jazz, as much as he did the drone. Besides foregrounding music from the

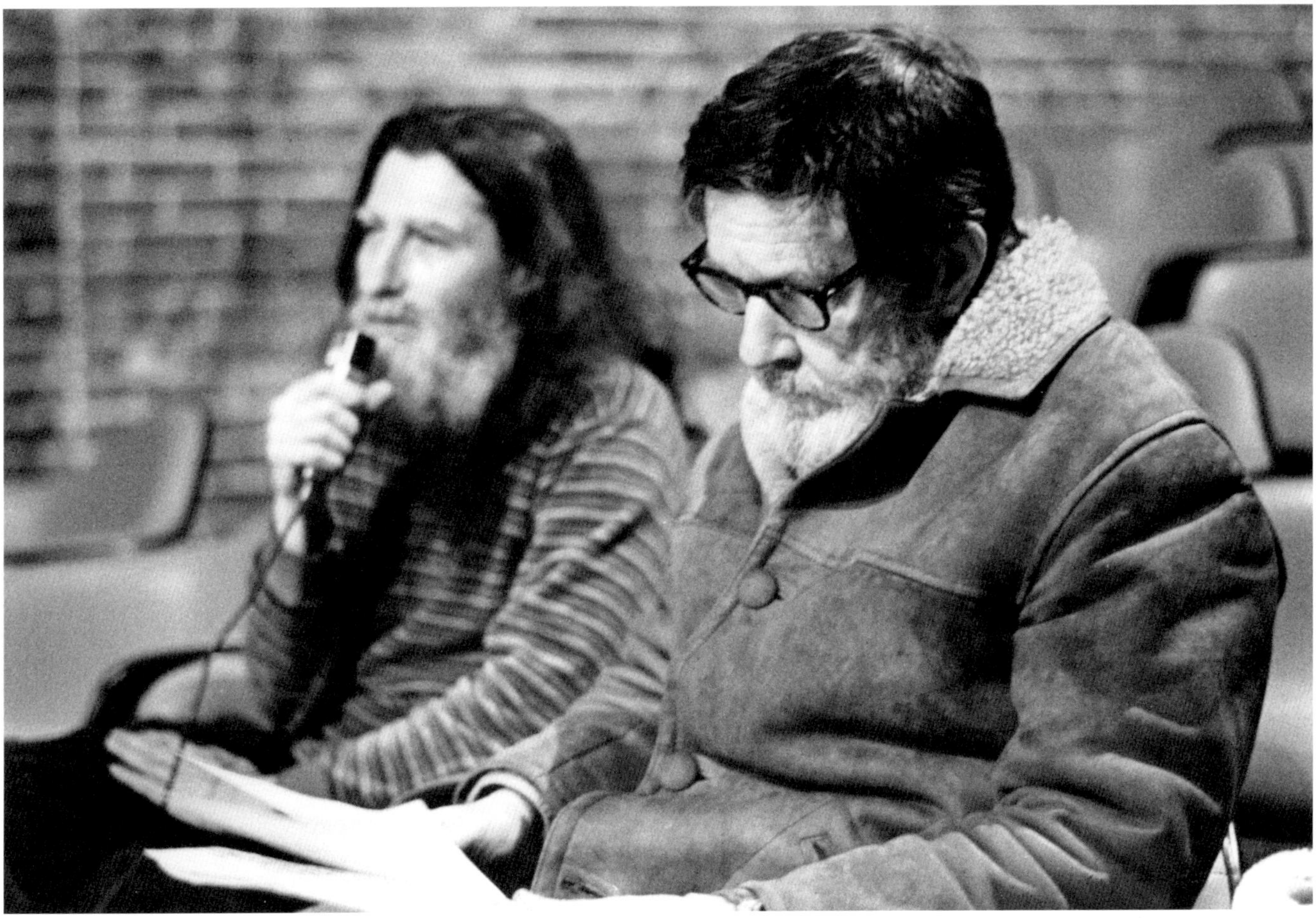

John Cage and Jackson Mac Low at the Film-Makers' Cinematheque, 1968.

37 Mekas, program notes for *Walden*, first draft. The Kreeping Kreplach Non-Profit Cultural International Foundation of Purple People Art Combine had a fluctuating membership, including Barbara Rubin, Andy Warhol, Jonas Mekas, Allen Ginsberg, Peter Orlovsky, Tuli Kupferberg and Ed Sanders (poets and cofounders of the band The Fugs), Gerard Malanga, the rock writer Al G. Aronowitz, Ronna Page (a writer and actress in Warhol films), and Walter Bowart (writer for the *East Village Other*). Ginsberg explained the purpose of the Kreeping Kreplach as "to expedite matters of international cultural exchange . . . by paying the expenses of visiting artists in America and England. [After expenses, the money made from] film, poetry readings, concerts, or exhibitions, will be put into a fund in the country where the performance is held and applied to the expenses of the next performance." Tom McNamara, "Kreplach to Invade London," *East Village Other*, June 7, 1966, 6.

38 Mekas's son, Sebastian, recalled that he was also "very much influenced by the taste of [the Fluxus artist] George Maciunas who was tremendously versed in the history of music literature—especially early music. He was not so much fond of Mozart or Mahler; he would have rather chosen Pergolesi and was a huge fan of Monteverdi. . . . Some of that music landed in the background of Jonas's work. George also introduced him to the musical endeavors of Ezra Pound, better known as a poet, notably his opera, *Le Testament de Villon*, written under the influence of the troubadour tradition." Sebastian Mekas, quoted in Šumila, "New York Scenes and Echoes from Lithuania."

39 Mekas's film *Requiem* was born out of a co-commissioned invitation by the Shed in New York and Festspielhaus Baden-Baden, Germany. The *Requiem* performances, for which Currentzis conducted a one-hundred-member orchestra and eighty-member chorus from Russia, ran at the Shed, November 19–24, 2019, https://theshed.org/program/series/18-requiem.

40 Hans Ulrich Obrist, senior program adviser for the Shed, *Jonas Mekas's Legacy*, video interview, November 19, 2019, https://www.facebook.com/watch/?v=1121924594676463.

Velvet Underground, John Lennon, Yoko Ono, and Chopin, and sound from the street and subway for *Walden*'s soundtrack, he also included an eclectic mix of Lithuanian folk music, psychedelic rock, Viennese music, jazz, accordion music (improvised by himself), the Jim Kweskin Jug Band, banjo, camera clicks, ambient noise ("leaves in the wind," "birds and skating rink music," "ocean waves"), radio, chanting by a Hare Krishna group and many voices, including Mekas's, members of the Film-Makers' Coop, and the Kreeping Kreplach.[37] He also sampled classical composers such as Lili Boulanger (one of Stan Brakhage's favorite French composers) and Dietrich Buxtehude, a Danish-German Baroque organist and composer. In other films, he borrowed snippets of music from the Italian madrigal composers of the late Renaissance, such as Monteverdi.[38]

Almost all Mekas's films use some form of chance, particularly in the way a relationship is established between music, sound, silence, and image. But his last, grand work, *Requiem* (2019), was, in many ways, the most chance-centered work of his oeuvre. It was screened with a live performance of a new interpretation of Verdi's *Requiem* (1874) by the daring Greek conductor Teodor Currentzis.[39] According to Mekas's editor, Elle Burchill, he agreed to this project mostly because he was an admirer of the poet and novelist Alessandro Manzoni, whose death inspired Verdi's *Requiem*. The venture "grew very organically out of the interest Mekas always has had in music and the way he connected music and cinema," explains one of the commissioning curators. Mekas was "fascinated also by Currentzis's work and he was really listening a lot to Currentzis's recordings."[40] Burchill offers a different view, that Mekas's process of editing *Requiem* was conducted primarily without sound of any kind: "The piece was edited without the score, as are all of his works when there is music involved. Also, the natural sound was turned off as well.

41 Elle Burchill, email to author, February 9, 2020.

42 This merging of political and personal cinema—images of state crimes such as the mass murder of millions of Jews and political dissidents in concentration camps across Europe, alongside poetic, quotidian human moments—points back to Mekas's utopian dream of realizing a contemporary avant-garde form of newsreel (intended as an alternative to commercial news). "We are here [approximately 20 people were present, i.e. filmmakers, journalists, full-time activists] to . . . "discuss and practically establish . . . vaguely, very vaguely maybe we could understand what we are talking about if we call it a CONTEMPORARY NEWS REEL. That is, that footage that many of us pick up every day at demonstrations and pickets and, sometimes, at some more quiet moments . . . and it is there . . . something is happening, and we think it should be seen across the country." Jonas Mekas, *I Seem to Live*, 821.

43 *Requiem*'s cumulative (of images of everydayness and destruction) and, ultimately, composer-driven structure is reminiscent of Godfrey Reggio's film *Koyaanisqatsi: Life Out of Balance* (1982), for which Philip Glass wrote the lush, relentless, pulse-patterned soundtrack. In other ways, they are vastly different, especially in terms of the context of their content: Reggio's barrage of repetitive images is a direct critique, a filmic assault, on American consumer society.

It was just about the rhythm of the visuals. He likes chance." In a sense, *Requiem* is a kind of retrospective of his video work from the late 1980s until his death on January 23, 2019. As Burchill describes: "Although some sections appear in other Mekas videos or diaries, like *365 Day Project* (his daily web diaries, 2007), *Sleepless Nights Stories* (2011), etc., none are edited the same. The original footage was transferred [from these other works] and edited on its own in the context of this work," *Requiem*.[41] Mekas worked on it for more than two years, right up until 10:00 PM the night before he died. Thus, in many ways, it is not only a tribute to Manzoni, as Verdi had intended, but also a *chance requiem* to himself.

After the first rough edit, Mekas simply dropped Currentzis's recording of Verdi's *Requiem* into the image sequences of his film, allowing the music to align with the visuals by Cagean chance. The results were satisfying, even thrilling: hardly any of the images accentuated or amplified Verdi's sweeping, grand gestures in typical or predictable ways. When they did, Mekas instructed Burchill to edit ever so slightly, cutting a frame or two in order to alter any "ridiculous" associations, such as a dolphin rising out of the water during Verdi's Dies Irae (Days of Wrath) section. Often even the most dramatic musical sequences are paired with the most mundane of images, very much in the spirit of his earlier films: flowers, city streets, rain-drenched sidewalks, snow-covered trees, gardens, parks, ponds, and meadows. But the work is also punctuated, even punctured, by repeated scenes of disaster: archival footage of the fires caused by Hurricane Sandy in New York in 2012; images of torture and degradation in World War II concentration camps; photographs of starving children; as well as footage of the destruction by the massive tsunami that flooded Honshu Island in Japan in 2011.[42] Emergence, as a technique in the work of Reich and Glass, haunts Mekas's visual montage—especially present in the relentless repetition of hundreds and hundreds of images of flowers (shot across four different continents). In a sense, Mekas achieves visually—albeit with much less precision—what Glass accomplishes aurally, a gradually evolving temporal subject-in-process.[43]

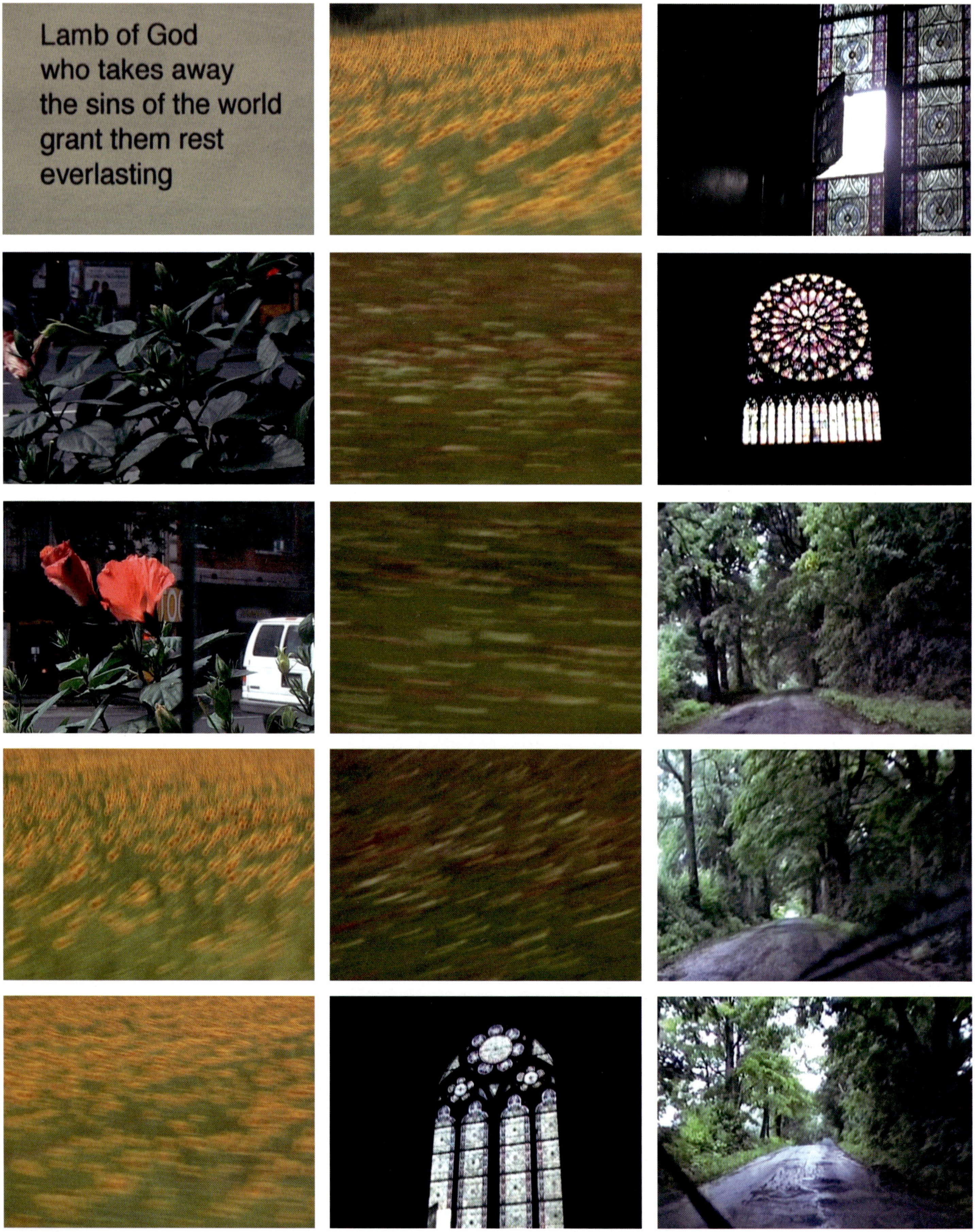

Stills from *Requiem*, 2019.

44 Don McClean, "Deliverance and Compositional Design in the 'Libera me' of Verdi's Messa da Requiem," in *Explorations in Schenkerian Analysis*, ed. David Beach and Su Yin Mak (Rochester, NY: University of Rochester Press, 2016), 253.

45 *Breathless* was one of the key early films that inspired Mekas to become a filmmaker. Irresistible is the comparison between Verdi's ambivalent relationship to his own liturgical score (he was an atheist) and Godard's (as represented by Michel in *Breathless*) cynical relationship to any system of judgment. As Mekas said to the moral critics of *Breathless* in 1961: "*Breathless* is empty, *Breathless* is immoral, they say. But, say, what other recent movie has succeeded in freeing itself from dubious values as perfectly as *Breathless*, both in form and content?" Jonas Mekas, "On Values, Godard, and a Woman's Toe," in *Movie Journal*, 39. On Verdi's religious skepticism in his *Requiem*, see McClean, quoting Charles Osborne: "The question of whether or not the end of the *Requiem* is optimistic or pessimistic, or whether it is at best ambiguous or even ambivalent, might understandably be linked to our awareness of Verdi's own religious views. . . . [He was] not a believer, but an atheist, willing in his more contemplative moments to soften his attitude to one of agnosticism." McClean, "Deliverance and Compositional Design," 275.

Mekas's largely chance-determined, audio-to-image work decenters and unsettles our relationship to Verdi's vertiginous score. Mekas delivers a complex compendium of the most tender documentary images of the environment side by side with the most horrific images of natural and culturally constructed disasters: for example, footage of the mass murder of Jews and political dissidents by their own government alongside a poetic, quotidian human moment such as Mekas's hand touching a delicate hyacinth blossom.

Although Mekas set the footage of his *Requiem* to the Verdi score, he used both chance and touches of editing to undermine the coupling of dramatic television footage (urban fires, war, flooding) with the escalating "orchestral thunderclaps" or "lightning cascades" of Verdi's *Requiem*.[44] During such dramatic musical moments, Mekas shows a swan gliding on a river or rain-wet autumn leaves emitting luminous bronze light on New York City sidewalks. The work is filled with such sound-image relations that undo commonplace cinematic expectations for how a score should function.

Another clever subversion of Verdi's liturgical score is Mekas's insertion of both subtle and overt references to avant-garde and independent film history. For instance, at one point he inserts an intertitle taken from the Agnus Dei choral sequence in Verdi's composition: "Lamb of God, who takes away the sins of the world, grant them rest everlasting." Immediately after, we see an image of a movie theater nestled next to a tattoo parlor, with marquees announcing the current film playing. (It is a long shot, so the film titles are indiscernible.) This is followed by stunning rolling frames of fields of sunflowers, and then poppies (apparently in the South of France), which blur into kinetic abstraction. Then a mist-filled landscape comes into brief focus, followed by interior shots of the Cathedral of Notre Dame in Paris, with a slow build-up of shots that lead to a grand, sweeping image of the renowned south rose window. Subsequently, viewers are given the point of view of a driver in a car, cruising down a tree-lined street perhaps in Marseille. This sequence is recognizable as an abstracted replay of one of the opening scenes of Jean-Luc Godard's *Breathless* (1960), one of the most iconic movies of the French New Wave: Michel, in a stolen car, drives down a tree-lined road in the countryside, singing and talking to himself.[45] After

46 Gregory Markopoulos, "Towards a New Narrative Film Form," *Film Culture* 31 (Winter 1963–64): 11. Markopoulos is describing his own approach, readily mappable to Mekas.

47 Ibid.

48 Jonas Mekas, "I Seem to Live" manuscript, 1492.

shooting a cop in a kind of hyperreal trance, he drives back to Paris—Notre Dame is one of the first buildings he passes. Mekas's entire Godard-inspired montage is accidentally, but nevertheless ironically, accompanied by contemplative soprano and mezzo-soprano voices, singing in unison about salvation from worldly sins.

Requiem presented an opportunity for Mekas to assert, one last time, his unwavering belief in the fragment or phrase of film as one of the most important metrics of our temporal existence. He was invested in a system of filmmaking that involved the "fusion of classic montage technique with a more abstract system."[46] One way to develop such an abstract system was to think of film as the material of cognition, that is, as a "thought image" (or passage of sound), in which "each film phrase is composed of certain select frames that are similar to the harmonic units found in musical composition."[47] Mekas wanted to see these filmic phrases or fragments collected in as many different indexes as possible—an anthology, a diary, a newsreel, even a requiem.

> My theory of the history of art (and cinema) is very simple: We should see and show absolutely everything that has survived and has been passed to us. What we know about art (and cinema) of the Past are tiny fragments of it—the fragments that are left, that have survived by a pure Cage-ian chance after all the wars, pestilences, dictatorships, fires, earthquakes, Hitlers, Stalins, Attilas have passed through; everything that hasn't fallen to dust.[48]

Finally, while Mekas incorporated various strategies of post–World War II experimental music, such as duration, emergence, and chance, into the fabric of his audiovisual work, he also injected their Minimalist, more rule-based forms with the anarchy of historical, political, and affective content. He developed shattered sonic and visual narratives of alienation, intrigue, rabble-rousing, and romance, as well as the simple, almost imperceptible gestures of everyday filmic poetry in order to unsettle and challenge structural sobriety.

ZEFIRO TORNA OR SCENES FROM THE LIFE OF GEORGE MACIUNAS, 1992

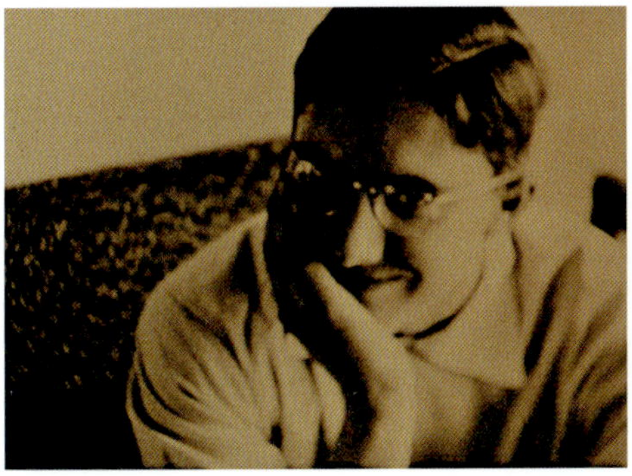

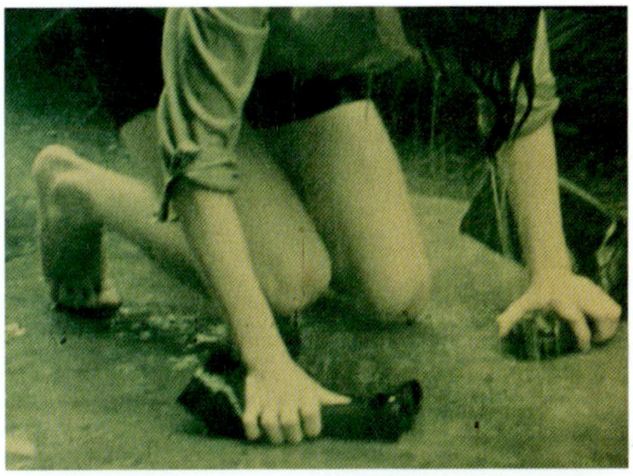

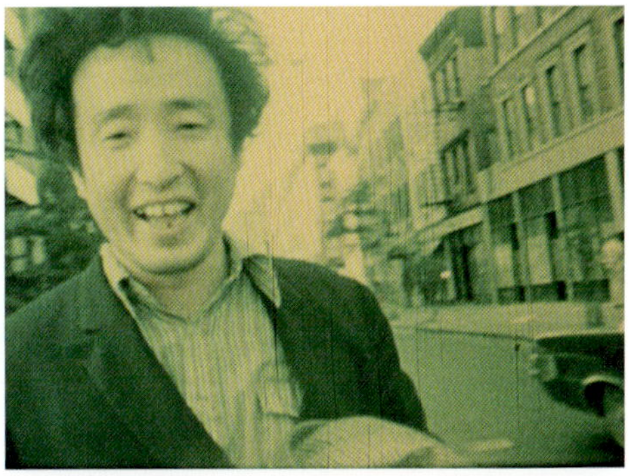

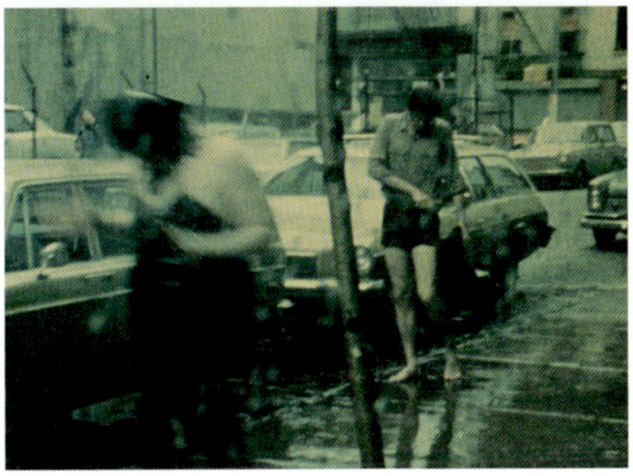

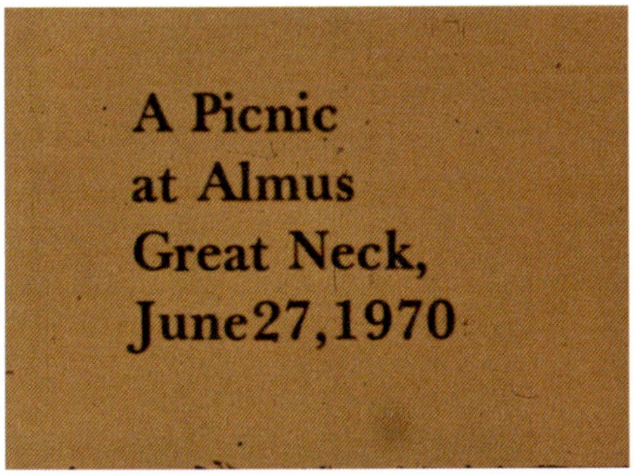

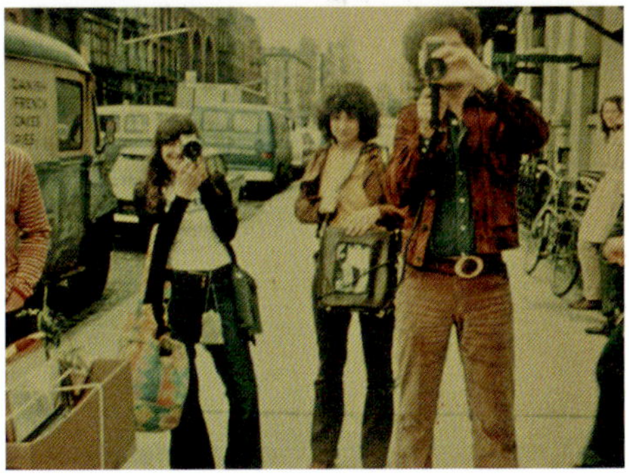

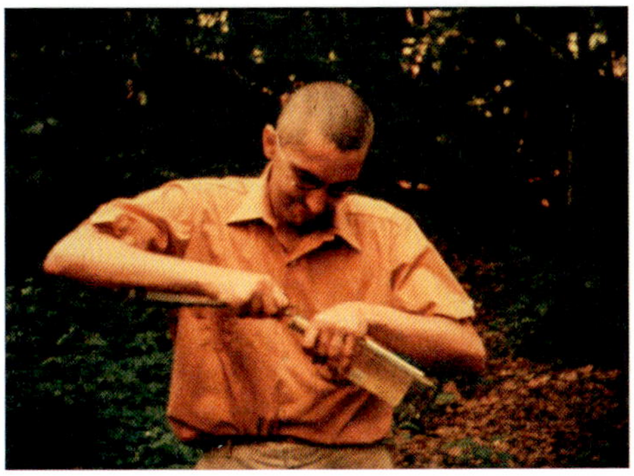

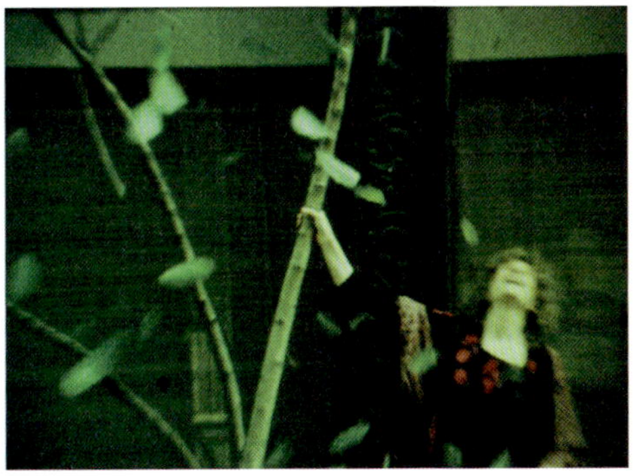

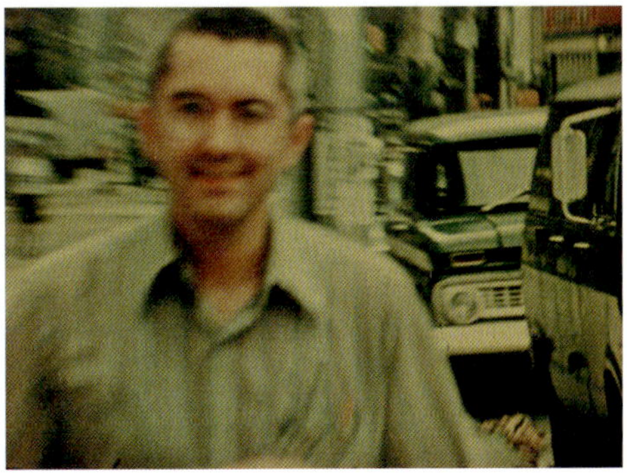

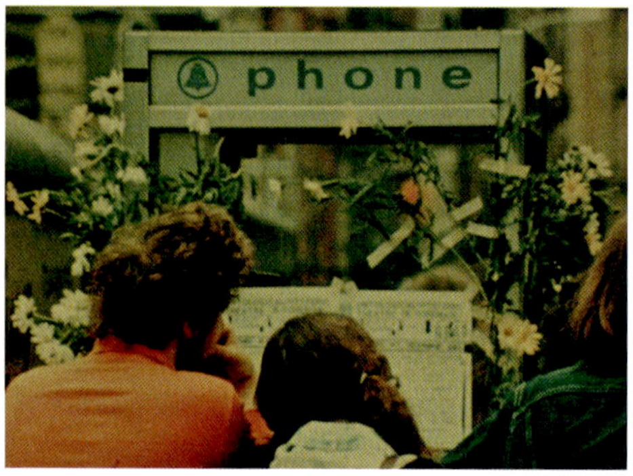
phone

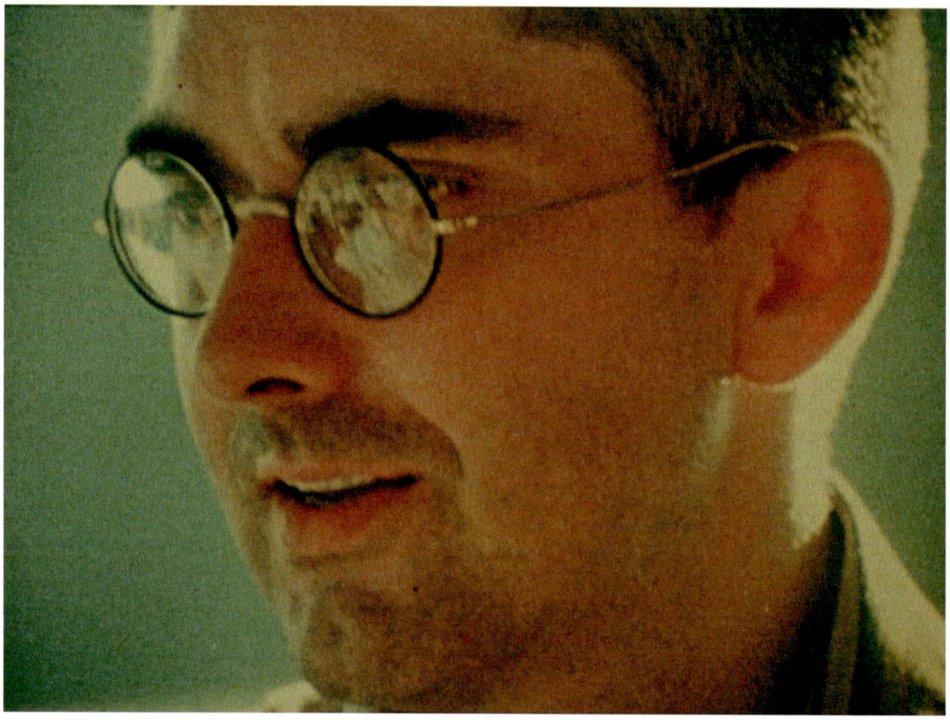

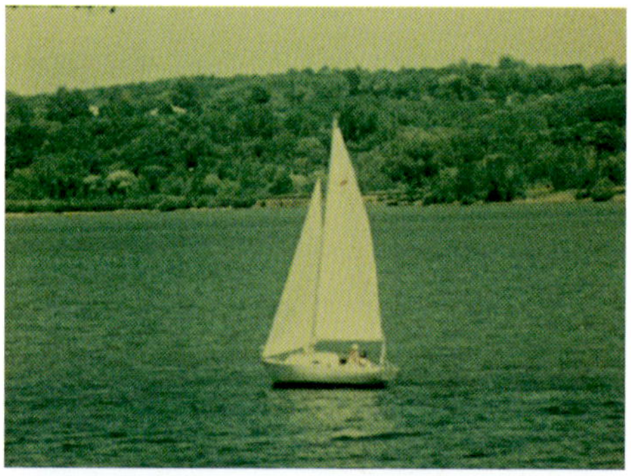

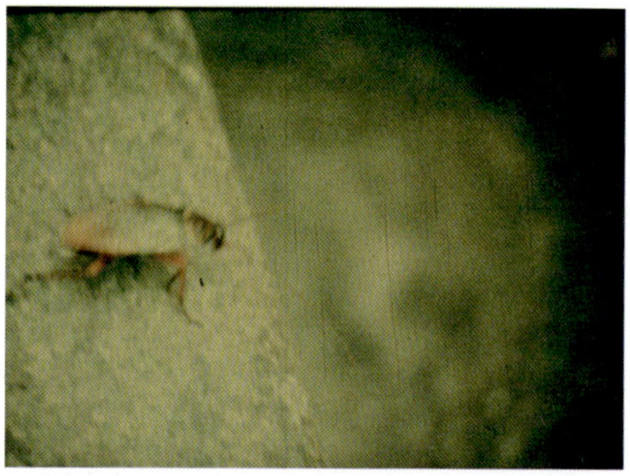

George's door
80 Wooster
May 11,1975

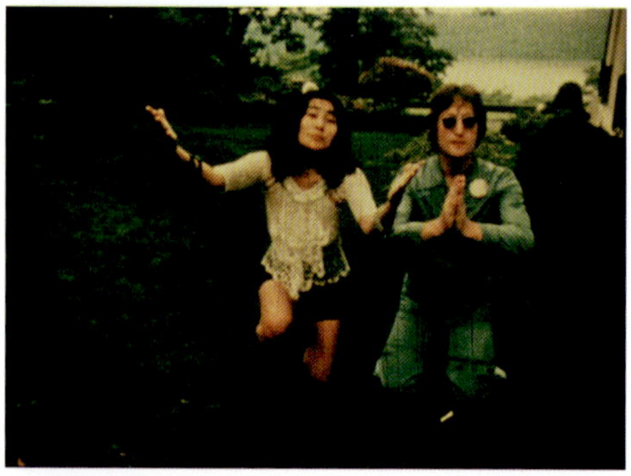

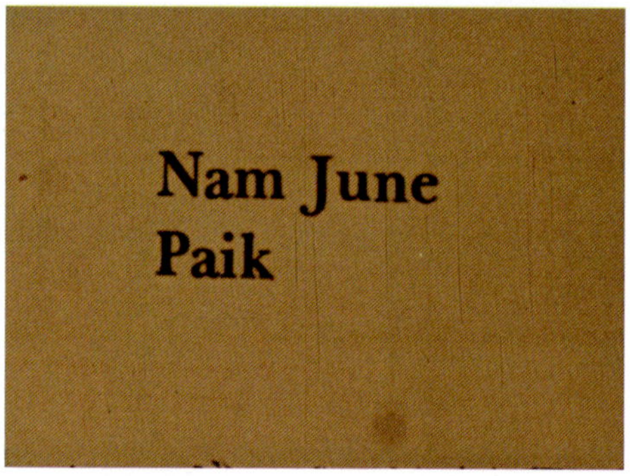
Nam June
Paik

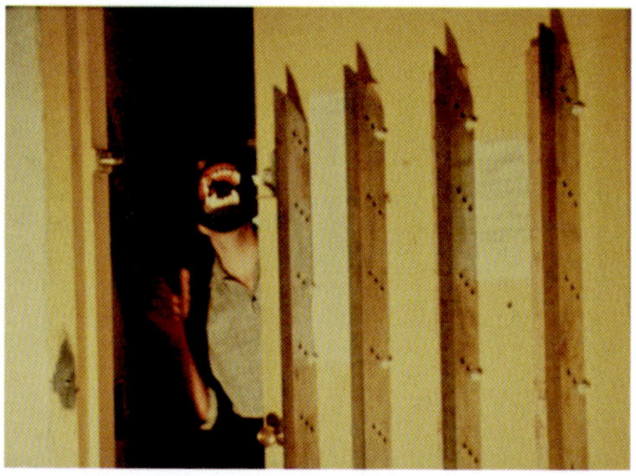

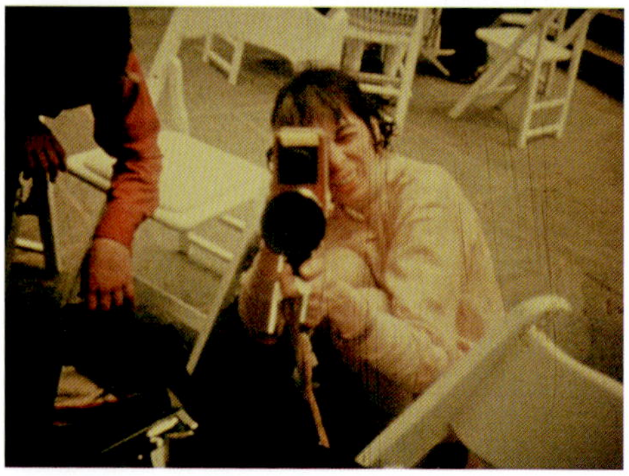

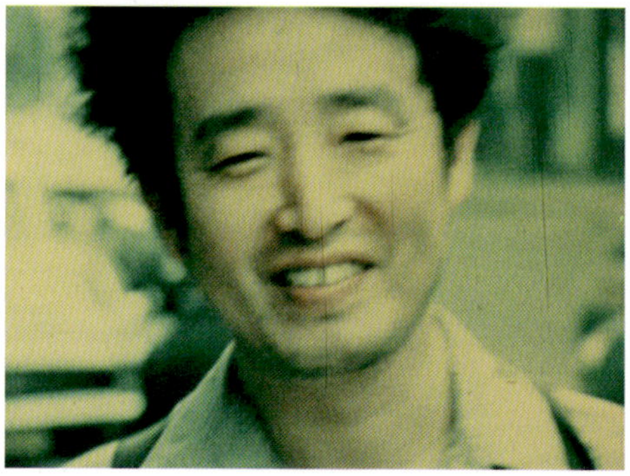

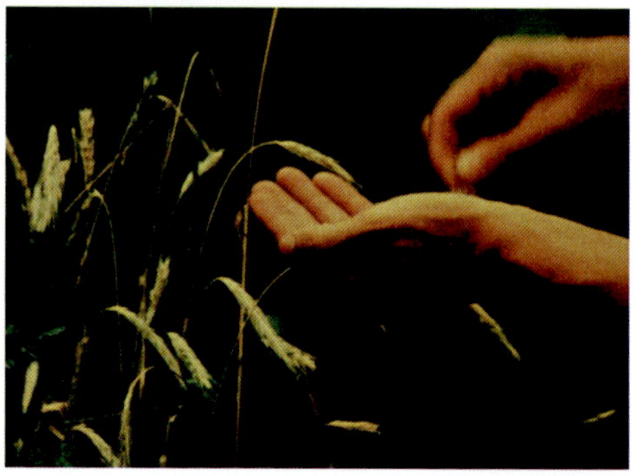

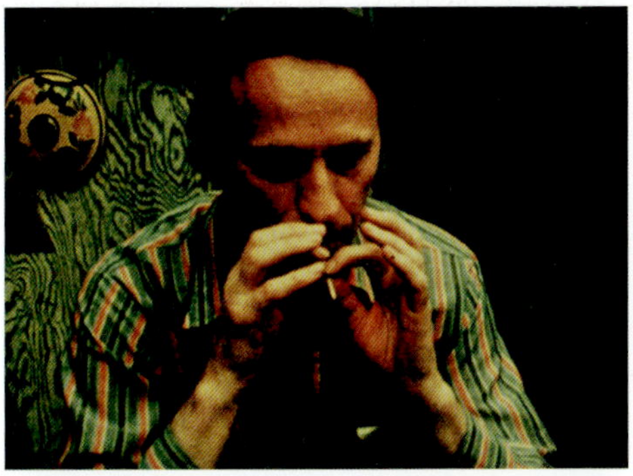
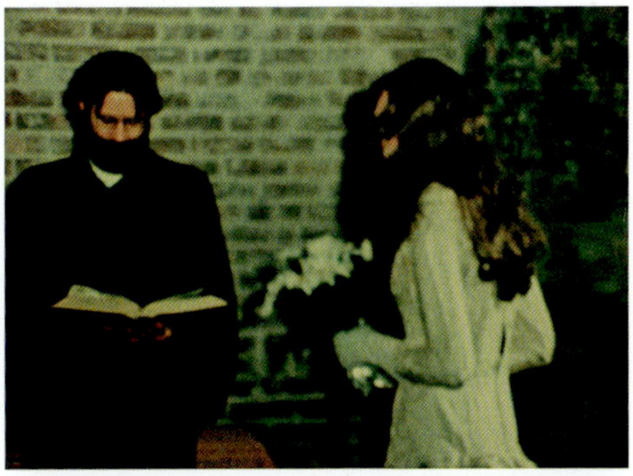
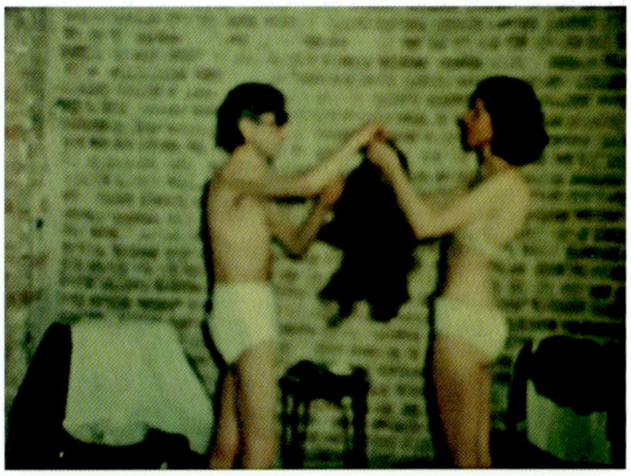
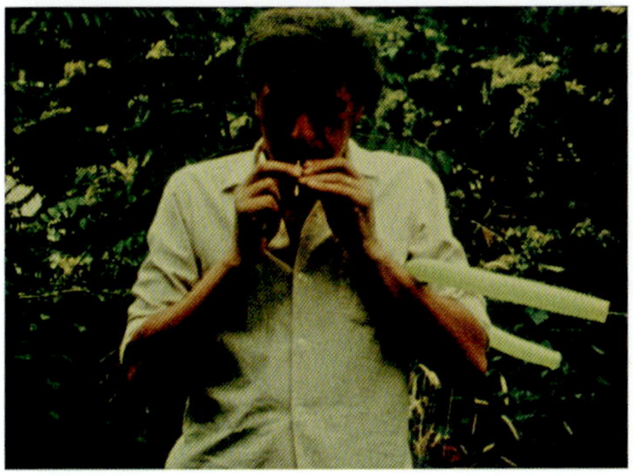
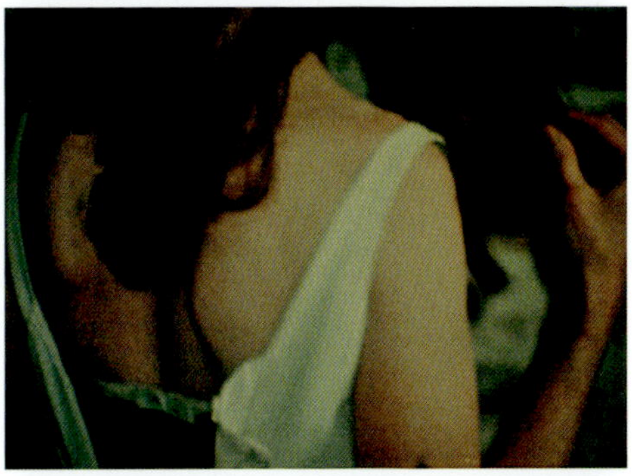
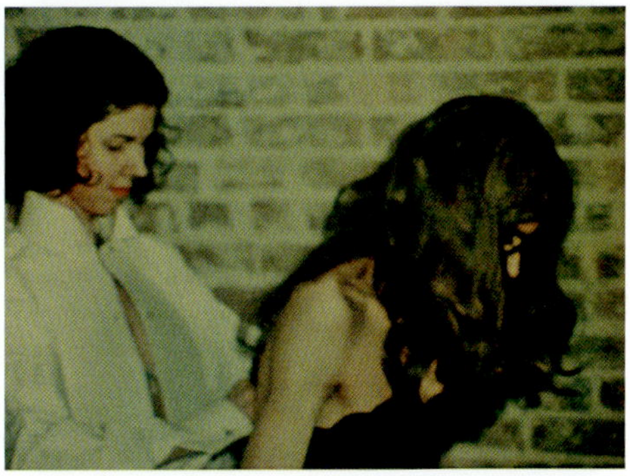
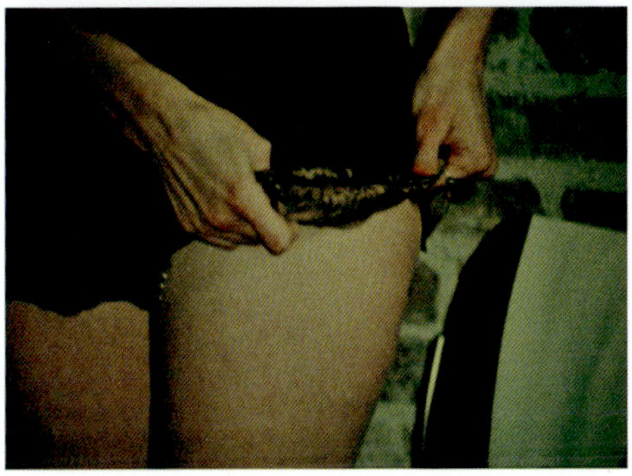
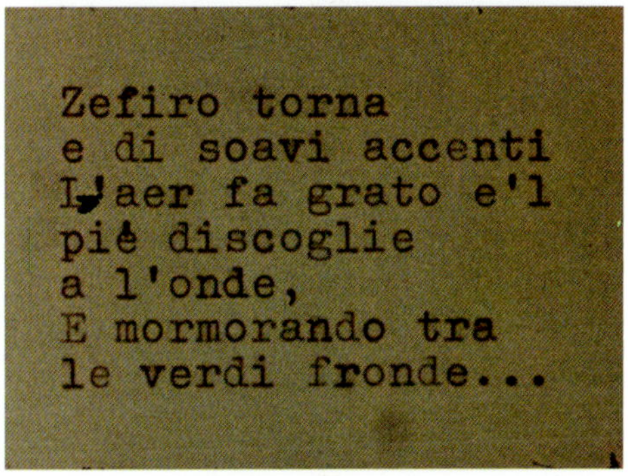

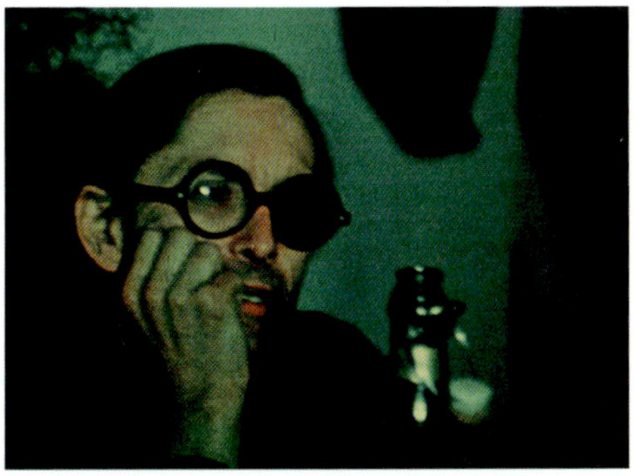
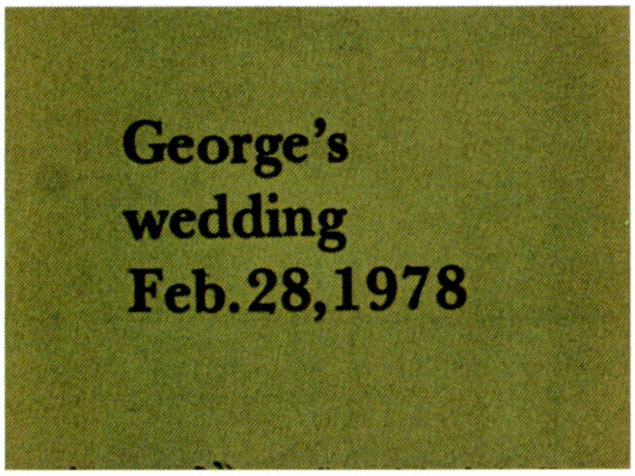

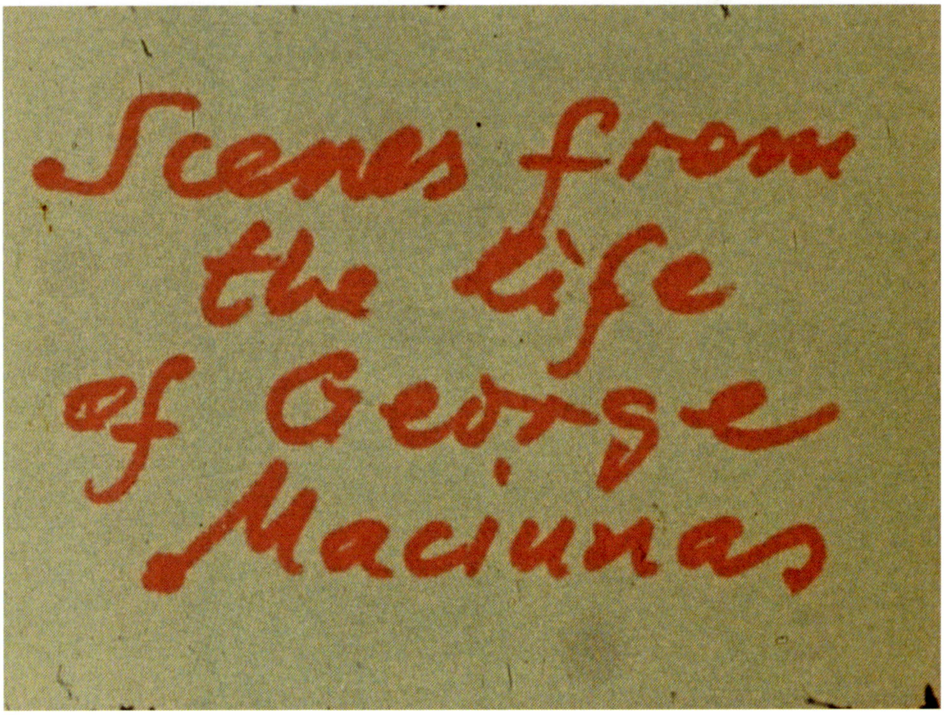

 COLOR, BLACK AND WHITE SOUND 34 MIN

THIS SIDE OF PARADISE, 1999

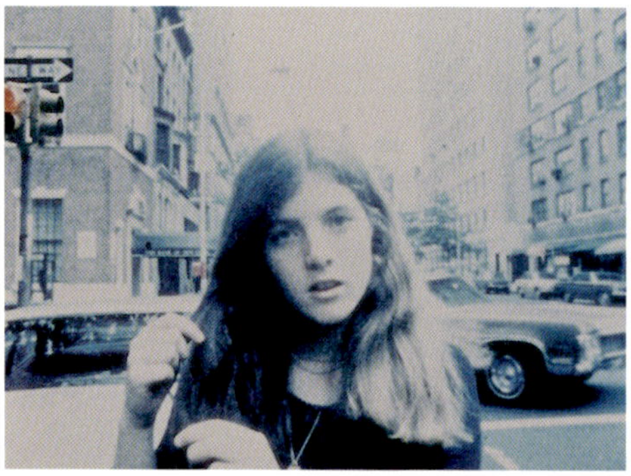

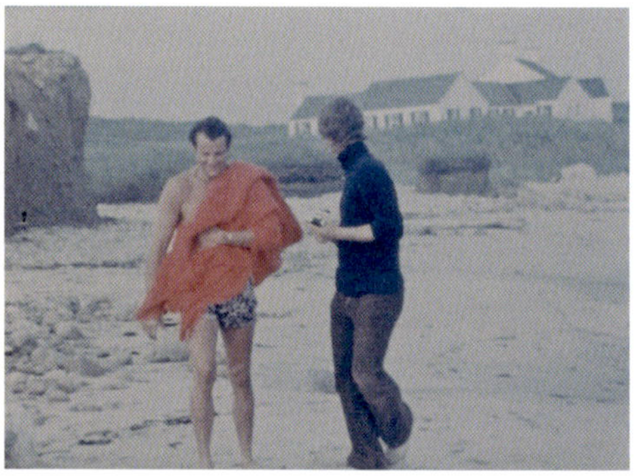

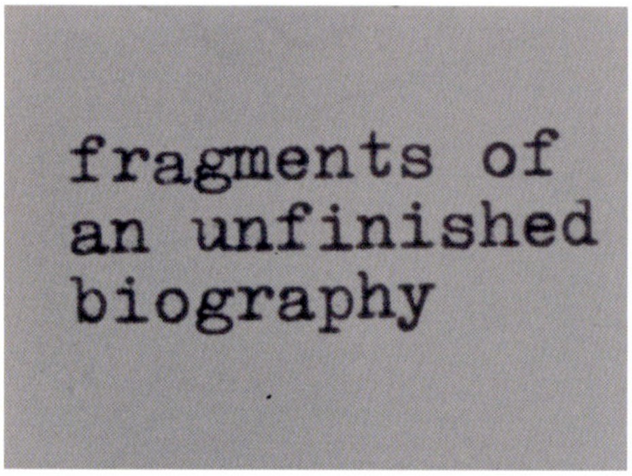

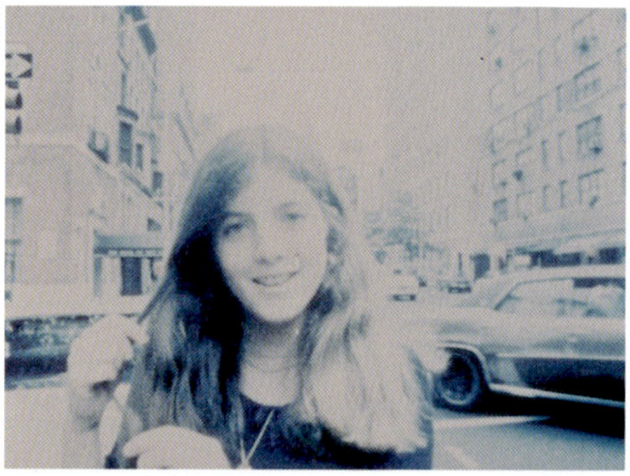

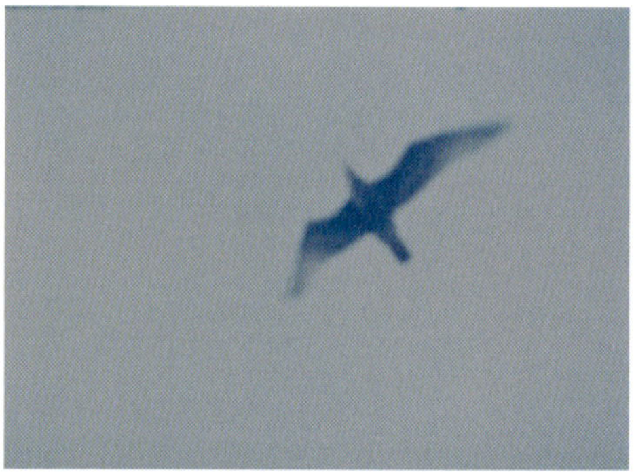

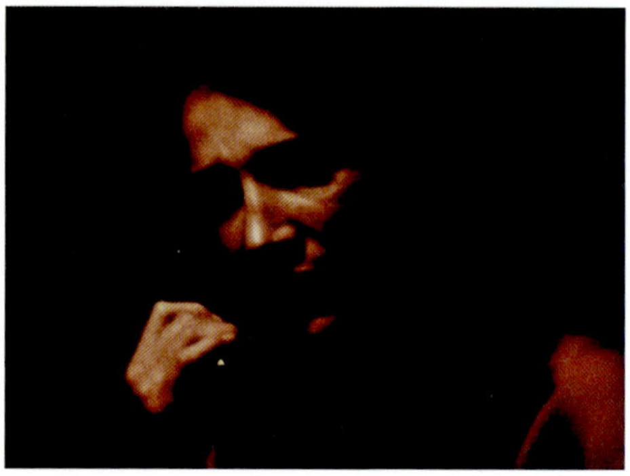

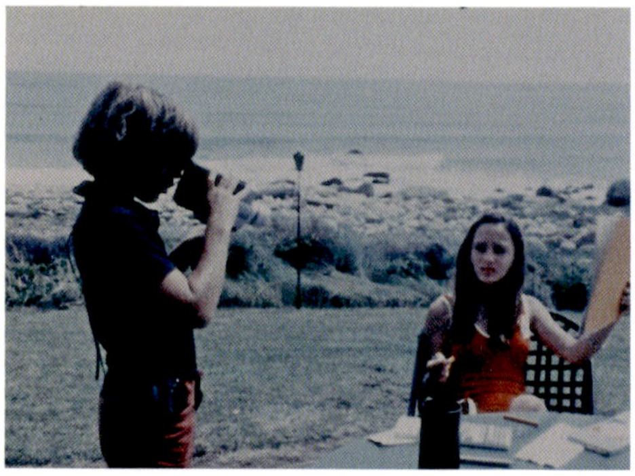

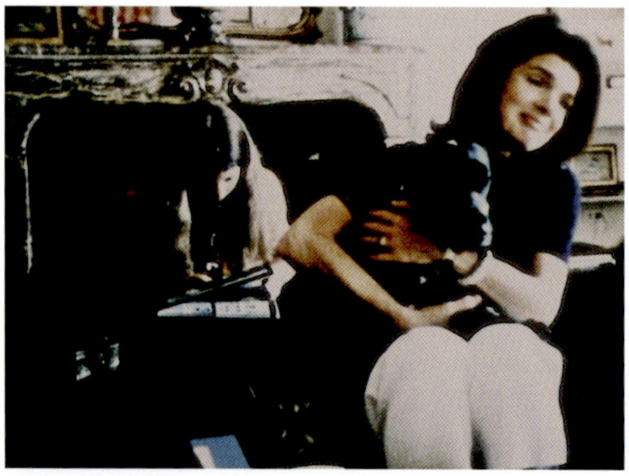

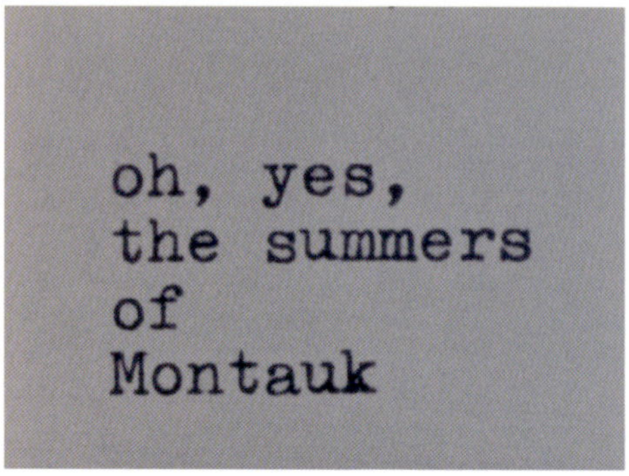

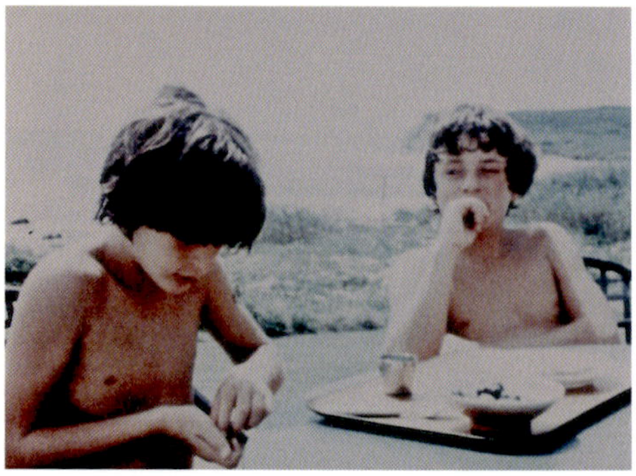

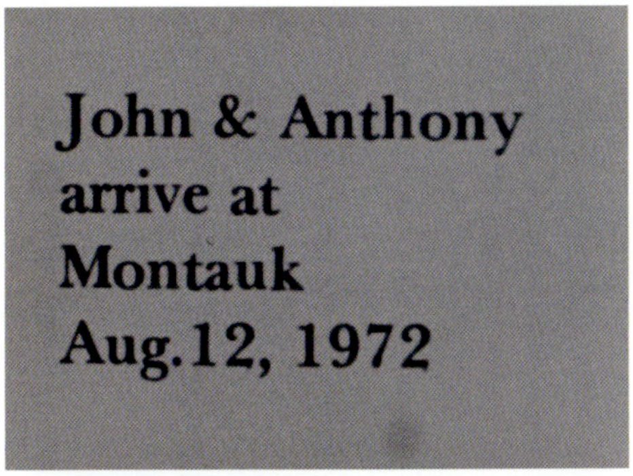

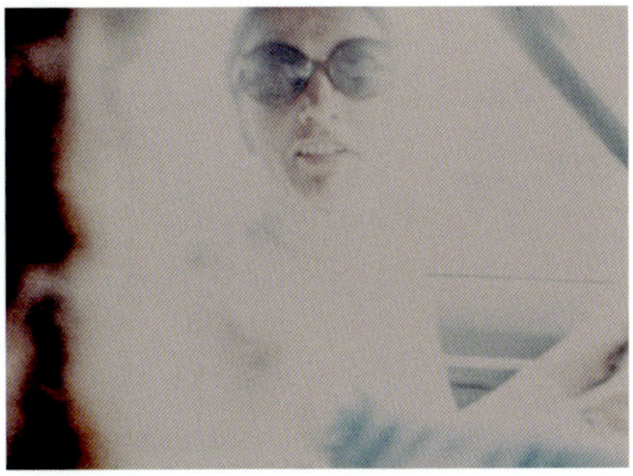

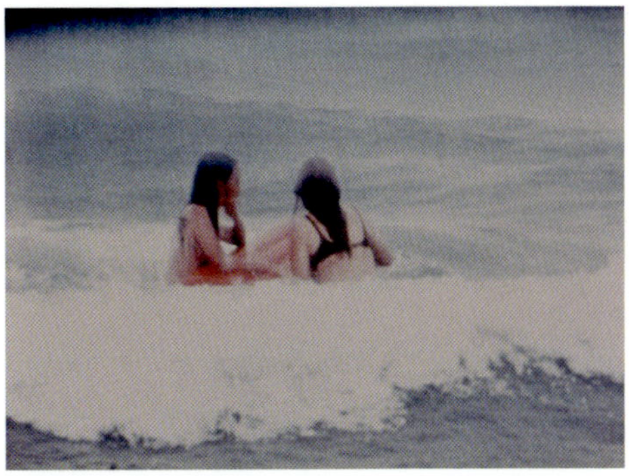

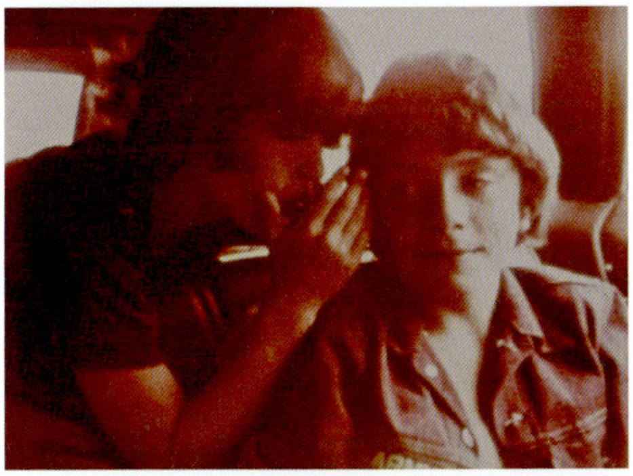

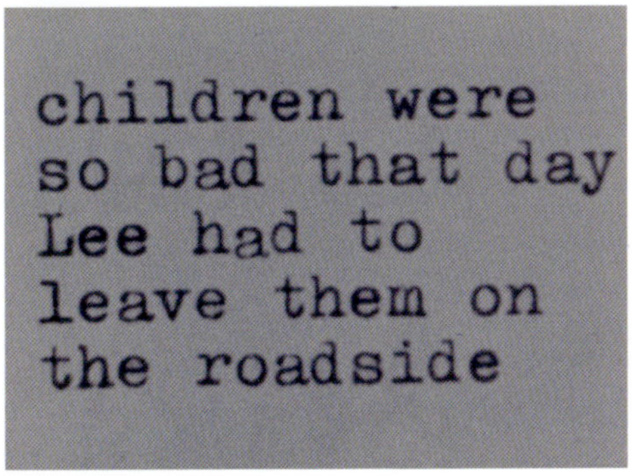

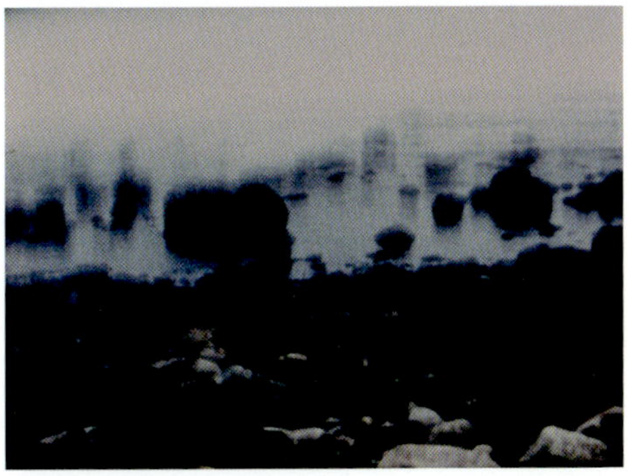

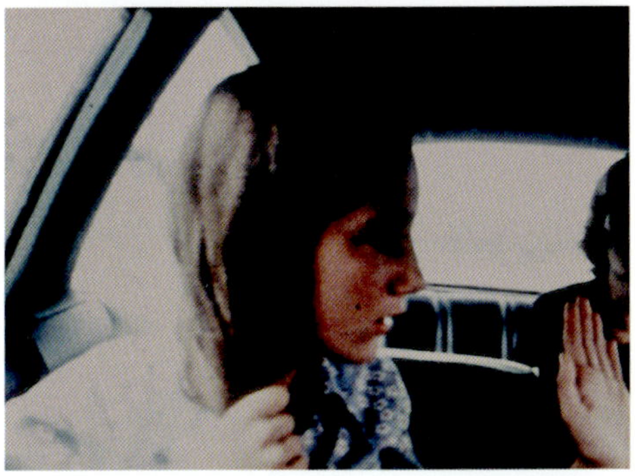

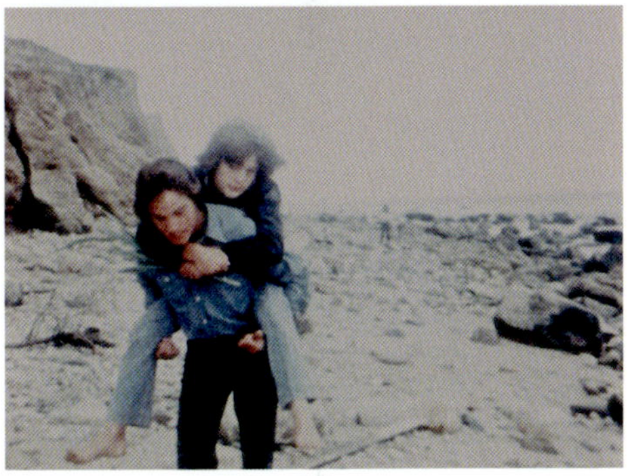

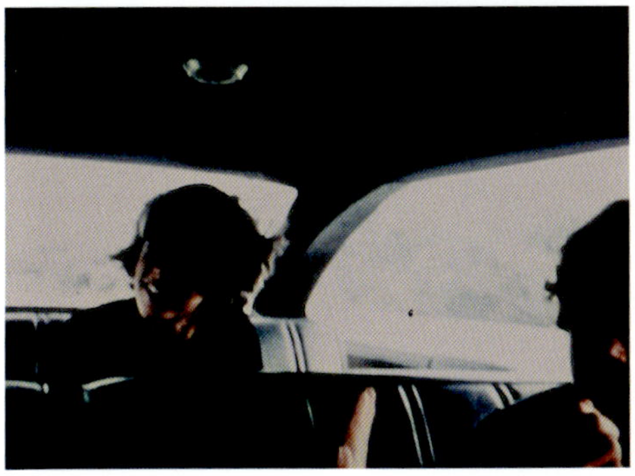

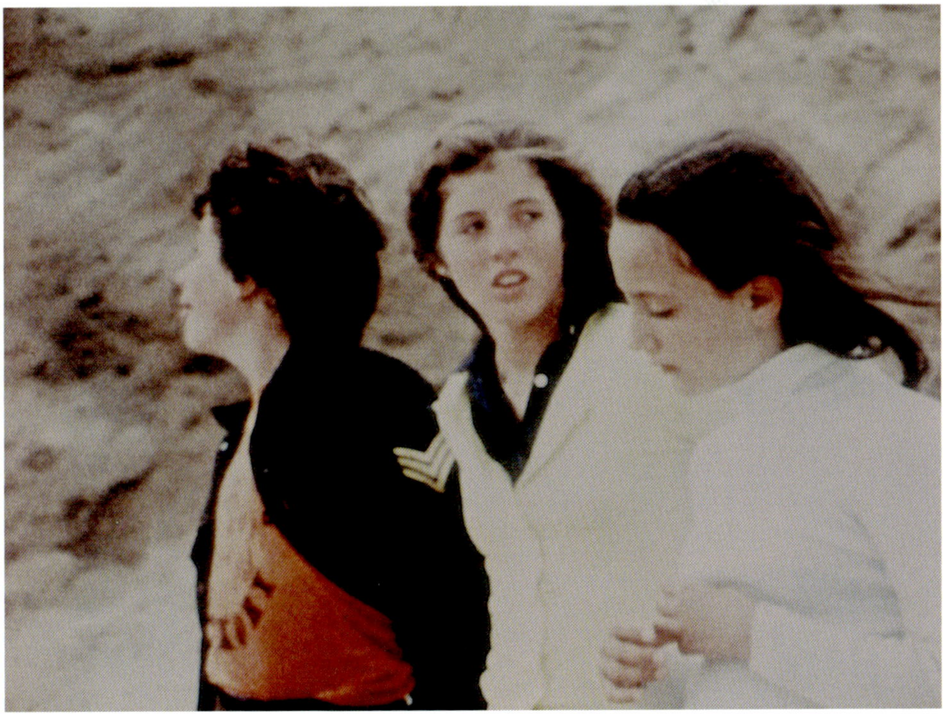

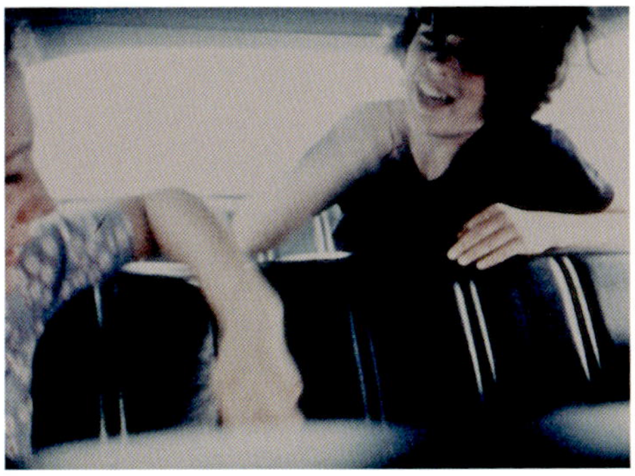

COLOR, BLACK AND WHITE SOUND 35 MIN

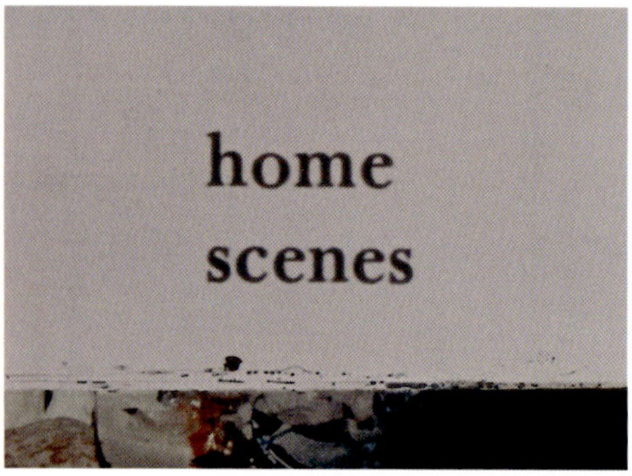
home
scenes

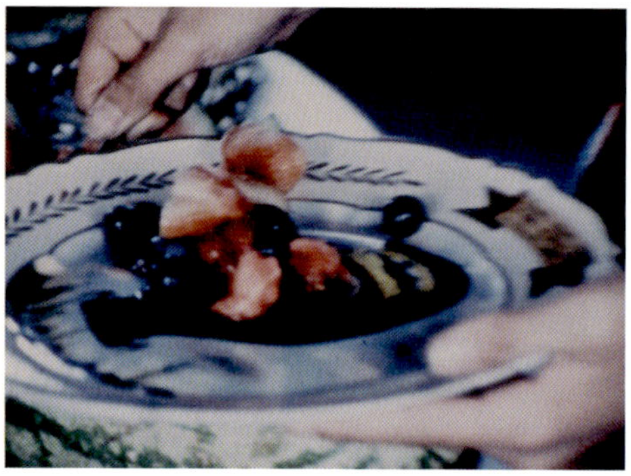

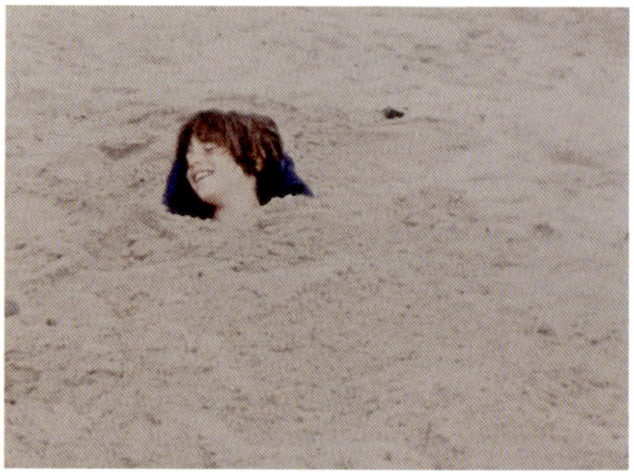

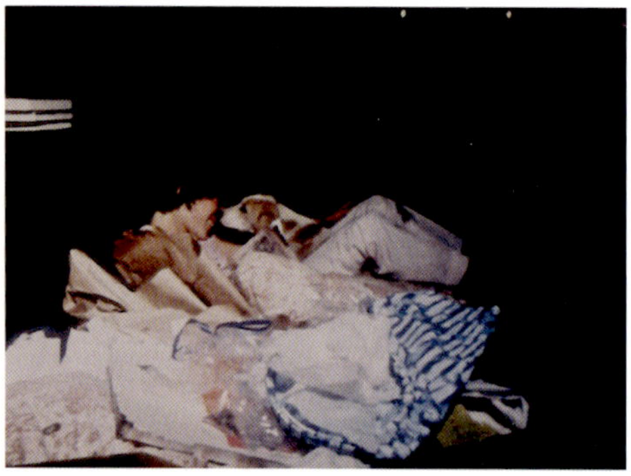

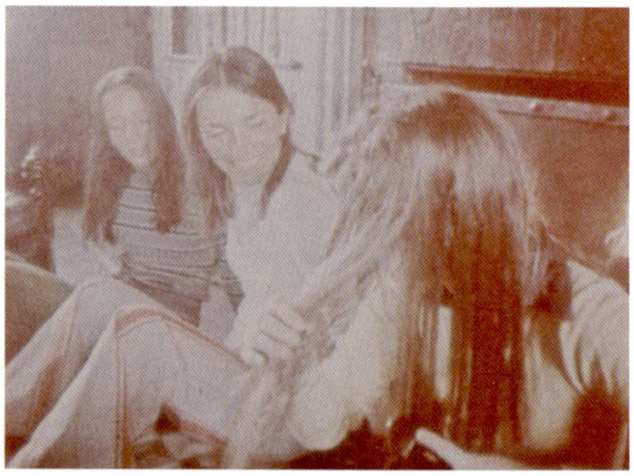

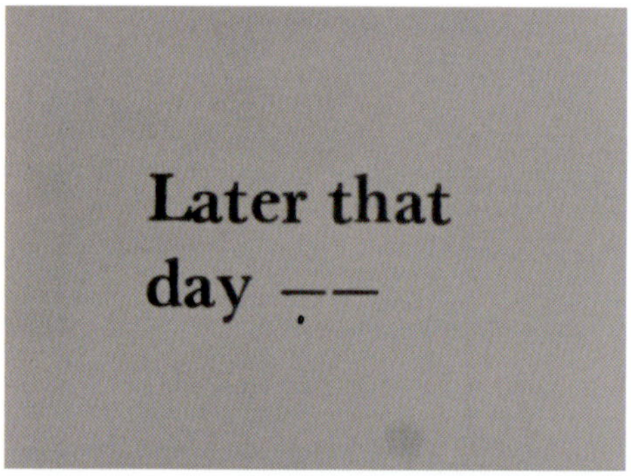
Later that
day --

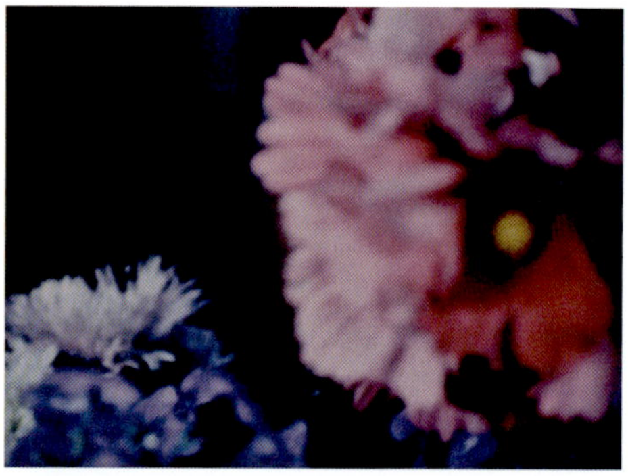

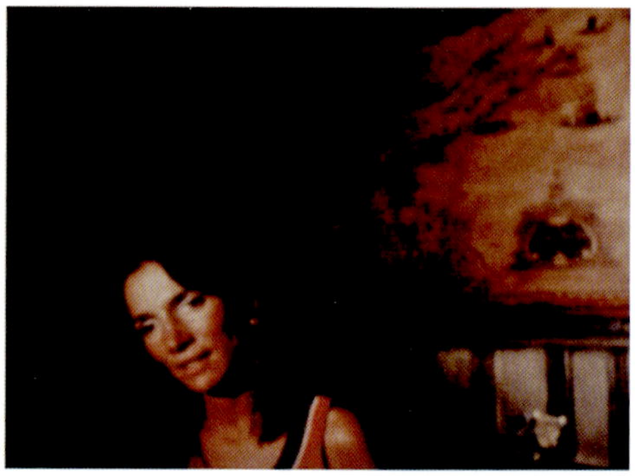

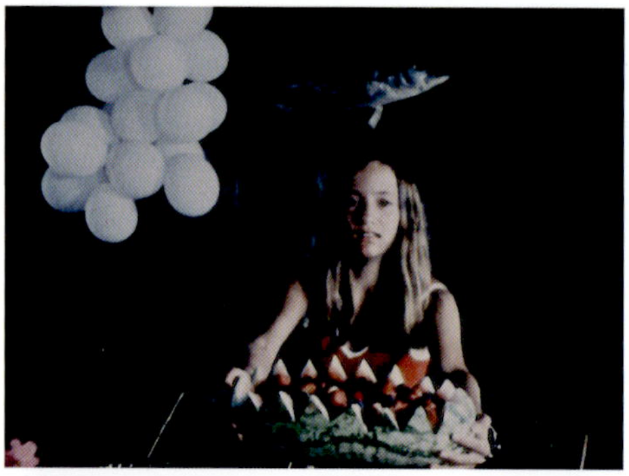

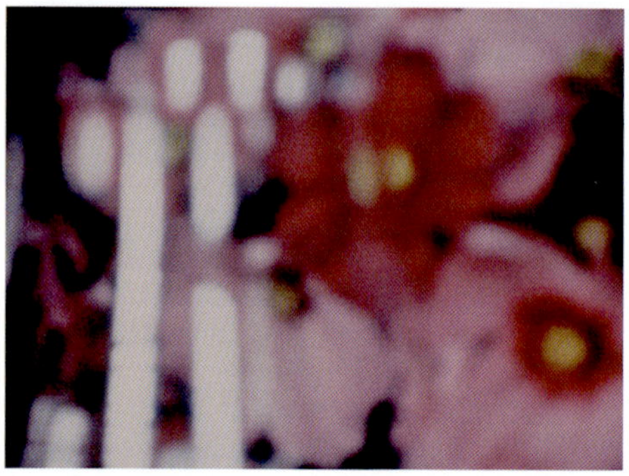

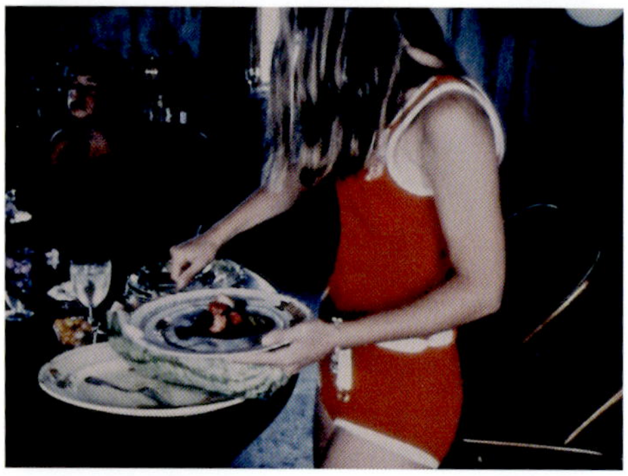

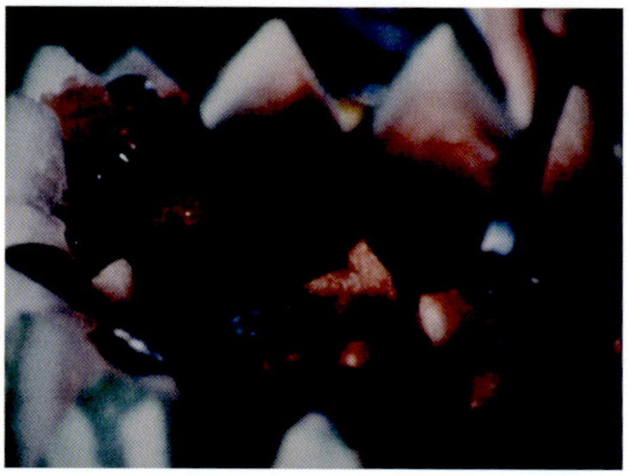

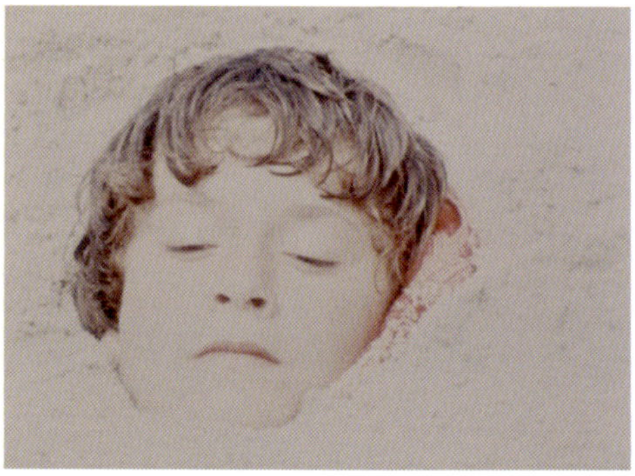

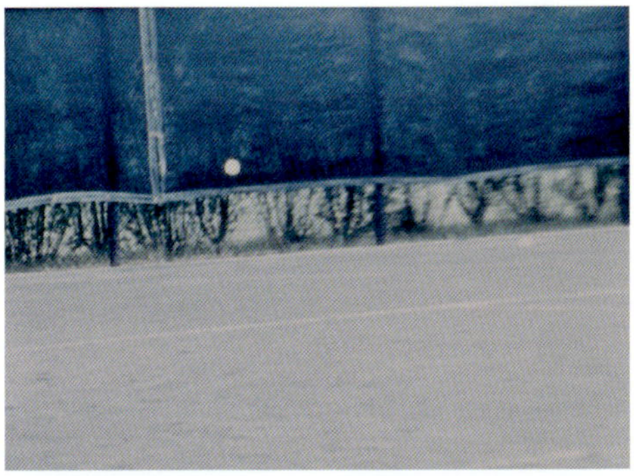

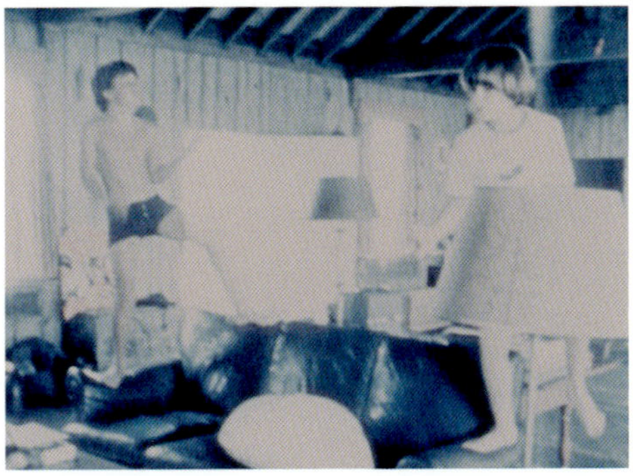

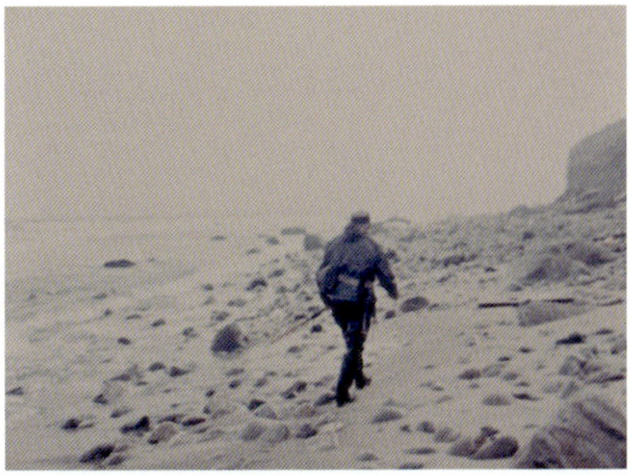

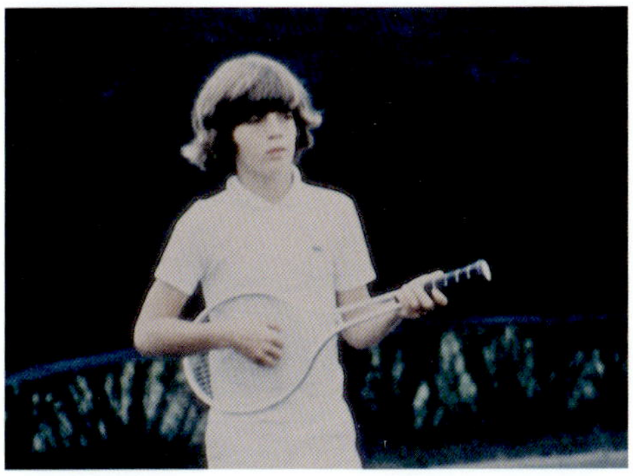

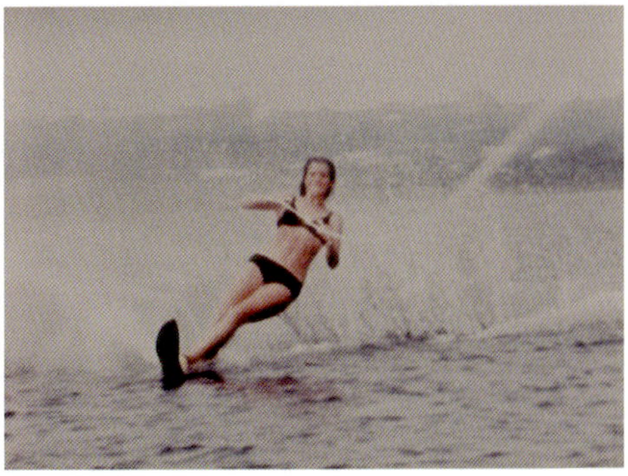

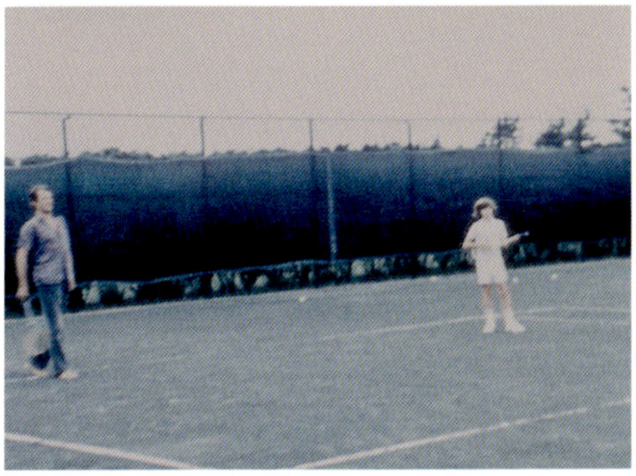

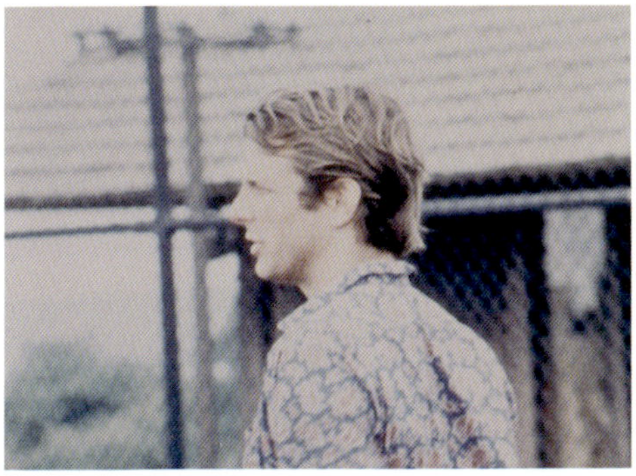

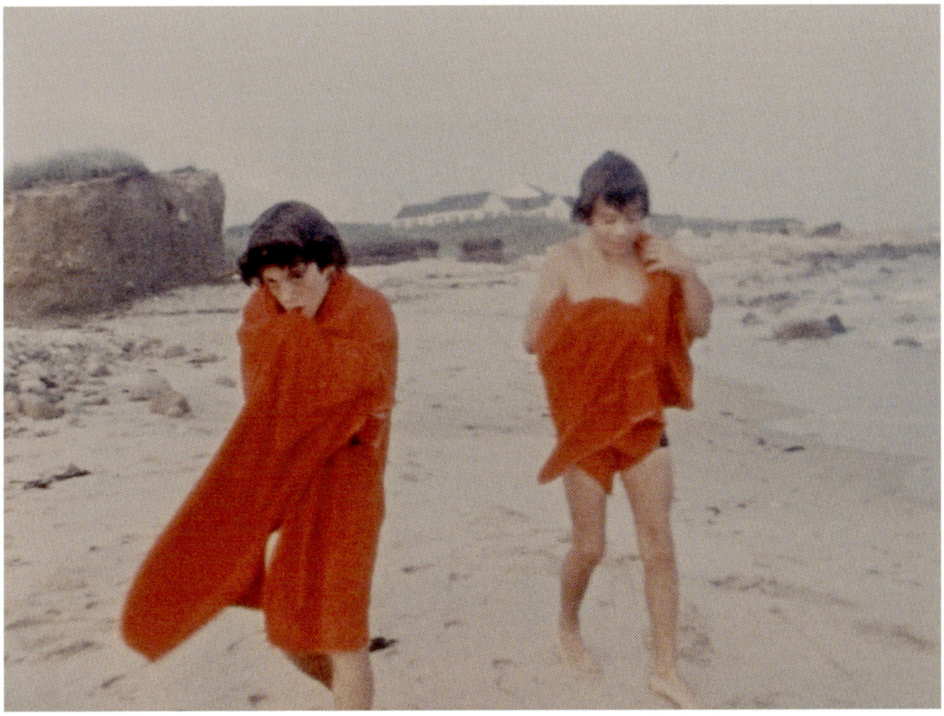

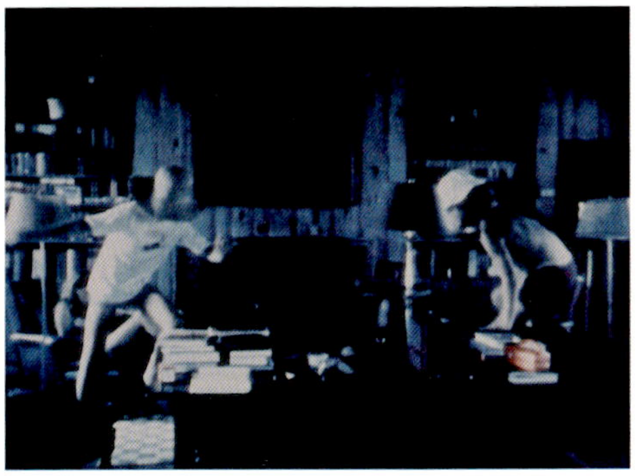

COLOR, BLACK AND WHITE SOUND 35 MIN

AS I WAS MOVING AHEAD OCCASIONALLY I SAW BRIEF GLIMPSES OF BEAUTY, 2000

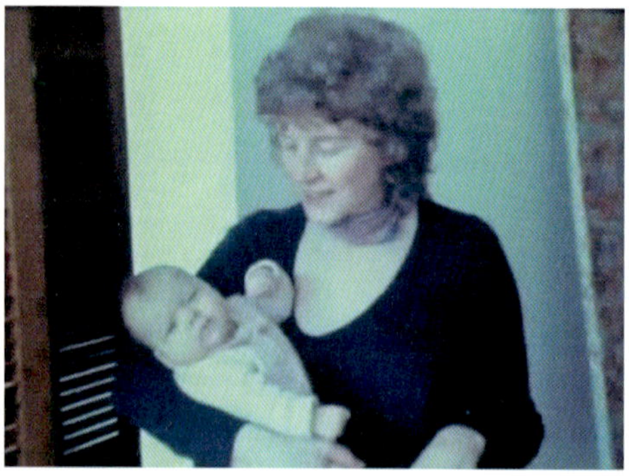

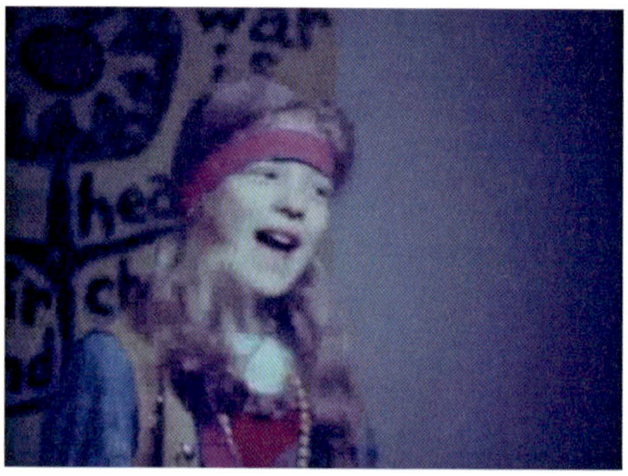

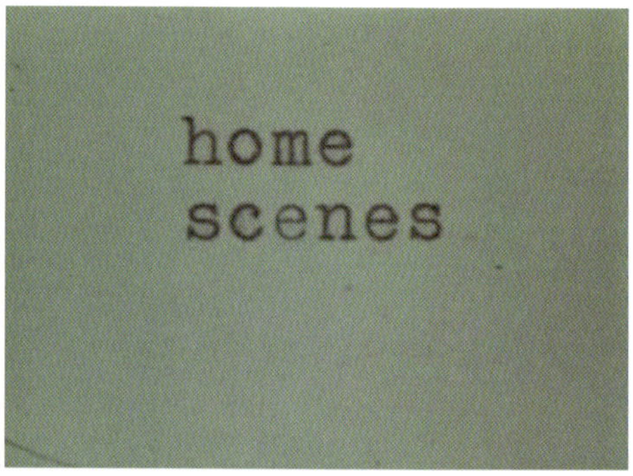

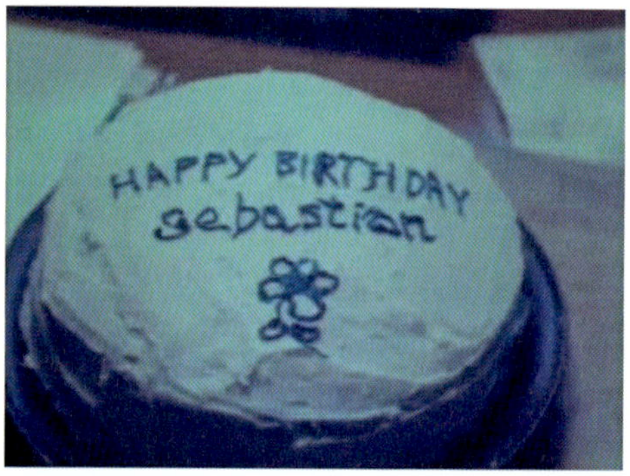

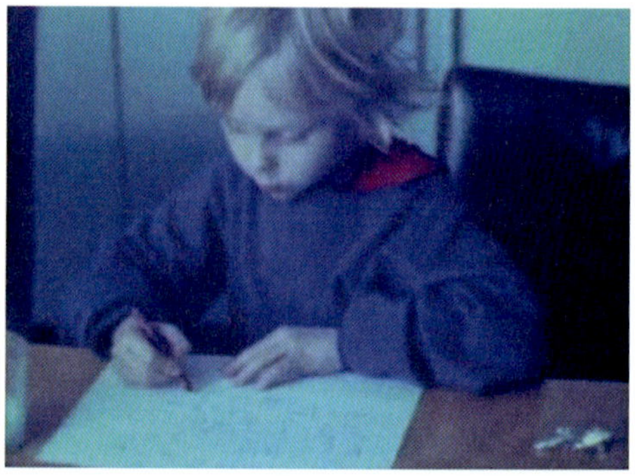

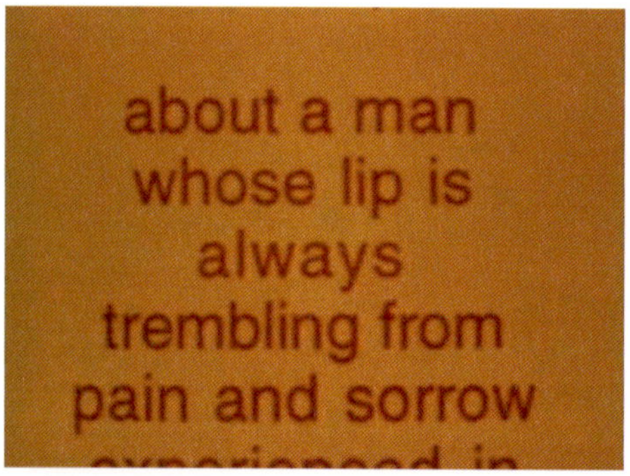

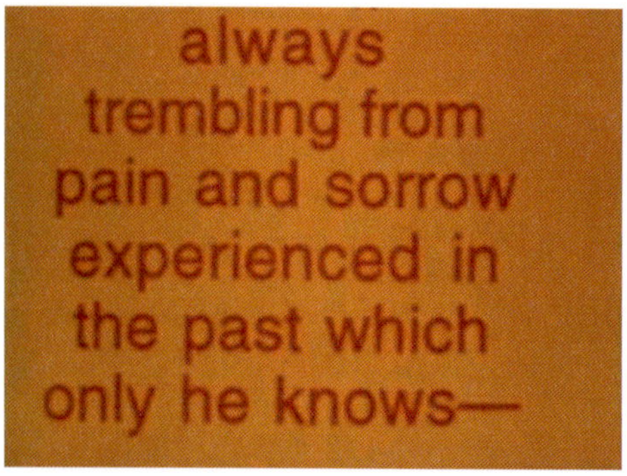

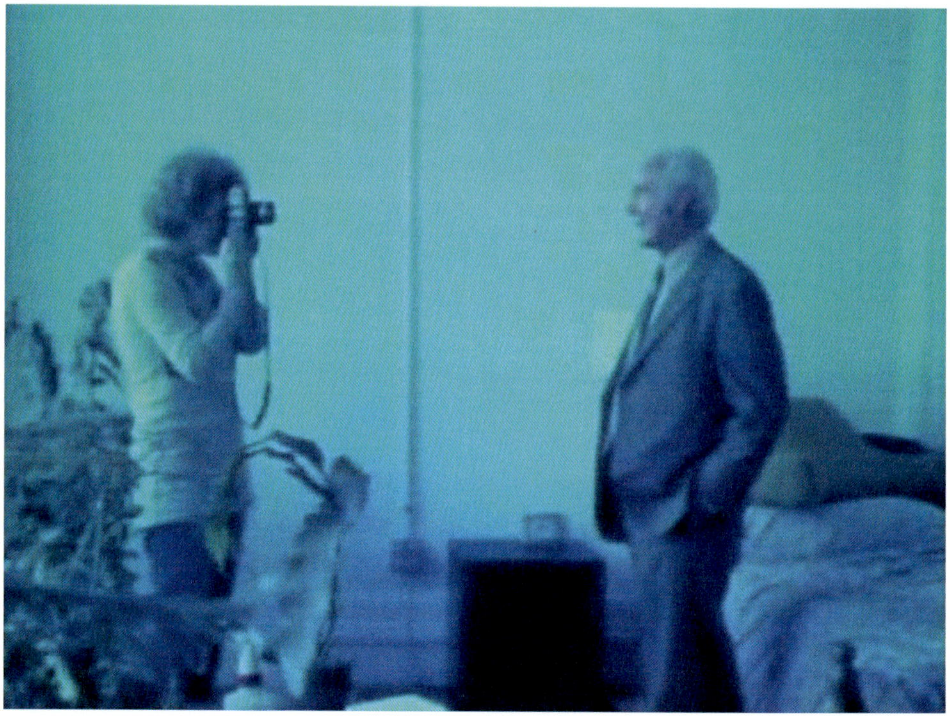

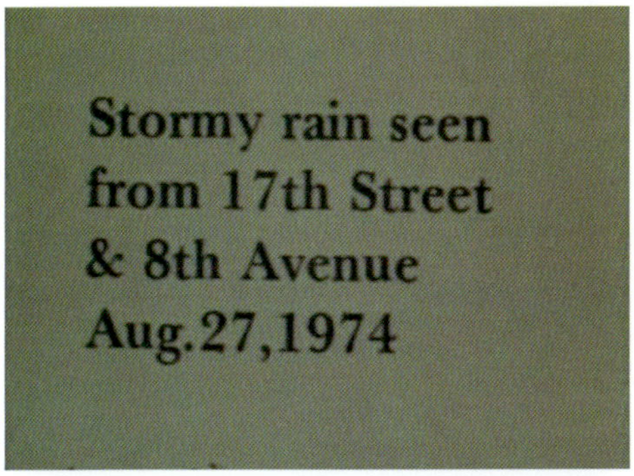
Stormy rain seen
from 17th Street
& 8th Avenue
Aug.27,1974

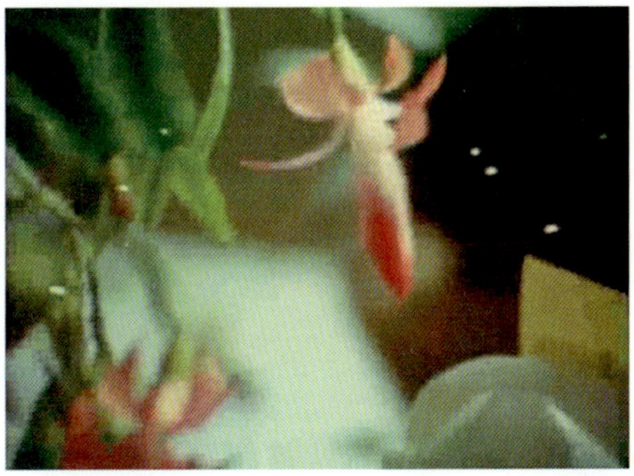

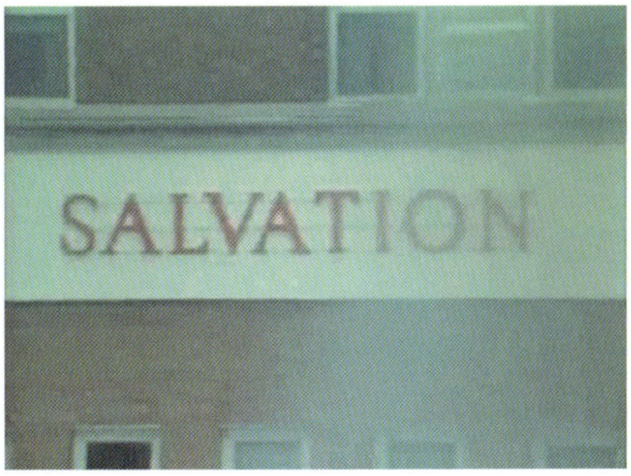
SALVATION

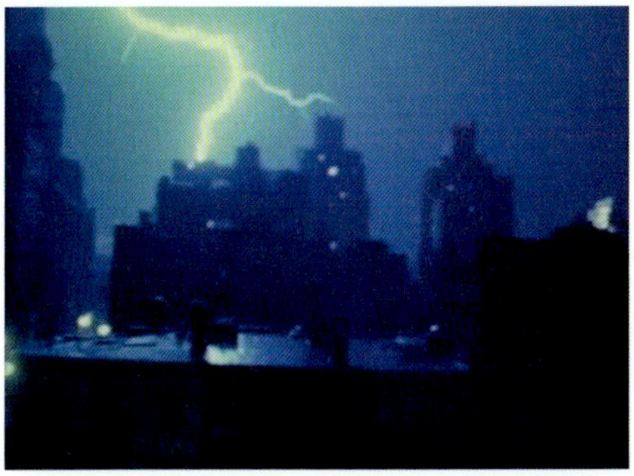

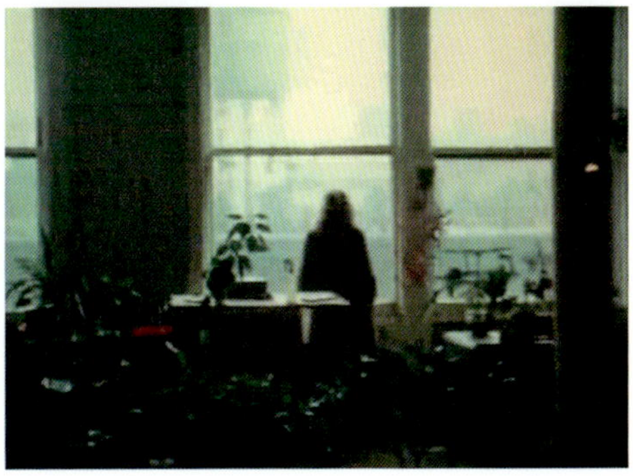

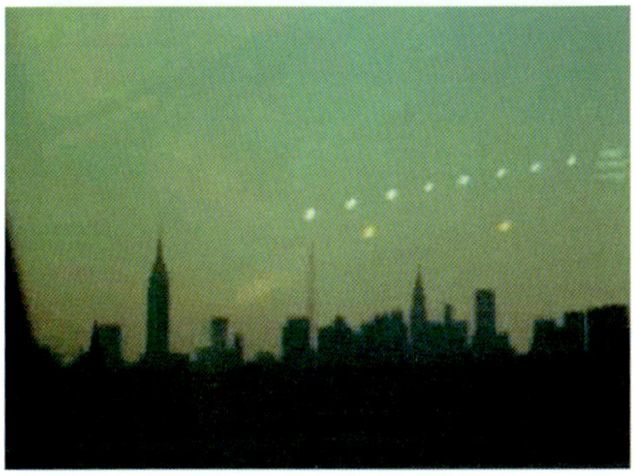

this is a
political
film

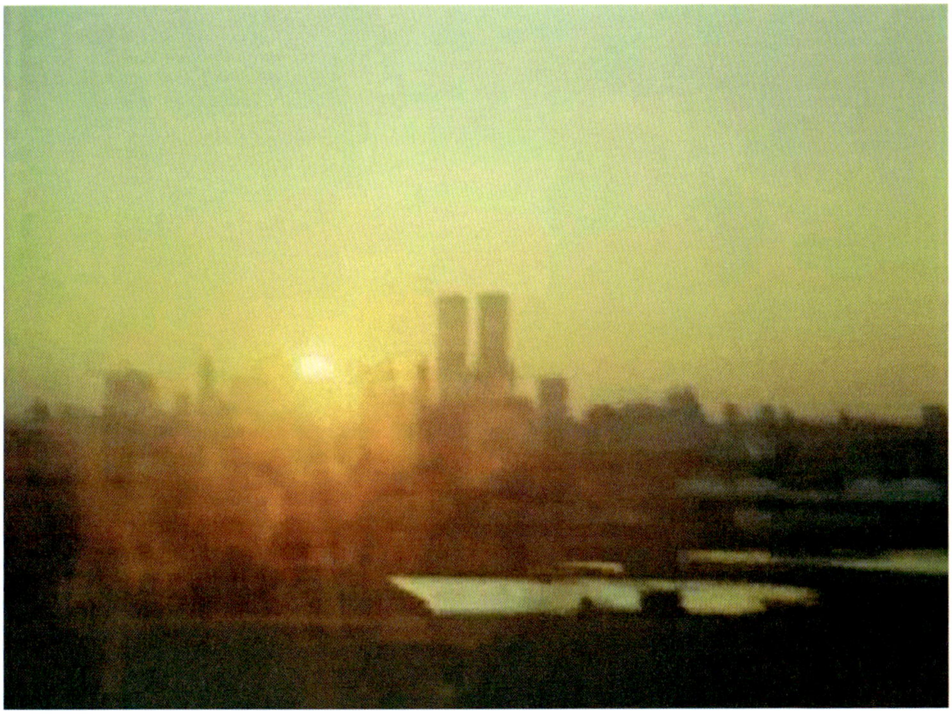

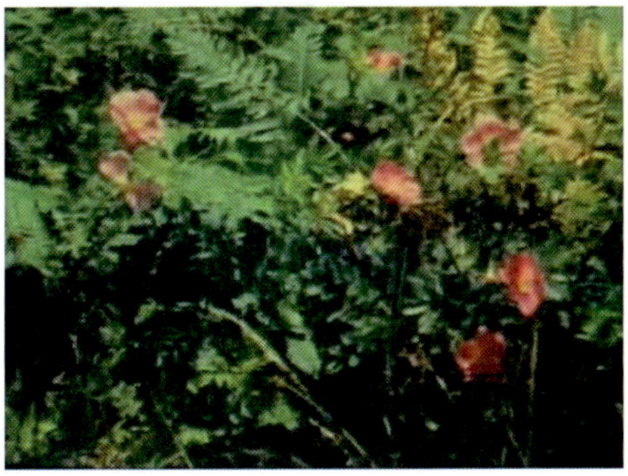

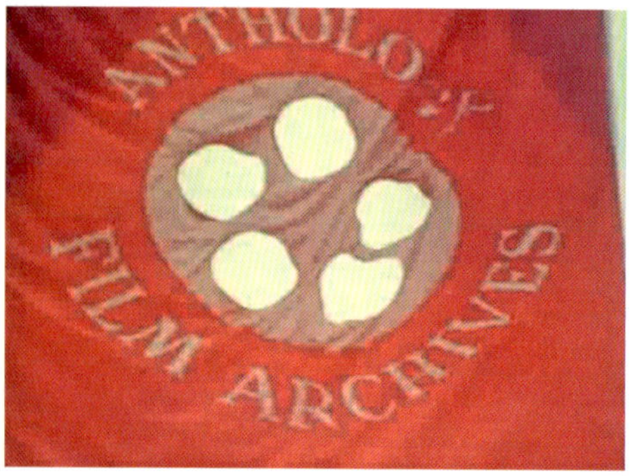
FILM ARCHIVES

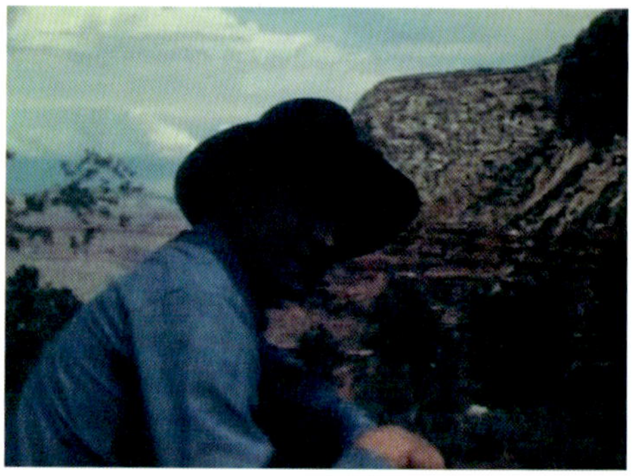

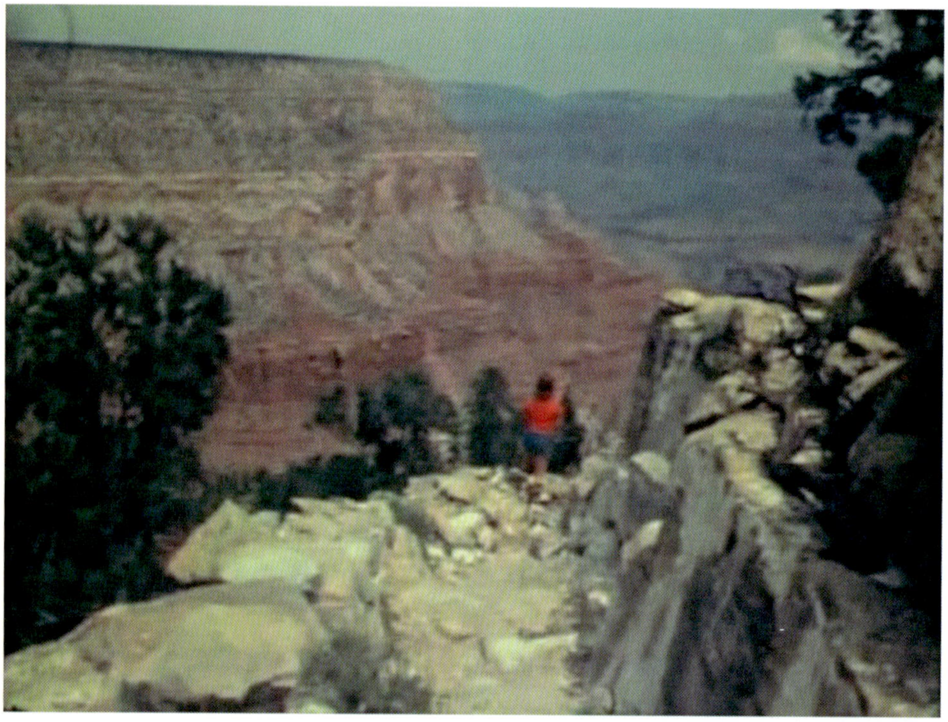

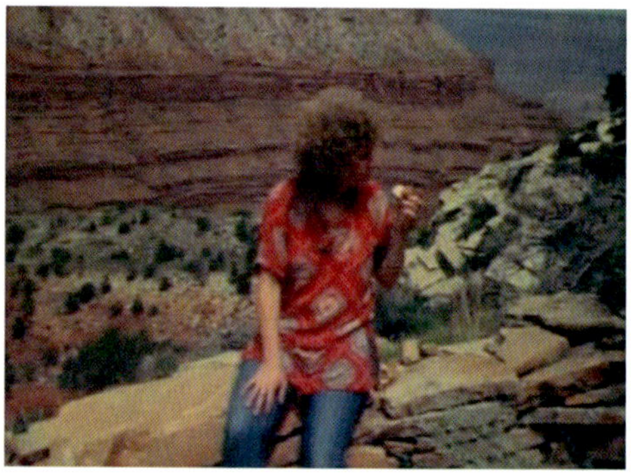

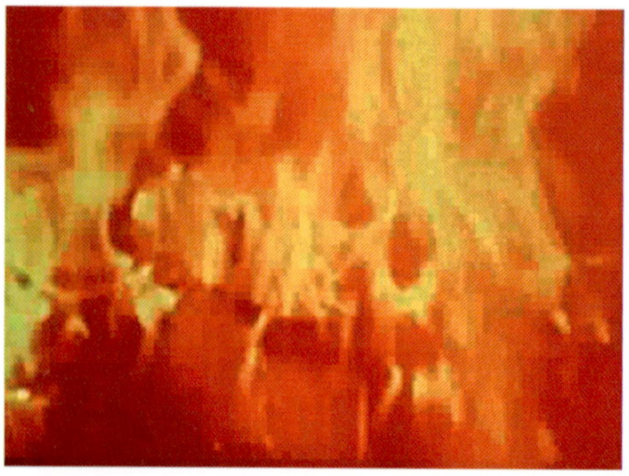

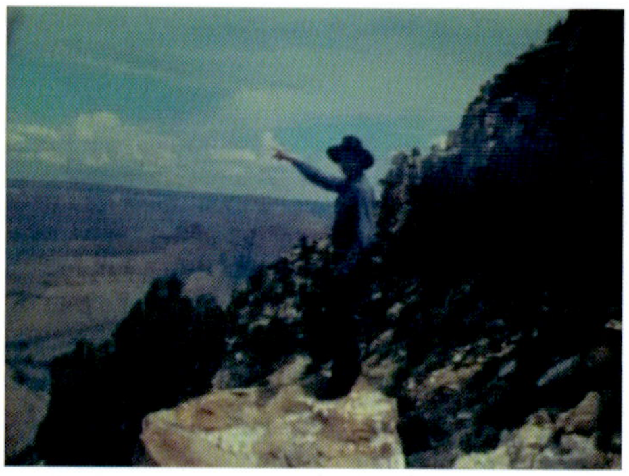

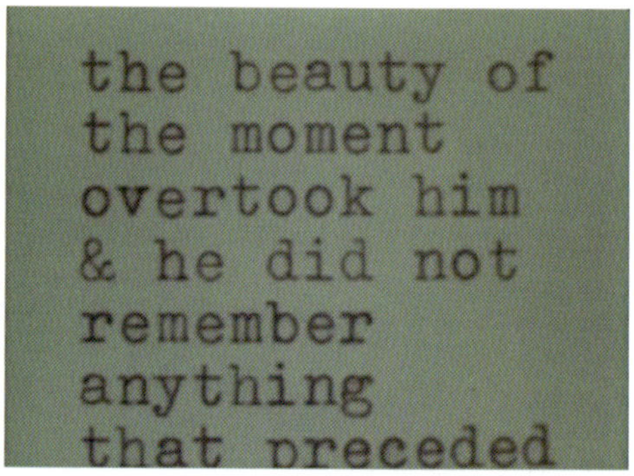
the beauty of
the moment
overtook him
& he did not
remember
anything

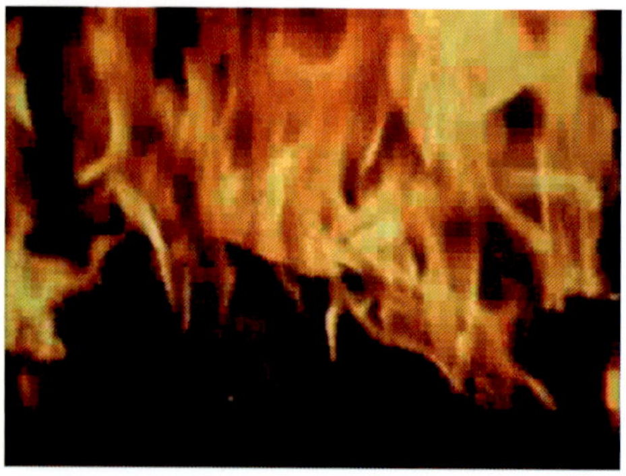

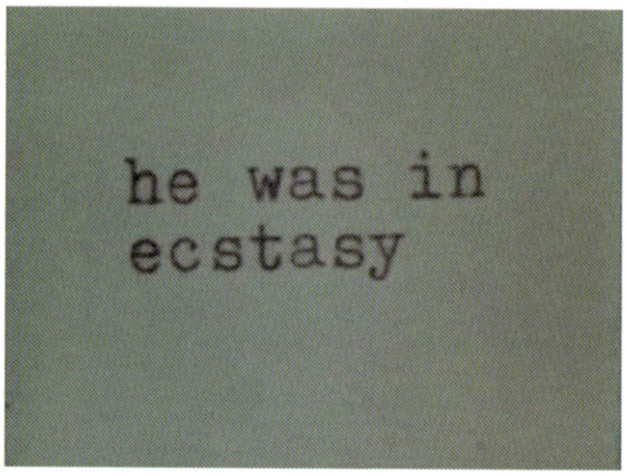
he was in
ecstasy

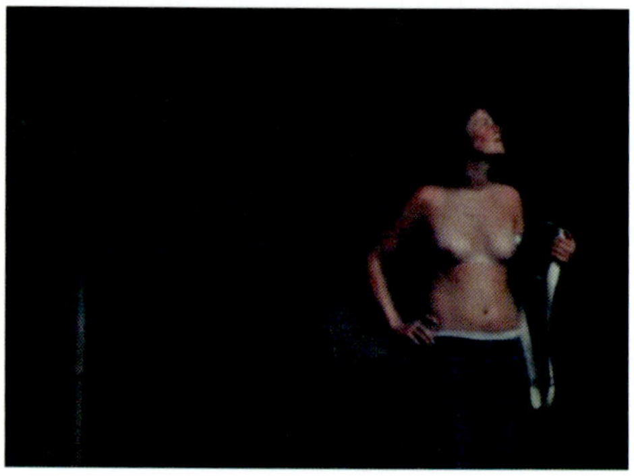

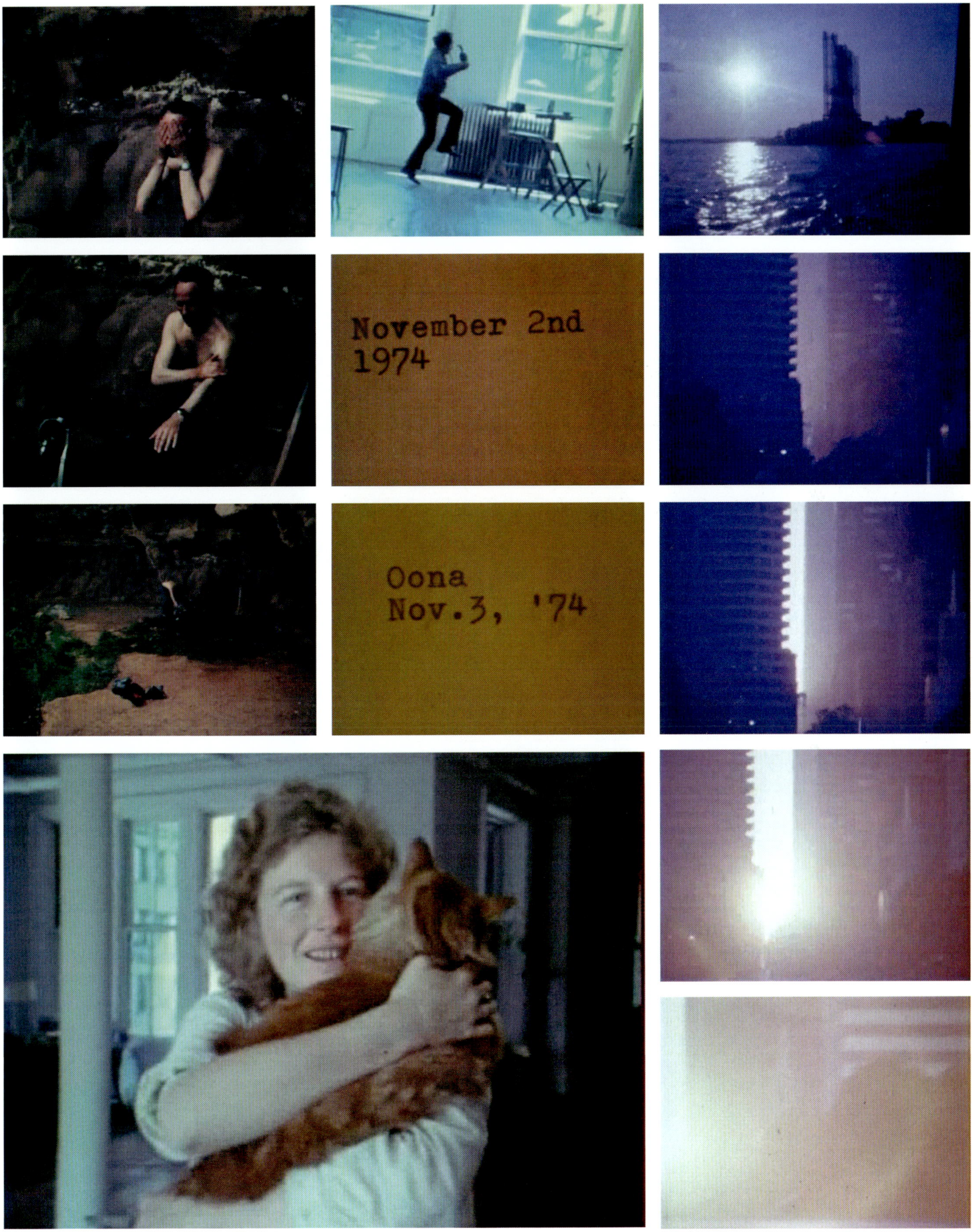
November 2nd
1974
Oona
Nov.3, '74

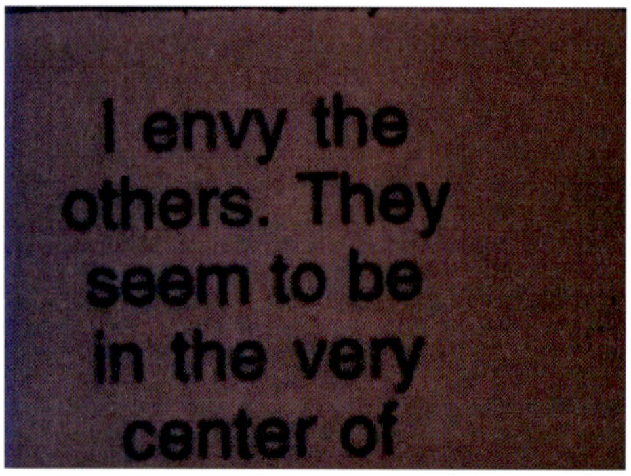
I envy the
others. They
seem to be
in the very
center of

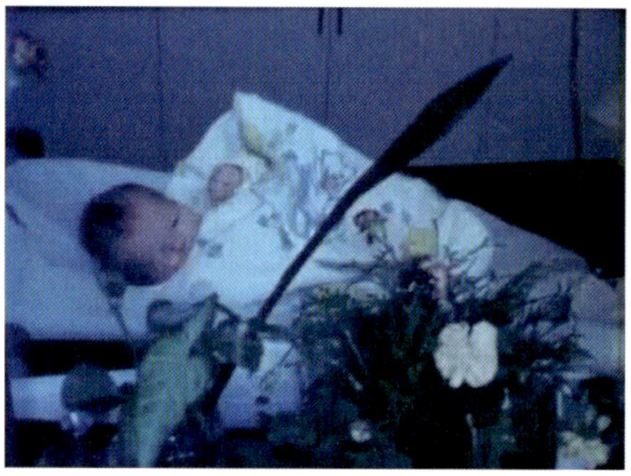

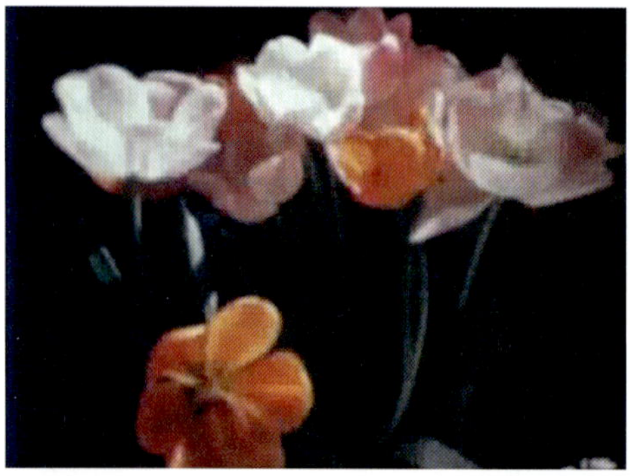

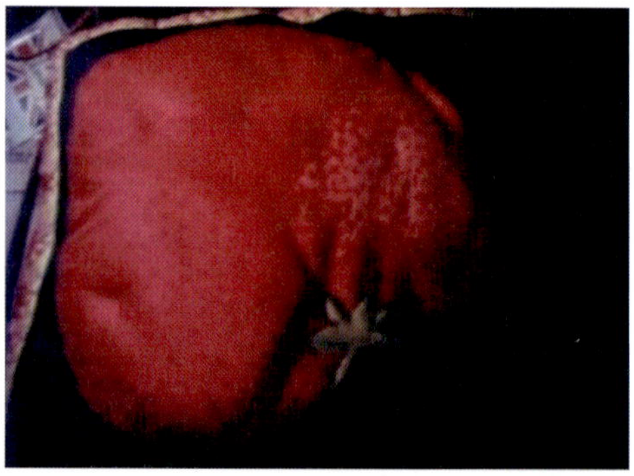

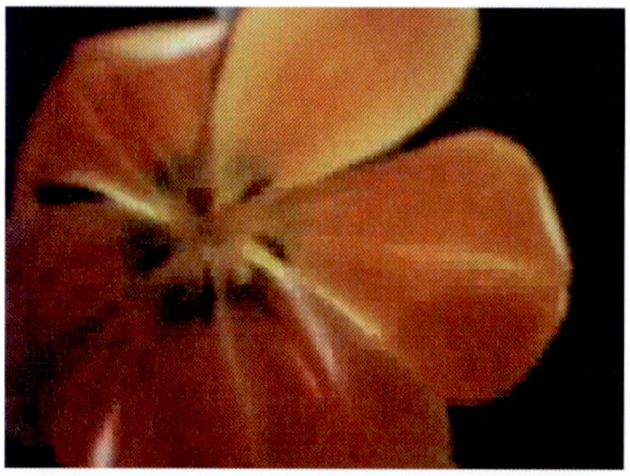

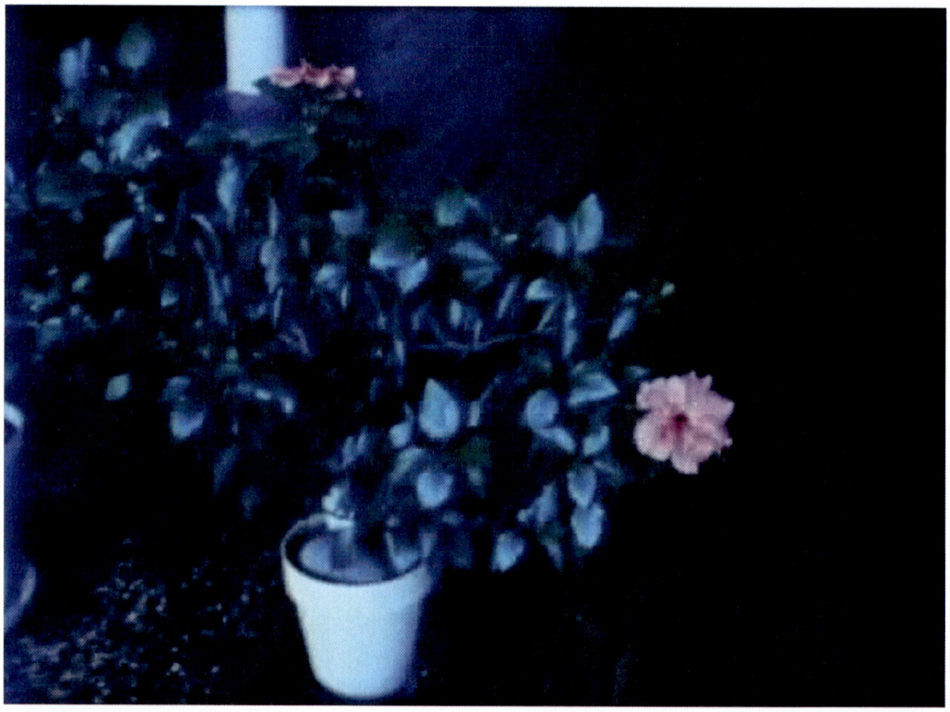

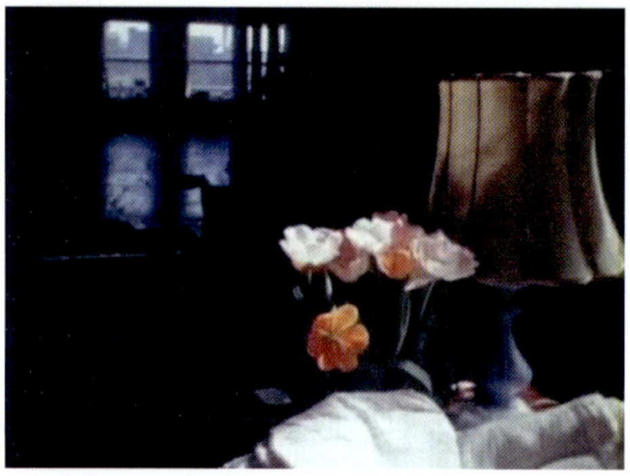

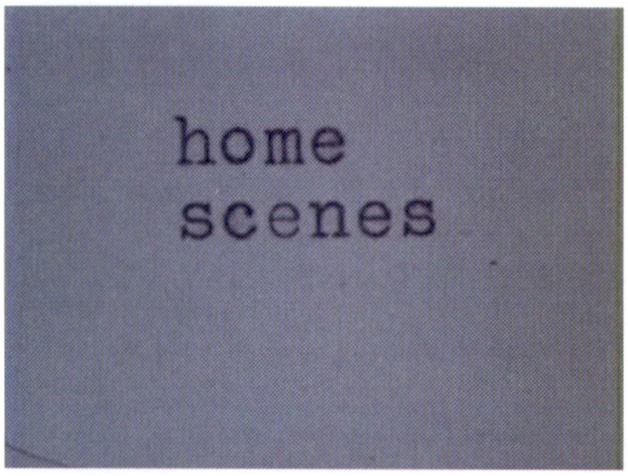
home
scenes

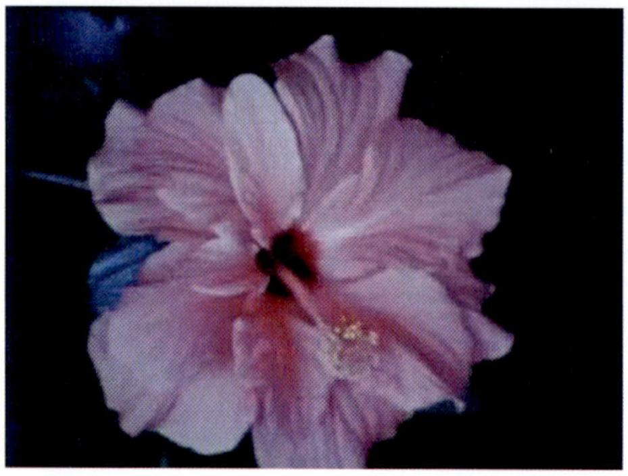

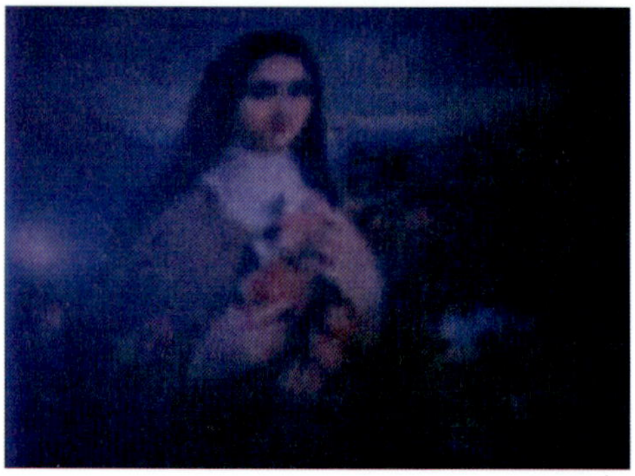

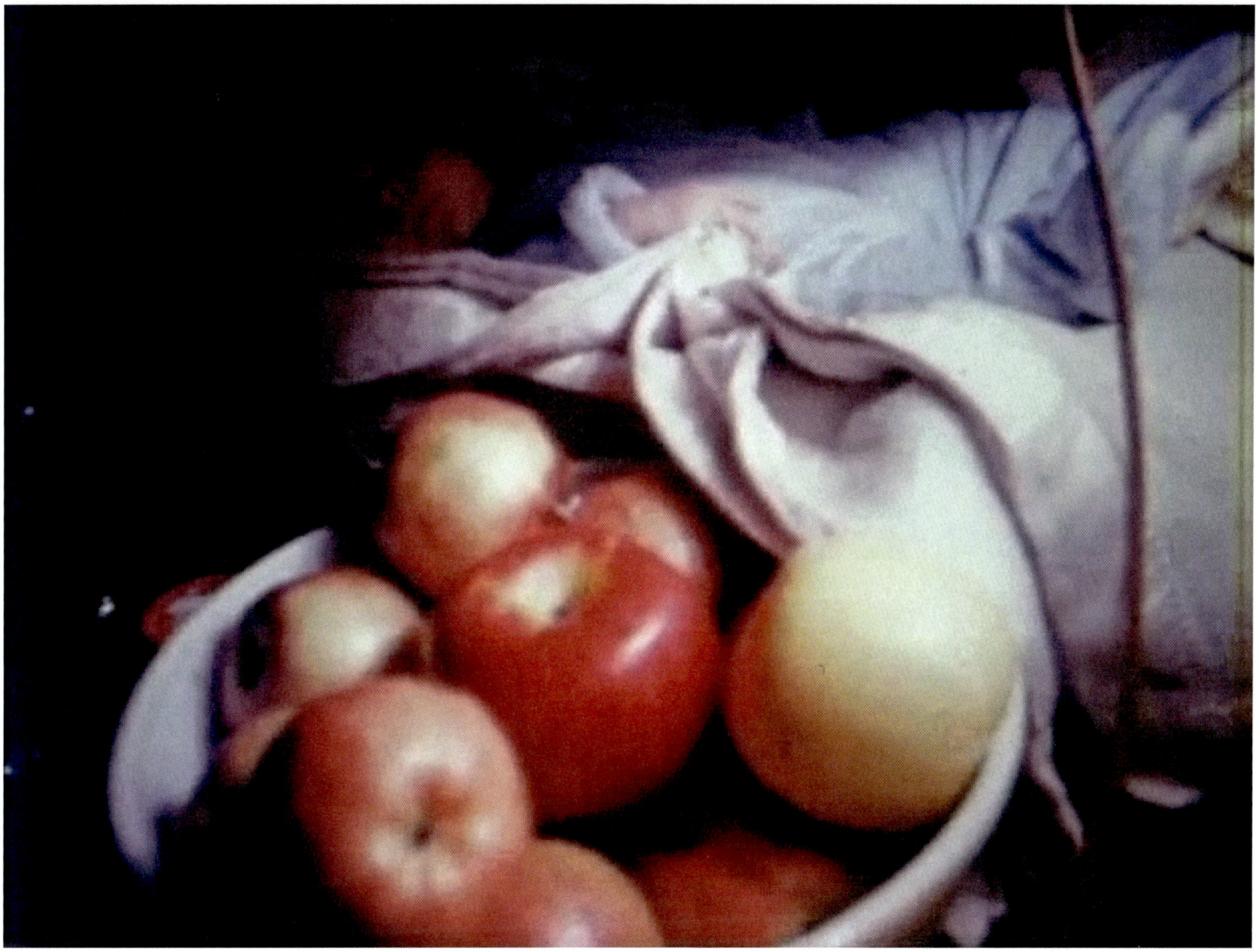

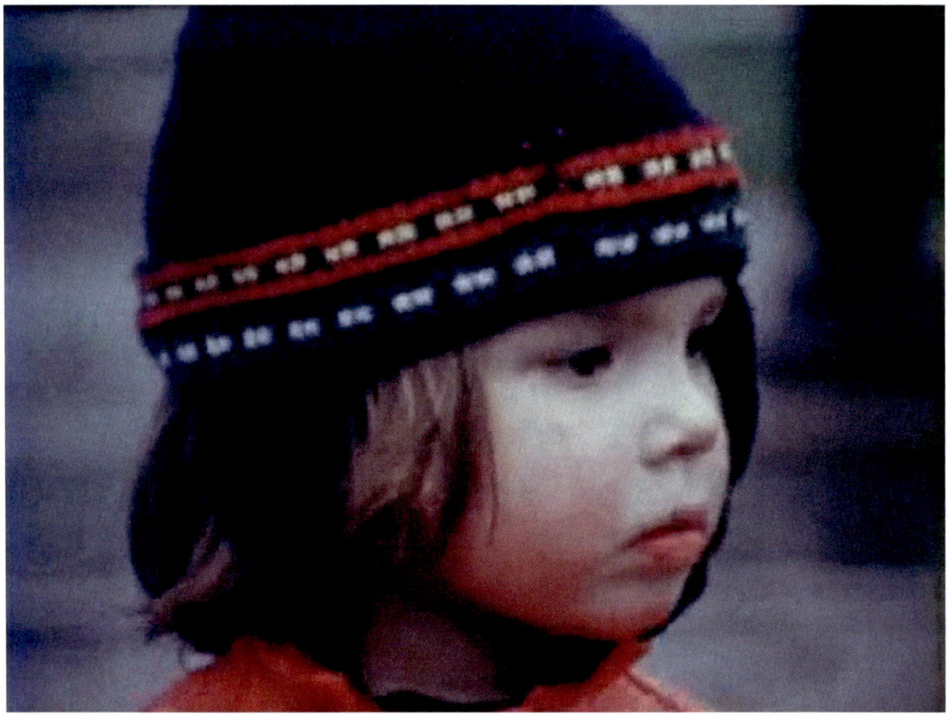

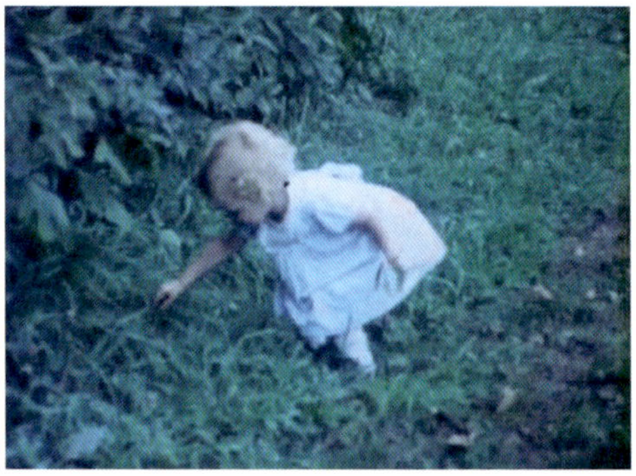

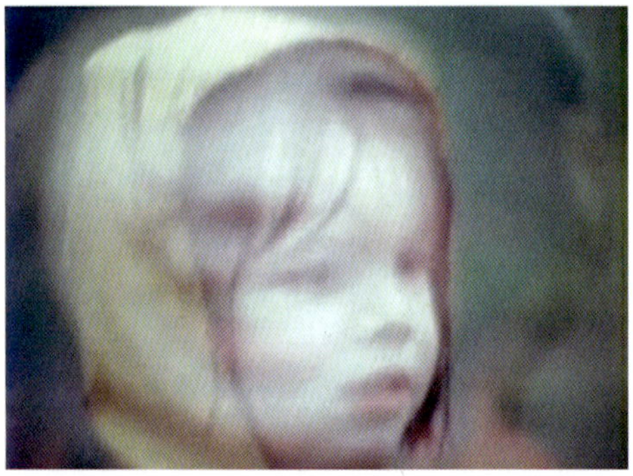

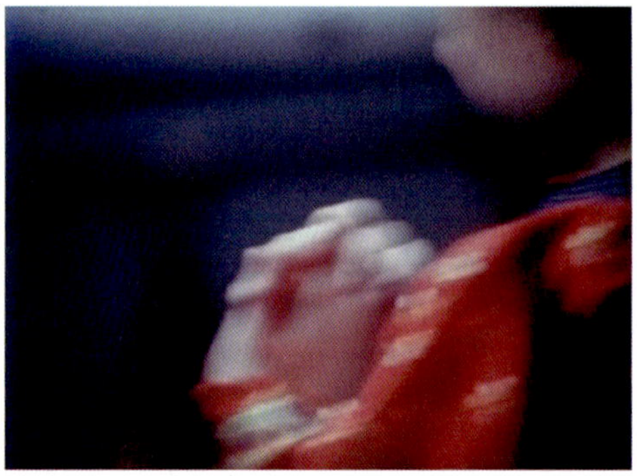

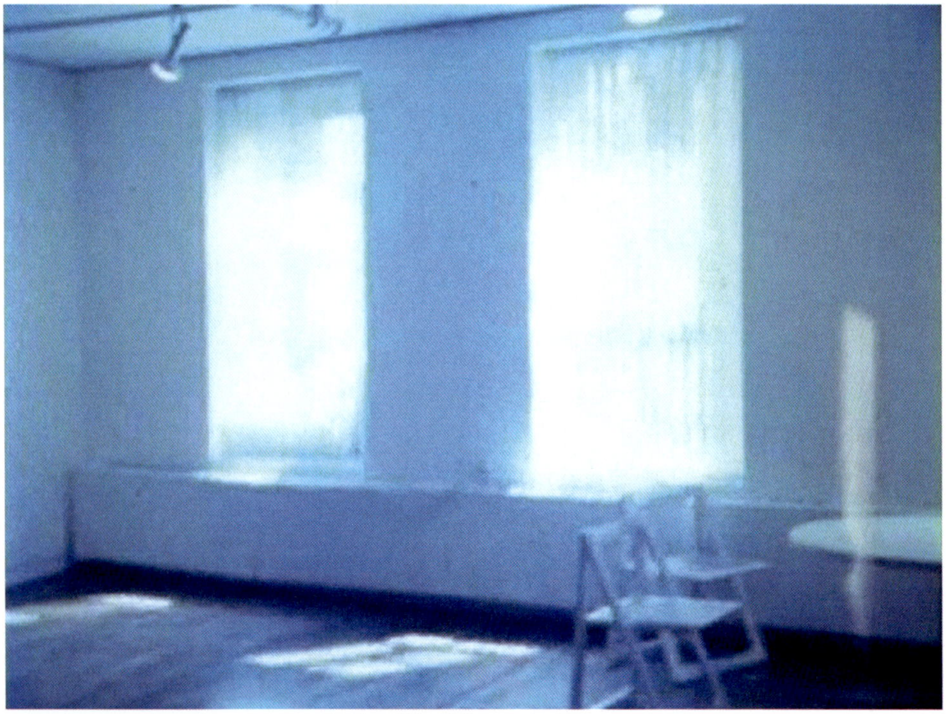

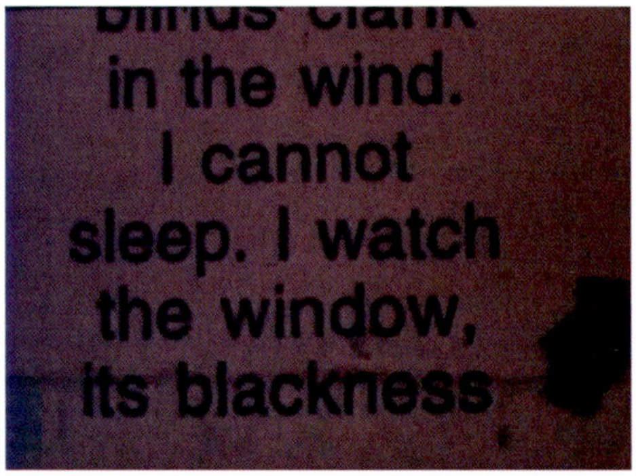

AS I WAS MOVING AHEAD 16MM 2000

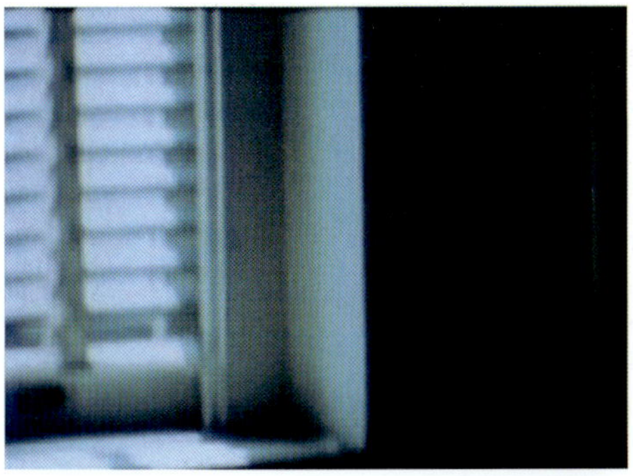
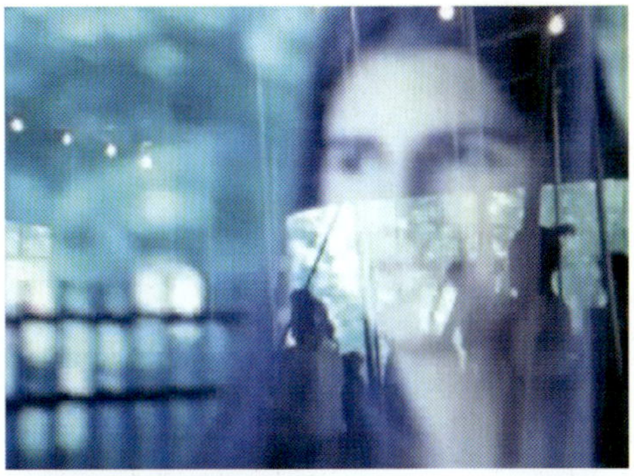
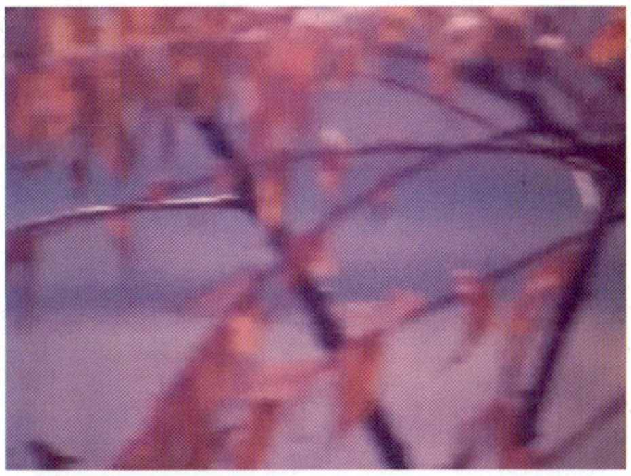
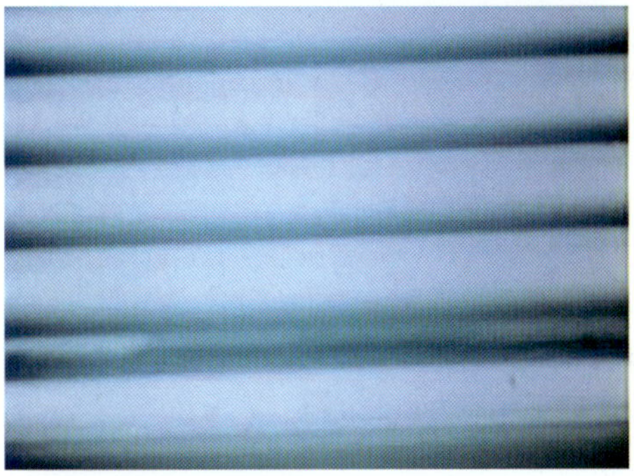
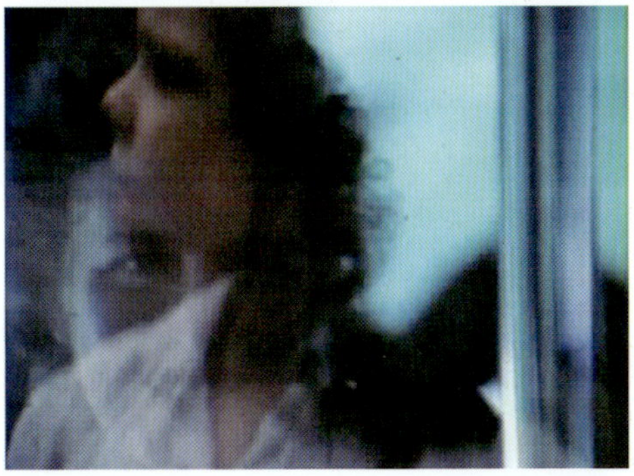
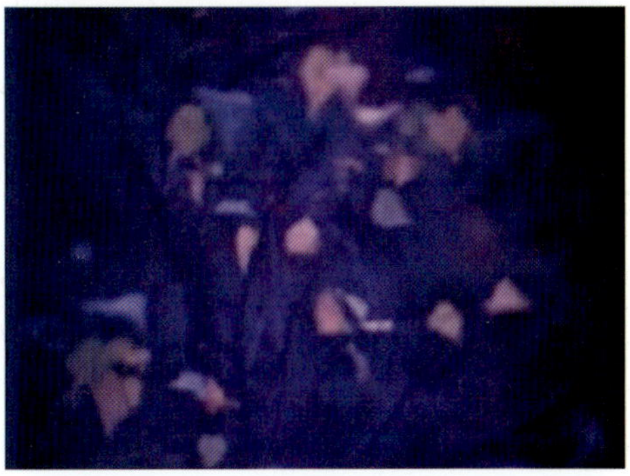
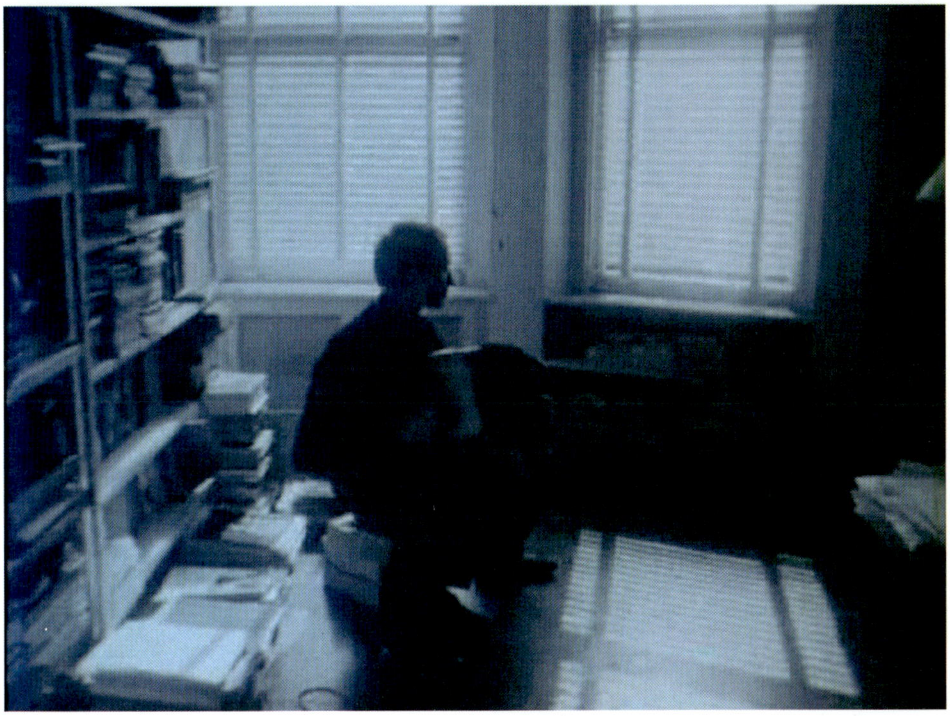
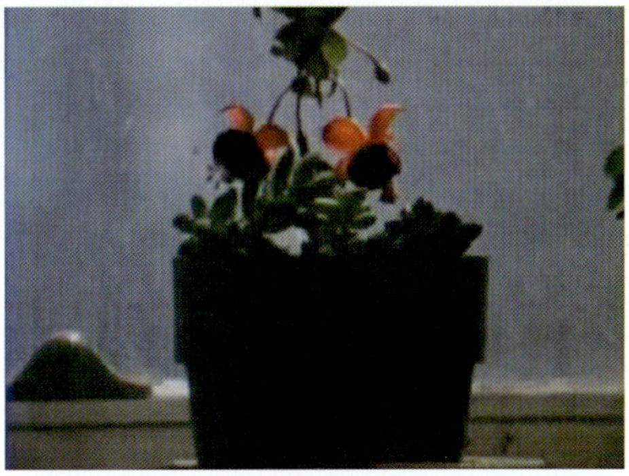
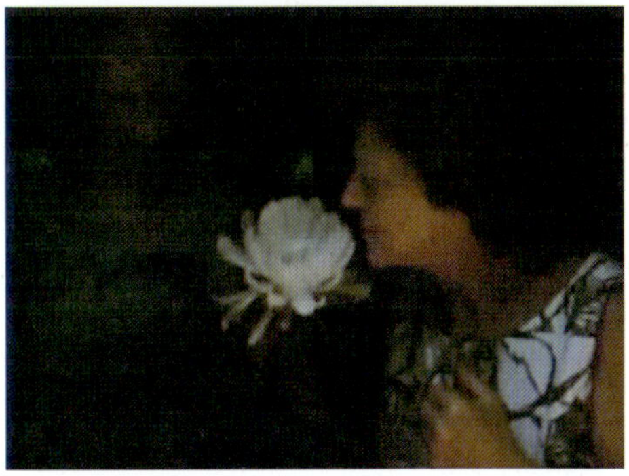
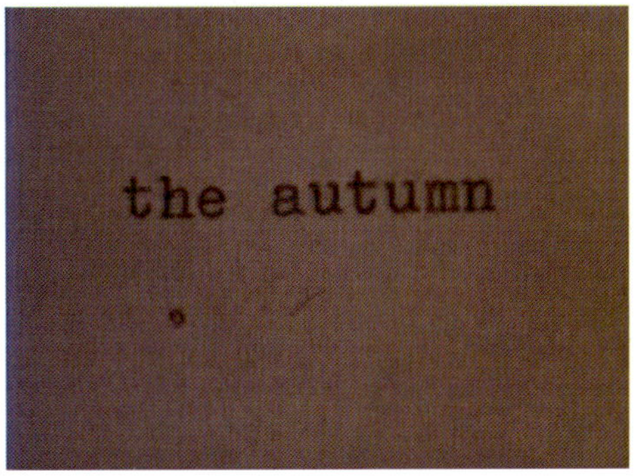

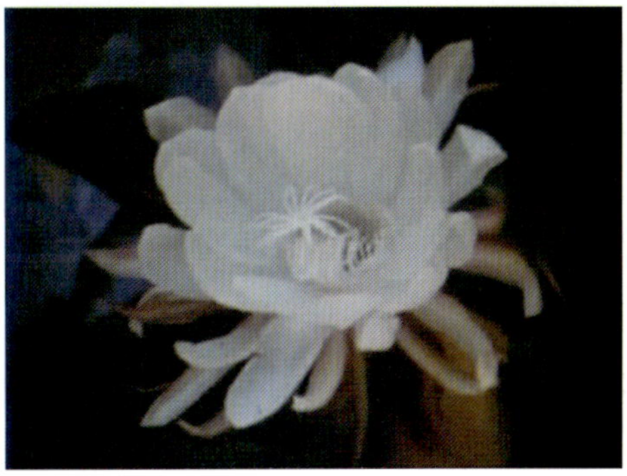

 COLOR, BLACK AND WHITE SOUND 288 MIN

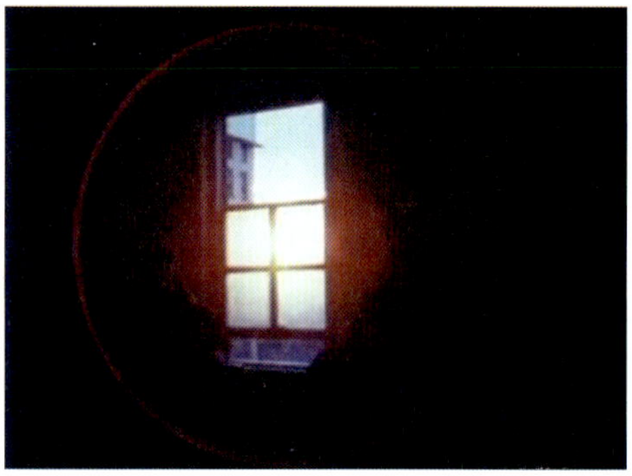

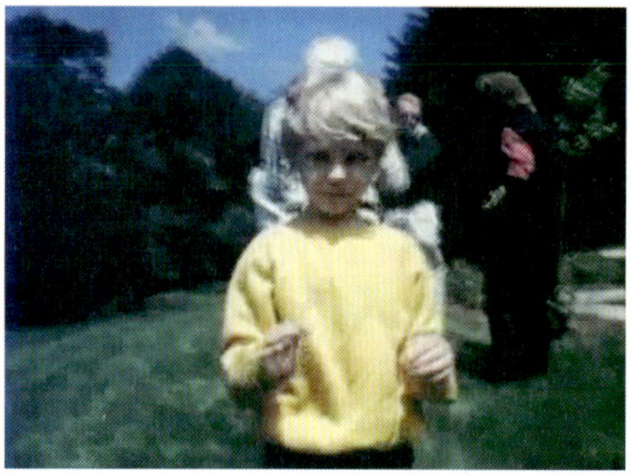

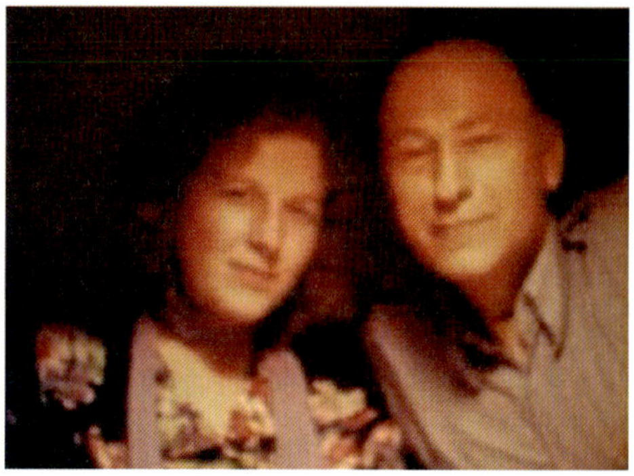

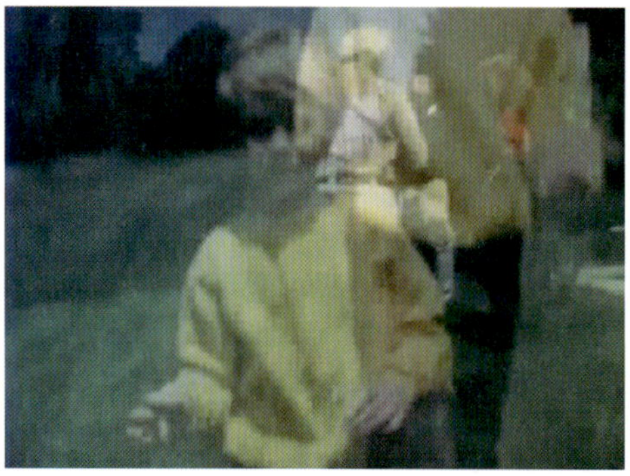

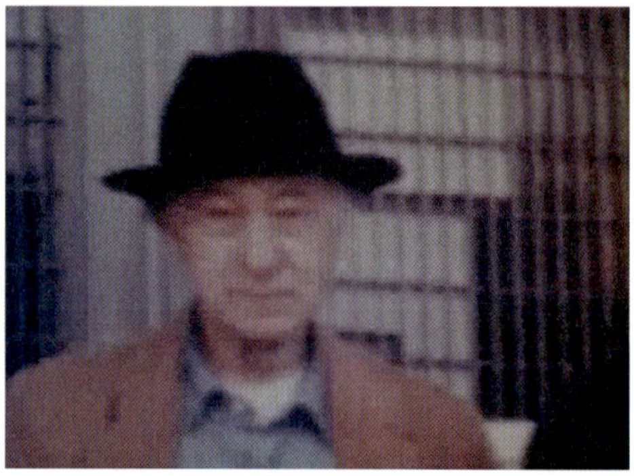

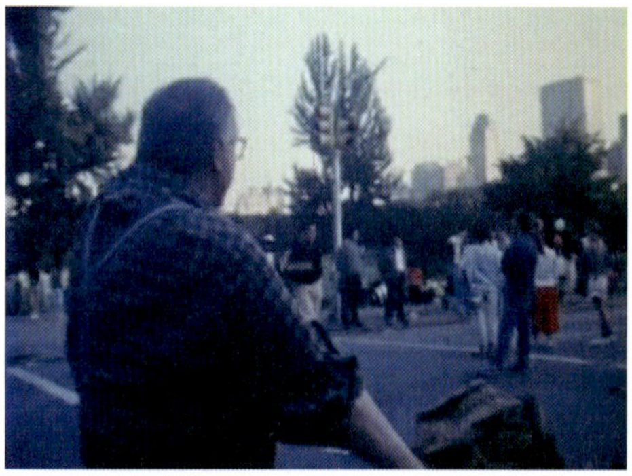

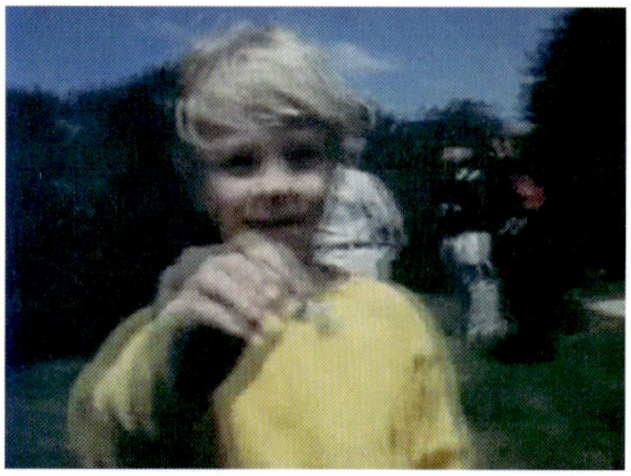

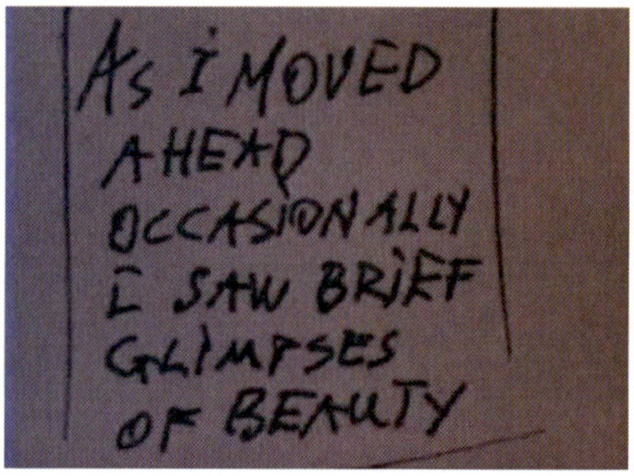
As I MOVED
AHEAD
OCCASIONALLY
I SAW BRIEF
GLIMPSES
OF BEAUTY

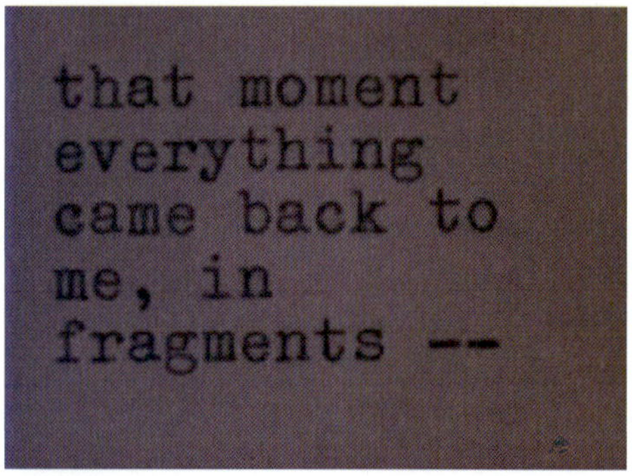
that moment
everything
came back to
me, in
fragments --

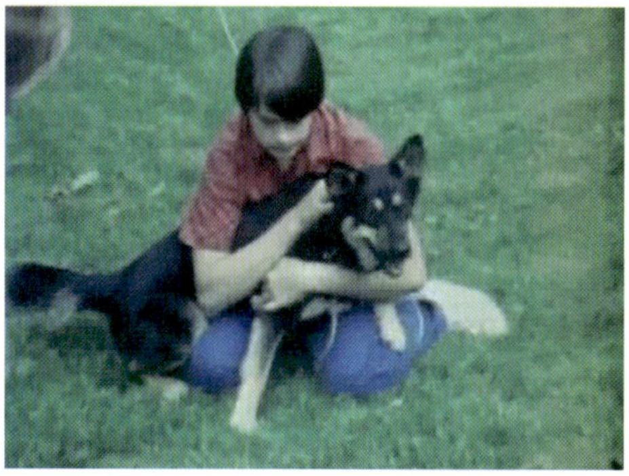

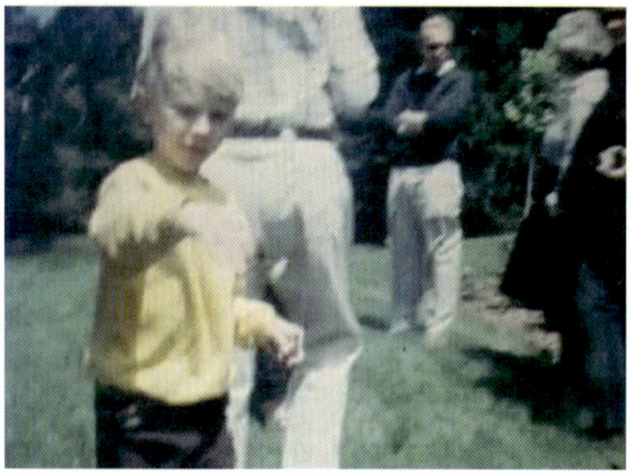

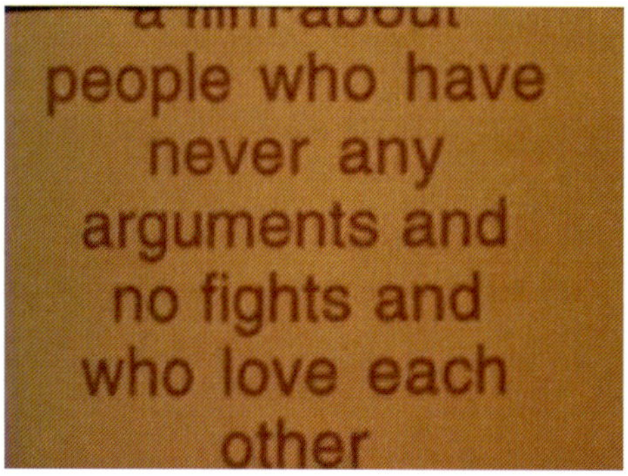
people who have
never any
arguments and
no fights and
who love each
other

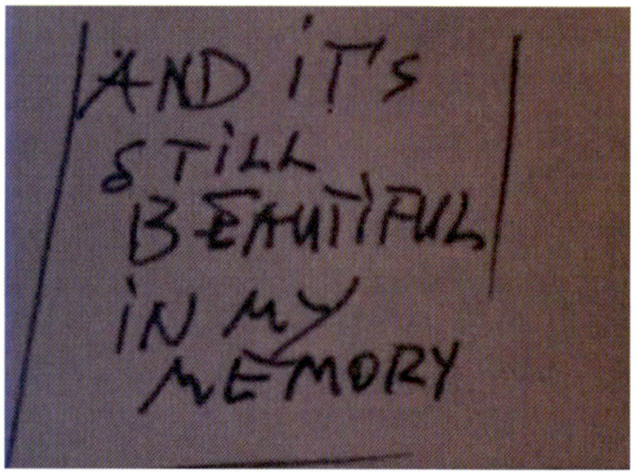
AND IT'S
STILL
BEAUTIFUL
IN MY
MEMORY

EPHEMERA

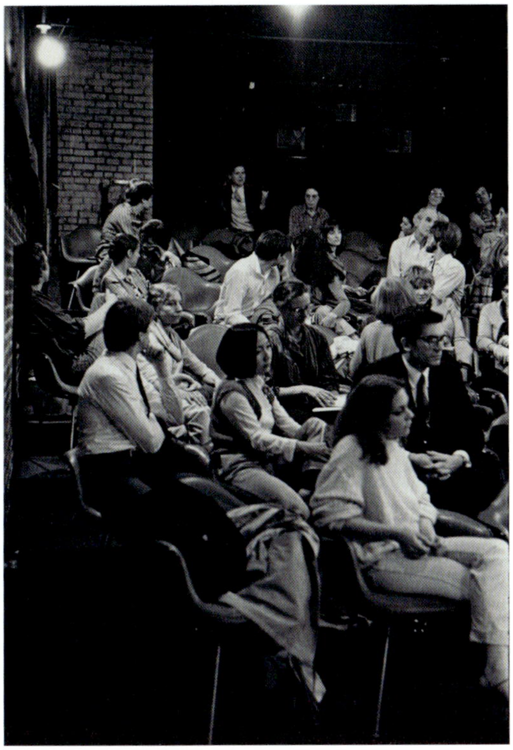

Lecture at Anthology Film Archives, undated photograph.

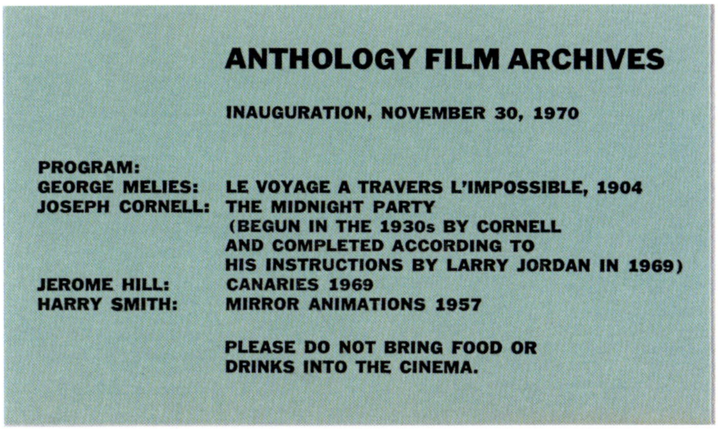

ANTHOLOGY FILM ARCHIVES

INAUGURATION, NOVEMBER 30, 1970

PROGRAM:
GEORGE MELIES: LE VOYAGE A TRAVERS L'IMPOSSIBLE, 1904
JOSEPH CORNELL: THE MIDNIGHT PARTY
(BEGUN IN THE 1930s BY CORNELL
AND COMPLETED ACCORDING TO
HIS INSTRUCTIONS BY LARRY JORDAN IN 1969)
JEROME HILL: CANARIES 1969
HARRY SMITH: MIRROR ANIMATIONS 1957

PLEASE DO NOT BRING FOOD OR
DRINKS INTO THE CINEMA.

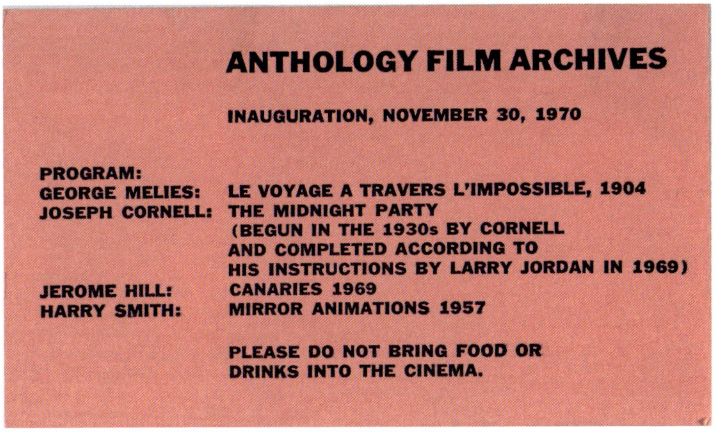

ANTHOLOGY FILM ARCHIVES

INAUGURATION, NOVEMBER 30, 1970

PROGRAM:
GEORGE MELIES: LE VOYAGE A TRAVERS L'IMPOSSIBLE, 1904
JOSEPH CORNELL: THE MIDNIGHT PARTY
(BEGUN IN THE 1930s BY CORNELL
AND COMPLETED ACCORDING TO
HIS INSTRUCTIONS BY LARRY JORDAN IN 1969)
JEROME HILL: CANARIES 1969
HARRY SMITH: MIRROR ANIMATIONS 1957

PLEASE DO NOT BRING FOOD OR
DRINKS INTO THE CINEMA.

Invitations to the inauguration of Anthology Film Archives at 425 Lafayette Street, November 30, 1970.

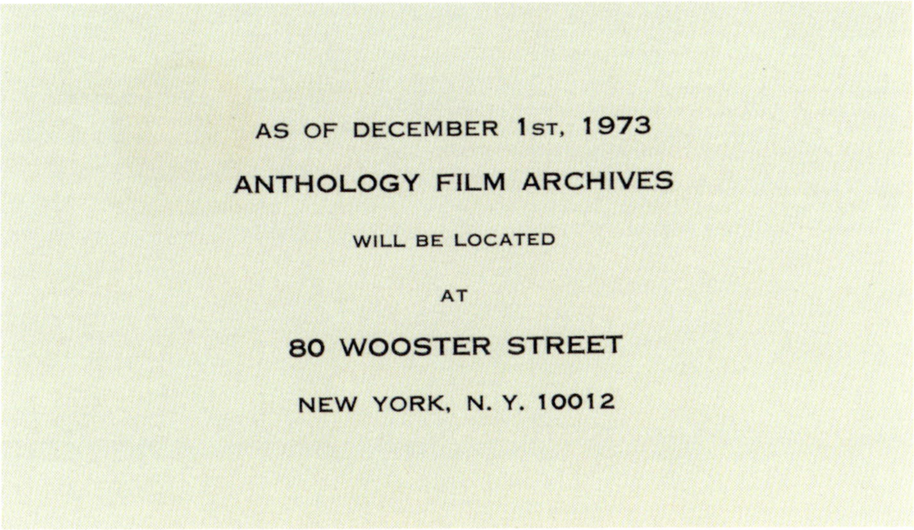

AS OF DECEMBER 1ST, 1973

ANTHOLOGY FILM ARCHIVES

WILL BE LOCATED

AT

80 WOOSTER STREET

NEW YORK, N. Y. 10012

Notice of Anthology Film Archives' relocation to 80 Wooster Street, 1973.

Section 2
Sunday, November 29, 1970

The New York Times

ARTS AND LEISURE

Now You Can See Invisible Cinema

By VINCENT CANBY

A COUPLE of major motion picture companies are teetering on the brink of insolvency. The film Society of Lincoln Center is desperately trying to find ways by which it can cut costs and continue the annual New York Film Festival. The New York City Center of Music and Drama is raising funds to support its planned New York equivalent to Henri Langlois's Cinémathèque Française of Paris. And tomorrow night, without any apparent financial problems Anthology Film Archives, a museum devoted exclusively to what its founders call "the film as an art," will have its invitational opening in the Public Theater, the beautifully remodeled old Astor Library, 425 Lafayette Street, the home of Joseph Papp's New York Shakespeare Festival, which is one of the sponsors of the movie project.

Mark the name well, for Anthology Film Archives is a unique undertaking and one that is bound to stir up a lot more of the kind of controversy that has attended the rise and rise of Jonas Mekas, editor (Film Culture), critic (Village Voice), filmmaker ("The Brig"), underground film evangelist and fund-raiser extraordinary.

Anthology Film Archives, which occupies a sizable portion of the north end of the Public Theater, consists of offices as totally carpeted and as Danishly modern as any to be found in a major film company headquarters uptown, a library devoted to film, and small projection and cutting rooms. Most important, it includes a new 90-seat theater of precedental design called the Invisible Cinema where, starting Tuesday, the museum will screen three different programs a day, seven days a week, 52 weeks a year, with the purpose of giving students, as well as members of the general public, "a concentrated history of the art of the film within a period of four or five weeks." The price of admission is $1.

At the present time, the museum's archives include the works of about 60 filmmakers that will be shown in repertory, in alphabetical order, beginning with a film by James Agee, in collaboration with Helen Levitt and Janice Loeb, "In the Street," and winding up with films by John and James Whitney, "Film Exercises." Among the other programs, there will be the complete works of Kenneth Anger, what seem to be the complete works of Stan Brakhage and Gregory Markopoulos, six of the 10 features made by Robert Bresson, four films by Luis Buñuel, extensive selections from the works of Chaplin, Cocteau, Dovzhenko, Dreyer, Méliès, the Lumière brothers, Eisenstein, Warhol, and one film each by Renoir ("Rules of the Game"), Griffith ("Intolerance"), Murnau ("Sunrise"), Welles ("Citizen Kane"), and Mekas ("Diaries, Notes and Sketches, 1965-1969").

In addition to Mr. Mekas, the two other filmmaking members of the museum's five-man selection committee also have works in the museum's repertory—James Broughton, the San Francisco poet-teacher, and Peter Kubelka, who is also a co-founder and co-director of the Oesterreichisches Filmmuseum in Vienna.

The non-filmmaking members of the selection committee are Ken Kelman, the dramatist and film critic, and P. Adams Sitney, the film theoretician who, with Mr. Mekas, has been a tireless promoter of the American film underground and a staunch worker on behalf of such other underground organizations as the Filmmakers' Cinémathèque and Filmmakers' Distribution Center.

When, in the course of a recent preview visit to Lafayette Street, I brought up the matter of the inclusion of films by Mr. Mekas, Mr. Broughton and Mr. Kubelka, Mr. Sitney said that since the filmmakers on the committee are first-rate filmmakers, it is only natural that some of their films would be included in a definition of film as an art. (One can't very well question that without debating assumptions, which I wasn't prepared to do.)

The purpose of Anthology Film Archives, he was careful to emphasize, is not to present a history of the cinema as either a social or commercial phenomenon. Rather, the museum is oriented toward what the members of the selection committee call the "pure" film, and in being so oriented, its purposes are polemic, to "form a new generation of film understanding," to counterbalance conventional film criticism and its historical bias in favor of the feature film (at the expense of the short film), as well as to "increase the sensual enjoyment of cinema." This last quote was supplied

BINDER 10 AFA on LAFAYETTE

Clipping of Vincent Canby, "Now You Can See Invisible Cinema," *New York Times*, November 29, 1970. Canby discusses the opening of Anthology Film Archives and its "new 90-seat theater of precedental design called the Invisible Cinema."

Following pages: some of Manhattan's most notable cultural and political figures wrote letters in support of Anthology Film Archives' purchase of the Second Avenue Courthouse, which became the organization's permanent home.

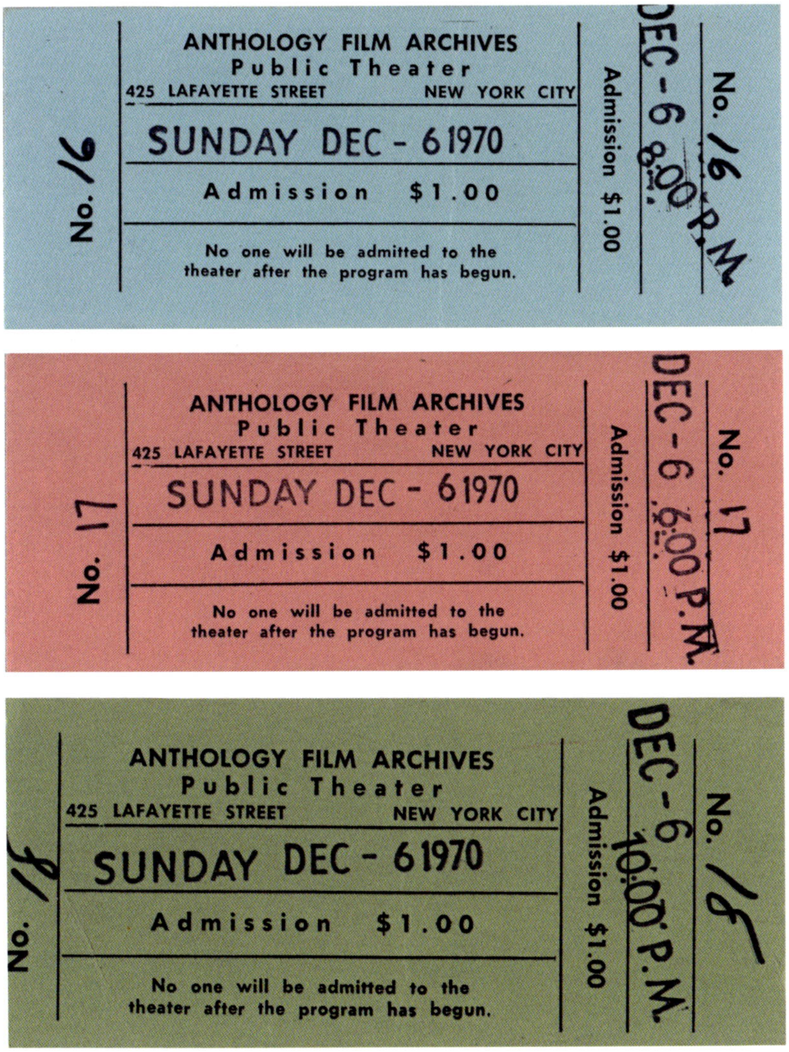

Tickets to Anthology Film Archives screenings at the Public Theater, December 6, 1970.

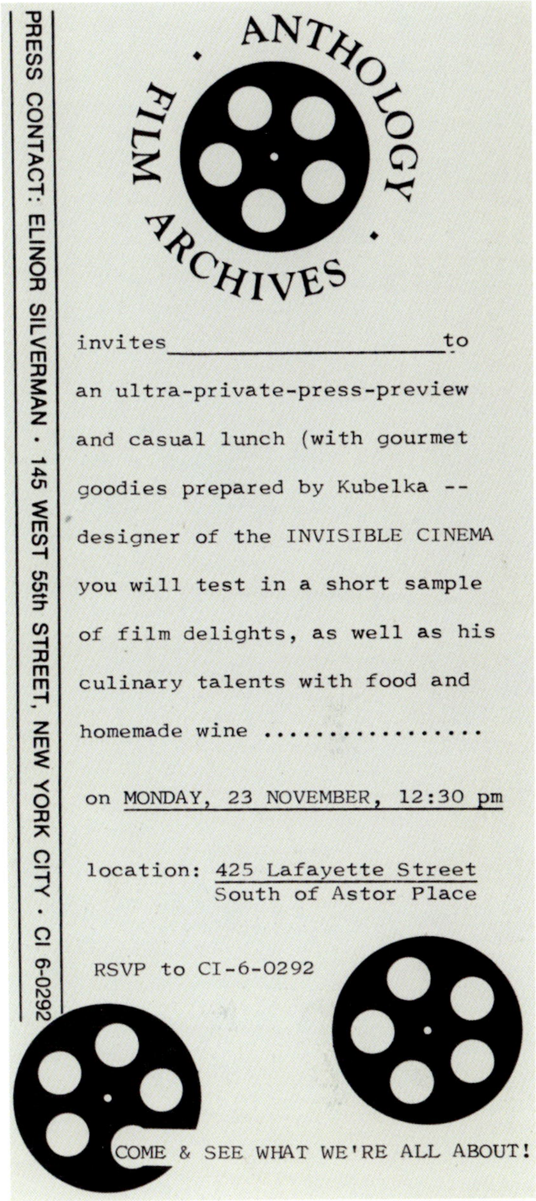

ANTHOLOGY FILM ARCHIVES

PRESS CONTACT: ELINOR SILVERMAN · 145 WEST 55th STREET, NEW YORK CITY · CI 6-0292

invites ______________________ to
an ultra-private-press-preview
and casual lunch (with gourmet
goodies prepared by Kubelka --
designer of the INVISIBLE CINEMA
you will test in a short sample
of film delights, as well as his
culinary talents with food and
homemade wine ....

on MONDAY, 23 NOVEMBER, 12:30 pm

location: 425 Lafayette Street
South of Astor Place

RSVP to CI-6-0292

COME & SEE WHAT WE'RE ALL ABOUT!

Invitation to an "ultra-private-press-preview" of Anthology Film Archives on November 23, 1970.

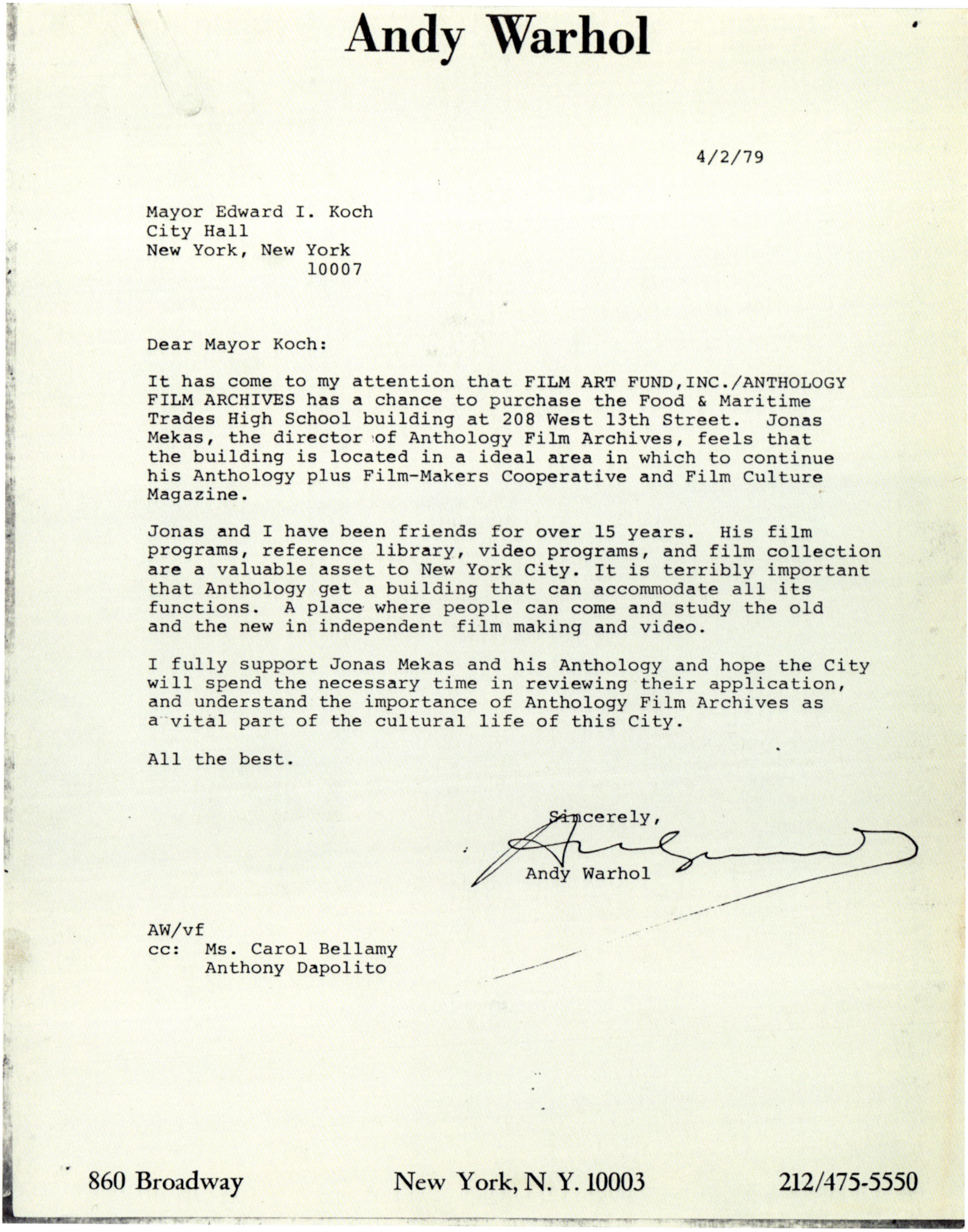

Andy Warhol

4/2/79

Mayor Edward I. Koch
City Hall
New York, New York
10007

Dear Mayor Koch:

It has come to my attention that FILM ART FUND, INC./ANTHOLOGY FILM ARCHIVES has a chance to purchase the Food & Maritime Trades High School building at 208 West 13th Street. Jonas Mekas, the director of Anthology Film Archives, feels that the building is located in a ideal area in which to continue his Anthology plus Film-Makers Cooperative and Film Culture Magazine.

Jonas and I have been friends for over 15 years. His film programs, reference library, video programs, and film collection are a valuable asset to New York City. It is terribly important that Anthology get a building that can accommodate all its functions. A place where people can come and study the old and the new in independent film making and video.

I fully support Jonas Mekas and his Anthology and hope the City will spend the necessary time in reviewing their application, and understand the importance of Anthology Film Archives as a vital part of the cultural life of this City.

All the best.

Sincerely,

Andy Warhol

AW/vf
cc: Ms. Carol Bellamy
Anthony Dapolito

860 Broadway New York, N. Y. 10003 212/475-5550

Letter from Andy Warhol to Mayor Edward I. Koch in support of Anthology Film Archives' proposed purchase of the Food and Maritime Trades High School, April 2, 1979.

American Zoetrope

The Sentinel Building
916 Kearny Street
San Francisco, CA 94133
(415) 788-7500
Telex 340226

April 12 1979

Mayor Edward I. Koch
City Hall
New York, New York 10007

Dear Mayor Koch:

I understand that the Anthology Film Archive has applied to the City of New York to purchase an available, empty building located at 208 West 13th Street, the former Food and Maritime Trade High School.

I am writing to you in support of their need to exist in a functional public space in New York, to continue their valuable work in the preservation, presentation and study of classic and avant-garde works of film art. The Anthology Film Archive, under the direction of the poet and film-maker Jonas Mekas, is a unique institution with an international reputation for its tireless dedication to the independent film-maker throughout the history of film: it is currently the only study and exhibition center in the world specialising in the avant-garde/experimental cinema , and as such plays a vital role in the cultural life of New York.

I am sure that Mr. Mekas and his colleagues would make creative use of this space in their plans to offer a continuous daily repertory of cinema art to the public, and in their related programs of film study, film distribution, video exhibition, and mixed media performance art.

Sincerely,

Francis Coppola

cc: Jonas Mekas
Andrew Stein
Carol Bellamy
Anthology Film Archive

Letter from Francis Coppola to Mayor Edward I. Koch in support of Anthology Film Archives' proposed purchase of the Food and Maritime Trades High School, April 12, 1979.

MARTIN SCORSESE

May 20, 1980

Jonas Mekas
Anthology Film Archives
80 Wooster Street
New York, New York 10012

Dear Jonas,

I wanted you to know that I support your venture into the preservation of independent films, entrusted to Anthology Film Archives, completely and entirely. As you know, I have gotten very involved in the preservation of color film negatives, in so far as all of our work is endangered by the fading of colr film sotck. However, my work in this area has been limited to those films produced under the auspices of the Hollywood system. Thus, I am delighted and encouraged that you have taken the initiative to extend this concern to all films, particularly the independents.

Without a doubt, I and many of my colleagues, owe our basic film understanding to the independent filmmakers. Independents, such as Kenneth Anger and Stan Brakhage, were instrumental in my personal development as a filmmaker -- and, I am certain their importance will continue, for future generations of directors, cinematographers and actors. Thus, the urgency to preserve their work is obvious. Since cold storage seems to be the only feasible method of preservation available to us presently, I urge everyone to support your courageous project. Anthology Film Archives will set the example of the first necessary step we must all take to preserve our color film.

Best Regards,

Martin Scorsese

Letter from Martin Scorsese to Jonas Mekas in support of his cold-storage film-preservation project, May 20, 1980.

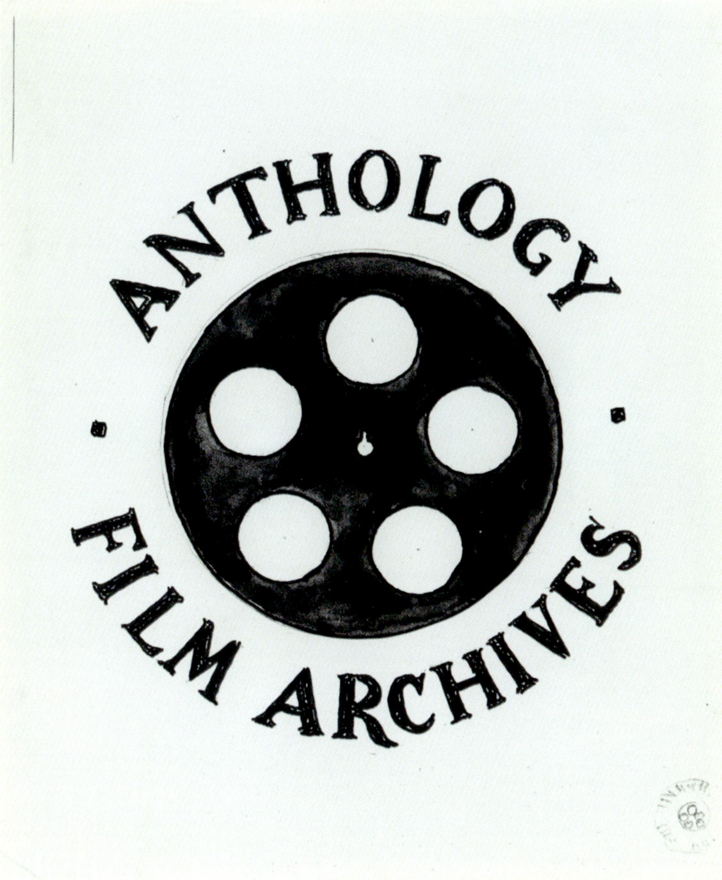

Logo of Anthology Film Archives.

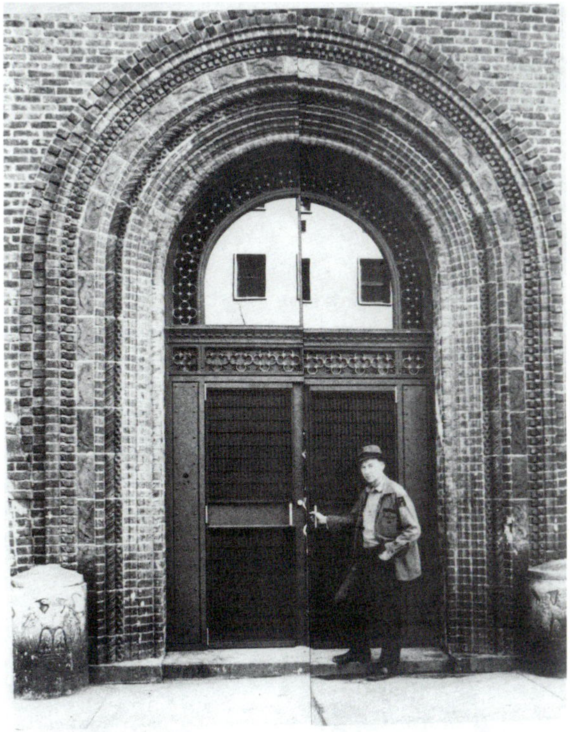

Jonas Mekas at the doors of the Second Avenue Courthouse, the future Anthology Film Archives, photographed by Hollis Melton, undated.

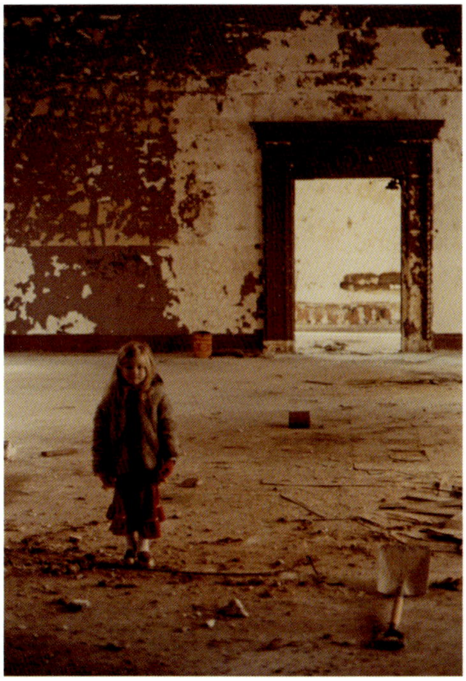

Portrait of Oona Mekas in the Second Avenue Courthouse, 1977.

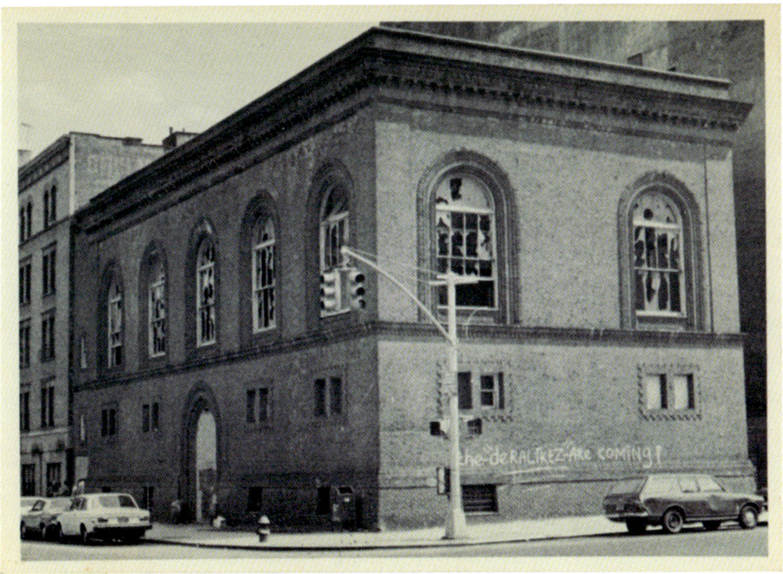

Postcard announcing the purchase of the Second Avenue Courthouse, photographed by Hollis Melton, 1979.

The Metropolitan Museum of Art

PERSONAL

CHAIRMAN FOR SPECIAL PROJECTS

June 22, 1978

Honorable Carol Bellamy
President, City Council
City Hall
New York, NY 10007

Dear Ms. Bellamy:

The Film Art Fund, Inc., Anthology of Film Archives would like to rehabilitate the abandoned and vandalized courthouse at 32-34 Second Avenue, in order to make it a Center for independent, avant-garde film-makers and mixed-media artists. This building would be exceedingly suitable for this project.

I am writing to you today to express encouragement for this exciting project and urge you to support the Anthology of Film Archives' request.

Sincerely,

Karl Katz

KK:jr

Letter from Karl Katz, chairman for Special Projects at the Metropolitan Museum of Art, to City Council President Carol Bellamy in support of Anthology Film Archives' proposed purchase of the Second Avenue Courthouse, June 22, 1978.

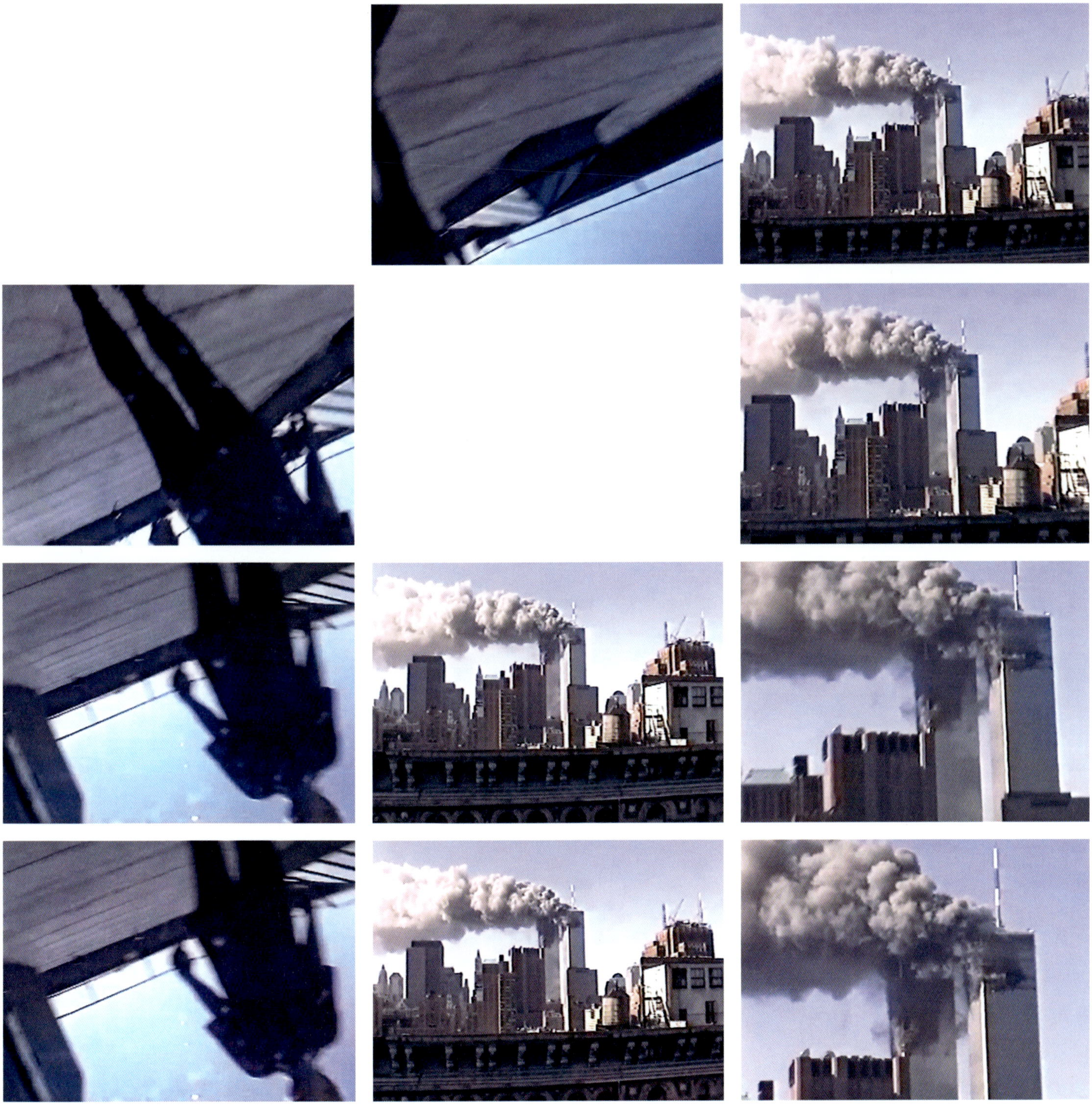

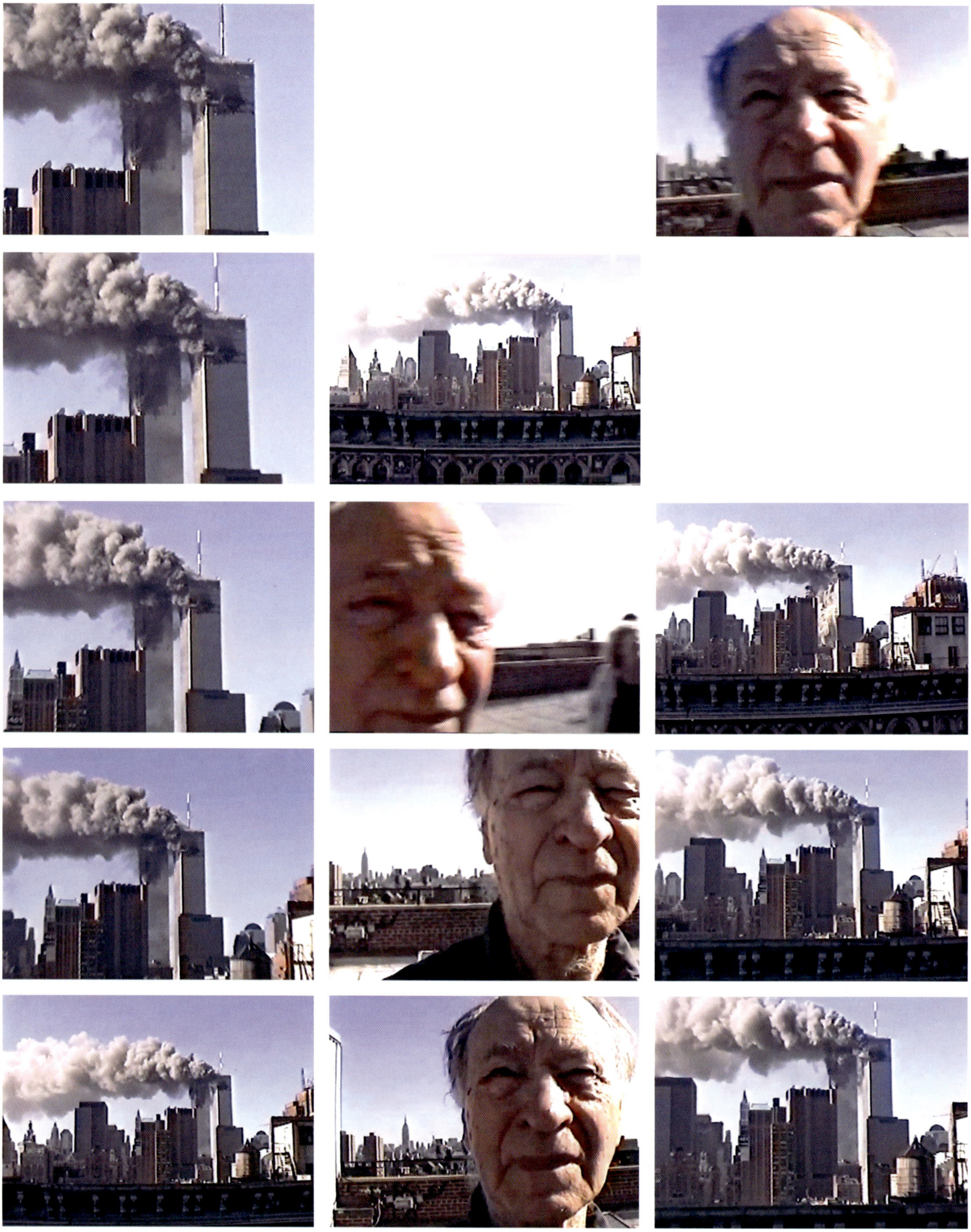

MY 9/11 FOOTAGE VIDEO 2001

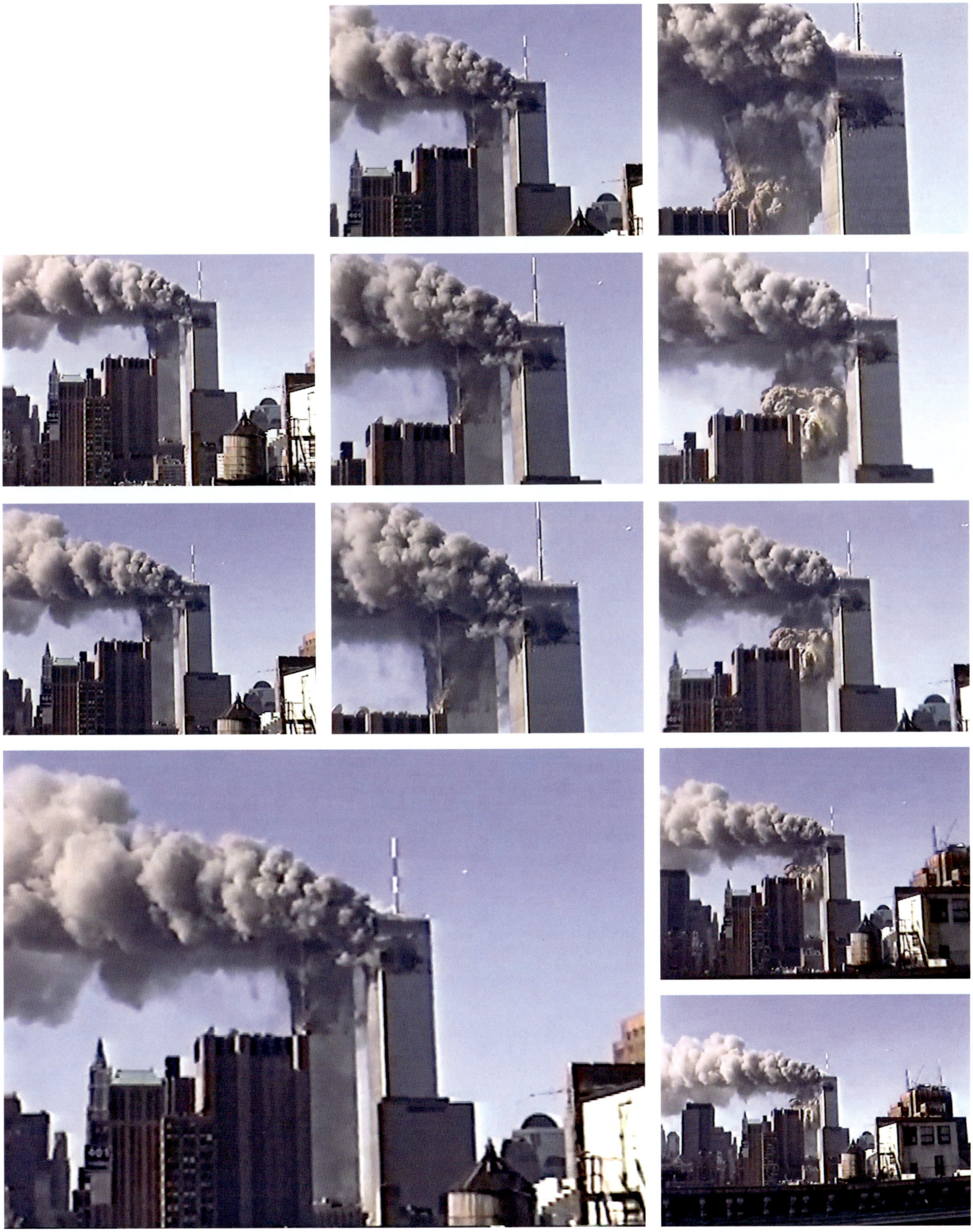

A LETTER FROM GREENPOINT, 2004

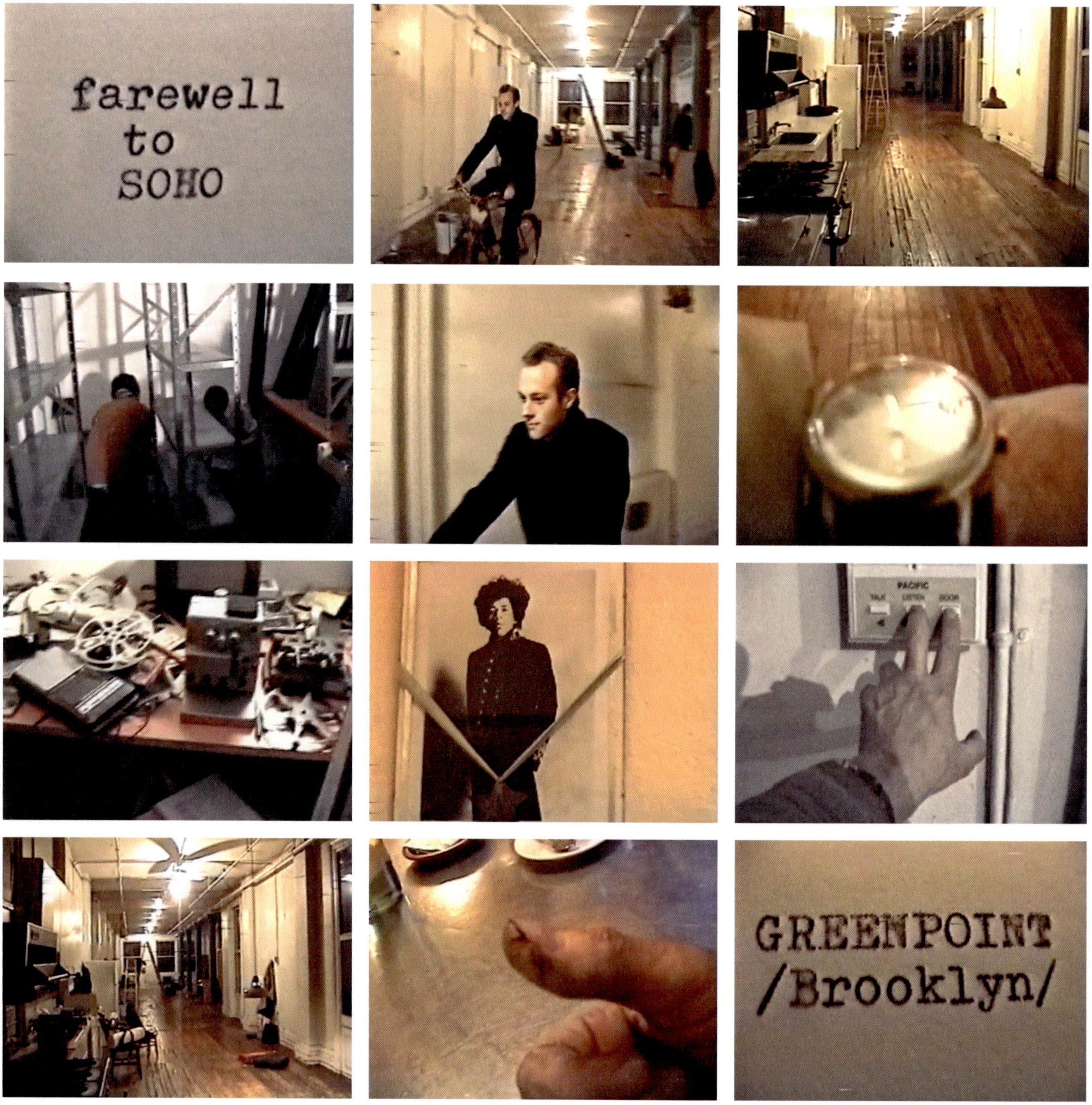

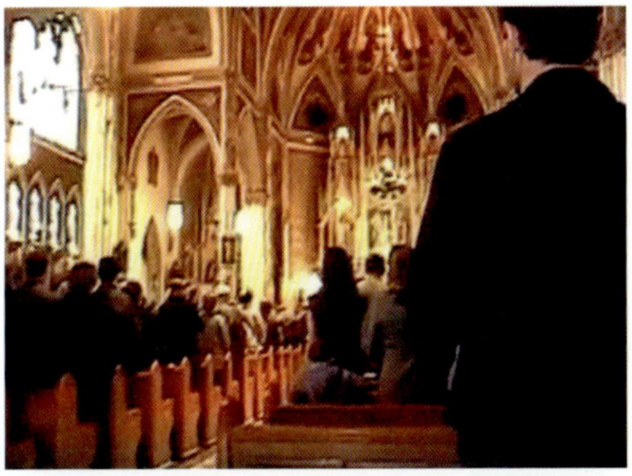
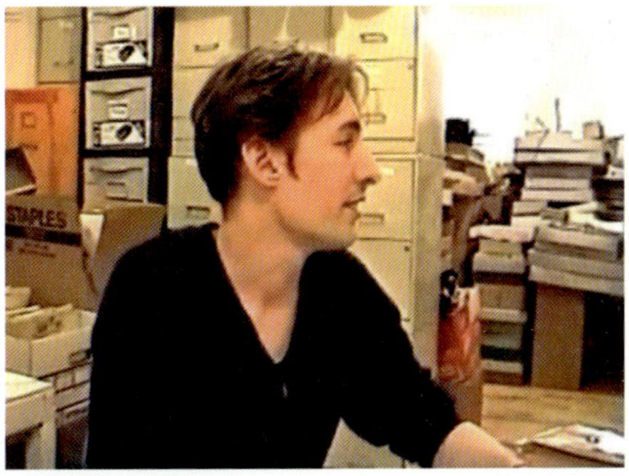
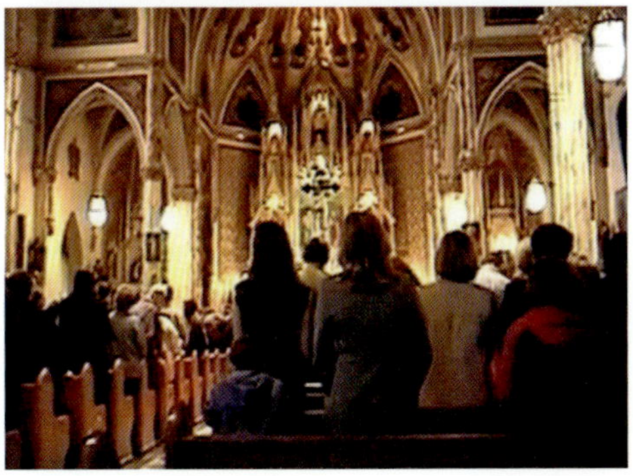
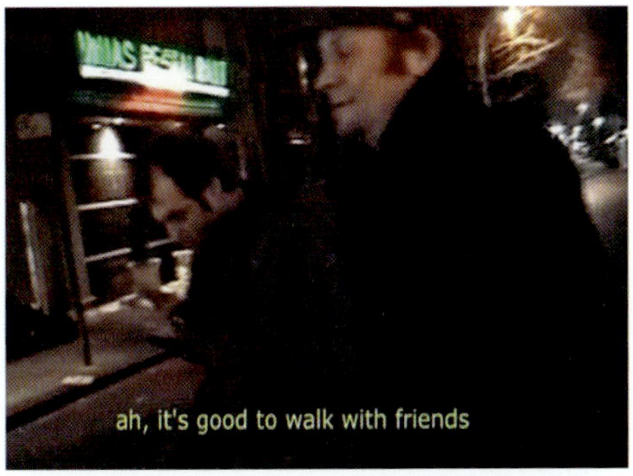

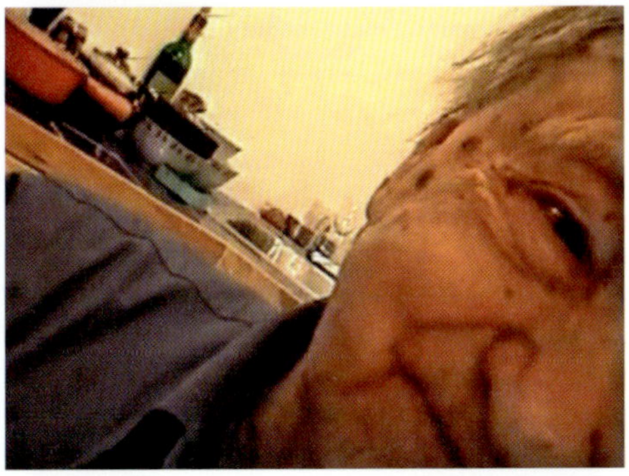
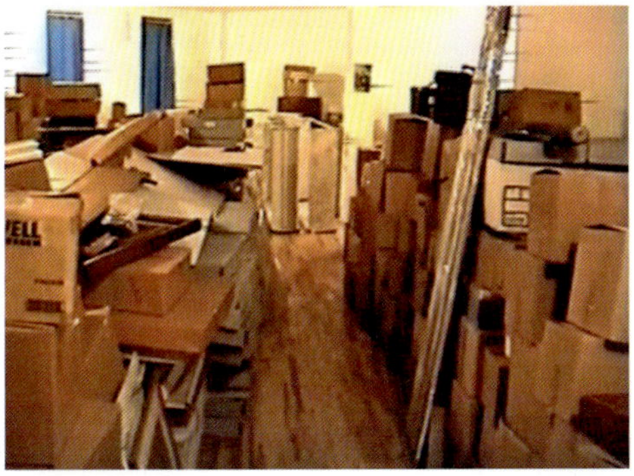
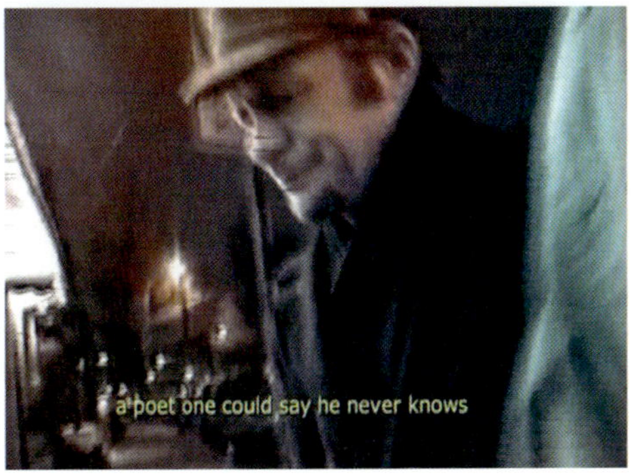

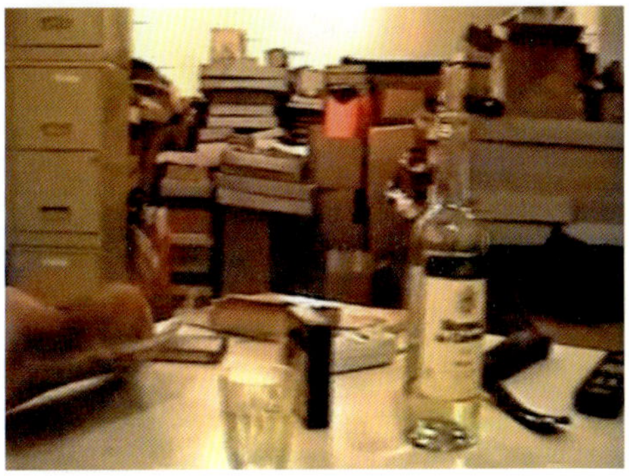
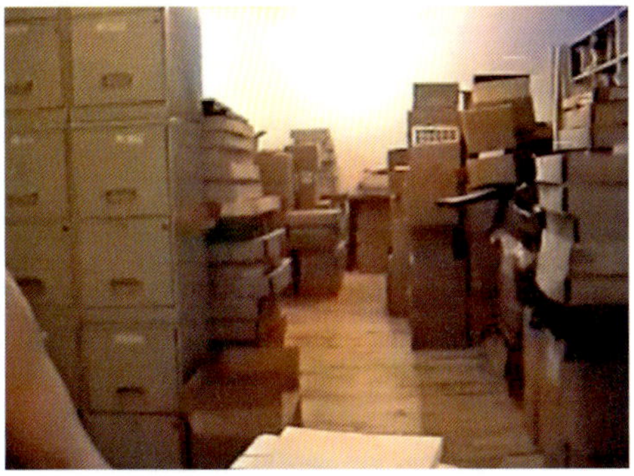
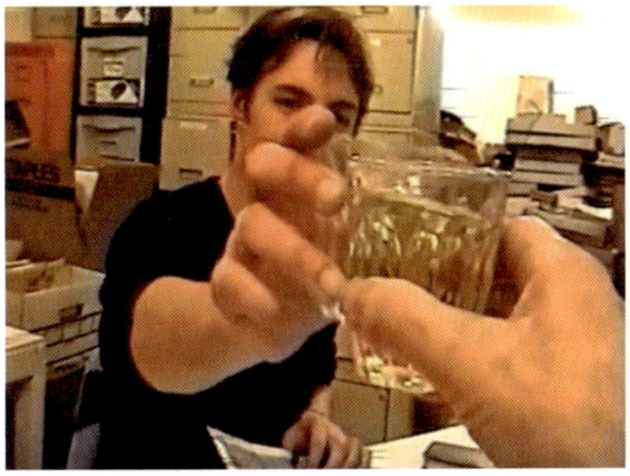

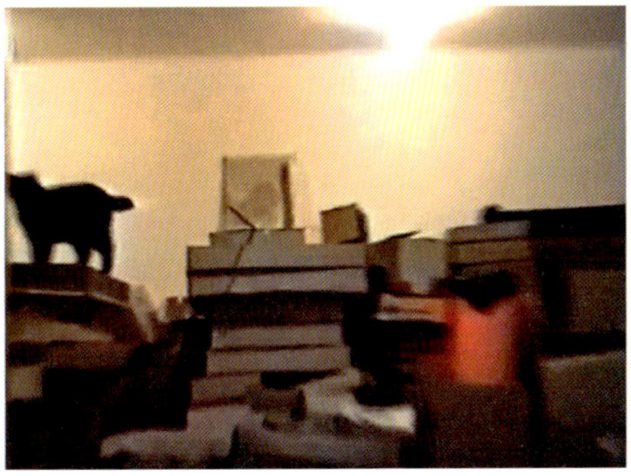
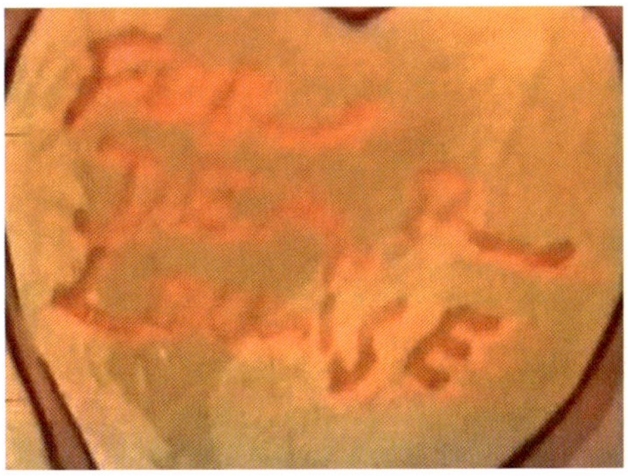

 FILMS COLOR SOUND 80 MIN

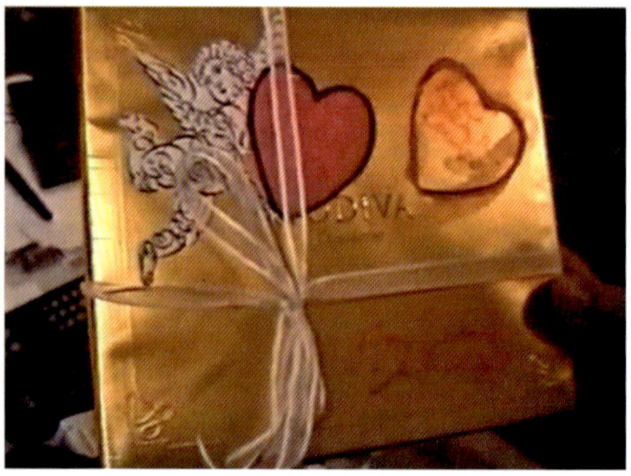
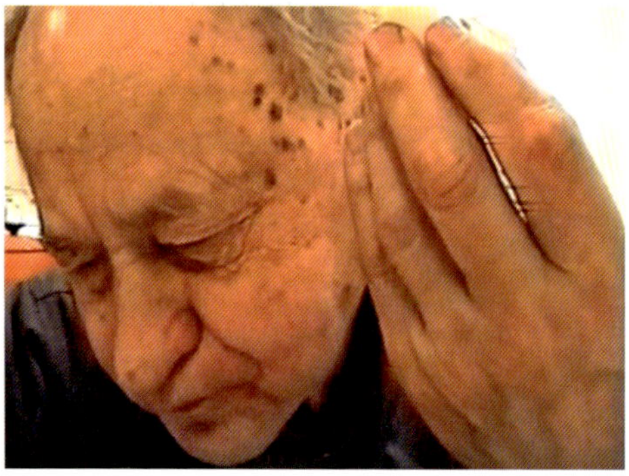
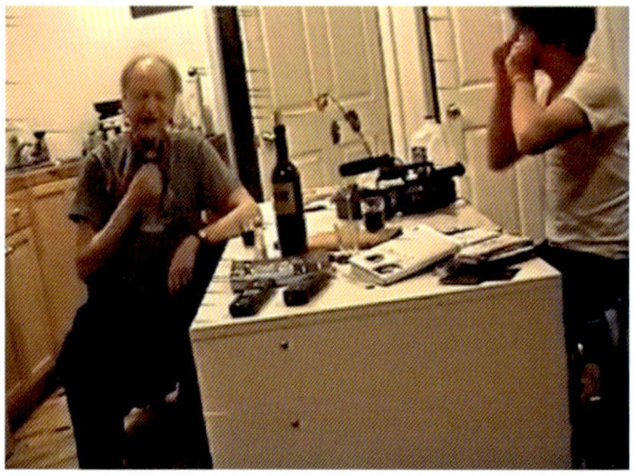
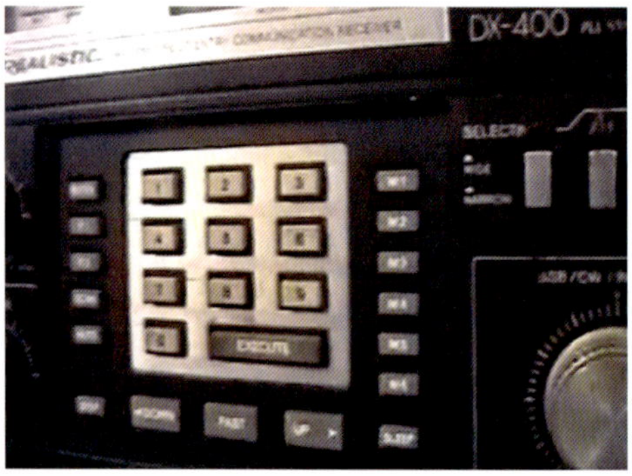
DX-400
EXECUTE
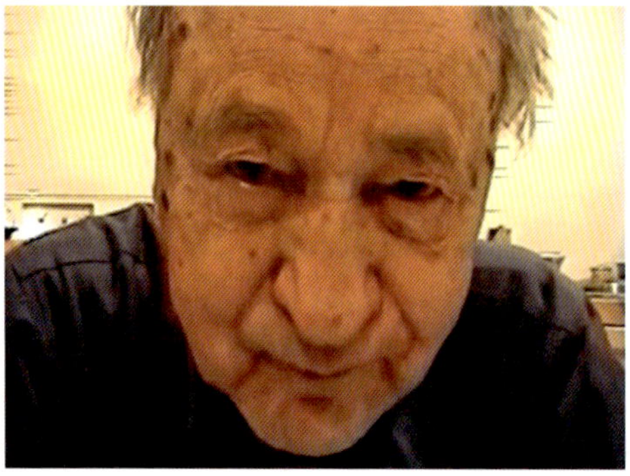
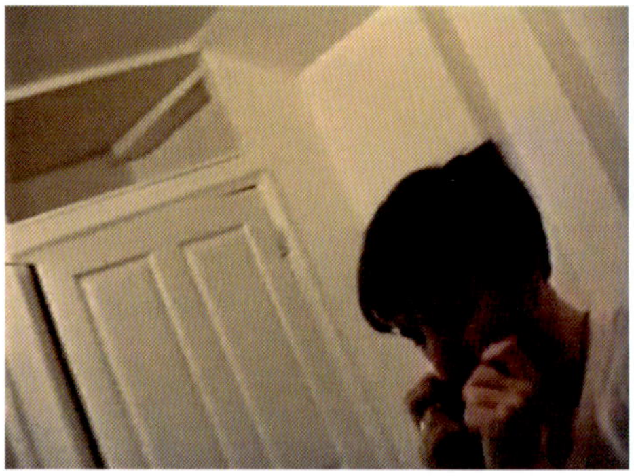
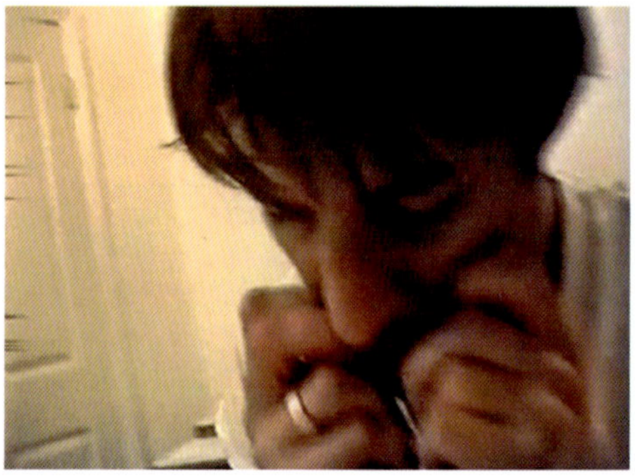
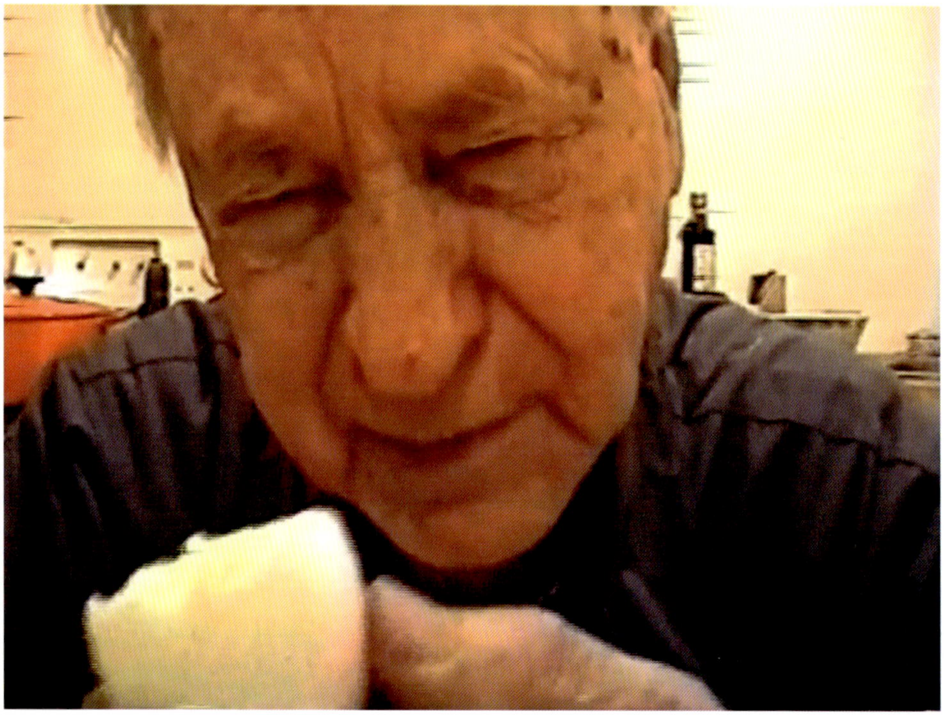
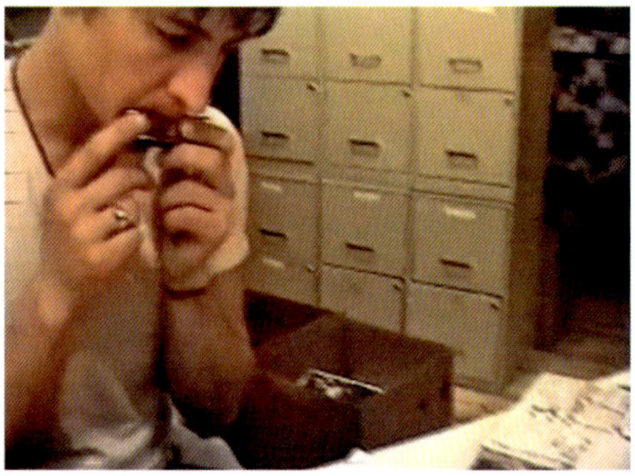

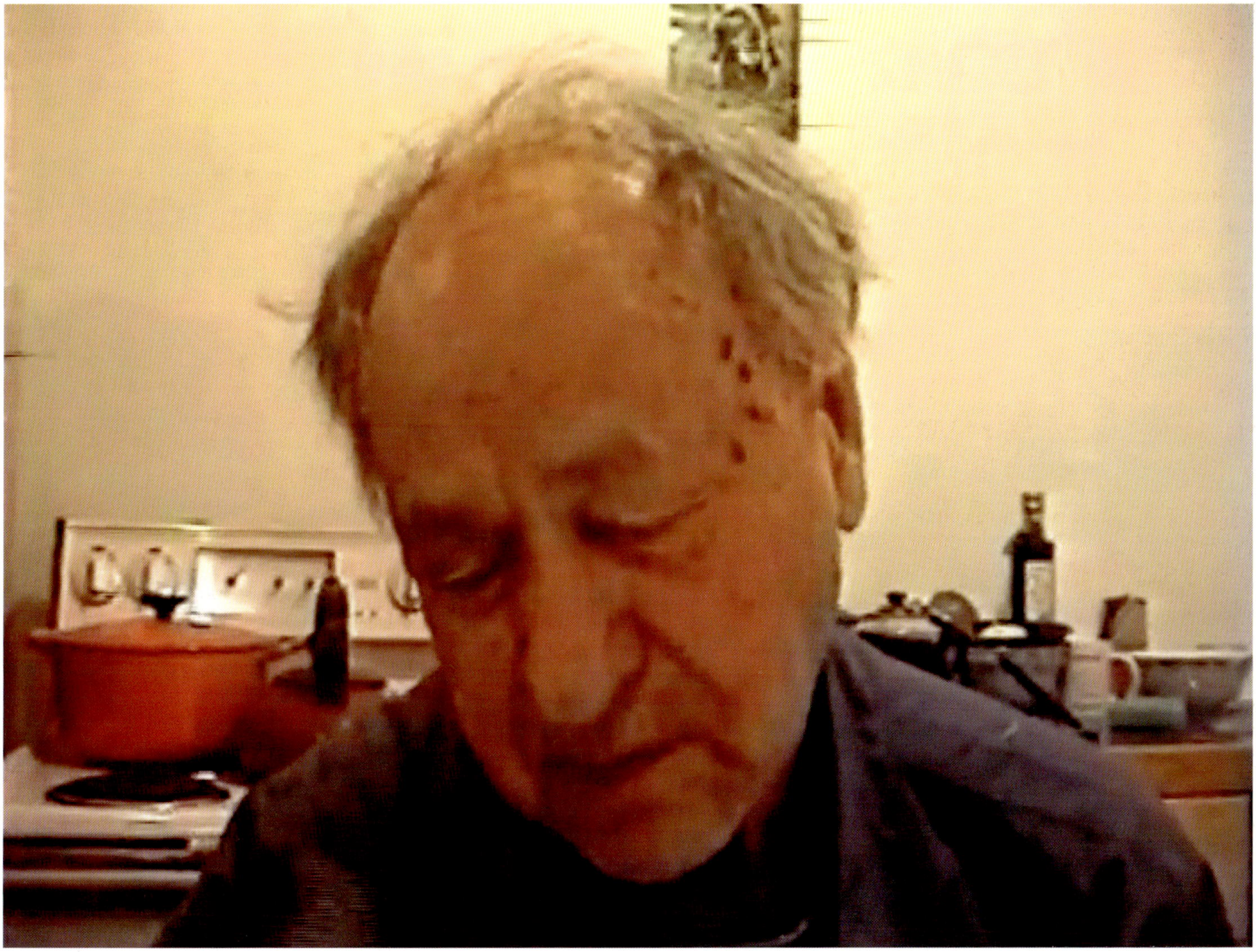

 FILMS COLOR SOUND 80 MIN

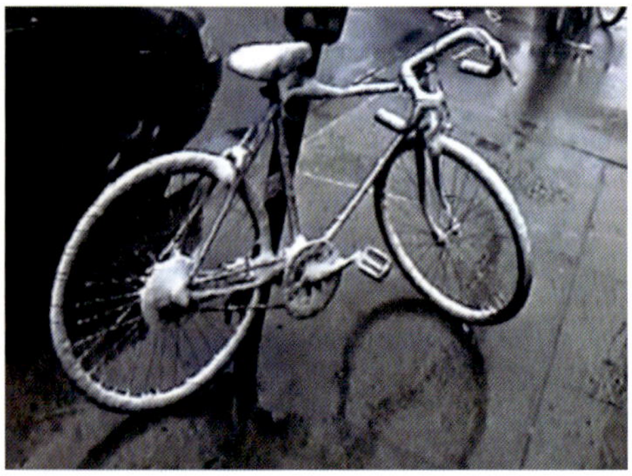
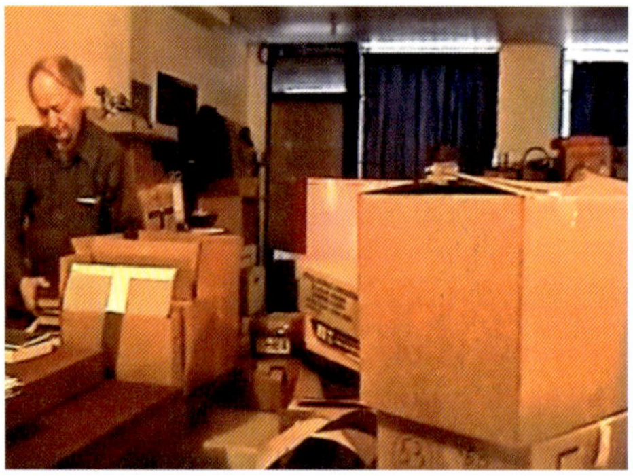
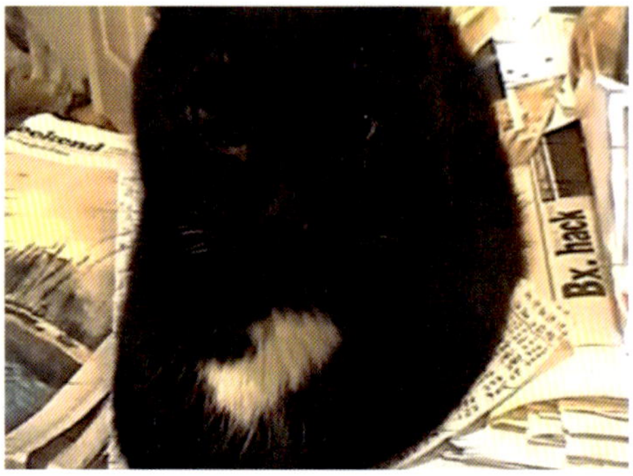
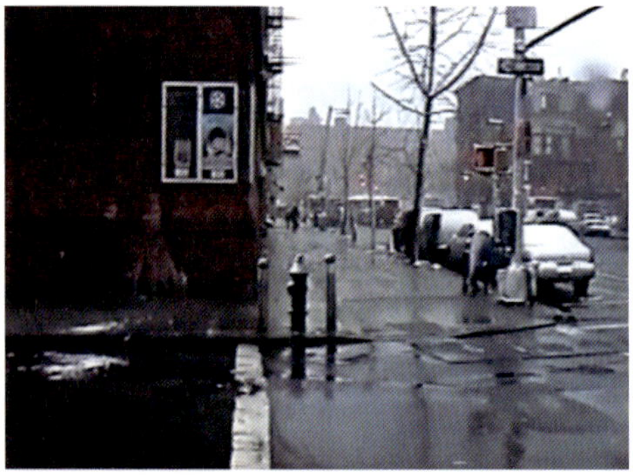
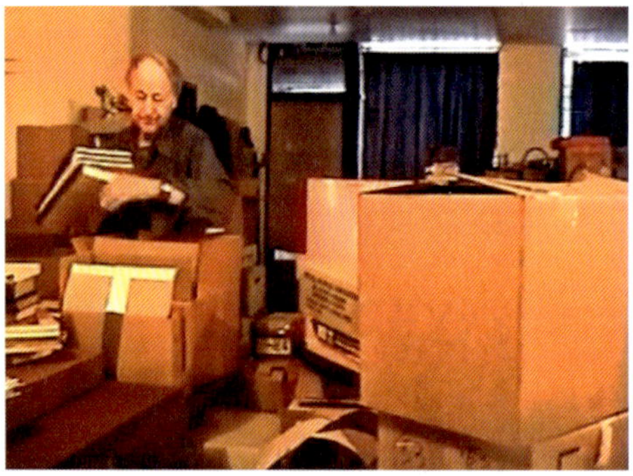
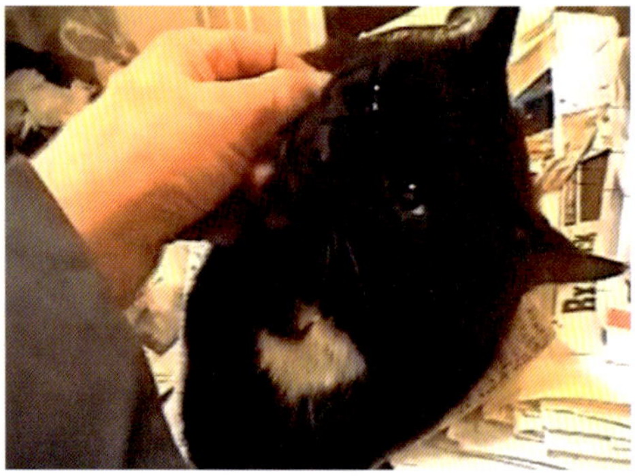
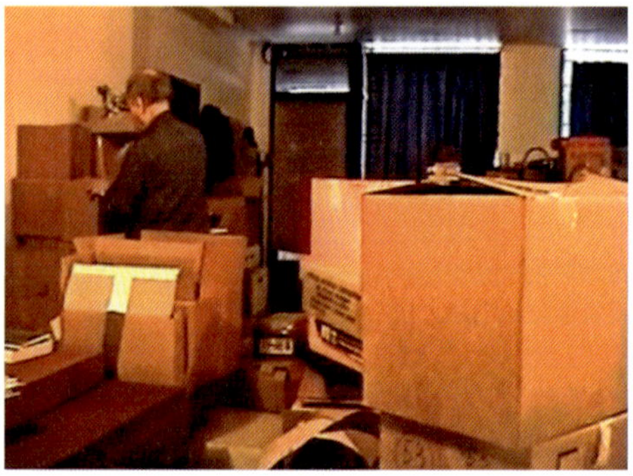
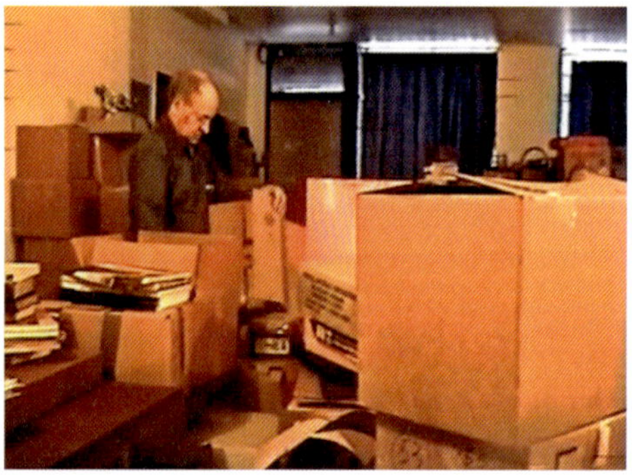
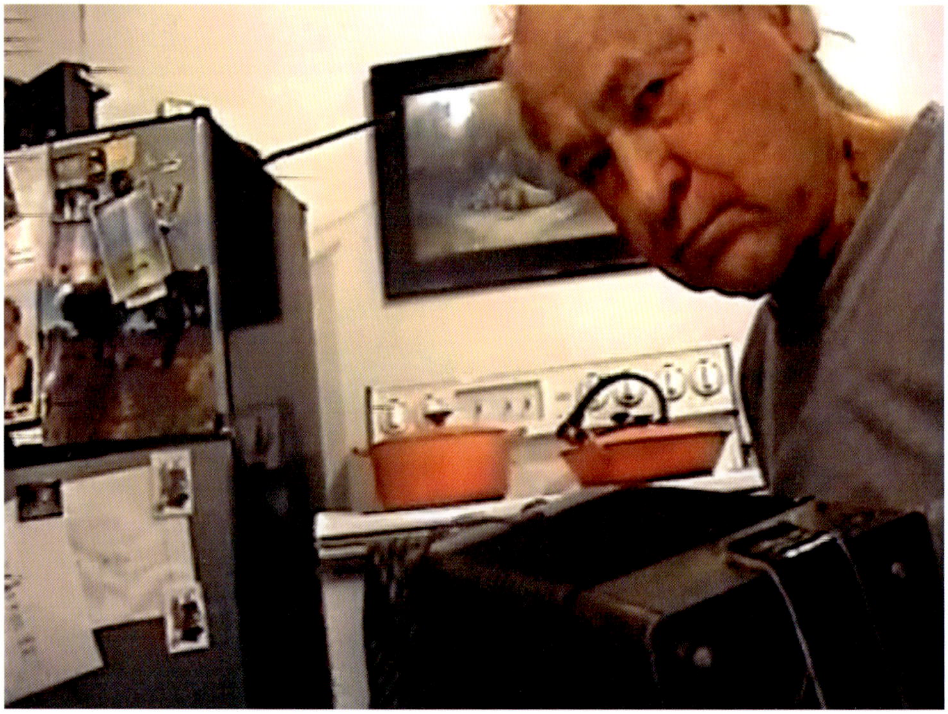
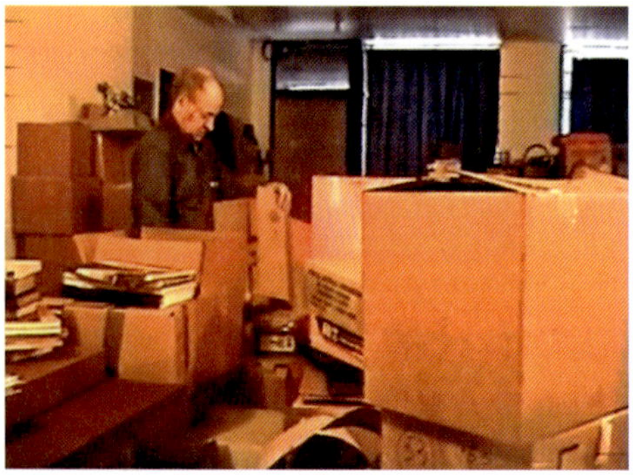

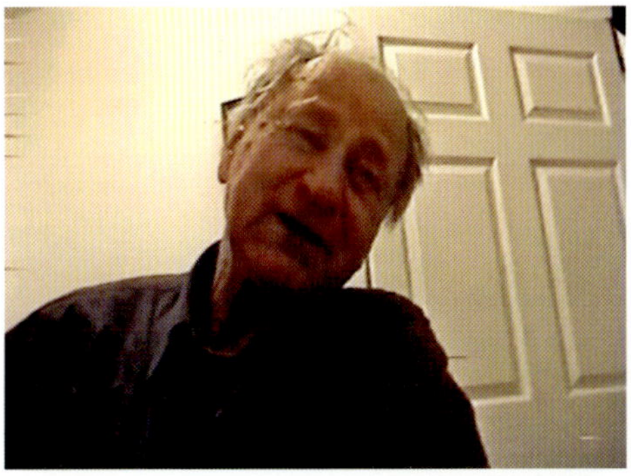

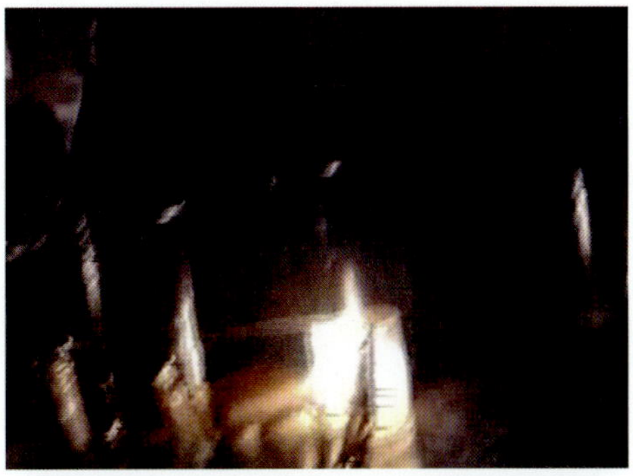

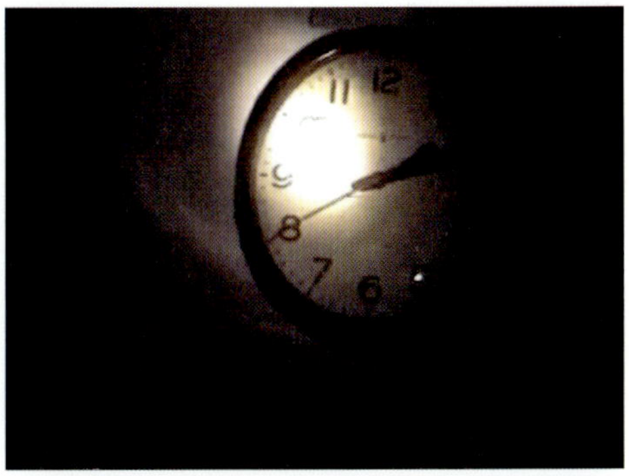

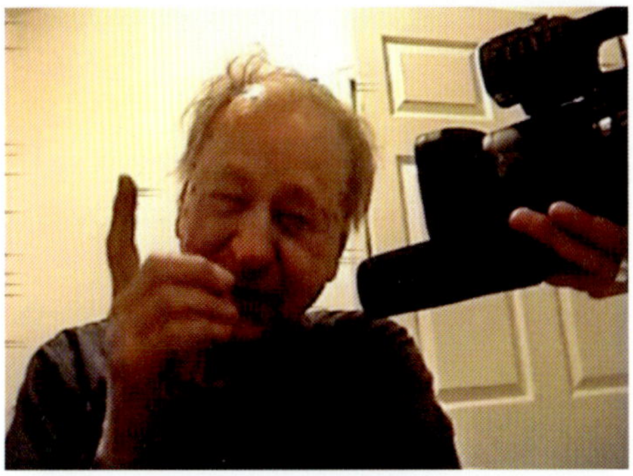

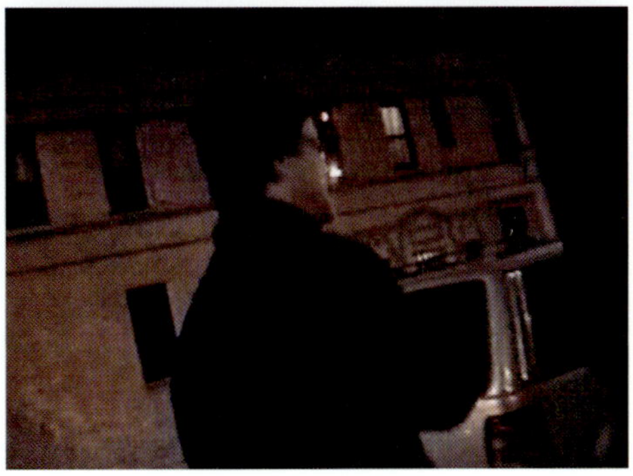

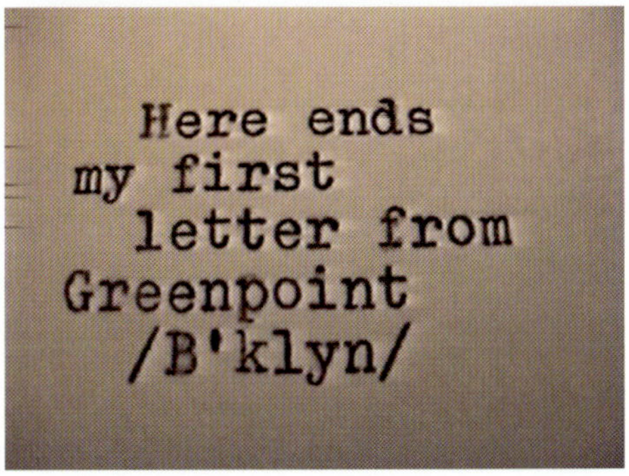
Here ends
my first
letter from
Greenpoint
/B'klyn/

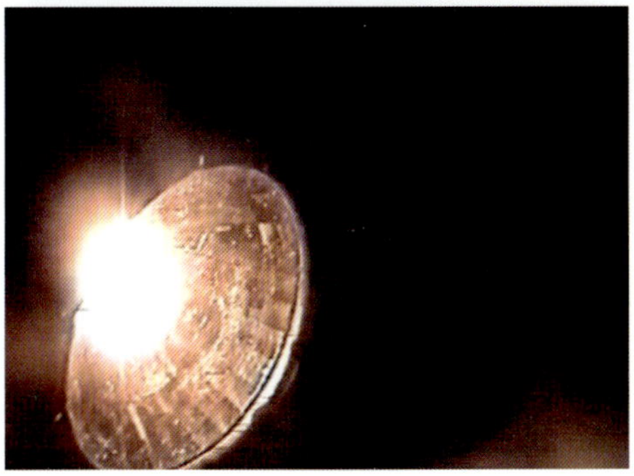

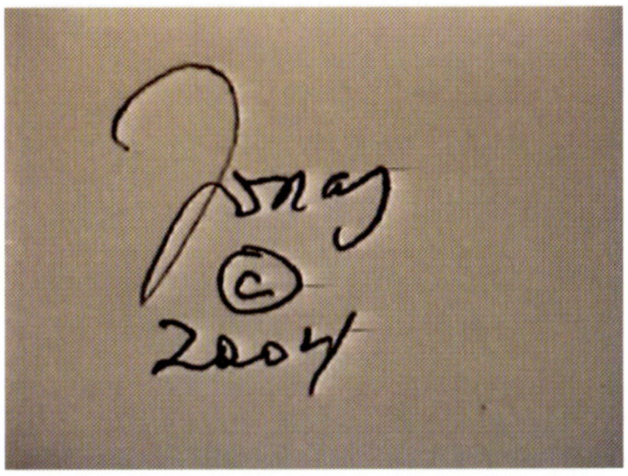
Jonas
©
2004

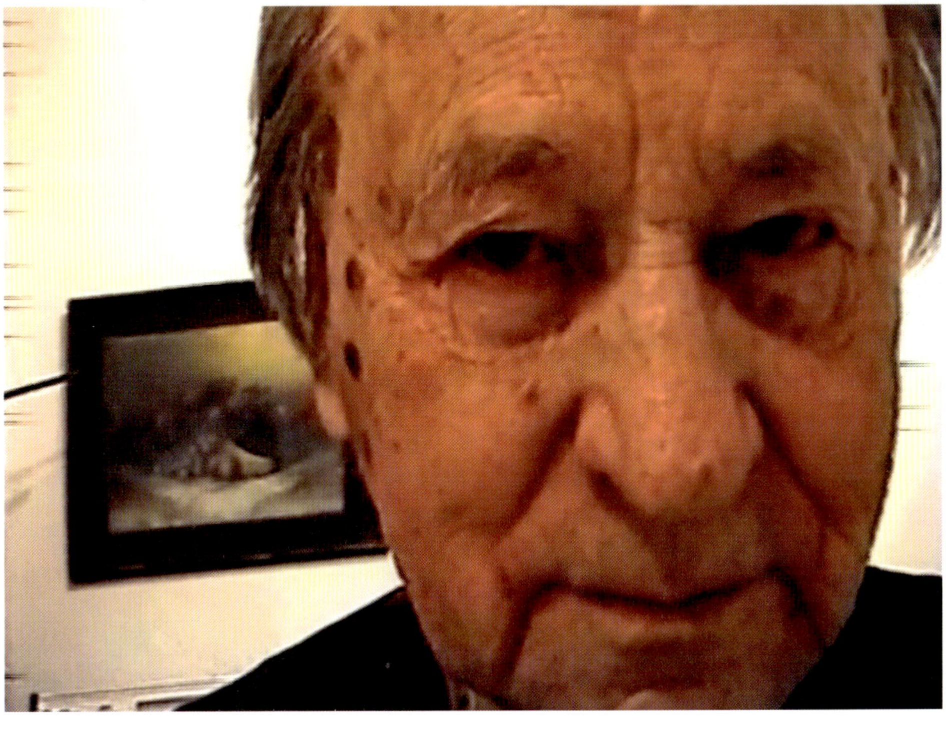

365 DAY PROJECT, 2007

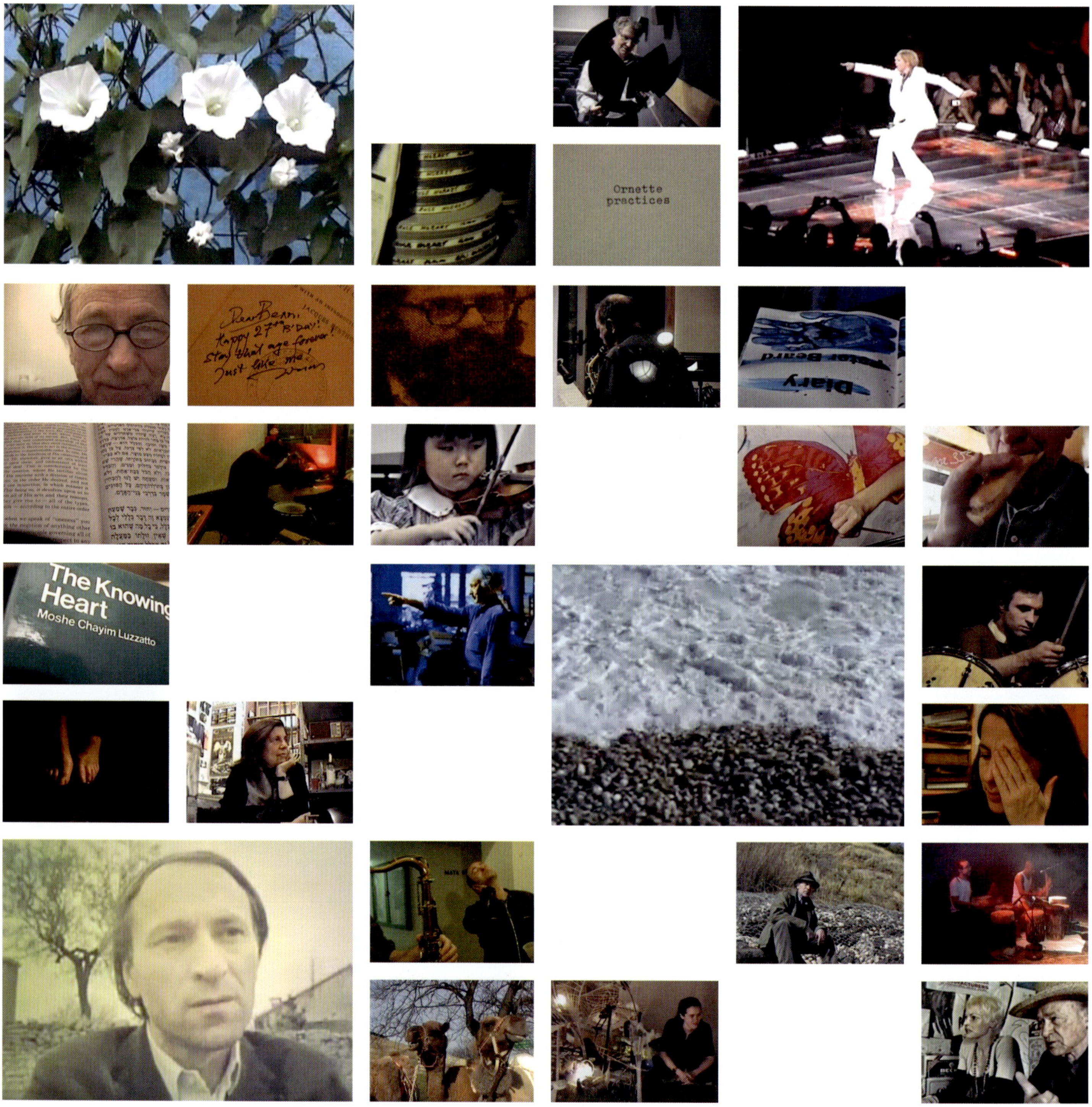

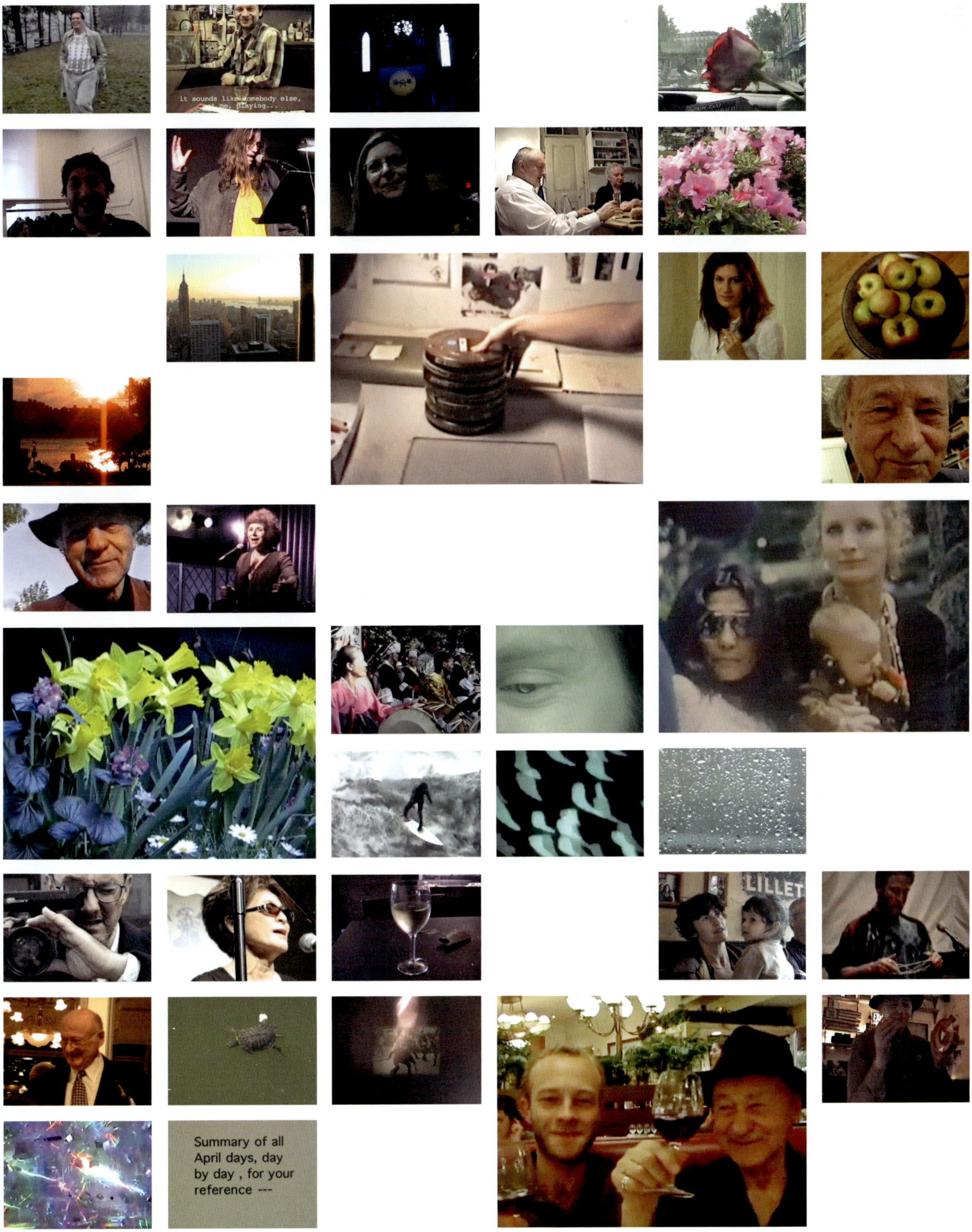
it sounds like somebody else,
Summary of all
April days, day
by day , for your
reference ---

I WORK AT
ANTHOLOGY
FILM
ARCHIVES

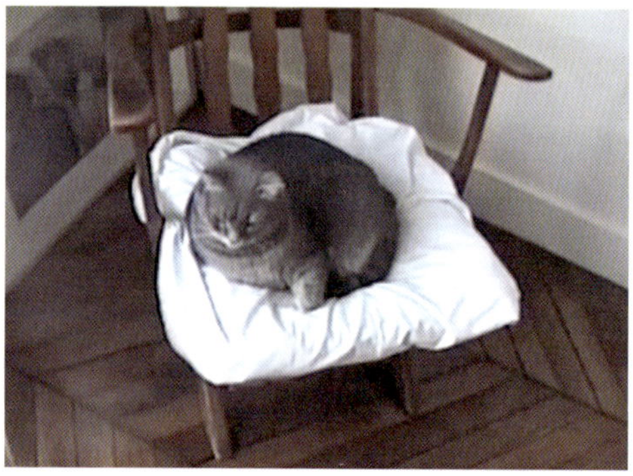

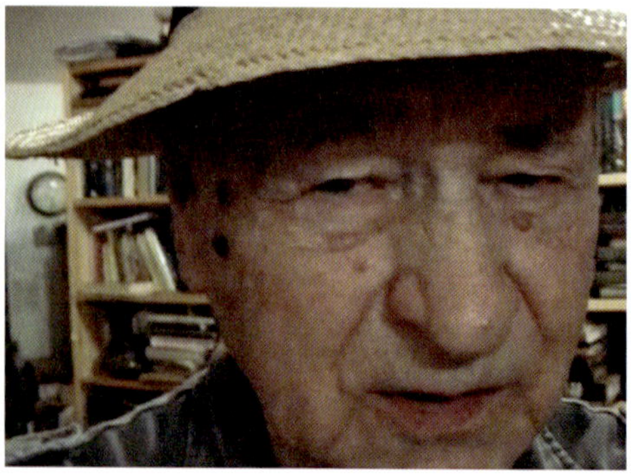

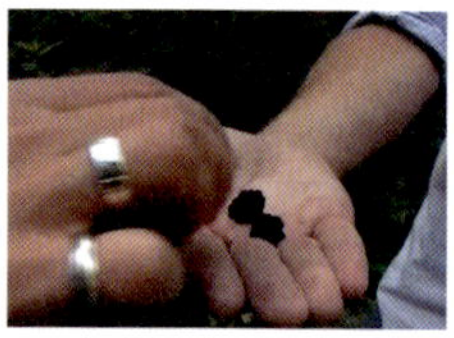

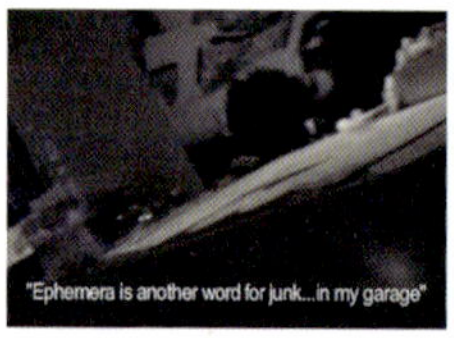
"Ephemera is another word for junk...in my garage"

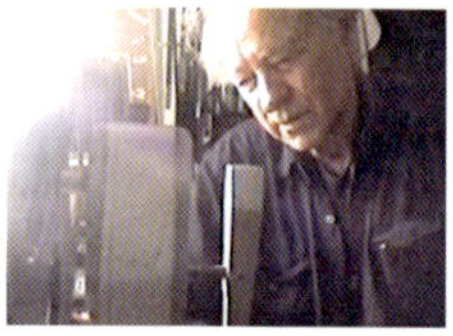

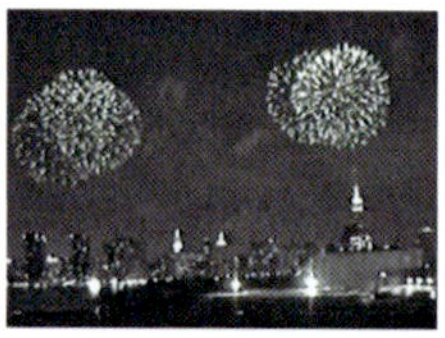

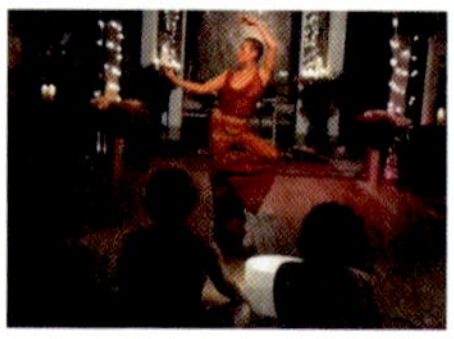

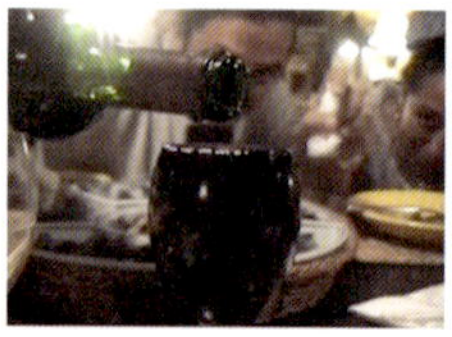

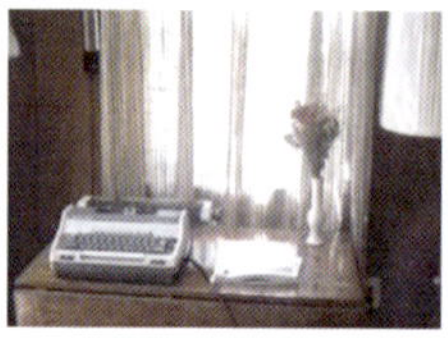

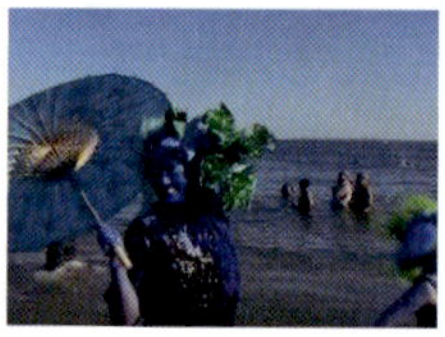

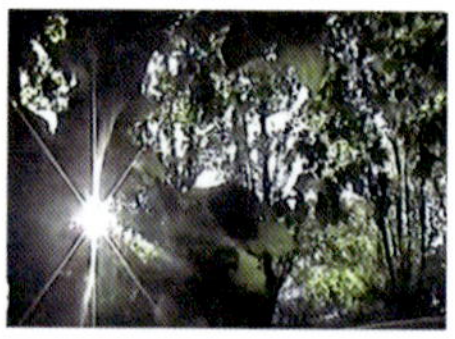

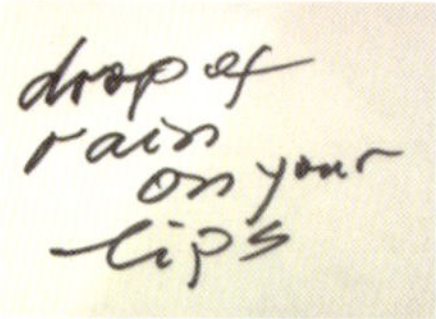
drop of
rain
on your
lips

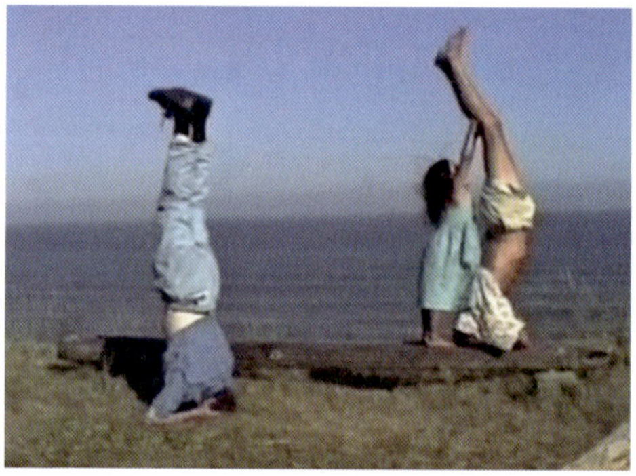

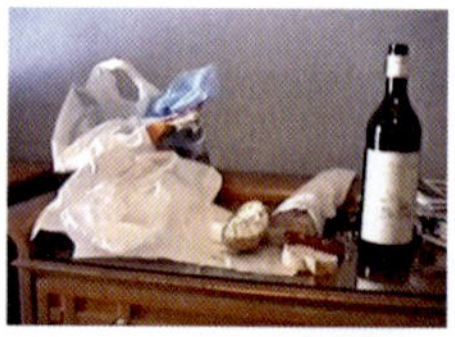

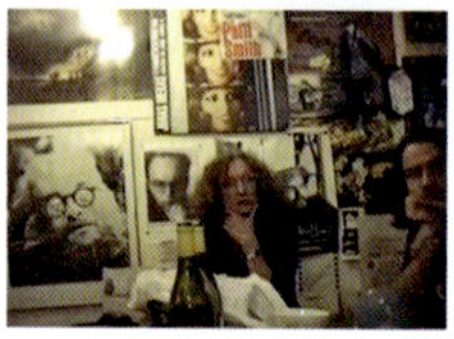

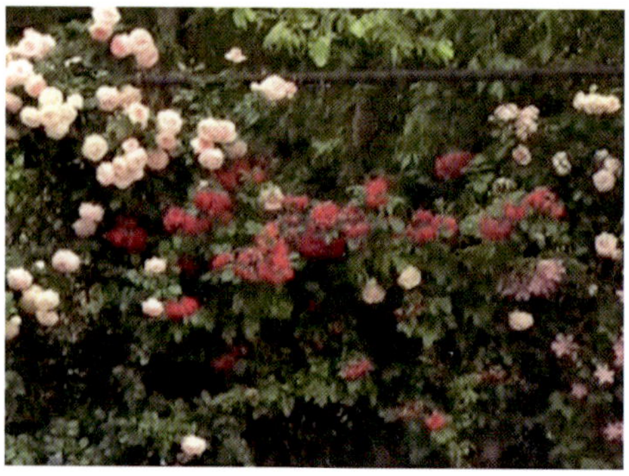

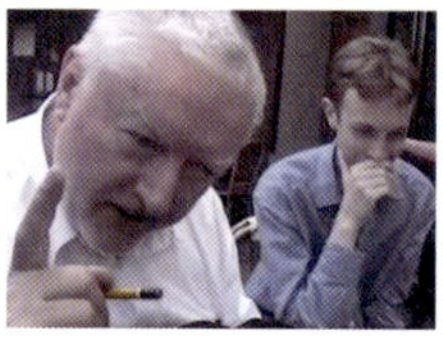

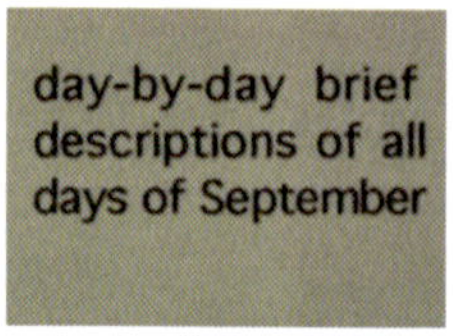
day-by-day brief
descriptions of all
days of September

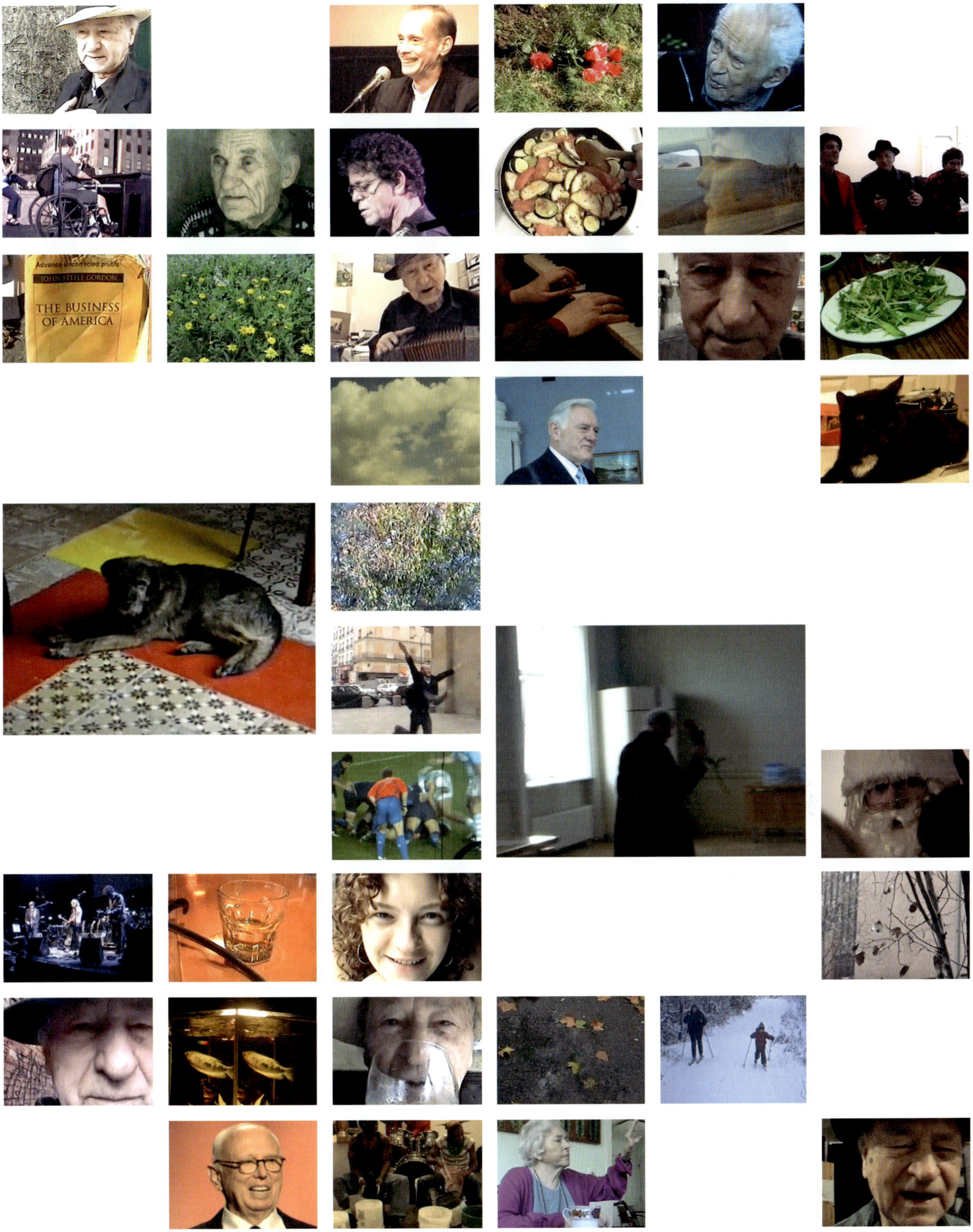

FILMS COLOR SOUND BETWEEN 2 AND 15 MIN EACH

REQUIEM, 2019

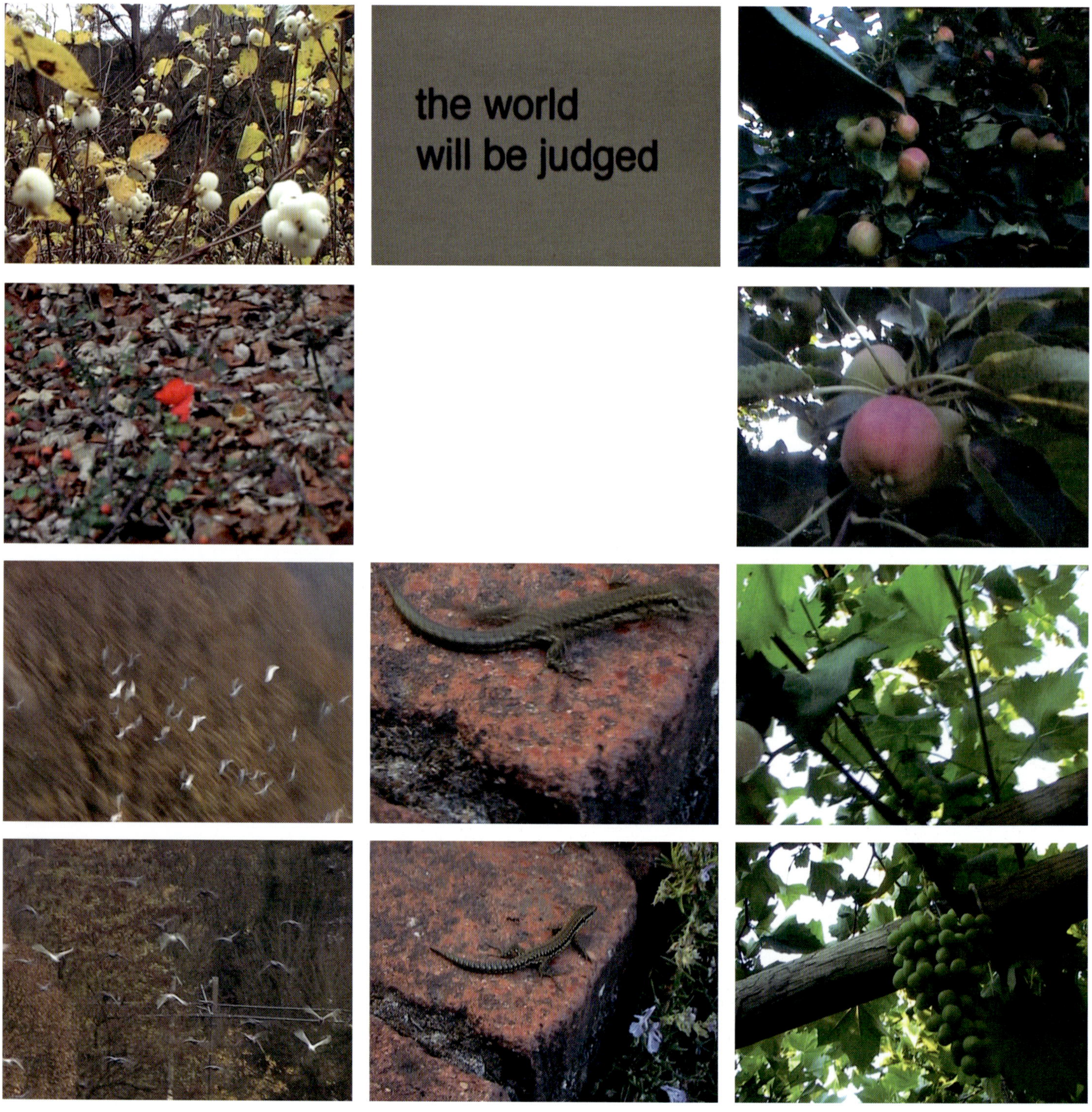

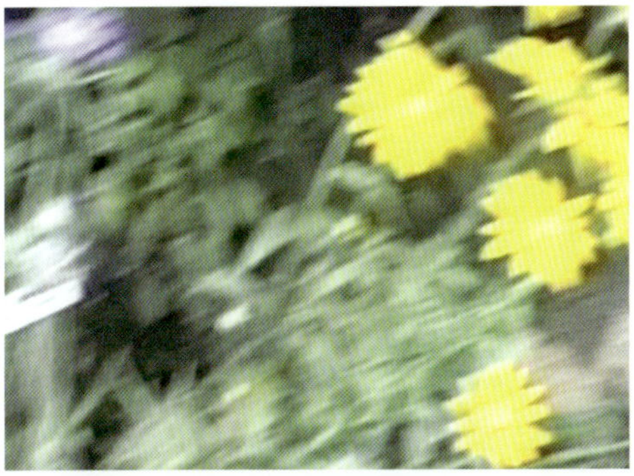
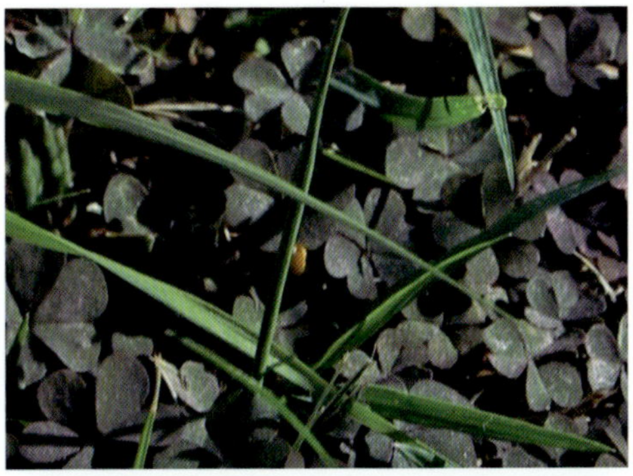
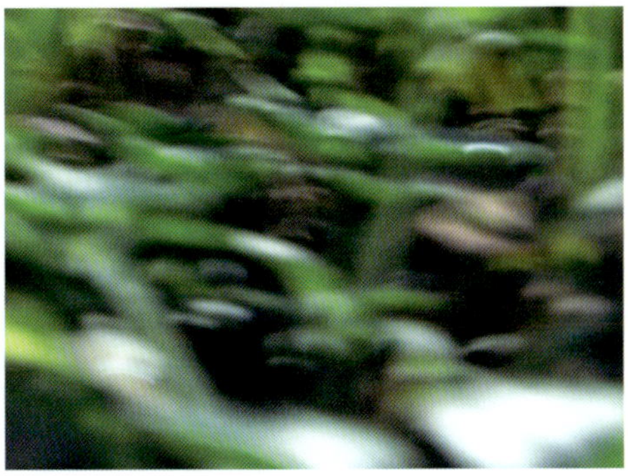
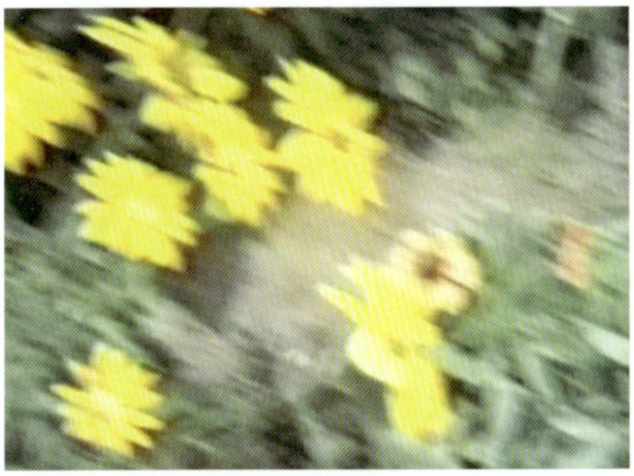
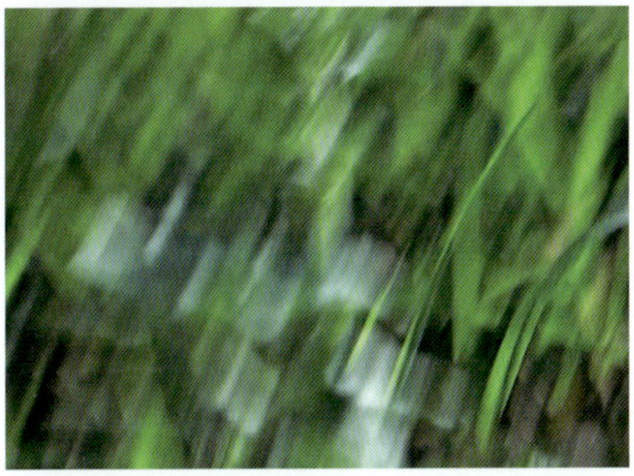
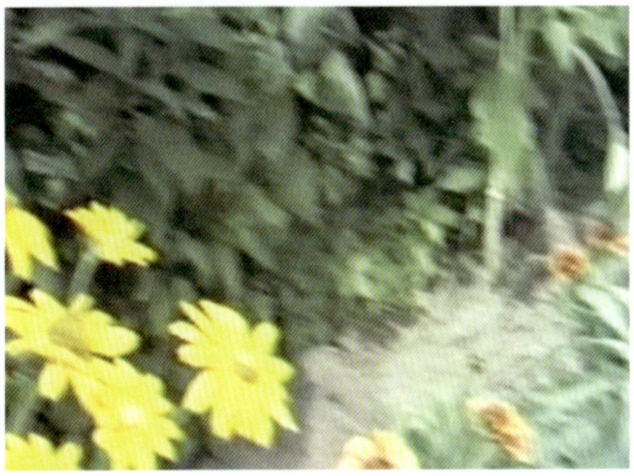
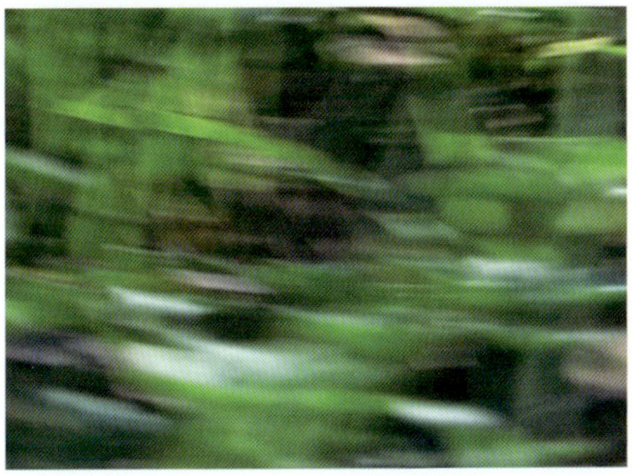
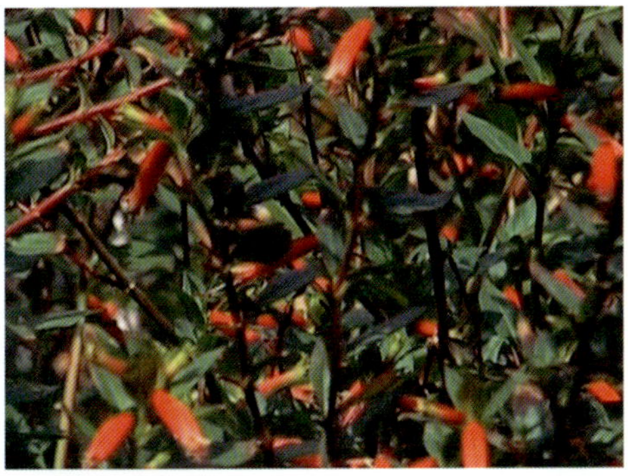
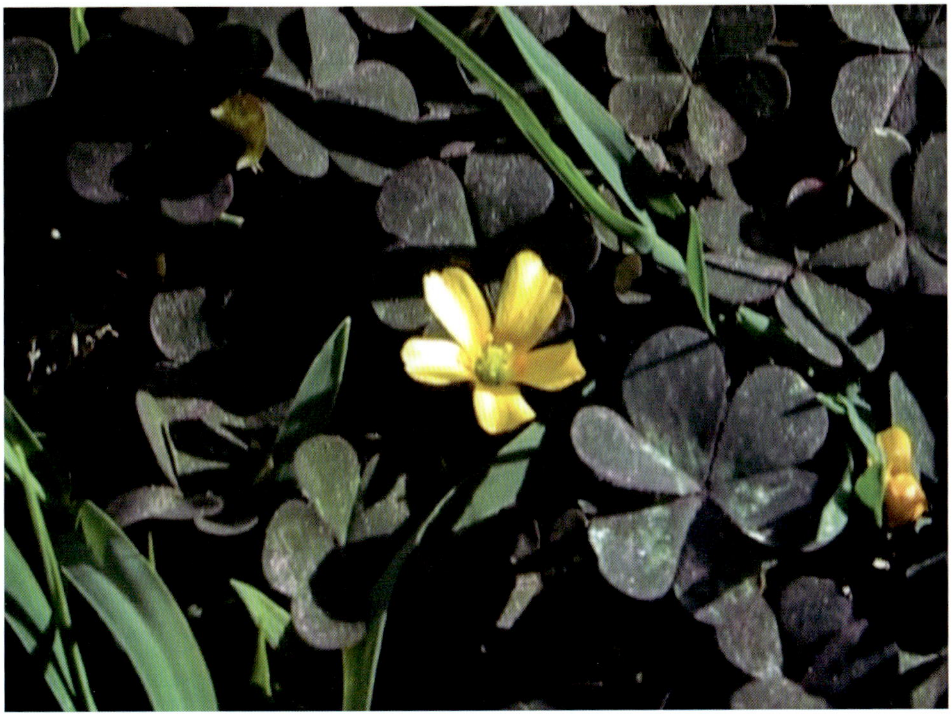
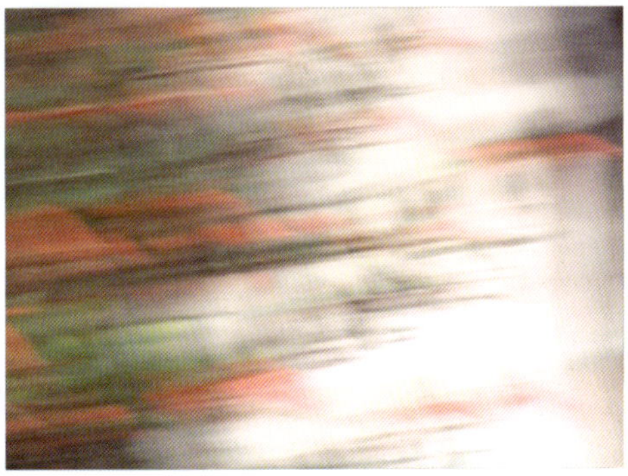
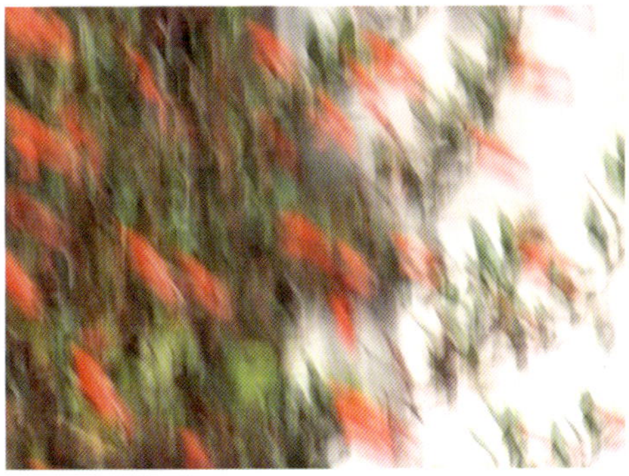

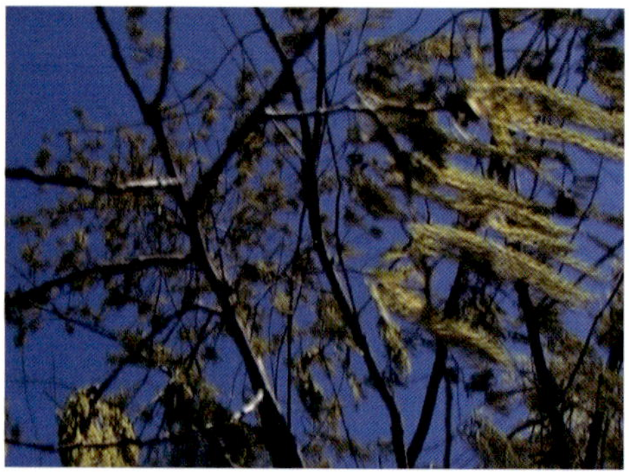
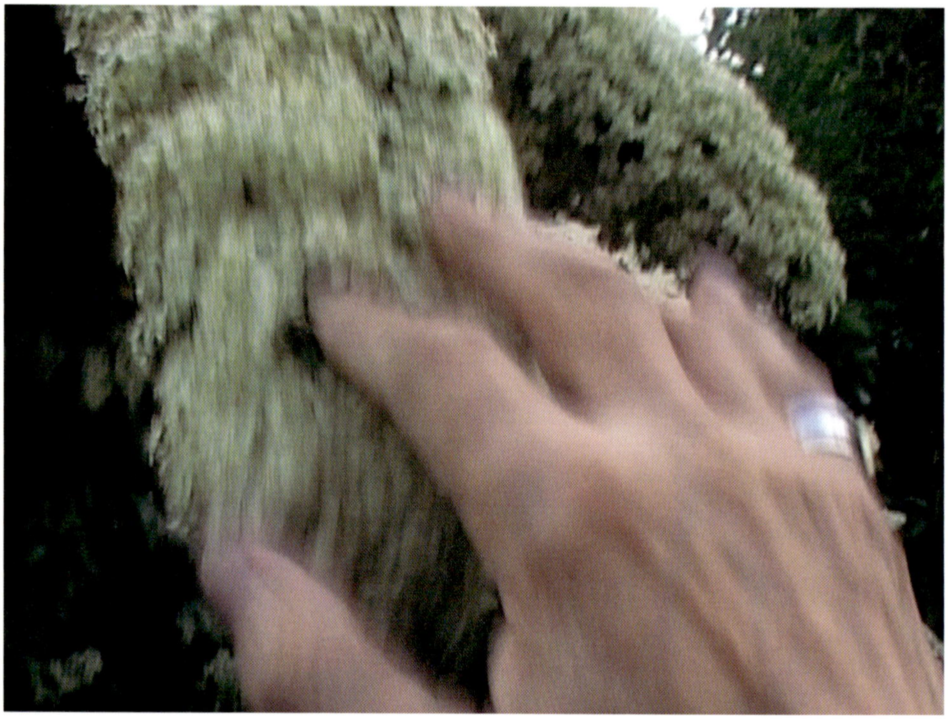
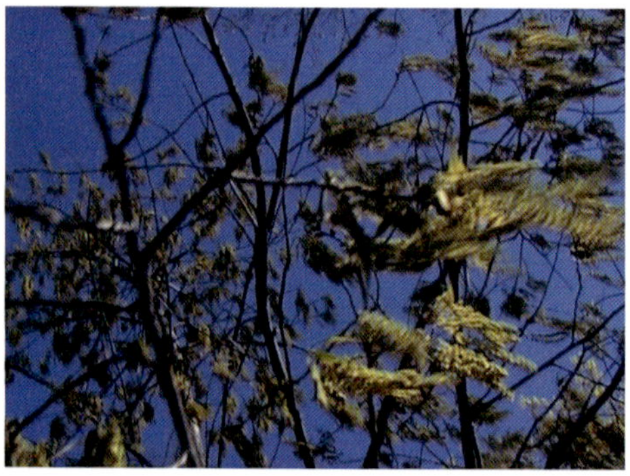
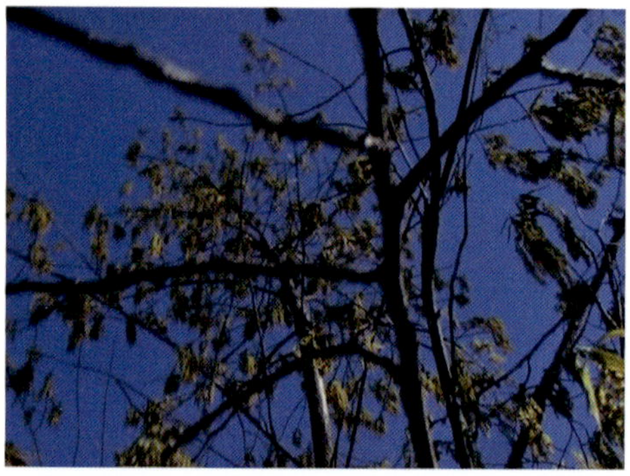
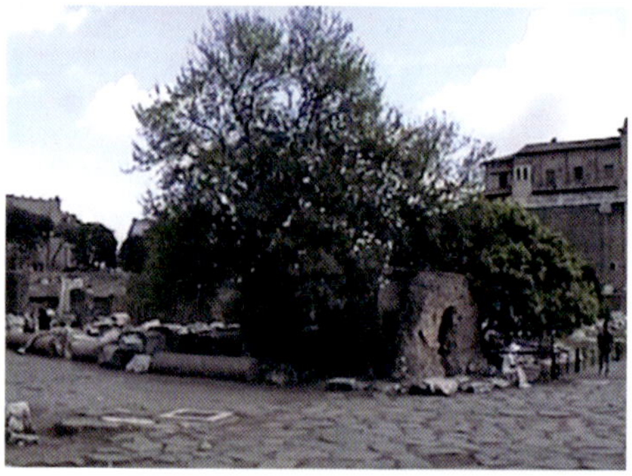
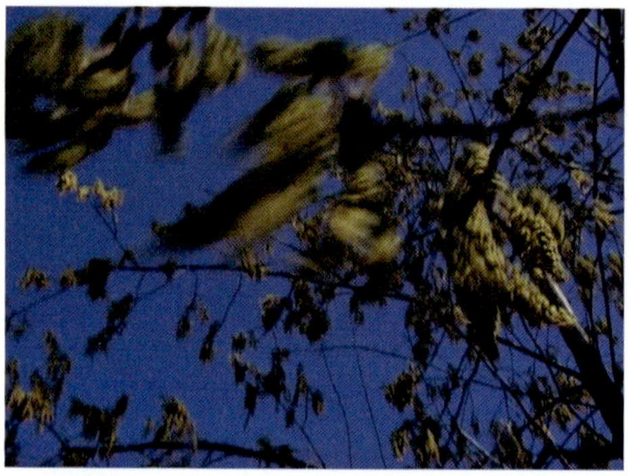
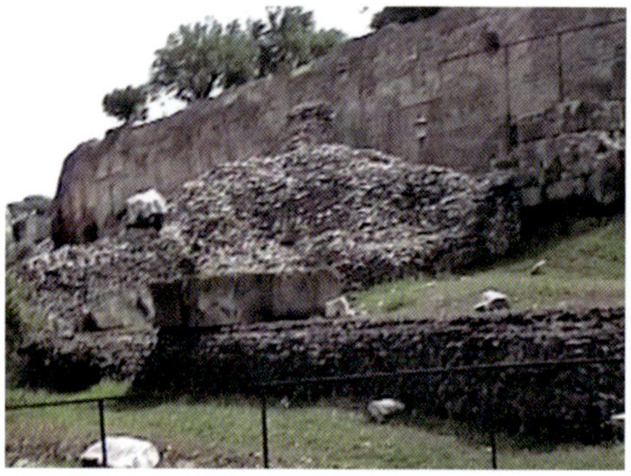
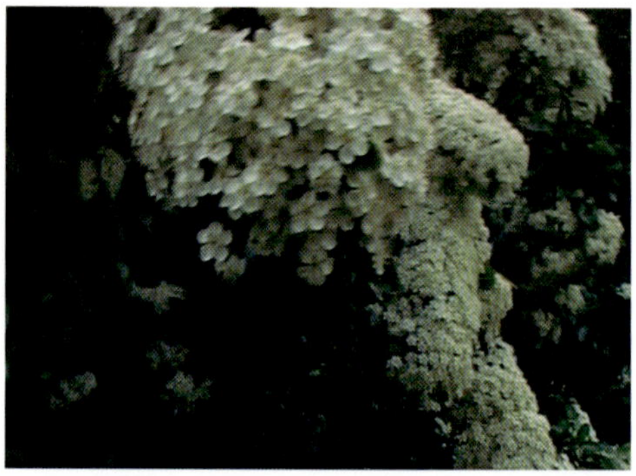
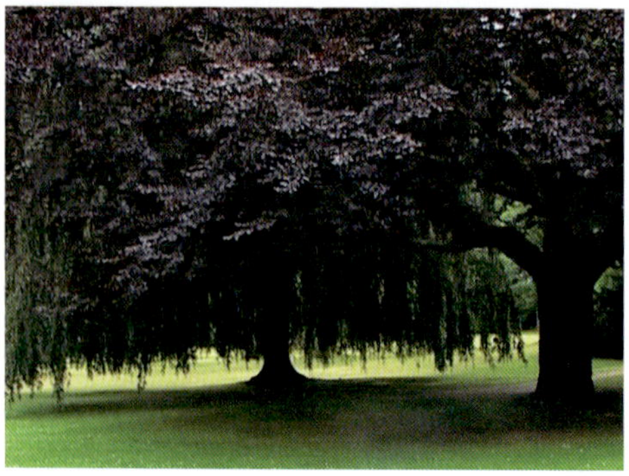
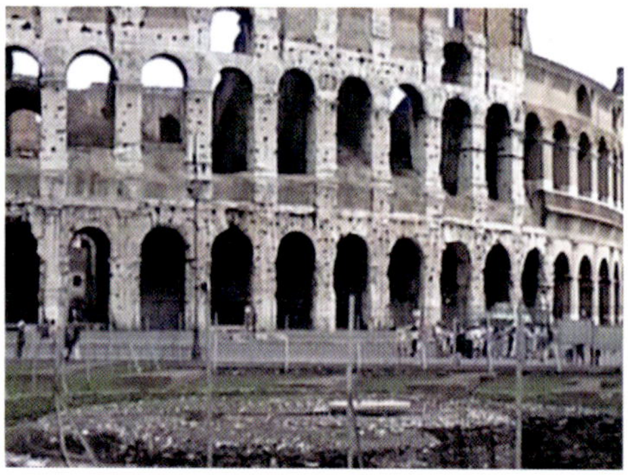
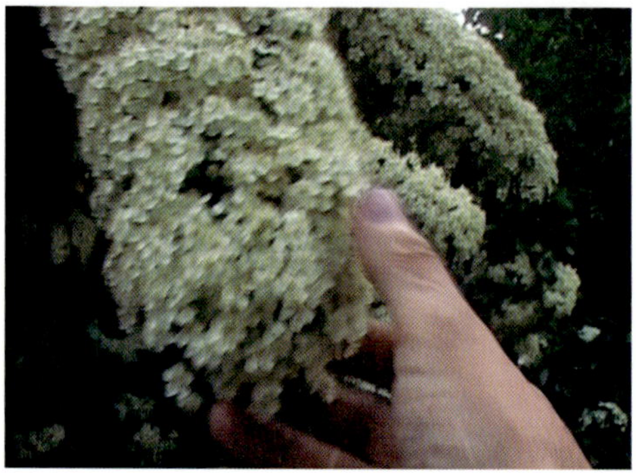

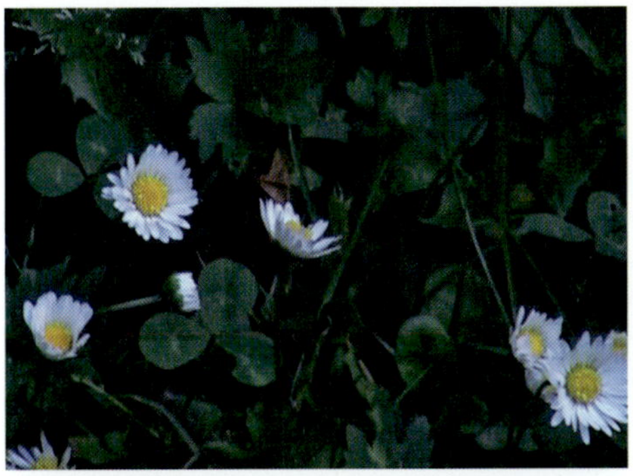
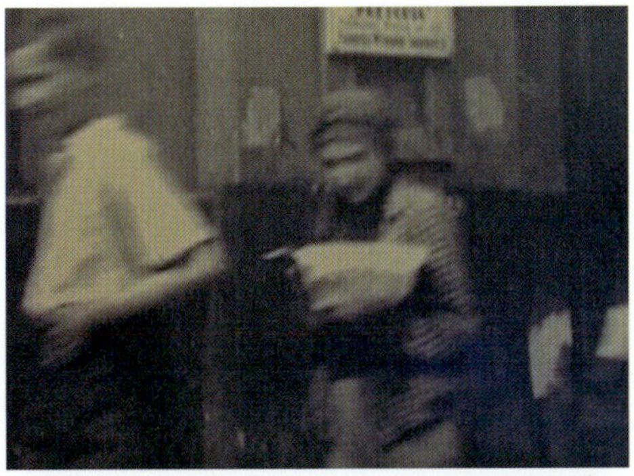
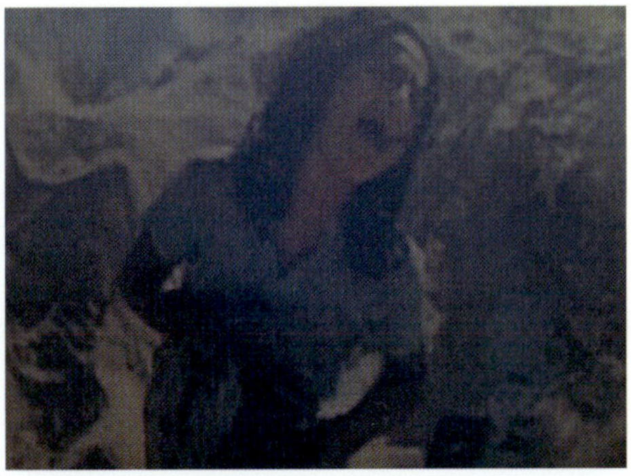
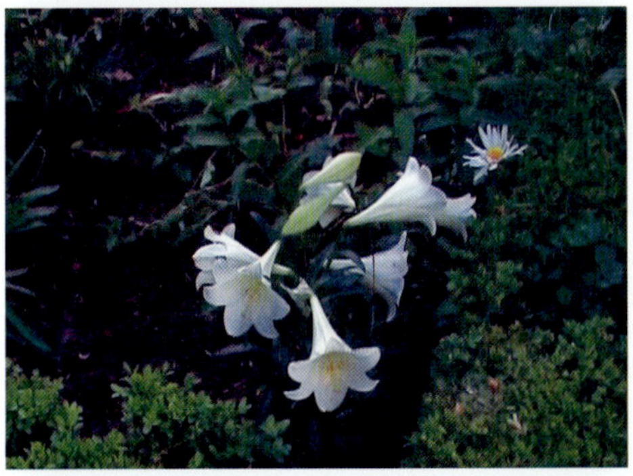
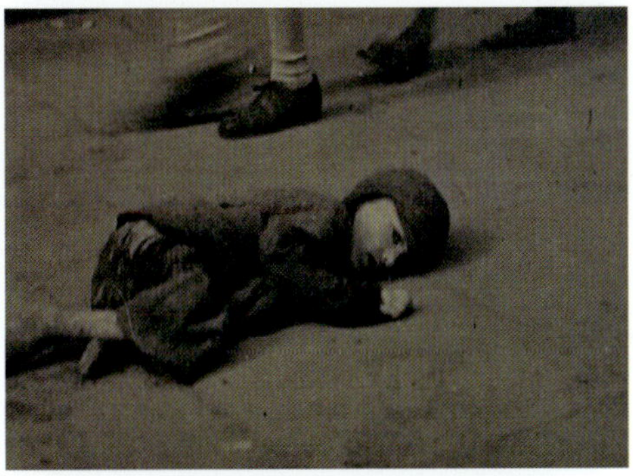
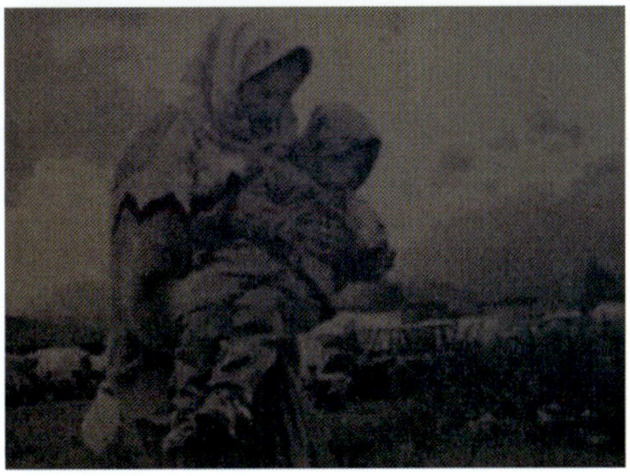
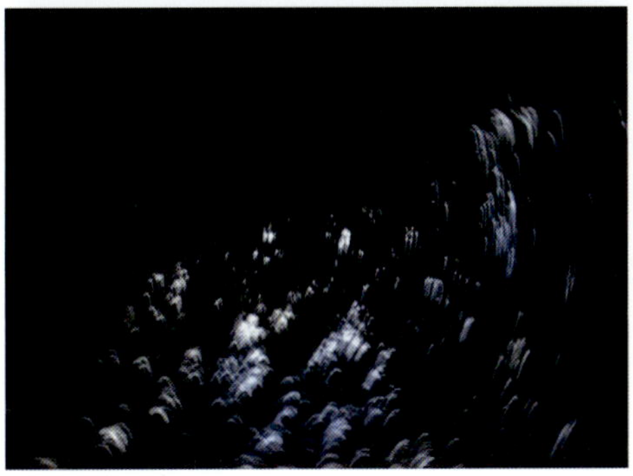
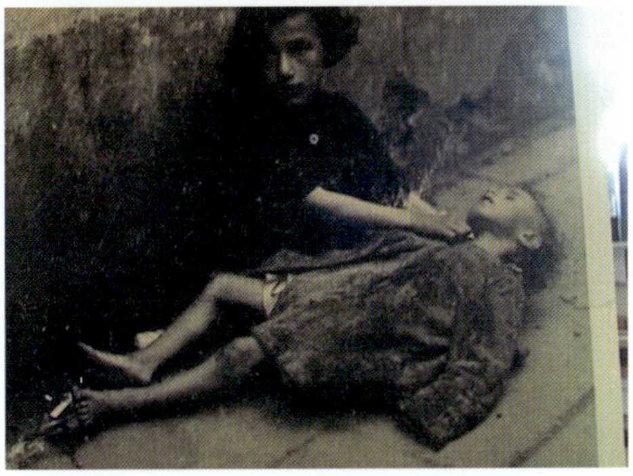
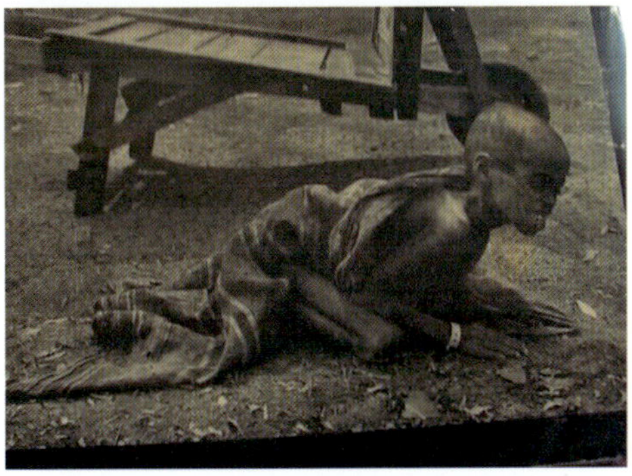
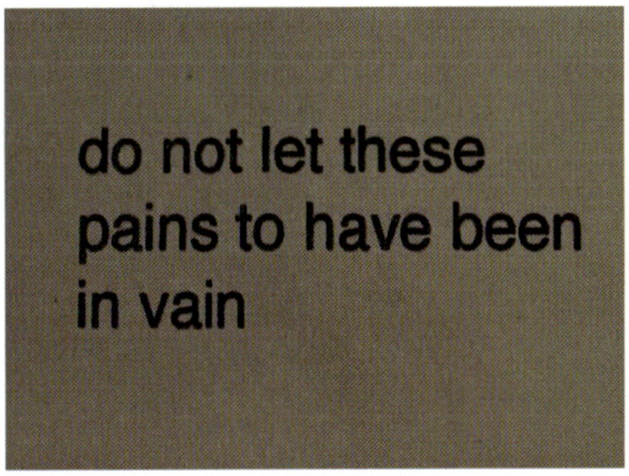
do not let these
pains to have been
in vain
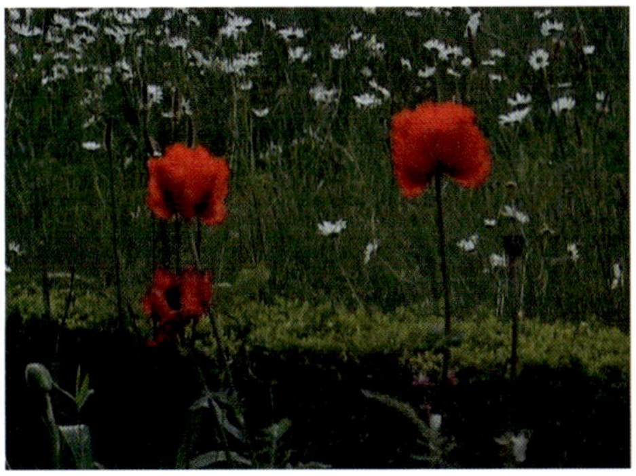
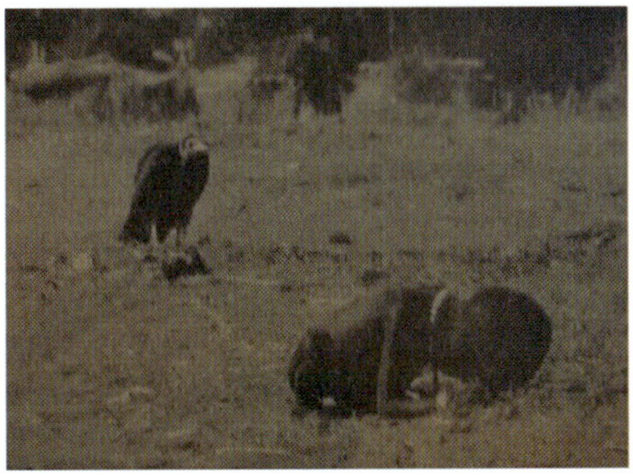

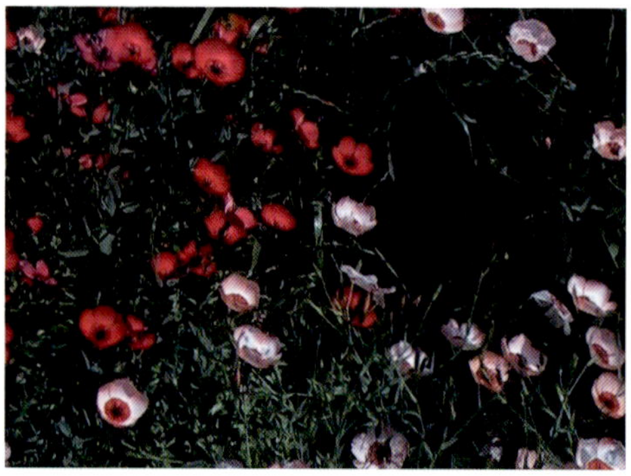
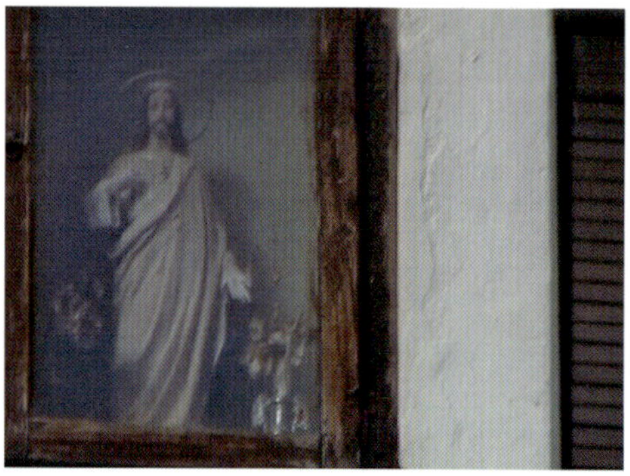
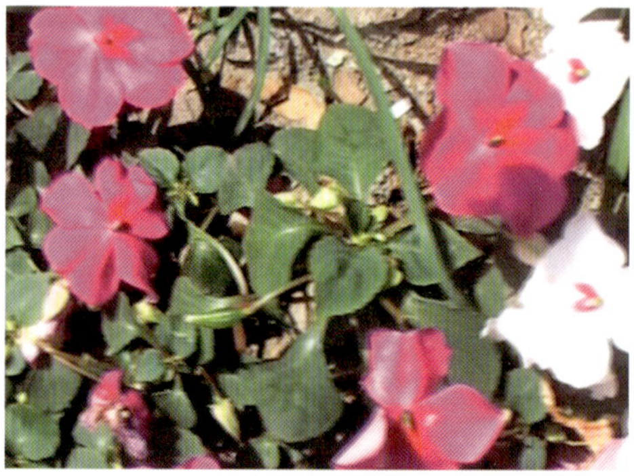
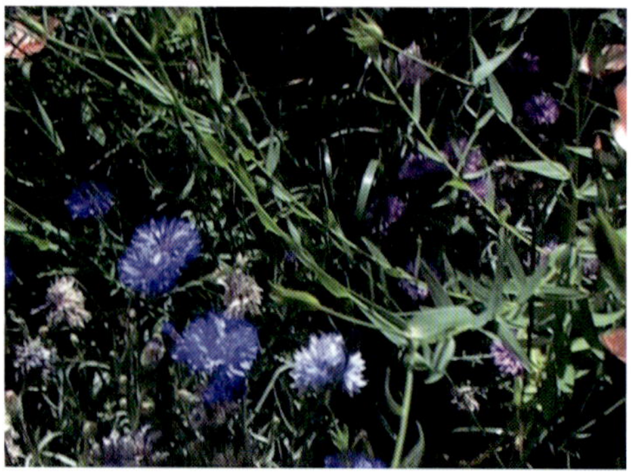
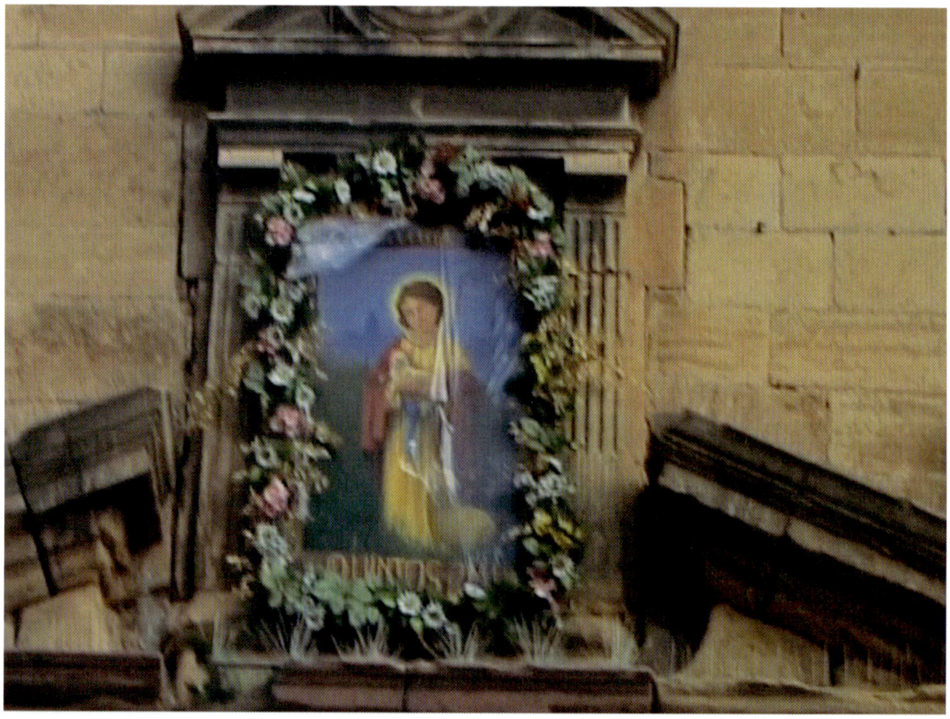
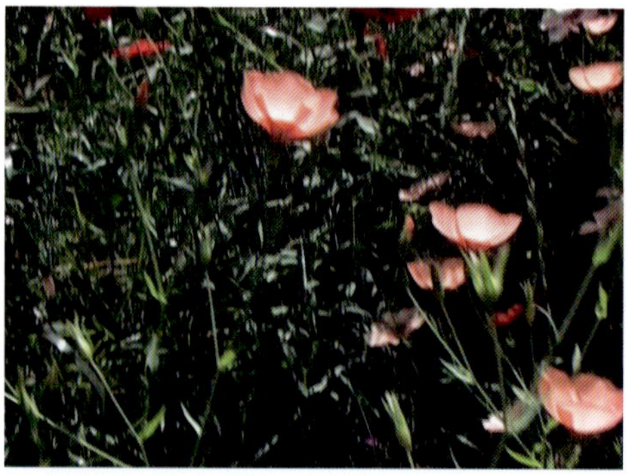
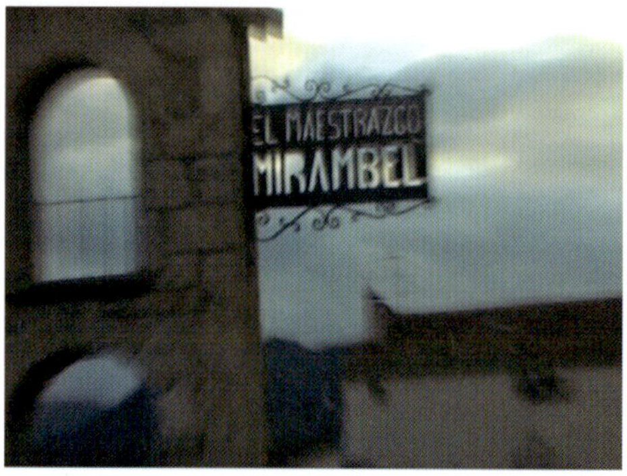
EL MAESTRAZGO
MIRAMBEL
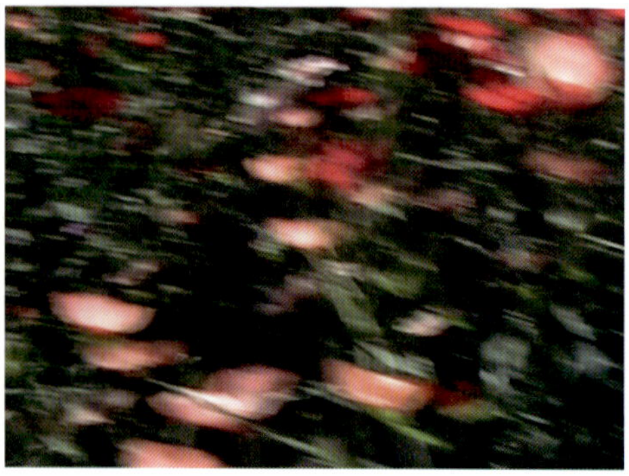
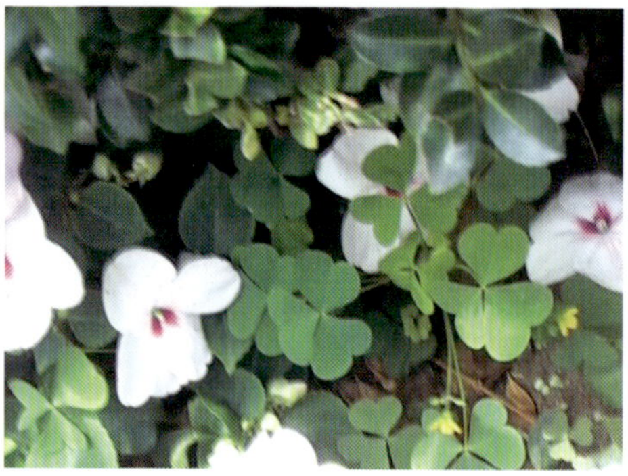
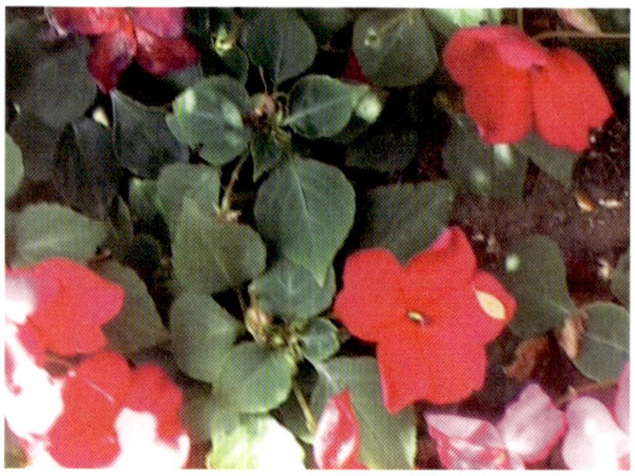

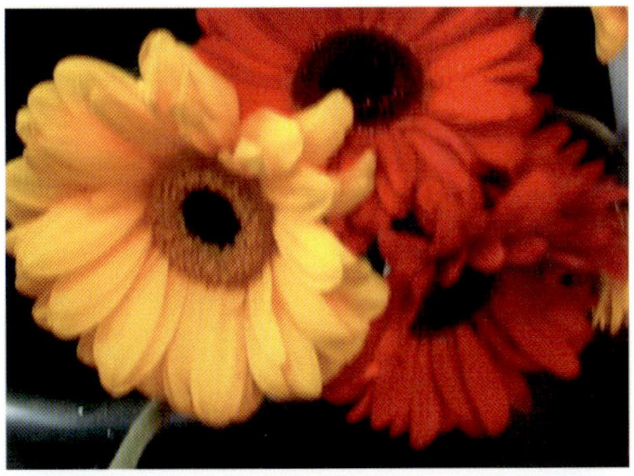
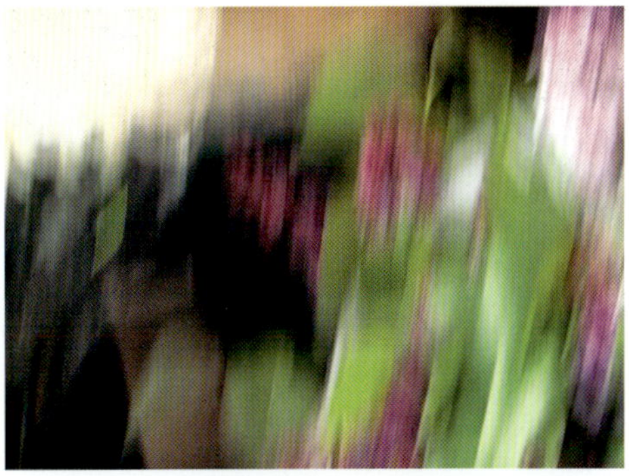
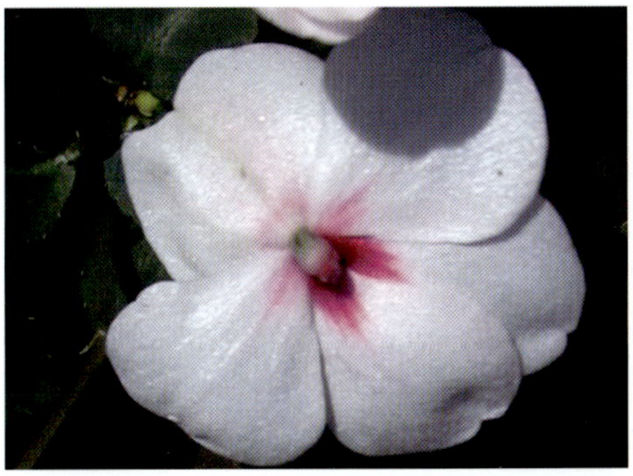
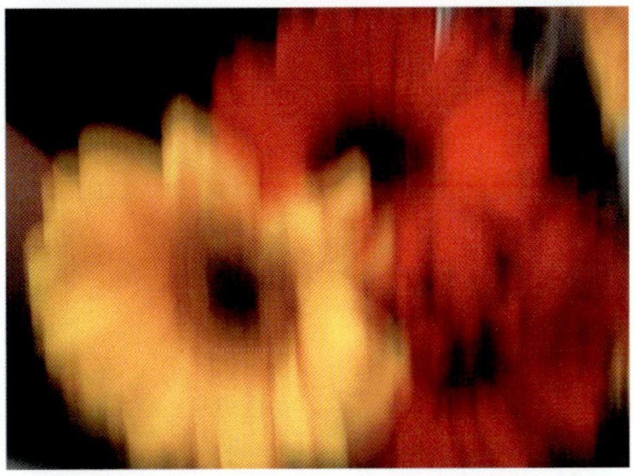
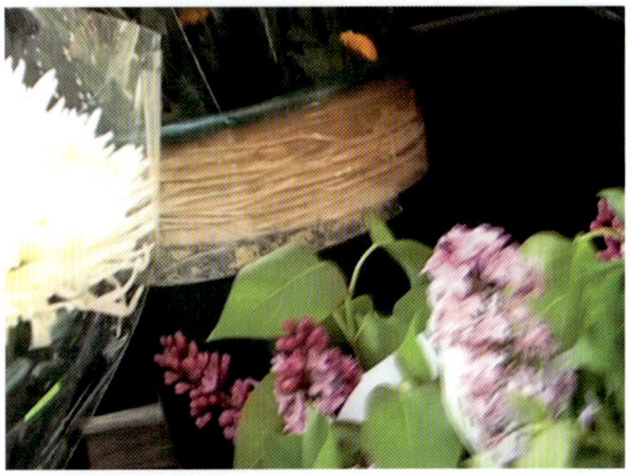
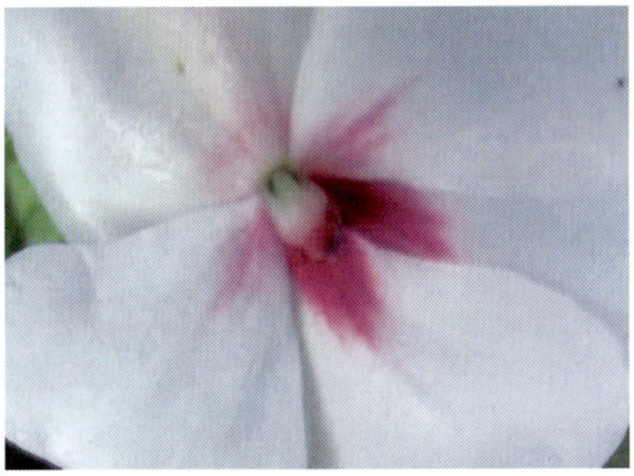
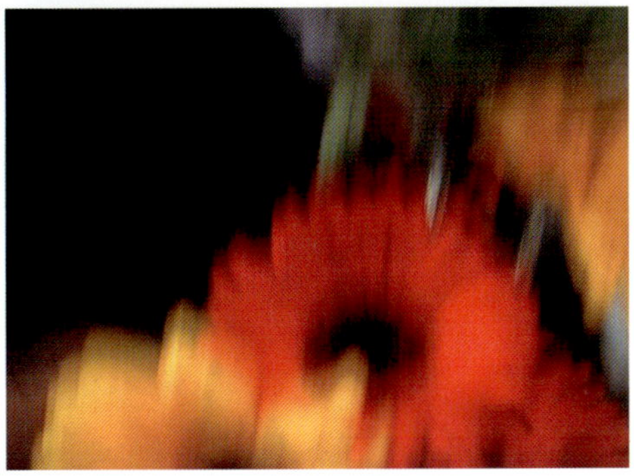
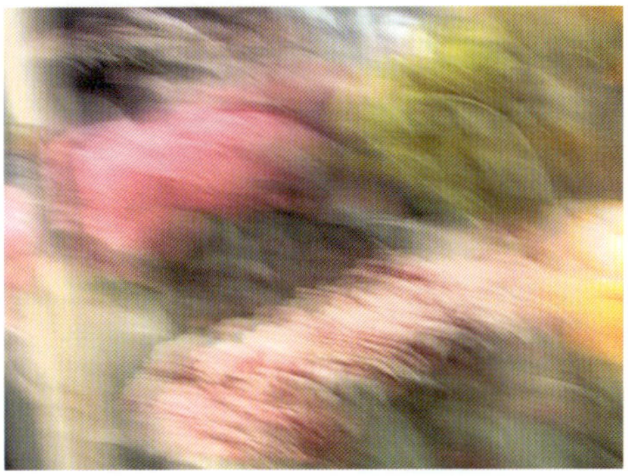
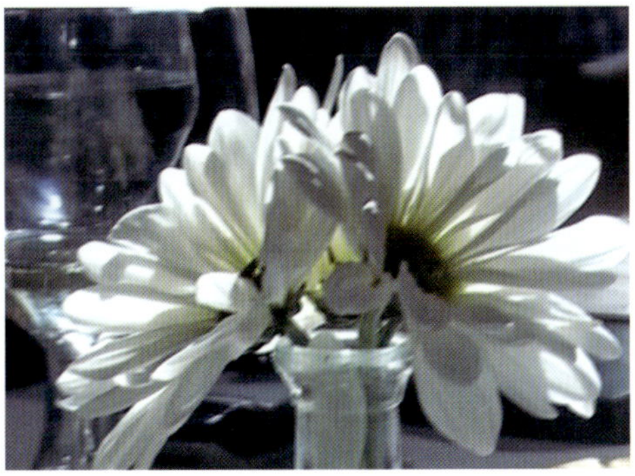
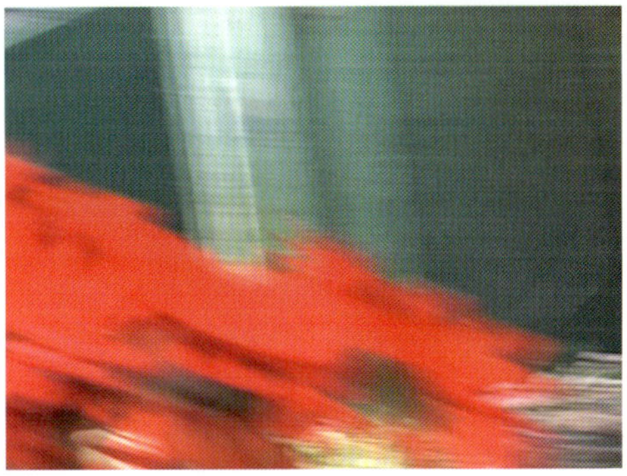
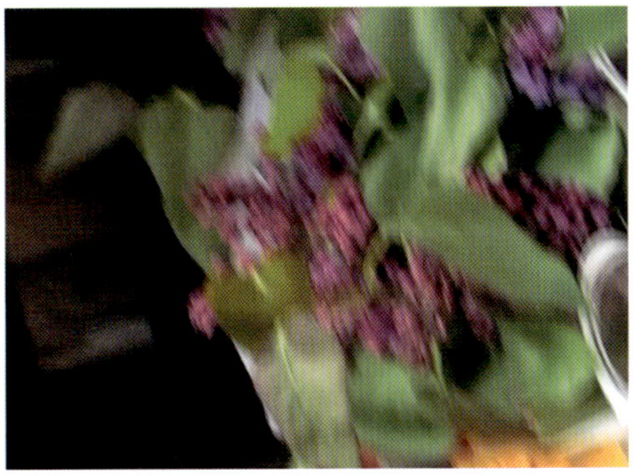
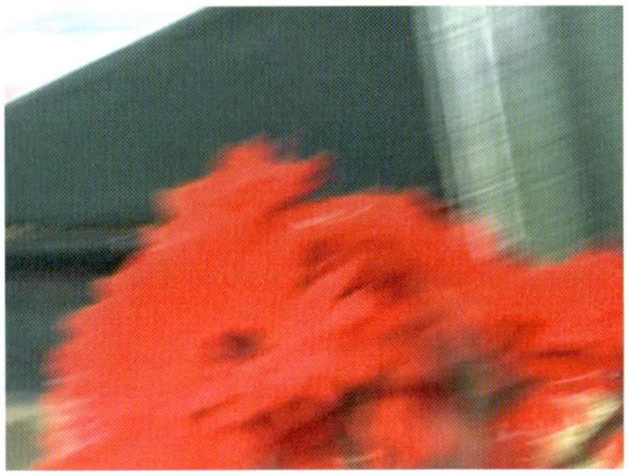

 FILMS COLOR SOUND 84 MIN

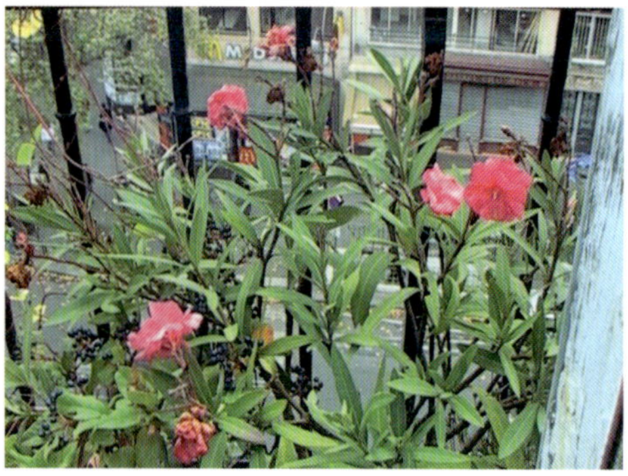

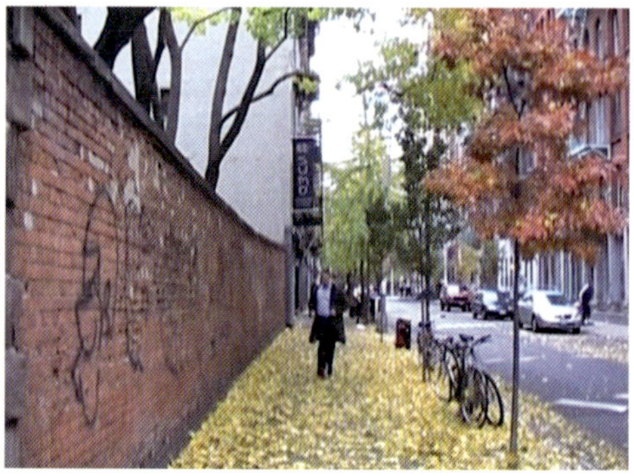

spare the supplicant
O God

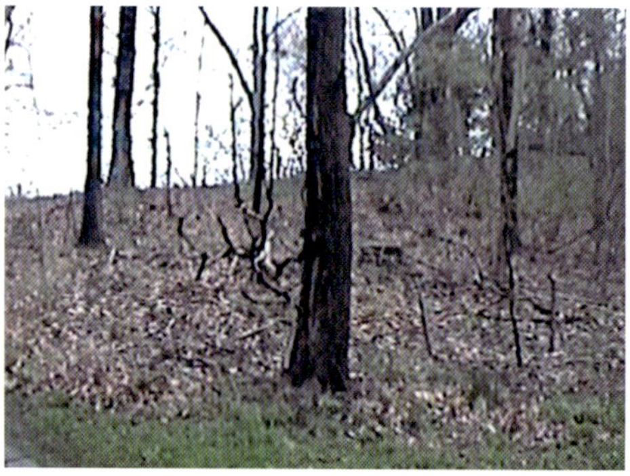

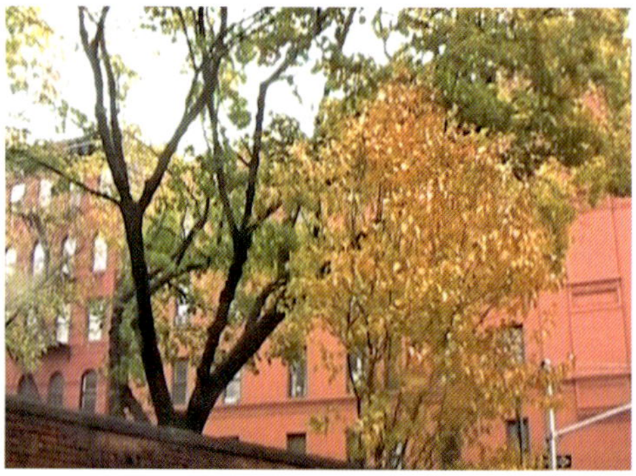

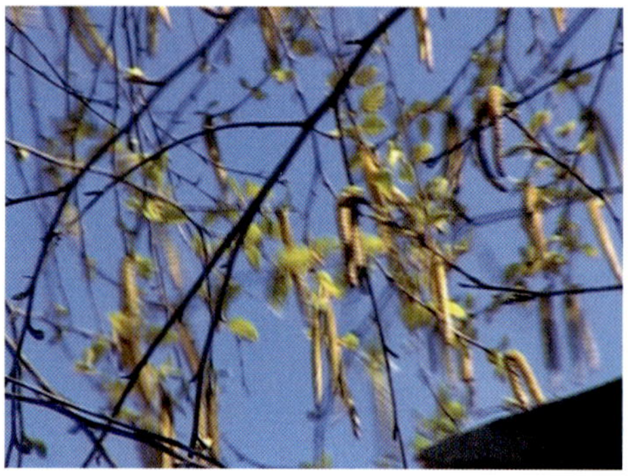

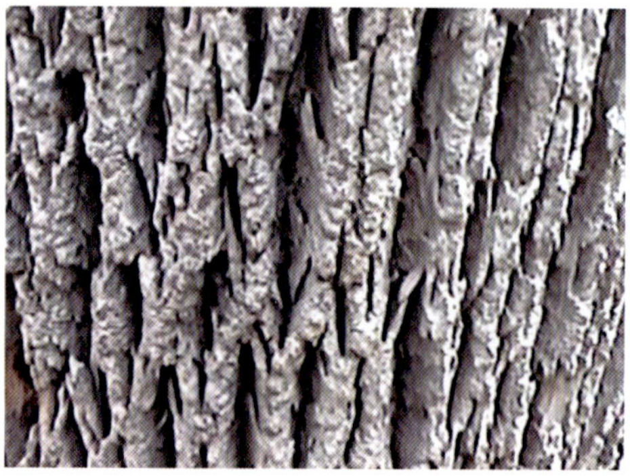

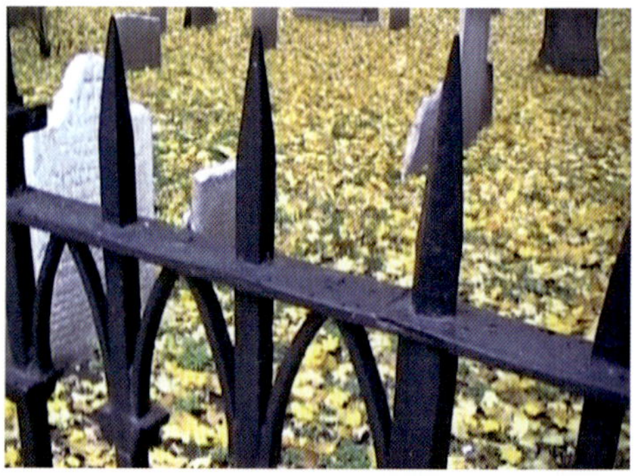

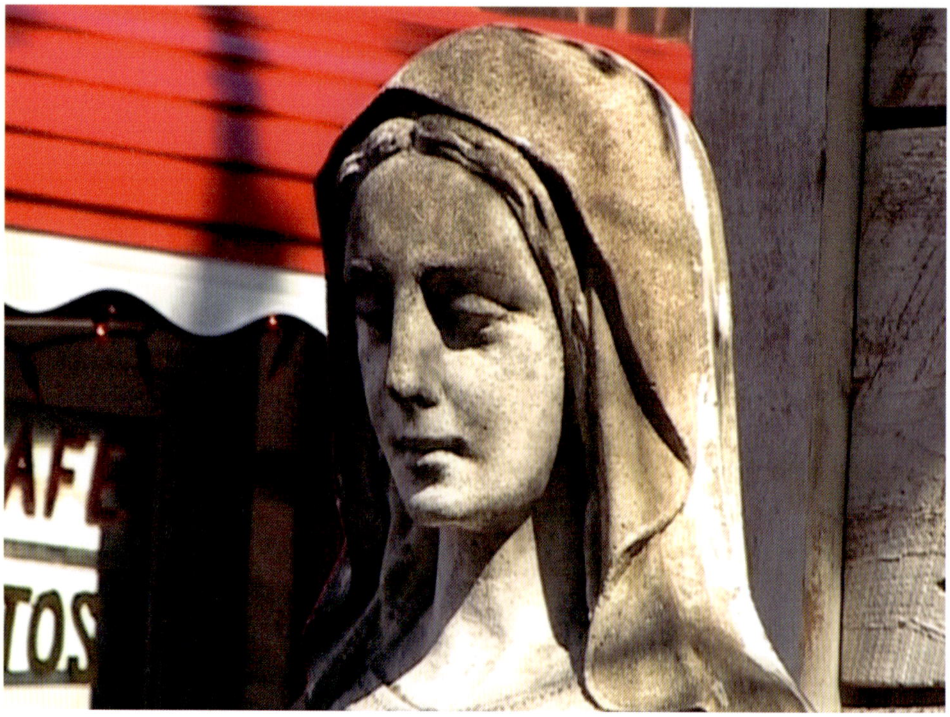

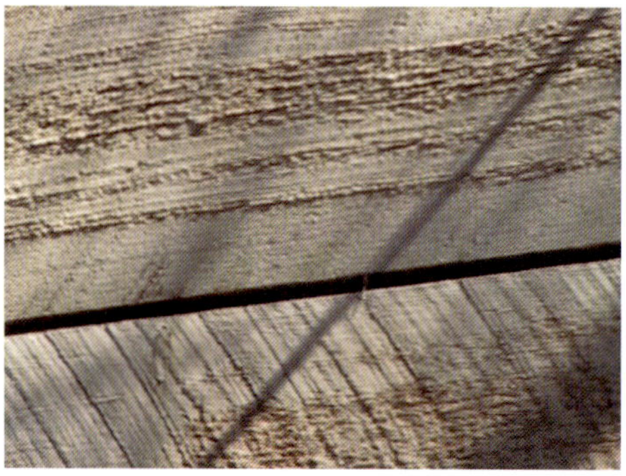

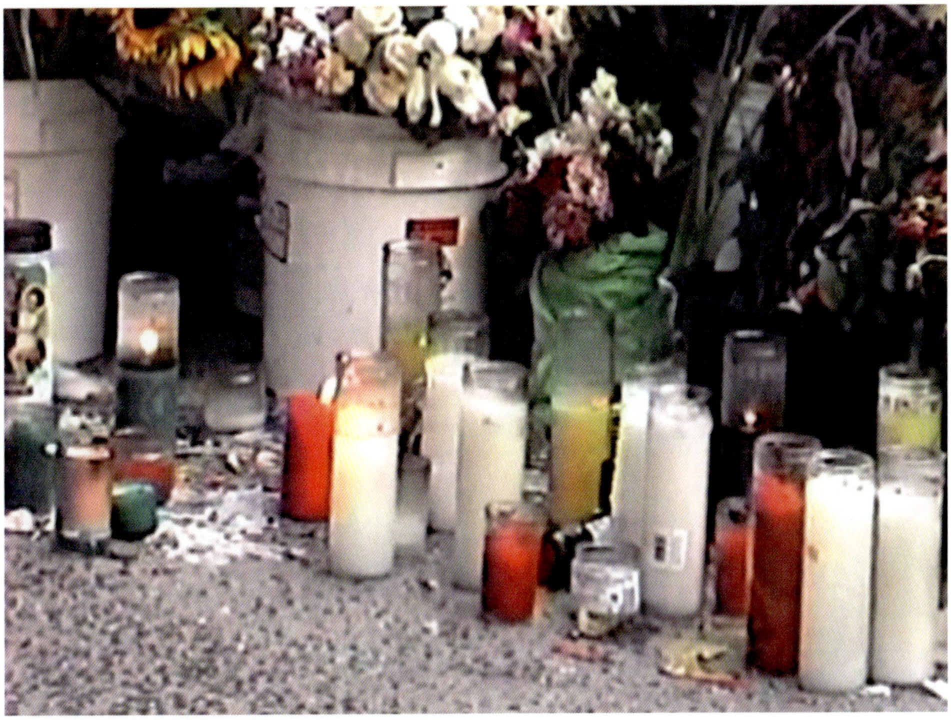

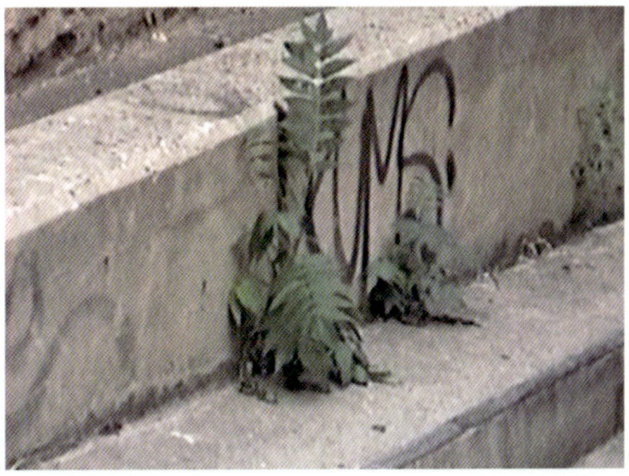

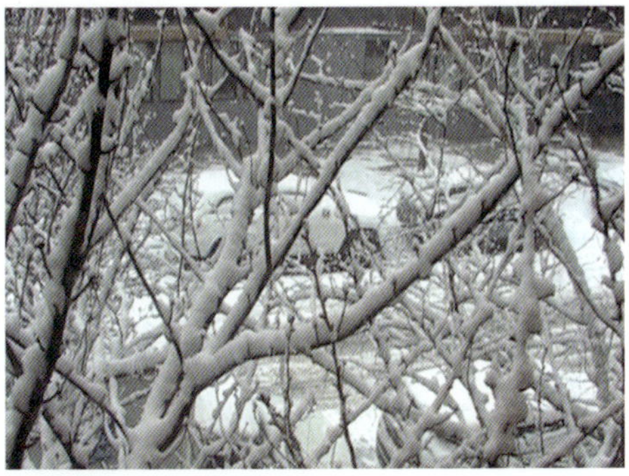

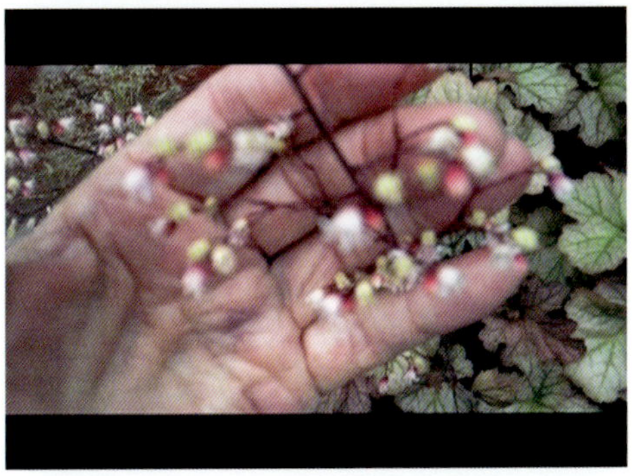

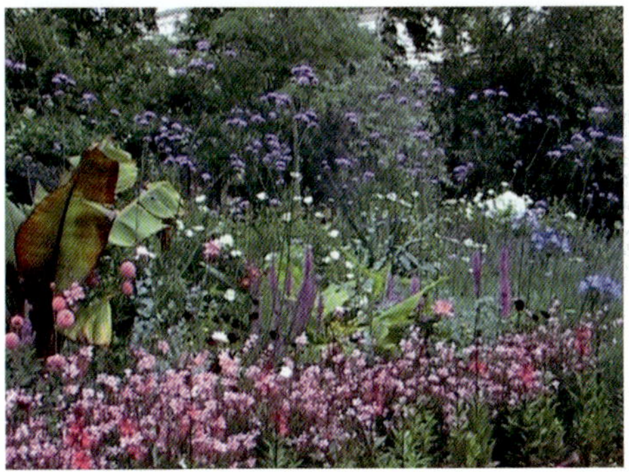

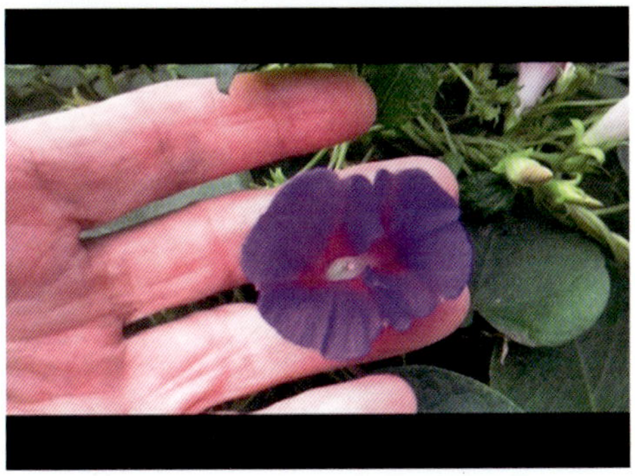

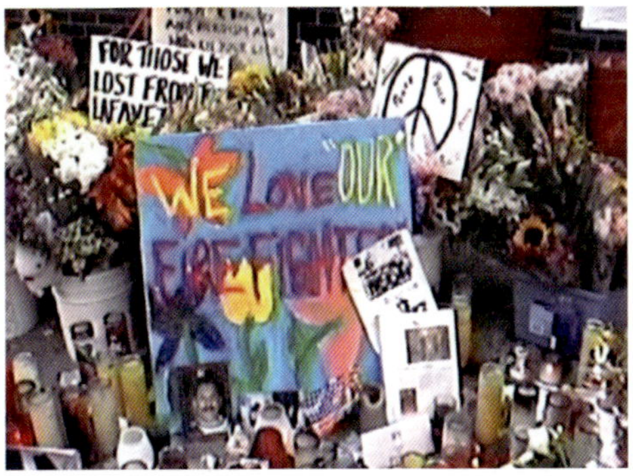
FOR THOSE WE
LOST FROM
WE LOVE "OUR"

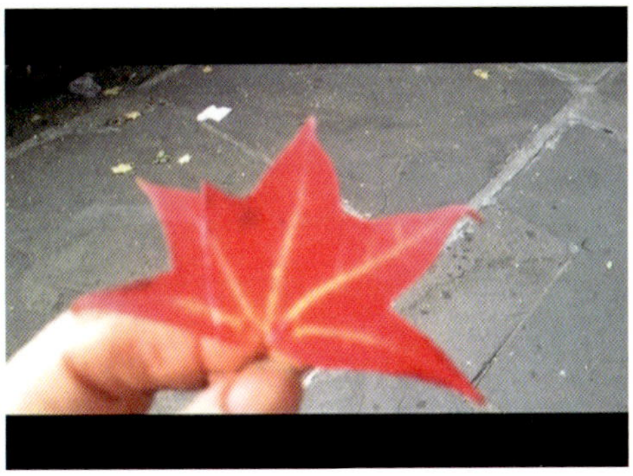

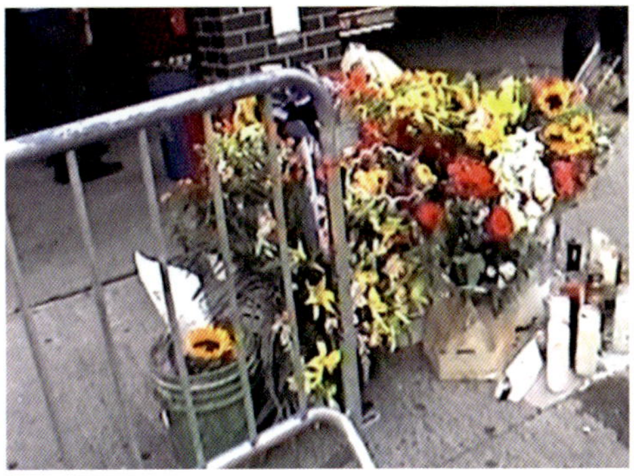

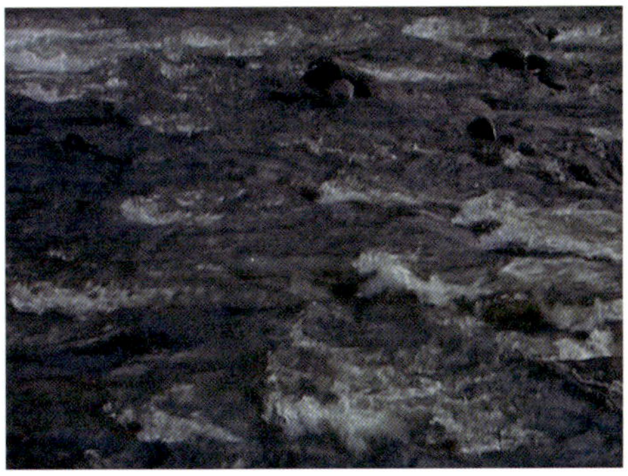

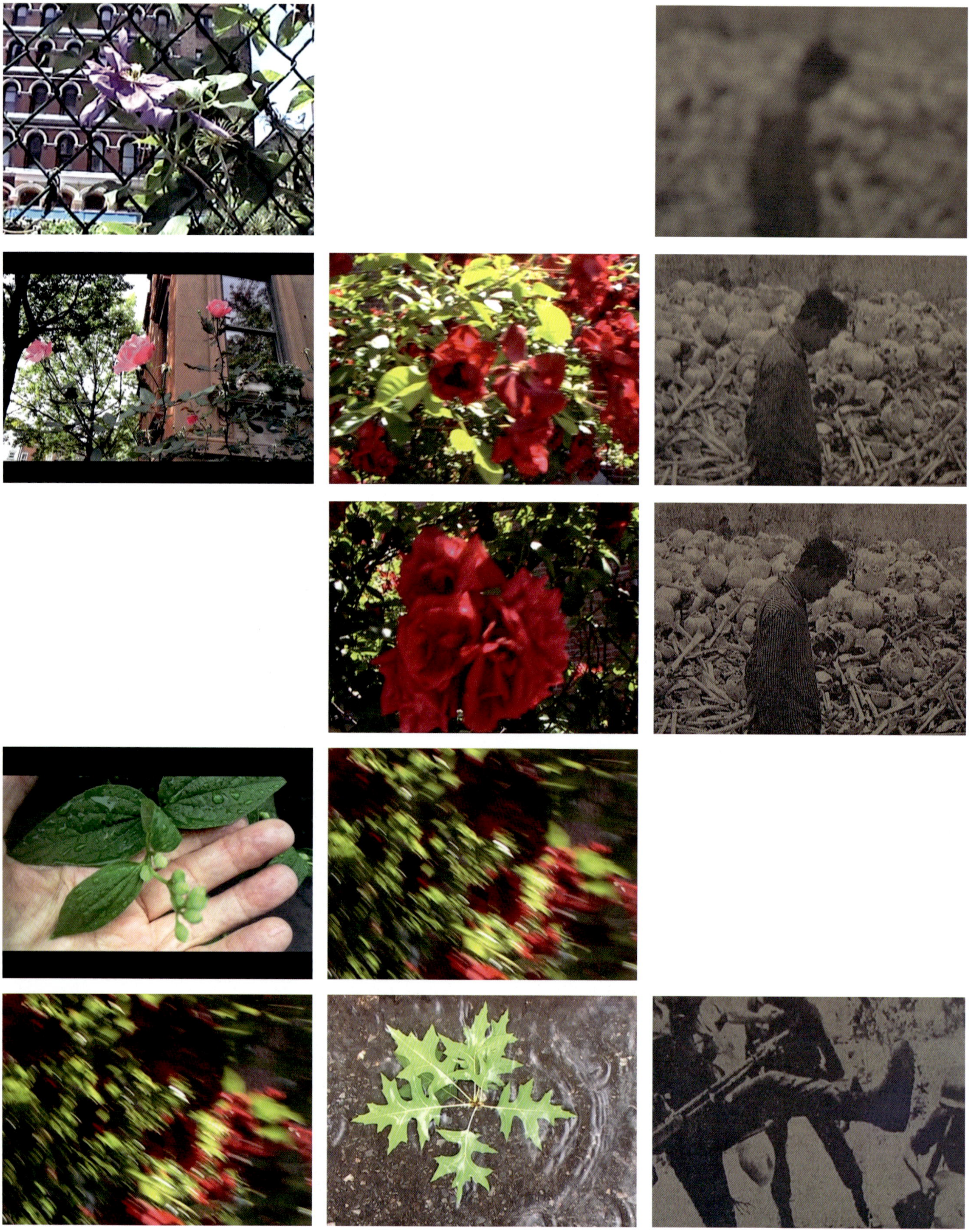

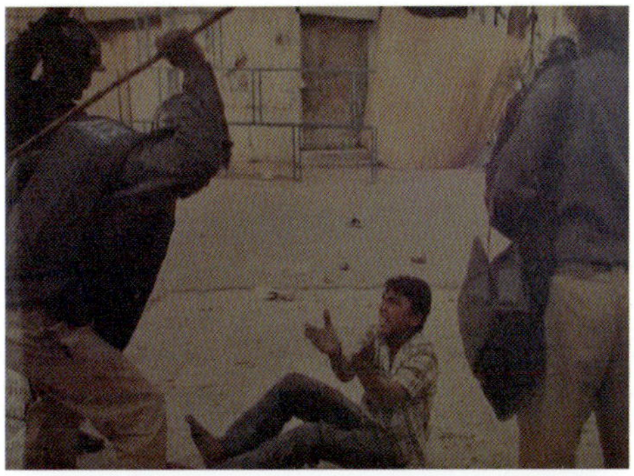

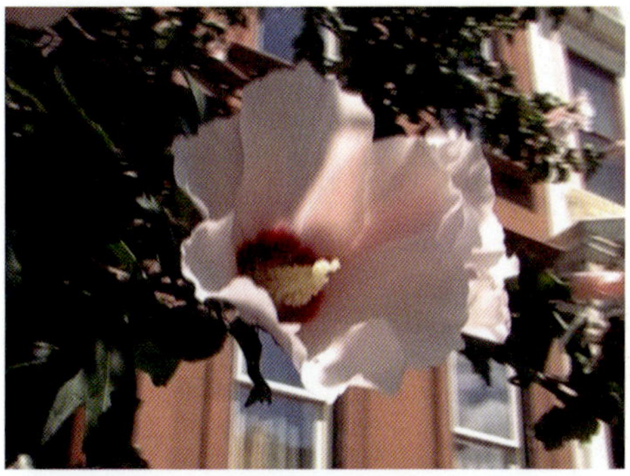

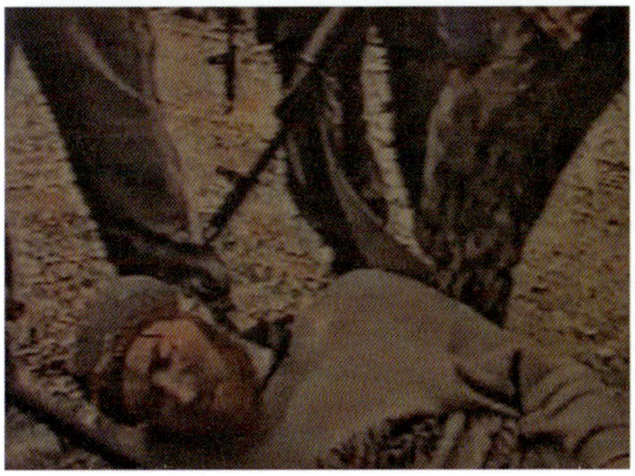

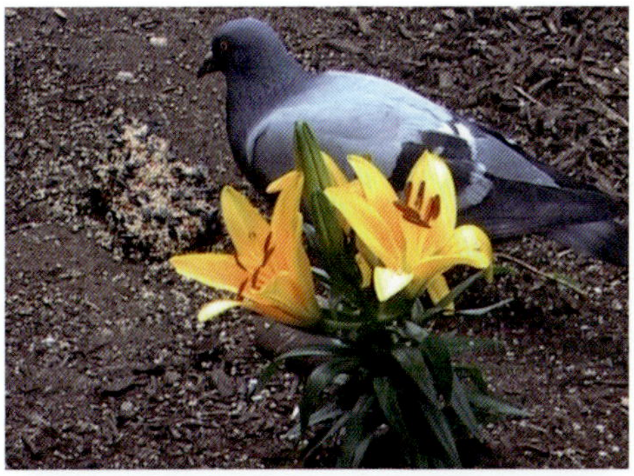

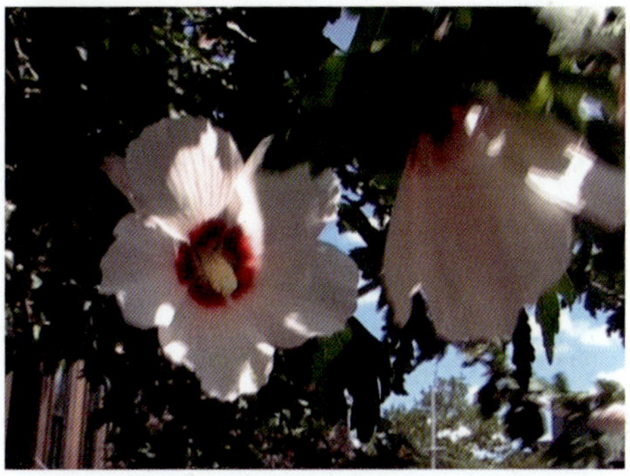

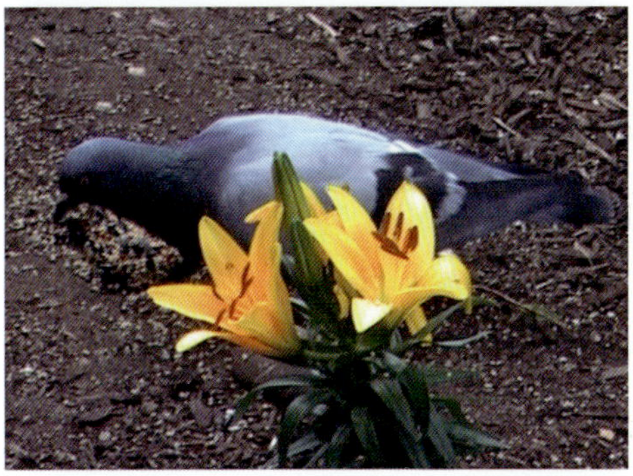

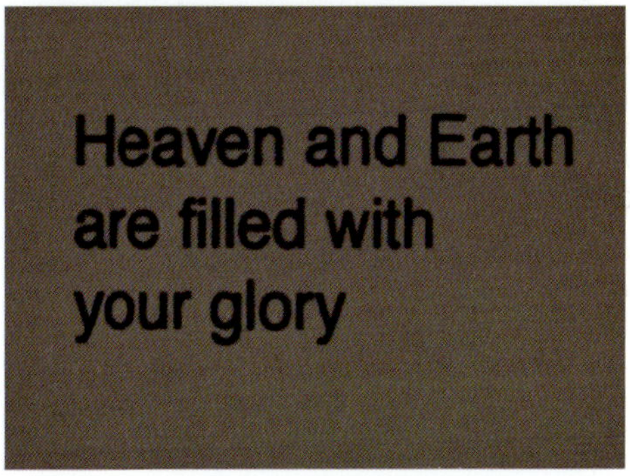
Heaven and Earth
are filled with
your glory

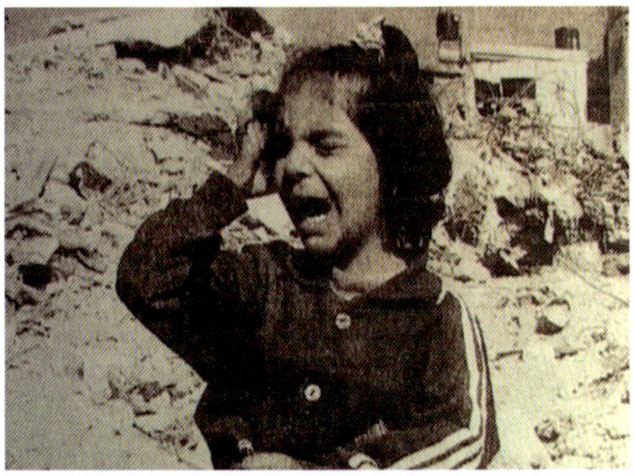

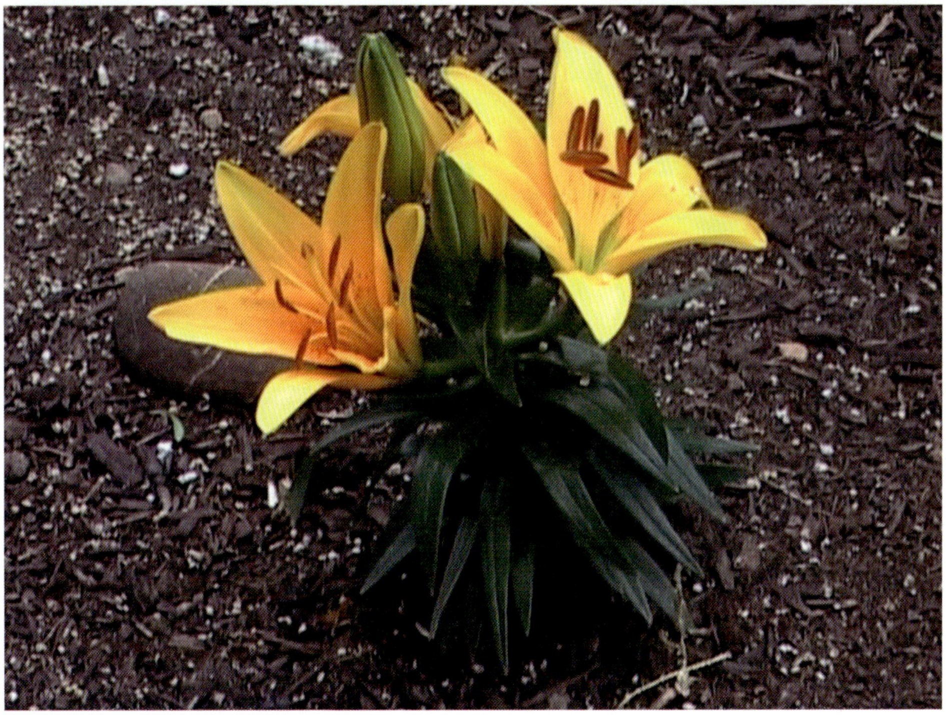

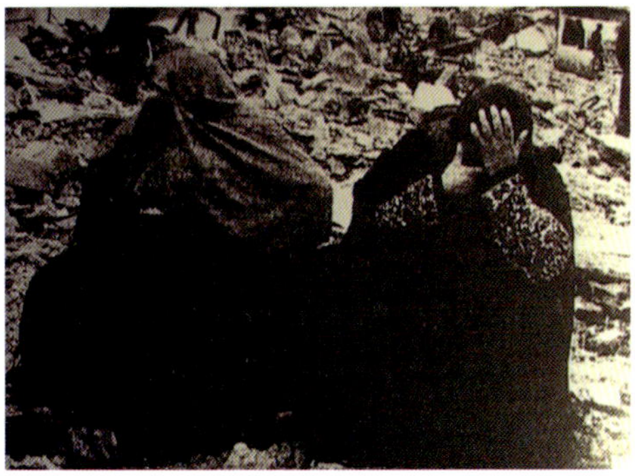

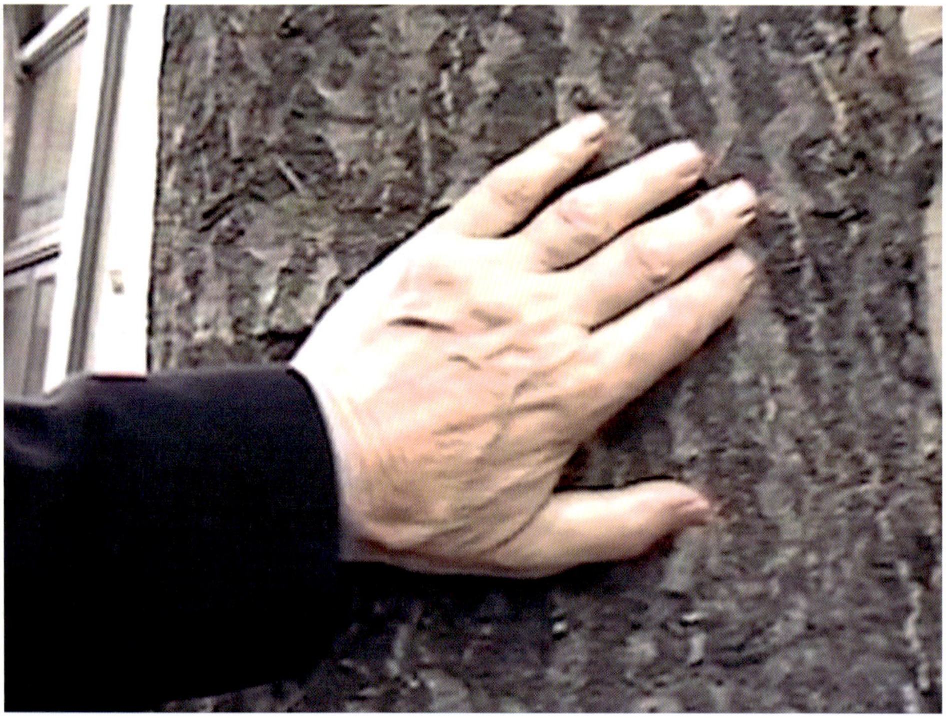
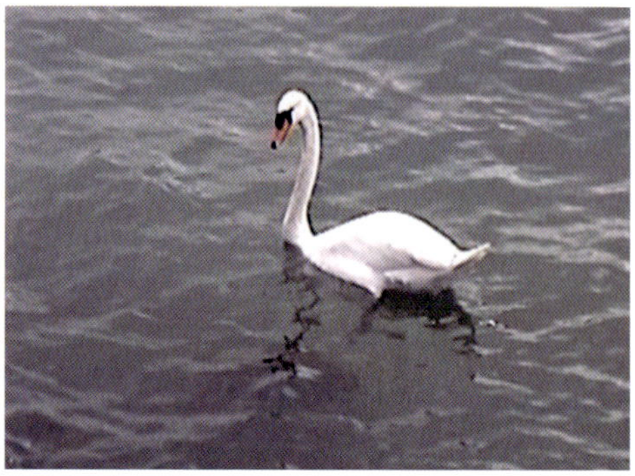
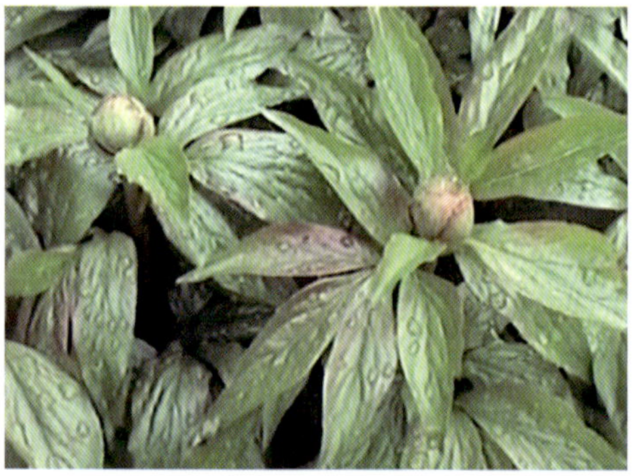
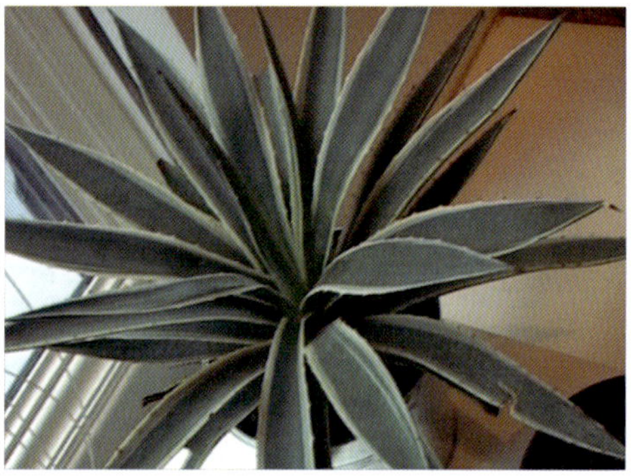
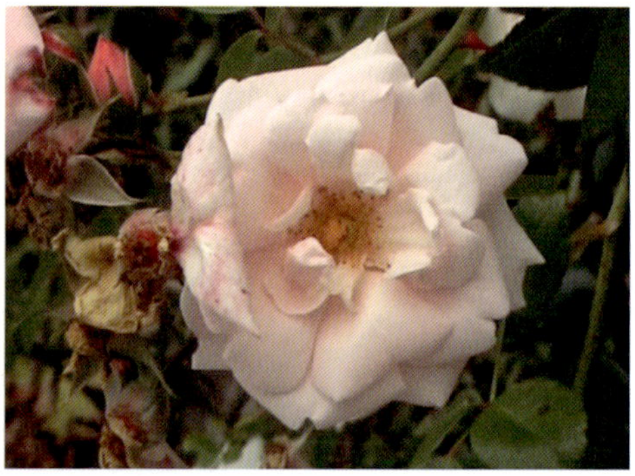
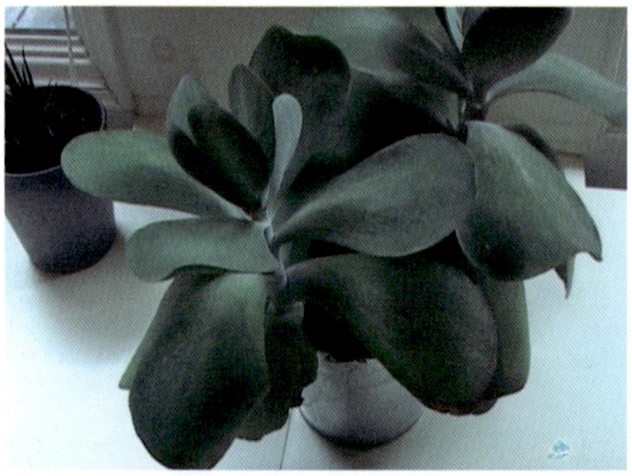
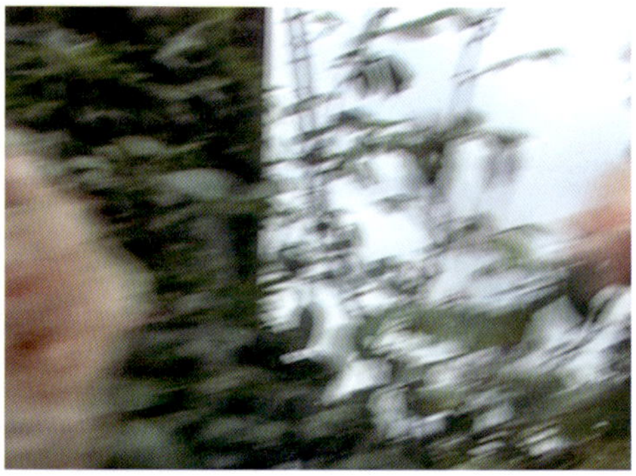
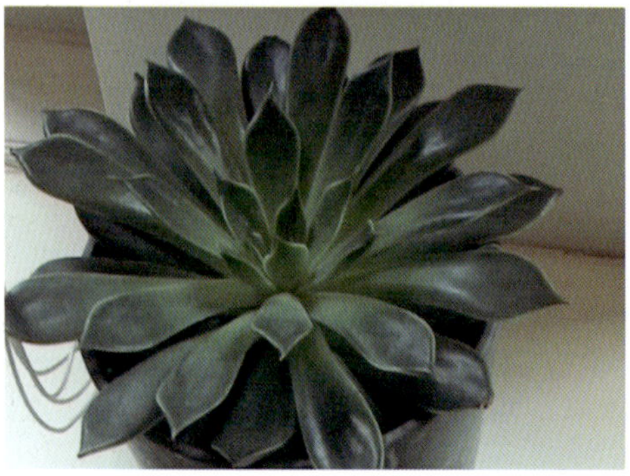
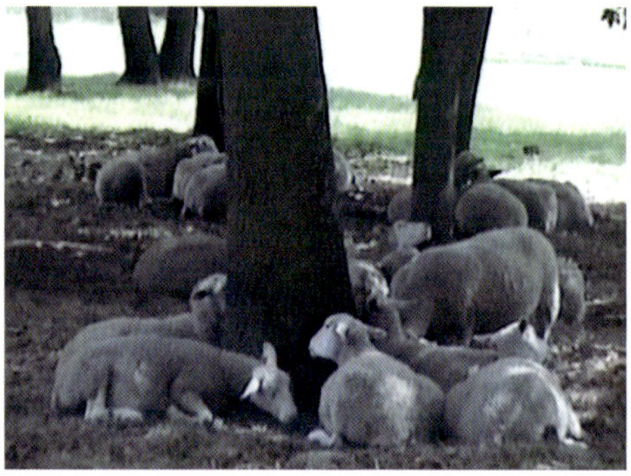
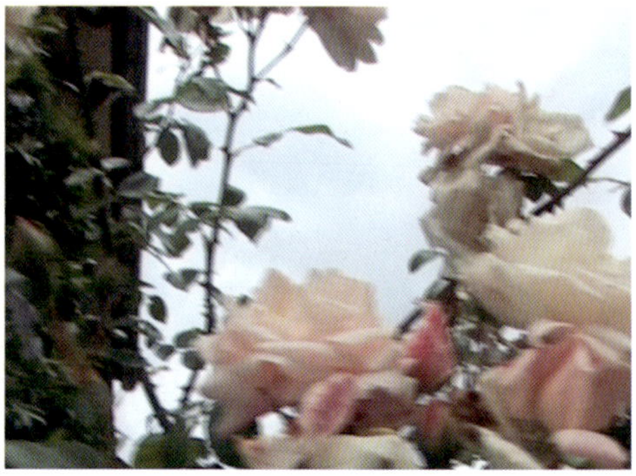

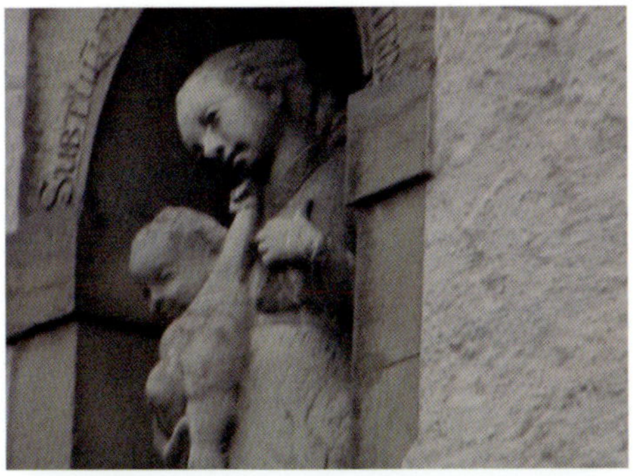
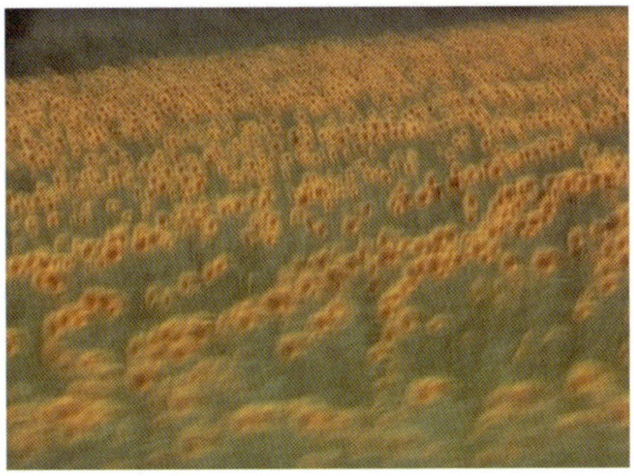
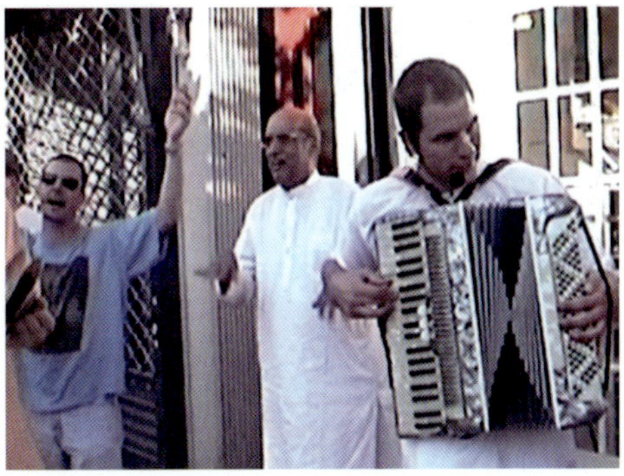
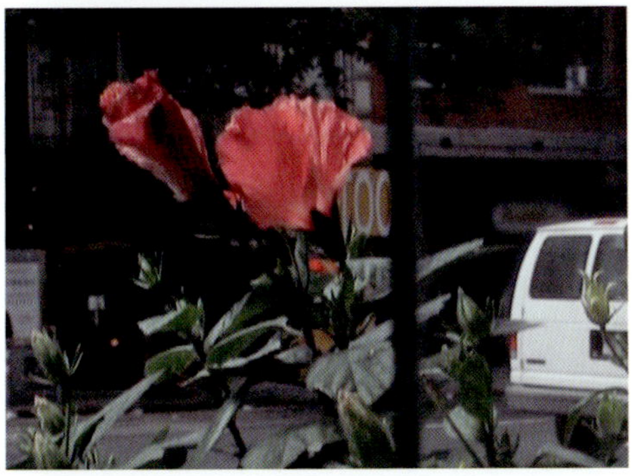
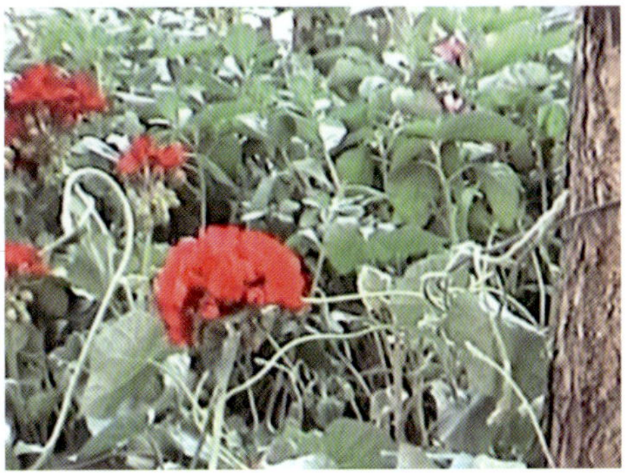
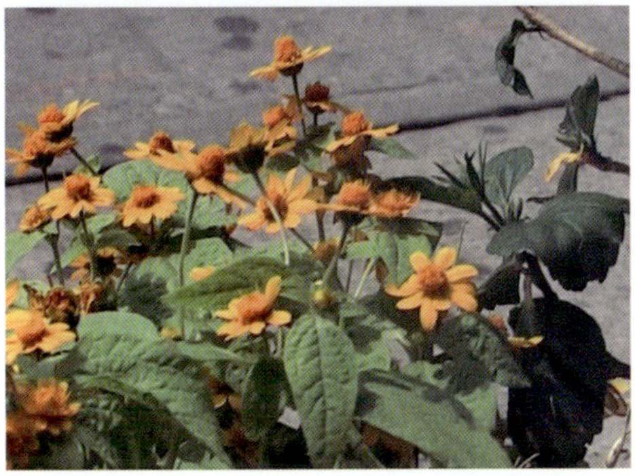
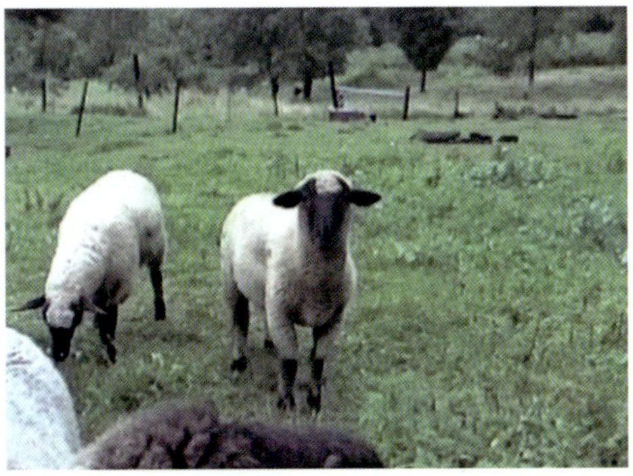

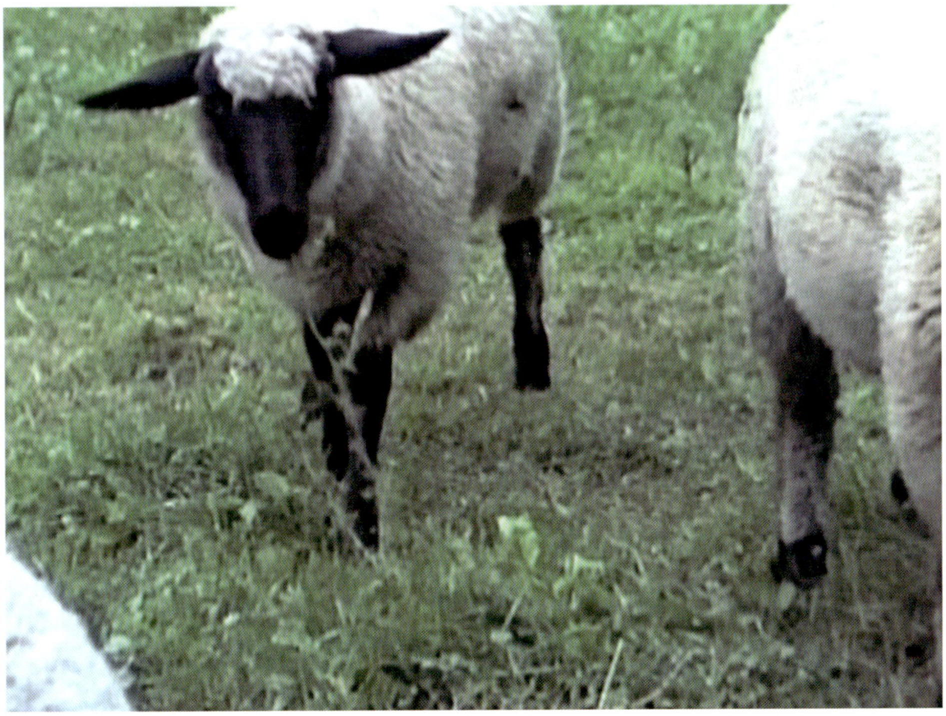
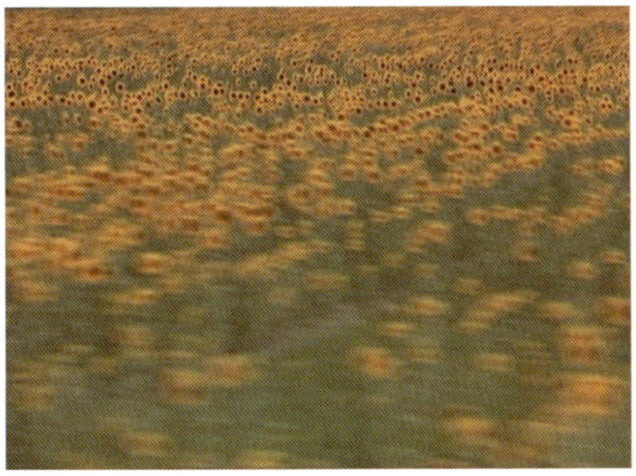

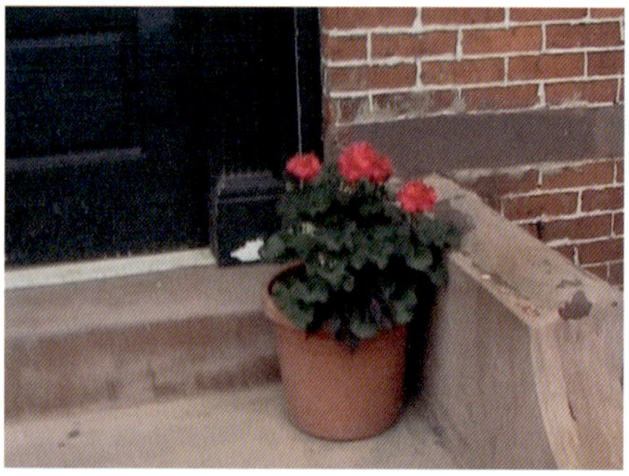
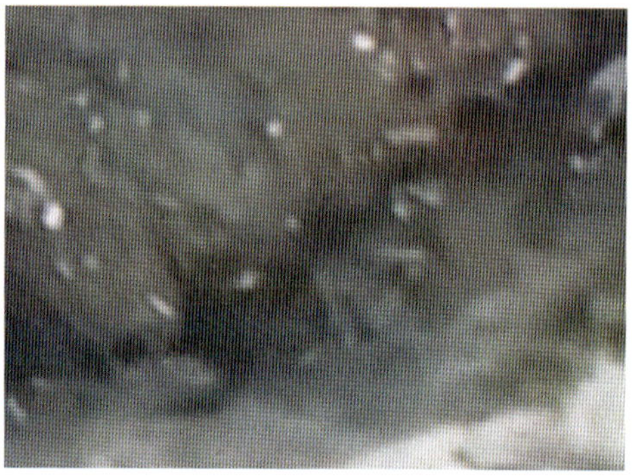
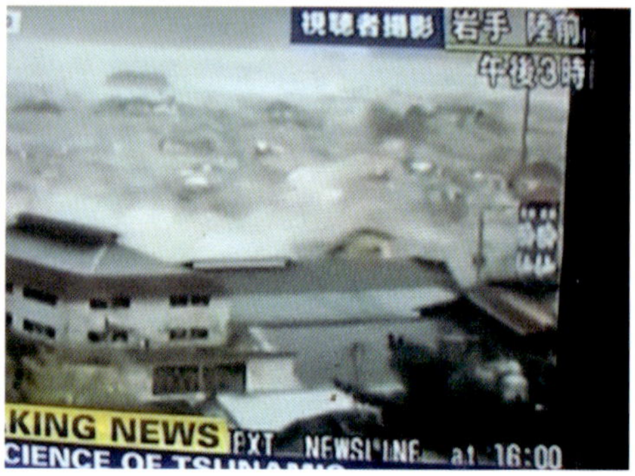
視聴者撮影
岩手 陸前
午後3時
KING NEWS
at 16:00
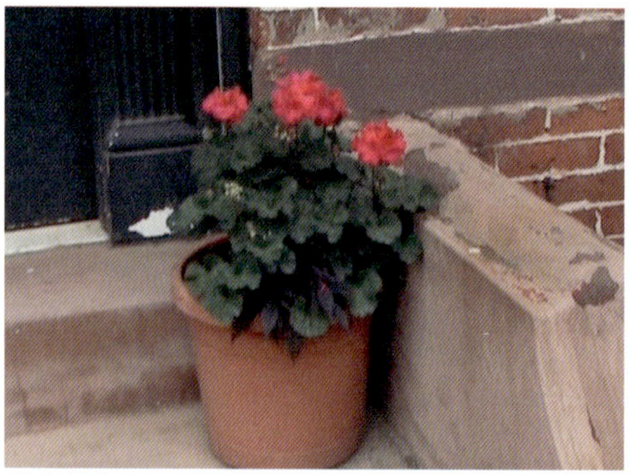
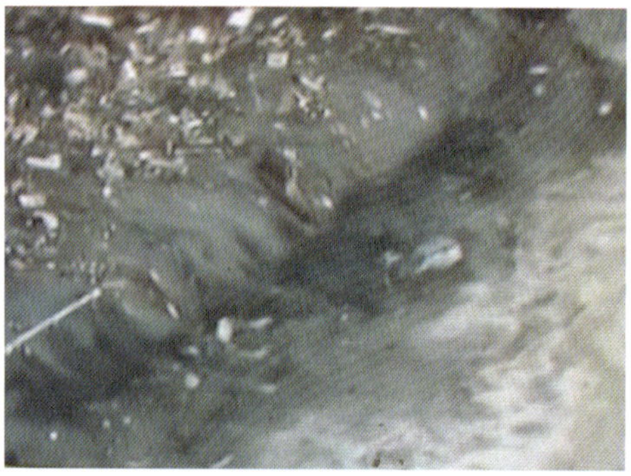
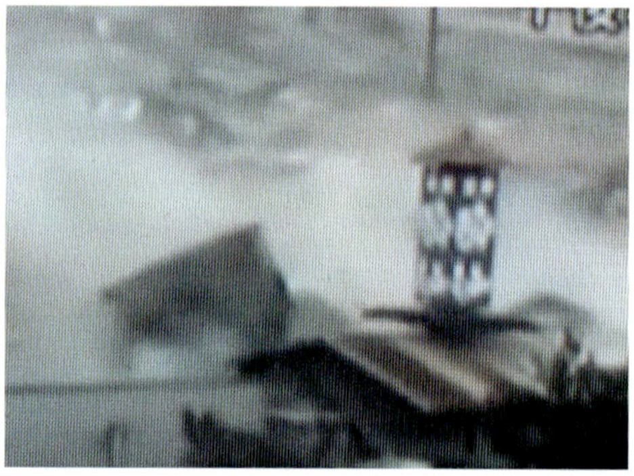
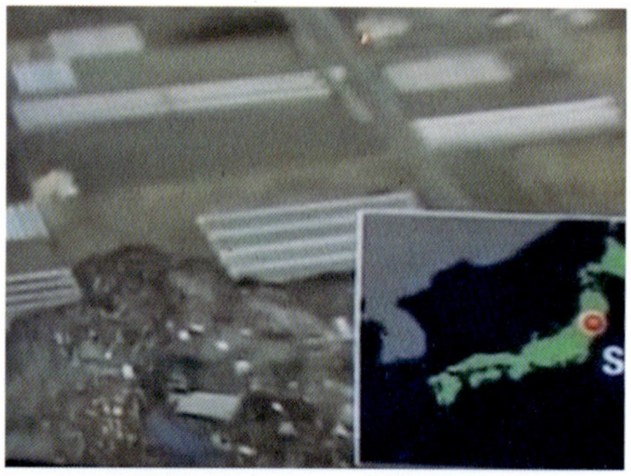
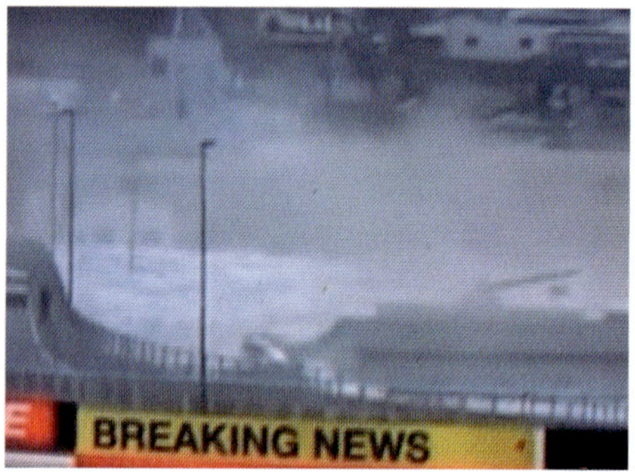
BREAKING NEWS
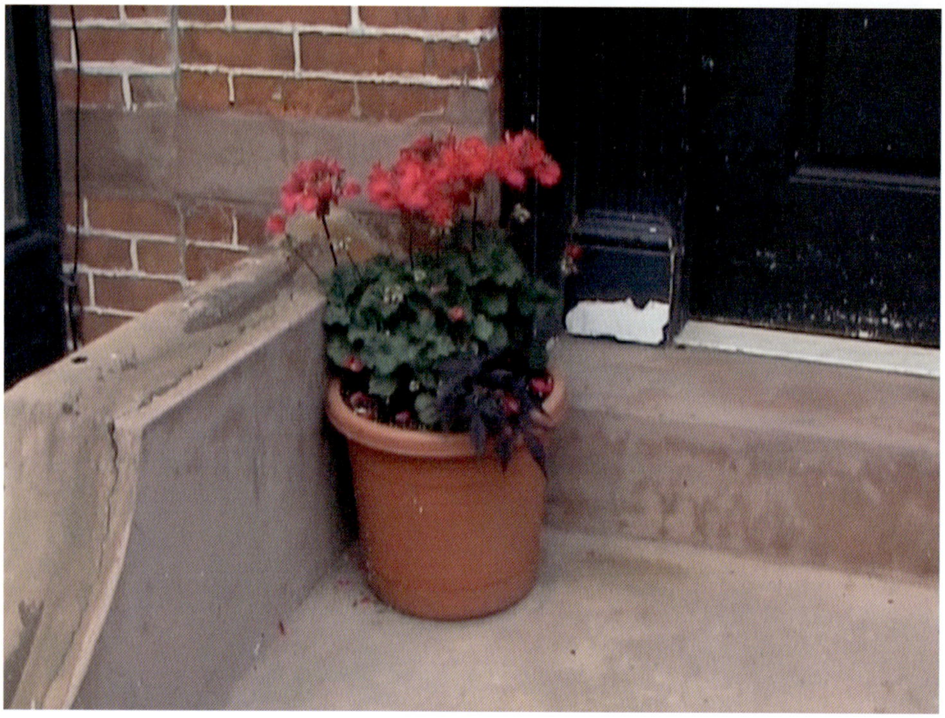
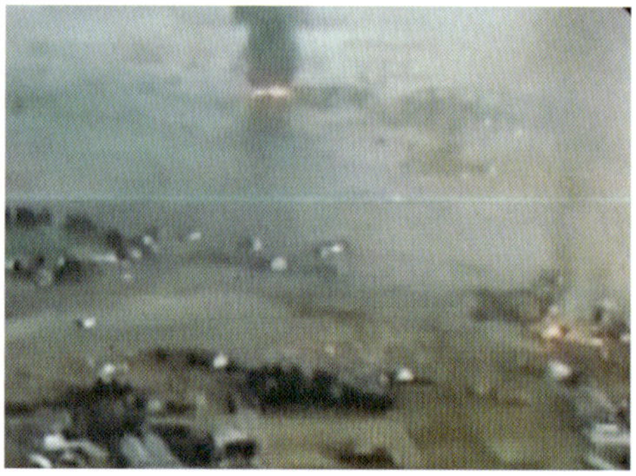

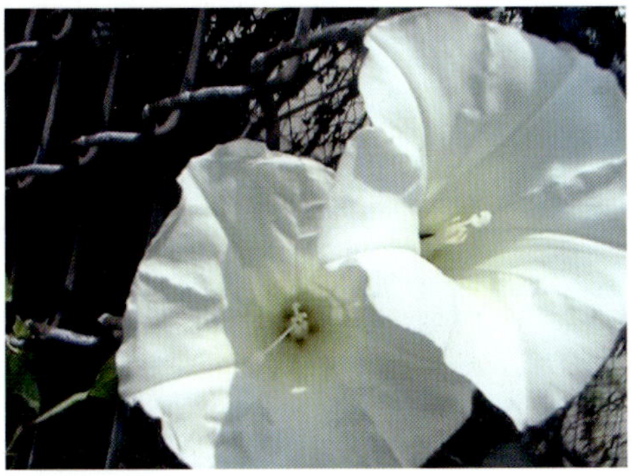
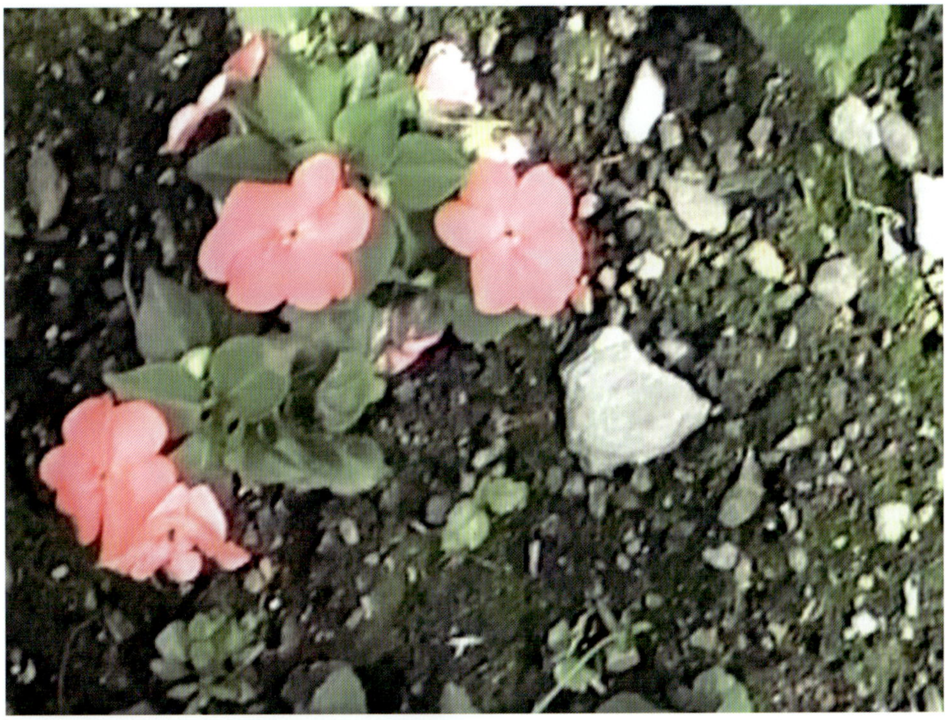
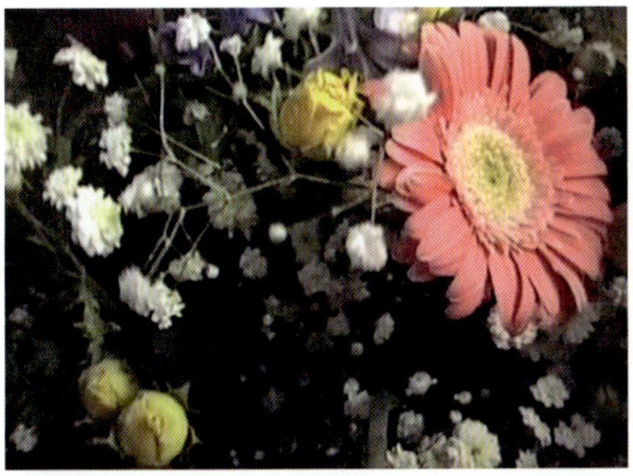
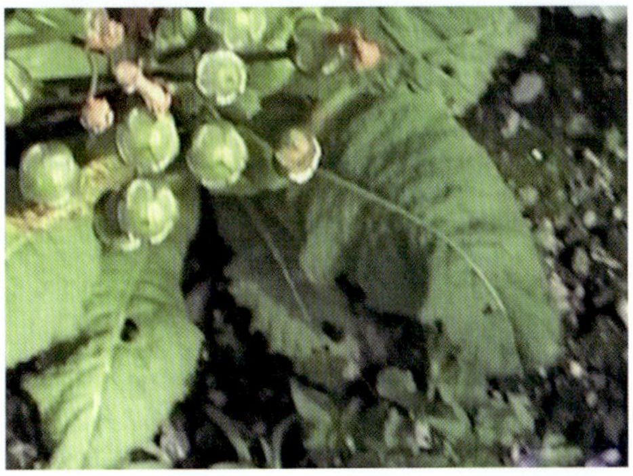
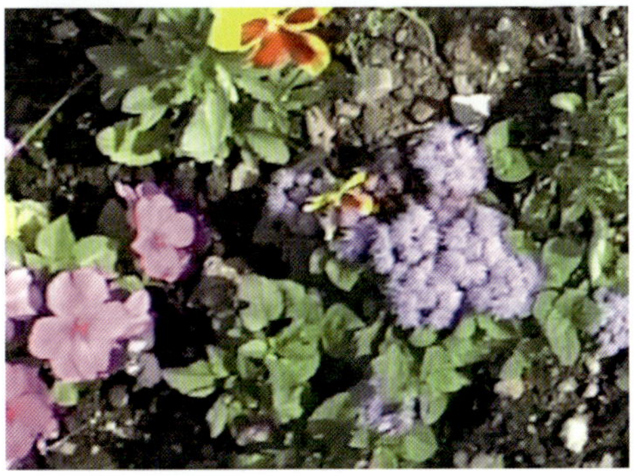
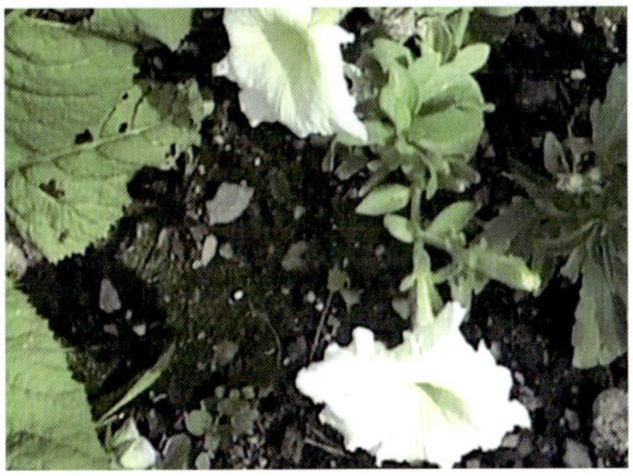
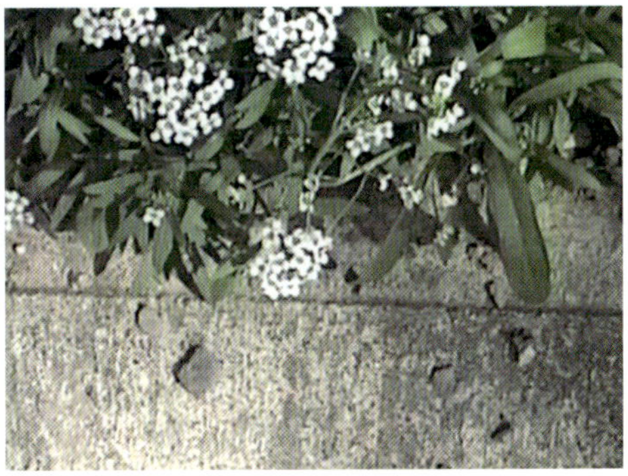
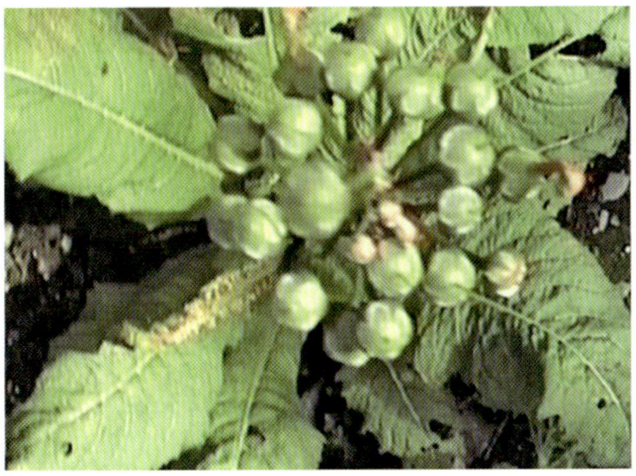
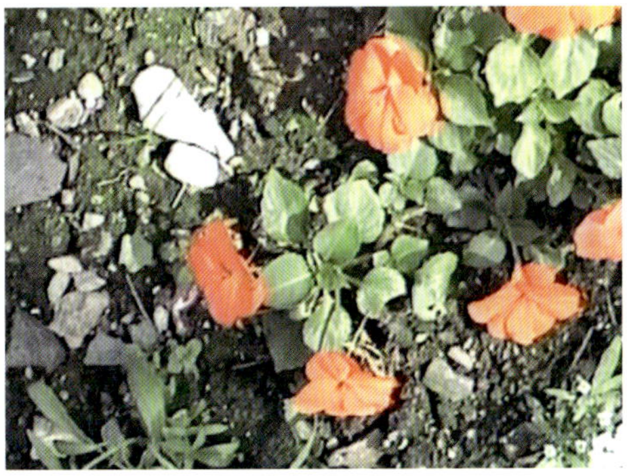

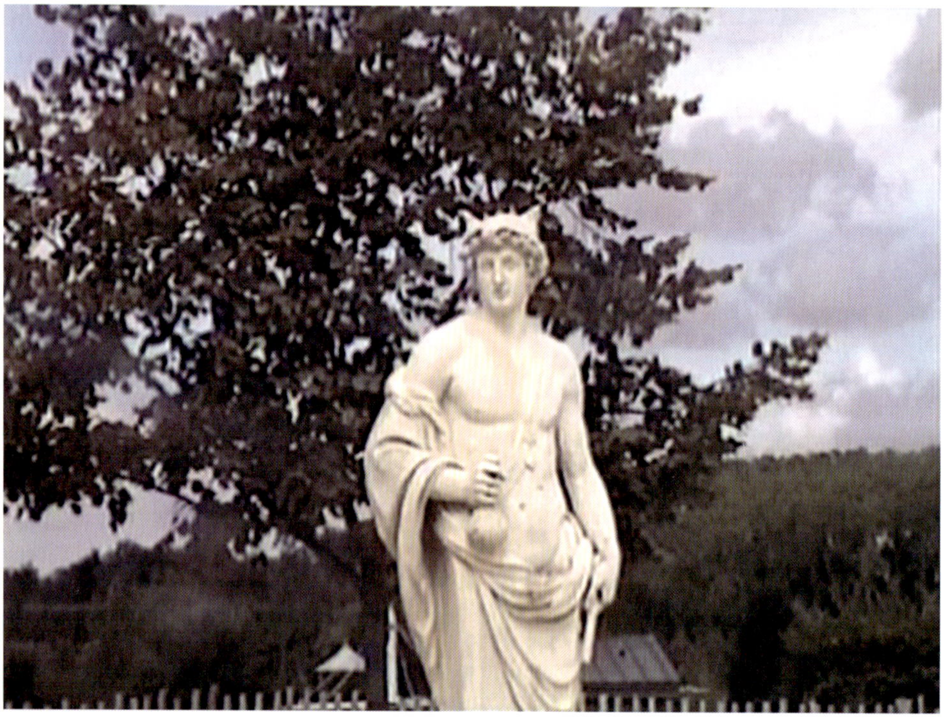

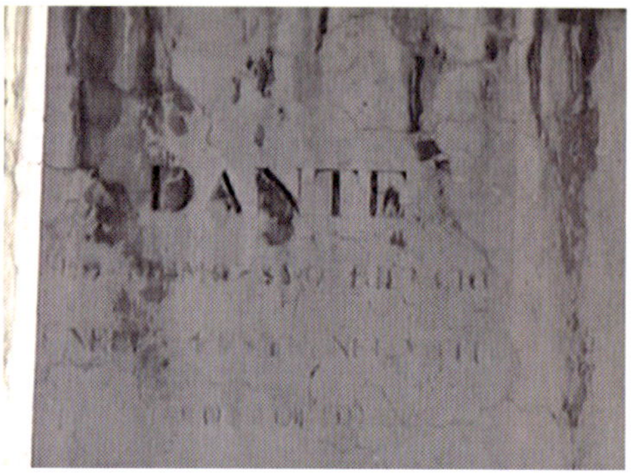
DANTE

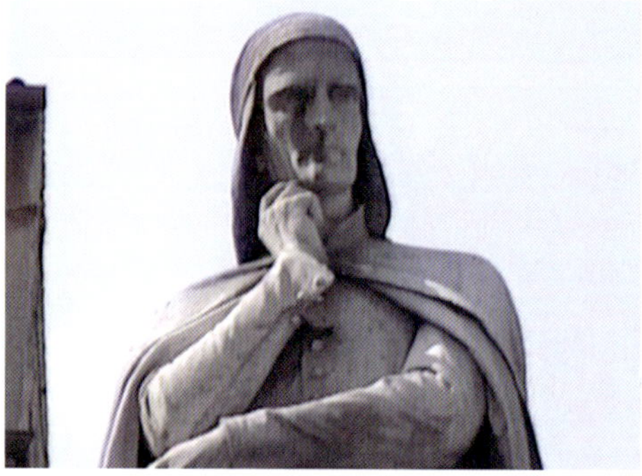

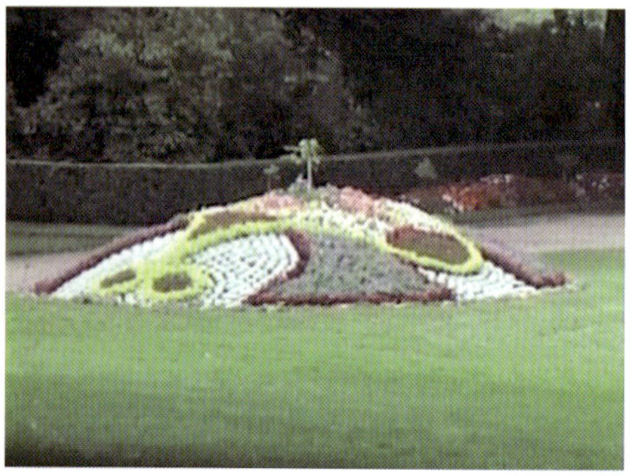

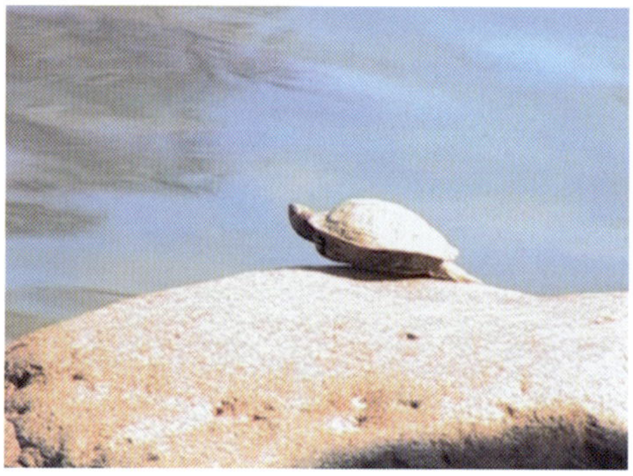

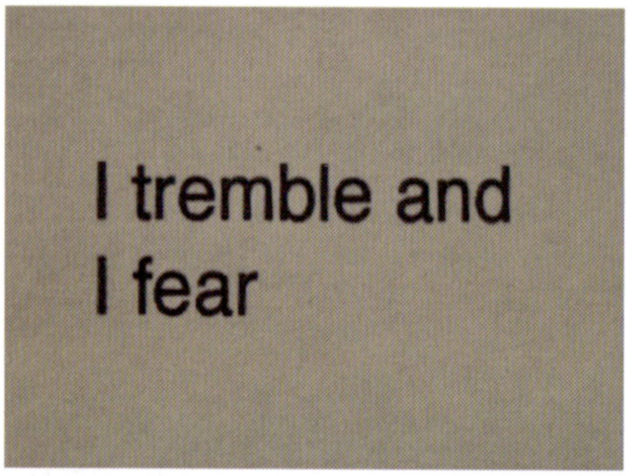
I tremble and
I fear

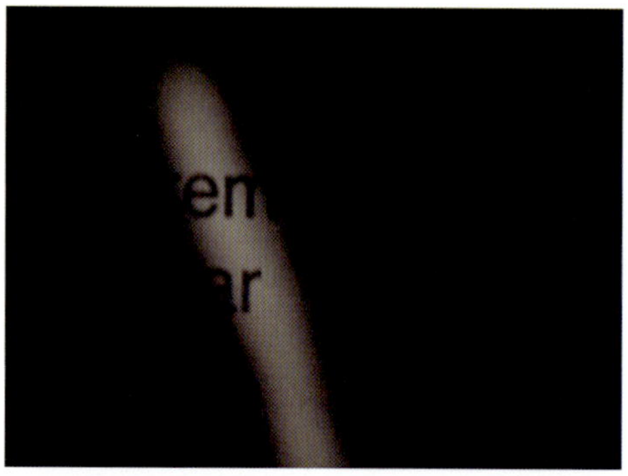

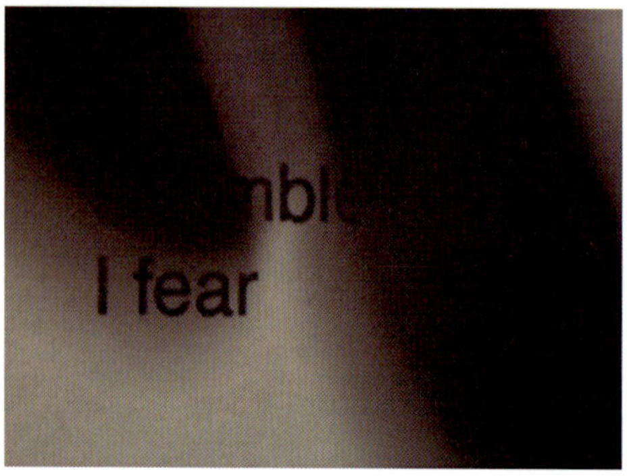
I fear

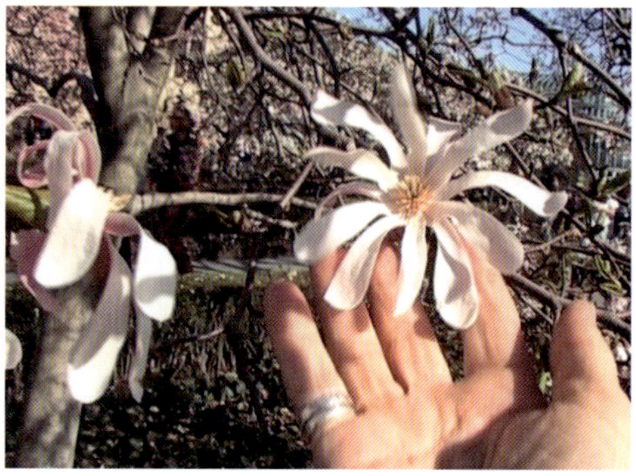

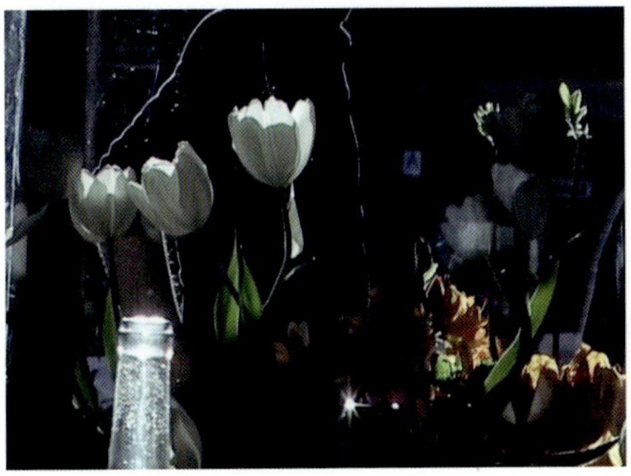
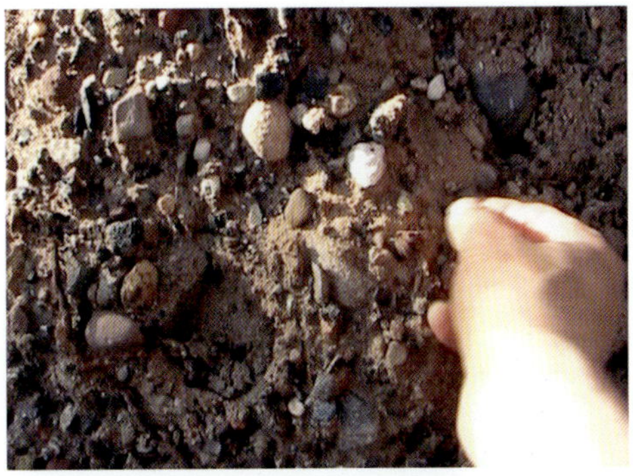
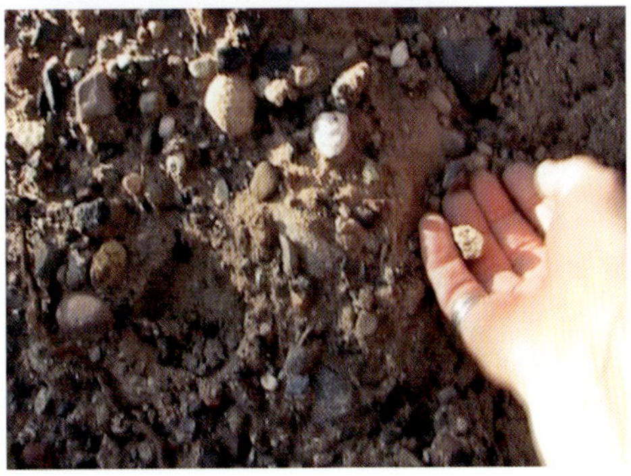
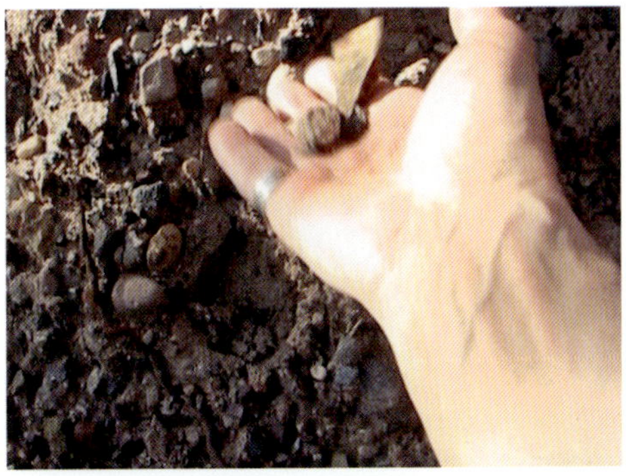
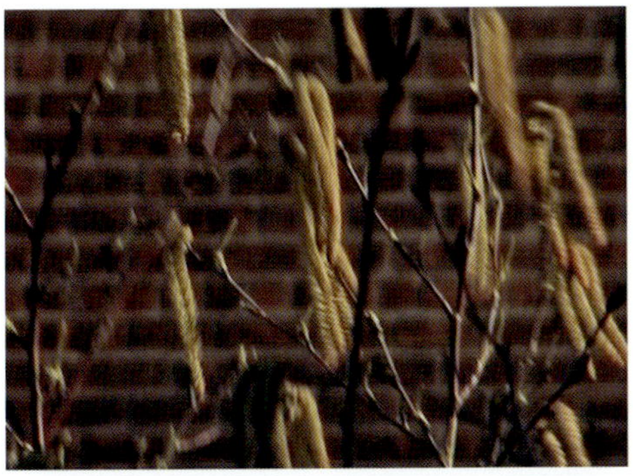
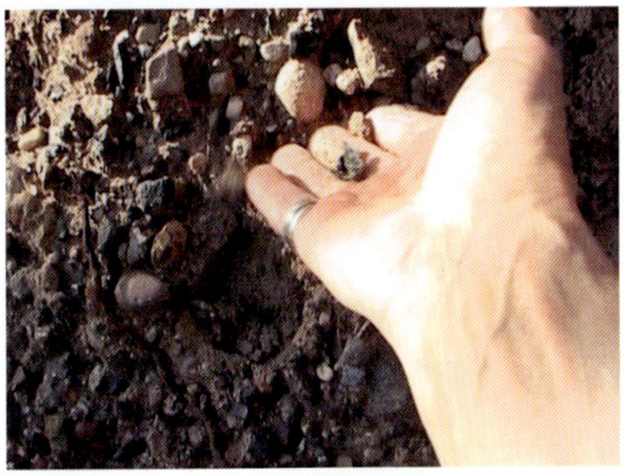
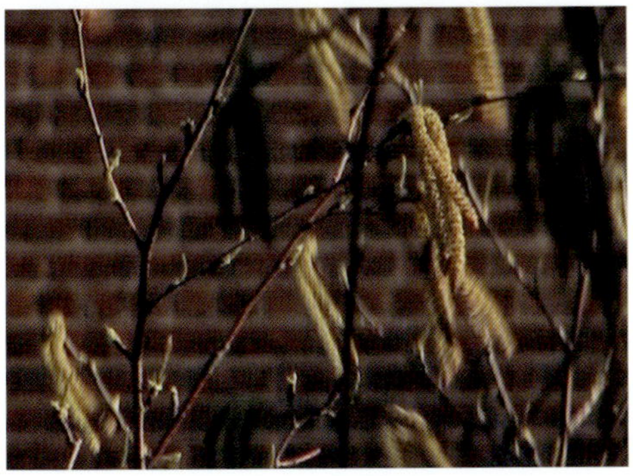
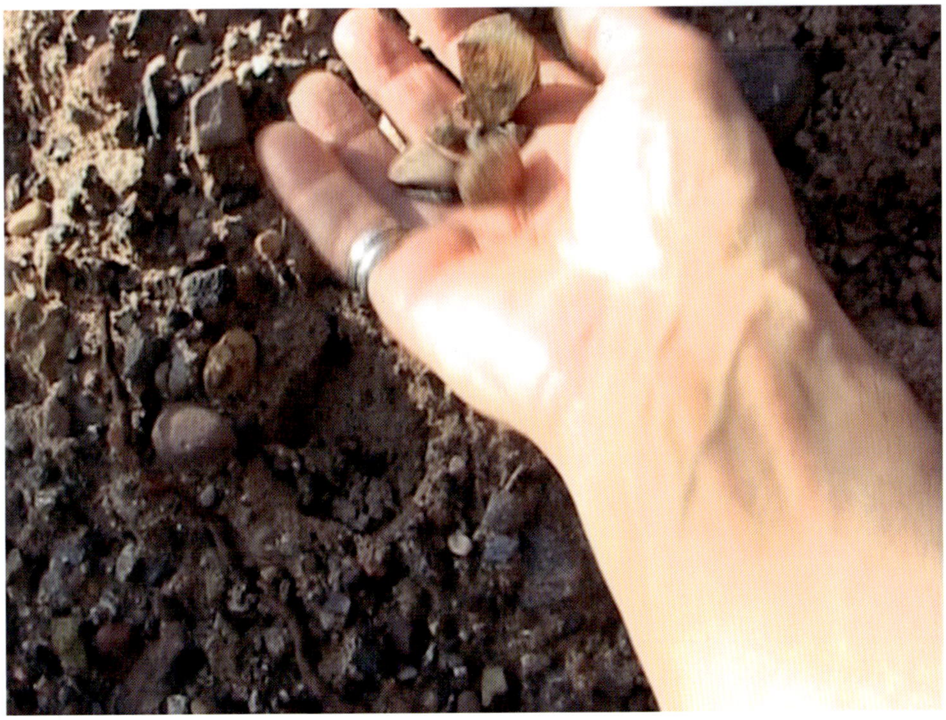
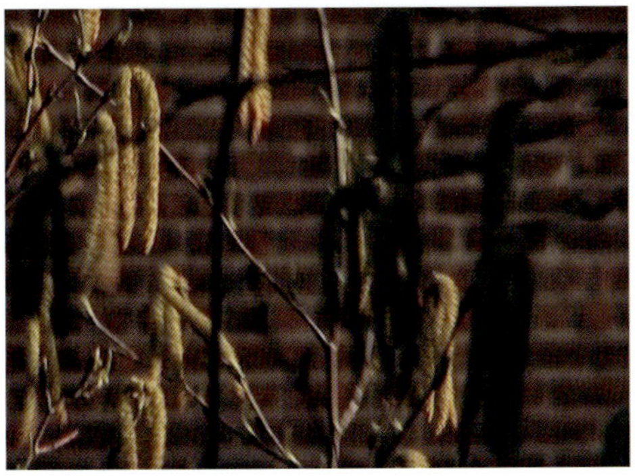

TIMELINE

1922

December 24
Jonas Mekas is born to Elžbieta and Povilas Mekas, farmers in the rural village of Semeniškiai, in northeast Lithuania, 20 miles from the Latvian border. He has four older siblings: Elžbieta, Povilas, Petras, and Kostas.

In Jonas's childhood, twenty families lived in Semeniškiai.

1925

September 30
The Mekases' youngest son, Adolfas, is born.

1926

December 17
After a coup d'état, Lithuania's democratically elected government is replaced with a conservative, authoritarian regime led by Antanas Smetona. Lithuania signs a nonaggression treaty with the Soviet Union.

1933

Fall
Jonas enters primary school in Laužadiškis, 4 miles from his home. His enrollment had been delayed because he was needed to work on the family farm.

1936

May
Jonas graduates from primary school.

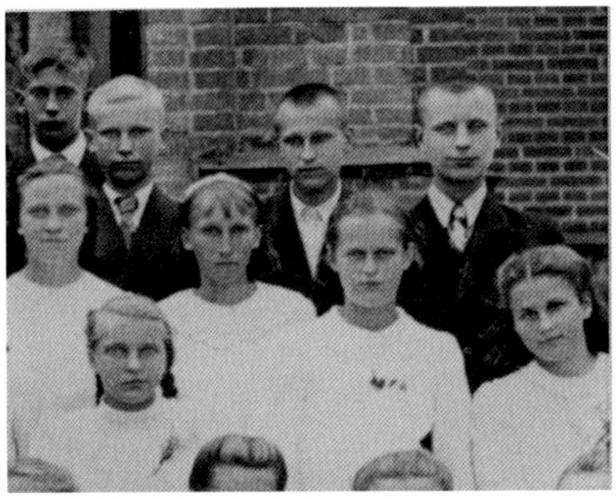

School photograph showing Jonas Mekas in the last row, center, 1940.

1937

Fall
Jonas continues his education in Papilys, 5 miles from Biržai. He edits the school newspaper.

1938

Fall
Adolfas attends high school in Biržai. Jonas joins him there and attempts to enroll, but is rejected because he is too old to be a first-year student.

1939

August 23
Germany and the Soviet Union sign a nonaggression pact that divides eastern Europe into two spheres of influence. Lithuania falls within the Soviet sphere.

September 1
Germany invades Poland; World War II begins.

1940

May
After tutoring himself the previous winter, Jonas passes the high school entrance exams and enrolls as a sixth-term student.

June 15–17
The Soviets invade Lithuania, Estonia, and Latvia and outlaw all non-Soviet political parties.

Jonas receives a still camera from his older brother Povilas. Sometime in June a Soviet cavalcade passes his family's farm, and Jonas runs out to take a picture. A soldier approaches,takes the camera from his hands, rips out the film, and throws it to the ground, destroying it.

July
In Lithuania, the puppet government|installed by the Soviets begins to arrest some 2,000 "enemies of the people." These include politically active citizens, former leaders, and members of outlawed political parties.

August 3
The Soviet annexation of Lithuania is completed.

1941

June
The exiled German filmmaker Hans Richter takes charge of the Institute for Film Techniques at the City College of New York, serving as its director until 1957. The first documentary film school in the United States, the institute had been founded earlier in the year by Irving Jacoby as a way to train students in response to the Nazis' effective use of propaganda films.

First mass deportation in Lithuania. About 18,000 Lithuanians are deported to labor camps in Siberia and Russia. Most are former military officers, police, political figures, religious leaders, intelligentsia, and their families, as well as thousands of Jews.

1942

In the Jewish ghetto of Vilnius, the poets Abraham Sutzkever and Shmerke Kaczerginski lead an effort against the Einsatzstab Reichsleiter Rosenberg (Reichsleiter Rosenberg Task Force), a Nazi organization charged with appropriating cultural property. The task force plans to loot the Strashun Library, known as a "Jewish public library," and the Yiddish Scientific Institute. With the help of twelve volunteers, the two men smuggle Jewish cultural items and the archives of the institute back to the ghetto and bury them for excavation after the war. The event is now known as the "Paper Brigade."

June 22–28
The German army invades the Soviet Union and takes control of the territory of Lithuania within a week. Initially, many Lithuanians believe Germany will restore their independence.

June 22–23
The Lithuanian Activist Front, an antisemitic organization, organizes the June Uprising against the Soviet Union.

June 23
Nazi death squads, aided by Lithuanian troops and partisans, begin mass murdering Jews. By the end of the war, 90 percent of Lithuanian Jews have been killed.

Fall
Jonas assists in the layout of *Biržų Žinios* (Biržai News), a local newspaper in which he publishes several poems.

1943

Spring
Jonas graduates from high school with the honor of "Best Student of the Year."

November
Jonas and Adolfas establish Biržų Teatro ir Dramos Studijos (Biržai Theater and Drama Studio), the first dramatic theater in Biržai.

1944

January
Jonas moves to Panevėžys, about 42 miles from Biržai, where he works as assistant editor of a local

newpaper, *Panevėžio Balsas* (The Voice of Panevėžys). All newspapers are controlled by the Nazis and, in addition to local news and literary works, publish anti-semitic propaganda.

July
Jonas is the typist for a resistance group that publishes a weekly bulletin featuring transcripts of BBC and other news broadcasts. One morning, he discovers that his typewriter is missing from its hiding place and reports the theft to the group. As pamphleteers are traced by matching typefaces to typewriters, everyone decides that Jonas must flee. His uncle procures false documents stating that Jonas has tuberculosis and is unfit for military service, as well as papers for him and Adolfas to travel by train to Vienna to attend university. Their plan was to continue from Austria to Switzerland.

Mid-July
Soviet forces drive the Nazis from Vilnius.

July 12
Jonas and Adolfas board a train for Vienna.

July 20
Jonas and Adolfas reach Elmshorn (a suburb of Hamburg), where their train, which is hitched to cars carrying Russian and Polish prisoners of war, is stopped. Everyone is taken to a Nazi labor camp. The brothers protest but, according to Jonas, "The Germans looked at us and laughed. . . . Germany doesn't need students: Germany needs workers. Every wheel for the victory!"

1945

March
The Elmshorn factory is shut down, and Jonas and Adolfas are reassigned to Kiel, in northern Germany. The brothers plan an escape to Sweden by way of Denmark, but after a false start they are assigned to work on the farm of Otto Thiessen, in the village of Neuhof, where they remain until the end of the war.

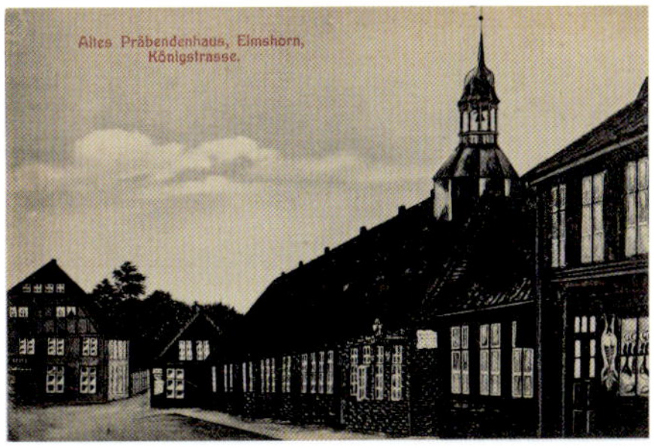

Postcard of Elmshorn, Germany, site of a D.P. camp, undated.

May 8
World War II ends in Europe.

May 29
As the war comes to a close, Jonas and Adolfas are assigned to Camp Murwick, a displaced-persons camp in Flensburg, in northern Germany. D.P. camps were established by the Allied forces to accommodate 8,000,000 forced laborers—like the Mekases—as well as concentration camp survivors, war prisoners, and political refugees.

August
Jonas and Adolfas transfer to a D.P. camp in Wiesbaden and settle in with nearly 2,000 Lithuanian refugees. Jonas edits the daily *Wiesbaden Naujienos* (Wiesbaden news).

October
Jonas volunteers to be the camp's liaison of artistic activities. He organizes music and literary evenings, and edits a daily bulletin that contains camp news and news heard over the radio. The bulletin includes a literary supplement on Saturdays.

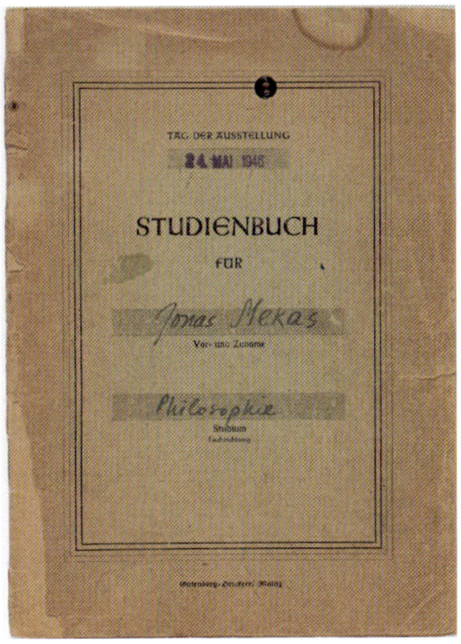

Jonas Mekas's academic transcript, University of Mainz, 1946.

1946

May
Jonas and Adolfas register to study philosophy and literature at the University of Mainz.

Giedra, a Wiesbaden-based publisher, releases Jonas and Adolfas's *Trys broliai ir kitos pasakos* (Three Brothers, and Other Tales), a book of children's stories.

1947

The Mekas brothers write *Knyga apie karalius ir žmones* (A Book on Kings and Men), filled with literary sketches, fairy tales, and poems. The book is published by Patria, one of many publishing houses established in D.P. camps that focus on Lithuanian literature. Giedra also publishes their book *Iš pasaku krašto: Rinktinės įvairių tantų pasakos* (From Fairyland: A Collection of Tales of Different Nations).

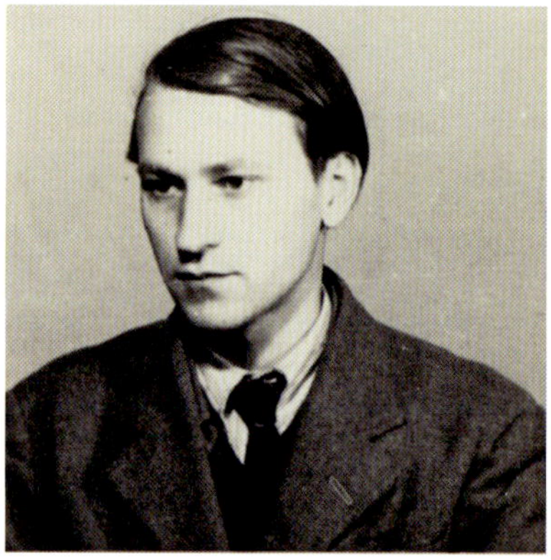

Jonas Mekas, 1947.

In New York, Amos and Marcia Vogel establish Cinema 16 (active until 1963) to screen and distribute independent cinema. It becomes one of the largest and most influential film societies in North America.

August
The Wiesbaden D.P. camp closes, and Jonas and Adolfas transfer to a D.P. camp in Mattenberg, a suburb of Kassel, Germany.

1948

Jonas and Adolfas establish an avant-garde literary journal called *Žvilgsniai* (Glimpses) while living in the D.P. camp. Jonas releases *Semeniškių idilės* (Idylls of Semeniškiai), a book of pastoral poetry that includes illustrations by the poet and artist Leonas Lėtas.

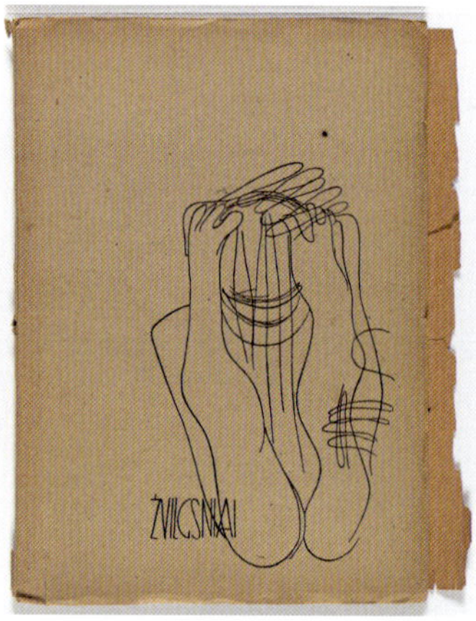

Cover of *Žvilgsniai* (Glimpses) 3, 1948.

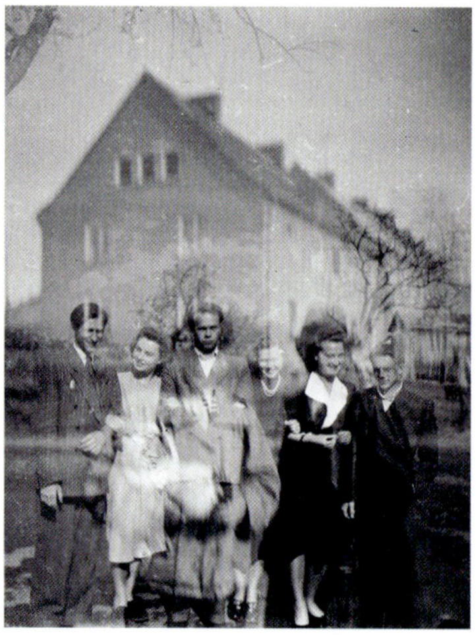

Jonas's caption: "I am in it, somewhere . . . in this picture . . . Kassel/Mattenberg D.P. Camp, 1948," photograph.

1949

April
Povilas Variakojis, a friend of Jonas's uncle Jašinskas, secures jobs in a Chicago bakery for the brothers so that they can apply for U.S. visas.

June 3
The Mekases are transferred to a D.P. camp in Schwäbisch Gmünd, in southern Germany.

October 29
Through the International Refugee Organization, Jonas and Adolfas immigrate to the United States, docking in New York City while en route to Chicago. Instead of continuing on, they decide to remain in New York. Jonas recounted, "That's a very, very, very important date, because that's where my life begins."

Jonas and Adolfas room on Meserole Street in Brooklyn with Algis Landsbergis, a friend from the D.P. camps and fellow contributor to *Žvilgsniai*.

November
Jonas is hired as an assembly worker at the GM Manufacturing Company in Queens.

The brothers move to South 3rd Street in the south Williamsburg section of Brooklyn.

1950

Jonas and Adolfas begin attending screenings at Cinema 16, which Jonas describes as his Sunday church and university.

April 29
Jonas and Adolfas put a deposit on their first Bolex at Peerless Camera Stores. Povilas Klybas, the former mayor of Biržai, serves as guarantor.

May
Jonas, Adolfas, and Leonas Lėtas move to 58-85 Maspeth Avenue in Queens. Jonas works at a neighborhood laundromat ironing clothes.

June
Jonas starts working at a plumbing company on East 4th Street in Manhattan.

July–August
Jonas works as a machine operator at L.W. Machines in Bushwick, Brooklyn.

September
Jonas holds a job cleaning ship parts on 44th Avenue in Long Island City, Queens.

December
Jonas is hired as a messenger boy by Graphic Studios, at 126 West 22nd Street. Later, he is employed there as a cameraman.

1951

Jonas meets George Maciunas, a fellow Lithuanian émigré and Cooper Union art student, through George's sister, Nijole Maciunas.

1952

Spring
Jonas and Adolfas move to 123 Linden Street, Brooklyn.

August
Jonas writes to Hans Richter to ask about enrolling in the Institute for Film Techniques. Richter allows Mekas to attend for free. There Jonas meets the filmmaker Shirley Clarke, the film theorist and critic Gideon Bachmann, and the poet and filmmaker Frank Kuenstler.

Jonas serves as program director of the Film Study Group with Gideon Bachmann, organizing screenings and talks.

1953

Maya Deren establishes the Film Artists Society (later renamed Independent Filmakers Association, or IFA). Mekas attends the meetings of the society, which is foundational to his own work.

Shirley Clarke's first short film, *Dance in the Sun*, is released. An adaptation of Daniel Nagrin's dance of the same name, it is screened at the Museum of Modern Art as the best dance film of the year.

Spring
Jonas and Adolfas move to 95 Orchard Street in Manhattan. Mekas wrote, "When I escaped from Brooklyn to Manhattan's Lower East Side, I was entering the Paradise Regained."

October–December
Jonas, Adolfas, and Louis Brigante begin organizing film screenings for Gallery East at 7 Avenue A. The artist-run cooperative was founded by Joel Baxter, Louis Brigante, and Storm de Hirsch.

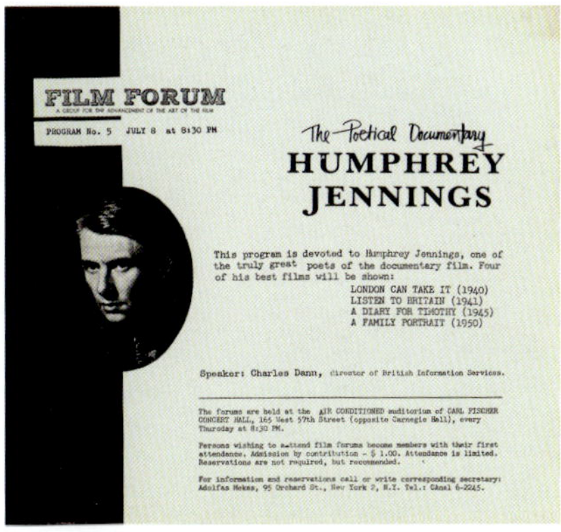
FILM FORUM
A GROUP FOR THE ADVANCEMENT OF THE ART OF THE FILM
PROGRAM No. 5 JULY 8 at 8:30 PM

The Poetical Documentary
HUMPHREY JENNINGS

This program is devoted to Humphrey Jennings, one of the truly great poets of the documentary film. Four of his best films will be shown:
LONDON CAN TAKE IT (1940)
LISTEN TO BRITAIN (1941)
A DIARY FOR TIMOTHY (1945)
A FAMILY PORTRAIT (1950)

Speaker: Charles Dann, director of British Information Services.

The forums are held at the AIR CONDITIONED auditorium of CARL FISCHER CONCERT HALL, 165 West 57th Street (opposite Carnegie Hall), every Thursday at 8:30 PM.

Persons wishing to attend film forums become members with their first attendance. Admission by contribution – $ 1.00. Attendance is limited. Reservations are not required, but recommended.

For information and reservations call or write corresponding secretary: Adolfas Mekas, 95 Orchard St., New York 2, N.Y. Tel.: CAnal 6-2245.

Flyer for the Film Forum screening of "The Poetical Documentary: Humphrey Jennings," July 1954.

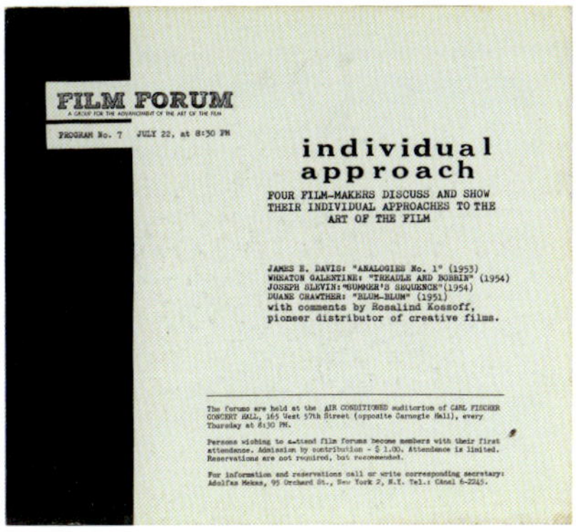
FILM FORUM
A GROUP FOR THE ADVANCEMENT OF THE ART OF THE FILM
PROGRAM No. 7 JULY 22, at 8:30 PM

individual approach
FOUR FILM-MAKERS DISCUSS AND SHOW THEIR INDIVIDUAL APPROACHES TO THE ART OF THE FILM

JAMES E. DAVIS: "ANALOGIES No. 1" (1953)
WHEATON GALENTINE: "TREADLE AND BOBBIN" (1954)
JOSEPH SLEVIN: "SUMMER'S SEQUENCE" (1954)
DUANE CRAWTHER: "BLUM-BLUM" (1951)
with comments by Rosalind Kossoff, pioneer distributor of creative films.

The forums are held at the AIR CONDITIONED auditorium of CARL FISCHER CONCERT HALL, 165 West 57th Street (opposite Carnegie Hall), every Thursday at 8:30 PM.

Persons wishing to attend film forums become members with their first attendance. Admission by contribution – $ 1.00. Attendance is limited. Reservations are not required, but recommended.

For information and reservations call or write corresponding secretary: Adolfas Mekas, 95 Orchard St., New York 2, N.Y. Tel.: CAnal 6-2245.

Flyer for the Film Forum screening of "Individual Approach," 1954.

1954

June
Jonas, Adolfas, and George Capsis organize Film Forum, a group for the advancement of the art of film. The first screening is on June 5. Films are shown every Saturday at 8:00 PM in the auditorium of the Food Trades Vocational High School at 208 West 13th Street, and admission is one dollar. A series of films around the theme of "The Poetical Documentary" is presented on June 19.

July
Film Forum screenings move to Thursdays at 8:30 PM in the Carl Fischer Concert Hall at 165 West 57th Street.

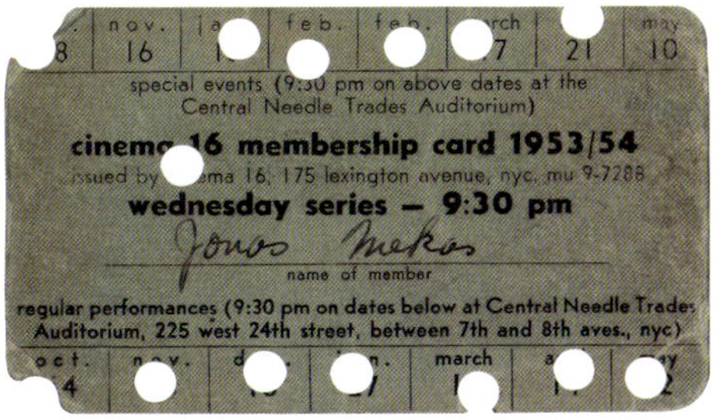

Jonas Mekas's membership card to Cinema 16, 1953–54.

December
Jonas and Adolfas establish *Film Culture*, the first internationally distributed magazine for American experimental cinema. George Maciunas contributes to the design and layout. Jonas is the editor in chief with George Fenin, Andrew Sarris, Eugene Archer, Adolfas Mekas, Arlene Croce, and Édouard de Laurot serving as the editorial board.

1955

January
The first issue of *Film Culture* is released. Orson Welles features on the cover, with articles by Welles, Erich von Stroheim, Hans Richter, Édouard de Laurot, Herman Weinberg, George Fenin, William K. Everson, and others.

April
Jonas and Adolfas move to 16 West 109th Street, Manhattan.

A second edition of *Semeniškių idilės* (Idylls of Semeniškiai) is published in New York by *Aidai* (Echoes), a magazine run by Lithuanian émigrés who also arrived in 1949.

Maya Deren founds the Creative Film Foundation as a network for experimental filmmakers. It provides awards to independent filmmakers in collaboration with Cinema 16 until 1961.

1956

November 1
Allen Ginsberg's *Howl and Other Poems* is published by Lawrence Ferlinghetti's City Lights Publishers.

1957

Jonas begins writing film reviews for *Intro Bulletin*, an arts magazine established by Louis Brigante and Storm de Hirsch.

June
Jonas publishes two poems, "The Wolf" and "The Man on San Ysidro," in *Lituanus*, an English-language journal dedicated to Lithuanian culture, literature, and history.

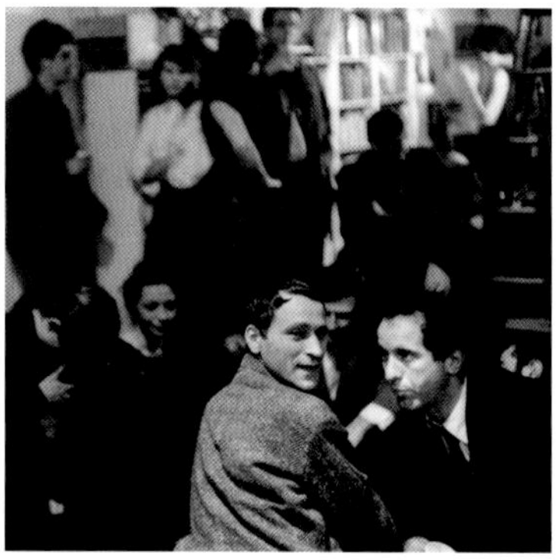

Jonas Mekas and Robert Frank on the set of Frank and Alfred Leslie's *Pull My Daisy*, 1959.

1958

November
Jonas pitches a film-review column to Jerry Tallmer at the *Village Voice*, and Tallmer agrees to the idea. Mekas returns the next day with a review of the film *Pather Panchali* (1955) by Satyajit Ray. With his column "Movie Journal," Mekas becomes the newspaper's first full-time film critic.

1959

Jonas and Adolfas move to 515 East 13th Street.

February 2
The Very Eye of Night, Maya Deren's last completed film, has its U.S. premiere at the Living Theatre. It had premiered in Port-au-Prince, Haiti, in 1955.

February 25
Mekas reviews *The Very Eye of Night* in "Movie Journal," writing that it is "a very thought-out film, clear and crystalline. Maya Deren differs from most of the other experimentalists through her clarity of purpose, clarity of images, universality of symbols."

October 4–10
Allan Kaprow debuts *18 Happenings in 6 Parts* at the Reuben Gallery in Manhattan. It is the first documented use of the term "Happening" in reference to early performance artwork.

November 11
Pull My Daisy, a short film by Robert Frank and Alfred Leslie, premieres at Cinema 16. The film stars Jack Kerouac, Allen Ginsberg, Gregory Corso, Larry Rivers, Delphine Seyrig, and Peter Orlovsky.

November 18
Mekas reviews *Pull My Daisy* in "Movie Journal": "I don't see how

I can review any film after *Pull My Daisy* without using it as a signpost. . . . Robert Frank has succeeded in transplanting life—and in his very first film. And that is the highest praise I can think of. Directorially, *Pull My Daisy* is returning to where true cinema first began, to where Lumière left off."

1960

April 4
Lionel Rogosin opens Bleecker Street Cinema at 144 Bleecker Street, with a premiere of his film *Come Back, Africa* (1959).

Summer
Jonas begins filming *Guns of the Trees*, his first feature, which he describes as dealing "with the thoughts, feelings and anguished strivings of my generation faced with the moral perplexity of our times." Mekas's script is a poetic sketch consisting of thirty short, nonlinear scenes. Jonas is the writer, director, and cinematographer. Adolfas, Frances Stillman, Ben Carruthers, Argus Spear Juillard, Frank Kuenstler, and Louis Brigante constitute the cast, and Allen Ginsberg is the narrator.

While Jonas is filming, Maya Deren fills in on "Movie Journal," contributing a series of statements on cinema, including "Of Critics and Creators" (July 14) and "Some Metaphors for the Creative Process" (July 21).

September 28
At a meeting at the Producers Theatre at 135 West 36th Street, a group of filmmakers, led by Jonas, formulates the idea of the New American Cinema Group (NACG). Attendees of this first meeting include Adolfas, Lionel Rogosin, Peter Bogdanovich, Robert Frank, Alfred Leslie, Édouard de Laurot, Ben Carruthers, Argus Spear Juillard, Emile de Antonio, Lewis Allen, Shirley Clarke, Gregory Markopoulos, Daniel Talbot, Guy Thomajan, Louis Brigante, Harold Humes, Bert Stern, Don Gillin, Walter Gutman, Jack Perlman, David C. Stone, Sheldon Rochlin, and Edward Bland.

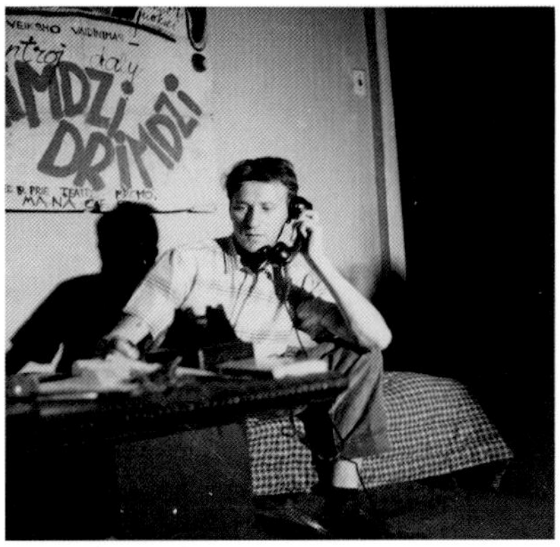

Jonas Mekas, May 1, 1960.

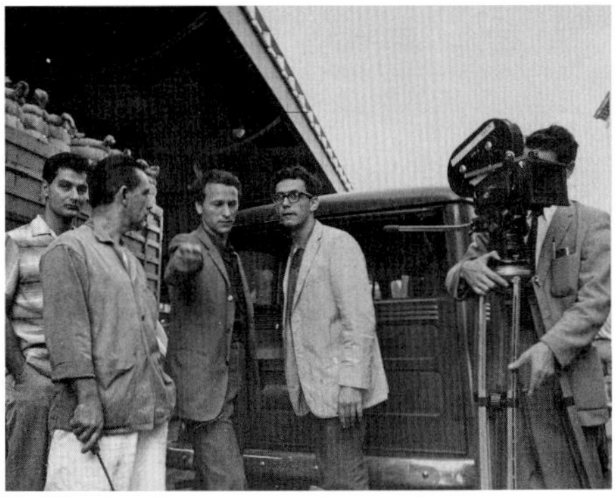

Jonas Mekas filming *Guns of the Trees*, 1960.

September 30
The second meeting of the NACG takes place at the Bleecker Street Cinema. The group releases its first statement, which proclaims the existence of a New American Cinema movement that rejects the "slickness" and superficiality of "official cinema" in favor of one that is "rough, unpolished, but alive."

1961

March
George Maciunas and a fellow Lithuanian, Almus Salcius, found AG Gallery at 925 Madison Avenue.

July 14
The New American Cinema Group (NACG) is formally established.

August
Guns of the Trees premieres at an invitation-only midnight screening at the Bleecker Street Cinema.

November 1
The demonstration Women Strike for Peace, organized by Bella Abzug and Dagmar Wilson, occurs in sixty cities throughout the United States. Jonas records the New York protest and includes footage in his film *Lost, Lost, Lost* (1976).

November 2
Jonas begins "Open House" screenings at the Charles Theatre, owned by Edwin Stein and Walter Langsford, at 12th Street and Avenue B.

1962

The first performances are held at the Judson Dance Theater, an influential avant-garde dance collective housed in Judson Memorial Church at 55 Washington Square.

January 7
The Film-Makers' Cooperative is established as a subsidiary of the NACG to distribute avant-garde and experimental films. Both the Coop and *Film Culture* magazine are headquartered in Jonas's live/work loft at 414 Park Avenue South.

Andy Warhol attends screenings at the loft and meets Jonas through their mutual friend, the filmmaker Naomi Levine.

January 29
The first of many demonstrations calling for a World-Wide General Strike for Peace takes place, sponsored by the New York Committee for the General Strike for Peace. More than three hundred people march down 5th Avenue. Jonas films the event and includes footage in *Lost, Lost, Lost*.

Spring
Jonas hires Barbara Rubin to assist at the Film-Makers' Cooperative.

June 29
The Filmmakers Festival presents twenty-five films at the Charles Theatre, including Stan VanDerBeek's *Wheeeeels 2*.

July 7
Guns of the Trees wins grand prize at the Second International Free Cinema Festival in Porretta Terme, Italy.

July 9
Andy Warhol's first solo exhibition, at Ferus Gallery, Los Angeles, debuts his soup can paintings.

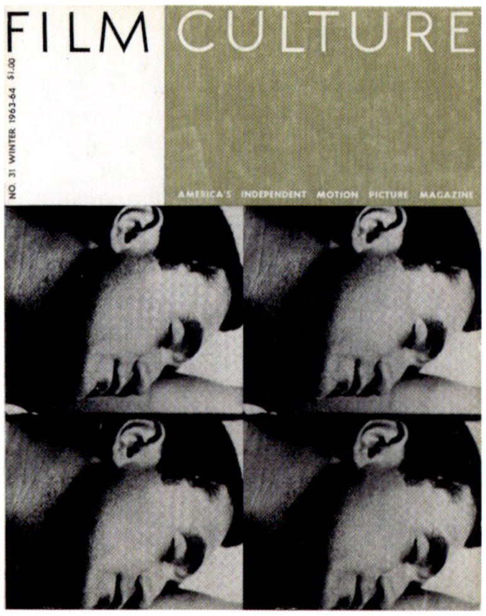

Cover of *Film Culture* 31, Winter 1963–64, featuring stills from Andy Warhol's *Sleep*, 1963–64.

1963

George Maciunas publishes the *Fluxus Manifesto* to "PROMOTE A REVOLUTIONARY FLOOD AND TIDE IN ART, promote living art, anti-art, promote NON ART REALITY to be fully grasped by all peoples, not only critics, dilettantes and professionals."

April 29
Jack Smith's *Flaming Creatures* (1963) premieres at the Bleecker Street Cinema as part of the Coop's Film-Makers' Showcase. The film is screened at midnight along with Smith's *Scotch Tape* (1963).

June
Using Mekas's Bolex camera, Barbara Rubin shoots her film *Christmas on Earth* at an apartment on Ludlow Street.

1964

January 1
Jonas and Barbara Rubin hold an illegal screening of Jack Smith's *Flaming Creatures* at the Third Experimental Film Festival in Knokke-le-Zoute, Belgium, by detaining the projectionist and forcibly seizing the projection booth. Mekas is a juror for the festival.

January 17
The Film-Makers' Coop premieres Warhol's *Sleep* at the Gramercy Arts Theatre.

Late February
The night after the final performance of Kenneth H. Brown's play *The Brig*, produced by Judith Malina, Julian Beck, and the cast of the Living Theatre, Jonas and the troupe break into the Midway Theatre. Mekas was overwhelmed by *The Brig*'s dehumanizing depiction of military life and the Living Theatre's sparse set and

brutal acting. He decided to create a record of the performance as though making a documentary of a real event, stating, “I wanted to see it with my camera. I had to film it, not knowing what will come next, like real life . . . not an adaptation of a play . . . a record of my eye and my temperament lost in the play.”

February 24
The Film-Makers’ Cooperative produces a Film-Makers’ Showcase series at the New Bowery Theatre. Warhol’s *Tarzan and Jane Regained Sort Of*, starring Naomi Levine and Taylor Mead, is the first film shown.

February 25
Detectives attend a Coop screening of *Flaming Creatures* at the New Bowery Theatre.

March 3
The Coop screens *Flaming Creatures* for a second time at the New Bowery Theatre. Ticket seller Florence Karpe, ticket taker Jerry Sims, and projectionist Ken Jacobs are arrested. Jonas arrives and demands that he also be arrested as the film’s distributor, in solidarity with the group. They spend the night in jail and are charged with showing and distributing obscenity.

March 7
Jonas and Pierre Cottrell are arrested at the Writers Stage Theatre for screening Jean Genet’s film *Un Chant d’Amour* (1950). The film’s scenes of erotic homosexuality are considered obscene by the police.

June 12
The obscenity trial relating to *Flaming Creatures* begins. Susan Sontag and Allen Ginsberg are among those who testify on behalf of the film’s artistic and cinematic merit. Mekas, Ken Jacobs, and Florence Karpe are found guilty and receive suspended sentences.

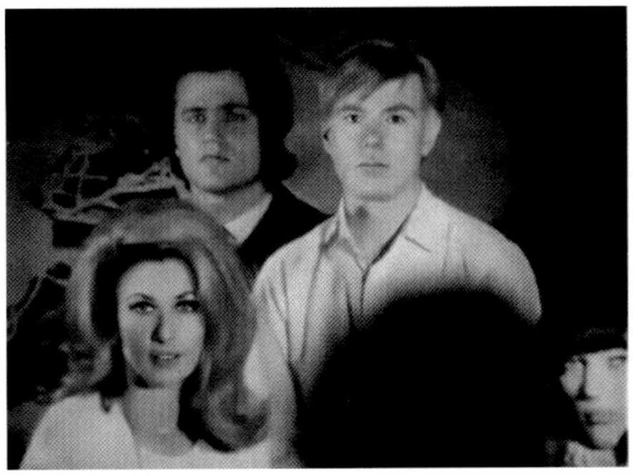

Still from Jonas Mekas’s *Award Presentation to Andy Warhol*, 1964.

July 24–25
Mekas, Warhol, John Palmer, Gerard Malanga, and Henry Geldzahler film *Empire* between 8:00 PM and 2:30 AM. Jonas is the cinematographer. The 485-minute film captures an illuminated Empire State Building in a single, continuous, black-and-white shot.

August 27–September 10
The Brig wins grand prize for Best Documentary at the Venice Film Festival.

September 14–26
The Brig is shown at the New York Film Festival.

November 30–December 21
A series of Film-Makers’ Cinematheque screenings takes place at the New Yorker Theater, 89th Street and Broadway, featuring films by Robert Breer, Ken Jacobs, Naomi Levine, Marie Menken, and Andy Warhol.

December
Jonas films *Award Presentation to Andy Warhol* at the Factory, which depicts Mekas presenting *Film Culture*’s Sixth Independent Film Award to the artist and Factory regulars Jane Holzer, Ivy Nicholson, Gerard Malanga, Gregory Battcock, and Gregory Markopoulos.

1965

January 18–26
Film-Makers’ Cinematheque screenings move to the Maidman Theatre. During this time Gregory Markopolous screens his three-part film *Du Sang, de la Volupté et de la Mort* (1947–48).

January 25–May 31
Film-Makers’ Cinematheque screenings are held at City Hall Cinema.

March 6
Andy Warhol's *Empire* premieres at City Hall Cinema.

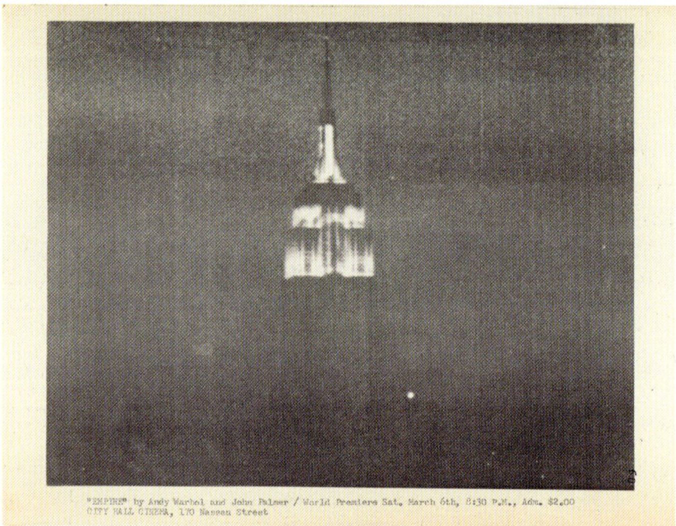

Invitation to the premiere of Andy Warhol and John Palmer's *Empire*, 1964. The inscription reads: "'EMPIRE' by Andy Warhol and John Palmer / World Premiere Sat. March 6th, 8:30 P.M., Adm. $2.00 CITY HALL CINEMA, 170 Nassau Street."

June 4–November
Film-Makers' Cinematheque screenings move to Astor Street Playhouse.

November–December
The Film-Makers' Cinematheque presents the first Festival of Expanded Cinema (also called the New Cinema Festival 1) at the 41st Street Theatre. The monthlong festival is devoted to experiments and new developments in cinema, light, and sound, and presents multimedia and "intermedia" productions by artists including Robert Rauschenberg, Claes Oldenburg, Robert Whitman, Stan VanDerBeek, Jack Smith, Andy Warhol, Carolee Schneemann, and Nam June Paik. On December 1, 2, and 3 Rauschenberg presents *Map Room II* (1965), an interaction between people, animals, and everyday objects featuring Trisha Brown, Alex Hay, Deborah Hay, and Steve Paxton.

December
At Café Bizarre in Greenwich Village, Barbara Rubin introduces Andy Warhol to the Velvet Underground, a rock band with Lou Reed, John Cale, Sterling Morrison, and Moe Tucker. Warhol serves as the band's manager until 1967.

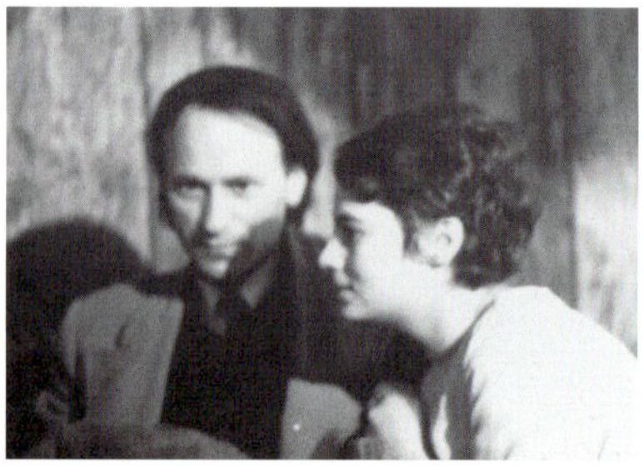

Jonas Mekas and Barbara Rubin at Café Bizarre, photographed by Adam Ritchie, 1965.

1966

Jonas creates three short films, *Hare Krishna*, *Notes on the Circus*, and *Cassis*. They eventually become part of *Walden (Diaries, Notes, and Sketches)* (1969).

January 13
Jonas and Barbara Rubin film the Velvet Underground's first performance at the New York Society for Clinical Psychiatry's annual banquet, held at the Hotel Delmonico. Jonas incorporates the footage into *Walden (Diaries, Notes, and Sketches)*.

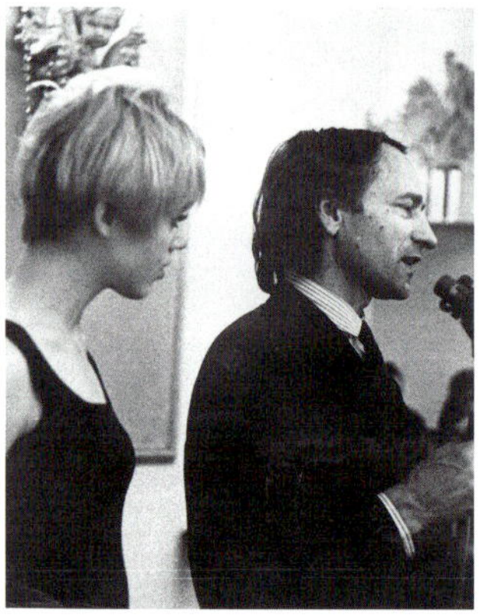

Edie Sedgwick and Jonas Mekas introduce the debut performance of the Velvet Underground at the Hotel Delmonico, New York, January 13, 1966.

June 11
Jonas is honored with a gold medal by the Philadelphia College of Art for his "devotion, passion, and selfless dedication to the rediscovery of the newest art." In his acceptance speech, he states, "This award doesn't, really, go to me; it goes to the new cinema—to all those avant garde artists who are trying to bring some beauty into a world full of sadness and horror. . . .We could continue expressing our own surroundings, being mirrors of the dirty cities, the black dailiness. But we have done that job already. There is pain in the arts of the last few decades. The whole period of so-called modern art is nothing but the pain of our ending civilization, the last decades of the Christian Era. Now we are looking, we are being pulled by a desire for something beautiful deep within us, deep in the stars, and we want to bring it down to earth so that it will change our cities, our faces, our movements, our voices, our souls—we want an art of light."

1967

February 18–March 2
Barbara Rubin organizes Caterpillar Changes, a two-week multimedia festival at the Film-Makers' Cinematheque, which includes live music and projections. Through a built environment of torn sheets and streamers, Rubin screens films by Storm de Hirsch, Harry Smith, Stan VanDerBeek, and Marie Menken, among others.

March 12
The Velvet Underground, featuring Lou Reed, John Cale, Sterling Morrison, and Moe Tucker, releases its first album, *The Velvet Underground and Nico.* Andy Warhol produces the album. The Underground soon becomes the house band for Warhol's Factory.

August
George Maciunas develops a "Fluxhouse" at 80 Wooster Street in SoHo. Fluxhouses were nonprofit housing cooperatives that offered affordable live/work spaces to artists.

December
The Film-Makers' Cinematheque opens Cinematheque I on the ground floor of 80 Wooster Street. The space offers an experimental showcase to anyone who would like to screen films or present mixed-media events.

1968

March
Jonas and Nam June Paik stage a political Fluxus performance at the University of Cincinnati. To remind audiences of human rights as defined in the United Nations Charter, Jonas reads and translates the text into Lithuanian and Nam June does the same in Korean. Jonas says, "We did a horrible job of translation. But, of course, nobody knew it—the audience spoke neither Lithuanian nor Korean. But we didn't care about that. We had to make our political statement and we did it in a Fluxus sort of way."

November 12
The Film-Makers' Cinematheque begins Avantgarde Film Tuesdays at the Jewish Museum, highlighting "American films of the last decade, the most fruitful period of the avant-garde film." Kenneth Anger's *Eaux d'Artifice* (1953) and *Inauguration of the Pleasure Dome* (1954) are screened at 5:30 and 7:00 PM, followed by a conversation with the filmmaker.

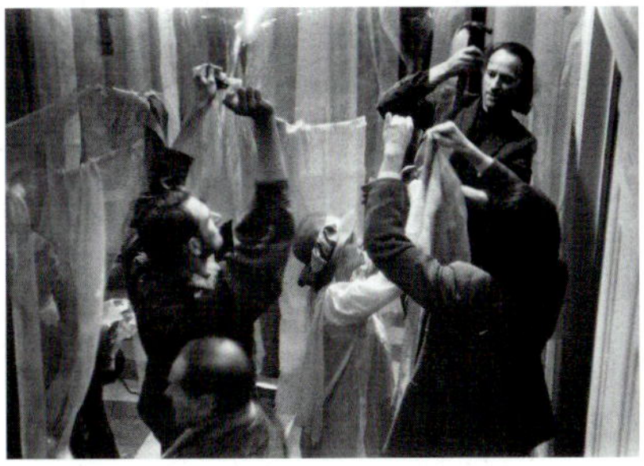

Jonas Mekas, Jack Smith, and Barbara Rubin at the Film-Makers' Cinematheque, February 18, 1967.

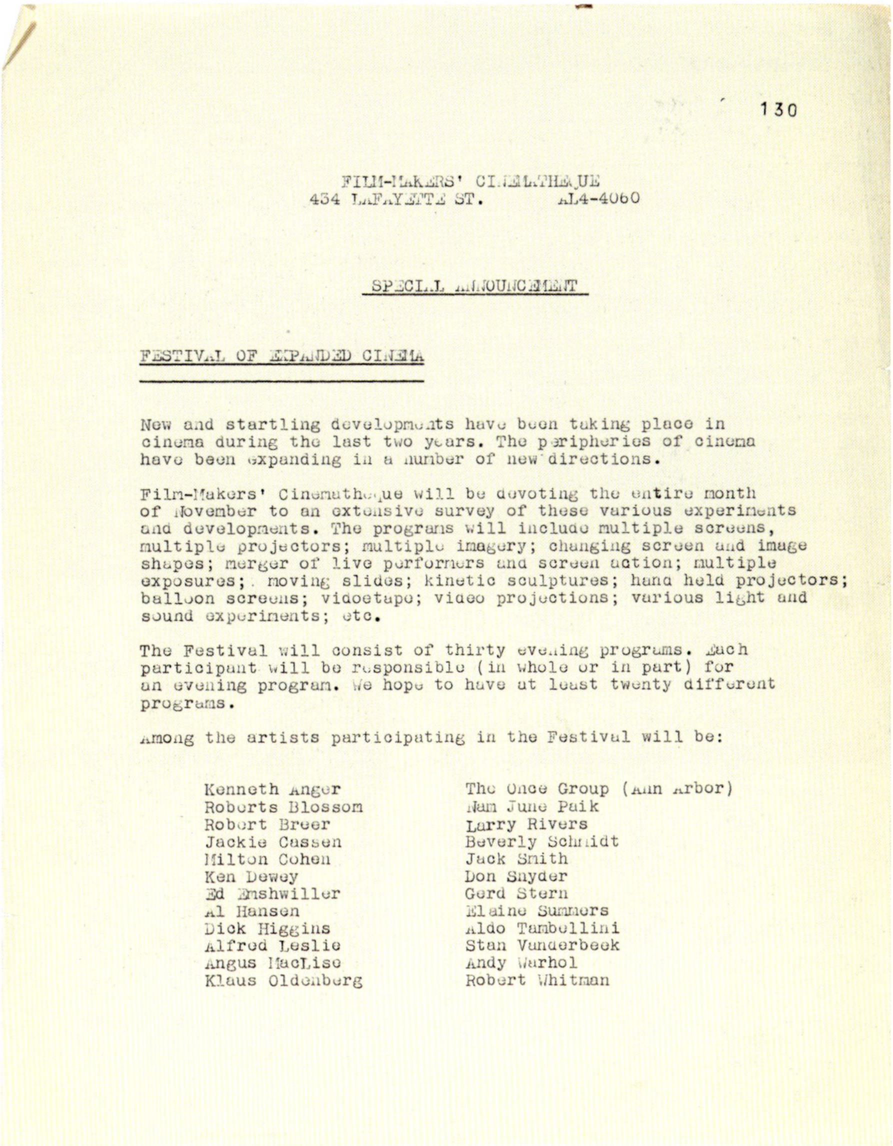

130

FILM-MAKERS' CINEMATHEQUE
434 LAFAYETTE ST. AL4-4060

SPECIAL ANNOUNCEMENT

FESTIVAL OF EXPANDED CINEMA

New and startling developments have been taking place in cinema during the last two years. The peripheries of cinema have been expanding in a number of new directions.

Film-Makers' Cinematheque will be devoting the entire month of November to an extensive survey of these various experiments and developments. The programs will include multiple screens, multiple projectors; multiple imagery; changing screen and image shapes; merger of live performers and screen action; multiple exposures; moving slides; kinetic sculptures; hand held projectors; balloon screens; videotape; video projections; various light and sound experiments; etc.

The Festival will consist of thirty evening programs. Each participant will be responsible (in whole or in part) for an evening program. We hope to have at least twenty different programs.

Among the artists participating in the Festival will be:

Kenneth Anger	The Once Group (Ann Arbor)
Roberts Blossom	Nam June Paik
Robert Breer	Larry Rivers
Jackie Cassen	Beverly Schmidt
Milton Cohen	Jack Smith
Ken Dewey	Don Snyder
Ed Emshwiller	Gerd Stern
Al Hansen	Elaine Summers
Dick Higgins	Aldo Tambellini
Alfred Leslie	Stan Vanderbeek
Angus MacLise	Andy Warhol
Klaus Oldenburg	Robert Whitman

Flyer for the Festival of Expanded Cinema, 1965.

1969

January 26–March 23
Film-Makers' Cinematheque screenings are presented at the Elgin Theater on Eighth Avenue and 19th Street. Jack Smith's *No President* premieres on February 2.

January 31–February 28
Film-Makers' Cinematheque screenings are presented at the Gotham Art Theater.

March 1
Film-Makers' Cinematheque screenings are presented at the Gallery of Modern Art.

March 25–31, May 26–June 1
John Lennon and Yoko Ono stage their first weeklong Bed-In for Peace at the Hilton Hotel in Amsterdam to promote world peace. The press is invited into their honeymoon suite, where for 12 hours a day they protest the war by staying in bed, speaking to the press, calling for an end to the Vietnam War, and growing their hair. Their second Bed-In, in May, is at the Queen Elizabeth Hotel in Montreal. Jonas visits and films. Other celebrity attendees include Timothy Leary, Dick Gregory, and Allen Ginsberg.

Spring
Jonas Mekas, Jerome Hill, P. Adams Sitney, Peter Kubelka, and Stan Brakhage begin to draw up plans for "Anthology Cinema," which will become Anthology Film Archives.

December 20 and 24
Jonas's first, complete diary film, *Walden (Diaries, Notes, and Sketches)*, premieres at the Elgin Theater.

1970

November 30
Anthology Film Archives opens at Joseph Papp's Public Theater at 425 Lafayette Street. Jonas and the film theorist P. Adams Sitney serve as codirectors. It includes a 90-seat theater called the Invisible Cinema, designed by filmmaker and architect Peter Kubelka, and shows three films daily, 365 days a year. Admission is $1.

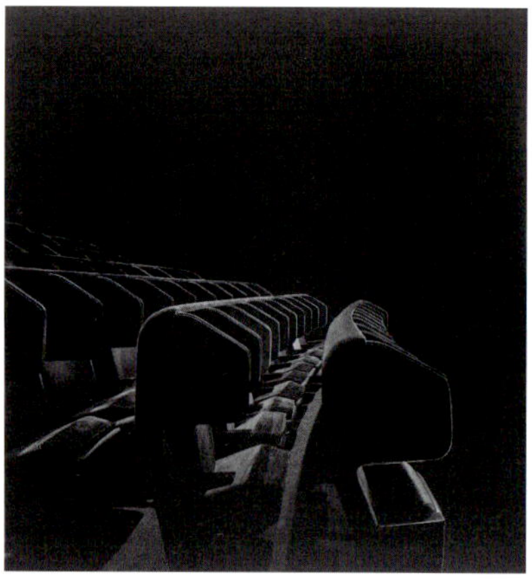

The Invisible Cinema, the theater at Anthology Film Archives.

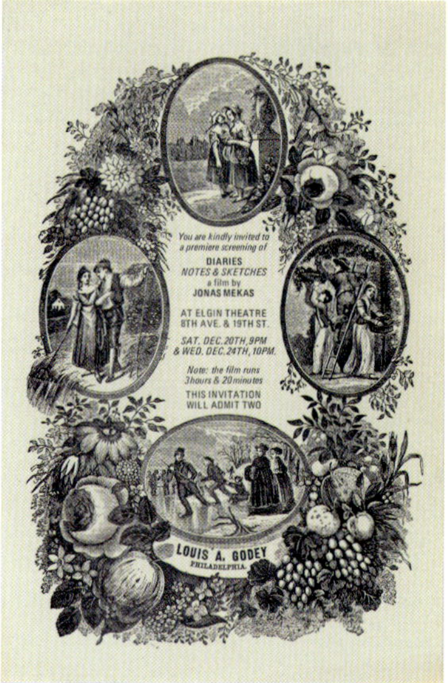

Invitation to the premiere of *Walden* at the Elgin Theater, 1969.

1971

Adolfas establishes the film program at Bard College, which he directs for thirty years.

Summer
Jonas and Adolfas return to their hometown of Semeniškiai, Lithuania, for the first time since fleeing in 1944. The visit becomes the basis for the film *Reminiscences of a Journey to Lithuania* (1972).

1972

Summer
Jonas teaches photography and filmmaking to Jackie Kennedy's children, John and Caroline, at Warhol's home in Montauk. They are accompanied by Lee Radziwill and her children Anthony and Christina, Peter Beard, and a rotating cast of characters that includes Elia Kazan, Mick Jagger, and Warhol. Footage from this summer becomes *This Side of Paradise* (1999).

October 4
Reminiscences of a Journey to Lithuania premieres at the 10th New York Film Festival. It is screened with Adolfas Mekas's film *Going Home* (1972), on the same subject.

1974

Anthology Film Archives relocates to 80 Wooster Street. Shegeko Kubota becomes its first curator of video under Jonas (until 1982).

June
Jonas marries Hollis Melton, a photographer.

November 3
Daughter, Oona, is born.

Fall
The Mekas family moves to 491 Broadway in SoHo, the last Fluxhouse.

1975

Jonas ceases publication of "Movie Journal" in the *Village Voice*.

1976

September 15
Lost, Lost, Lost premieres at the New American Filmmakers series at the Whitney Museum of American Art.

1977

Jonas receives a Guggenheim Fellowship.

Jonas teaches the course "The New York Avant-Garde Film Scene" at the New School for Social Research.

1978

Jonas teaches the workshop "Documentary Methods and Theory" at Massachusetts Institute of Technology in Cambridge.

1979

August 21
Jonas purchases the Second Avenue Courthouse for $50,000

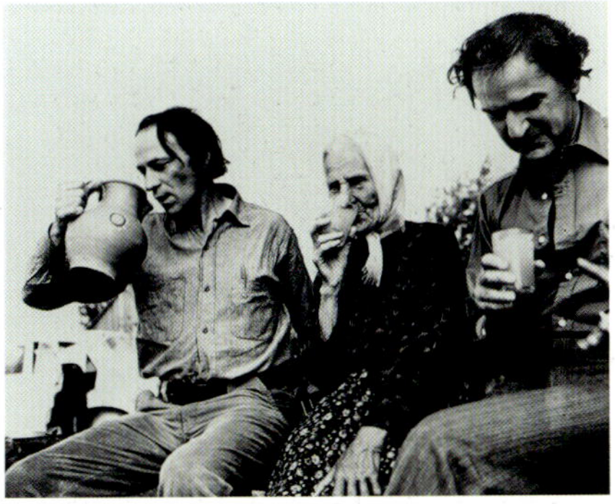

Jonas and Adolfas Mekas drinking homemade beer with their mother during their visit to Lithuania, 1971.

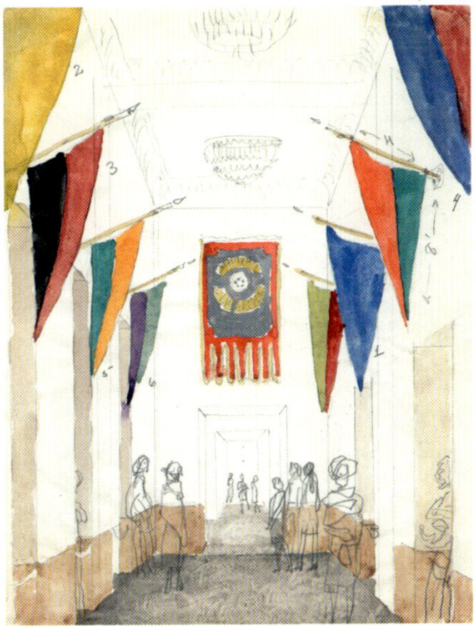

Watercolor of the lobby of Anthology Film Archives by Jerome Hill, undated.

as the permanent home of Anthology Film Archives (AFA). To do so, he and his colleagues persuade the city to restrict the sale of the courthouse to a nonprofit, and then petition the mayor's office for the right to purchase. Friends and supporters of Mekas and AFA, such as Andy Warhol and director Francis Coppola, write letters in support of the organization.

1981

December 9
Son, Sebastian, is born.

1987

Jonas receives a video camera from Sony and begins experimenting with the medium.

1988

October 12
Anthology Film Archives opens in the courthouse building after a decade-long renovation. The space houses two theaters, an archive, and a library.

1989

Jonas is given the 33rd Annual Creative Arts Award by Brandeis University. Louise Bourgeois and Martin Puryear also receive awards.

1990

Scenes from the Life of Andy Warhol is released.

1991

The first edition of Jonas's postwar diary *I Had Nowhere to Go* is published by Black Thistle Press.

1992

Jonas is honored as a Chevalier de l'Ordre des Arts et des Lettres by the French Ministry of Culture.

1996

Black Thistle Press publishes *There Is No Ithaca*, which contains two cycles of Jonas's poetry: *Idylls of Semeniškiai* and *Reminiscences*. It is the first English publication of these works, which were translated by Vyt Bakaitis.

1997

April 5
Allen Ginsberg dies. Jonas records his friend's Buddhist wake, and the footage becomes *Scenes from Allen's Last Three Days on Earth as a Spirit* (1997).

1998

Anthology Film Archives launches The NewFilmmakers series. It begins as an opportunity for New York University students to project their work in a theater; today, it is a yearlong, bicoastal series that highlights emerging filmmakers of different backgrounds with programs in New York and Los Angeles.

2000

Jonas is honored as an Officier de l'Ordre des Arts et des Lettres by the French Ministry of Culture.

November 4
As I Was Moving Ahead Occasionally I Saw Brief Glimpses of Beauty, Jonas's last 16mm film, premieres at the London Film Festival. The nearly five-hour chronicle presents joyful moments from his family life, mixing together three decades of footage.

2001

September 11
Jonas records the attacks on the Twin Towers from his rooftop at 491 Broadway in SoHo.

2003

July 2–September 28
The exhibition *Jonas Mekas: A Camera for Jonas* is held at the Musée d'Art Moderne de la Ville de Paris.

2004

January
491 Broadway is sold and Jonas moves to Greenpoint, Brooklyn. The event becomes the subject of *A Letter from Greenpoint* (2004). After fifteen years of experimentation with the format, Jonas considers this his first mature video work.

2005

January 1–April 17
The exhibition *Jonas Mekas: Farewell to SoHo* is on view at the Moderna Museet, Stockholm.

June 12–November 6
Jonas represents Lithuania at the 51st Venice Biennale with *Celebration of the Small and Personal in the Time of Bigness*, organized by Liutauras Psibilskis, Lolita Jablonskienė, and the Lithuanian National Art Museum, Vilnius.

2006

Reminiscences of a Journey to Lithuania joins the Library of Congress's National Film Registry.

Jonas accepts an award from the Directors Guild of America honoring Anthology Film Archives for "preserving and promoting independent and avant-garde filmmaking."

January 27–March 19
The exhibition *Jonas Mekas* at the Contemporary Art Centre, Vilnius, presents films from different periods of his life, some shown for the first time in Lithuania.

2007

Jonas undertakes the *365 Day Project*, in which he releases a short (2–15 min.) video each day on his website, jonasmekas.com. The footage dates from the late 1980s to 2007. The project is inspired by Petrarch's collection of 366 poems, *Il Canzoniere* (Song Book).

November 4
The Jonas Mekas Visual Arts Center, an archive and gallery dedicated to the artist and his circle, opens in Vilnius and presents its first exhibition, *The Avant-Garde: From Futurism to Fluxus* (November 5, 2007–February 3, 2008).

2008

Jonas receives the Baltic Cultural Achievement Award.

November 8, 2008–March 1, 2009 The exhibition *Jonas Mekas* at the Museum Ludwig, Cologne, is the artist's first retrospective in Germany.

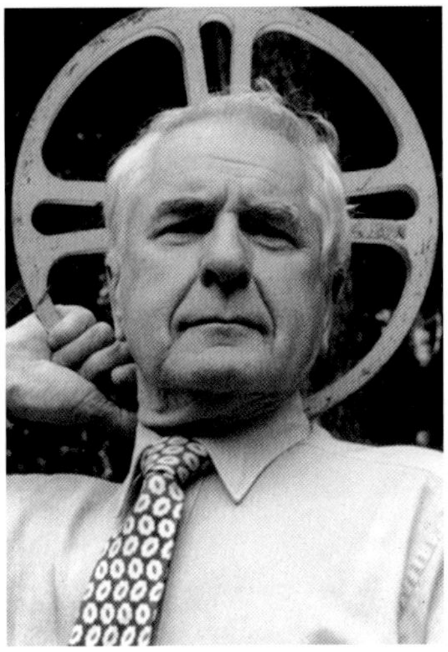

Adolfas Mekas, photographed by L. Syd M Johnson, early 1990s.

2011

February 18
Jonas's video *Sleepless Nights Stories*, composed of twenty-five vignettes of his life and inspired by *One Thousand and One Nights*, premieres at the Berlin Film Festival.

May 31
Adolfas Mekas dies.

December 15
Sleepless Nights Stories has its U.S. premiere at Anthology Film Archives.

2013

January 15
Jonas receives the Commandeur de l'Ordre des Arts et des Lettres from the French Ministry of Culture at a ceremony in New York.

October 18, 2013–January 26, 2014
The exhibition *Jonas Mekas/The Fluxus Wall*, organized by the Lithuanian Art Museum in Vilnius, is on view at Bozar, Brussels.

2016

Douglas Gordon produces the film *I Had Nowhere to Go* about Mekas's life.

September 16, 2016–
February 5, 2017
Jonas is included in the exhibition *Take Me (I'm Yours)* at the Jewish Museum, New York.

2017

Jonas is elected to the Academy of Motion Picture Arts and Sciences.

November 8–July 16
Gordon's film *I Had Nowhere to Go* premieres at Documenta 14.

Also included are Mekas's film *Reminiscences of a Journey to Lithuania* (1972) and the series *Images Out of Darkness*, forty-two photographs taken between 1945 and 1949 while Jonas and Adolfas were in the D.P. camps.

The New York City Landmarks Preservation Commission approves an expansion of Anthology Film Archives to include a new floor, library, and cafe.

November 8, 2017–March 4, 2018
The exhibition *Again, Again, It All Comes Back to Me in Brief Glimpses*, at the National Museum of Modern and Contemporary Art, Seoul, is a retrospective of Mekas's work.

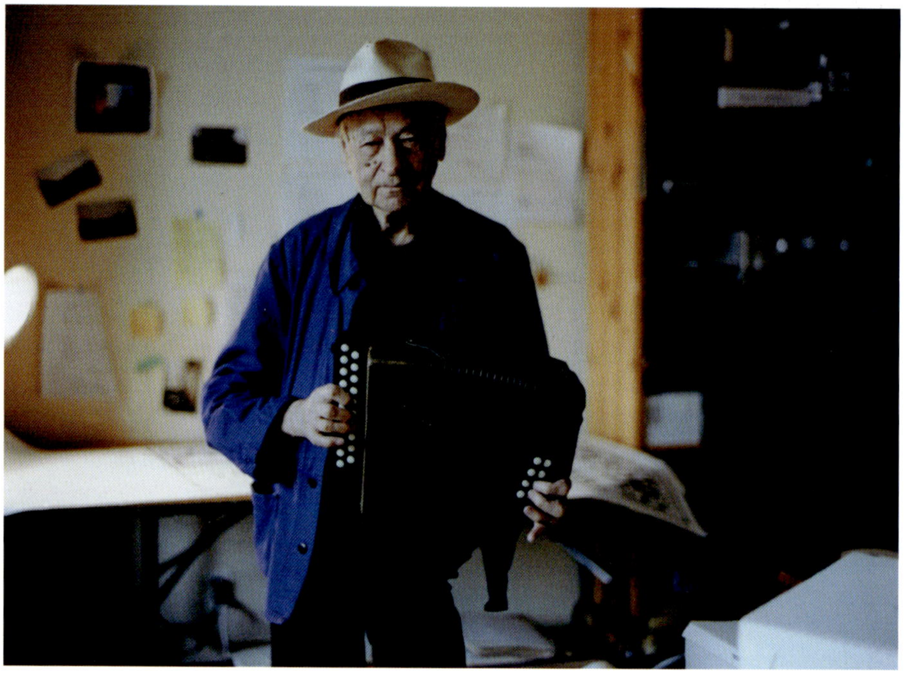
Jonas Mekas photographed by Barbara Anastacio, 2012.

2018

June 29 and July 1
Jonas conducts a six-hour interview with Ina Navazelskis for the United States Holocaust Memorial Museum's oral history project.

2019

January 23
Jonas dies at his home in Brooklyn at age ninety-six.

June 21–July 21
The exhibition *Jonas Mekas: Let Me Dream Utopias* is on view at the Rupert, Vilnius. The project, proposed by Mekas before his death, focuses on his poetry as an ever-present practice and influence, and features many previously unpublished poems spanning sixty years.

November 1
Jonas's final work, *Requiem*, premieres at the Shed, New York. It is projected to accompany a performance of Giuseppe Verdi's *Messa da Requiem*, conducted by Teodor Currentzis and played by the musicAeterna orchestra and choir.

2021

November 19, 2021–
February 20, 2022
The exhibition *Jonas Mekas and the New York Avant-Garde,* at The Lithuanian National Museum of Art / National Gallery of Art, Vilnius, is the first comprehensive exhibition in Lithuania on Mekas's multifaceted activities and his milieu.

2022

February 18–June 5
The exhibition *Jonas Mekas: The Camera Was Always Running*, at the Jewish Museum, New York, is the filmmaker's first museum survey in the United States.

INDEX

Page numbers in *italics* refer to illustrations.

D

E

F

G

H

N

JEWISH MUSEUM BOARD OF TRUSTEES, 2021

This book has been published in conjunction with the exhibitions *Jonas Mekas and the New York Avant-Garde*, at the National Gallery of Art, Vilnius, organized by The Lithuanian National Museum of Art, November 19, 2021–February 20, 2022, and *Jonas Mekas: The Camera Was Always Running*, Jewish Museum, New York, February 18–June 5, 2022.

Jewish Museum, New York
Curator: Kelly Taxter
Director of Publications: Eve Sinaiko
Editor: Susan Higman Larsen
Editorial Assistant: Amelia Kutschbach
Rights Manager: Taylor Catalana
Editorial Production: Tina Henderson

The Lithuanian National Museum of Art / National Gallery of Art, Vilnius
Curators: Inesa Brašiškė and Lukas Brasiskis
Chief Curator: Lolita Jablonskienė
Head of Exhibitions: Giedrius Gulbinas

Yale University Press
Editor, Art and Architecture: Amy Canonico
Production Manager: Sarah Henry

Designed by Mark Owens with David Wise

Set in Display Grotesk (Chi-Long Trieu), Syndicat Grotesk (Adrien Menard), and Times New Roman Seven

Printed in Singapore

Jewish Museum
1109 Fifth Avenue
New York, New York 10128
thejewishmuseum.org

The Lithuanian National Museum of Art
Didžioji st. 4, LT-01128
Vilnius, Lithuania
lndm.lt

Yale University Press
P.O. Box 209040
New Haven, Connecticut 06520–9040
yalebooks.com/art

Library of Congress Control Number: 2021939811
ISBN 978-0-300-25307-8

A catalogue record for this book is available from the British Library.

The paper in this book meets the requirements of ANSI/NISO Z 39.48-1992 (Permanence of Paper).
10 9 8 7 6 5 4 3 2 1

Cover: Jonas Mekas at the doors of the Second Avenue Courthouse, the future Anthology Film Archives, photographed by Hollis Melton, undated (see page 201).
Frontispiece: Jonas Mekas, "The Tree of Jonas," drawing, c. 1997 or 1998.
Endpapers: Portraits of Jonas Mekas by Christine Ljubanovic, Paris, 2003.

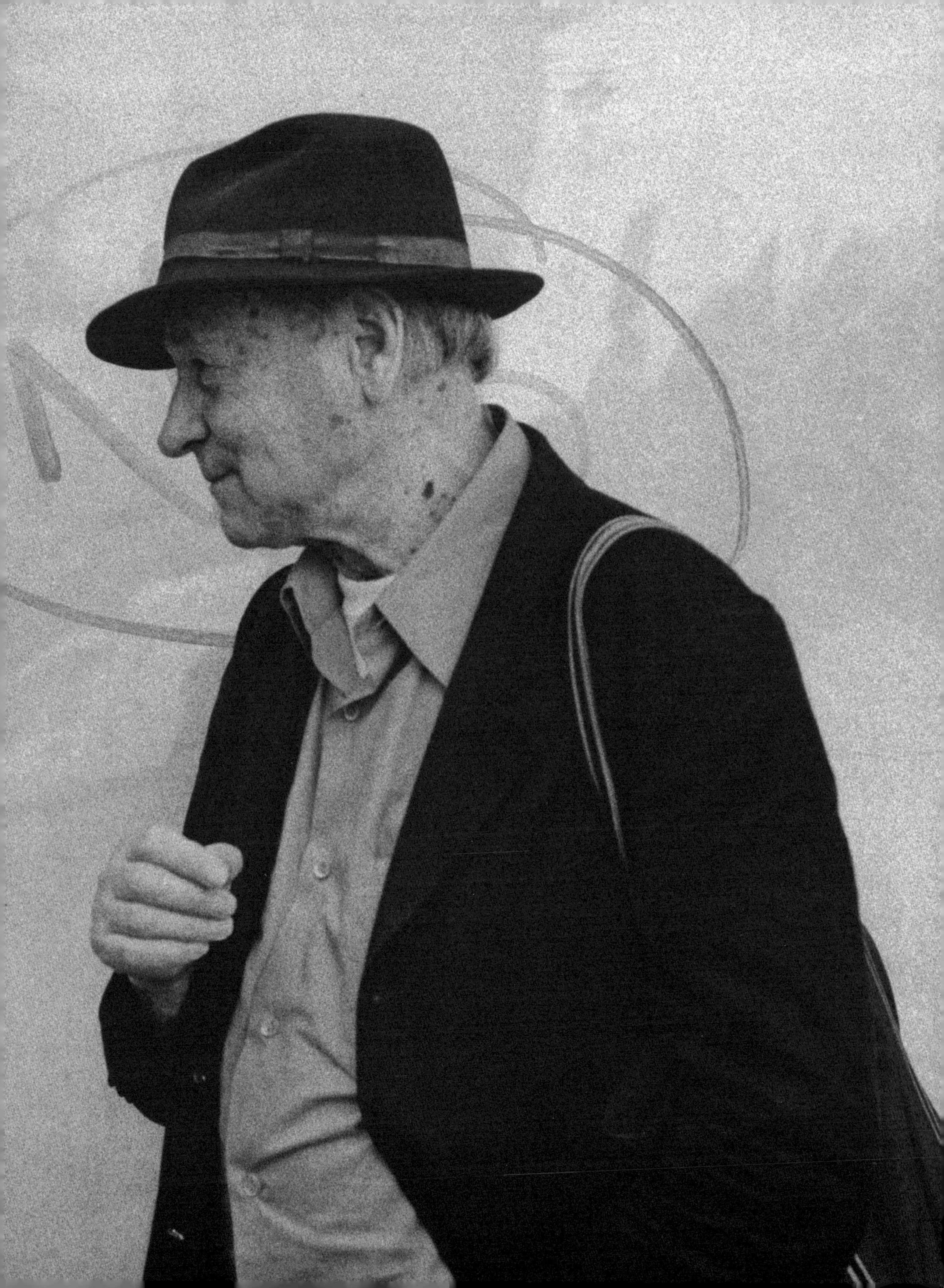